HUGH GAITSKELL

For Mridul

HUGH GAITSKELL

BRIAN BRIVATI

RICHARD COHEN BOOKS · London

British Library Cataloguing in Publication Data:
A catalogue record for this book is available from the British Library

Copyright © 1997 by Brian Brivati

ISBN 1 86066 115 7

First published in Great Britain in 1996 by
Richard Cohen Books
7 Manchester Square
London W1M 5RE

Design by Margaret Fraser

Typeset in Bembo by Rowland Phototypesetting Ltd,
Bury St Edmunds, Suffolk

Printed in Great Britain by
Mackays of Chatham plc

Contents

List of Illustrations

Acknowledgements

A full statement of personal and professional gratitude to the many people who helped with the research, writing and production of this book is contained in the first edition. In addition to the people listed there I would like to thank a number of reviewers who pointed out minor errors in the text, in particular, Roy Jenkins, Anthony Howard and Alan Watkins. The main text of this edition remains the same; I have revised and updated the introduction to take account of Labour's victory in the 1997 general election. Any comments or further response to this work can be emailed to me at B.Brivati@ Kingston.ac.uk.

Brian Brivati
Stoke Newington, London
July 1997

The author and publishers are grateful to the following for permission to reproduce printed matter:

Mrs Julia McNeal and Mrs Cressida Wasserman for material from the estate of Hugh Gaitskell; Dr Stephen Byrd for material from the Labour Party Archive at the National Museum of Labour History; the Master and Fellows of University College, Oxford for the papers of Earl Attlee; the Rt Hon Michael Foot for the publications of Richard Crossman, John Murray Limited for extracts from 'Summoned by Bells' by John Betjeman, Professor Elizabeth Durbin for the papers of Evan Durbin; The Controller of Her Majesty's Stationery Office for Crown copyright material; the West Yorkshire Archive Service for material from the Leeds South Constituency Labour Party Papers and Mark Amory for the letters of Ann Fleming.

Where extensive quotations appear from a single source every effort has been made to contact the copyright holder.

The author and publishers are grateful to the following for permission to reproduce illustrations:

PLATE SECTION

Mrs Julia McNeal and Mrs Cressida Wasserman for Gaitskell family photographs; Camera Press: 13, 19; The Dragon School, Oxford: 2, 3; Hulton Getty Collection: 4, 5, 6, 9, 11, 12, 14, 17, 18; NMPFT/ Science & Society Picture Library: 15; Popperfoto: 1, 7, 8, 10, 20, 23, 24, 25

TEXT PAGES

Emmwood, *Sunday Dispatch*, Solo Syndication 345; Illingworth, *Punch*, 271, 285; Vicky, *Daily Mirror*, Centre for the Study of Cartoons and Caricature, University of Kent 207; Giles, *Daily Express*, 179

Introduction

When in 1962 Hugh Gaitskell sat down at the end of his speech to the Labour Party Conference he was the dominant political personality in British politics. By so forcefully opposing UK membership of the European Community he united the Labour Party behind his leadership and eclipsed the Conservative Prime Minister, Harold Macmillan. It was the apex of his political career. The poignancy of the story of Gaitskell's life is simply that 108 days later he was dead. Though it is a story that has been told before, Gaitskell remains a relatively neglected figure. The official biography published in 1979 was very much an authorised life and strictly a political one. With a little more distance of time and relationship to the subject, this book, while still generally supportive, is more critical and explores aspects of Gaitskell's life previously neglected; there is not even a hint in the official life of Gaitskell's affair with Ann Fleming. Nor does it discuss the most important male relationships of Gaitskell's life, with Hugh Dalton, Evan Durbin and Anthony Crosland, friendships based on intense feelings on both sides. Gaitskell tried throughout his life to maintain the separation of the personal and the political, and many people found the man they encountered in private life difficult to square with the public persona. The gap between the dry, pedantic Wykehamist Minister and the warm, passionate friend and lover is the central paradox of Gaitskell's life, the source of an extraordinary tension between the two sides of his personality. Occasionally the barriers were breached and the intense feelings flooded into the political sphere with electrifying effect, but more often the two were kept strictly apart by the discipline of convention and upbringing.

The nature of a political reputation and our perception of particular political figures fluctuate through time. When Roy Jenkins was reviewing the eruption of biographies of Wilson in 1993, he concluded that he would now be buying Wilsons and selling Majors. The shifts in the leadership of the Labour Party over the last decade provoke the question: should we now be buying Gaitskells and selling Bevans, perhaps slowing down our purchases of Wilsons? Neil Kinnock employed Gaitskellite qualities of leadership but did not completely abandon his loyalties to an older socialism represented by Nye Bevan. John Smith deployed Wilsonian guile in bringing unity but lacked the revisionist zeal to move the party at the speed and in the direction that Tony Blair has done. In 1996, Roy Jenkins, the most distinguished living Gaitskellite, endorsed Tony Blair as leader of the Labour Party, completing a circle as many of those who launched the SDP came back into the Labour Party fold. However, while many Gaitskellites have been eager to see Blair as the heir to Gaitskell's mantle, the Blairites have noticeably refrained from embracing Gaitskell's memory. Gaitskell's name is absent from Peter Mandelson and Roger Liddle's study of the Blair revolution. The reluctance to associate the new revisionist leader with the old has two elements. First, the Prime Minister has been careful generally to embrace all aspects of his party's history. Second, he has resisted being specific about the particular means he endorses from the past, while espousing a complicated set of 'eternal' Labour values.

Blair has paid tribute to both the old Gaitskellite and the old Bevanite traditions. In his introduction to Tony Wright and Matt Carter's *The People's Party* (the new edition of the Thames and Hudson history of the Labour Party) he talks of the party's youth and ability to modernise. In his contribution to some of the Nye Bevan centenary tributes he acknowledges the role of the champion of the radical wing of the party. As many modernisers claim a Bevanite genealogy or came through Bennite groups, this endorsement of the left's old hero is understandable. Indeed, Blair himself is a self-confessed fan of Barbara Castle. The old revisionists amongst the new Blair government, such as Bernard Donoughue, are either the Gaitskellites who stayed in the Party after 1981 or those who took the more tortuous root from Labour to SDP to Liberal Democrats to New Labour. For them, the 1997 government is part of Gaitskell's legacy. Yet another group of modernisers, which is growing as the number of old Gaitskellites and old Bevanities declines, are those for whom the history of the Labour Party is at best an irrelevance, at worst an encumbrance to the speed of change. The relatively comfortable coexistence at the heart of the administration of the two once bitterly opposed traditions with this new anti-historical one is a clear indication that New Labour's claims of inclusiveness are well founded.

However, this general endorsement of the radical heritage of the party is deliberately light on detail. Take for example the notion of a renewed 'unity' of the left with the coming together of the Liberal and socialist traditions – a return to the Lib-Lab era of the 1890s. The idea that a short-term and contingent electoral cooperation was in fact a golden age of radical togetherness which predates the creation of the Labour Party was popular before the election when modernisers thought they might need Liberal Democratic votes; it soon disappeared when the size of the Labour majority became clear. The distinct radical and socialist tradition that forged the ideology of the Labour Party in opposition to the timidity of Gladstonian and New Liberalism had been conveniently forgotten. Similarly, lip service has been paid to the spirit of the 1945 victory, a spirit which inspired Gaitskell throughout his life, but the detail of the 1945 programme and the objectives for which the administration existed – aside from certain values – has been consciously ignored.

This is the context of the omission of 'equality' as a political objective from Tony Blair's political vocabulary. To compare Blair and Gaitskell is to associate the Prime Minister with a politics of secular but ethical collectivism whose objective was greater equality, the underlying purpose of the 1945 government. There are, nevertheless, parallels between Blair and Gaitskell, indeed, Tony Blair can be seen as Gaitskell writ large. The Prime Minister leads from the front, relishing power and office, and was prepared before the 1997 election to extend the boundaries of modernisation beyond all that was formerly sacred within his own party and is now intent on making a lasting impact on the country. In this sense, Labour leadership has flowed back to the stream of change and reform that Gaitskell represented, but there are extremely important distinctions – beyond the obvious ones of period and circumstances – between the two figures which have been emphasised by the General Election of 1997.

The extent of Labour's landslide victory in May 1997 has forced a reappraisal of the history of the Labour Party. The assumption that Labour was a narrow class-based party doomed, by what A. H. Halsey has called the politics of an affluent culture, to be permanently excluded from office has been flatly contradicted. The historical entity that was the British Labour Party founded in 1900 has been returned to power and seems set, at the time of writing, for an extensive period in office. The architects of that victory, especially

Tony Blair and Peter Mandelson, had set out to modernise the country. The hardback edition of this biography was published in September 1996, while the phoney war which preceded the general election proper was in full swing, but after the main elements of the modernisation of the Labour Party had been put in place. The book's argument, which has if anything been strengthened by the size of Labour's victory, was that Hugh Gaitskell was the grandfather of the Blair revolution; his life had significant lessons for the contemporary modernisers and the underlying differences between his political philosophy and the direction in which New Labour has travelled reflect the nature of the change in the times.

The first actions of the new Labour government have underscored the nature of these changes and have implied that the historical entity that was the Labour Party is in the advanced stages of a metamorphosis into a substantially new political party; the type of change more usually associated with the Conservative Party's reinventions of itself for electoral advantage. Such a conclusion requires a reappraisal of the conventional perception of Gaitskell's leadership in several significant respects.

Now that the Labour government has abandoned any intention of using progressive taxation for the redistribution of wealth as distinct from controlling consumer demand, the long-running battles over public ownership, which are conventionally presented as being central to Labour's ideological direction, appear now as so much bickering over inessentials characterised by a profound confusion of means (public ownership) and ends (greater equality). Moreover, the other long-running internal battle, over the global position of Britain, expressed either in a desire to see Britain dominant through political leadership or through moral leadership, now appears complacent and delusional. Moreover, the essence of Labour's victory in 1997 was the abandonment of the notion that economic intervention was superior to market allocation for managing the economy. At the heart of Gaitskell's socialism was a belief in equality and a faith that the Labour Party contained the people best able to promote equality by the effective management of the economy coupled with deep patriotism – a conviction that Britain was a great country that had a global role to play. Deep in the debates over policy was the belief that there was a key to the successful running of the economy and that economists held that key – one of Gaitskell's favourite dismissive lines was that someone was 'not much good at economics'. He agreed much more with his major political opponents during his lifetime than he would do with the current generation of leaders of the Labour Party. But the contemporary state of British politics would have given him temporary pause for reflection and a certain enjoyment, though here too the great distances that New Labour and the world have travelled would have been quickly apparent.

When Hugh Gaitskell found out that he was to be asked to replace Stafford Cripps as Chancellor of the Exchequer, he told William Armstrong – the Chancellor's private secretary – that politics in Britain would gradually become a competition over competence. It would resemble the politics of the United States and the Labour Party would evolve into a British version of the American Democratic Party. The current convergence of interest and policy between Clinton's New Democrats and Blair's New Labour would have given him pleasure. Despite this superficial continuity, the detail of the ideological underpinning of that convergence would also have troubled him. For Gaitskell in the 1950s, the special relationship was based on the unity of the democracies against the Communist world, but the differences between Britain and America remained real because it was the Labour Party that set the terms of the political debate in the UK and it was collectivism that set the context within which politics would take place. The party-political battle, he firmly believed, would be fought out on the ground prepared by the Labour Party: an interventionist state, a progressive tax system designed to redistribute wealth in the name of greater equality, public ownership of a substantial section of British industry and a global military and strategic role as a key partner to the US in the anti-communist Western alliance.

The contrast with cooperation between New Labour and the New Democrats is striking. Clinton's 'triangulation' of positions separate from either the Democrats or the Republicans is based on an acceptance of the Reaganite-neo-liberal shift away from Roosevelt's New Deal and the use of Federal government powers. The New Labour government seems to have developed a similar position which is based neither on Gaitskell's collectivist faith nor on a full-blown endorsement of neo-liberalism. New Labour's third position comprises two key elements. First an acceptance of the broad direction of the management of the economy derived from the Thatcher years, including a complete acceptance of the defeat and irrelevance of public ownership as a form of planning that is desirable to correct market failure or necessary to promote equality. Second, a radical rejection of Conservative definitions of the British constitution and sovereignty. The latter will involve a devolution of power and resources that might eventually open the door to a renewed sense of the efficacy of state action, but this will be at local and regional rather than national levels.

The politics Gaitskell espoused are primarily of historical interest now. The argument in the 1950s was entirely within the terms of reference of collectivism. He did not believe in the efficacy of markets; he believed in planning. His opponents within the party went further. In the debate on Clause 4 in 1959, Nye Bevan stated that Britain faced an economic challenge from countries that are 'at long last being able to reap the material fruits of economic planning and public ownership'. Top of his list was Russia: do not worry about the USA or Germany, he said, with their market economies; worry about the command economies. A few years later, Harold Wilson evoked the white heat of technological revolution so that Britain could keep up with the material and scientific advances of the Soviet Union. Faith in the efficacy of the state and in the rightness of the aim of equality permeated political debate.

The contemporary Labour Party leadership does not operate in an intellectual environment it has shaped, nor does it believe it has the economic answers to contemporary questions: in essence Tony Blair is 'playing catch-up' to a revolution in political economy insti-gated from the right. Collectivism is largely a dead political idea; planning is no longer seen as economically relevant; the market mechanism is seen as the economic 'truth' of the 1990s. The econ-omic ambitions of the contemporary Labour government are modest, the radical emphasis has shifted to constitutional reform and a remaking of the British nation state. The emphasis of a Gaitskell government would have been the other way round: constitutionally moderate, economically interventionist. The shadow of the Attlee governments fell over Gaitskell's years as leader, for the achievement of those years underpinned his faith in what he was doing. The contemporary Labour Party operates in the shadow of the Thatcher revolution. In the long run historians might judge that revolution to have been partial and limited in scope, but to have achieved one not inconsiderable success: the Labour Party has abandoned equality as an objective and in so doing it resembles the 'historic' Labour Party founded in 1900 in name alone.

Introduction

There is, clearly, a vast, though contested, difference in the overall context of the UK economy in the late 1990s from that of the 1950s. Much of the underlying argument for the shift away from nationalisation, use of progressive taxation, support for universal benefits and so on comes from the notion of the global economy. Though the impact of this global economy, particularly the free and instantaneous movement of capital, is contested and frequently used as a political cover for inaction, nevertheless it would be ludicrous to argue that the Labour Party should, or could, have stayed still in 1963 or indeed that Gaitskell's own beliefs would not have changed and evolved had he lived. The purpose of this book is not to win a counter-factual contest about what might have been if Gaitskell had lived. Nor is it to claim posthumous endorsement or condemnation by Gaitskell for contemporary polical positions, but rather to contribute to a better understanding of the Labour Party by examining the ideology of a leader who shared Blair's instinct for power and modernisation, but placed different limits on what he was prepared to change.

In these respects the differences tend to be more profound than the continuities between the party of Gaitskell and that of Blair. However, similarities of approach between the two leaders do exist. They share modernising instincts – and, of course, Gaitskell tried and failed to ditch Clause 4 in favour of a new statement of aims: he was the first moderniser. The styles of the two leaders also invite comparison, with each other and with Mrs Thatcher. Ironically, Gaitskell would have resembled Thatcher in some ways: his dedication to work, his clarity of objectives and his pedantic attention to detail would have given him many of the strengths and the weaknesses of a Thatcher-style premier. However, the leader he resembled more, as John Campbell has pointed out, was the Conservative Prime Minister, Ted Heath. They shared that mid-century technocratic love of the machinery of state and, in Gaitskell's more than Heath's case, the mechanics of economic policy. They shared a positivist faith in the ability to find solutions to human problems. Gaitskell might not have been able to bend to the wind of industrial militancy in the way Heath did, but then the context would have been different.

Gaitskell embodied a strand of British politics now extinct, but he was also an intriguing human being: he never stopped struggling with his upbringing, his class and, finally, the constraints of the public life he had chosen. Initially he sought ways of escaping his background by rebelling against it; later he rebelled against the constraints his political life had placed on his ability to have fun by making a point of having it. Personally, this seeking out of fun took the form of a love of food, alcohol, jazz and dancing. At times the intensity of his pleasure-seeking could draw criticism, and the closeness of his relationship with women such as his lover, Ann Fleming, provoked some to question his commitment to the working class; but more often people remarked on his capacity for friendship and on his extraordinarily warm private persona. Politically, each time it appeared that he had found his level he transcended it, and confounded people's expectations. He slowly resolved a number of deep-rooted private battles – for instance, between the demands of the Wykehamist code and his deep emotional needs – and seemed to be on the threshold of fulfilling a life of intense hard work when he died. This is the story of the man who was for many the last great democratic socialist leader of the Labour Party.

Chronology

1928	MacDonald elected for Seaham Harbour
1929	General Election
	Bevan elected MP for Ebbw Vale
June 1929–	Second Labour Government:
Aug 1931	MacDonald Prime Minister
Oct 1931–	National Government:
June 1935	MacDonald Prime Minister
1932	Socialist League formed
1934	Bevan marries Jennie Lee, former MP for North Lanark
1935	General Election: National Government
	MacDonald elected MP for the Scottish Universities
	MacDonald Lord President of the Council
	Attlee leader of Labour Party
1937	MacDonald dies
	Gaitskell marries Dora Frost (nee Creditor)
1939	Popular Front against fascism advocated
	Expulsion of Stafford Cripps, Bevan and others from Labour Party for support of Popular Front
1940–45	Bevan editor of *Tribune*
May 1940	Formation of Coalition Government
	Attlee Lord Privy Seal
1942	Attlee Deputy Prime Minister
1945	General Election: Labour Government: Attlee PM
	Gaitskell elected for Leeds South
1950	Attlee elected for West Walthamstow
Oct 1950	Gaitskell Chancellor of Exchequer
April 1951	Resignation of Bevan as Minister of Labour, and John Freeman and Harold Wilson
Oct 1951	General Election: Conservative Government
Nov 1955	Resignation of Attlee as leader of Labour Party
Dec 1955	Election of Gaitskell as leader of Labour Party
1959	General Election: Conservative Government
	Bevan elected deputy leader of Labour Party
1960	Nye Bevan dies
	LP Conference: unilateral disarmament debate
Jan 1963	Gaitskell dies
	Election of Wilson
Oct 1964	General Election: Labour Government

1

Dragon, Wykehamist, Socialist, 1906–1928

Once more we biked the hedge –
   And darker seemed the hawthorn caves
And lonelier the water's edge,
   And we were sad returning slaves
To bell and rule and smell of school
   Beyond the high cow-parsley waves.
                    John Betjeman, *Summoned by Bells*, 1960

He made his weight felt by quiet determination and a certain
sweet reasonableness and sense of justice.
                    Housemaster, Winchester, 1951

From now on my future is with the working class.
                    Gaitskell, Oxford, 1926

Hugh Gaitskell was born in Kensington, London, on 9 April 1906.
He was named after his godfather who, like his father, was in the
Indian Civil Service. His father's family, which came from Cumber-
land, had a military tradition dating back to the Napoleonic Wars.
His paternal grandfather had been a colonel but his father dropped
out of university to join the Indian Civil Service, arriving in Burma
at the age of nineteen in 1889. His mother, Addie Mary Jamieson,
was a daughter of the Consul-General in Shanghai and came from
a Scottish farming background. Hugh Gaitskell, who was soon nick-
named Sam – the photographs of him at the time show an extremely
engaging child who seems to suit the name better than Hugh – was
not born into the labour movement; his world was defined by the
British Empire. By the time Sam entered this world it was already
characterised by a lightly fading privilege and dusty gentility.

   From the moment of his birth he was materially secure, never
rich but, equally, never having to worry. No one would ever say,
'I'm sure there's no one in this wide world was ever poorer', as a

1

contemporary remarked of Ernest Bevin and his mother.[1] If not quite sterling silver, the spoon in Sam's mouth was silver-plated. But although this was a middle-class world it was not the middle class of industrialists and capitalists; it was the middle class of largely state employment, in public service of various kinds. It was not an unusual family background for the time; indeed, R. A. Butler, later Gaitskell's political opponent, had almost exactly the same origins.[2]

Hugh later told a friend at Oxford that he had had a conventionally happy childhood.[3] This is a deeply revealing phrase, echoed by Clement Attlee about his childhood; but whereas Attlee had in many ways a conventional family life, in a house with an attentive mother and a father who went to work each day, Sam did not. He may well have rationalised it in such a way, and indeed for the time and for his class this may have been the case: his father was capable of being very warm, especially to Hugh's sister Dorothy, and as the baby of the family Sam was loved and protected. But from the outside it appears a dislocated childhood and an increasingly lonely, isolated adolescence, the influence of which was profound. Years later, Gaitskell told his mentor Hugh Dalton that to love and to be loved was the biggest thing in the world.[4] The absences of his youth influenced this desire to give and receive affection. It was a childhood shaped by the nineteenth century, by the demands of the Empire and the English public school system. For all his later love of modernity and radicalism, at root Gaitskell was made by the England of privilege, conformity and the silent bourgeois struggle between the needs of convention and the demands of emotion: until well into the 1920s Hugh had the probably endearing habit of blushing when speaking.

His background was of that unique middle-class internationalism which the Empire created. Not only was Sam's family defined by the Empire; he experienced it at first hand. He spent the first winter of his life in Burma and stayed there for a memorable year when he was five. Burma and the Empire were integral parts of his family life. His brother Arthur worked from 1923 to 1952 in the Gezira irrigation scheme in the Sudan; in 1952 he was chairman of the mission to the Bechuanaland Protectorate to investigate the possibilities of economic development in the western Kalahari and in 1953–5 a member of the East Africa Royal Commission. Hugh's father, Arthur 'Tiger' Gaitskell, spent much of his short life in Burma and ended up as Commissioner for Settlement and Land Records in

Rangoon. His mother was younger, livelier and warmer than his father. She once mixed up all the road signs in Rangoon, and, at a time when the races did not intermingle socially, made a large number of Burmese friends. Addie Gaitskell seems to have had that combination of gaiety and conformity with which Gaitskell struggled for so much of his life; she eventually became a Labour supporter and lived until 1956.

Years later, in the last great political debate of his life, Gaitskell opposed the terms of British entry to the European Economic Community. His objections did not stem from his early experiences in Burma, but he did have an emotional attachment to the idea of the Commonwealth that flowed from him in that speech. Few at the time could understand where that feeling came from. In the *Periodic Table* Primo Levi describes his ancestors as the 'inert gases'. For Sam, the inert gases in his emotional formation were Burma, his beloved ayah, Mary, and the appearances and absences of his parents, which mingled to form his background. Rather than having no influence on his actions and his policy decisions, the Empire was simply part of him. It is impossible to isolate the precise effect it had, but in his speech to the Labour Party Conference in October 1962 the inert gases of his past came flooding out.

Sam's father was a high-minded, conventional product of his class and time; there is no hint of the genteel radicalism of Attlee's father.[5] He believed in service and integrity; but there was also a romantic streak in him and a certain impetuousness – leaving New College, Oxford, to travel across the world is not the action of an entirely cautious man. Moreover, when he met Addie on the boat taking him to England for leave in 1898, he fell in love with her and pursued her all the way to Scotland to ask her to marry him. They had three children: Dorothy, in 1899, who stayed very much in her class and married the Conservative MP, Hubert Ashton – later Parliamentary Private Secretary to R. A. Butler; Arthur, in 1900, who followed the family career pattern; and lastly Hugh, the baby of the family by six years.

Sam was a slow starter, not learning to talk until he was two, but becoming an argumentative and precocious child once he began. His mother taught him bridge at the age of six – a game his father had given up when he began to win too much money – and even as a small boy he played golf and cards.[6] He seems to have been a fairly typical youngest child: a little spoilt, a little stubborn, and adored by all. Having had Sam in England, Addie returned with him to Burma for a year before he came back for good, bringing with him his ayah, Mary. The style of Gaitskell's childhood disappeared with the Empire; but his distant and spasmodic relationship with his absentee 'working' parents did not. Since they were away for much of the time, he revelled in their attention when they appeared. But in the main it was a childhood spent on the move, staying with various relatives and then boarding at school; it was that English brand of family life that breeds self-reliance and emotional confusion; moreover, it meant there was no single house or place of which Sam could say, 'That is where I come from.'

In 1915 Arthur Gaitskell died from a tropical disease at the age of forty-five. Hugh was nine. In place of his father he came to idolise his brother. Hugh was in the shadow of his brother Arthur at school and then at New College, Oxford. He later wrote to a friend, 'When I was a boy I loved my brother, no one else, no one else would do.' Subsequently, at a time of general revolt against his family's values he also attacked Arthur's values, and lack of rebellion, but the two brothers remained close throughout their lives.

The Empire was at its height in April 1906 when Gaitskell was born. Two months before, the Liberal Party, led by Sir Henry Campbell-Bannerman, had won a landslide election victory. There were two kinds of 'dangerous radicalism' in the domestic politics of Sam's nursery years: socialism and suffragettes. The Liberal government was regarded as extremely radical when it passed a Trades Disputes Act to give trade unions a privileged legal position, setting in place one of the foundation stones of the labour movement. David Lloyd George and Winston Churchill were the radicals of the ruling party, new liberalism – with its interventionist tendencies – the wave of the future. Twenty-nine Labour MPs had been elected in the 1906 election, another one joined just after, and as Parliament assembled the Labour Representation Committee took the name Labour Party and elected Keir Hardie as chair. The membership of the party was nearing a million, and was dominated by the National Union of Mineworkers. In the election Labour had polled 329,748 votes. Since no progress had been made towards votes for women, the Prime Minister advised a delegation of suffragettes to 'go on pestering' and they would have their way.[7] None of these developments would have been welcomed in the Gaitskell family.

Hugh's early years were spent in Oxford with a cousin of his father's, Mrs Pike, in whose household 'one pot of jam had to last a week'. Arthur, who was five years older, was already at the Dragon School. With his father only returning from Burma for his leaves, and with more frequent but still rare visits from his mother, Gaitskell usually lived with relatives or boarded at school. Until 1919 summer holidays were spent in Norfolk with his brilliant grandfather, George Jamieson, an accomplished Chinese scholar who once won a world prize for an essay on bimetallism. Easter and Christmas vacations were spent in Scotland with his mother's uncle. Gaitskell later wrote: 'Some of my happiest memories are of night train journeys to Scotland, of breakfast in the train crossing the Forth Bridge ... [and] playing for hours beside a burn that splashed down the hillside into the Spey.'[8]

His preparatory school, the Dragon School in Oxford, had been founded to educate the sons of Oxford dons, when they were allowed to be married after the 1870s reforms. It was more liberal and interesting than the other Oxford prep school, Summerfields, which Harold Macmillan left in the year of Sam's birth. From six to eight Hugh was a day boy and from eight he was a boarder.[9] The Dragon School was dominated by 'Skipper' Lynam, who was dedicated to the memory of William Gladstone. In keeping with his somewhat slow start, Hugh was a good but not outstanding pupil at the Dragon, a school with extremely high standards. He won prizes and ended up fifth out of some 200. One of his prizes was for a divinity exam and he was also awarded 6d. for not missing a 'single cold plunge bath in the winter'. He once recited Kipling's 'For All We Have and Are' to school assembly. The poem, typical of the time, represents another kind of inert gas from Gaitskell's childhood. It begins:

> For all we have and are,
> For all our children's fate,
> Stand up and take the war.
> The Hun is at the gate!

and ends:

> No easy hope or lies
> Shall bring us to our goal,
> But iron sacrifice
> Of body, will and soul.
> There is but one task for all –
> One life for each to give.

5

What stands if Freedom fall?
Who dies if England live?[10]

At the Dragon, games played a large part in school life: Sam learned to box and play rugby, and captained the second eleven cricket team – probably, he thought in 1951, 'because of vague qualities of leadership rather than any ability to hit the ball'.[11] He best loved tennis and later golf, at which he became proficient. In addition he played rugby and was in the back row of the scrum, with the younger Mallalieu as scrum half. He took part in sport but he did not become a fan; there was no obsessive collection of cricket statistics.

Skipper Lynam was an 'ardent radical' with a taste for loud ties and boating. Gaitskell followed the Skipper's lead and started a vogue for colourful neckties among the boys; he continued wearing them for the rest of his life. Whenever he could he would get out of playing cricket and go boating and swimming – a lifelong pleasure. His friends were Charles Plumb, who later went to the Board of Trade and shared his enthusiasm for colourful ties; Colin Clark, a rival economist for many years; and the Mallalieu brothers – J. P. Mallalieu once defeated Hugh in a speech competition. John Betjeman remembers Gaitskell as 'mild and friendly and very correct' and claims to have seen him walking through South Kensington at the age of twelve 'impeccably dressed with a bowler hat and a stick'. Gaitskell questioned the bowler hat and retorted: 'By Betjeman's standards, then and since, almost everyone else but Betjeman would have been described as very correct.'[12] The tone of tolerance set by the headmaster permeated the school. There were occasional beatings but these were much less frequent than elsewhere. The First World War also gave the school a sense of unreality. In assembly the Dragons who had been killed would be announced by the Skipper:

> The latest names of those who'd lost their lives
> For King and Country and the Dragon School.
> Sometimes his gruff old voice was full of tears
> When a particular favourite had been killed.[13]

Four years after his father's death, in 1919, Hugh's mother married Gilbert Wodehouse, a cousin of P.G., and they returned together to Burma while Hugh followed his brother Arthur to Winchester. He was twelve years old and still at the Dragon when his future was decided. Walking through Oxford one day, he ran into the father of a friend from school and told him where he was going on to school. The man – in later life Hugh could only remember that his name was Fawcett – told the schoolboy: 'You don't know how lucky you are – only one boy in ten thousand has the chance of an education like that.' This shocked him, Gaitskell claimed later, into 'the first awareness of a social problem'.[14]

William of Wykeham, Bishop of Winchester, founded New College, Oxford, in 1379 and Winchester College in 1382. On foundation it was specified that scholars should be poor but could also be relatives of Wykeham; 'for a number of years the scholars included virtually no one else.'[15] Both institutions were part of the same educational idea, to counter 'fewness of the clergy, arising from pestilence, wars and other miseries'. They would take 'poor and indigent scholars' and turn them into 'men of great learning, fruitful to the church . . . King and realm'. The administrators of the church and of the state would be forged in these institutions, both built at one go, New College setting the architectural style for later colleges and the relationship being copied by Eton when it was founded with King's College, Cambridge, in 1442.[16] By the time Sam left the Dragon and took over his brother's nickname, 'the goat',* at Winchester, it had become the most intellectual of the English public schools, with its own linguistic tradition and the 'Notions', 'a 38-page booklet of rules, terminology and traditions to be learnt by every new boy at Winchester and on which he is tested, and if necessary retested, after his first week in the school'.[17] Thus were Wykehamists produced.

Richard Crossman was the star of Winchester at the time, and caught the spirit and nature of the experience years later:

> The secret of Winchester . . . is that it imposes on a boy's mind a complex structure of rules, a rigid hierarchy of values, and a system of taboos, privileges and obligations utterly remote from his home life or from the world outside. Any boy who entered Winchester had to accept them at once as protective colouring of his individual personality. Then he learnt to use them as an instrument for self-advancement. I suspect that the majority of boys – even at Winchester, where the entrance exam requires scholarship standard – assimilate very little of the classical tradition. They take from it merely its external forms, in particular that blend of intellectual

---

* It is not clear why Arthur was known as 'the goat'.

arrogance and conventional good manners which is so much resented by those who do not qualify for the old school tie.

The 'blend of intellectual arrogance and conventional good manners' captures something of Gaitskell in later life. Crossman's sense of superiority comes through clearly in his own analysis of the school, particularly that group which, he felt, most clearly reflected a successful transition from Winchester:

> As for the few who have the ability to master its esoteric secrets, they fall into three groups. Most of these very able boys are mentally dehydrated by the rigours of the classical discipline and uncritically accept its scale of values as the ultimate of truth, beauty and goodness. These are the permanent Wykehamists, who remain all their lives spiritually at school, although their careers may well make them in their fifties Permanent Under-Secretaries, Chancery Judges, Vice-Chancellors or Archdeacons ... Others accept the tradition with varying degrees of sceptical detachment ... they alternate the reverent Amen with a snigger, which makes them feel that they are now grown men with open minds. A few – their minds sharpened by six years of mental struggle with the tradition but in lifelong reaction against it – remain grateful to Winchester for teaching them that all institutions, laws and persons in authority may well turn out to be as bizarre a mixture of the good and the fraudulent as their old Headmaster. They are radical throw-outs of the Public School system; and some of them even become 'traitors to their class'.[18]

Perhaps a fourth set would be those who, while they are in lifelong reaction to the tradition of the school, have also been imbued with its values. Richard Crossman's mischievous nature was a true reflection of a reaction against Winchester; Hugh Gaitskell, more critically than his friend Douglas Jay, reacted against but also to an extent embraced the idea of it. They might have been traitors to their class, but they were not traitors to their school. Mrs Thatcher is supposed to have once said that all men are weak, public school men are weaker and Wykehamists are the weakest of the lot.[19] Even the motto of the school, 'Manners Makyth Man', implies a certain high-mindedness of behaviour over action. But Gaitskell was only ever a Wykehamist to a limited extent; he felt little sympathy with the school and though it influenced him he was in no sense a weak man or an excessively polite politician: in personal matters he was considerate and polite to a fault, but in political matters he had a streak of very un-Wykehamist ruthlessness.

Soon after he went to Winchester, Hugh's grandfather died and holidays were spent either with his aunt at Brancaster or on Exmoor, where his stepfather had been a vicar. His mother had returned to Burma and his sister Dorothy followed her in 1921. In 1922 his brother went to the Sudan and thereafter Hugh holidayed with his sister Dorothy when she was in England, but in the main he was now on his own.

His career at Winchester began with a disappointment when he tried for a scholarship and failed; but it was the only school he wanted to attend because Arthur was there, so his family paid. The bad start worsened when he contracted mumps and started his schooldays in the infirmary. However, his natural competitiveness showed itself and with determination and hard work he did well in his first two years, being promoted every term and then spending a year in a form full of scholars. The other boys, including the star, Richard Crossman, whom Hugh sat next to,[20] were better at Latin and Greek, and although Hugh worked hard his career at Winchester, after his bright start, was unremarkable. In the opinion of his biographer, Tam Dalyell, Crossman never really stopped seeing Gaitskell as the 'amiable and ineffective schoolboy who, in glaring contrast to himself, had made not the slightest impact while he was at Winchester'.[21] Roy Jenkins concurs: 'He was a much less successful Wykehamist than either of his Labour Party contemporaries, Richard Crossman or Douglas Jay, and retained no great feeling for the place.'[22] His former housemaster told the *Picture Post* in 1951 that Gaitskell was 'a quiet, modest, studious and undemonstrative boy, of whom nobody could have predicted his future . . . He made his weight felt [as a prefect] by quiet determination and a certain sweet reasonableness and sense of justice – still highly typical, I should say.'[23] His interest in sport continued; Philip Williams records him 'playing football with and other sports without enthusiasm, but . . . he much preferred individual games such as golf and tennis.'[24] As Hugh wrote to his mother: 'I may have felt that "esprit de corps" feeling half a dozen times . . . but not more. It is very much an illusion.'[25] He also rowed twice for his house and raced in cross-country running. Douglas Jay's first perception of the young Gaitskell was that he had failed in a race that he was tipped to win.[26]

As he wasn't a scholar in college, he spent only five years at the school, where some of his contemporaries such as Dick Crossman and Douglas Jay spent six. Just below the sixth form, however, he closed the gap with Dick Crossman and lay in second place behind him. William Hayter (in 1963 Warden of New College, Oxford) and John Sparrow (in 1963 Warden of All Souls College, Oxford), who was editing John Donne's sermons in his spare time, were in the same form.

Hugh's finest moment at Winchester was winning a prize for an essay on international arbitration; he had a keen interest in international affairs and was responsible for founding a branch of the League of Nations at the school. In recollecting this, he inflated his standing in the school; obviously he still felt relish at his achievement but perhaps a little insecurity about his time there. He recalled that he used 'his influence with the leading figures in the school – the popular games-playing element, school prefects etc. – to induce them to join. This made it fashionable and before long it had membership of over 100.'[27] Perhaps his sister proved useful in this respect, as the Ashtons were the sporting stars of the school and one of them later married Dorothy. The essay prize was sponsored by Stafford Cripps, already a well-established lawyer and later Chancellor in the Attlee government.

> Gaitskell read up [international arbitration] in the *Encyclopaedia Britannica*, entered and won, beating Colin Clark and another boy who had beaten him for the two top scholarships to Winchester. The result was his first meeting with Cripps. He waited in the dreary legal chambers: Cripps was delayed so long in court that he could only suggest that Gaitskell came with him in the taxi to Paddington, where he was due to catch a train. Talking in the taxi, Cripps said that the only hope he could see for lasting peace was a union of the Christian Churches in the world; and Gaitskell felt a sense of disappointment in his hero. 'I did not think it was quite adequate,' he says.[28]

Gaitskell's upper-middle-class childhood left him with a strong relationship with his mother and an even stronger independence. By the time he left Winchester in 1924 he had learned to be self-reliant, and to choose what he read and where he spent holidays. Roy Jenkins and Philip Williams both play down the impact of his childhood and early life, Jenkins concluding that Gaitskell's father had no impact and that this was 'to some extent true of all his family'.[29] However, the nature of his childhood and his experience at school does go some way towards explaining aspects of his character.

In 1970 Lucille Iremonger published *The Fiery Chariot: A Study of British Prime Ministers and the Search for Love*. This book put forward the hypothesis that the drive and ambition required to get to the very top of British politics are based on an unhappy childhood, particularly the loss of one or more parents at an early age.[30] Sam did not lack normal affection in his upbringing – indeed, his brother and sister were very fond of him – but he had hardly seen his father before his death in 1915 and he saw his mother infrequently. When he did she swamped him in attention. Hugh Berrington, in assessing Iremonger's work, concluded:

> It is easy to find fault with Mrs Iremonger's book. Her statistics are marred by error and, like most commentators in this field, she exploits every ambiguous report or equivocal event in a way to favour her own hypothesis. Yet these shortcomings must be set against her considerable achievement. She has shown for the first time in a systematic way the extraordinary degree to which the highest political office in Britain has, paradoxically, summoned to it men who might by temperament have been deemed to be singularly unfitted to bear some of its burdens ... political candidacy at this level draws towards it men who are exceptional both in their high abilities and in their strong needs.[31]

Sam grew up into a man with enormous ability and highly developed needs: in this he was not untypical of those who reach the top of Disraeli's greasy pole.

Until he reached Oxford, although generally said to have been a pleasant and friendly child, he was often alone; as a result his character combined a deep self-reliance with a need for company and for fun. At times in his life the quiet, self-contained and determined aspects of his character predominated and he could appear austere, distant and something of a pedant. On such occasions the part of his inner self that had been made hard and resilient in his youth came through. Upon this foundation were laid the expectations and strictures of Winchester and, later, a certain driven quality in dealing with all tasks, however mundane, with equal energy. The other compartment was the side that had been indulged as the youngest child on the visits from his parents – the side of his character that was to discover dancing and seek out fun with the same energy with which he could redraft a speech. That the two sides remained separate, and that in the main he kept apart the people who appealed to the two sides for much of his life, was not an accident; it was a consequence of his childhood.

The public and private kept separate, the emotional and the analytical divided: Gaitskell's growth as a politician, as a communicator and, perhaps, as a person was shaped by the way in which the

11

cool, detached, pedantic man influenced by Winchester and a lonely adolescence increasingly let in, or could not prevent, the warm, passionate, intimate man formed in reaction against these experiences – the way in which the emotion pushed its way through into the public persona. While it is easy to identify these sides to his character, and the evidence for them is plentiful, connecting them to particular elements in his life is more difficult. He had a conventional upper-middle-class upbringing but suffered the early death of his father. He developed at an early age considerable self-reliance, in turn enhanced by his experience at a public school he did not like but which had a strong set of standards and values. He idealised his brother Arthur, following him to school and college, competing with him and emulating him until he developed an independent personality.

He was also Sam, the youngest son, with a deeply emotional mother who smothered him in love on her visits to England and then remarried after the death of his father. It would not stretch our tolerance of psychoanalysis from a distance to say that this left him with a deep need for affection and a corresponding ability to give it, but that his school then tried to train affection and warmth out of him through the classic English public school emotional lobotomy of a loving child; yet what effect did this have? It resulted in the unique combination of private charisma, courage and intense emotion, and the public attempt to control all these feelings and behaviour as a Wykehamist should. He left Winchester in 1924 – the year of the first minority Labour government – a fairly typical, and typically confused, product of his social background.

As with Winchester, Gaitskell's career at Oxford started under something of a personal cloud when again he failed to win a scholarship; he was offered an exhibition at Hertford but refused, preferring to follow his brother and father and countless generations of Wykehamists to New College.

Hugh now felt the freedom from the constraints of school opening up before him and, with a little money of his own, he set about having fun.[32] His ambitions at this stage amounted to no more than winning a golf blue. It was at Oxford, though, that he made a number of friendships that were to be of lasting importance, the most significant being with Evan Durbin. There is a remarkable similarity to the careers of Durbin and Gaitskell, which underpinned many shared attitudes and beliefs. Durbin came up to New College in the same term as Hugh, but took a first degree in zoology and left Oxford two years after him. Both trained as economists, served on the wartime home front and were elected MPs in 1945. They were, though, very different characters. Durbin was the son of a Baptist minister and planned to become a minister too, but 'Socialism became his earthly mission'. Frank Pakenham, later Lord Longford, who was also at New College at this time and was on the same staircase as Durbin, recalled him making a big impression because he was a socialist: 'I remember Evan Durbin saying to me, "Man, have you ever been hungry?" '[33]

Durbin represented the characteristics of moral certainty and the fringes of theology; Pakenham, then a Conservative, was also a pillar of what we might call the moral majority of the college. They were neither hearties nor aesthetes, but earnest young men who took themselves and their degrees seriously. Gaitskell became more like them as his university career developed. Initially, however, he set about having fun with all the stubborn determination and self-discipline that he was later to apply to getting a First. However, on balance, university sustained the process of emotional repression that was to continue until the last decade of his life, when he rediscovered fun.

He was not yet a socialist but had developed an awareness, somewhat dim and often obscured by golf, of the social problems in British society. In his first two years at Oxford he combined pursuing a golf blue, reading Lawrence and Proust and moving in a fast, fashionable and predominantly homosexual set – which included Maurice Bowra, John Sparrow, John Betjeman and W. H. Auden – with a gradually increasing intellectual horizon and close friendships with a serious, often socialist and academic set which included Evan Durbin and later the leading Oxford socialists of the age, George Douglas Howard (G. D. H.) Cole and Margaret Cole. In his final year Gaitskell shared a house with two Conservatives, Frank Pakenham and Roger Nickalls. In later years Nickalls reminded Pakenham of Gaitskell's tremendous sense of right and wrong: 'I had forgotten it really, but it didn't strike me, he seemed like other undergraduates – very nice, very popular – but Nickalls remembered that he used to say, "It's not right." In 1952 Nickalls heard Gaitskell say, "It's not fair", on the radio; it reminded him of Hugh at Oxford.'

Gaitskell became increasingly rebellious as he rejected the lifestyle and many of the values of his family. He experimented intellectually and sexually but always retained a strong sense of self and the ability to move with ease in different kinds of circles. His personal experience of liberation from school was mirrored in the dominant philosophy and social trends of the time. This was the 1920s, the jazz age, the outpouring of a generation emerging from war; it was also the age of the Vienna School of logical positivism – the pursuit of truth and answers based on rationality – all of which had a powerful influence on the young Gaitskell. As he later wrote, 'It was a brief, blessed interval when the lives of the young were neither overshadowed by the consequences of the last war nor dominated by the fear of a future one.'[34]

Gaitskell never belonged to any group or set exclusively, enjoying the atmosphere of the salon around Maurice Bowra as well as the company of Pakenham and Durbin. Through Bowra he met W. H. Auden and John Sparrow, renewed his friendship with John Betjeman, and met a Maryland undergraduate, Jim Orrick, whom he took for long walks as a cure for being too much of an aesthete. The avant-garde fashion at Oxford was homosexuality. Many years later Ann Fleming, the society hostess and wife of Ian Fleming, the creator of James Bond, described a reunion of aesthetes from Gaitskell's time at Oxford:

> I have had one dinner-party enjoyed by no one except me. John Sparrow, – and Hugh Gaitskell read Yeats aloud, they all sat in a row holding hands because in early life they loved each other in the same set . . . Ian arrived in the middle, very intoxicated . . . he temporarily silenced the eminent 'homos', they did not look pleased. The Duke and Duchess of Devonshire were very bored and went home.[35]

Perhaps Gaitskell experimented sexually. A friend from those days certainly thought that he did, and there is a legend that John Betjeman once asked if he could touch Hugh's bottom, to which Hugh replied, 'Oh well, if you must.' However, it is more likely that, because he was affectionate and unstuffy, people naturally assumed he was bisexual or gay. Aside from the particular sexual experiences he had at this time, two characteristics stand out. First, he loved his friends with a commitment and strength that was unusual, and there was certainly an element of homo-eroticism in these feelings and in this Oxford world. Second, this intensity of feeling was also a reaction against his upbringing. It is significant as part of his general rebellion, which was to culminate in his conversion to socialism, that he was attracted by whatever was unconventional at the time.

As he worked out his ideas, he rejected the existence of God and organised religion and embraced the ideas of the Vienna School. In 1927 he wrote to his mother:

> I think sentimentality is implied in any kind of strong belief whether it be religion, patriotism, socialism, or any thing like that – forcing oneself to believe things for fear of living with no beliefs, I suppose I'm just the same in believing in the truth only.[36]

After this dramatic rejection of all systems other than 'the truth', Gaitskell later developed a strong faith in two out of the three 'isms' he had rejected as an undergraduate; what did not return was a belief in God or organised religion. At Oxford he also began a lifelong habit of trying to improve people. Elizabeth Longford met him in the third term of her first year at Oxford. She was living next door to his first cousin, Audrey Townsend, at Lady Margaret Hall and they got on immediately. Gaitskell introduced her to 'all sorts of very exciting people'. She remembers him as a born teacher, keen to introduce her to all his passions. However, before becoming friends she had to pass a special test. He asked what she thought of Oscar Wilde and she, in saying that she loved his work, gave the right response. Later he told her that if she had given the wrong answer he would have dropped her. But his tendency to keep separate the different parts of his life meant that he never talked about politics with her. Elizabeth remarked that he had little

> to do with my political education but what he did was quite enough. He was a real teacher, he liked instructing people and getting them more sensible . . . he was very delicate: he never suggested that we should sleep together – in those days people never did or rarely – he once suggested that we should get engaged to be married in order to be able to see each other without other people interfering, but that was the only reason he gave. I can see now that would have been inhuman and he must have thought this was a good strategy. I was told afterwards that when we went to Paris in a little group for fun one weekend he was going to propose to me but it all went wrong and he never did.[37]

Though the romance never really came off, the friendship flourished, and remained close until his death.

Gaitskell's great concern was with authenticity of experience; he despised any sort of dramatising of emotion or argument and frequently deplored sentimentality. Any remark that did not measure up to his view of what constituted 'strict reality' he would pounce

15

on. 'He gave practical advice as to how to live.' He also enjoyed a healthy diet of fine food and wine and above all sought lively conversation. As Bowra remembered:

> He was drawn to people with lively minds and an active taste for living, and he was never at home with the solemn or the pompous. Nor in the last resort was he much interested in the subtler refinements of psychology. For him there was quite enough to be done with ordinary human beings without troubling about such enquiries.[38]

Gradually, as Oxford engaged his mind as much as his other appetites, he studied harder. Pakenham and he were both reading Modern Greats – a new and at the time adventurously contemporary combination of politics, philosophy and economics. They were tutored together by H. K. Salvensen and engaged in lively debates. History essays were written for H. A. L. Fisher, and 'the treatment was competent, high-minded and far from radical.'[39]

While Gaitskell was still in the Bowra circle and enjoying the reading and life of an Oxford he later described as 'gay, frivolous, stimulating and tremendously alive', events in the wider world were about to have a major impact and pull him more towards Durbin. The syndicalist turn in trade union politics, inspired in part by the Bolshevik Revolution, reached its climax and its eclipse between 3 and 12 May 1926. For this brief moment some in the industrial wing of the labour movement became intoxicated with the syndicalist notion of taking over capitalism by means of strike action and for the only time in its history the British trade union movement attempted a general strike. As the events unfolded on the national stage, Gaitskell was unusually susceptible to the influence of the flourishing of militancy that so quickly withered on government intransigence and the TUC's mistrust of the whole idea. In the period immediately before, he had been reading R. H. Tawney, Sidney and Beatrice Webb, Karl Marx, J. A. Hobson and Hugh Dalton. The mixture of ideas gleaned from them and his natural favouring of the underdog pushed him on to the side of the miners and made him a lifelong democratic socialist. The nature of the long-term impact of the strike, like the events of 1931, was somewhat obscured by the initial burst of enthusiasm. The genuine emotion in his response was also characteristic: 'The impact of the strike was sharp and sudden, a little like a war, in that everybody's lives were suddenly affected by a new unprecedented situation, which forced us to abandon plans for pleasure, to change our values and adjust our priorities. Above all we had to make a choice. And how we chose was a clear test of our political outlook.' For some, like John Betjeman, it was a great lark; but for Gaitskell it was a defining experience and entirely shifted his priorities: Lord Longford remembers him saying at the time, 'I doubt if I will ever play golf again.'[40]

In early 1926, Gaitskell was becoming more interested in politics and was already intent on teaching people to be aware of the injustices of the world: one Oxford friend remembers him as 'set on improving the human race, beginning with me'; another remembers his clear sense of right and wrong, and a third his natural egalitarianism. Thus, when the general strike broke, the combination of the emotional force of the miners' case, his ability to drive very fast for the Trades Union Congress and his proud declaration to an aunt, 'My future is with the working class', was almost irresistible. Though he ultimately rejected the strike, syndicalism and guild socialism (the more moderate version of workers combining to take over capitalism industry by industry) as anti-rational movements that would lead nowhere – the general strike was eventually, to him, the last spark of a firework that went off in 1921 when the wave of industrial unrest had begun – the events were important in bringing to a head a number of strands in his slowly maturing personality. He was not born a socialist but he chose socialism and in turn socialism allowed him to combine features of his character successfully; it gave him an identity that liberated him from his family and his class, while combining strong rational arguments for change with strong emotional attachments and moral certainty that his cause was just; and it offered the possibility of a secular life of service to others.

But initially he contemplated helping the government. He wrote to his mother on 5 May 1926:

> I finally decided on not enlisting in the Govt Volunteers when the Govt abruptly broke off all negotiations . . . & in fact practically declared war on the strikers . . . If one joins the Govt, be it only originally to maintain supplies, one is pretty well under orders & if things develop . . . it would be difficult to get out of what will practically be an Army. Anyway I have offered my services through the University Labour Club to the Trades Union people in Oxford.[41]

He turned up at Douglas and Margaret Cole's house and offered to help:

17

What could I do? Precious little. Speak to meetings? God forbid [!!].
Organize? Absolutely no experience. Had I got a car? No. Could I by
any chance drive a car? Yes, I had learnt the year before. Then perhaps
I could drive John Dugdale's . . . as he was taking Schools in a few weeks
he could not spare much time.[42]

They got him a union card – it is not clear but he seems to have
joined the Labour Party at this point as well – and he became the
Coles' driver, 'competent' but 'with a disconcerting speed at corners'.
They were most exciting days. The main task was to drive between
London and Oxford carrying messages and text for the strike papers.
The village of Benson – halfway between Henley and Oxford on
the London road – had nine right-angled bends, and Gaitskell had
to take them all at speed to get back into New College before it
closed; he could not afford to be gated. Once they had to wait
for the papers from the TUC and called on Tawney at his flat in
Mecklenburgh Square in London. While Hugh did the washing up,
Tawney, in his sergeant's jacket, schemed with Margaret Cole. Then
on to Clement's Inn to collect an editorial for the *Lansbury Labour
Weekly* from the journalist Aylmer Vallance. Then back to collect
Will Thorne of the General Workers' Union from Eccleston Square
and take him to the House of Commons. Gaitskell was introduced
to the labour movement in the space of a few frantic days.

After the general strike, Gaitskell got down to serious work and
chose G. D. H. Cole's special subject of the labour movement for
his extended essay, published some years later by the Workers' Educational Association. It provides a snapshot of Gaitskell's beliefs in
his early twenties. His writing is clear and has an underlying passion
that traces a radical ancestry from the 1780s through to the Chartist
movement. The aristocracy and the factory owners are the villains;
the people – Tom Paine and William Godwin, and the middle-class
radicals William Cobbett and Henry Hunt – the heroes. Although
there is a certain admiration for the working-class radicals, the conclusions reject revolution in favour of a moderate policy based on
an alliance between classes.

> The success of the middle class alliance depended on the acceptance by
> the working class element of middle class leadership and middle class
> ideas. To begin with, a moderate policy, and probably one which did
> not go so far as the Charter was essential . . . in a revolution the chances
> would have been tremendously against the rebels. To begin with every
> swing to the left lost them support in the country. It was not only the

middle class who feared bloodshed . . . Chartism, in its beginning the last and most violent protest of the new proletariat, reveals in its conclusion the triumph of a new bourgeoisie.[43]

The years after the essay on Chartism was written saw the Wall Street crash, rising unemployment and political extremism. Gaitskell responded by advocating the class struggle. This was in part because he had been searching in vain for an economic alternative to capitalism. He was never very much at home with Marxism, and though he defended the Soviet Union to his friend Evan Durbin – who was always bitterly opposed – he could not reconcile the Marxist approach to the central importance he gave to the individual. In the *Chartism* essay he had written, 'If the temper behind a political agitation is almost revolutionary, we may be sure that, until human nature has changed a great deal, there are economic grievances in the background which the achievement of the immediate political aim is expected to remove.' These grievances were those much more of the individual than of the class; individual fulfilment was the only way, he argued to Cole, that a sustained change in the nature of capitalism could be achieved. It was the principle that the government could intervene to stimulate demand and thereby reduce unemployment contained in Keynesian economics which gradually through the 1930s gave him the economic ideas that he believed could eradicate collective economic injustice and provide individual fulfilment. Despite his belief in the importance of the individual, he retained, for the rest of his life, a basic faith in the ability of the state to act; thus his individualism was of a very particular kind.

Along with writing about Chartism, Gaitskell got down to hard work. He kept up some of his social activity from the first two years but now concentrated on his studies; he set out to get a First and attached himself to G. D. H. Cole. Cole appreciated him for three main reasons: first because of his command of English, 'a quality still, alas, not over-common among economists'[44] – he was, Cole said, the only student who could write properly; second, because he was generally interested in culture; and, third, because he would argue back. Working regular hours and making no secret of his ambition, he achieved a good First in an unexceptional year. Just after the general strike had ended he visited an aunt in Cheltenham and all the excitement of the previous days crystallised as he contemplated his future: '3 days at Cheltenham made me quite convinced that I must make up my own mind about my life. It's too absurd to think of just doing what people of 70 or so want you to do.'

He wrote to his mother that if his interest in politics lasted he would try to get some sort of job with the Workers' Educational Association: 'I should be more useful there than anywhere else.'[45] Dining with Cole in Soho after graduating, he was offered either the chance to write a life of the Chartist leader, Feargus O'Connor, or a job with the WEA in the Nottinghamshire coalfield. Despite violent rows with his mother, who wanted him to go to India in the Indian Civil Service, he jumped at the chance of the WEA job.[46]

Gaitskell's time in Nottingham, from the summer of 1927 until the autumn of 1928, provided a depth to his experience and confirmed his social as well as political rebellion against his family and class. But it also made him see perhaps more clearly that the life he had led at Oxford was not all that he thought it was. Elizabeth Longford remembers him coming to see her after he had moved to Nottingham and admitting that the Oxford of 'Maurice Bowra, John Betjeman, Harold Acton – all this group that had seemed to him so glamorous – had lost its charm because now he thought he was in real politics through going to Nottingham.'[47]

With his family scattered around the world, and finding many of his Oxford friends increasingly unsatisfactory, Gaitskell looked to two slightly older men as father figures and friends; it was a pattern that was to be repeated. The first was George Martelli, who had been in the navy; Gaitskell congratulated him when he left. 'Hugh looked on him as extremely sophisticated and mature compared with himself',[48] and it was Martelli, Frank Longford thinks, who introduced Gaitskell to one of his enduring interests, the writings of D. H. Lawrence. The second figure who became a firm friend in Nottingham was an unemployed miner called George Keeling. Together they wrote Gaitskell's first published article on conditions in the coalfield and Keeling watched this rather affected Oxford undergraduate grow into a socialist. He told Philip Williams that the shy youth who had arrived in Nottingham 'was almost unrecognisable when he went back to London ... as if he [came] seeking something, and now he had found something to fight for'. Both these men, along with the miners whom Gaitskell travelled around the county to teach, became vitally important symbols to him of the class to which he had decided to dedicate his political allegiance. But they also satisfied his hunger for straight talking, for authenticity and a clear and unambiguous identity, which he felt was lacking in the Oxford of Maurice Bowra. As he wrote to his brother, the miners were 'the nicest sort of people – indeed I like very much all the working people I have met . . . more honest and natural than the Middle Class who are always trying to be something they aren't & who are never quite sure whether they are saying the right thing.'[49]

The experience of teaching the working class confirmed Gaitskell in his political convictions but the discovery of the directness and bluntness of the Nottinghamshire miners did not lead him to ape any working-class characteristics. Gaitskell was always self-evidently from the 'Top Drawer'; he did not patronise the people he met by adopting their accents or modes of expression – something which endeared him to the Notts miners and, later, his constituents in South Leeds. Yet in his first tentative steps he also encountered conservatism among the working class. After a talk in which he rambled on about his ideas on truth, emotion, sentimentality, religion, morality and sex, six questioners attacked him for talking irreligious nonsense.[50]

Beyond the realm of politics, he was also discovering the benefits of the freedom of his own flat. On one of his trips to Brancaster while an undergraduate Gaitskell discovered what would become a lifelong passion – dancing – and achieved his greatest sporting success by winning the Prince of Wales golf cup at the Royal West Norfolk Golf Club. In Nottingham the golf was replaced by tennis but the dancing continued at his characteristically frantic pace. With the dancing came his first mature encounters with women.

He seems to have had a considerable success, and it is not hard to imagine the kind of figure he cut. He was never a very handsome man but he was always great fun; and in Nottingham at this time, with his background, accent and position, he must have presented a somewhat exotic figure. There were a string of girlfriends, whom he took for long walks and to his rather squalid flat in the centre of town; he worried in a letter to his brother that his 'existence here is becoming too much sex without the essential intellect'.[51] But after a while he settled into a steady relationship. The woman was a 'very nice Notts girl' and for a time they lived together. Bearing in mind that chaperons had not entirely disappeared from Oxford and that Gaitskell had suggested engagement to Elizabeth so they could be alone, the freedom of this lifestyle was a wonderful release for him.

The relationship, however, did not continue for long, once Gaitskell returned to London.

Based in the extramural department at Nottingham University, he despised the institutional conservatism of the university and the stuffiness of his colleagues, but he loved his WEA teaching. Speaking to a hall full of working and unemployed miners was utterly different from his attempts at teaching his fellow undergraduates. He learned to make his material accessible and relevant and also to speak in public. He already had well-developed debating techniques; he was already skilled at explaining and analysing, but lecturing to the WEA students taught him how to think on his feet and deal with direct and pointed questioning. He greatly enjoyed the experience, though it served to accentuate the somewhat romanticised and almost abstract view he had of the working class. He was described at this time as a William Morris socialist, and one could sum up his time in Nottingham as fulfilling the Morris side of his politics at work and the D. H. Lawrence side of his emotions at play. For the rest of his life he looked back on the year in Nottingham as a sort of national service in socialism and on his affairs with a certain wistfulness; when a Minister he once wondered why his Nottinghamshire lover did not write to him.

While Nottingham was important and marks a key stage in his political and emotional development, it was also simply a stepping stone. Gaitskell was rarely ambitious in a blatant or underhand way; he was often very open and straight about his intentions. He was, nevertheless, highly ambitious for himself and for his newly acquired set of beliefs. Nottingham could be no more than a stepping stone if he was genuinely serious about making a difference and about being independent from his family and his background. For all its earthy pleasures, Nottingham was a small provincial town dominated by the coalfield; it was not at the centre of things. As the new decade approached, the speed and extent of change in the world of politics and economics, the greater social fluidity and the dim beginnings of foreboding combined to push Gaitskell towards London. Moreover, Gaitskell was essentially a metropolitan figure; despite his avowed disapproval of the Oxford scene, he had continued to attend Bowra's dinner parties and to travel to London. He wrote to his brother: 'I see tremendous danger of stagnating here . . . I went to London a few days ago. The difference is quite remarkable – there is so much more vigour and better taste and better intelligence and more personality in the atmosphere.'[52] But he was torn between the pleasure of life in Nottingham and the urge to settle into a proper career. He wrote to his mother:

> Also I shall probably not become an Academic for (a) I dislike the academics and their attitude and their bourgeoisieness (b) I am likely to continue my association with the Labour movement, I have seen enough of Working Class conditions, industrial war and Class war here to make it probable that on and off through my life . . . I shall be taking part in the Working Class movement . . . The point is that the London job is a means not an end. I shall work hard and learn and learn and learn and teach a little . . . and then perhaps gradually move with Journalism and Politics.[53]

When he had gone up to Oxford the atmosphere had been remarkably open as the shadow of the First World War receded. The aesthetic climate, the irreverence and the frivolity placed an emphasis on feelings and genuineness of experience, but the nature of the experience seemed increasingly banal to Gaitskell. He enjoyed the first couple of years and never lost the capacity for pleasure, even a little hedonism. But his initial searching for authentic experience through the Bowra group did not satisfy him. After the general strike, with the national and international situation darkening, he followed his beliefs to Nottingham. There the search for authenticity was realised in the working-class people he encountered and the frivolity was further buried.

The nature of Hugh Gaitskell's birth and early life raises the question: are democratic socialists born or are they made? If they are born then Gaitskell had an inauspicious start. He was not altogether unusual in this respect: Attlee and Dalton both came from backgrounds with as much privilege; others in the Labour Party, on both left and right, had backgrounds with even more. Does birth determine one's right to be a socialist? At least one of Gaitskell's schoolfriends remembers him as a natural egalitarian. Despite his class, despite his upbringing, or perhaps, like Dalton, in revolt against his upbringing and his class, Gaitskell became a socialist. The point is that he could have gone in a number of different directions from this beginning.

The motivations and influences that made people like Gaitskell socialists are complex. For a Nye Bevan or a George Brown, democratic socialism was a route out of poverty, by way of a trade union. The labour movement – trade unions, the Workers' Educational

Association and the Labour Party – was the social cradle of a community, which was a fixed place in time and class: a Welsh mining village, an East End street. But there was much in that phrase that Nye Bevan used about the grown-up Gaitskell, that 'he was young in the movement', which was in essence true. He did not come from a mining village or an East End street. There are many tales of journeys from slums to the Palace of Westminster, journeys involving the acquisition of intellectual and cultural gifts and the pursuit of political office and fame. There are fewer tales of the journey from a position of privilege to the leadership of a working-class movement. Some features of his childhood might lend themselves to being seen as foundations of a socialist character, but they might also have led in other directions. Gaitskell was a socialist who was made and not born: he chose the Labour Party.

2

An Unorthodox Academic,
1928–1939

If Dora were free I'd marry her.

Gaitskell, 1933

The only way to combat fascism was to stand firmly by
democracy.

Gaitskell, 1934

There will be a war and we shall win it in the end.

Gaitskell, 1938

Of all the areas of central London, the university district has perhaps
changed the least in character if not in appearance since the 1930s.
University College, London (UCL), where Gaitskell arrived in the
autumn of 1928, is situated in the heart of the district, adjacent to
the Union and the Senate House Library and the British Museum.
The imposing architecture and interior courtyards give UCL, alone
of all the London colleges save King's, the feel of an Oxford college.
Gaitskell came to a tiny economics department, overshadowed in
the capital by the London School of Economics (LSE), which Hugh
Dalton had done so much to build up, and in the country by the
Cambridge of John Maynard Keynes.

Gaitskell was initially a little reluctant to take up the London post.
Noel Hall had asked A. J. Jenkinson, one of Gaitskell's examiners,
to recommend someone as an assistant lecturer in the economics
department. Jenkinson suggested he see Gaitskell. They arranged
lunch in Charlotte Street and Hall offered Gaitskell the job. The
young WEA lecturer now had doubts about the appeal of London.
He considered staying another year and enjoying the freedom of
Nottingham but his old warden at New College, H. A. L. Fisher,
warned him not to stay too long in Nottingham; then his old economics tutor, Lionel Robbins, and his mentor, G. D. H. Cole, also

25

urged him to take the post. Not surprisingly he took the advice of Fisher, the most famous liberal historian of the age, Robbins, one of the most influential economists of the time, and Cole, the leading socialist intellectual of the day, and became a lecturer at UCL.

He wrote to his brother, 'I am quite aware that I have no exceptional ability so that there really is no reason why I should be successful . . . But I want vitality.'[1] The move to London was crucial in giving him access to this 'vitality' and connecting him with the means to achieve something for his beliefs. Most important of all, it brought Gaitskell into regular contact with Hugh Dalton.

Gaitskell had first met Hugh Dalton while he was in Nottingham. Dalton found him 'very emphatic and delightfully unrespectful. He was out to change society from top to bottom. He was against all privilege and social injustice.'[2] In turn Dalton impressed fellow economist Nicholas Davenport as towering over lesser mortals. 'When seated,' said Davenport of Dalton, 'his great bald dome dominated the table, and when he was plied with good wine his talk became lively and amusing, but he always boomed.'[3] The two Hughs renewed their acquaintance later through Dalton's student contemporary Eileen Power. 'During the 1930s Dalton's circle of political friends moved away from his own generation. This was partly because there were few leading Labour contemporaries whose company he enjoyed; partly because of his emotional preference for young men; and partly because, early in the decade, he encountered a group of particularly able and stimulating political aspirants who looked to him for guidance.' Indeed, 'he made a hobby and a crusade of seeking out, encouraging and nurturing the socialist leaders of the future.'[4] At a dinner party in 1930, Dalton and Tawney were matched by Eileen Power with Gaitskell and Durbin. Michael Postan, who was also present, remembered having to defend himself from the Dalton 'boom' after the two young economists had left: 'why had they been hoarding these charming young socialists?'[5]

Dalton now took them up and introduced them to other young economists and to the XYZ Club. The key circle comprised Hugh Gaitskell, Evan Durbin, who was at the LSE, Colin Clark, who was also an economist, and John Wilmot, victor of a by-election in Fulham in 1933. The LSE and Cambridge were two opposing citadels of economic approaches. What was the difference in this great economic debate? Some have seen the young economists of the XYZ Club as the first Keynesians. Indeed Colin Clark, one of the

XYZ group, played a walk-on part in the debates that raged around the writing of Keynes's revolutionary 'general theory' when he helped Richard Kahn with his work on a central item, 'the multiplier',[6] whilst James Meade fed the Labour Party's think tank, the Fabian Research Bureau, with information on the debates.[7] Others maintain that they were in fact too influenced by Dalton's rather more conventional theories. The difference was in the role of the state: for Keynes the question was not ownership and control but effective monetary policy to manage demand; Dalton's main insight was somewhat different in character.

Writing in 1956, Gaitskell heaped praise on his old master's achievement. He credits Dalton with identifying the importance of the question of differences of distribution of wealth between persons rather than between factors of production.[8] Dalton's first book – *The Inequality of Incomes in Modern Communities* - published in 1920, Gaitskell observed,

reflects both the influence of modern economic teaching and his own concern with practical reforms. Like Professor Tawney, he vigorously attacked the traditional arguments in defence of inequality, especially those put forward by some of his fellow economists. But his main contributions in this book were first a most penetrating analysis of the causes of the distribution of income, secondly his concentration on the distribution of income between persons – in contrast with the distribution between 'factors of production' i.e. labour, capital and land – thirdly the emphasis which he rightly placed upon the significance of inheritance, and finally his suggestion for reducing inequality by fiscal policy ... As we have seen, earlier Socialist writers had been inclined to base their criticism of capitalism on the nature of the payments made, on the wrongness of rent, interest and profits as such, which they thereby treated as the cause of inequality, rather than in any analysis of why one man got more than another. To the Marxists who believed that society was rigidly divided into classes, between those who had property, and those who had to work for wages, the distinction did not matter much. And revolutionaries who desired to overthrow the system at a single blow and abolish private property in the means of production altogether, did not need to bother with the details of distribution between persons ... The Classical economists, equally absorbed with the problem of how in a competitive individualistic economy the level of rent, wages and interest came to be settled, had neglected the question of personal distribution, perhaps because it was not 'economics' as then understood, perhaps because subconsciously they disliked an inquiry which might challenge one of the basic

27

assumptions of their system – the right of inheritance. The one notable exception was John Stuart Mill, whose outlook became more and more socialist, and whose discussion of inherited wealth was described by Mr Dalton, as 'his most important contribution to economic thought'.[9]

Beyond the detailed assessment of the advances that he felt Dalton had made, Gaitskell also summed up something of the approach to economics that was to characterise the main contribution of the young Labour economists:

> to a modern economist who understood the nature of the pricing system, who was not hopelessly prejudiced against a market economy as such, who realised that the class structure was a great deal more complicated than the Marxists supposed, who was nevertheless shocked by the social and economic injustice which he saw around him, but being a democrat wished to proceed gradually to remove them, to such a man the realistic analysis of why some individuals were richer than other individuals was of great importance.

However, Dalton's economic outline was always open to influence and, though stubborn about his own achievements, he was also open to new ideas. Durbin and Gaitskell's influence in this period was mainly in their ability to bring Keynes's ideas to the attention of people like Dalton and to cut through some of the personal and professional rivalry that poisoned relations between Cambridge, London and Oxford.

It was in these years at UCL that Gaitskell came to know Hugh Dalton well. Gaitskell was Dalton's most successful protégé. From Gaitskell's point of view it was encouraging to have the backing of such an eminent socialist, but Dalton also offered a male figure whom Gaitskell could approach for emotional as well as political support.

Elizabeth Durbin, in her analysis of the making of the democratic socialist approach to economic policy in the 1930s, has written that the combination of new economics and the depression 'raised fundamental questions about the role of the Labour Party, for it seemed as though the only choice was between capitulation to the market forces of capitalism or preparation for drastic take-over of the economic system'.[10] It is impossible to over-emphasise the significance of this dilemma for the democratic socialists. Not only was the economic fate of the class they sought to represent threatened but also the democratic means they cherished seemed for a moment inadequate to the task they faced. For many this led to an embrace of communism, or communistic strategies, and for the young at Oxford it was a reflex response as much as anything else. As Denis Healey has written: 'Almost any undergraduate who wanted to stop Hitler was then easy game for the Communists.'[11] Yet some already equated the fascist and the communist regimes, as did Christopher Mayhew, later a close colleague and friend of Gaitskell, who fought a battle against the communists, and what he still termed the fellow travellers in 1991, by establishing a democratic Labour club.

In the grown-up Labour Party the battle was joined for the dominance of the rump left by the débâcle of 1931. In the struggle to articulate an alternative there is what Ben Pimlott has called the other side of the 'Red Decade': 'While Cambridge Apostles dreamed of revolution and joined Stalin's secret service, their Oxford equivalents planned to transform capitalism, and helped to bring about a revolution in socialist thought.'[12] It was an intellectual battle which the democrats began at a considerable disadvantage.

Keynes's theories were beginning to trickle out; in America, F. D. Roosevelt's election in 1932 brought some glimpses of the alternative, but the New Deal was slow in coming. The battle was between those, like Harold Laski, bewitched by 'the profoundest historical forces that have affected any people since the French Revolution',[13] and those who felt that there was little to choose between the two forms of totalitarianism: the real issue for them was the survival of democracy. On the one hand were those such as John Strachey who reacted against the events of 1931 by condemning the democratic labour movements: 'By a tragic paradox, at the very moment when socialism has been securely established on the face of the earth for the first time in history, and when the conditions of human life in the rest of the world cry aloud for the socialist solution, some of the oldest and most powerful socialist movements, such as the British, have allowed themselves to become confused, to lose direction and so to slacken their efforts to produce a living realisation of the necessity of social change in the minds of men.'[14] On the other hand were those, like Gaitskell and Dalton, who tried to rebuild the Labour Party on a firmer set of specific policy positions. For Gaitskell the events of 1931 created a crisis within democratic strategies, not a crisis of the democratic strategy. Gaitskell was first and foremost a party loyalist who did not believe that there was an alternative to the Labour Party.

Under the guidance of Dalton, Gaitskell was thrown into the

29

thick of the reconstruction of Labour economic policy. He concentrated on combating ignorance of the operation of the City of London, assessing the relevance of economic planning and politicising the emerging Keynesian analysis. It was real politics on a higher level and a more interesting stage than the politics of the Nottinghamshire coalfield. Dalton's star had risen with the divisions of 1931, and his central role in the web of committees, formal groupings and informal networks that developed in the 1930s also gave Gaitskell an increasingly central role. However, Evan Durbin and another young Winchester and Oxford economist, Douglas Jay, had a greater direct impact on the development of ideas – Jay through his 1937 book *The Socialist Case* and Durbin through numerous articles and pamphlets brought together in *The Politics of Democratic Socialism*, published in 1940.

The informal side of this life was fun, and Durbin initially took the lead. Durbin was meticulous about money. (He kept neat and detailed accounts of his income and expenditure from 1929 until his death, and he even drew a graph based on these figures to show gross and regular income and expenditure. In 1941–2 he recorded an illness which cost him £35; in 1931–2 he spent £15 on his wedding and £35 on his honeymoon – although top of his list of extras was election, £10.[15]) In 1931, in order to supplement his income as an academic, he persuaded friends to invest in 'Bogey's Bar, a small café in the basement of the Royal Hotel, just off Russell Square'. Durbin had been impressed by Colin Clark's success at supplementing his income from pig farming and was setting out to do the same with the café. The partnership lasted about five years and, although they never made a profit, the location, about five minutes from Gaitskell's flat on Great Ormond Street, down the road from Durbin's and within easy walking distance of UCL and the LSE, made it an ideal place to meet and talk. As Elizabeth Durbin records: 'Sir Michael Postan recalled going there for a series of gatherings organized by Hugh and Evan in 1931 to discuss the economics of a socialist society, some of which were attended by James Meade and Roy Harrod.'[16]

Just north of Russell Square, on Mecklenburgh Square, lived Michael Postan and Eileen Power, whose flat acted as another centre for informal socialist discussion. 'In 1932 they formed a group to discuss the sociological and historical implications of economic problems', and it was during these sessions that Gaitskell worked through his attachment to Marxism. This brief Marxist phase is an intriguing one. In 1929 he joined the 1917 Club, 'a cheap social and political centre named after the earlier non-Bolshevik revolution' and, in 1930, with Solly Zuckerman and G. P. Wells helped found Tots and Quots, a 'small dining club of scientists and other intellectuals, many of whom were committed Marxists',[17] which met 'regularly to discuss the social aspects of scientific affairs from a broadly left-wing perspective'. Tots and Quots was reincarnated in the 1950s as the Gaitskell Group on Science, by then having lost much of its Marxist content.[18] At various times during the early 1930s, Gaitskell advocated the abolition of the House of Lords, talked much about the class struggle, and even recommended the 'liquidation' of opponents.

The three main forums for debate and drafting of policy outside the Labour Party were Cole's short-lived Society for Socialist Inquiry and Propaganda (SSIP), founded in June 1931 and lasting little more than a year, the New Fabian Research Bureau (NFRB), set up by Cole but kept separate from SSIP in March 1931, and the XYZ Club, founded in January 1932 to encourage links between the Labour Party and the City. Within the party, Hugh Dalton chaired the NEC sub-committee on Finance and Trade and in 1936 co-opted Gaitskell and Durbin on to this body. These groups in the early 1930s have been described as Low Bloomsbury, in contrast to the Edwardian and post-war Bloomsbury circles where experimentation in artistic and sexual life was based on a passionate optimism. In the moment between the ending of one war and the foreboding of the next, the old Bloomsbury spirit had a last flowering. Gaitskell's Bloomsbury was an altogether more serious affair. The times did not demand aesthetic exploration but action and the Bloomsbury of the 1930s reflected this. 'It was a world . . . of continuing discussion, of tube journeys to and from the meetings of informal groups, often in the upstairs rooms of cheaper Soho restaurants.'[19] Gaitskell loved it and flourished intellectually, politically and personally.

The most interesting and innovative of the groups in which Gaitskell became involved was the XYZ Club, also known as the City Group. Francis Williams later regarded the XYZ as the group with the greatest influence on government policy 'in the most private manner'.[20] The secrecy was necessary because the labour movement feared too close an involvement with the City and bankers, given the events of 1931, and because the City figures were frightened that association with the Labour Party might affect their careers. Yet the XYZ Club was born out of the perceived need to prevent another 1931 by educating the party in the ways of the City. Secrecy was also politically useful to Dalton, who championed XYZ, not least because their meetings were more convivial than those of some of the other groups, and because he could refer loftily to his 'experts' at meetings of the NEC of the Labour Party.[21]

The XYZ Club was founded by the banker Vaughan Berry in January 1932:

> I invited a few men to dinner to discuss the possibility of forming a small group which would meet regularly to discuss financial problems from a socialist point of view, and be ready to offer its help to the Labour Party. I was myself at that time an assistant manager of the Union Discount Company ... I had been horrified by the Labour Party's ignorance of the city machinery and their complete lack of contacts with the banking world. I felt that something must be done to break this apartheid.[22]

As he found it hard to muster City people, he invited City editors instead. The membership seems to have fluctuated but had a core of Nicholas Davenport, a columnist on the *New Statesman* who later claimed to have founded the club himself; Williamson, an accountant; Quigley, a statistician with the Central Electricity Commission; Francis Williams, City editor of the *Daily Herald*; George Strauss of Strauss & Co.; C. F. Chance, a stockbroker; John Wilmot, a Labour MP; Charles Latham, chairman of the finance committee of the London County Council (LCC); George Wansbrough, director of Robert Benson & Co.; and James Lawrie from Lloyds Bank. In 1934, at the prompting of Dalton, Durbin, Gaitskell and Jay were brought in, Gaitskell becoming the secretary. The meetings took place in private rooms, at the Craven Hotel, in members' houses or occasionally in the House of Commons. Sometimes figures from the Labour Party's headquarters at Transport House would attend, and Dalton was a frequent presence. Members would read papers and there would be lengthy debates. The XYZ was more fun than the NFRB, more 'business-like, and more urbane'.[23]

In the spring of 1929, Hugh popped into Kleinfeld's, a pub on Charlotte Street – now the Fitzroy Tavern – to refresh himself before an open-air meeting during a by-election in Marylebone. In the pub was Dora Frost. Dora was the daughter of Jewish refugees from the Bolshevik Revolution: her father, Leon Creditor, was a writer; and her mother, in typically immigrant style, pushed Dora towards a profession, trying to steer her away from English literature and towards medicine. But Dora, as she was to show time and again over the years, had immense strength of character. At eighteen she married a doctor, David Isaac Frost, securing her future, and no doubt appeasing her mother, and then took a job in publishing, pursuing her literary interests. The Frosts had a son, Raymond, who was four years old when Hugh and Dora met.

Dora and her husband maintained separate groups of friends, and Gaitskell became a member of her lively Bloomsbury set. She was also working on the by-election campaign and was an old friend of the Labour candidate Amyas Ross. Dora was small, dark and five years older than Hugh. She had joined the Labour Party at the age of sixteen and was a regular at Kleinfeld's, where she was completely at home, in contrast to Hugh who, although appearing unconventional as a don at UCL, looked like a Wykehamist among the writers and artists in Kleinfeld's. By this stage Gaitskell had overcome his aversion to psychology and, with a shared interest in Freud and in the Labour Party, he and Dora soon became friends. The sexual attraction does not seem to have been immediate. Hugh was regularly dancing late at the Cave of Harmony at the Seven Dials in Covent Garden, later the Gargoyle Club, and often spoke to friends against the institution of marriage. The Frosts took a large house on the north side of Regent's Park and Hugh rented a room there for a time before a trip to Austria. Eventually, he and Dora became lovers. It is difficult to imagine anyone further removed from Gaitskell's family and background than Dora; this, and the fact that she was a little older, made her extremely appealing to him. In 1933 he confided to Peggy Ross, 'If Dora were free I'd marry her.' Whatever other qualities Dora had, and there were many, part of her appeal to Hugh was the way she personified the rejection of his family and the constraints of his upbringing.

The atmosphere of Bloomsbury in those days was one in which many of Gaitskell's debating and analytical skills, improved in Nottingham, were further refined. Through the various groups and committees Dalton and his experts made an impact on the left inside the Labour Party.

Few were more responsible for defeating Laski's efforts in the 1930s to move Labour left than Hugh Dalton, who in his position on the National Executive Committee dominated the party's policy-making process.

Under his patronage young Oxford economists like Hugh Gaitskell, Evan Durbin and Douglas Jay were busy in NEC committees, in the New Fabian Research Bureau [NFRB] and in the XYZ Club, which brought together Labour intellectuals and city radical sympathisers, formulating the alternative vision of socialism focused on state management of a still largely capitalist economy where a public sector dominated, but run by experts not by workers. Like Keynes, these new Fabians tended to be more interested with fine-tuning prosperity than in crafting a new society based on new social, economic and, ultimately, human relationships.[24]

Elizabeth Durbin's *New Jerusalem* captures the mood of this exciting and lively period:

In crowded classrooms and leisurely senior common rooms, in stuffy committee rooms and the freezing NFRB office, in pubs and restaurants and coffee shops, in welcoming homes and country cottages, another, largely unheralded, Bloomsbury group argued out the economics and politics of democratic socialism.[25]

Gaitskell's role in this 'last great flowering of . . . intellectual discourse, of social responsibility and of collective idealism', developed slowly. Looking back from 1955 when he became Labour Party leader, it is tempting to overplay his role in these groups and accentuate the importance of his contribution. In fact, this role developed only slowly and he was in many ways less influential or well known in the 1930s than Colin Clark, Douglas Jay or Evan Durbin. Indeed it was Durbin who was often the leader and the instigator, and Gaitskell who followed. In the early 1930s Gaitskell was somewhat compromised in Dalton's eyes by his association with G. D. H. Cole and by his brief Marxist period. In contrast, Durbin had always made a comparison between the fascist and the Soviet style of politics, refusing even to join Tots and Quots or the 1917 Club because they contained too many Marxists, and had worked out a coherent theory of democratic socialism which he published in 1940; whereas Gaitskell defended the Soviet Union and published no single work of theory in his lifetime.

What is striking in Durbin's historical essays and lectures is the almost whiggishness of his interpretations of British history and the way he uses history to attack Marxism.

III Criticism of Marxist Thesis
I think the thesis is not borne out by historical evidence.
Consider this country:

(a) the transfer of economic power in England – from the landed aristocracy – to the capitalist bourgeoisie – in the struggle of 1832 (the fate of
agrarian class sealed then and consolidated in 1846).
(b) the transfer of political power – from the narrow circle enfranchised
in 1832 – to the modern universal electorate (a century to complete) –
but nevertheless a transfer of political power from class to class.
Both these transfers – not without struggle – but without bloodshed –
are a supersession of democracy.
(c) We were brought near to civil war – by the struggle over Northern
Ireland – not a class or economic issue: the economic position of English
Conservatives never in question.[26]

So Durbin argued that Marxism was wrong not because of a fault
in the logic but because the experience of the British states did not
support the conclusions of Marxism. Yet he acknowledged that 'there
is a class struggle' but thought it did not 'at all times occupy the
central causal position'. He further condemned the Marxist thesis
on the grounds that men are motivated to fight for various reasons
and not just money, and that the dictatorship of the proletariat would
in fact be dictatorship of the party machine. It was a position that
Gaitskell initially rejected, though he later decided that Durbin had
been correct all along.

The shift began when Gaitskell returned from Austria and together
with the rest of the Labour Party abandoned revolutionary rhetoric.
He had won a Rockefeller scholarship to study in Austria in 1934
and at the age of twenty-seven he fell in love with Vienna and
with the socialist movement there. He took to Viennese student life
immediately, writing to his brother, in a passage strangely reminiscent
of his view of Nottingham, 'there is probably no place in Europe
where the standard of women's looks is so high and their morals at
the same time pleasantly loose . . . so that one's path is really rather
strewn with primroses'.[27] As Hugh and Dora were by now lovers,
he confided to his brother, 'if I were not attracted to Dora or if she
were here, I should not want to go back to England.'

Behind the seductive exterior, the political situation in Vienna
was darkening. Since 1925 unemployment had been increasing and
both the National Socialist and the Socialist parties had increasingly
adopted paramilitary organisations. The Socialist Party had withdrawn from national government and established separate communities guarded by the *Schutzbund*; one of their strongholds was Vienna.
As the depression deepened the political situation worsened. On 4

March 1933 parliamentary government ended in Austria and power was concentrated in the hands of the Chancellor, Engelbert Dollfuss. That summer Gaitskell arrived for a holiday and then stayed for the following academic year to complete his Rockefeller fellowship.

In April 1933 the Dollfuss government confiscated 22 million schillings from the Socialist municipal government in Vienna. The municipality appealed to the courts, but nothing was done. Walter Citrine, the head of the British TUC, urged the British government to demand the recall of the Austrian Parliament or withhold loans. The British government refused. In the autumn the joint TUC-Labour Party National Council recommended that 'the Government should urge upon the Austrian Chancellor the due observance of the provisions of the peace treaties which guarantee freedom of association for the workers.'[28] No action was taken. Dollfuss was now resolved on removing the socialists.

On 11 February 1934 Gaitskell noticed machine-gun positions being set up in the streets of Vienna. On 12 February the socialists in Linz resisted a weapons search, the Socialist Party called a general strike, and fighting broke out in Vienna, Linz, Steyr and Upper Styria. The strike failed. Dollfuss declared martial law and artillery opened fire on the workers' flats in Vienna. The Social Democrat Party was declared illegal and 1,500 people were killed. Historian E. H. Carr, then a Foreign Office official, minuted: 'Independent Austria is dead, and the heir to her estate must be either Italy or Germany.'[29]

As soon as the bombardment ended Gaitskell went to the *Daily Herald* offices and telephoned the Coles. He arranged with them to send a Labour delegation to visit the prisoners and start collecting money for a relief and defence fund.[30] From there he escorted three socialist leaders to safety in Prague, and arranged escape routes with professional pepper smugglers and a young socialist leader, Josef Simon. Naomi Mitchison, the novelist (and wife of the Labour activitist Dick Mitchison, with whom Gaitskell stayed sometimes in Scotland) who was rather in love with him at the time, reached him in Vienna by telephone on the 23rd. He urged her to come to Vienna to see what was happening so that reports could be published in the British papers, but warned her that the situation was pretty rough and dangerous. In the diary that she kept of the whole affair, and later published, Naomi speculated on what this meant. 'I wonder what he wants me to do? I hope not anything complicated or illegal.'[31]

Naomi arrived on 25 February and Gaitskell met her from the train, bringing her to meet two socialist leaders in the lobby of a hotel. They sat whispering, afraid of being overheard – Gaitskell was regularly followed by the secret police and could have been arrested and deported at any time. He distributed the money she had brought with her. All active socialists were operating underground: 'People are constantly being arrested through the treachery of their neighbours, who betray them to the police, perhaps for pay, but mainly so that they themselves will not be arrested'. Gaitskell worked tirelessly: 'he was a leader, a counsellor, who constantly accompanied delegations into town halls and prisons. He was the organiser of innumerable secret meetings.'[32] They used the money Naomi brought from England for legal defence, drafted petitions and arranged for messages to be passed out of Austria and across Vienna. Whenever they got any sort of tip or lead they would tell the socialists in hiding to move, with the aim of preventing another comrade from being arrested or beaten up. As Naomi noted, there was an element in what they were doing which was fun – 'what a boy-scout, red-Indian business it all is'[33] – but in the main it was highly dangerous. Though an Englishman was 'almost beyond suspicion' there was always the possibility that if caught he could have incriminated others. A young Austrian socialist, Ilsa Kulscar, came across Gaitskell one day 'in his shirt sleeves, carrying a laundry-basket. "I'm turning into a stoker," he said. He was taking a load of compromising papers from [his] centrally-heated flat . . . to his former digs . . . where there were honest stoves to burn them in.'[34] On other occasions Gaitskell would wait on a street corner and a courier would pass by twice before returning to slip him a letter.[35]

By the time he left, 170 socialists had escaped through Gaitskell's network, many on false papers that he had helped to arrange and through bribes that he had paid with money from London. Articles began appearing in the British and American papers. Naomi returned to Britain in April and published her account. The labour movement responded but the battle had already been lost by the socialists waiting for the revolution. Gaitskell returned to Britain in the summer of 1934 and the steel in his character was now more evident than the boyishness. Noel Hall, his professor at UCL, remarked that you could no longer joke about politics with him. He was twenty-eight years old; in the streets of Vienna he had come of age, personally and politically.

It was an exceptional exposure to the realities of the fight against fascism and it made Gaitskell an early, consistent and passionate anti-appeaser. In reaction to the events in Austria he abandoned his former revolutionary rhetoric, and began to advocate the rearmament of the democracies in the face of fascism and a war he saw as inevitable. Austria also stamped out the last vestiges of frivolity in his character; this did not mean that he ceased to enjoy dancing or non-political conversation, but it did mean that he re-intensified his focus on politics.

Dora and Gaitskell were now deeply involved with each other. Divorce in the 1930s presented many difficulties and Gaitskell's developing political career was also a potential problem. Dora separated from her husband in 1933 but it was another four years before they could marry. In the meantime they shared a house in Harley Road, near Swiss Cottage, and Gaitskell settled down into the central relationship of his life. Dora was an active political wife and the centre of the settled family existence that he had never enjoyed and which he came slowly to appreciate: he gradually dropped his anti-domesticity rhetoric as he began to esteem family life. Eventually Dora's divorce came through and on 9 April 1937 they married at Hampstead Town Hall. Hugh was thirty-one, Dora five years older. Many of Gaitskell's family stayed away and disapproved of the marriage, partly because Dora was divorced but more, one suspects, because she was a metropolitan Jewish intellectual. The qualities that attracted Hugh were also the features that his family disapproved of. In marrying Dora, Hugh was becoming his own person and becoming secure enough in himself to leave behind gestures of rebellion. He had found his way of being, and after his marriage to Dora he no longer expressed the rather posed radicalism of his early twenties: he began to conform more, but on his own terms.

Two symbols sum up this coming to terms with himself and his family. First, he and Dora bought a cottage in the village of Milland near Hugh's mother, and, second, the radical anti-respectability, anti-bourgeois Gaitskell discovered the delights of gardening. After this the layers of a settled existence came thick and fast: their financial future was assured a year later when Hugh inherited £14,000 from an aunt. In April 1939 their first daughter, Julia, was born; three years later Cressida was born. Hugh's mother slowly came round to the marriage, the birth of the daughters no doubt helping, and later lived with Hugh and Dora. With his private life stabilising and his personality maturing, politics came back to centre stage.

He had been adopted as prospective Labour Party candidate at Chatham in 1931 while going through one of his left-wing phases: in fact the Chatham party had adopted him because he was more left-wing than either Durbin or Colin Clark. From the time of his adoption he began to make regular speeches, going to Chatham every Friday and taking part in three open-air meetings. At one regular spot he was always introduced as 'Mr Huge Gaitskell'. He was highly active with the local youth section and showed the conscientiousness and effort that were characteristic of his relations with local parties for the remainder of his career. But Chatham was a safe Conservative seat, and though Gaitskell increased the Labour vote by 2,500 at the general election of 1935 he still lost:

| Capt. L. Plugge (Con.) | 19,212 |
| H. Gaitskell (Lab.) | 13,315 |

A year or so later, George Brett, the election agent in South Leeds, realised that his sitting member was nearing retirement age. For years public meetings had taken place at Cross Flatts Park every Sunday morning – lively political debates which often led to people getting home late for lunch. Dick Mitchison, Naomi's husband, spoke at one of these in the autumn of 1936 and discovered that George needed a new MP. The result was a letter from John Parker, an MP and secretary of the NFRB, suggesting:

a. Hugh Gaitskell, a lecturer at University College, London. A first-rate speaker; the runner-up in the recent selection conference for Clay Cross. He fought Chatham in the last election. An authority on finance, foreign and colonial questions.

b. E. F. M. Durbin, a lecturer at the London School of Economics. An economist and authority on credit questions and planning. He fought Gillingham in the last election . . .

[Two others, T. Reid and Lady Noel Buxton.]

e. Dr Edith Summerskill who is a good speaker and a live and active woman. If there are many Catholics in the division, however, I should not recommend her as she is a strong advocate of birth control.[36]

George Brett and his daughter Marjorie went through the list. As there were a large number of Catholics in the constituency, that ruled out Edith Summerskill. George decided to find out more about

Gaitskell and asked Dalton when he came to speak in Leeds a month or so later. Dalton, of course, gave a highly favourable report.

As if on cue, when the Gaitskells returned from their honeymoon in April 1937, a letter was waiting from George Brett asking if they could meet. After the 1935 election Gaitskell had been a little ambivalent about his future in politics. Dora, though taking her time to develop a public role in the 1950s, was not reclusive and was independently dedicated to the party. UCL had been understanding about the election. For a moment Gaitskell had hesitated about politics; but Leeds was a different prospect to the safe Tory seats he had tried for before, so he replied:

> I am very sorry to have missed you when you were in London last week. Mr Parker will probable have told you that I was away on my honeymoon. I understand from him that you will be coming up again on 22nd May. If you have time I should be very glad to have a talk with you.

They met; Gaitskell spoke at Cross Flatts in August and George Brett became his champion in the seat. He was at a disadvantage because he was not sponsored. Because MPs were only paid a small salary many constituencies preferred candidates sponsored by trade unions, who would provide election expenses and support for the MP's work. The most powerful union in the constituency was the National Union of Railwaymen. Luckily for Gaitskell the local NUR behaved in a rather heavy-handed manner, insisting on an NUR-only short list, and the local party members asserted their independence. After an abortive selection conference because of a mistake by Brett, there were two names on the short list, Gaitskell and the NUR candidate. The meeting was packed with trade-unionists and Gaitskell won by only a couple of votes. After he had won he told them he would be donating money to party funds to keep George on. From November 1937 Gaitskell began to nurse his new constituency:

> He spoke frequently in Cross Flatts Park and at other meetings in the division. He attended social evenings, whist drives, fête days and summer outings to Scarborough and the Lake District. He tried to meet personally in the homes of the leading party members all the active people in South Leeds Labour Party and he paid the first of many visits to the working-men's clubs where he met men who were not active in politics and learnt what they thought about current problems.[37]

Gaitskell had been selected for a safe Labour seat, his reputation was growing, and he was promoted to a readership at UCL. Within the Labour Party circles in which he moved, and in particular in his relationship with Dalton, one other factor was increasingly making him stand out: his dedicated anti-appeasement stance. Douglas Jay, who watched the growth in Gaitskell's character with increasing interest as the decade progressed, pinpoints one instance in which he saw the 'will like a driving spear':

> We had all been anti-appeasers, Hugh Gaitskell the strongest of the lot, more deeply even than Dalton, not so loudly of course because Hugh Gaitskell was deep rather than loud. In the fortnight after Munich, Hugh Dalton held a meeting at his flat with Leonard Woolf, with Philip Noel-Baker, with John Wilmot, with Hugh Gaitskell, Evan Durbin, me, Robert Fraser [also present were Kingsley Martin, Herbert Morrison, Ivor Thomas, Dick Crossman] . . . we discussed what the situation was and what we and the Labour Party were to do next. And Dalton went round the room at the end . . . and the question was do we resist? or do we now try to make some bargain or deal? The only people round the room [who said we should resist] were Hugh Gaitskell and myself and Philip Noel-Baker strangely enough . . . We left to go home and I said to Hugh, 'Of course this is right and this is what we ought to do but it fills me with despair . . . We, the Labour opposition, are the only people who can correct this now . . . we are the one section [of the Labour Party] who are neither corrupted by Chamberlain nor pacifist in the face of Hitler and yet even of us, eight out of ten are in favour of capitulation in effect.' We only had the distance between Victoria station and Charing Cross station where we would change on to different tubes. And Hugh Gaitskell said 'Not at all, there will be a war and we shall win it in the end. We shall strengthen our party and somehow the Labour opposition will combine with Churchill and strengthen the government, and we shall go to war and in the end we shall bring the United States in on our side and we shall win.'[38]

For Jay this was a defining moment in his relationship with Gaitskell: the moment he became the first Gaitskellite.

Two main points were fixed in Gaitskell's political philosophy by the end of the 1930s. First, it was essential for the Labour Party to pursue the democratic route; to do this it had to ensure that it was independent. If it did form alliances then those alliances could only be with democratic parties, not with the communists. Secondly, in international relations the democracies had to negotiate from a position of strength. Gaitskell was an early and consistent anti-appeaser. Power was what mattered in this situation. Gaitskell had learned his politics in the age of power and this had two main impacts on his thinking. On the domestic front the impotence of the Labour Party after the split of 1931 made unity and realism his paramount political principles – unity in the sense that the party had to follow its leader, but also that the leader could only take the party so far; realism in the need to adopt electorally relevant policies. In international relations his natural inclination towards internationalism was challenged somewhat by the feebleness of the League of Nations and the democracies' inability to work together against the dictators.

The process whereby Gaitskell formulated his response to the collapse of the second Labour government and the increasing polarisation of the international scene were mirrored more broadly in the wider labour movement. As a result of the political and ideological bankruptcy of the labour movement in the face of the financial crisis and the steadily increasing unemployment of the early 1930s, many extreme positions were adopted and the party itself passed through a phase of impassioned rhetoric at the same time as Gaitskell. Douglas Jay regarded this as part of a long-term pattern in the Labour Party's response to defeat:

> There is a certain rhythm or see-saw, whatever you call it, by which the Labour Party after losing an election always has a bad time and a great deal of recrimination. Then after a year, or a little more, it recovers from it; and you remember after the 1931 defeat there was a very bad and acrimonious conference which passed resolutions to abolish the monarchy, the House of Lords and everything else. I remember thinking myself at the time that the party was getting a bit crazy. But it wore off and by 1935 things were about back to where they had started.[39]

By the time the party had righted itself it had also begun the process of working out a more mature form of economic and political analysis that was to carry it to power in 1945. The basis of that approach was intervention and the heart of the policy was to be full employment but, before Labour was given the chance of putting these ideas to the electorate, Britain, Europe and the world were plunged into war; all political debate, and any development of ideas, were relegated below the effort to defeat Hitler and his allies.

3

Whitehall Irregular, 1939–1945

Put away your books! War has been declared.
>   Denis Healey's mother, 1939

This 'democratic international' must use many different methods,
including industrial and military sabotage, Labour agitation and
strikes, continuous propaganda, terrorist acts against traitors and
German leaders, boycotts and riots.
>   Hugh Dalton, 1940

I do not think there have been any very exciting developments
in the Board of Trade.
>   Hugh Gaitskell to Christopher Mayhew, 1943

Eleven days after Hitler invaded the Rhineland in March 1936,
Whitehall had tentatively begun to plan mobilisation if war were to
come. As part of this plan, the vice-chancellors and professors in
British universities were asked for lists of experts who might be
useful. The emphasis was very much on the scientists, those who
became the code breakers, but writers and other scholars – even
economists – had their uses in total war. The Central Register,
created to collate the information with Michael Postan's formidable
sister-in-law, Beryl Power, as keeper, sent out thousands of 'little
forms' saying 'Do you undertake to go wherever you are sent in
the event of a national emergency?' At the suggestion of his old boss
from University College, Noel Hall, Gaitskell was recruited into the
Ministry of Economic Warfare and there became one of the Whitehall irregulars who revolutionised, albeit temporarily, the Whitehall
machine.[1]

Fighting on the home front, in the early part of the war at least,
carried perhaps more physical risk than many in the active services
felt. It also seemed a little surreal. The novelist Graham Greene,
Gaitskell's near contemporary at Oxford, was in the Ministry of
Information at this time. In a short story written in 1940, 'Men at
Work', he captures something of the atmosphere of Whitehall during

the war. The main character, Skate, is living in town and visiting his wife and family in the country twice a week, sleeping on a camp bed; his whole world has become the Ministry. Amid the Battle of Britain after the fall of France, Skate has to chair the Book Committee.

On Skate's agenda was written:

1. Arising from the Minutes.
2. Pamphlet in Welsh on German labour conditions.
3. Facilities for Wilkinson to visit the ATS.
4. Objections to proposed Bone pamphlet.
5. Suggestion for a leaflet from Meat Marketing Board.
6. The Problem of India.

The meeting meanders around various topics until a late arriver brings news of a daylight raid in which fifty Nazi planes had been shot down. The meeting resumes:

> 'We must really get Bone's pamphlet out,' Hill said. Skate suddenly, to his surprise, said savagely, 'That'll show them,' and then sat down in humble collapse as though he had been caught out in treachery.[2]

Sometimes Gaitskell wished that he had been suitable for active service. There were no savage outbursts like Skate's but an occasional wistfulness and, in later years, perhaps some regret. While he realised it would not have made the best use of his talents – he had learnt German at Oxford and travelled there half a dozen times before spending a year in Austria and he was also, of course, an economist – he also felt somewhat jealous of those like Christopher Mayhew who started out at home but then went abroad to fight. In a letter to Mayhew in September 1943 the feeling comes across:

> I wonder where you are. I made all sorts of guesses but the few indications you gave in your letter of where you had been were not enough. Probably you went round Africa! But is it now India? or Persia? or Egypt? or are you one of those British Officers who, we are told, are organising guerrilla warfare in Greece and Yugoslavia? Or did you perhaps come west (or go east) and are now in Italy? . . . I do not think there have been any very exciting developments in the Board of Trade.[3]

While it was probably true that his 'over-rational mind never allowed the problem to pose itself' because 'he could be more use where he was' than in the services,[4] the question of whether or not he had a 'good war' matters in relation to his peers and in terms of how he experienced it at the time and subsequently.

Some of his later political contemporaries and friends could have avoided active service or served on the home front but, like Tony Crosland, chose to fight:

> Undergraduates were exempted from military service until they had taken their degrees. Tony had started as a classics scholar, a four-year course at Oxford. He had a year to go. Walking down Piccadilly late in June 1940, he noticed two soldiers with a black flash emblazoned on the back of their tunics. Five black ribbons – which a century earlier would have bound the soldiers' hair in a queue – each 2 inches wide (9½ inches for officers, 7½ inches for other ranks), spread like a fan from the collar of the tunic. Tony maintained his sole reason for joining the Royal Welch Fusiliers, which he did a few days later, was to wear their emblem, the flash.[5]

Denis Healey's mother called upstairs, 'Put away your books! War has been declared.' Healey volunteered but was sent back to Oxford to finish his degree.[6] Both Healey and Crosland were younger, and both had good military wars; others of Gaitskell's generation like Douglas Jay and Evan Durbin served alongside him on the home front. Harold Wilson, then acting as William Beveridge's research assistant, 'registered at the local employment exchange under the Military Service Act. He was categorised as a specialist, but there was no immediate demand for his specialism. At the end of the war, Wilson was keen to stress that he had "tried to volunteer for the Services" but the recruitment board ordered him to do Government Department Work. His efforts to get into uniform, however, do not appear to have been particularly strenuous.'[7] Wilson had a 'good' war, establishing his reputation and sliding into a parliamentary seat; the lack of military service never seemed to bother him.

For Gaitskell, though knowing that he was serving his country the best way he could, the energy and drive he exhibited suggests a somewhat more troubled view. For someone so dedicated to the effort against Hitler and with his first-hand experience of the suppression of the Austrian socialists, the desk-bound jobs of the war years must have caused some frustration. Indeed, at times he clearly found the institutional bickering and departmental manoeuvring infuriating. But he compensated for his lack of military service with a strident militancy of attitude towards how the war should be fought.

This militancy chimed with an increasing dissatisfaction with

Neville Chamberlain, the Conservative Prime Minister. Hampered by his close association with the failed policy of appeasement, Chamberlain was increasingly under attack as the first days of the war were filled with news of successive German victories. The Labour Party was advocating the full mobilisation of the country for war and supporting Churchill, the staunchest opponent of appeasement, as the best wartime leader available. Hugh Dalton was campaigning vigorously on Churchill's behalf and had been in intermittent talks with the anti-appeasers on the government benches since Munich; his object was some kind of coalition with Churchill as Prime Minister. When war was declared, Chamberlain brought Churchill into the government as First Lord of the Admiralty and thereby limited his room for manoeuvre; in fact, Churchill served Chamberlain loyally. Dalton, however, did not stop attacking the inadequacy of the Chamberlain government and matters came to ahead with the failed Norwegian campaign in 1940.

Between September 1939 and 14 May 1940 Gaitskell served in the intelligence branch of the Ministry of Economic Warfare; he turned up on the first Monday the Ministry was founded. The new name, 'economic warfare', covered both the blockade of Germany in the accepted sense and other activities which took the economic war behind the enemy's battle-lines. Of these the area bombing of industrial targets was the most important, but sabotage, psychological warfare and other unconventional experiments were pursued with varying degrees of success or disappointment during the war. It was hoped, too, that the new name would create and express a new conception of economic attack as a fighting service.[8]

The problem with implementing the blockade was the conflict between the need to wage the economic war effectively and the need to keep lines of communication and diplomacy open with the neutrals. In March 1939 Major Desmond Morton, a friend of Winston Churchill, established the Industrial Intelligence Centre (IIC). It provided the research and ideas on which the Ministry of Economic Warfare attempted to act when war came.[9] After initially being in the neutral countries section, the intelligence branch of the Ministry was reorganised; Noel Hall became head of the Economic Warfare Intelligence Department with a slight change in responsibilities. A memorandum prepared in December 1939 summarised the new personnel and the purpose of the intelligence branch of this new kind of warfare:

MEMORANDUM

The Intelligence Branch of the Ministry of Economic Warfare under Mr Morton has now been organised in two Departments as follows:

'Blockade Intelligence' Department
Head: Hon Cecil Farrer (also Deputy Head of Intelligence)
Sections:
Statistics and Rationing Head: Mr R. Spicer
Black List Head: Mr E. L. Mercier
Commodities Head: Mr S. J. Johnstone

Economic Warfare Intelligence Department
Head: Mr Noel Hall
Sections:
Enemy Countries Intelligence Head: Mr H. T. N. Gaitskell
Neutral Countries Intelligence Head: Hon. T. H. Brand
Liaison and Censorship Head: Mr F. F. Clively

The function of the 'Blockade Intelligence' Department is to collect, collate and present information necessary for the prevention of traffic to or from the enemy. The function of the Economic Warfare Intelligence Department is to collate and present information relative to the wider questions of economic warfare including those relating to the economic condition of Germany. The Heads of each intelligence Department may draw directly on each other's subsections for any information which they require.
(Sgd.) G. Mounsey
Ministry of Economic Warfare, 18 December 1939.[10]

The months of the 'phoney war' were a period of intense political activity in the run-up to the formation of the coalition government and the ousting of Chamberlain as Prime Minister. Gaitskell argued within his department for the vigorous waging of the economic war and leaked material to Dalton to be used as ammunition in his campaign against Chamberlain and for a new National Government on 'the widest possible basis'. Thus Gaitskell, a temporary civil servant, was leaking material for Dalton to use in meetings with his own ministerial boss, Ronald Cross, who according to Dalton approved the contacts. 'H.G. suggests that with Cross I might converse as follows. Pre-emption. What is happening about Rumanian oil? Have we got it? And how about oil cake and oil seed from the Balkans?'[11] Such problems were caused by the conflicting needs of the different departments concerned with external affairs. The Foreign Office wanted to keep the neutrals sweet and therefore resisted antagonising them too much while the Ministry of Economic Warfare (MEW) was trying to starve the German war economy. Gaitskell summed up the problem: 'What can we do? The Foreign Office won't let us bully any of the neutrals and the Treasury won't let us bribe them.'[12]

As 1940 wore on, the need for some sort of military action against the Germans deepened. From the outset of war the officials in the MEW were aware of the supply of iron ore and other products reaching Germany through Norwegian territorial waters, particularly through the port of Narvik. This was the background to the abortive Allied strike at Norway. The MEW was asked to prepare a memo on the effect of cutting off ore from Sweden to Germany; Gaitskell had a walk-on part in the Norwegian campaign, since he helped draft the memo.

A certain Hermann Brassert in the United States had a long talk with a British agent, Dr Karl Otto, who reported to Sir Robert Vansittart at the Foreign Office that Hitler regarded a threat to the supply of iron ore as the greatest danger facing Germany. If Swedish supplies could be curtailed then this could damage Germany severely. This report found its way to the MEW.[13] The British plan was to land in Norway, seize the Norwegian supply lines and then attack Sweden; but before it could be put into operation the Germans attacked Denmark and Norway. British troops were nevertheless landed at Namsos and Andalsnes on 14 and 17 April but only held out against the German Luftwaffe until 3 May. The force sent against Narvik had to wait for the snows to melt and although they took the port on 28 May they had to withdraw on 8 June.

By then the Chamberlain government had fallen and the first, somewhat unsatisfactory phase of Gaitskell's war was over. His real war began with the restructuring of the government as a coalition, with Labour Ministers in the Cabinet and elections suspended for the duration. At 6 p.m. on 14 May, Hugh Dalton received a telephone call from Winston Churchill, now safely installed as the Prime Minister of a coalition government: 'Your friends tell me that you have been making a considerable study of Economic Warfare. Will you take the Ministry?'[14] Six hours later Gaitskell was summoned to Dalton's flat, and asked to be the new Minister's private secretary, 'more like a chef de Cabinet' and fully in his confidence. Gaitskell accepted the next morning. Neither appointment was made without some opposition. Dalton's posting ruffled feathers in Churchill's entourage, while Gaitskell's disrupted the 'tidy minds' of those running the Whitehall irregulars. In fact, Gaitskell's appointment resulted in a piece of Whitehall farce straight from *Yes, Minister*. Noel Hall told the story to Dalton's biographer, Ben Pimlott. Hall was summoned to the office of Leith Ross, the Permanent Secretary, and told, 'You will get a minute from me saying that Gaitskell is to be appointed to Dalton's Office. You will reply that, regrettably, he cannot be spared from his present duties.' Noel Hall refused and Gaitskell began his period of closest direct partnership with Dalton.

Life for Dalton's private secretary involved rapidly learning considerable diplomatic skill to deal with the consequences of the Minister's restless energy and the mundane administration of a blockade increasingly becoming irrelevant to the war. Gaitskell continued to work closely with Noel Hall, helping him to prepare monthly reports of MEW activities, such as the following, not unusual, example, from this period in the war. Gaitskell's corrections, as indicated on the draft, have been left in the quotations that follow:

> 13/2/1941
> Dear Noel
> The Minister asked me to cut down your draft monthly report a bit. I hope I have done it on the lines you would like and that it now meets with your approval.
> HG
>
> HG
> I think it is a grand job – wood and trees decently distinguished
> NH
> 13/2

The Gaitskell/Noel report began: 'There were no important developments in economic warfare during January, though some progress was made in tidying up trade agreements and rationing schemes with the remaining adjacent neutrals. Further tightening of the blockade now chiefly depends on American decisions which have been held during the passage of the Lend and Lease Bill.' Ten French vessels were detained at Gibraltar in January but the inward movement of 147,000 tons was slightly higher than in December; the outward, at 163,000 tons, was slightly lower. The department monitored the French steamship services between Marseilles and

> (1) the Antilles, with transshipment to Baltimore and New York, (2) Indo-China, and (3) Morocco, Senegal, Guinea, Dahomey and the Ivory

Coast. Up to the present, American exports have not arrived in the Antilles in large quantities for reshipment to France. The detention of the SS Mendoza appears to have caused the other French vessels which were ready to sail from the Plate to postpone their departure.

A recurrent question was the granting or withholding of Navicerts – the documents given to ships to allow them to pass through the blockade. In January 1941 they refused Navicerts for edible oils for Spain because part of the olive oil crop was to be sold to Italy and Germany, but the Spanish government agreed that copper and cocoa may not be exported or re-exported from, or transported through, Spain. In such a struggle this constituted a small victory.

> HRM's personal approach to Dr Salazar [the Portuguese dictator], and our willingness to rely upon his personal assurances, appear to have brought us within sight of a final settlement of questions outstanding with Portugal and there are hopes that a war trade agreement may shortly be reached. Little progress has been made in negotiations with the Swiss. But the lack of shipping and the closing of the port of Genoa to foreign vessels has, in any case, reduced Swiss seaborne imports to negligible amounts.

Minor concessions designed to speed up deliveries were made to Yugoslavia.

> Navicerts and certificates of origin will shortly ~~in operation~~ be required in the Persian Gulf, details having been worked out to control contraband trade though [sic] Iran and Iraq. The Navy appears to have interfered successfully with an increasing contraband trade across the Red Sea into Eritrea. Good progress has been made in the negotiations with the Netherlands Government ~~which~~ who, despite the delicate state of their negotiations with Japan, have refused to allow certain exports from the Netherlands East Indies which were suspected to be for re-export to the enemy and have agreed to institute a general control of Netherlands East Indies exports ~~which will~~ to be operated in harmony with our export licensing arrangements.

At the beginning of January, the United States had placed copper, brass, zinc, nickel and potash on the Export Licensing List – goods which needed licences to be sold and could therefore be controlled – but in spite of this goods were still getting through.

> Procrastination in Washington in carrying out proposals, some of which were actually made to us by the Administration, is now becoming serious. It has characterised our negotiations not only about financial and shipping control, but also in regard to export licensing. In particular, the US

administration has shown reluctance to curtail their trade with the USSR despite the evidence which we have adduced that the Soviet [*sic*] are importing war commodities from the USA to replace domestic supplies which they are exporting to Germany [in brackets and in pencil] (more recently there has been an improvement in the US attitude).

It was like an elaborate game of chess across continents. The MEW devised new methods of indirect control which gradually became known to the enemy and to unfriendly neutrals, and they in turn devised methods to get round them.

It now seems possible that a Pacific Club, designed to supply Japan and Russia, ~~will~~ may be organised to compete with our Ships Warrant Scheme: and the loyalty of those American firms who have voluntarily entered into agreements with us not to participate in dangerous trade is heavily strained when business is passed to their competitors.

In the absence of even tacit consent from Washington, we have been reluctant to press for contraband control in the Caribbean and, in spite of several reports from the CIC, American and West Indies Station, that uncertified items of cargo are being over-stowed in ships from Lisbon, we have been unable to ask for hold-back guarantees in the United States as HMR Washington is unable to guarantee that these would be respected.

A recurrent problem, until the USA entered the war, was the attitude of the US State Department, which was described as 'definitely unhelpful'. Gaitskell felt the Americans did not realise the importance of the blockade 'to our whole war effort of stopping the trade between Germany and South America'.

The position has been put frankly to Mr Hopkins and it may be hoped that on his return to Washington, he may be able to reinforce the efforts which Lord Halifax has been making to secure greater cooperation over the whole field of our economic warfare activities.[15]

Gaitskell's work for Dalton often consisted of routine private-office tasks and he dealt with the full range of MEW propaganda. The role of the MEW reflected its place as the interface between the official and the secret elements of the propaganda wars. Much of the management of this role involved complex departmental relations and a great deal of private-office diplomacy. Above and beyond the routine paper-chase there was also his boss to manage.

Dalton was restless and trying to find ways to increase his empire. 'As early as 25 May 1940 the chiefs of staff submitted to the War

Cabinet that if France did collapse Germany might still be defeated by economic pressure, by a combination of air attack on economic objectives in Germany and on German morale and the creation of widespread revolt in her conquered territories.'[16] Following discussion and intrigues, concentrated by the pressure of the times into days rather than weeks, the Special Operations Executive (SOE) was born. Dalton had written to the Foreign Secretary, Lord Halifax, on 2 July 1940:

> We have got to organise movements in enemy-occupied territory comparable to the Sinn Fein movement in Ireland, to the Chinese Guerrillas now operating against Japan, to the Spanish Irregulars who played a notable part in Wellington's campaign or – one might as well admit it – to the organisations which the Nazis themselves have developed so remarkably in almost every country in the world. This 'democratic international' must use many different methods, including industrial and military sabotage, Labour agitation and strikes, continuous propaganda, terrorist acts against traitors and German leaders, boycotts and riots.[17]

The combination of economic and political warfare under one ministerial head, liaising with the armed forces and the Foreign Office, was a considerable undertaking that cut across a number of established administrative empires. There seems to have been general agreement with Dalton's assessment of what was needed but some profound doubts whether Dalton was the best person to head the Ministry. Despite misgivings, Churchill was won over by a combination of Clement Attlee who became Lord Privy Seal on the formation of the coalition and Deputy Prime Minister in 1942 (and had been vigorously lobbied by Dalton) and Alexander Cadogan, the Permanent Secretary at the Foreign Office. On 22 July 1940 Churchill finally agreed to the new organisation, and political, or 'black', warfare came under the control of the Minister of Economic Warfare. This new style of warfare was summed up in Churchill's famous order to Dalton: 'And now set Europe ablaze.'

Part of the reorganisation had brought the clandestine operations under Dalton's control. Gaitskell was given the responsibility of organising the research wing – known as SO3 – which was not a success.

> SO3, organized in research 'bureaux' on a regional and country basis, was to have formed the planning and intelligence staff for SO2. The idea was borrowed from MI(R) [the secret section of the War Office], which

had launched a group of bureaux of junior staff officers, loosely co-ordinated by Quintin Hogg, to study particular countries – one of the bureaux was for France; but shortly afterwards MI(R) closed down. Within two months SO3 was moribund, for lack of forceful personalities to sustain it; its more promising officers were absorbed into the country sections of SO2, and it was finally abolished on 17 January 1941.

The historian of the SOE, M. R. D. Foot, summed up SO3 as 'a transient and embarrassed organisation planted by Hugh Gaitskell that wilted instead of taking root'.[18]

With the surge of energy that Dalton brought to the task, Gait-skell's life became less like that of Graham Greene's Skate. After the first few months as Minister, Dalton had the MEW running as he desired and concentrated more and more on the work of the SOE. His drive quickly established the pattern of the next few years for Gaitskell – ceaseless activity, frequent rows, followed by periods of calm. Dalton's paranoia and zeal placed an enormous pressure on his private secretary, but Gaitskell was not alone. John Wilmot, a colleague from inter-war Labour politics, was the PPS (Parliamentary Private Secretary) and the Liberal MP Dingle Foot – 'my foot', as Dalton called him – was Parliamentary Secretary. The Earl of Drogheda and Noel Hall were made joint directors of MEW. On the operational SO2 side, Gladwyn Jebb, who as Cadogan's secretary had fed Dalton with information on the security services, and Sir Frank Nelson, a former Conservative MP, were key figures and Colin Gubbins, a career soldier, ran the overseas network. Dalton worked closely, in different ways, with each; Gladwyn Jebb was, according to Dalton's biographer, the closest; and in many ways the work of SOE appealed to Dalton more than that of the MEW. On the domestic side, SO1 was put under Reginald Leeper, head of the Foreign Office Political Intelligence Department, and was eventually absorbed by the Political Warfare Executive, under Robert Bruce Lockhart, who in peacetime had been a writer.

Personal battles developed between Jebb and Leeper over the conduct of policy but Gaitskell was less concerned at this than with the management of his Minister. However, like the good private secretary that he was becoming, he was watchful of disagreements and reported his impressions to Dalton. The main conflict was with the MEW, between the established view of the Foreign Office and the permanent Civil Service of the way things should be done and the view held by the temporaries and Jebb – the warmongers.

But personalities and suspected or real slights were as much a part of the scene as real differences of substance. Richard Crossman, a key player in the development of black propaganda during the war, maintained that the whole set-up should have been under the control of the Chiefs of Staff because 'Psychological warriors tended to be prima donnas'.[19] Perhaps the biggest prima donna of all was Gaitskell's Minister but he was soon to meet his match.

The reorganisation of propaganda was initiated on Brendan Bracken's appointment as Minister of Information in July 1941. Under the previous Minister, Duff Cooper, there had been an armed truce between the black and the white propaganda organisations: officials from the different departments were simply told not to associate with each other. With Churchill's appointment of his crony, the newspaper owner Bracken, there was some hope that this truce would be resolved into a peace. Dalton thought they might be able to work together through the joint committee comprising the two Ministers and Anthony Eden, who had replaced Lord Halifax as Foreign Seceretary. However, Bracken was as forceful a personality and shared many of the same characteristics of bluff and bluster as the head of the MEW. The weekly meetings slowly became contests. Robert Bruce Lockhart sent Anthony Eden a progress report in August 1941:

> The Dalton-Bracken Conversations: I prepared no progress report last week, because the situation was too fluid for solidification. Throughout the negotiations Mr Bracken has been forceful, sometimes pugnacious, sometimes impulsive, yet adroitly skilful in tactics, always good humoured and always tractable. Above all, by quick-fire speech he has proved himself at least the equal of Dr Dalton in argument. From the beginning Dr Dalton has been on the defensive and even today, when agreement has been reached, probably interprets 'joint ministerial control' in his own way. The scientific definition of Daltonism is inability to distinguish between green and red, and I doubt very much if he has seen any danger signal to himself . . . To you sir, who have achieved final agreement, both ministers are grateful, and your role as mediator must have been admirable played, for both ministers claim you as an ally . . . The Irishman [Bracken] and the Englishman [Dalton] both believe that they have won a victory.[20]

In his diary Dalton recorded Gaitskell's comments on one of the many flare-ups:

R.L. is much too suspicious. He thinks that G[ladwyn Jebb] despises him
and realises that G always gets the best of any argument, having a much
quicker and more incisive mind. Also he is jealous of the fact that G sees
much more of me [Dalton] than he does and realises that I think much
more of G than of him . . . [Gaitskell] does not think G realises that he
sometimes antagonises people by his rather offhand manner and his apparent lack of interest in what they are saying.[21]

The disputes at ministerial level rumbled on, and the arguments
between the Minister and the heads of different sections, and between
the heads themselves, rarely let up. Dalton thrived on it all but
Gaitskell was less sanguine, observing to Dalton one day, 'I had no
idea it would be like this.'[22]

In the later part of his relationship with G. D. H. Cole it was the
young Gaitskell who led the older man away from guild socialism;
with Maurice Bowra it was the younger man who moved away and
became independent; with Evan Durbin in the inter-war period it
was Gaitskell who again initially followed but slowly became more
equal and, on appeasement, led; but with Hugh Dalton it was a
different kind of attachment. Gaitskell was inspired and much assisted
by Dalton; and he did not seem to come out from Dalton's shadow
until the middle of the 1950s – not in overt or public terms but in
the essence of the relationship. Gaitskell could, and did, stand up to
him and shouted back when Dalton boomed at him, but while the
two worked together Dalton was the dominant personality as well
as the boss. It was the defining political relationship of Gaitskell's
life. At crucial moments throughout his career Dalton was there,
scheming and campaigning, not always helpfully it has to be said,
on behalf of his protégé. As the balance of the relationship shifted,
Dalton's evolution from boss to sponsor was remarkable. Dalton did
not make Gaitskell, but Dalton was one central cause of Gaitskell's
rapid rise in politics. If the first half of Gaitskell's career was characterised by elder brothers to learn from and supersede, the second half
had a number of vitally important fathers to sponsor, promote and
support. Dalton was the first and the most important (indeed Keynes's
nickname for Dalton was 'Daddy').[23]

In the first phase of their war work together Gaitskell learned
from Dalton and served him loyally; he also took a great deal from
him. When Dalton died in 1962 Gaitskell remembered this phase
of their relationship thus:

exhausting, exhilarating and instructive. He taught me a lot, especially how to write Cabinet papers and draft letters. He hated slipshod English, sentences that meant little and added nothing . . . He used to keep a 'prod list' on his desk so that he could follow up all the things he had started. Many ministers I have known have bright ideas but no follow through. This was not true of Dalton . . . He had tremendous drive. He enjoyed power and getting things done. He was impatient with difficulties . . . He could be exceedingly bad tempered. He was apt to bully and shout at people. He got angry unreasonably when it was not really the fault of the officials. I found an easy way of dealing with this. I just shouted back. I remember once we had a shouting match; it must have lasted at least 5 minutes. At the end of it a sly grin spread over his face. 'Well, well,' he would say, 'perhaps there is something in your point of view.' He liked this sort of encounter and respected people who stood up to him.[24]

But few did and Dalton suffered as a result, despite Gaitskell's attempts to smooth the way and occasionally reprimand Dalton: 'Look here, Hugh, you are not to talk to civil servants like that – I won't have it.' Such a rebuke must have endeared him to the civil servants present.

Apart from this work as eyes and ears, as buffer between Minister and officials, and as intellectual sounding-board, in the main Gaitskell's tasks were those of a private secretary and after the failure of SO3 they became somewhat mundane. Then, with no real prospect of Bracken and Dalton finding common ground through the ministerial committee, Churchill finally decided to promote Dalton out of the situation. A year earlier, Dalton had considered and rejected the idea of the Board of Trade but now he accepted. His first move was to bring Gaitskell with him. This gave Gaitskell something of a problem. He had just been offered a job in what would become the British part of the United Nations Relief and Rehabilitation Administration (UNRRA). There was a strong pull on his colonial roots and away from the political path he had taken since Oxford. It would have offered a constructive way of implementing socialist principles in an international setting and would have made him a permanent member of the international Civil Service which developed in the post-war period. That Gaitskell seriously considered it as an option shows the extent to which the war had unsettled his fixed convictions on a political career and the extent to which the administrative process had come to interest him. That he did not accept was due to Dalton.

Although Gaitskell accepted Dalton's offer of the move to the

Board of Trade, there were certain terms: the UNRRA job was to stay open for three months, he was to be personal assistant and there were to be no more late nights with Dalton. Dalton recalled the 'treaty' a little differently: not too many late nights and the chance of promotion after a month. Gaitskell stayed for six months before being promoted to Principal Assistant Secretary. It was an eventful six months.

If Dalton had succeeded in removing the Labour MP D. R. Grenfell from his position as Minister responsible for mines, then events might have turned out differently. But the failure of one of his frequent and frequently ineffective intrigues left Grenfell in place and Dalton responsible for dealing with a crisis. The battle over coal in 1942 was a partial defeat for Dalton, although it did not change the fate of the coal industry in the long run. It was also the most openly party-political dispute of the war so far.

Rumbling in the background of Gaitskell and Dalton's work at the MEW had been the political charge that the propaganda they were producing was socialist propaganda – a charge they had resisted. Now, in the worst year of the war for Churchill, there was a more serious political accusation: Dalton was trying to nationalise the coal-mines through the back door. The problem was the ever-increasing demand for coal. 'Virtually all heavy manufacturing industry ran on coal', but 'nowhere were labour relations worse than in the mines.'[25] 1942 saw a sharp rise in consumption and the expectation of a shortage in the following year – although shortage of fuel never affected wartime production.[26] Churchill saw the response of the President of the Board of Trade as a political challenge.

When Gaitskell became Dalton's personal assistant at the Board of Trade in February 1942, his first task was to prepare a report on the Mines Department and its personnel. He identified the central problems as coal production, the call for nationalisation ('There is no need for me to say anything about the politics of this'), transportation and the problem of rationing: 'Can you ration fuel? This is the biggest question you have to face, and you will have to go into it in great detail yourself.'[27] Dalton went to work on Gaitskell's advice with characteristic crudeness. Gaitskell had identified Sir Alfred Hurst, the Under-Secretary, as a major obstacle to change, and Dalton sent a memo to the head of the Civil Service demanding his removal within twenty-four hours. He then asked William Beveridge to draft a report on how to implement rationing. (Many of the figures in the report were prepared by a young statistician who had worked with Beveridge in Oxford and who was now in the Mines Department. Gaitskell's report on the mines singled out this young man for special praise as 'extraordinarily able' and 'one of the most brilliant young men about'; the young man was Harold Wilson.)

Five weeks later Beveridge reported and on 21 April the President of the Board of Trade presented to the House a comprehensive scheme of fuel rationing; coal, coke, paraffin, gas and electricity were all included. The Conservative backbenchers reacted ferociously and it soon developed into a full-blown political row. Churchill, who had accepted the proposal after the Lord President's Committee had approved it, then moved against.[28] In the War Cabinet he suggested that the plan should be held in reserve or dropped.[29] At this point a series of strikes broke out in the coalfields, especially in Kent, where at one point 100,000 summonses were issued for the arrest of striking miners.[30] Churchill hardened in his resolve against rationing and Dalton withdrew to his house at West Leaze – overlooking the Marlborough Downs in Wiltshire – to contemplate resignation. Stafford Cripps, the Leader of the House, supported Dalton strongly and told him he would be prepared to resign on the issue.[31] Instead the focus shifted to reorganisation and, although rationing was never introduced, the miners received a national minimum wage, 'substantial state' intervention in the form of dual control and regional organisation in which the State worked with groups of mine owners to direct production. Once the threat of rationing – and by extension nationalisation – was removed, Churchill urged that 'something must be done to improve the miners' wages. The treasury must not be difficult about this.'[32]

Apart from the broad political implications of these events, the episode brought Gaitskell into contact with many key figures in the mining industry. Ben Pimlott in his biography of Wilson hints that his decision to take the Mines Department job was partly motivated by the political possibility of making contacts in one of the strongest Labour unions with key seats at their disposal.[33] Gaitskell, without the calculation, achieved the same result.

In the first half of his war service, up to his promotion to Principal Assistant Secretary in the autumn of 1942, Gaitskell had been more of a 'political' temporary than a fully 'Civil Service' temporary. He had a profoundly political master, who, though keen on waging war, kept an eye on the politics of the jobs he was doing – who believed passionately that propaganda should be run by a man of the left and clearly understood the political implications of the coal dispute. Therefore Gaitskell had to walk a particularly narrow tightrope between the unpolitical nature of the Civil Service and the political instincts of his boss and himself. However, Gaitskell shouldered the burden, learned from the experience and charmed many of those he came into contact with. He could make sharp and biting assessments of people – Grenfell, the Labour Minister of Mines, or Eady (at the Treasury), for example – but he could also smooth the path of his Minister, defend the civil servants from the worst excesses of Dalton's bullying and won many friends among the temporary and the permanent staff. His ability to do this was of course helped by the circumstances: everyone was, in the end, in the same fight and, especially among the temporaries, everyone was learning on the job. The pedantry and the desire to provoke a fight, sometimes seemingly for the sake of a principle not obviously important, seems to have been largely lacking in this period. The ability to improve a draft, the position of having the Minister's ear and a natural and striking sense of fairness in his dealings with people all marked him out as a successful temporary. He was discreet but his continuing political ambitions were obvious, he was a team player in a period which demanded team play and he was tireless in his physical capacity for work.

In the second half of the war, the nature of the work sometimes suited him less, and seemed of less obvious value. However, as the tide turned in favour of the Allies from late 1942 onwards, the meaning of the battle on the home front became less clear. In the early desperate days of running the blockade or establishing the SOE, the motivation for spending twelve or fourteen hours a day in the Ministry six or seven days a week was clear. The energy was also kept flowing by the threat of the Blitz and the constant worry about the next turn the war would take. As the war went on and the balance of the conflict switched to the Allies, much of the stimulus and the sense of urgency was removed. The physical danger also receded a little until the arrival of the V-weapons in 1944. In conjunction with this shift in the balance of the war, Gaitskell broke free of his boss and took a more independent and properly Civil Service position: his role was now, until 1945, more that of a civil servant temporary. In this period he became, to use Roy Jenkins's phrase, somewhat intoxicated with administration and he did not let up in the pace of work that he set himself. Even the nature of the work and the urgency of the course had somewhat altered. Perhaps it was more difficult then to recognise the broader shifts that had taken place, but perhaps too he was driven because he was compensating for not taking a direct part in the armed conflict.

The main concerns of Gaitskell, the independent civil servant, in the closing years of the war were price control, the location of industry and the retail trade; the most interesting matters were reconstruction – particularly in terms of consumer demand and slowly increasing his political contact with his South Leeds constituency and work with the film industry. In his duties at the Board he remained in close touch with Dalton and still worked hard but there were more weekends with the family. However, being out of private office had the disadvantage of cutting him off slightly from some of his formerly close colleagues. His record in these last years was sound, if unexciting. He seemed to enjoy the administrative process particularly if it involved concrete decisions and he seems to have impressed the people he came into contact with in the film industry.

The major problem for the British Film Industry was the access to studio space and resources necessary to compete with the cheap American imports that flooded the market. Gaitskell was sympathetic to the idea of resisting American cultural influence, gave much practical help in negotiations and was fascinated by the movie world. The work side of this involvement paid off richly and he wrote to his brother Arthur about having lunch with Vivien Leigh and Ingrid Bergman. He and Dora also attended gala openings and met Alexander Korda and J. Arthur Rank – the two key players in the golden age of British films in the 1940s and 1950s.

As the war drew to a close and speculation increased about the likelihood of victory, the bubble of tensions and pressures that had been kept up since 1940 seemed to burst. The adrenaline that had sustained him in virtually constant activity since the outbreak of war was sapped and the effort took its toll. For six years he had worked unceasingly in a series of jobs of increasing responsibility; for four years before that he had worked as a full-time academic and political intellectual. Gaitskell ended the war ill and exhausted.

He seemed set on the road to a political career but there were plenty of alternatives. The offer of the UNRRA job was renewed, UCL was inviting him to take a Chair in Economics (an invitation left open until after the election), and there was the option of staying in the Civil Service. Although weighing up the attractions of these different courses at least once,[34] Gaitskell decided that if South Leeds would have him he would still fight the election.

The war did not change Hugh Gaitskell as much as it did many others of his generation, nor was it the making of him in the way it was for many. In the intensity of war the slow development of his intellectual self-confidence and emotional maturity that had begun in the last years of peace was speeded up and heightened but not created. A combination of hard work, natural intelligence and competence, good manners and tact had made him an excellent private secretary to a very demanding boss. Similar characteristics with a somewhat enhanced independence of mind made him a competent administrator and a successful wartime temporary. The quality that marked him out, what one would have noticed, was his extraordinary level of commitment. It was a quiet sort of commitment that suggested a passionate belief in fighting for what he thought was right. This quiet passion became increasingly characteristic of the mature Gaitskell and could either attract people or repel them in perhaps equal measure. In the hothouse atmosphere of the war years, on balance it drew more people towards him, yet some considered him too concerned with detail and insufficiently skilled at delegation to be a department head, and others thought he never seemed to relax or gossip.[35] Overall, however, Gaitskell seems to have made a good impression as a temporary wartime civil servant.

4

Building the New Jerusalem,
1945–1949

It is surprising how many people hold me personally responsible
for what happens in their coal cellars.

Gaitskell in 1948

I live with the Minister of Fuel and Power and as far as I know
he never has any baths at all!

Durbin in 1948

In May 1945 Clement Attlee, a little against his own inclination,
endorsed the decision of the party's National Executive Committee
(NEC) to take Labour out of the wartime coalition. It was a matter
of months before the party would face the first general election for
a decade. Much of the policy work of Gaitskell's XYZ Club and
other groups in the inter-war period had centred on the attempt to
politicise the Keynesian approach to economic management, some
of which had found its way into the policy document, *Labour's
Immediate Programme of 1937*. This was suspended in favour of nationalisation at the Party Conference of 1944.

The 1944 conference had been in militant mood, and the future
left-wing MP Ian Mikardo made a dramatic speech demanding
that the party manifesto spell out the particular industries that
were to be nationalised. The historian of the Attlee governments,
Peter Hennessy, tracked down the party member who actually
drafted the resolution adopted at this Conference. He was Wilf
Canon, a Labour activist from Reading (Mikardo's constituency),
the man who 'in his own way, did for nationalisation in the late
1940s what Ralph Harris and Arthur Seldon of the Institute of
Economic Affairs did for privatisation in the 1980s'. The vote
was taken on a show of hands and the resolution spelling out a
programme of extending the public sector was adopted. Mikardo,
who moved the motion, was sought out by Morrison after the vote.

'You realise, don't you,' said Morrison, 'that you've lost us the election?'[1]

Reflecting the power of Conference at this time, the front bench accepted the vote and included some, but not all, of the industries specified in the party programme of 1945, *Let Us Face the Future*. This was then taken back to the pre-election Conference and 'duly authorised'; 'it became Labour's election Manifesto.'[2] That event determined Gaitskell's political life in the Attlee government. Indeed, he spent much of his first years as a Minister implementing Wilf Canon's resolution.

The elevation of nationalisation to the forefront of Labour policy suggests the extent to which debate in the Labour Party centred on the question of ownership rather than management. To be a radical in 1945 was to advocate not the demand management of Keynes but nationalisation on what was to become the Morrisonian model – a public corporation of usually natural monopolies, particularly the utilities, that had no workers' control but simply substituted private owners and managers with state ownership and publicly appointed managers. Gaitskell's work in the 1930s, his interest during the last years of the war in intervening in the economy to stimulate demand and prevent unemployment and his involvement with issues of consumer choice were submerged in the wave of nationalisation. As a result, his somewhat crude faith in state controls came to dominate his approach and his interest in modernising socialism lay dormant until the late 1950s.

A broad consensus on the desirability of nationalisation cloaked disagreement over the form the new public corporations should take. Gaitskell strongly favoured decentralisation in the electricity industry, for example, while Morrison always advocated a highly centralised model. Interestingly, Gaitskell's preference was for decentralised regional boards with autonomous financial controls, because he wanted to encourage competition between them and give responsibilities to the managers. However, the debate on the best form of the policy was deferred. In 1945 the party was dedicated to making permanent the wartime shift in the balance of the economy from private to public, and the only way they saw of doing this was by physically changing the nature of ownership and attempting rationally to plan the economy.

With the policy document in place, the Labour Party embarked upon the general election campaign. It was a curious affair: with the war in Asia still raging, many voters were only half concerned with the party-political battle; and the focus of the campaign was unusually ideological for a British election. On the one hand was a collectivism founded on the central idea of fair shares but diluted by a continuing support for a private sector and limited private profit. On the other was an economic liberalism diluted by state intervention to achieve reconstruction and maintain low levels of unemployment. One indication that the post-war general election would be a profound ideological confrontation was the publication on 10 March 1944 of F. A. Hayek's attack on the collectivist movement in politics, *The Road to Serfdom*. Its publication caused a considerable popular stir and gave Churchill the 'unifying theme' for his election campaign.[3] The essence of Hayek's case, and the part which became central to the election, was that planning and freedom were incompatible. It gave the Conservative Party the distance they wanted to differentiate themselves from the Labour Party. Although there is no direct evidence that Churchill read *The Road to Serfdom*,[4] the tone of his election campaign suggested that he was conversant with the ideas it contained. The famous Gestapo broadcast with which he opened his campaign was centred on the claim that socialism required a secret police to carry out its planning policies.*

Hayek, diverted from attacking the wartime Allies of the Soviet Union – to whom his analysis applied more readily – had used many of his illustrations from the case of Germany.[5] In Attlee's brilliant, understated response to Churchill, he said he had understood Churchill's purpose: '[Churchill] wanted the electors to understand how great was the difference between Winston Churchill the great leader in war of a united nation and Mr Churchill, the party leader of the Conservatives. He feared lest those who had accepted his leadership in war might have been tempted out of gratitude for having followed him further. I thank him for having disillusioned them so thoroughly.'[6] Attlee also condemned Churchill's use of a 'second-hand version of the academic views of an Austrian professor Friedrich August von Hayek'.[7]

Evan Durbin and Hugh Gaitskell's long discussions in the 1930s

---

* There is an alternative and more colourful explanation of this speech. A 'figure from the intelligence world' once told Peter Hennessy that the root of the Gestapo speech was in fact Hugh Dalton's use of SOE equipment to bug Arthur Greenwood, a fellow Labour Minister in the Coalition, during the war. See Hennessy, *Never Again* (Cape, 1992), p. 83.

about the need to reconcile freedom and planning were also challenged by Hayek's book. Gaitskell had a greater initial ambivalence about the ability of democracy to withstand the assault from totalitarianism. But both shared the view that socialism without democracy was unsustainable in the long run. In 1937 Durbin had begun a lecture on the causes of war with 'The Faith of a Social Democrat': '1. That freedom is as important as equality. 2. That where Democratic Machinery is working properly – it should be used unremittingly – and should be protected.'[8] Durbin now replied forcefully to Hayek's challenge, saying that he did not sufficiently differentiate between kinds of intervention: central planning on the British model had been married to liberalism and democracy and was entirely different from the command economies of the communist world. Both Durbin and Gaitskell argued that planning was not incompatible with freedom within the context of democratic government. Controls imposed on the population needed explanation; the case had to be made to people on moral and economic grounds, but ultimately the people could vote the controllers out of power. The task of explaining planning and control was to dominate Gaitskell's ministerial career in the Attlee government. Much of what he did was a vivid refutation of the limitations of Hayek's critique of democratic socialism and a vindication of the compatibility of planning and freedom.

The obscure Wilf Canon's resolution and the famous Professor Hayek's attack on collectivism set the terms of Gaitskell's first mature political challenges. Rising to those challenges was, however, to be delayed. After a prolonged period of overwork, in early March 1945 he and Dora escaped for an evening's dancing at the Gargoyle Club in Soho. His usually frantic pace on the dance floor must have taken its toll because he ended the night with pains in his chest which returned whenever he exerted himself. At first they thought it was neuralgia, but he visited a heart specialist in April who told him he had suffered a minor coronary thrombosis. In other words, at the age of just thirty-eight Gaitskell had worked himself into an early heart attack.

Dora took charge. She suggested they consult Lord Horder. One of the most distinguished doctors of the period, Thomas Horder had known Gaitskell for fifteen years. Horder, who was physician to George VI and a consultant at St Bartholomew's, where the Gaitskells probably saw him, ordered that Hugh have complete rest. Dora therefore wrote on her husband's behalf to his agent in South Leeds describing the condition: 'one of the blood vessels supplying my heart is not functioning properly. This produces a sort of cramp which brings on the pains and sensations and seems to have caused some damage.' George Brett replied that all would be well with the constituency.[9]

Despite the order to rest they travelled north together in the weeks before the election so that Hugh could be close to his constituency. Dora also let him draft his own election address. One suspects that, aside from this concession, she enforced the doctor's orders that he rest and carried the political and familial strain of a difficult period. A general management committee (GMC) in South Leeds endorsed his candidature and his party workers agreed to fight with or without a candidate. The bulk of the burden for the campaign fell on Brett and the small band of loyal Gaitskellites which was beginning to develop in South Leeds. After a mild and well-mannered campaign, Brett was able to tell him that he had been elected to Parliament by a comfortable majority.

H. Gaitskell	17,899
A. Ramsden (Cons.)	7,497
W. Barford (Lib.)	3,933
Majority	10,402

Gaitskell's account of the moment in his diary, like much else, is matter of fact. He made his acceptance speech, 'the usual sort', and then listened to a long speech from the defeated Liberal, who was 'foolish enough to end his much too long speech by talking about "national socialism". Of course he was booed heavily by the crowd.'[10]

The national election result was announced on 26 July 1945:

Labour	393
Conservative	213
Liberal	12
Communist	2
Commonwealth	1
Others	19

An overall Labour majority of 146 seats. Clement Attlee, stop-gap Labour leader from the troubled 1930s, accepted Ernest Bevin's advice to ignore the intrigues of Morrison – 'If the King asks you to form a Government you say "Yes" or "No", not "I'll let you know later!"' – and accepted the invitation from the Palace. 'At 7 p.m. Churchill set off for Buckingham Palace in a chauffeur-driven Rolls, to tender his resignation, and at 7.30 p.m. Attlee arrived at the Palace in a Standard Ten driven by his wife.' The conversation between the King and Attlee is supposed to have been as follows:

Attlee: I've won the election.
George VI: I know. I heard it on the Six O'Clock News.[11]

Michael Foot caught the moment perfectly: 'No Socialist who saw it will forget the blissful dawn of July 1945. The great war in Europe had ended; the lesser war in Asia might be ending soon. This background to the scene in Britain naturally deepened the sense of release and breath-taking opportunity.'[12] The 1945 general election, in purely party-political terms, represented the coming-of-age of the British Labour Party.

The point was powerfully made in the contemporary press reaction to Labour's landslide victory. The *New Statesman* for 28 July 1945 summed up the impact of the result: 'The 10,000 votes cast for a "freak" candidate against Mr Churchill at Woodford measure the failure of the Tory attempt to turn the election into a personal plebiscite in favour of the Prime Minister . . . the British people . . . plumped for a party which dealt in a sober and practical way with the issues which touch closely their everyday life . . . The country, in short, has voted for socialism.'[13] But in the same breath the *Statesman* identified the storm clouds which quickly gathered around the new government: the disquiet in America; the acute difficulties of the economic situation; and the need to bring the people along with the government's plans. It was also clear that progress would take time. After listing all the difficulties and tasks of the government, under a headline quote from Morrison, 'Bold, Decisive and Sensible', the *Statesman* predicted success but warned: 'In a word, it must keep its promises.'[14] The *Spectator* greeted the first King's Speech with the words: 'neither the Country nor Stock Exchange need alarm itself very gravely yet.'[15] This was a far cry from the women dining in the Savoy Hotel on 26 July who proclaimed, 'But this is terrible – they've elected a Labour Government, the *country* will never stand for that.'[16] Both left- and right-wing periodicals like the *Statesman* and the *Spectator* expressed the immense weight of expectation or trepidation felt by friends and enemies of the government and a certain degree of uncertainty as to what a majority Labour government would be like. When Disraeli passed the 1867 Reform Act and increased the franchise, he had feared that the body politic was taking a leap in the dark. The election of the first majority Labour government represented the same body politic landing.

The government Attlee formed was impressive at every level. It was headed by a Cabinet which, because of the wartime coalition, was the most experienced and talented Labour Cabinet of the century. Attlee was the unifying figure, who led by a combination of being consistently underrated by his opponents, of effectively delegating to his subordinates, and of having the powerful backing of Ernest Bevin. Bevin wielded power within the labour movement by means of his personality, his crucial wartime role, his inter-war leadership and as the virtual creator of the largest single trade union – the Transport and General Workers' Union (TGWU). In the 1945 Cabinet he took the Foreign Office and was outwardly the dominant figure of the government in the early years. Hugh Dalton, Gaitskell's champion, became Chancellor of the Exchequer. Herbert Morrison, Attlee's most verbal political opponent, was appointed Lord President of the Council, with an uneasy overlord role on economic policy that was grand on paper but, not being directly tied to a department, left him floundering somewhat without a power base. A moderate loyalist Chuter Ede, was made Home Secretary. Stafford Cripps went to the Board of Trade and Nye Bevan to Health. All wings of the party were represented and all the main players benefited from six years on-the-job experience.

But the quality did not stop at the top. The largest and most important new intake of Labour MPs of the twentieth century was elected in 1945. Partly because of the sheer numbers of freshers – 227 new Labour MPs in 1945 – and partly because of the political legacy of the previous decade, the reserve of talent from which Labour could draw was uniquely gifted. In the House of Commons the class of 1945 included two future Prime Ministers (James Callaghan and Harold Wilson), three future Foreign Secretaries (George Brown, Patrick Gordon Walker and Michael Stewart), and a host of other future Labour Ministers, leading figures and mavericks. A representative but not exhaustive list would include Richard Crossman, one of the foremost political diarists of the post-war period; Michael Foot, a future leader of the Labour Party and a radical unilateralist; Barbara Castle, a formidable politician and radical; Woodrow Wyatt, at this stage a promising young left-winger; Christopher Mayhew, a close friend and colleague of Gaitskell whose semi-detached approach to politics meant that he did not rise as high as his early promise and skill in the new medium of television suggested; and Ian Mikardo – the quintessential troublesome backbench Labour MP.

Outside the House there was also a generation of talented political thinkers, candidates, policy-makers and politicians who would soon make different kinds of impacts on the Labour Party, including Denis Healey, Peter Shore, Anthony Crosland, Roy Jenkins and Douglas Jay. This political generation with experience of war was about to forge the most successful period of democratic socialist government in the twentieth century, the government which established the basic framework of British politics up to the mid-1980s. It was also a generation of exceptional political and intellectual ability which has produced more of the classic texts on twentieth-century British politics than any other. Beyond all this, they were a generation who believed they could make a difference to the basic structures of society so that it could function more equitably. This belief was not held as a forlorn or idealistic objective but as something tangible and practical that the war had shown was possible, and, perhaps uniquely for a generation with such definite plans, most of the goals were achieved and the consequent institutions lasted for most of their lifetimes. It was this gilded group which Hugh Gaitskell first impressed, then dominated and finally led. In the process some of them became his dedicated followers, others his concerted and bitter enemies; but all eventually had to acknowledge that he came top of the class of 1945. If one considers the leading Ministers at the top of the greasy pole in 1945, the achievement becomes even more marked. There were two figures well established, with long records and deep roots in the party, who were natural choices for top jobs when Labour was first elected – Herbert Morrison and Nye Bevan. Both thought that once the 'little man', Attlee, was out of the way the leadership would be theirs; neither counted on Gaitskell. In sum, Gaitskell came from nowhere to dominate a political generation whose young men and women were the stars of the future and whose established figures were seemingly unassailable champions of the left and right.

Initially, however, Gaitskell and Evan Durbin were deflated by

69

Dalton's insistence that no newly elected members 'would or could get jobs' in the government. (In fact Wilson, Hilary Marquand and George Lingren all got jobs.) Gaitskell also picked up gossip from Dalton on his appointment as Chancellor and on Herbert Morrison's desperate bid to force Clem Attlee from the leadership. Gaitskell's comment was dry, to the point: 'Ambition driving the most intelligent people mad as usual, I suppose.'[17]

Durbin and Gaitskell, close since the 1920s, now entered Parliament together. Durbin was a quieter character than Gaitskell, calmer but just as talented a thinker and debater. Their natural affinity extended beyond politics to a personal friendship rare in political life. They shared holidays together with their families, spending the first summer as MPs in Durbin's Cornish farmhouse writing letters to their respective constituents about demobilisation. The following summer the Gaitskells moved from Well Walk, next to Hampstead Heath, to 18 Frognal Gardens – a large house at the end of a private drive on the top of Hampstead Hill. The Durbins became their tenants. In its time 18 Frognal Gardens was as famous a political house as any in the country, and it gave Gaitskell a base for an active social life: many parties which ended with the carpets being rolled up for dancing, and many meetings, like the Clause 4 weekend of 1959. In 1946, however, with his fellow MP and closest friend as a lodger, it set a Spartan example – a home for Crippsian austerity. As the post-war shortages worsened and rationing had to be extended, Gaitskell turned his garden into a productive vegetable patch; this interest born of necessity continued for the rest of his life. But it was Dora, in the main, who had to manage this austerity, trying to provide hot water for the various lodgers and her own family from the Gaitskell coke ration. The early post-war years were difficult for many. The Gaitskells, though financially secure, suffered along with the rest. The constraints of the war years were continued, and the pace of Gaitskell's career was also soon to be speeded up again, renewing and in some cases extending the pressure on his family life.

When Attlee first formed the government, Gaitskell had to rule himself out, even if a job had been offered, because of his health. He was, though, clearly considered at the highest level for an immediate position. As he was walking into the House for the first session of the new government, Stafford Cripps, his boyhood hero and the new President of the Board of Trade, approached and 'asked me searching questions about my health' – to which Gaitskell honestly replied that he still needed time to recover. 'Is it a matter of a few weeks' rest only?' Gaitskell gave the wonderfully naïve reply that it would be considerably longer until he was fully fit but that he would help in any way he could. To which Cripps responded: 'It really depends on your health.'[18]

Despite his failure to get into the government first time round, he picked up the threads of the XYZ immediately and began drafting work on the bill to nationalise the Bank of England. Moreover, his experience of film at the Board of Trade worked in his immediate favour and he became, after consulting Dalton and Cripps, a paid vice-president of the British Film Producers' Association at £1,000 a year.[19] This combination of easy access to the leading figures of the government and extensive contacts developed during the war meant that Gaitskell was never an ordinary backbencher.

On 1 August he again visited Lord Horder, this time with the Chancellor, and it was confirmed that he was not ready for office. Though he had no choice but to accept the advice, it must have been frustrating to see less able men being appointed. Five days after Gaitskell had visited Horder, the end of the war in Asia became inevitable. 'Exactly fifteen minutes past eight in the morning, on August 6th, 1945, Japanese time . . . the atomic bomb flashed above Hiroshima.'[20] In his diary for 8 August, Gaitskell recorded a rather detached entry more concerned with Evan Durbin's reaction than with his own: 'Everything for the moment is overshadowed by the atomic bomb which we also discussed. Most people are depressed, except for the immediate value in the Japanese war. Evan is now saying Europe is finished, possibly parts of North and South America may survive. He also suggests that if only the U.S.A. were more imperialistically minded the thing for them to do would be to govern the world.'[21] There was no moral outrage at the event, no feeling that the world was changed for ever and that only this counted from now on. It was a significant omission: the bomb, it suggests, did not elicit a profound shift in his thinking or beliefs or represent a defining moment for him; though it was later to engulf his political career, the beginning of the atomic age barely registers a response in his diary.

A week later he was walking through the Central Lobby of the House of Commons when a fellow backbencher, Ellis Smith, came up and told him that the Speaker had called his name to give his maiden speech. Gaitskell was naturally panic-stricken because he had assumed it would be weeks before he was called. He rushed off to find the Speaker and managed to delay it for a week. He finally made his maiden speech, after rehearsing it in front of Dora – the only speech she ever heard like this – on 21 August. His main focus was on the hard work of the Civil Service but he also praised the opposition for being moderate in their hostility to coal nationalisation, suggested action against monopolies, and supported the nationalisation of the Bank of England. The opposition benches were empty and he 'felt it went off rather well' but that Evan Durbin's speech was better and more off the cuff.[22]

Durbin had suffered a similar fate of not being appointed straight away. They had to endure the cycle of gossip about who was in and out, who was resigning or retiring, who had not been up to the job; each week brought hopes raised and dashed. But both had much more access to leading members of the Cabinet than the average backbencher and could make their presence felt through XYZ dinners and meetings with Dalton. During the first weeks of the Attlee government Gaitskell occasionally offered advice to Dalton; he was not sparing in his judgements of some of those who had entered the government and some of the Treasury mandarins he had encountered during the war.

Hugh Dalton was always trying to promote his favourites among the younger MPs. As he expressed it in his diary, 'We must get our good young men on. I am always hammering at the PM on this.'[23] In early May 1946 during an all-night sitting, he led Gaitskell into the lobby, where he told him that the Prime Minister had asked if Gaitskell was fit, and that he, Dalton, had said that he was. The Chancellor then strongly hinted that there would be a place in the government and that he should take whatever was offered. Gaitskell replied that he had already decided on this course: he would not repeat the political naïvety he had shown to Cripps the year before.

The latest rumour was that the sixty-year-old Will Foster, Parliamentary Secretary to Emmanuel Shinwell at the Ministry of Fuel and Power, was resigning – possibly due to ill health. Harold Wilson's Minister, George Tomlinson, at the Ministry of Works, told Wilson to expect a move to Fuel and Power, saying that Gaitskell would get Wilson's old job at the Department of Works. Such a move would have confirmed Wilson's small lead over Gaitskell in the ministerial horse race. The prize, in political terms, was the Fuel and

Power job, because, as Dalton noted, 'They have more nationalisation and post-nationalisation work in this Ministry than in any other in the next two years.' There was also a growing awareness of possible shortages and the Minister, Manny Shinwell, was felt to be in need of expert support. Wilson was therefore 'delighted' with the offer and cancelled an official trip in 'anticipation of a call from Downing Street'.[24]

Instead – unknown to Wilson – Gaitskell was told to see the Chief Whip at 2.15 p.m. In the morning before the meeting, Gaitskell ran into Wilson, who said, 'I hear you're going to a place I'm interested in.' Gaitskell thought he meant Fuel and Power; but Wilson meant that Gaitskell would get his old job at Works. When he arrived to see the Chief Whip, Gaitskell was told he would be offered the post at Fuel and Power. Because his expertise in mines was not as developed as Wilson's, Gaitskell mischievously recorded in his diary, 'Shinwell objected to [Wilson] and chose me because he did not want anyone who was supposed to know about mining to be his Parliamentary Secretary.' Wilson stayed where he was. Shinwell later denied that he knew Wilson had been offered the job, arguing that he had, in fact, been keen on getting Wilson as a PPS the year before. Perhaps a clue to why Gaitskell was offered the post is contained in Dalton's judgement of the appointment: 'He may find personal relations difficult with Shinbad [Dalton's nickname for Shinwell] but, on the other hand, he is very skilled at handling such things.' Perhaps it was Gaitskell's abundant charm and tact – qualities that had served him well during the war – that convinced Attlee he would be able to work effectively with the often difficult Shinwell.

The short interview with the Prime Minister was typical of Attlee's style. Attlee, who had first met Gaitskell in the 1930s, had been impressed by his charm, and he would have made him an Under-Secretary in the government on its formation but for his ill health. Now he brought him into the government as a junior Minister at the age of forty. The PM said, 'I understand you are now well; I wish to have you in the government. Will you take "Mines"?' Then added: 'But this doesn't mean going down mines all the time; there's Gas and Electricity, and the Bills coming along.' Gaitskell was to start on Monday and to get in touch with Shinwell at once. Thus, as soon as his health had improved and a job had become available, he entered the government and he was back in the fast stream.

After the meeting with Attlee, Gaitskell rang up Shinwell and had a similarly monosyllabic introduction to life as a government Minister:

> 'I understand you're going to be my new Parliamentary Secretary.'
> 'Yes, I understand so.'
> (after a pause) 'Well, that's all right. We've got this Bill on Monday but you won't be able to do much.'
> 'No, I suppose not.'
> 'There's a meeting this evening with the Attorney-General and the Financial Secretary – you can come if you like.'
> I said 'I did like.'[25]

Harold Wilson went straight into the Attlee government as a junior Minister and was later skilful at managing the cumbersome Parliamentary Labour Party; Michael Foot spent decades campaigning at the grass roots and from the back benches but as Labour leader had extreme difficulty controlling the party: so a long period on the back benches is no guarantee of successful leadership. Nevertheless, perhaps a little longer on the back benches would have given Gaitskell a greater feel for the party, although there are other possible reasons for Gaitskell's later relative failure as a party manager. The real problem created by his short stay on the back benches was that he did not throw off the administrative film he had acquired during the war and reconnect with the more radical phase that had come just before. A little longer on the outside might have allowed him more time to develop that independence of mind and judgement so characteristic of his last years but somewhat lacking in the Attlee period. But this is merely speculation. With his experience and competence, Gaitskell would have been wasted as lobby fodder and he had no compensating campaigning gifts that would have enabled him to serve the party as, to use Roy Jenkins's phrase, a 'politician at large'.

The Mines appointment had a particular importance. The Labour government's economic policy was directed across two broad and difficult fronts: the reconstruction of Britain's industrial base, which required an emphasis on production; and the construction of a welfare state, which required an emphasis on welfare provision. Significantly, the Labour government did not believe you could have one without the other. As Douglas Jay recorded in his memoirs: 'A myth has grown up since then that the Attlee Government after 1945 plunged into vast expensive welfare schemes and ignored the hard economic base of production and exports which could alone support

them. This is almost the reverse of the truth.'[26] The case has been
well argued by Jim Tomlinson, among others: 'One question to be
asked is whether a benign dictator, with the knowledge available at
the time, and concerned to maximize the long-run growth of the
British economy, would have accorded these industries priority. For
coal, iron and steel, and electricity the answer would perhaps have
been "yes" – at that time these three industries looked crucial to
any industrial expansion.'[27] In fact Labour made many hard and
successful economic decisions in these years and welfare simply has
not been proved to be among the causes of post-war Britain's relative
economic decline. One way of grasping the extent of Labour's commitment to the supply side of economic management is simply to
read a list of the industries nationalised by the government. It brings
home both the pace and the extent of the change:

1946	The Bank of England
	The coal industry
	Civil aviation
1947	Electricity
1948	Railways and canals
	Gas
1949	Iron and steel

It was to electricity, oil and coal that Gaitskell now directed his
energy. Gaitskell was actually well qualified for the job and in all
the technical – parliamentary and administrative – aspects he was a
success; in selling the government's austerity policy in the bleak
winter of 1947 he was less sure of himself and had much more
to learn. His expertise was based on personal experience of the
Nottinghamshire coalfield from the 1920s and, more importantly,
his work at the Board of Trade for Hugh Dalton. In 1942 he had
told Dalton that the biggest question he would face as president was:
'Can you ration fuel? . . . and you will have to go into it in great
detail yourself.' The question came back to haunt Gaitskell.

His first task was to help steer the passage of the Coal Nationalisation Bill through the House of Commons. In his first week in the
job he impressed many by taking some of the amendments in the
House. Despite the picture that is sometimes presented, the opposition was bitter and later, when facing Brendan Bracken, he felt it:

'I have to sit in a committee of the House, opposite Mr Brendan Bracken, listening to every kind of taunt and insult and not being able to reply because it would prolong the debate. We are the scapegoats for everything. It is surprising how many people hold me personally responsible for what happens in their coal cellars.'[28] But this was the future. First Gaitskell had to get himself back into the coal industry and prepare for what his close friend Douglas Jay was warning would be a coming disaster.

Gaitskell's political position was a little exposed. Shinwell may have blocked Wilson because of his expertise, but it is more surprising that he did not block Gaitskell because of his closeness to Dalton. Shinwell and Dalton hated each other. George Wigg, a Shinwell supporter who attacks Dalton repeatedly in his account of the situation, had only praise for Gaitskell: 'A pleasant memory was that Gaitskell, Dalton's nominee in the Ministry, did his job ably and faithfully. He was in continuous session presiding over the committee, tackling problems as they arose, improvising and generally making the best of a bad job.'[29] The 'bad job' had some similarities to the 1942 situation but many important differences.

The reliance on coal had not let up and the loan which Keynes had secured from America and Canada to bail Britain out in 1945 when the Lend–Lease wartime credit system had been withdrawn provided only a temporary respite. Britain was facing, in Keynes's words, a financial Dunkirk. The initial strength of the legislative programme had only partially alleviated the potential collapse of the basic economic infrastructure of Britain. Moreover, although Gaitskell's health had improved, he was not fully recovered and other members of the government were beginning to feel the strain of six years of war followed by the daunting workload of the peace. For the Under-Secretary at Fuel and Power the problem was how to achieve the economy of fuel consumption needed within the framework of a peacetime set of controls. The task called for a combination of administrative expertise inside the corridors of the Ministry and public relations expertise in selling constraint to the British public; in the former Gaitskell excelled, in the latter he floundered.

The significance of what Gaitskell was doing in these years should not be overlooked. As Peter Hennessy puts it in *Never Again*, 'Coal never lost its symbolic, almost romantic, place in the Labour movement as the industry where the excesses of capitalism had left blood in the seams.' It was Hugh Gaitskell who carried the brunt of the committee stage and wound up the final debate on nationalising this industry; and it was Gaitskell who wound up the second reading debate on electricity nationalisation: reported as being 'the most accomplished performance by a junior minister in this Parliament'. It was Gaitskell who shouldered much of the ministerial burden of the 1947 fuel crisis when the systems created by the Nationalisation Act virtually collapsed in the face of a sudden freeze. Douglas Jay and James Meade had been warning Gaitskell for months of the possible problems and Gaitskell had tried to get this through to Manny Shinwell – who dismissed him as a Wykehamist who did not know the miners. Finally, on Thursday 6 February, Shinwell had to ask the Cabinet to close down the power stations – blaming the Minister of Transport for the crisis. Gaitskell was in his constituency when the crisis struck. He organised lorry convoys of Yorkshire coal into stricken Lancashire, rising, as in Austria years before, to the practical challenge of an emergency. On his return to London, it was Gaitskell who ran the key committee that decided where the coal should go. His administrative decisiveness and skill made a considerable impression throughout the department and the Cabinet.[30]

Unfortunately, the relationship with Shinwell was strained almost to breaking point by Gaitskell's competence. The younger Minister tried to fulfil Dalton's hope that his charm would work, but confided to his diary that Shinwell 'walks alone one feels because he has never been able to fully trust anyone. The cause? Basically no doubt being Jewish. But there are plenty of Jews who are not suspicious. "He always had to fight." He always *fought* but may not that too have been his preference? No, without knowledge of his childhood and boyhood I can offer no further plausible explanation.' He found Shinwell suspicious, competitive and somewhat neurotic: ' "Passing the buck" is frequent enough between Ministers. But Shinwell did not pass it. He picked it up and hurled it.'[31] Those characteristics bred insecurity and actually fed the attacks that Shinwell feared; but it was administrative failure rather than personality faults that led to his being demoted, to Minister of War outside the Cabinet – which Shinwell took badly. The reconstruction of the government led to a challenge from Stafford Cripps, the inter-war maverick who had became an extremely popular figure during the war, to Attlee's leadership. This was resolved, with Bevin's weight behind the PM, by moving Cripps to be an economic overlord and Gaitskell's own promotion to number one at Fuel and Power on 7 October 1947.

Gaitskell had another interview with the Prime Minister. Attlee began in his usual clipped tones, 'I am reconstructing the government. I want you to be Fuel and Power.' Gaitskell replied, 'Oh! Well!' Attlee: 'It is not a bed of roses.' Gaitskell: 'I know that already.' So Gaitskell was made a full Minister, but outside the Cabinet. He had to keep the news private for three or four days and travelled to his constituency. On the day the reshuffle was made public he was speaking in Swadlincote, a mile from the location of one of his old WEA classes. A former pupil was showing him round and he met Tom Baxter, the regional organiser who had been Evan Durbin's agent in East Grinstead in 1931 and who had first persuaded Gaitskell to go forward as a candidate for Chatham. Returning to the department after the announcement had been made, he found a general welcome and a good response in the press. In the country the first headlines the new Minister attracted were not the ones he would have chosen. But for people of a certain generation, Hugh Gaitskell is particularly remembered for his first speech as Minister of Fuel and Power.

Having won an award at school for never missing a cold plunge bath perhaps Gaitskell had developed an adult aversion; whatever the cause the speech illustrated the amount he still had to learn about political communication. He had set out on a series of speeches urging fuel economy. In Hastings he was appealing for electricity economy in the home and said: 'Personally, I've never had a great many baths myself. And I can assure those who are in the habit of having a great many baths that it does not make a great deal of difference to their health if they have less. And as for your appearance most of that is underneath and nobody sees it.' In private, Herbert Morrison told him later that the Labour Party was rather touchy on the subject and did not like being considered dirtier than the Tories.[32] In public, Gaitskell was made to pay bitterly for the speech. At the end of the Gas Bill Committee stage he was summing up with the words 'When we look at the faces of hon. Members opposite it is easy to think of various bits of animal life, but we do not want to follow the Opposition . . .' Brendan Bracken interrupted, 'At any rate, they wash.'[33] At a dinner party a little after the baths speech, Evan Durbin added the perfect postscript: 'You all call it a joke, but I can assure you it is statement of fact. I live with the Minister of Fuel and Power and as far as I know he never has any baths at all!'[34]

There are few phrases that one associates directly with Gaitskell before 1960 and unfortunately this is one of them.

Sub-Churchillian speech-making was much in vogue. In August 1946 Gaitskell had called the miners the 'fighter pilots of 1946' and declared that the fate of the country was in their hands; this must have endeared him to the mineworkers, a group that was fast becoming a bedrock of his support, and the phrase was picked up and used by senior Ministers, though it has a somewhat hollow ring.[35] Other attempts at eloquence were also rather lame. On 28 February 1948, speaking in Blackpool, Gaitskell stressed that the country was nearing the exhaustion of its reserves and could not rely on the help of others. He then launched into a tortuous oration: 'We are like a man climbing a mountain. There is a strong wind blowing across our path – blowing towards a dangerous precipice which lies one side [sic]. We do not control the wind. And now it is blowing more strongly. We have got to get past that precipice to the easier uplands that lie beyond. And to do it we still need all the qualities that made our Nation great.'[36] He was actually a better speaker when quietly but firmly putting a complex case: he could carry much before him simply by his confidence in his argument and was especially good at explaining complex matters.

Gaitskell was to discover the many hazards of government office. Ministers had to keep a careful watch on their own behaviour because any hint that they might be receiving special treatment would be pounced on by a press enjoying its regained freedom and savouring the return of the cut and thrust of party politics. A sense of the atmosphere of the time and of the care with which Labour Ministers had to lead by example can be gleaned from two stories, one concerning the consumption of two bread rolls, the other about alleged preferential treatment for Ministers on the newly nationalised British Railways.

In July 1948 Gaitskell attended a luncheon, and the shocked press reported: 'Both Ministers and chairman [of the meeting] had bread with their three course meal, though restrictions on the serving of bread at restaurants do not end till tomorrow.' Thankfully a major scandal was averted because 'Neither they nor the Connaught Rooms were breaking the law. A member had arrived armed with some rolls, two of which he deposited on the top table.'[37] The point of this story is that bread rationing had not yet ended and the rhetoric of fair shares had to be constantly lived up to: the reconciliation of planning and freedom was based, in a concrete and day-to-day sense, on equality of sacrifice. It was especially important for Gaitskell, who was shifting the government's emphasis away from Wilson's developing line that there should be a huge bonfire of controls, and towards the view that some controls would have to be maintained permanently.

The second incident occurred in May 1949 and concerns the prospective Liberal candidate in Hugh's South Leeds seat, Mr R. D. Broughton, who first contacted the press with the story. Gaitskell was travelling to London by train and sitting reading a two-shilling novel, *Where the Pavement Ends* – the first but not the last rather unlikely feature of this story – in the first-class dining carriage. Mr R. D. Broughton spotted him and sat down opposite him. Gaitskell then beckoned to the car superintendent and indicated Mr Broughton. At once the attendant approached Mr Broughton and asked, 'Would you please mind moving to another seat?' Mr Broughton replied: 'Why should I? I am perfectly comfortable where I am.' The attendant said, 'Well, sir, as a special favour would you mind moving? I will see that you get the very best service in the car.' After Mr Broughton had moved, the attendant claimed that the railway workers had very strict guidelines about preventing government Ministers from being bothered by the general public. On 22 May the papers carried Gaitskell's and British Railways' denials that the incident ever took place. A statement issued from the Ministry of Fuel and Power said, 'He has never read the book mentioned, and has never asked the railway authorities to make special arrangements for his dining car facilities.'

Despite these moments of bad publicity, Gaitskell stuck to his guns: in January 1948 he told the Electrical Association for Women that they could 'do a great deal by teaching the women of the country how and when, and when not, to use electricity'. In speech after speech he urged economy and saving of power: he told stokers to be careful and praised the growth of open-cast mining; and he consistently defended the heads of nationalised industry against smears, sneers and innuendo about their levels of pay, calling the accusers 'mudslingers'.[38]

His difficult campaign on fuel economy, on which he had been working hard as Under-Secretary, was made even more daunting by the Cabinet's decision, made just as he was promoted, to stop all supply of domestic petrol. There were 2,232,270 licences for cars in 1946, and although their owners were predominantly middle class the expected saving of £36 million was at the price of upsetting a geographically even spread of voters in the vital Midlands and southern seats that made up a precious element of the Labour government's majority.

Gaitskell did all he could to alleviate the impact of the ration, ensuring that the backlog of complaints was answered and agreeing six out of seven applications for 'supplementary rations'. The *Manchester Guardian* praised the 'sweet reasonableness, manly sympathy, confidential frankness and firm hand' with which he put across the government's case. However, not all his efforts were so successful. Having lobbied hard to make a broadcast on the BBC about the petrol ration, he was then approached by Movietone News, who wanted to feature him in a cinema newsreel. He checked with Clem Leslie, the head of the Treasury Information Department, who offered the following advice: 'Be careful and insist on seeing the film before it is released. It can be a very dangerous medium.' Gaitskell wanted his script to be written up on a blackboard like a teleprompter but the technicians insisted the lights would prevent him from being able to read, so he had to learn the script. It was hot, the lights were blinding and he had no producer. After he had consulted Leslie's people about watching the film in advance, they agreed that it could be released. The following Thursday, 22 January, Gaitskell went to the first night of Alexander Korda's *Anna Karenina* starring Vivien Leigh. The newsreel came on and he watched himself looking 'terribly serious' and 'blinking a lot'. The audience began to boo and hiss and, worse, there was some laughter. 'I felt horribly embarrassed and really suffered agony for some time, not because of the booing so much as because I felt the film was ridiculous and cursed myself for agreeing to its release.'[39]

Cutting off the ration for petrol was not the most significant intervention Gaitskell made in the oil industry. In 1939, 80 per cent of petroleum products had reached the UK in refined forms: there was no British refining industry to speak of. The British oil industry had developed only slowly since the turn of the century when the Admiralty had begun to substitute oil for coal in their battleships. The key players in the industry became the Burmah Oil Company – exploiting 'the only part of the empire with significant proved oil deposits' and exporting for the Admiralty through Rangoon, where Gaitskell's father had been Commissioner for Settlement and Land

Records – and Burmah's subsidiary, the Anglo-Persian Oil Company, which became British Petroleum. In addition to the two main companies there was the largely Dutch-owned Shell. The Petroleum Department, created in the First World War, had been in virtual abeyance until 1936, when as part of the rearmament process it was strengthened and then transferred to the Ministry of Fuel and Power in 1942 and thus came under Gaitskell's control in 1947.

He launched an extensive review of the existing situation and discovered the main contribution of the oil companies to the UK balance of payments. 'When the results were tabulated, some Ministers thought that two or three noughts must have been added to them by mistake. It was realised that the earnings of these three companies were a major factor in the UK balance of payments and the strength of sterling, and that by a policy of "substituting" sterling for dollar oil, and also by building refineries in the UK and sterling area, a further major easement of Britain's economic difficulties was achieved.'[40] As the historian of Burmah Oil has written, the other objective was to encourage 'a petrochemical industry, as well as domestic manufacturing facilities for refining equipment, hitherto obtainable only from the US' – the result being that 'by 1960 about 77 per cent of Britain's oil needs were imported in crude form'.[41] In this, Gaitskell's ministerial role was crucial, effective and far-sighted. But the real work on this took place in closed, élite circles: in private meetings and through ministerial and private-sector channels, getting the oil companies acquainted with the government and vice versa.

When dealing with the general public, Gaitskell was more effective in small groups and in impromptu situations, since he tended to be stilted if speaking from the platform. Sometimes, however, the pressure he was under and his strong attachment to the Labour government's cause could make his speech break through into open emotion. It was on these occasions that Gaitskell made a major impact and marked himself out from the run-of-the-mill Ministers – not always in a positive way.

On the first of the few instances when the quiet passion burst through, although not intended for any political effect, it was immensely powerful. The occasion was a speech at a coalfield visit. He began confidently enough, speaking of this 'moment of supreme crisis': 'We don't know what the election result will be – I don't know whether you will be able to ask me to your conference next

82

year – but nobody could have been a member of our government in these last years with all its worries without having an immense feeling of pride.' The Nottinghamshire coalfield, the pressure of the 1947 winter fuel crisis, the long hours of travel and work, the possibility of failure – all perhaps came seeping through as his voice broke: 'I am proud particularly of the experience I have had with you. Whatever happens I shall never forget these coalfield visits.'[42] Gaitskell grasped a tumbler of water to hide his emotions; his face was deathly white, and for a moment he staggered as if he were about to collapse. Clearly the emotional breakdown deeply embarrassed the old Wykehamist, for he kept repeating apologies for his emotions to the miners' leaders long after the conference had broken up. But the miners' leaders assured him that the impact had been electric. He confided to his diary; 'For the first time in my public life, tears came into my eyes and I had to stop speaking for a few seconds and have a drink of water. From the point of view of the speech it was, I suppose, extremely effective. Emotion is infectious, and as somebody said to me afterward when I apologised, it was what really made the speech.'[43] It was the first time in his public life that he had failed to maintain the façade of his public persona and it was the most significant public intervention Gaitskell had thus far made in his career.

Gaitskell's first major role as a politician was to create and then deal with the failure of nationalised industries. He believed in nationalisation not only on grounds of efficiency, economies of scale and rationalisation of production, but as morally right; yet he was also aware of the limitations and, though he defended the structure of the industries to the hilt, he was somewhat ambiguous in describing how the public corporation had been devised. The problem was that Gaitskell, like the rest of the Labour government, put far too much faith in the nationalisation programme. The result could hardly be presented as the socialisation of industry or, indeed, anything very much to do with socialism – no workers' control or involvement and no real change in management structure – but Gaitskell's real hope for the industries was that the relationship between workers and bosses would be transformed. It was a hope that was never realised.

Gaitskell spent much of the middle and late 1950s persuading his party that the Morrisonian model of nationalisation – the centralised public corporation – should not have been seen as the main feature of a socialist economic policy. These battles were more constructive and less vitriolic than the corresponding foreign and defence policy battles of the 1950s, and they succeeded in moving the party away from shopping-list nationalisations, back towards the broader range of policies that had been debated at length in those Bloomsbury groups of the 1930s and in part developed by the Attlee government. However, they did not move the Labour Party towards the market – which was still fundamentally regarded as the cause of unemployment, inefficiency and inequality. His stance in all these debates was grounded in as much, if not more, direct experience of the industries than any leading Labour politician.

The year 1949 was when Gaitskell made his greatest strides forward and ahead of the pack. David Marquand summed up the significance of his actions thus: 'He played the key part in persuading the economically "tone-deaf" Attlee that the run on the reserves which developed in the summer of 1949 should be halted by devaluing sterling rather than by the orthodox methods that had destroyed MacDonald's Labour Government in 1931.'[44] It was a group of young Ministers who were crucial to bringing to a head, in the absence of the Chancellor, a debate on changing the value of sterling that had first surfaced among officials in 1942.

Douglas Jay decided on the need for devaluation on Sunday 17 July 1949 as he walked across Hampstead Heath – persuaded by the possible gains in exports. Gaitskell, at home on the other side of the Heath, made the same decision on the same day. On Monday morning they met and told each other the way their minds were moving, then lunched with the economist Nicholas Kaldor, who urged them to support devaluation. After lunch, Attlee announced that Wilson, Gaitskell, Jay and another Labour Minister, W. G. Hall, would be deputising for the Chancellor, Stafford Cripps. On Wednesday 20 July, the Wykehamists made a full confession to each other and worked out their case in detail before having dinner and persuading Aneurin Bevan, John Strachey and George Strauss of the case. They extended the lobbying to Wilson, who hedged – agreeing with the need for devaluation but unsure of the timing. The three young Ministers – Gaitskell, Jay and Wilson – then had a series of meetings with senior members of the government: Jay urged immediate action, Wilson argued for a delay until after the regular meeting of the IMF in September and Gaitskell steered a diplomatic course between the two, taking the lead in the presentations. Attlee agreed with him that the devaluation should take place before the IMF meeting in Washington but after Cripps's return to England from Zurich, where he was recovering from an illness.

The decision to devalue was finally reached on Thursday 28 July, and Wilson offered to take the news to the Chancellor in Zurich. Attlee, however, decided that Wilson should take Cripps a letter, and this was drafted by Douglas Jay. Jay's first draft, which set out the case for action, was redrafted by Sir Edward Bridges so that more emphasis was placed on waiting until after the meeting in Washington. When Gaitskell saw this he exploded and insisted they return to the original draft – which, with some amendments, they did. Wilson then took the letter to Cripps. Later Wilson tried to claim that he had swayed the government to this course and that he was the only person who could inform the Chancellor, because they were so close. In fact, Attlee's insistence on the letter made Wilson simply a message carrier. Douglas Jay alleges that Wilson went out of his way to make it appear that he was the critical factor in the decision, when in fact he reserved his judgement on numerous occasions and had generally dithered. Jay never trusted Wilson again after the devaluation episode, and senior Ministers also seem to have been unimpressed. Moreover, Jay, who as the leading Treasury Minister involved should have been the natural choice to take the lead, had tended to defer to Gaitskell.

Thus it was Gaitskell who consolidated his position as the leader of the three young economists by the straightforwardness of his approach, by the way he stood up to officials and by the two memoranda he prepared in the space between the decision and Cripps's return. The first was a ten-page summary of the case for devaluation and the second a shorter note in favour of an early election before the short-run effects of the devaluation could be felt or a much later election after the benefits had flowed. One point was made forcefully in the memoranda: 'The essential thing to keep firmly in mind in face of the cataract of advice and propaganda pouring in upon us is *that the only major economic problem is the dollar gap*. Employment is high, production is high, the overall balance of payments is not bad, there is inflationary pressure, but no runaway inflation. If it were not for this dollar gap we should have little to worry about.'[45] At heart, then, the only economic problem for Britain was caused by the rapid expansion of the protected American economy, producing the dollar gap, because the new forms of intervention had solved the other economic problems. Thus in the dark days of the Attlee governments the profound optimism on which the 1950s revisionist approach to Labour's economic policy – the idea that the difficulty was in distributing the benefits of economic growth and not in creating that growth – was born.

On Cripps's return the Prime Minister invited Wilson and Gaitskell to join him, Cripps and Bevin to discuss the matter. Cripps eventually agreed with the necessity for action. Devaluation was delayed until September, not because of the case for waiting until after the American trip but because of Cripps's health. Bevin and Cripps decided on the rate while in the USA and on Sunday 19 September 1949 the pound was devalued by 30 per cent from $4.03 to $2.80. Though this was later and more than Gaitskell had argued for, his conduct during the devaluation crisis was crucial in his appointment as Chancellor, which in turn ensured that he became the leading political figure of his generation – something that earlier had by no means been obvious.

This was the technical Gaitskell, the administrator, the master of a brief; this was the Wykehamist who in private argument could use skills of analysis and conversation and the force of his charisma to dominate a situation. But a deep personal sadness afflicted his life at this time, the aftermath of a tragedy the previous year which Gaitskell recorded, with characteristic precision and feeling, in his diary:

> We had just come back from a long walk to Abbotsbury – a walk with Ronnie Edwards and his wife, an old colleague of Evan's, and had just finished dinner when the telephone rang for me. It was Miss Bolton [a private secretary] who gave me the news. She said that she thought I would not have wished to hear it on the nine o'clock radio.

It was a windy day in the cottage in Cornwall in which the Gaitskells and the Durbins had all stayed on that first holiday after becoming MPs. Evan Durbin was staying there in the summer of 1948 with his family and friends.

> Evan wanted to bathe, and particularly to bathe at Strangles Beach . . . he persuaded them and the whole party went, taking lunch with them and intending to go back to tea. Marjorie came last with Geoffrey whom she had to carry down the cliffpath. As she went down Evan, Jossie and a child called Tessa Algar (father is the propaganda man in Transport House), plus Nadine and Tom Marshall, were all going in. Marjorie says that she saw that the left hand side of the beach was all right, there were

big rollers coming in but they were breaking evenly ... But the right hand side was horrible, all potholes and whirlpools ... The children then started to come in and moved diagonally (this was the fatal thing) across the beach to where their clothes were; thus passing through the nasty part where they soon got into difficulties ... Evan got hold of Jossie ... and managed to get her into shallower and safer water.

Then Evan Durbin turned to find that the other child had been swept out of her depth and he swam towards her. Exhausted, he managed to save her by getting close to some rocks and his wife Marjorie whisked the girl out, but, when she turned, Durbin had gone.

I still cannot get it firmly into my head that he has gone. Every now and then I think about it again. I suppose one's personal loss declines as time passes, at least one will feel it less frequently. But the full loss to his friends and to the country will be there, sure enough. There is nobody else who had his pecular combination of theoretical and practical knowledge of Labour policy and the intelligence and will-power needed. And, there is nobody else in my life whom I can consult on the most fundamental issues, knowing that I shall get the guidance that I want.[46]

Most of all perhaps, Durbin was Gaitskell's first political friend, his first socialist friend and the closest to his beliefs politically – indeed, they seem to have influenced each other and grown together in those beliefs. In such a relationship of growth there are unspoken bonds of mutual respect that cannot be matched in relationships that develop later in life: such a friend can tell you truths and argue with you from a point of real equality. Gaitskell found it hard to control the tears in the days that followed. While one can never really know these things it is surely true that Durbin was his closest male friend and his subsequent close ties with men like Crosland and Jenkins were on a much less equitable basis. More than this, a phase of Gaitskell's life ended with the death of Durbin.

5

Chancellor for Dentures and Defence, 1949–1951

I am not an actor, but he is.

Edwin Plowden, 1950

I think the appointment of Gaitskell to be a great mistake.

Nye Bevan, 1950

He rose a comparative tyro and sat down an acknowledged star.

Glasgow Herald, 11 April 1951

Aside from the brief rest in 1945 – forced by illness – Gaitskell had worked tirelessly in peace and war for the whole of the 1940s. In many ways his life was a typical 1940s story: hard work, a dislocated home life, the beginning of a young family, maturity and success accelerated by the intensity of war. The difference was that Gaitskell had moved through the upper echelons of the wartime Civil Service and into the upper reaches of the Labour government. Eating at his desk, frequently working three weekends out of four, living through personal austerity and rationing (often items on which he had himself put limits), having to explain this continued hardship and sacrifice to a nation who had endured the war and seemed to be getting few of the benefits of the peace: this was an unrelenting task. In the 1940s there was less fun, less good food – it is noticeable how often good meals crop up in his diary as noteworthy in the late 1940s – compared to the mid-1950s,[1] and obviously less relaxation than in the 1930s. His home life was happy and settled, and he could be relaxed and playful with his young daughters, climbing over the cliffs of Jersey with them on one summer holiday in 1949.[2] Dora was a good political wife and champion, the 1945 election campaign was one of many trying times which she coped with, and they were occasionally able to escape to Dorset or out for a night's dancing.

The 1940s were a patchwork decade with dreary expanses of hard work, austerity and war, interspersed with brightly coloured patches of exhilaration, achievement and even some popular recognition. They ended with an extraordinary combination of personal tragedy and political triumph. The 1950s began with Gaitskell's ascent to fourth place on the greasy pole of political success.

By the summer of 1949 the Attlee government was approaching the twilight of the Parliament – the curious period in which, because of the lack of fixed terms in the British system, the timing of the election is left to the Prime Minister. Labour governments have suffered from the ambiguities of the system since the war. In 1964 the Conservative Prime Minister, Alec Douglas-Home, nearly confounded everyone by hanging on until the very end of the Parliament. When deciding the date of the 1970 election, Harold Wilson did not allow for the inclusion of two jumbo jets in the trade figures and Britain's defeat in the football World Cup and so unexpectedly lost. James Callaghan delayed the 1979 election until almost the last possible moment and thereby endured the explosion of trade union militancy which buried his government in the so-called 'winter of discontent'. In each case different timing might have helped. The trend was set in 1950 by Clem Attlee.

Gaitskell's 'Political Strategy' memo to the leading members of the Cabinet of 18 August 1949 had concluded: 'The Foreign Secretary has suggested, I believe, that we ought to go to the country as "the government that weathered the storm". It is an attractive idea. But let us be reasonably sure that if we pin ourselves down to next June, we shall have weathered the storm by then and not missed a convenient lull which seems highly probable this November.'[3] Either November or June seemed to the Minister of Fuel and Power the best option, but not any time in between. Attlee summoned his Ministers to discuss the issue on 7 December. Cripps refused, on moral[4] and tactical[5] grounds, to introduce another Budget before the next election.[6] The date was therefore fixed for 23 February 1950 and announced on 10 January. This timetable created a long campaign, which gave the government's enemies time to muster their attack, and produced the first election since 1906 held in the depths of winter.[7] (On that occasion the Liberal opposition had won a landslide against a somewhat exhausted Conservative government.)

Gaitskell's initial feeling was that the government's majority would be reduced to under 50. He feared the impact of redistribution of seats by the boundary commission and, more interestingly, felt that 'one other factor cannot be ignored. The Government interferes so much in people's lives these days that the swing of the pendulum is likely to be far greater than ever before. This may lead to a surprise. Only a very small proportion of votes have to change over to make such a big difference in the number of seats.'

At Cripps's New Year party – 'there was no drink except sherry and apple juice. The meal was pretty foul and conversation, not surprisingly, drab and commonplace'[8] – they relieved the boredom by all writing down predictions of the result. Gaitskell's was the second most pessimistic after Douglas Jay's: Gaitskell went for a majority of 30, somewhat down on his earlier guess, and Jay predicted losing the election by 30. When Gaitskell's guess was read out, Bevan commented that with such a low majority 'I would rather not be in power at all.'[9]

With a date he had advised strongly against, and in a pessimistic mood about the result, Gaitskell launched himself into his first defence of South Leeds in a general election. He found the time passing slowly and the endless repetitive speech-making tedious.[10] He spent longer in South Leeds in 1950 than in his subsequent elections, but still made frequent journeys to neighbouring constituencies to speak for fellow candidates. His main emphasis was on his departmental field, stressing that coal production was going to break all records. When he spoke on broader themes it was to stress that the Tories and private enterprise could not be trusted on full employment.

> So this is the choice. Freedom for sectional interests or Full Employment for the People. You cannot have both. Tory policy is to favour the sectional interests every time and it is to these interests that their whole appeal is addressed. The Labour Party believes that controls which are needed to ensure work for all should be kept on because this is an essential foundation for the true liberty which depends on economic security.[11]

This reflected his abiding faith in physical controls which, according to a contemporary historian, would ensure the 'balance of payments of equilibrium, and . . . avoid inflation' but 'were designed for economic stabilization rather than modernization, hence their negative character'.[12] As in 1945, there was a solid ideological underpinning to the election campaign. It was not expressed in such extreme language as at the earlier contest but it was certainly evident.

Many meetings in 1950 gave Gaitskell trouble but some also gave him special pleasure. An untypical meeting took place in the Oxford Union supporting Elizabeth Pakenham, who was the Oxford City Labour Party candidate. Though Elizabeth was not optimistic about winning the seat – 'The fight would be a "propaganda" fight'[13] – she put up a good show against Quintin Hogg. Frank Pakenham spoke too and it was a good knockabout political meeting. There were not as many hecklers as in Gaitskell's meeting at Enfield the previous night[14] but they asked him hard questions about the quality of coal that was being supplied to the home market and the increase in the price of domestic coal. Gaitskell enjoyed the evening: 'They were very sweet and flattering about my speech and one could not help feeling what a pleasure it was to have such friends in the middle of all this political struggle.'[15]

But Oxford was the exception to the regular grind of the election. In Coalville and Molesey, where he fielded questions on the nationalisation of sugar and cement, he had an off-night, giving some feeble answers.[16] The next day at his adoption meeting in South Leeds he was back on form and hitting hard on his key themes: 'It is not enough for the Tories just to want full employment. It cannot be done without economic planning and planning cannot be effective without the use of economic, industrial, and financial controls. These are the controls that the Tories are never tired of denouncing as vexatious, bureaucratic tyranny.'[17] His performance was always measured but the tone was damning. He wrapped himself in the ministerial shroud and though sometimes there was a little too much of the 'Whitehall knows best' about him, often he could command an audience with the force of his words. He was not a powerful platform speaker at this time, and often came over as a cross between a slightly awkward don and an over-briefed civil servant.

However, he did show his mettle in one exchange during the campaign when he let slip glimpses of the more substantial politician that the donnish civil servant was keeping tightly repressed. It was the only time he made a national impact in the 1950 battle and it was in response to attacks from Winston Churchill. Gaitskell's views on Churchill were entirely conventional. In 1940 he helped Dalton scheme for the formation of a coalition under Churchill and fully endorsed the view of him as a great wartime leader. He also realised that Churchill was a partisan opponent and never gave him excessive respect. Churchill's role in 1950 was more diluted than it had been in 1945 but he had asserted that the Conservatives had been kept in the dark about petrol rationing. Gaitskell dismissed the claim out of hand: 'The only information that was kept back was the volume of reserves and this was for security reasons.'[18] He defended the rationing of petrol in terms of the dollar gap and pledged that it would be lifted as soon as possible. But he also warned that the rationing might be extended: 'We would rather keep motorists a bit short than stop the factories and mills and throw the workers on the street, and it is better to go easy on petrol than be short of bread.'[19] The next day, speaking at Hemsworth in Yorkshire, he compared unemployment in Germany and Italy with Labour's Britain, claiming that it was lower in the UK because of controls, and also stressed the great strides made in increasing wages; then on to Barnsley, Huddersfield, Cleckheaton and back to Leeds. On 16 February he was again attacking Churchill's claims on the petrol position with detailed and strident denials. Churchill had claimed that there was plenty of oil in the sterling area.[20] It was a spirited series of responses from a junior Minister to the leader of the opposition and was widely reported.

At Barnsley there were arguments about whether Gaitskell could be entertained by the municipality as part of the election rather than as a Minister of the Crown; at Cleckheaton there had been a rumpus about whether or not the Americans were jealous of the British social security system.[21] In the Barnsley meeting Gaitskell also expressed his fears for the future of the nationalised industries if the Conservatives were elected. Generally, it was the competent performance of a politician feeling his way into the front rank but not quite there yet in terms of public recognition or the ability to capture the headlines. He made neither any great gaffes nor any great impact.

In contrast, his main rival had a rough and bad campaign. Nye Bevan was wrong about the date of the election and much was made of his speech in 1948 in which he had said that the Tories were lower than vermin (even Harold Laski criticised it) and of a later one in which he had claimed that the middle class liked servants so that they could have someone to order about.[22] Bevan was kept isolated during the campaign itself and was blamed for frightening the middle-class voters who would have maintained the Labour Party's dominance of the Commons.

Gaitskell's election in his own South Leeds seat was a comfortable victory in one of the few Labour areas that had benefited from a national redistribution of seats. Overall, Labour lost out, since constituency boundaries had been redrawn to reflect movements in population. Gaitskell's first two general election results were both comfortable wins: in 1950 he increased his 1945 majority from 10,402 to 15,359. As usual Gaitskell donated £100 towards his own election expenses, which totalled £690 8s. 4d.; the divisional party made up the vast bulk of this, £450 8s. 4d.,[23] a proportion that was never repeated. The Labour Party was at the height of its membership and influence at a local as well as a national level and this was reflected in a small way by the large amount the divisional party managed to raise in 1950.

The Labour Party suffered one of the worst electoral reversals ever inflicted by the inequities of the first-past-the-post system.* The total number of Labour votes increased from 11,995,152 to 13,266,592, but the number of seats was slashed from 393 to 315. Labour's core support had increased by 1.27 million but the spread was concentrated and the losses came in the seats that the high tide of 1945 had swept to Labour with small majorities. Above and beyond this, Labour had a majority over the Conservatives of 764,025 votes.

Two unfortunate pieces of rhetoric from Bevan could not really be blamed for such an outcome. Gaitskell concluded that the result 'of the election seemed to suggest that the Morrison policy of going slow and retrenchment – a move to the right rather than to the left – would have been appropriate'.[24] But there was no real move to the left in the final years of the first administration and Gaitskell's earlier judgement, that the effect of the government was being felt more by the middle- and lower-middle-class voters who decided the key marginals, was probably nearer the mark.

Kenneth Younger made a strikingly similar judgement in his Grimsby constituency: 'We have done badly in the prosperous Home Counties and suburban seats. That was partly expected. Those are the areas that never really knew the slump, and consequently they resent the minor annoyances of the last few years and cannot compare them, as the north can, with serious hardships before the war.'[25] Dalton thought the result just about the worst of all possible worlds. 'If we had lost 10 seats more, Tories would have had bare majority, and would have had to form a powerless government; if we had lost 10 seats less we would have had a majority between 20 and 30 and

---

* Worse was to come, of course, in 1951.

could have scraped along for a bit. As it is, we have office without authority or power, and it is difficult to see how we can improve our position.'[26] The combination of the British first-past-the-post system and the general feeling that the state had interfered for too long and by too much, and that the Conservatives were the party of freeing the country from controls – the opposite of the mood of 1945 – decimated the party in the south and Midlands and left the government with a majority of 5. The 1950 election provided a crucial series of lessons for Gaitskell about what the Labour Party had to be to win and hold on to power.

In September 1946 the American Ambassador in London had filed one of his regular reports home on the state of British politics: 'The most promising of the younger Ministers are Hector McNeil, John Strachey, Geoffrey de Freitas, J. H. Wilson and Hugh Gaitskell . . . Except for McNeil, it is impossible to say yet which of the others have the capacity to develop into astute and wise political leaders to complement their ability.'[27] One could have added, of course, Nye Bevan, Douglas Jay and Evan Durbin. By 1949 the future leaders had progressed: Bevan was still in the Cabinet, where he had been joined by Wilson at the Board of Trade. Outside the Cabinet, John Strachey was at Food, Hector McNeil at the Foreign Office, Geoffrey de Freitas at the Home Office and Douglas Jay at the Treasury. Hugh Gaitskell was at Fuel and Power and was about to pull clear of the pack.

Political fallout from the devaluation decision was immense and its consequences for the government's survival profound. Gaitskell's consistency, toughness and command of the situation was generally noted. If anyone at the top of the Labour government had missed the full significance of Gaitskell's role, the Dalton 'boom' was there to make sure they understood it. 'Cripps was absolutely irreplaceable as Chancellor', Dalton boomed at Attlee at the start of the 1950 campaign:

> No one else could do it, until, in due course, one came down the line to the 'young economists' . . . But Cripps had too much to do – old Treasury + new Planning + constant travelling abroad. He should have a Minister of State, who could relieve him of some of this . . . Gaitskell was the man for the job.[28]

Attlee agreed and said that he had already been discussing this with Bridges. The PM and Dalton agreed that Gaitskell was better than

Wilson or Jay. Wilson continued to disappoint Dalton, and a year later he summed up his view of the future Prime Minister: 'Harold Wilson is not a great success. He is a weak and conceited minister.'[29] Douglas Jay's problem was less his ability than his personality: he 'had not always good judgement, and wasn't very personable.'[30] Dalton pressed home the point and told Attlee that Gaitskell had a great gift of concentration, of clear thought and argument; his recent paper on controls had been 'quite masterly'. In due course, 'he probably should be Chancellor of the Exchequer.'[31]

Gaitskell's strong political performance on devaluation, together with such powerful advocacy, resulted in his second interview with Attlee. The Prime Minister asked him to go and help Stafford Cripps and then – at least so Gaitskell felt – he was tested as to his commitment to the government. 'There is one snag about it,' said Attlee. 'I am afraid you will have to accept a cut in salary. A Minister of State only gets three thousand.' Gaitskell was surprised, because he had been earning the full Minister's salary as head of Fuel and Power. 'Well, I naturally don't welcome that, but it does not worry me much. The only thing is the question of status. Will not that be rather awkward – will not everyone say I have been demoted?' 'Oh! That is certainly not the case and I will make it quite clear in the announcement.' Was it, as Gaitskell thought, 'a deliberate test of my loyalty – rather like the King and the good prince in the fairy stories'? If so, he passed, and anyway Attlee was mistaken: Gaitskell did not have to take a cut in salary. However, if it was a test, it gives a striking insight into how Attlee viewed one of his rising 'intellectuals'. He admired Gaitskell's ability and liked his charm but was never able to muster much enthusiasm for him; he promoted him because of his obvious competence and seems to have been rather surprised by his later success. In this little episode, however, there are the seeds of that view of Gaitskell and his relationship to the party that was to become much more open in the 1950s: was he in some sense semi-detached? Moreover, the fact that Gaitskell believed he had been tested reveals an insecurity.

In February 1950 Gaitskell became Minister of State at the Treasury. Backing up Shinwell and then running the Ministry of Fuel and Power had been a challenge of administrative skill and endeavour. He had been a moderate success in what was essentially an administrative and organisational challenge – with some political content – while at Fuel and Power. However, it was not what he had achieved at that Ministry that pushed him forward. It was his expertise as an economist and the force of personality and consistency that he had shown over devaluation that now propelled him to the Treasury. The job of Cripps's deputy was a test of his actual professional training.

Soon he was deputising for Cripps, who was increasingly ill and absent. In March 1950 he took the press conference on the Economic Survey – the annual report on Britain's economic performance. The press reports said that he had handled things well, never tried to dodge a question, and, when asked something that he could scarcely be expected to answer, said so frankly.* It was part of a generally good press for his ministerial performances. Gaitskell was always good at consuming and following a brief. On this occasion the brief was itself excellent. A similar good press was received for a speech in June on the profits tax. The *Manchester Guardian* reported his more realistic approach compared to that of Stafford Cripps, and praised his recognition of the need for investment. Gaitskell observed, 'We should build up institutions which are prepared to invest money in risk-bearing enterprises which find difficulty in getting funds from other sources.'[32] Such statements and illustrations of independent judgement caused the odd minor tussle with Cripps but in the main their relationship was smooth.

The following month he scored a similar success with a speech to the United Nations Economic and Social Council in Geneva. He went representing the Cabinet and made a speech on full employment, in response to a report by five economists including Nicholas Kaldor. He liked Geneva and was struck by Mont Blanc 'coming out in the evening after it had been hidden in a haze during the day', but felt that the ECOSOC was simply a talking shop.[33] On his return to London he found he had made a good impression and received his first public backing for the top. 'Of all Mr Attlee's "young" Ministers, Winchester-educated Mr Gaitskell is the man in favour at the moment. Westminster sees him as a future Chancellor or Foreign Secretary.'[34] He also started to do better in the House of Commons. 'For more than an hour Mr Hugh Gaitskell lectured the

---

* *Evening Standard*, 30 March 1950. The piece also accused him of being forty-five minutes late for the press conference. He wasn't; the journalist got the time wrong, and actually printed an apology saying the 'black mark is on me'.

House on the economic consequences of rearmament. It was a good, efficient and at times brilliant performance.'[35]

The pressure on family life was acute. In 1948 Gaitskell had already been feeling the strain. 'I am grossly overworked again. Everything is happening at once. The Gas Bill – now three days a week, mornings and afternoons in Committee; the new petrol scheme and all its repercussions; a crisis in the Coal Board; some horrible problems of coal quality and exports and rather a heavy list of speaking engagements. And then finally the grim world oil situation with all its repercussions on our plans here.'[36] By 1950, when he had switched jobs, the burden was even greater. With Cripps's frequent absences and his own unrelenting commitment to work, the pressure was immense. He lamented to his diary that he and Dora had not been to a night club for 'years and years'.[37] He could occasionally combine work and social life and tried hard to include Dora when he could. They went to Paris together when he had to attend a series of meetings and enjoyed the evenings together; but his normal rhythm of life comprised long periods of unrelenting work and rare escapes with family or friends.

The family holiday in 1950 illustrated the extent to which the ministerial career could intrude on their life and relationship. The initial plan had been for a three-week trip to Cornwall in a rented cottage, but Cripps fell ill and Gaitskell had to deputise at the IMF meetings, which clashed with the first two weeks of the holiday. So they changed to a week in Abbotsbury in Dorset – a long-time favourite haunt – and a week in Exmouth. Then the rest of the family would go to Cornwall, while Gaitskell went to the IMF.

This complicated plan was further disrupted when the Foreign Secretary telephoned him at Abbotsbury to ask him to go to France with Shinwell, by now back in the Cabinet as Defence Secretary. The British planned to raise conscription to two years and the government wanted to put pressure on the French to do the same. A car arrived at the hotel at 6 a.m. Gaitskell had got up, shaved, had breakfast on his own in the still-sleeping hotel, then found that the front door was locked. So the Minister of State at the Treasury climbed through a window. He managed to make it to his plane and flew most of the way to the meeting, developing air sickness and then having a run of unsatisfactory talks with the French before flying back to Abbotsbury and arriving at 10 p.m. He left again soon afterwards for Paris. While that holiday was a particularly difficult one, this level of intrusion in their personal lives was fairly typical.

By now he was filling in for Cripps constantly and had moved into the Chancellor's office whenever Cripps was away for an extended period. Indeed, Gaitskell often spoke as an equal rather than as a deputy.[38] But many in the press tended to treat him as the 'stop-gap new boy' who would be superseded in a matter of time, not as the fully fledged understudy who would get his chance to become the star.[39] Dalton had told Attlee that a crucial factor in the appointment would be the Minister's ability to exhibit not only 'quick intelligence, or bright ideas, or diligence or methodical administration, but power to resist high-powered advice'.[40] Gaitskell was also in a position to offer advice to his new boss. One of the first suggestions he made to Cripps was to cut taxes in expectation of an imminent second election.[41]

The scale of the challenge at the Treasury was larger, the ethos of the institution itself being a large part of the problem of becoming a successful Minister. The way Gaitskell set about being a Treasury Minister did not please some officials: he knew his subject and was able to 'match them in objectivity and analytical power'. He fulfilled Dalton's hope that he could say no when the need arose: 'It was the adroit Eric Johnston who remarked after his unsatisfactory film negotiation that Mr Gaitskell could say "no" even more charmingly than other Englishmen.'[42]

Gaitskell always got on well with civil servants. He received many letters from people within the Fuel and Power department when his move was announced. Though some of the older ones resented his independence of judgement, most seemed to look on their Minister favourably: 'We get rare pleasure out of seeing you take hold of all sorts of bowling,' wrote one admirer.[43] Whether such platitudes from civil servants are actually what democratic socialist Ministers should receive on leaving office is of course an awkward question. Such praise might well imply a lack of radicalism. As for Gaitskell, he sometimes seems to have regarded the relationship between himself and civil servants too much as one of equality; he was, after all, their political boss. In reviewing his progress at the Treasury in May 1950 he identified Sir Harry Wilson-Smith, head of the Overseas Finance Division, as his chief opponent on the question of a European Payments Union and on the fundamentals of overseas economic policy. 'But,' wrote Gaitskell the Minister, 'I think I can claim to have won both battles. On E.P.U. he has retired from the field and left it all to me; and on the fundamentals also the Chancellor ruled in our favour.'[44]

It is intriguing to speculate on who the 'we' are in this entry. Gaitskell sees himself not as being on the side of the Chancellor but as competing for the approval of the political boss with other powerful civil servants. Many junior Ministers find themselves in such a situation; but, when coupled to Gaitskell's civil-servant-like devotion to detail, his attitude casts doubt on his ability to lead at the highest level. The inner core of confidence and determination had begun to emerge but his tendency to adopt the colours of his department never completely disappeared in his ministerial career, and call into question quite how effective a Prime Minister he could have made.

On a more personal level, Gaitskell was a very pleasant boss. All his private office staff seemed to have liked him. He did tend to flirt, jovially and gently, with female staff, but there is no record of any problems caused by this. He was honest and direct with senior civil servants, understanding the way they worked and not being intimidated by their social or political confidence, as some of the other new Labour ministers seem to have been.

The first great set piece of Gaitskell's political career was the Mansion House speech in 1950. Gaitskell was the first Minister not holding the office of Chancellor to make the speech in over fifty years. He had a good set of figures to announce, so he again received a positive response and a good press; the *Daily Worker* took particular pleasure in recording the warmth of the bankers' welcome.

A few days after the Mansion House speech he left for the United States for his first visit. Gaitskell was committed to the idea of the Atlantic alliance and dedicated to the new North Atlantic Treaty Organisation, created in 1949. These beliefs were based on a deep sense of patriotism and a great affection for America and Americans; occasionally it is difficult to separate the two, but the patriotism tended to come first. 'I think it must be an event in anybody's life when he first crosses the Atlantic' – and it was an event that Gaitskell was determined to make happen when he reached the Treasury.[45]

When Ernest Bevin died in April 1951, Gaitskell praised him in terms that suggested that his primary achievement had been to fulfil the needs and desires of ordinary British people: 'Ernest Bevin was first and foremost a great Englishman, forthright and courageous, an idealist, but an eminently practical one. He understood the people of this country which he loved and I believe he interpreted the British idea with great fidelity. He was a great Labour leader; he understood instinctively the reactions of the ordinary man and woman.'[46] It was Bevin who set the broad terms of Gaitskell's foreign policy ideas. It was also Bevin who personified, for Gaitskell, the idea of being in tune with the aspirations of ordinary 'English' people. This desire is something that is present in all the great foreign policy battles of Gaitskell's career. Thus his political attachment to the American alliance was based both on his patriotism and on his belief that Britain had a world role to play: different, modernised and not founded on colonial exploitation, but a world role nevertheless. This vision of Britain's place was founded on the not unreasonable conviction that it was only through the Atlantic alliance that Britain stood a chance of continuing in its global role. This view was shaped largely by the war and there is little evidence for it from the inter-war period: it became a fixed idea and because of the primacy this patriotism came to take he was prepared to sacrifice virtually anything to policies that he believed would sustain the world role. In part at least this was because that is what he believed most ordinary British people wanted. Gaitskell's first visit to the United States, in October 1950, crystallised the connection between his patriotism and his pro-Americanism. It was to have profound political significance for the remainder of his life.

Apart from politics, it was in America that he apparently found people who combined personal and political seriousness and positivism with an emotional and even hedonistic ability to enjoy themselves. Americans also appealed to his liking for authenticity and honesty. Moreover, as he was first discovering the United States while Britain was enduring rationing and austerity, the contrast with American affluence was striking. He was not the first Englishman to find relaxed, approachable Americans congenial company, but for Gaitskell the uncomplicated way in which they seemed to resolve the split between public control and private emotion was captivating.

He spent four days in Washington, between 8 and 12 October, but had mixed feelings about it as a city:

> It is an attractive place; more especially in its domestic architecture, a pleasing Georgian, Colonial style house built in the wooded country outside; and then again the fact that the many, many big white Ministry buildings stand in a kind of Park; and then the trees, mostly fully grown and just autumn tints on them, were I think very beautiful. There was

nothing much impressive about the shops. It is, as everyone knows, a capital city. Civil servants, politicians, diplomats – the same sort of people whom I tend to meet in London; highly intelligent, cultured, very friendly.

From Washington he went into talks with the Canadian Prime Minister and Finance Minister before returning to New York. He had a few days off and spent them enjoying New York. 'I liked this best of all.' He was struck by two things more than anything else:

(a) Negroes – quite smartly dressed Negresses looking after the lifts for example. (b) Above all the cars – endless streams on the roads even on Sunday afternoon.

Thoughts of the petrol rationing back home must have made an uncanny contrast. He also liked the feel of the city:

a very vital city, but friendly too. You do not have a feeling of fuss and bother. People seem to take things in their stride, and I like the way when you said, 'Thank you!' [they replied] 'You're welcome!'

Returning to his hotel late one night he received a message to phone the Canadian High Commission. He instantly thought he had made some appalling blunder. In fact it was time for his third interview with Mr Attlee, this time via the High Commissioner in Ottawa: 'Prepare yourself for a shock. I have a message for you from the P.M.' Gaitskell continues his account in the diary, too excited to write down the exact words.

Stafford was not going back for a year and that after consulting with his colleagues, the P.M. wanted me to take his place. 'Would I agree to having my name submitted to the King?' I can never think of the right thing to say without notice on these sort of occasions. So I just said, 'I suppose he wants to know quickly. You had better say "Yes I will do it and I will send him a message myself soon."'

An old colleague from UCL was with Gaitskell in his hotel room when he took the call. Gaitskell turned round to him, drank some whisky, and said, 'Well! I am to be Chancellor.'

Stuck in New York with only his officials for company he forced them, rather manically, to go out and celebrate. He got Edwin Plowden, the central Whitehall figure in post-war economic planning who was the key official on the trip, out of bed and dragged him along to the Blue Angel night club. The hostesses greeted them at the door and because of their accents asked if they were actors.

101

Plowden replied, 'I am not an actor, but he is.' The whiskies were $10 each and with insufficient hard currency for a second round they had to leave. Only later did they discover that the cabaret and several drinks were included in the price. Gaitskell accused Plowden of excessive Crippsian austerity.[47]

The next evening began with a cocktail party among the glitterati of the Democratic Party. After leaving this he linked up with an old Oxford friend, Jim Orrick, and went to Greenwich Village. At the Vanguard night club, he danced with Orrick's sister-in-law to a jazz band. He remembered a story about Lord Birkenhead when Lord Chancellor being seen in Nice with a chorus girl on each knee. 'I would not do that because it would upset my wife, I did like the idea of dancing in Greenwich Village as well as the reality.' He danced until 4.30 a.m. When he emerged later in the morning to have lunch with the International City Bank – 'very nice and friendly too and I thought more intelligent than our bankers' – he found reporters waiting for a statement, which he duly delivered: 'I am extremely sorry to hear that Sir Stafford has been obliged to resign ... There will be a most serious loss to the British government and people. He was both the main architect of and the driving force behind our remarkable recovery.'

After lunch, as he was about to hurry into a hired car on the way to the airport, a group of photographers caught him in the lobby. Before taking his picture the photographers insisted on removing his hat and straightening his tie. Though this seemed to surprise him he submitted gracefully, and in his diary he described the photographs as horrible. Gaitskell had not been able to speak to Dora directly from New York but when he landed in London on 22 October, she came on the plane, kissed him congratulations and walked down the stairs with him to face more waiting reporters. Journalists and the full glare of publicity would remain with them for the rest of his life.

The response to his promotion was decidedly mixed. Until his appointment as Chancellor of the Exchequer he had clashed with Bevan in private over departmental differences but these conflicts had usually been reconciled at Cripps's regular dinners. However, after Gaitskell was made Chancellor, the thin lines of mutal respect between them were broken. Bevan's hostile reaction was due partly to petulance and partly to ideology. The petulance was less understandable than the ideology. Though the press had been hedging its bets as to Gaitskell's chances of succeeding Cripps, privately it was generally assumed that the deputy Chancellor would succeed. What rankled was that Cripps had been to Bevan, as Dalton had been to Gaitskell, in Foot's words, 'father-confessor and father-promoter',[48] though perhaps 'father-controller' would be more apt. As Attlee commented, Bevan 'had great ability, and as a matter of fact we had no trouble with him while Stafford Cripps was alive. He had great respect for Stafford. Stafford had a very good influence on him.'[49] Now that Gaitskell had inherited the Crippsian mantle, Bevan may not, as Foot claims, have seen himself as the next Chancellor, but equally he could not quite stomach Gaitskell in the job.

Ideology also played a part. Gaitskell, Bevan judged, was rooted in gradualism and would always choose the middle-of-the-road option. This was connected to Bevan's view of Gaitskell's place in the party: 'Political leaders in a democracy, particularly in the Labour movement, should represent something and somebody; they must speak for the major sections of the movement.' Gaitskell, in Bevan's estimation, 'represented nothing, unless it was the civil service-cum-middle class which was already over-represented at Westminster and had no business to wrest the leadership from the working class'.[50] Putting to one side the extent to which it is difficult to separate the personal and the political in this kind of charge, Foot and Bevan had a point. It was one of Gaitskell's great problems that he reached the top of the greasy pole before he had built up the national following to sustain him there. The early 1950s were to be spent building up the foundations for his leading place in the party.

Bevan dashed off a letter full of hurt pride to the Prime Minister, angry that he had not been consulted and concerned that the appointment might backfire on the government.

> I am sure you will agree that it is impossible to give advice and counsel about Government policy when only a part at a time is disclosed to me . . . you will, I hope, appreciate that it is only possible to be of service in an atmosphere of candour and trust . . . I feel bound to tell you that for my part I think the appointment of Gaitskell to be a great mistake. I should have thought myself that it was essential to find out whether the holder of this great office would commend himself to the main elements and current of opinion in the party.[51]

Harold Wilson was a little more realistic in his appraisal. Though he told one friend that it 'had been a great blow when Hugh got it',[52] he must have realised that the die was cast when Gaitskell had been appointed Minister of State. However, Gaitskell was sure that Wilson was burning with jealousy[53] and, as Wilson's biographer put it, 'Wilson could consider himself better qualified academically than Gaitskell, and was senior to him in the Government. The Chancellorship had been his childhood fantasy. These were reasons enough.'[54] Gaitskell realised that any initial reactions were 'premature because the real struggle will come when we try and settle expenditure policy'.

There were some very positive responses to Gaitskell's appointment: apart from friends, like Pakenham and Jay, Jim Callaghan found 'not a single word of criticism about your appointment, because it is regarded as a natural and inevitable step. There is no one else. That is a remarkable tribute.'[55] Harold Hutchinson in the *Daily Mirror,* later a key champion of Gaitskell as leader, reported the accession to the Chancellorship with a glowing report and profile. 'For six months he had been deputising for [Cripps] in London, Paris and Washington. He was on probation. He passed all the tests. To the onlooker he was smiling and charming but behind that exterior was a tough, clear mind.' Hutchinson stressed the extent to which his time as Minister of Fuel had convinced many in the trade unions of his ability: 'He may be a professor – but not just another professor. He knows what he's talking about,' a miner told Hutchinson. His lunch was taken at his desk; as was his dinner, accompanied by a glass of light ale.

Another journalist obtained the first interview with Dora at Frognal Gardens while Hugh was flying across the Atlantic. Under the headline 'Who was the Chancellor in the Gaitskell House' Dora told the *Evening Standard* reporter, 'I receive an allowance for the housekeeping. And I see we live inside it.' She 'dresses quietly, wears loose-fitting coats and dresses, and the centre of her life is her home. "I hope our new conditions will mean little alteration to that," she says.'[56] The promotion actually made little material difference to their lives; except that Gaitskell probably worked even harder than ever.

Financially their position had steadily improved since the war. As a Principal Assistant Secretary (civil servant) at the Board of Trade his salary had been £1,800 a year, cut to £1,000 a year when he was elected as an MP. As a Parliamentary Secretary at the Ministry of Fuel and Power from May 1946 he received £1,500. With his promotion to Minister of State of Fuel and Power in October 1947 this rose to £3,500. On joining the Treasury as Minister of State for Economic Affairs his salary was increased to match the Chancellor's at £5,000 a year. It remained at £5,000 with his new job. After an initial hesitation they decided not to move from Frognal Gardens to Number 11 Downing Street. They both enjoyed their garden and the Hampstead house was not too far from Downing Street and the House of Commons to be inconvenient, whilst maintaining a certain distance; Dora was always conscious of trying to protect her family life from Hugh's political life.

Gaitskell's own reflections on the moment at which he became the fourth figure in the government, a point he made sure to clarify with Attlee, were acute:

> At first it was very strange – one could not get used to the idea of being Chancellor. One did not feel any different, and one could not, so to speak, modify one's idea of the office to fit in with one's idea of oneself. Now I am beginning to get used to it a bit more, and I suppose that in a few months' time if I am here there will be nothing strange about it at all. But we certainly face some very, very difficult problems arising out of inflation and rearmament, more difficult in some ways, though less critical, than the 1947–9 problems. So far everybody is being very nice but that will not last for long.[57]

It did not. Bevan's private rumblings of discontent had broadened out to become generalised fears on the left of the party that the appointment marked a decisive move to the right.

Gaitskell's first Cabinet as Chancellor of the Exchequer took place on Monday 23 October 1950 at 11 a.m., just twenty-four hours after his return from the US.[58] The agenda included some key issues that would crop up repeatedly throughout the remainder of his political career: German rearmament, the Soviet Union, the United Nations, European unity and nationalisation.[59] But top of the agenda was the issue that was to dominate the rest of Gaitskell's ministerial career: defence expenditure. Its prime importance was an illustration of the extent to which the Attlee government had been almost overwhelmed by the Cold War.

Four months before Gaitskell became Chancellor, an event had occurred on the other side of the world which shifted the axis of the government. On 25 June 1950, North Korean forces had attacked

South Korean positions south of the 38th parallel which divided the two states created from Korea. The Security Council of the United Nations had adopted a resolution calling for the withdrawal of troops the next day. On 27 June, President Harry S. Truman had given a military pledge of support to South Korea and the Security Council called on member states to help.

The British Cabinet had responded by arranging time for debating the matter in the Commons on the afternoon of 5 July. The Cabinet met in the morning to consider its position. After discussing the legality of the decision to intervene on behalf of South Korea (the Soviet Union had not been present at the meeting of the Security Council which made the decision), the Cabinet considered a memo presented by Kenneth Younger, the Minister of State at the Foreign Office, on the 'economic action which might be taken in support of the military operations in Korea'. The memo argued that the only practical action open to the UK was to prevent the shipment of goods from Hong Kong to North Korea. It further argued that 'to strengthen the hands of the Hong Kong government the export of goods from the UK to North Korea should also be prohibited.' Some months earlier the Attlee government had recognised Communist China, causing a breach with their American allies. They now responded to the call for American aid: it was 'the price British governments occasionally have to pay for the "special relationship"'.[60] But the British also explored diplomatic responses to the crisis.[61] The government's commitment to supporting UN-led, but American-dominated, intervention was mixed at Cabinet level and lukewarm to hostile in other sections of the party.

In the last week of July the American Ambassador, Lew Douglas, met with Clem Attlee and asked what specific actions Britain would take to support the new North Atlantic Treaty Organisation and UN involvement in Korea. He also stressed that American aid would be available to help in the switching of production from exports to armaments.[62] In response the Treasury put together a programme, 'Defence requirements and United States Assistance',[63] which the Cabinet considered in the following days. Simultaneously there was a debate in the House of Commons on an increase of £100 million in defence expenditure caused by the creation of NATO.[64] The US request had been direct and 'somewhat out of the blue'; the American government wanted to know, by 5 August 1950, 'the nature and extent of the increased effort both as regards increases in forces and increases in military production which His Majesty's Government as a North Atlantic Treaty Power are willing and able to undertake.' The Cabinet had already authorised additional defence expenditure of £100 million, of which about £30 million would be incurred in 1950–1 and £70 million in 1951–2. They had also approved in principle a civil defence programme costing £137 million over the next four years. In addition, for the same period it was planned to improve the pay and extend the size of the armed forces for which the Chancellor proposed to allow a further £100 million, £10 million in 1950–1 and £30 million in each of the three following years.

These decisions and proposals produced the following totals of defence expenditure over the four financial years 1950–4; all amounts are millions:

1950–1951	£820
1951–1952	£900
1952–1953	£840
1953–1954	£850

The supply department had been asked what additional expenditure on armaments would be physically possible during these four years. The proposed programmes, totalling £814 million, brought projected spending in the next four financial years to:

1950–1951	£824
1951–1952	£1,075
1952–1953	£1,133
1953–1954	£1,192

This produced a total paper figure of £4,224 million by the end of the financial year 1953–4.

Programmes of this magnitude could not be undertaken without substantial financial aid from the United States. Realising this, the Americans had also enquired what aid Britain would need. In Cabinet on 31 July 1950, Stafford Cripps had therefore proposed that Britain should take the following line:

> We should state that by decisions already taken or likely to be taken in the near future we were committed to a defence expenditure of about £820 million in 1950–51 and £900 million in 1951–52. We considered that on general economic grounds an annual expenditure of £950 million

on defence was the most we could afford in 1951–52 and in the following two years. If, therefore, we were to undertake the additional programme indicated above, we must ask for United States assistance to cover the difference between an expenditure of £2,850 million over the three years and the total programme of £3,400 million i.e. we should ask for United States aid to the extent of £550 million.[65]

The figure of £950 million was Gaitskell's. As Cripps's deputy he had been shown the initial response from the Civil Service to the US request and, as was his habit, questioned the detail. He examined the way in which the figure of £900 million had been arrived at, raised his questions with Bridges and Plowden and had the figure increased to £950 million. It was a small but important intervention: the increase was about twice the amount that could be raised by the imposition of National Health Service charges in a full financial year. The £950 million figure was also symbolic, because, according to Plowden, 'in terms of a percentage of national income' it 'put our defence expenditure on a par with the United States'.[66]

In Cabinet, when Cripps presented this figure, he stressed the fact that these proposals would commit the government, subject to parliamentary approval, to a net expenditure on defence at the rate of £950 million a year over the next three years: 'Ministers should recognise that the resources required for this additional production could not be provided without some reduction in Government expenditure, some additional taxation or some reduction in capital investment, or a combination of all three.'

Nye Bevan voiced his 'grave misgivings' about the implications of the proposals put forward by Cripps. The phrase 'grave misgivings' seems to have been a compromise between Bevan and Norman Brook, the Cabinet Secretary. Bevan wanted his 'opposition' recorded in the minutes but the Cabinet Secretary refused because that would have undermined collective responsibility and raised the question of resignation.[67] Bevan stated, somewhat oddly given the recent creation of NATO, that the Labour government's foreign policy up to this Cabinet meeting had been based on the view that the 'best method of defence against Russian imperialism was to improve the social and economic conditions of the countries threatened by Communist encroachment'. The US seemed now to be abandoning this social and political defence in favour of a military defence. Indeed, Manny Shinwell in the Commons debate introduced the notion that there were 175 Russian armoured divisions waiting for their moment to sweep through the West. Bevan believed that this change of policy, and of course by implication the ethos of NATO, was misjudged. He felt that Britain could withstand the pressure on its social and economic position but he questioned whether the same was true of France, and concluded:

> If as a result of this further military effort, their economic and social standards were still further reduced, their ability to resist the domestic threat of communism would be seriously prejudiced. If the Cabinet now endorsed the proposal in paragraph 10 of CP (50) 181 that the Government should commit themselves to defence expenditure at an annual rate of £950 million over the next three years, he foresaw very great difficulties for the Ministers responsible for the social services. They would be forced to accept reductions in the Government's civil programmes; their only freedom would be to decide which of those programmes should suffer first and most. If some increase in defence expenditure was inevitable, would it not be better to take the line that there could be no reduction in our existing level of expenditure on social services and capital investment, and to allocate to defence the increase in the national income which was expected to accrue from increased industrial productivity?

It was a skilful conclusion, and the battle-lines were drawn up. Bevan was defeated and the cabinet approved CP (50) 181. At the same Cabinet, Bevan's request for supplementary funding for capital projects for the NHS was also defeated.

Though the Labour Cabinet approved the initial programme, the Americans were dismayed when it was announced. As they had expected a programme that put the British economy on a virtual war footing, what Plowden now presented seemed to them 'a mandate to develop a rearmament programme with a strong "business as usual" flavour . . . involving the minimum economic dislocations'. They also felt that the request for £550 million aid was far beyond what they had had in mind.[68] Originally the United States had offered full aid to cover problems with balances of payments; now the Americans were indicating that only very limited aid would be available. In fact the US Congress had placed strict limits on the amount the administration could hand out. By October 1950 the Americans were offering a maximum aid programme of £200 million, but had proposed the idea of burden-sharing between the NATO allies according to a formula that would produce an equality of sacrifice.

It was at this point that Gaitskell went to Washington, to negotiate directly on the idea of a burden-sharing exercise. This is the crucial factor that must be kept in mind. America's launching of its rearmament programme was causing rapid increases in the prices of raw materials and thus undermining the British economy's post-devaluation success in building up reserves and improving general economic performance. Yet it was this successful economic performance that was the basis for the American rejection of further aid, either for rearmament or through the Marshall Aid programme. As Plowden puts it, 'In October 1950 they saw an economy with minimal inflation, full employment, a unique welfare system, large reserves, a strong currency and a policy of discrimination against the dollar in many areas'.[69] In such circumstances it was difficult for those individuals well disposed towards the British government, like Averell Harriman who was responsible for foreign aid, to argue their corner. There seems to have been a certain amount of ignorance on both sides. The British showed a lack of awareness of the intricacies of the American political system and the Americans did not fully appreciate the political and economic constraints on the British.

From these and other talks there emerged an acceptance of the idea of burden-sharing between the NATO allies but no agreement on the exact formula. There were several interrelated fears in the British camp: that the Americans would withdraw into isolationism; that they would demand more than Britain could afford; and that they would see Britain as just one among the European powers rather than as a special partner. Gaitskell's task was to balance Britain's economic position with the need, perhaps best expressed in the government's recent rejection of the Schuman Plan for the creation of a European Coal and Steel Community, to keep Britain ahead of the other European powers. One conclusion came home to Gaitskell forcibly: 'It was no longer a question of how aid from the USA was to be divided out, but simply how the common burden was to be shared.'[70] This concept was central, but the Americans had difficulty accepting it. In essence they needed to be able to present the aid they gave the NATO allies as entailing certain controls, but this would make the British idea of independence an illusion. In turn, for Gaitskell, unless Britain fully upheld its part of the programme, then the negotiating position with the Americans would be lost. With the concept of burden-sharing destroyed, either Britain would become a client state of the USA or the USA would withdraw from European defence.

The problems deepened after China entered the conflict and President Truman seemed to imply that he would be prepared to use atomic weapons. Attlee decided that he needed to go to the USA and speak directly to the American President. He arrived for the talks on 5 December 1950. Truman and Attlee got on well and the British obtained the assurances that atomic weapons would not be used – though Truman, despite a great deal of contingency planning, had never intended to use the weapons. However while the two leaders were reaching their understandings in high-level meetings there had been little progress on the issues of the prices of raw material or the burden-sharing formula. The Americans were a little more forthcoming than in October, agreeing to set up a joint committee on resources based on those that had operated in the Second World War, yet they were also demanding an even greater level of commitment to the NATO alliance. Attlee told the Cabinet on his return that an 'acceleration of the defence programme was now unavoidable' and that the British government had to take a lead in ensuring that others fulfilled their responsibilities in the context of the alliance.[71] This meant an increase in the total programme of defence expenditure to a projected £4,500 million, or 14 per cent of GDP, on the presumption that the burden-sharing exercise would cancel out some of the excessive British commitments with American aid.[72]

In Cabinet on 19 January 1951, Gaitskell was adamant that the cost of the programme should be placed as much as possible 'on current consumption rather than to burden the future by any serious reduction in investment.'[73] As he expressed it at a meeting at Leicester a few days later, 'We must ensure that the impact of rearmament does not fatally damage our future. We must try to carry it out by sacrificing what matters least – the luxuries of the present';[74] or as the *Daily Express* then reported, 'Gaitskell says: Cut out the luxuries.'[75] It was a responsible message that had immense political repercussions. It made sense in the broadening context of a global ideological conflict, summed up by Paul Nitze, a banker in 1951 but Director of Planning for the US Navy for much of the 1960s, when he drafted the policy document commonly known as NSC-68, 'a strategy for containing Communism by force if necessary', and in the UK by the Joint Intelligence Staff's report 'The Spread of Russian Communism'.[76]

The inherent message which Gaitskell accepted was that the West was some way behind Russia in military strength and needed the rearmament programme to achieve and maintain a position of strength. Gaitskell began his career as a Cold Warrior by pushing the case for the revised rearmament package at a public meeting in Birmingham in January 1951. Almost overnight a more mature and substantial national political figure emerged.

Until this speech, Gaitskell had generally focused on the economic aspects, or the need for sacrifice. In his Birmingham speech he spelt out a chilling message of ideological conflict between East and West that rivalled anything from the United States.

In this speech the influence of a combination of Ernest Bevin, Evan Durbin and the Americans he had known came through, as well as his own shrewd assessment of the Stalinist system. There was, he argued, a great disparity between the armed strength of Russia and that of the West 'which would not matter if the Russians could be trusted not to use armed force to solve disputes, but their record since the war means that any such presumption would be a gamble with our national safety.' He continued: 'I believe that the fundamental struggle of our time is between the democratic values and the false doctrines of totalitarianism, and it is this which lies behind the decision that we must now take to build up our defences.' He went on to explain the differences between the peoples and the systems that meant there could be 'no meeting of minds with them, no friendly easy intercourse; for between us stands inexorably and ruthlessly the Iron Curtain, so well named, so real the barrier imposed by the Soviet Government.'[77] It is a speech in which one can measure the distance that the Labour government had travelled since the wartime hope that left could talk to left. It also speaks volumes for the extent to which Gaitskell had embraced an uncompromising equation of totalitarianism of the left and right. Russia could be compared with Nazi Germany: 'In a police state, in a dictatorship, where a man fears his best friend, where he cannot speak his mind, where he is only allowed to read and hear and see one point of view, neither moral nor intellectual development is possible. As for happiness, that is corroded and withered away by suspicion, anxiety and fear.'[78] In many ways it could have been the pre-war Evan Durbin arguing with his friend in a Bloomsbury pub. It was now, however, the Chancellor of the Exchequer giving the full measure of the Labour government's commitment to the Cold War.

Forty years later Paul Nitze expressed his admiration for the rearmament programme upon which the British embarked: 'You can call it hubris or you can call it courage – I think we have much to admire the British for . . . [what] I consider to be breathtaking courage.'[79] Perhaps a little less courage would have been required if the burden-sharing arrangements, on which Gaitskell had pinned his hopes, had actually materialised. Instead, what had been a balance-of-payments surplus in 1950 moved month by month into deeper deficit and raw material prices continued to push up inflation. In this atmosphere Gaitskell started to prepare his first and only Budget.

The 1951 Budget did not lose the Labour government the election in October that year, but it did little or nothing to help the government win. Gaitskell was not in the business of delivering a reflation package; he placed what he saw as the national interest unequivocally above his party's interest. When he presented the outline of his proposals to Attlee, the PM's response was: 'Well, we shall not get many votes out of this.' Gaitskell replied that he could not expect votes in a rearmament year.[80] The question of votes was important, since the government had a slender majority and there was likely to be another election soon. The political judgement was very fine: there needed to be a rearmament Budget which would include unpopular tax increases, but did there need to be a Budget which actually forced Ministers out of the government? This calculation weighed heavily with senior Ministers in the months ahead as they tried to reconcile Bevan and Gaitskell. It is tempting to look back on 1951 and assume that the Labour government had run out of steam. However, a successful Budget, a unified party and careful timing might have produced a different result in 1951. In the event, not only was it an unpopular Budget – it also split the government.

The feature of the Budget which caused the enormous political fallout was the imposition of charges for false teeth and spectacles. This proposal was already an established bone of contention in the Cabinet. It represented a basic division between Ministers at the heart of the government on the priorities for democratic socialism, as well as being the pretext for a straightforward power struggle. When the argument became public it marked the beginning of post-war Bevanism and the culmination of the fairly consistent economic and political line that Gaitskell had been developing. The imposition of charges is seen either as a symbolic failure of the Attlee government to be properly socialist by 'attacking' its most central achievement, the NHS, or as evidence of the commitment of the Attlee government to Britain's world role.

There were reasons other than rearmament for favouring the imposition of charges. The argument against unlimited social expenditure was also based on the emphasis on the second front of the economic struggle: production. The extension of limitations on social expenditure to the NHS and the political victory of Gaitskell's line on this represented a significant indication of the actual as opposed to the rhetorical position of the Labour government. It is so often asserted that the NHS was the greatest achievement of the Attlee government that the meaning of the phrase is somewhat unconsidered. It was a great achievement; but did that mean it should be exempt from the financial control imposed on other great socialising achievements such as increases in state pensions, abolition of the means test, National Insurance, provisions of housing or education? Was it a greater achievement than full employment, or nationalisation, or the adoption of demand management?

Within a year of the founding of the NHS, Labour had realised that the blank cheque on social expenditure was not sustainable, and in 1949 a bill was taken through the House by Bevan to impose charges on false teeth and spectacles and put a shilling charge on prescriptions; but the legisation was not implemented because no date was fixed for the introduction of the charges and the measure was simply shelved. In the subsequent period Bevan had successfully fought off challenges to his inaction. After the 1950 election Gaitskell had lamented to his diary the failure to move Bevan from the Ministry of Health where he sat troll-like in his defence of the National Health Service. Gaitskell had tried to stiffen his Chancellor's resolve in the fight with Bevan: 'I begged Stafford to insist on two things. First, Treasury control should be established as effectively as it is over other Government expenditure and secondly there should be a definite limit placed on the total National Health Service expenditure. I would have liked this to have been below next year's estimates, so that we should be quietly committed up to the hilt to finding the rest of the money . . . by making charges.'[81] But Treasury control was slow in coming and Bevan, as was his habit, submitted a large supplementary estimate for 1949–50, continuing a gradual increase in the cost of the NHS by some £100 million. It was not just a case of a Minister defending his corner; Bevan believed that the free and universal National Health Service was a central socialist achievement and was viewed as such by states around the world.

The first round of the 1950 battle was fought to a draw in Cabinet on 13 March. The supplementary estimate was accepted but a ceiling £392 million was set for the next financial year and increased Treasury control was introduced. Bevan's supplementary estimate also resulted in a Cabinet committee being established to monitor the Minister of Health and ensure that the overshoot would definitely not be repeated. The initial mistake, Gaitskell thought, had been to send Bevan back to clear up the mess he had created, and in the second round the truth of this became clearer. Cripps came back to the issue when discussing proposals for his Budget in April 1950 and requested that charges be introduced to reduce the estimate from £392 million, as agreed in March, to £350 million. Bevan argued that such an imposition of charges would be a grave disappointment to socialists around the world. Cripps gave in on that occasion but the battle continued to be joined in the Cabinet committee. While the 'gut' feeling of the Cabinet was still markedly against the imposition of charges, Ministers in other spending departments felt, according to Morrison, that 'Nye was getting away with murder.'

The Cabinet committee was the first forum for conflict between Gaitskell and Bevan: Gaitskell as the Treasury interrogator, Bevan as defender of the Health Service and of his own weakness as an administrator – though it should be stressed that Bevan himself had asked for the committee. The battles over the NHS charges under Cripps ended as a draw. The Chancellor was perhaps reluctant to force the issue to Bevan's resignation, which was frequently offered. As for Gaitskell, the conflict between the two extended to private dinners. Cripps had assembled a regular dinner of Ministers on Thursday evenings. Gradually, these became dominated by arguments between Gaitskell and Bevan. Bevan would give Gaitskell a tongue lashing, while Gaitskell would reply coolly. Moreover Bevan maintained that Gaitskell kept raising the issue of NHS charges at these social occasions. From the various accounts that exist, it seems likely that sometimes Gaitskell was the aggressor, sometimes Bevan, but that slowly they became fixated on the issue; it became increasingly a personal dispute. The fundamental problem was that, while Gaitskell could understand the place of a figure like Bevan in the labour movement and could see the point of Bevan, Bevan found it hard to see the point of Gaitskell or what place he occupied in the labour movement. In his diary Gaitskell heaped praise on Bevan: 'He is so much the best debater; so much the most effective speaker on the Front Bench, indeed in the House, that he can always raise his prestige in the House by a performance.'[82] He had liked the fact that he could argue with him in Cabinet committee and then have a congenial dinner with him in the evening, though these became fewer as the Budget approached.

As for Bevan, he was challenged by John Strachey as to why he was intent on picking a fight with such a considerable member of the government, to which Bevan replied, 'Considerable? But he's nothing, nothing, nothing!' Strachey goes on, 'I tried to explain to Bevan that the quiet rather slight man who sat opposite him had a "will like a dividing spear". I might have saved my breath for all the effect I had on Bevan. I talked the thing over with Stafford Cripps, and with that curious fatalism about personal relations which he often exhibited, Stafford shrugged his shoulders and said there was nothing to be done.'[83] Though Michael Foot goes out of his way to claim that Bevan's dismissal of Gaitskell was not about personal relations but about 'policies, principles, political themes', he then contradicts this starkly by his analysis of what those themes were:

> He pictured several of his Cabinet colleagues, now assisted by this glorified civil servant, banded together, contentedly it seemed, to undermine the greatest Socialist achievement of the Labour Government. He noted not the will and courage but the other aspects of Gaitskellism: the parched political imagination, the pedantic insistence on lesser truths in the presence of great ones.[84]

It is a powerful indictment, the more so for being partially true – but there is much more in the contrast. The focus in Foot's and other accounts is very much on Gaitskell's pedantry and stubbornness; yet Bevan was just as pedantic and stubborn on this issue as Gaitskell. Bevan had already seen off Cripps by his own brand of pedantic stubbornness. Moreover, while there were fundamental principles at stake, there was also ministerial mismanagement of the NHS and a refusal to set limits to expenditure to prevent the need for further supplementary estimates: demands that other Ministers accepted. But the difference goes deeper: if the Bevanites, and Bevan himself, represented the poetry of politics, then Gaitskell was indeed pure prose; the mistake they made about each other was in not recognising the extent to which the Labour government needed both.

Gaitskell's main case for the pedantic insistence on the few million pounds of charges was that this was the only way in which the charges would ever be implemented and that they needed to be implemented if social expenditure were to be controlled. The rearmament package was a separate issue. Thus the substantial question on which the Labour government split was in two halves: first, whether the NHS could have been sustained without the imposition of charges; second, whether charges should have been imposed to help finance the rearmament programme – alongside an overall Budget that proposed wide-ranging tax increases. On the first question Gaitskell represented the technical consensus in the Cabinet as agreed in 1949 and in February 1950: welfare could not be an open-ended commitment, and this reflected the Labour government's dedication to production or supply issues as well as to welfare issues. On the second point – whether these charges had to be implemented at this moment, in this Budget, in this way, and with the possible political fallout resulting from resignations – Gaitskell simply forced the Cabinet to back him. Morrison and others repeatedly offered a compromise whereby the Budget would contain a ceiling on NHS spending but would not mention charges. Gaitskell consistently refused and made this the sticking point. He believed that it was necessary to adopt charges and that merely setting a ceiling was insufficient. Politically he needed to be backed by the Cabinet to assert his ascendency over Bevan.

The politics of the episode are fairly straightforward and there was definitely an element of jockeying for future position. When Gaitskell became Chancellor he was determined that the issue would no longer be shelved; that the NHS would be managed like any other part of the state and subject to the control of the Treasury. He might also have seen his chance to take a commanding lead at the head of his generation of Labour Ministers.

In his first Cabinet as Chancellor the issue surfaced in the discussion on the King's Speech to open the new session of Parliament. The previous version of the speech, which had warned of the possibility of the social and economic costs of rearmament, was toned down: the fear was that the PLP were likely to be 'disconcerted' by the reference, in the tenth paragraph of the draft, to the effects of increased defence expenditure on the government's social policy. It was agreed that this paragraph should be redrafted so as to make it clear that, despite the rearmament programme, the government would continue to give the same high priority to housing and would maintain the essentials of their social policy. It could then continue to the effect that Ministers would do their utmost to ensure that rearmament interfere as little as possible with the maintenance of stable costs and prices. In fact no mention of the possible social cost of rearmament was made in the King's Speech. But the first discussion of the new government rehearsed many of the key themes of the first public schism of the Attlee Cabinet.[85]

This was followed by Cabinets in February 1951 in which the imposition of charges had been reluctantly conceded. This initial agreement was critical to Gaitskell's case, but the imposition of charges on false teeth and spectacles was completely irrelevant to the short-run economic well-being of the country, to the ability of the country to fulfil the rearmament programme and even to the terms of the Treasury's own forecasts. The teeth and spectacles episode was a symbolic political struggle.

Bevan openly broke ranks with the rest of the government in response to a heckler in Bermondsey in the week before the Budget. He stated simply that he would not belong to a government that imposed charges on false teeth and spectacles. Hugh Dalton, now Minister of Town and Country Planning, visited the other Ministers he judged likely to resign in the week after Bermondsey. He found Harold Wilson worrying about his marginal seat and 'desperately jealous' of Gaitskell.[86] In contrast, John Freeman seemed focused very much on the issues and 'was sure our Rearmament was an excessive programme, could not, in fact, be carried out, and would, if attempted, cause great dislocation'.[87] Bevan was adamant in his talk with Dalton: 'If it is such a small thing, why not give way? The compensation of giving way would be me. Is that a very small thing? . . . unless at Monday's Cabinet the charges are withdrawn my resignation will be in the press at the same time as the report of the Budget Speech.' Gaitskell by this stage was also deep in his trench. Dalton had a last long talk with him on Thursday 5 April 1951:

> I told Hugh I had learned of Nye's intentions but did not tell him of my talk with Harold Wilson. I asked whether he had considered the consequences of Nye's resignation. He said 'Yes', and he was convinced that we must face these consequences. He was very firm and determined. He said we could not always be blackmailed and give way. If we didn't stand up to him, Nye would do to our Party what Lloyd George had done to the Liberals. It would, he thought, do us good in the country

to make a stand on this. Nye's influence was much exaggerated. When the case was put, he would have very little support . . . [Dalton] thought he seriously underestimated Nye and his potentialities for mischief. I thought that Hugh thought too little of the Party and too much, relatively, of the general body of the electorate . . . I said Strachey might go as well as Nye and Wilson. He said we'd be well rid of the three of them![88]

Monday 9 April 1951, his forty-fifth birthday, was one of the most hectic and momentous days of Gaitskell's life. It began with a morning Cabinet, starting at 10.30, in which Gaitskell presented the main points in his Budget.[89] These all passed quietly until he reached the health charges issue. They went over the ground one more time, Bevan pointedly asking if he was worth £23 million, Gaitskell responding that if he had a spare £23 million he would not spend it on false teeth and spectacles.[90] The Cabinet adjourned until 6.30 p.m.

Gaitskell returned to the Treasury, briefed the governor of the Bank of England on the main points in the Budget, drafted the peroration for the Budget speech he was still not sure he was going to deliver, then returned home briefly for his birthday party. Arriving home to find his family celebrating was simply too much for him and he broke down and had to leave. At 6.30 the Cabinet reconvened in the Prime Minister's room in the House of Commons. Aside from Bevan, Wilson and George Tomlinson – the Education Minister, who rather late in the day had come down against charges in the hope of trying to save Bevan – the Cabinet was formally united behind the Chancellor. In fact, most simply refused to go back on the decisions that had already been made and had no more enthusiasm for them now than before. Hugh Dalton, more out of personal loyalty than through any burning conviction, Manny Shinwell and Viscount Addison, the Lord Privy Seal, were Gaitskell's strongest backers – but others felt ambivalent and voted with the Chancellor out of loyalty and collective responsibility. Attlee, who was in hospital, Ernest Bevin and Herbert Morrison had all at one time or another urged restraint on both sides. Finally, however, the voices were taken and Gaitskell won the day. He returned home for an hour's rest, then his staff joined him to finish the speech, which they completed at 1 a.m. However, the Prime Minister had not yet formally agreed.

Gaitskell arrived back at his office the following morning – Tuesday 10 April, Budget Day – to be told that the Chief Whip was worried about the state of the party. At this stage even the Bevanites were worried. In the smoking room, Dalton ran into Crossman who told him that Ian Mikardo had been sent to have breakfast with Nye and persuade him not to resign. The only person in favour of his resigning was Michael Foot.[91] Bevan and Wilson visited Attlee in St Mary's Hospital, Paddington, at 10.30 a.m. Together they worked out a form of words that would be an acceptable compromise, similar to the compromise worked out with Cripps in March 1950, setting a ceiling on NHS spending and mentioning the need for charges but without giving a date for their implementation. Meanwhile, still at the Treasury, Gaitskell was rung up by Patrick Gordon Walker, who urged him to compromise by not referring to the charges in the speech but just mentioning the ceiling. Gaitskell refused. He then saw the Foreign Secretary, Ernest Bevin, and again refused to compromise: 'He said, "Well, you will have to argue it out with the P.M." '[92] At 11.30 Gaitskell arrived at the hospital where Attlee presented him with the form of words worked out with Bevan and Wilson. This involved the acceptance of a ceiling and of the possible need for charges in the future. Gaitskell rejected this – for the third time on that day alone. He had decided he must announce the charges or else resign. The PM tried for an hour to persuade him. Finally, Attlee murmured 'what I took to be "Very well, you will have to go." In a split second I realised he had said, "I am afraid they will have to go." ' Gaitskell was safe.

He returned to the Treasury at about 12.30 p.m. Sir Edward Bridges, the Treasury Permanent Secretary, came in and paid him a remarkable compliment: 'I want you to know that not only all those in the Treasury who know about it tremendously admire the stand you have made, but that all the others who do not at present know but will know will feel the same way. It is the best day we have had in the Treasury for ten years.' Dora arrived, they had lunch together in his office, then she joined his mother and Mrs Attlee in the public gallery. At 3.25 p.m. they went across to the House of Commons. Morrison came in and urged him to leave out the sentence which gave the date on which the charges would be announced. For some reason he and Gaitskell felt this might make the difference. It was the only concession the Chancellor was prepared to make and he struck out the sentence at 3.28 p.m. 'His private secretaries still shudder at the memory.'[93]

William Ewart Gladstone delivered thirteen Budget speeches and defined much of the ritual that Chancellors follow. His idea of

Budget-making was Olympian in all respects – four and three-quarter hours in the house, fifteen hours a day at his desk preparing it and three and a half hours briefing his Cabinet colleagues on its contents. Lloyd George was the only Chancellor to rival Gladstone's stamina – taking four hours to present the famous 'people's Budget' of 1909.

The other great Gladstonian contribution was the Gladstone box, in which Gaitskell now carried his papers. The House of Commons was customarily packed for the speech. Gaitskell was wearing a bright red carnation given to him by his first love from the days at the Royal Norfolk Golf Club, Felicity Cory-Wright. By coincidence this was the symbol of the Austrian socialists, who were very touched that he wore it.[94] Gladstone also established the precedent that the Chancellor could drink while delivering the speech – the only time alcohol is allowed in the Chamber. The Grand Old Man favoured a cocktail of egg and wine to fortify him. Hugh Dalton had drunk rum and milk from a silver teapot for his first two Budgets until he changed to a tankard for the third and final one. Stafford Cripps was teetotal. Gaitskell drank whisky during the two and a quarter hours that he spoke. He was nervous and must have been exhausted by the time he finally started. He set off too quickly and Churchill kindly intervened and urged him to slow down. That seemed to relax him and he grew in confidence as the speech went on. For the first time he commanded the House and produced a mature political performance.

Winston Churchill and Clement Davies, as leaders of the Conservative and Liberal parties, gave the customary compliments but both seemed to have been genuinely impressed. Ernest Bevin, four days away from death, sat through it all; Gaitskell recorded in his diary: 'when I sat down he said, "That was a great speech" and he held my hand for quite a long time.'[95] The speech was widely praised on all sides of the House for its intellectual brilliance, as a Tory paper put it: 'He rose a comparative tyro and sat down an acknowledged star.'[96] The London *Evening Standard* was also fulsome in its praise: 'The Chancellor made a speech so pleasing and so masterly that it is clear he is a new force in politics.'[97]

The Budget proposals centred on a heavy set of revenue-raising measures, the reception for which was not quite so positive. The standard rate of tax increased from 9*s.* (45p) to 9*s.* 6*d.* (47.5p) in the pound and the two lower rates of tax from 5*s.* (25p) to 5*s.* 6*d.* (27.5p) and from 2*s.* 6*d.* (12.5p) to 3*s.* (15p). Profits tax on the distributed profits of businesses was increased from 30 per cent to 50 per cent. Purchase tax was increased from one-third to two-thirds on certain luxury goods like television sets, cars and domestic appliances. Entertainment tax was increased on cinema tickets and, of course, NHS patients were to be charged 50 per cent of the cost of dentures and spectacles. Typically this meant a charge of £1 (£15.15 in today's money) for glasses and £4 for dentures. But there was no increase in the tax on cigarettes and drink, income tax allowances were increased for families, and a number of small items were removed from purchase tax. In his radio broadcast Gaitskell explained:

> In a sense everybody is being taxed at present by rising prices, many of them prices of necessities. That obviously matters most to people with small incomes who have least to spare for anything above absolute necessities. Besides the pension increases this is one reason why I haven't touched drinks and smokes.[98]

Overall, the Budget would raise £4,236 million in 1951–2, with expenditure at £4,197 million of which nearly £1,500 million would be dedicated to the defence programme. Gaitskell said he regretted imposing purchase taxes on the domestic appliances which made housework easier but it was necessary as part of the defence programme: 'The setting for this Budget is remote from this island. It is the clash and conflict between Soviet Imperialism and parliamentary democracy.'

The Budget brought Gaitskell close to a physical and emotional collapse. He concludes his diary entry on the false teeth and spectacles affair with a rather extraordinary admission:

> If I had realised that there were so many things which could have meant defeat, I might never have begun; or at least I would have surrendered early on . . . All the same I think I was right. I said in the middle of one discussion to Hugh Dalton, 'It is really a fight for the soul of the Labour Party.' More people understand that this was so now. But who will win it? No one can say as yet. I am afraid that if Bevan does we shall be out of power for years and years.[99]

Nye Bevan duly resigned from the government, followed by Harold Wilson and John Freeman. Bevan compounded his political error by making a violently abusive resignation speech; Wilson and Freeman probably gained a little from the resignation, though for many Wilson's reputation as untrustworthy was reconfirmed. Gaitskell, in political terms, having slipped neatly into Cripps's shoes, gained most. He established his credentials as a political actor in his own right, he forced his two main opponents – from his own generation – out of the government and he consolidated his standing among the leadership, who generally felt that Bevan was on the way out anyway.

Paradoxically, perhaps, Gaitskell – supporting a rearmament package for an anti-communist war in south-east Asia – emerged as the Labour government loyalist; while Bevan – supporting the idea of a free health service and opposing an over-ambitious rearmament package which squandered much of the post-war recovery in export trade – emerged as the government rebel and splitter. The teeth and spectacles episode was steeped in layers of irony.

6

The Road from 1951

And opportunity is carrying you forward on a great wave.
                                    Dalton to Gaitskell, September 1950

I love it. It's the power.
                                    Gaitskell on being in office, 1951

After their resignations, Nye Bevan, Harold Wilson and John Freeman combined with an assortment of rebels to form the Bevanite
group. The left-wingers who had been languishing on the back
benches since 1945 were infused with a burst of mental energy and
political credibility by the trio of ex-Ministers. The press, Gaitskell
and the rest of the government waited for a storm of criticism from
people who could no longer be dismissed as malcontents with frustrated ambitions, or as having little experience of the 'real' world of
government. But the 'Bevanites', as all the government's critics now
became known, did not proceed to launch an immediate public
offensive against the government's rearmament programme. The first
Bevanite pamphlet, *One Way Only*, was a moderate affair which
stressed the need for spending on colonial development rather than
armaments. It was hardly a broadside against the government's Atlanticism. Bevan's biographer, John Campbell, comments: 'By its tone
of reasoned argument, *One Way Only,* and Bevan's speeches in these
months, were a clear and commendable attempt to lift the level of
the debate.'[1]

Arguably of course such constraint came a little late for Bevan's
long-term prospects. Even though it was Gaitskell who had refused
to compromise, it was Bevan who had resigned. This broke a deep-
seated attachment to party unity which transcended the particular
debate concerned. Ironically, Bevan was to make similar mistakes in
the battles ahead, consistently underestimating the value the Labour
Party put on maintaining the correct 'form' in parliamentary and
political behaviour.

Even though Bevan, after his appalling resignation speech, seemed to sober up and behave himself, the problem for the government was his latent capacity for explosive rebellion. Moreover, while Bevan might have been conducting himself like a responsible ex-Minister, other rejuvenated critics of the government on the back benches, in sections of the press and in some parts of the rank-and-file labour movement did not share his sense of restraint towards the policies of the government he had done so much to make a success. There was a good deal of pent-up frustration with the moderation of the government's foreign policy. Bevan was immensely popular. There was always the possibility that others would kick up a fuss on his behalf and, once the argument was started again, there was never any way of telling which way Bevan would go. A general election could have been forced at any time; Attlee was being kept in power by MPs dragged in from their sick-beds to vote. In such a situation a Party Conference characterised by deep divisions on the rearmament programme and the Budget was a real possibility. The government's problems went even deeper: the rate of inflation climbed during the summer and there was anxiety about rapid increases in dividends sapping money from investment and undermining calls for wage restraint. A restless TUC, an unmuzzled left and a worsening economic situation combined to produce a thoroughly uncertain political future. The already gloomy picture darkened further when a crisis blew up in the Middle East.

Under Herbert Morrison's unsteady control as Foreign Secretary (he was appointed just before Bevin's death on 14 April), the Attlee government faced a profound challenge to British power in Iran in the spring and summer of 1951. After the assassination of one Prime Minister, the Shah of Iran had appointed Mohammed Mossadeqh. Dr Mossadeqh announced in March that he intended to nationalise the assets of the Anglo-Iranian Oil Company in the area. Attlee took the lead in urging caution and Gaitskell sided with the Prime Minister, trying to persuade the Minister of Defence, Manny Shinwell, of the need for a diplomatic solution. The Chancellor had family connections with the oil company through his brother-in-law, Hubert Ashton, and, because of his extensive work on refining while at Fuel and Power, knew more about the oil industry than virtually any other Minister.

As the crisis deepened, the crucial symbol became the largest oil refinery in the world at Abadan. Months of negotiation and argument followed. The Americans were keen for the British to allow the nationalisation to stand. There was no way in which the British could have kept control without the use of force to protect the refinery, but the talks on possible compensation had broken down in June. This became the crux of the argument. The hawks were demanding military intervention in defence of Abadan; Morrison as Foreign Secretary had dispatched a cruiser and backed by Shinwell was behaving, according to Dalton, like a latter-day Palmerston. On the other side of the Cabinet, the doves argued for the defence of personnel, if necessary by force, but only after full use of mediation through the United Nations. Attlee assured Dalton: 'I am handling Persia; I've made it quite clear that troops are to go in only to save lives.'[2]

With extensive military commitments in Korea, the projected rearmament which this and NATO membership entailed, and colonial police action in Malaya, a substantial or open-ended intervention in the Middle East would have stretched Britain's military resources almost to breaking point. The historical significance of non-intervention, given the events of 1956 in Suez, were of course profound.[3]

Attlee's role was crucial to the peaceful resolution of the crisis, but Gaitskell was also a key player. He had established a good working relationship with the European face of the Marshall Aid programme, Averell Harriman, during the long negotiations on the rearmament process. By coincidence, Gaitskell was due to be in Paris the day before Harriman would be passing through, and they arranged a secret meeting. Gaitskell had tried to meet the French Finance Minister Maurice Petsche the day before but had been unsuccessful because Petsche was trying to form a government; so the cover story was that the Chancellor had stayed on an extra day to make another attempt at meeting his French counterpart. Harriman's deputy, Milton Katz, a professor of law at Harvard, had a flat in Paris. Gaitskell called on Katz and waited for Harriman to join them there directly from the airport. They spent about forty minutes together, with Gaitskell pressing the case for the Americans to convince the Iranians that they could work with the British. The meeting went well; Gaitskell was then driven to a special airfield and flown in the military attaché's plane to Leeds for a constituency engagement.[4] Such contacts might have been a considerable help to Eden five years later.

Once the British had effectively lost control of the company, their secondary fear was that they would lose access to the supply of oil from Iran. When, partly through the American influence, this fear receded, the crisis trickled away. The British slowly evacuated their personnel from the refinery, and at Cabinet on 23 September the use of force was ruled out. Gradually the supply of oil from Iran restarted and in 1953 Mossadeqh was ousted in a CIA/MI6-aided coup which allowed the British oil company back into Iran as part of a consortium of oil companies.[5]

In the 1951 election campaign, Gaitskell made the government's case clearly and unequivocally. Perhaps repeating the speech on Iran at the outset of the Suez situation would have helped him at that later moment of crisis:

> The central issue is about the use of force – when it is and when it is not justified. However much the Conservatives may wriggle, this is the real question. We have never doubted that it would be justifiable to use force to protect the lives of British citizens if they were threatened by a serious outbreak of rioting and disturbance. We would have sent our troops in to rescue them and bring them out. That is why we had the troops ready and close at hand. Such a situation could easily have developed, but fortunately it did not. Should we, however, have used force to protect British property or to compel the Persians to allow the British employees of the company to remain? I do not think there is much doubt that this has been in the mind of many Conservatives all along. Indeed, Mr Churchill's recent attack on Mr Attlee makes it quite clear. I can understand this point of view though I do not share it. The argument runs like this: 'The Persian government have repudiated an important contract. They have been taken to the Hague court which made an interim recommendation which they at once flouted. They have rejected the reasonable offers we have made. They have stolen British property and expelled British citizens. We will not tolerate it. We have the power and we will use it.' It is all very tempting, but also very dangerous. Had we followed this course, we should have run the grave risk of war with Persia, with the possibility of wider and far more serious consequences. We should have been acting on our own without the backing of the Security Council before whom we should no doubt have been arraigned as aggressors. We should not have found it easy to justify our action, and I very much doubt if it would have led to any easy solution of the oil problem itself. We can fairly say that it is all wrong that a country tears up contracts, especially one made by the Persian government under the auspices of the League of Nations, and ignores the Hague court, that here is a real problem of enforcing a certain code of international conduct which has not yet been solved. But surely the right

course is to do as we have done and bring the whole matter to the Security Council.[6]

The point was well made: in a situation resembling the Suez crisis, Gaitskell argued in the Cabinet and in the country for the use of the United Nations Security Council and the international arbitration courts at the Hague against the threatened use of force, partly, though not only, because he judged that co-operation with the United States in the region was vital to Britain's national interests. Harriman in their Paris meeting reassured him that he too was very anxious to avoid an Anglo-American split.

On the home front Gaitskell's response to the government's precarious position was partly political and partly ideological: he contemplated a tax on dividends. Though he confessed to his diary that he did not feel strongly on the issue either way, he thought that the party needed a move to the left. After consulting widely among his colleagues he decided to propose some kind of control on dividends.[7] The proposal had a number of points in its favour. It would pacify the left of the party by representing an ideological move to the left, while at the same time easing the financial position marginally. It would also give the government a domestic rallying call of fair shares and equal sacrifice for the coming election. Moreover, it would do him no political harm to be associated with a left-wing measure for once. With this, and a series of other policy proposals, Gaitskell now favoured facing down the Bevanites at the Party Conference.[8] Forcing a vote on the defence issue was a means of establishing the Bevanites' real strength; and consolidating a partial leftward move on economic policy would motivate the party before the election. Gaitskell's fear was that the party would not be given the opportunity to fight out the Bevanite issue because Attlee would call the election before the Conference: 'He is tired, partly because the risks of hanging on are so great (that is the real argument in favour) and partly because he wants to get away from the conflict with the Bevanites and hopes that an Election Conference will smooth it all over.'[9]

In this atmosphere of uncertainty about the exact timing of the election and the amount of conflict at the Labour Party Conference, Gaitskell decided to speak at the Trades Union Congress. Initially he assumed he could just 'invite himself' but after the position was explained to him he managed to 'engineer' an invitation.[10] This was a significant personal political opportunity and an important occasion for the government. Characteristically, he left little to chance. The Treasury speech-writers were told to fill out his outline draft and send it to him in Jersey where he was taking his summer holiday with Dora and the girls. The official draft arrived and was rejected, so he spent two days of his holiday redrafting. Back in London the officials then had another go and in turn Gaitskell made more changes: 'I suppose by the time it was finished it had more time spent on it than any other speech, except the budget.'[11]

On 5 September at 10.45 a.m. he read the fifty-minute text to the TUC, and, according to the *Daily Mirror*, 'he broke the spell which the spectre of Aneurin Bevan had cast over this conference. Here at last was someone who would be a match for the flamboyant Welsh rebel.' The TUC decided, unusually, to print and circulate the speech: while urging restraint, and explaining the limited scope for improving wage increases by taxing profits, it also stated that 'the distribution of property is still far too uneven and undoubtedly a change here is essential if we are to have a truly just society.'[12] The combination of economics lecture and message of hope for more steps towards equality in an unspecified future had a considerable impact. Gaitskell himself was unsure of the reception as he spoke: the hall was silent as the conference delegates listened intently to an at times complex message, but at the end he felt it had been a 'pretty good reception, and all the people on the platform were overjoyed.' The miners cheered, and directly after the speech, or in the weeks that followed, a number of key union leaders congratulated him on the performance.[13] The *Daily Mirror* headline was direct: 'They were saying yesterday at Blackpool ... There goes our future Prime Minister.'

The Labour Party Conference itself was less significant because on 5 September, with Gaitskell away in the United States and Canada for more rearmament talks, Attlee told the King he would be dissolving Parliament in the first week of October for an election on 25 October. The influences on Attlee were a mixture of the political and the royal. Dalton had urged a quick announcement for a variety of practical reasons, including Conference arrangements and the manifesto, and for taking the wind out of the forthcoming Bevanite pamphlet, *Going our Way*.[14] Economically it was badly timed and, with the senior Ministers at the talks in Ottawa, there was no one of consequence in Cabinet, expect Dalton, to argue with Attlee. The King, however, had already informed his Prime Minister that he was reluctant to embark on an extended Commonwealth tour with the political situation in Britain so uncertain.[15] 'To Hugh', according to his private secretary William Armstrong, 'it came as a thunderclap. He was very upset by it.'[16] He and the other Ministers sent back messages begging that the decision not be announced while they were still negotiating on burden-sharing and the dollar trade. Morrison simply cabled, 'Still, no comment',[17] to show his disapproval at not being consulted about Attlee's decision.

The 1951 election was Gaitskell's second defence of his South Leeds seat. As Chancellor he was now a national figure and in contrast to 1950 spent much of the campaign speaking around the country on behalf of other candidates. He also made one of the party's radio broadcasts which entailed a visit from Labour's new radio adviser, who described the occasion: 'Gaitskell walked across from his desk to greet us, and as we were ushered in his smile was welcoming. We sat round his desk and he outlined to us the script that he proposed to deliver. He was immaculately dressed in a brown suit, with the very slightest aura of aftershave lotion and talcum powder about him.' Gaitskell listened, a little impatiently, as the young Anthony Wedgwood Benn, now MP, pressed him on the content of his speech, asking for whom it was intended and suggesting ways it could be directed at particular types of voters. The Chancellor replied that 'honest politics meant speaking the truth', and seemed rather bored and distant from the conversation.[18]

On his own ministerial ground of the economy, as Attlee had predicted when seeing the 1951 Budget, there were few possible vote-winning policies. Rearmament had made a significant dent in the balance of payments, and the Iranian crisis had made matters worse. The rate of increase in the volume of exports had slowed and the rate of inflation was rising. In such circumstances, Gaitskell and the party went on the offensive. In the Labour Party's election manifesto an 'elaborate "then" and "now" contrast was made between pre-war misery and present prosperity',[19] and the clear contention was that a vote for the Conservatives was a vote for a return to the bad old days: 'Forward with Labour or backwards with the Tories.' In private Gaitskell did not share this view; he recorded his own analysis in his diary: 'What the intelligent Tories will, of course, want to do is be able to say to the electorate when the election comes, "No war, no unemployment, no cuts in social service, just good government."'[20] In public he hit hard at the consequences of a Churchill administration. Speaking in Glasgow, he remarked that it was easy to call for cuts in public expenditure but that 'as soon as you get down to details . . . you see what nonsense that is. Public expenditure is not something remote from people's lives which can be cut without affecting them. Apart from such things as defence where a service is provided and paid for to protect the whole community, public expenditure includes the spending of a lot of money in payments to or for our fellow citizens whose standard of living is directly dependent upon them.' In general, Gaitkell played an effective and non-controversial role in the campaign.

Bevan had declared at the Party Conference: 'No matter what our differences we must never allow the British Labour Movement to become schismatic. We must avoid at all costs a repetition here of what has happened to continental socialist movements. That is why we must never carry doctrinaire difference to the point of schism.'[21] With this assurance the Bevan/Gaitskell battle did not figure in the election campaign and the party presented a more or less unified front. Gaitskell again expressed his boredom with the actual process of campaigning: 'There is really not much to say about the election . . . it is boring having to say more or less the same things so many times, even if the meetings are different.'[22] Having to follow the Defence Minister, Manny Shinwell, at some of the larger election rallies also irritated his sense of what politics should be about: 'They were so drunk by the emotional nonsense that Shinwell had talked that it was impossible to make them think at all.'[23]

The Labour government had looked increasingly tired as 1951 wore on and the rearmament Budget, as Attlee had feared, delivered few marginal seats. Recently divided at Cabinet level, and with many of the leading figures ill or having already succumbed to the pressures of over a decade's unrelenting toil, there was a national swing to the Conservatives. All things considered, Labour did remarkably well in 1951, increasing their total vote by 1,446,038 votes but losing 25 crucial seats. The Tories came in with an overall majority of 17. 'As to the result, we did rather better than I had expected, right at the beginning of the election I had told Dora privately that I expected they would get in with a majority of about 75.'

Significantly, the interesting aspect of this result was the lack of any sense of defeat. The surge in the Labour vote, and the solid set of legislative achievements, the feeling of maturity that the government had engendered in the party combined to give the outgoing administration a positive sense of the possibilities of the future rather than a despondency about entering opposition. Dalton felt that 'the election results are wonderful. We are out just at the right moment, and our casualties are wonderfully light.'[24]

The changeover between British governments is instant. Butler was well mannered and worked in the Parliamentary Secretary's office while Gaitskell tidied up his affairs. The outgoing Chancellor repeated his habit of trying to improve the reading habits of his officials by handing out novels and poetry as leaving presents. A few years earlier at the Ministry of Fuel and Power he had given one official whose 'literary tastes he found insufficiently developed' a dozen modern novels, including Somerset Maugham's *Of Human Bondage*, Virginia Woolf's *To the Lighthouse,* and James Joyce's *Portrait of the Artist as a Young Man*; to a secretary he had given John Bunyan's *Pilgrim's Progress* and Shakespeare's sonnets. On leaving the Treasury the pattern, partly charming and partly characteristically improving, was repeated, with A. E. Housman's poems, an Elizabeth Bowen novel and a Dostoevsky.[25] Then he walked out of the Treasury and away from the exercise of executive power for the rest of his life. Lord Roberthall, one of his advisers, had asked him how he endured the grind of political life. 'I love it. It's the power.'[26]

He never held real power again. Despite all the battles of Labour politics in the 1950s and 1960s it is impossible not to have the feeling, taking the rest of his life in the round, that this lack of power left a gap which he never really succeeded in filling.

When the Prime Minister backed Gaitskell over Bevan in April 1951, the history of the Labour Party shifted course. It took five years for this shift to become decisive, but the change in direction had begun. In backing Gaitskell, Attlee may simply have been acknowledging the political impossibility of sacking a Chancellor the day before he had to give his first Budget speech, but he was also anointing Labour's unlikely new star. Gaitskell's high-risk strategy for securing his position at the top of Labour's hierarchy was blessed in Attlee's hospital room in Paddington. Beyond Gaitskell's personal career considerations, Attlee's decision helped resolve a number of issues. Labour faced some critical choices on the road from 1951; it was now clear that Gaitskell would be a central part of the process of deciding the future of socialism.

Attlee identified Gaitskell as the alternative leader to Bevan, and the political positions associated with Gaitskell became defined as the alternative policy route to Bevanism. This road, the revisionist-Atlanticist-managerial road, came to dominate British democratic socialism from the mid-1950s to the early 1970s. But in 1951 the Gaitskellite road was only one option before the Labour Party. That it became the road the party took was largely due to Gaitskell. Before telling the story of the struggle between Bevan and Gaitskell, it is worth reflecting on just how far 'Sam' had travelled in his first forty-five years.

Gaitskell had been born into privilege yet chose the side of the underdog. As a young man he endeavoured to make himself different, and differently successful, from his effortlessly advancing brother, Arthur; he achieved this by rebelling against his family and his class, pushing himself, and striving, as he confessed to his mother, for recognition and fame. He also made much of his natural charm and abundant social gifts: 'he moved with an easy and entirely instinctive tact from one circle to another and was at home and welcome in all.'[27] Seeking emotional range and freedom from the constraints of his English public school upbringing, he found these through dancing and through – for his day – unconventionally liberal relationships, especially with women. At the same time as he sought honesty and authenticity in his relations with others he rejected the metaphysical, the unknowable and God. He looked for reality in people and ideas and increasingly found his various sets of Oxford friends unsatisfactory. It was only when he went to Nottingham and spent time with the miners that he thought he had found genuine and unstuffy people. Though he quickly tired of provincial life, the impression these working-class students made on him was immense.

In his twenties Gaitskell had been indelibly marked by the people, events and ideas that surrounded him at Oxford. These years painted different shades into his character which were rarely mixed up. Part of him was for ever Maurice Bowra's slim, curly-haired, fresh-faced, ebullient and intelligent young man: a cheerful undergraduate who mixed charm and urbanity with a noticeable drive to discover books and music; a healthy appetite for conversation and wit; and the disarming tendency to blush when speaking. Another part of him was for ever Evan Durbin's: propelled by intellectual curiosity and the momentous events of the time he become a serious socialist, interested in achievement and self-improvement, rejecting many of the values of his class and seeking, individually at first, then collectively, the improvement of others. It is no accident that Bowra, much to his great regret, never met Durbin.

The great defining point in the first phase of his adult life was the general strike. With the strike came the first full illustration of the extent to which the ideas that so appealed to him could be followed up by action, application and passion. The contrast between the different shades that his twenties left in him, the 'Bowraesque' and the 'Durbinesque', could also be seen in the other characteristics first shown in these years. On the one hand, in setting out to get a First, Gaitskell demonstrated his immense capacity for work. On the other hand, in learning to dance, he revealed a considerable aptitude for play. By a relatively early age he had developed an impressive range and depth of character and interests. With this came the 'will like a driving spear'; clear in the courage he showed in rejecting his family's values and politics, and in the tenacity with which he tried to improve his friends and teach them how to live. He never quite got over this desire to improve people and make an impression on their lives.

The second phase of his life as an economics don and political activist included his brief attachment to Marxism, formed mainly as an emotional response to the darkening international situation and worked through with characteristic thoroughness. It also saw his first serious relationships with women, overcoming the isolation and strangeness of those early months in Nottingham with a string of girlfriends. This period also neatly answered for him many of the questions that Oxford had posed, teaching him through direct experience about the possibilities and, one suspects, the limitations, of the authenticity of people. It also made his appreciation of the problems of the world a profoundly practical and non-utopian one.

If the first phase of his adult life had been dominated by his relationship with brothers, the second phase was concerned with fathers and lovers. The lovers began as adventures in his little flat in Nottingham, exploring the freedom of having his own place away from his family in what he described as the most libertarian town in England. They culminated in his friendship with Dora, leading to love and then marriage. The fathers began with G. D. H. Cole, initially Gaitskell's teacher and the first person to cultivate Gaitskell's socialism, Cole gradually became much more of an equal as Gaitskell rejected and then argued powerfully against Cole's ideas of guild socialism. The second more important father figure was Hugh Dalton, who was an extraordinarily doting father. Dalton was also a

134

decisive political patron, offering intellectual inspiration and practical assistance. He also loved, cherished and consistently believed in Gaitskell's star like no one else; he played an integral part in pushing Hugh quickly up the ministerial ladder; in inspiring him and in practically smoothing his path when needed.

Drafted as a Whitehall irregular as soon as the conflict started, Gaitskell followed Dalton and was pushed by him into challenging war work at a high level on the national stage. The war years were characterised by virtually uninterrupted effort and application, which illustrated for the first time Gaitskell's strengths and abilities as an administrator, manager and decision maker. However, this period also illustrated a major failure, which called into question his capacity for political leadership.

The wartime toil in the Civil Service proved he could have been a diligent, perhaps brilliant, Permanent Secretary, but it did not reveal much ability to discriminate or prioritise issues to be dealt with. For instance, retail price maintenance was, of course, a subject that deserved attention, but Gaitskell seems to have granted it in 1944 the same kind of dedication he gave to the blockade in 1940; it was spinning this seamless web of effort which cost him a heart attack at the age of just thirty-eight. Attlee commented years later, 'I am inclined to think that he worked too hard. This is no bad thing in itself but in the case of a possible Prime Minister there has to be a firm sense of priorities. He took a great many meetings. No doubt this was necessary in the earlier stages when he had yet to become well-known in the movement. But some retrenchment in engagements later would I think have been wise. I think this over-working was due to his great conscientiousness.'[28]

More personally, after 1948 there was also the memory of Durbin. At the point at which they were together beginning to influence events, Gaitskell lost his closest friend – the most important influence on him among his contempories, the person who more than any others had grown with him. When the time and opportunity presented itself to Gaitskell to get closer in touch with that part of himself that loved society, the 'Bowra' side, there was no Durbin to hold him back. In the following decade he was to look for and find an emotional outlet in a relationship with a woman who represented the social world that he had previously been forced by pressure of work and the demands of a political career to reject; it is possible that he would not have done so had Durbin lived. Beyond

this, the fact that his closest friend was robbed of the opportunity
to take part in the forging of the socialist commonwealth must have
been another unquantifiable but surely significant influence driving
the surviving friend on to political heights. But there is another side
to the pace at which Gaitskell pushed himself. Despite the public
school traits of superiority that the young Tony Benn noted in his
diary, in fact, things did not come easily or effortlessly to Gaitskell.
Part of the explanation for the unrelenting application to his career
was that it was necessary, or rather he felt it was necessary, to keep
ahead.

Ministerial office was the defining political experience of his life.
It was more important than even the general strike because it fixed
the single unshakeable conviction which underpinned much of what
was to come later: power was critical – power to put principles into
practice. He exercised power in the most successful administration
of the century. For the rest of his life he wanted it back.

It would be a mistake, however, to see Gaitskell as someone who
defined himself simply in terms of politics. When younger he had
said that the ideal would be either to be a creative artist or to be a
politician. He did not live and breathe the cut and thrust, the intrigue
and the battle, in the way that, say, Richard Crossman did. Though
he liked being famous and enjoyed the drama of the political theatre
he was not in politics primarily because he loved the game. After
all, here was a politician who found general elections boring. Following one rather bruising and embarrassing episode at Fuel and Power
he confided to his diary, 'Altogether I very much doubt if I am
really suited to this kind of thing.'[29] But in the winter of 1950 and
the spring of 1951 a political personality visibly took shape. Inhibitions were shed as he almost physically shifted the Attlee government behind him.

When he picked the fight over defence and dentures, leaving aside
all the questions of principle, he grew into a much more substantial
political figure virtually overnight. Bevan was the catalyst for this
change, the challenge that forced Gaitskell out into the open. He
could not fight the battle on the rearmament programme from
behind his desk in the Treasury, or in the Cabinet rooms. The issue
was too important to the survival of the government for that. He
had to attempt to communicate more broadly with the electorate.
In the 1930s when arguing the case against appeasement Gaitskell
had slowly become a leader among the small group of acolytes work-

ing with Dalton; and they in turn first felt the strength of his personality. It was not as yet a fully formed character that made this initial impact on a small circle of Labour economists – the character had not been rounded out by the experience of war, government and family life.

When defence issues returned to the forefront of British politics in 1950, as they had in 1938, Gaitskell again persuaded a small group to back him: but this time the small group was the Cabinet. Beyond the Cabinet, the trade unions had long been fighting the communists from branch level up but they had never had a champion on the issue at the top of the party. Gaitskell became their champion. In the constituencies too there was a largely silent block of rank-and-file party members who as the 1950s developed increasingly looked to Gaitskell as the leader of the governmental wing of the party.

Gaitskell's political growth progressed in almost imperceptible steps. In consequence he was not well known by the public for someone who held such high offices of state; more significantly he was something of an unknown quantity to many of his fellow politicians. Because so much of his political rise – the Board of Trade, the Ministry of Fuel and, indeed, even the Treasury – was due to the insider's knowledge of his competence and expertise, he suffered from a certain credibility gap with the party at large. However this might be phrased, it was something that annoyed his arch-rival Bevan. The fact that Bevan fundamentally underestimated his opponent in these years had much to do with the fact that Gaitskell seemed to come from nowhere. Even his friends were sometimes amazed by what he was capable of doing under pressure.

The political impact of the Attlee governments on Gaitskell in particular and on the labour movement in general was profound. The domestic programme had constituted a peaceful revolution in many spheres of life and economic activity. The government had reconciled intervention and freedom in the context of maintaining a democratic system. A significant shift in the role of the state, beginning in the inter-war period, had been extended and maintained. But the consequences of the Attlee governments were wider than simply the confirmation of certain shifts in political economy that had been developing in the inter-war period. The Attlee years changed the nature of the labour movement, particularly in terms of the Labour leaders' perceptions of the relationship between the party and the body politic of Britain. For the ministerial wing of the party, the period of protest was now over, and the period of government and responsibility had begun. In turn, this bred a particular kind of Labour nationalism and patriotism. This shift significantly marks out the immediate post-war generation from other generations of Labour politicians. Gaitskell was typical in the way in which his patriotism was consolidated by the war, and unique in the extent to which, by luck and design, so much of the rest of his political life was to be concerned with responding to perceived threats to his nation's role in the world.

In a sense, Nye Bevan was the making of Hugh Gaitskell. Without the false teeth and spectacles debate it is probable, though not certain, that Gaitskell would have stayed in his role as the insider, the expert, the 'glorified civil servant', who could operate on the technically difficult and (occasionally) politically important policy areas that made up so much of post-war politics. He would have stayed very much in the administrative track, safely within what were clearly his personal and intellectual limitations, and not risen to dominate the entire Labour political scene, and transcend those limitations. Without the hectoring, towering brilliance (and vanity) of Bevan to oppose, he might never have broken through the administrative exterior he had acquired during the Second World War. Without the battle on NHS charges, he might never have grown personally and politically into the front-rank politician who emerged, to the bemusement of many, in April 1951. Bevan dared Gaitskell to push himself through the limits his upbringing had placed on his political courage and persona, and he responded with extraordinary vigour to the challenge. Indeed, Gaitskell did not hesitate to pick the fight when it became clear there would be a conflict. But behind all this clashing of great egos the ideological argument between Bevan and Gaitskell was at heart about patriotism and nationalism. Bevanism represented a road for British democratic socialism which advocated an alternative to an alliance with either of the superpowers. It was Gaitskell more than any single individual who ensured that the British labour movement did not take the Bevanite road. This was either his greatest achievement or his greatest crime, depending on one's view of the politics of Bevanism. Whichever, it was the battleground on which Gaitskell grew into the left's greatest Cold Warrior.

For anyone educated and conditioned to the idea of a Conservative monopoly of patriotism, it often comes as a surprise to discover the extent to which it was the post-war Labour Party that initially tore itself apart over issues essentially concerned with sovereignty (atomic weapons), nationalism (the Atlantic alliance, German rearmament and the future of Europe) and patriotism (Britain's ability to be a leading nation). This was largely because the generation of Labour leaders, of both the left and the right, which came to power during this period took it for granted that Britain had a global role to play. The nature of this role was different at different times for different people. Gaitskell felt that Britain could lead only by trying to maintain the closest possible links with the Americans and by playing the most vigorous role possible in the Cold War; he believed, in short, in Britain's responsibility to provide political leadership for the Western world. Others, more usually on the left and to a limited extent Bevan himself, came to feel that it was only by offering an alternative to the superpowers – through, for example, the idea of a 'Third Way' or, later, unilateral nuclear disarmament, that Britain would keep its place in the world; in other words, that a socialist Britain would provide a form of moral leadership and intercession between the free world and the communist bloc. This idea of moral leadership was an important and recurring part of Bevan's philosophy though, as we shall see, unilateralism was not.

What is striking is that both Bevan and Gaitskell assumed that Britain would naturally be in a position of leadership. Gaitskell's world-view was infused with a sense of nationalism with respect to Britain's role as a nation-state among other nation-states and patriotism with respect to the singular qualities of the British people. British socialism was special because of the qualities of the British working class. Britain was special because of its history and its political system.

For Gaitskell, many of these feelings and beliefs were derived from his upbringing and schooling, but the war and the Attlee governments presented him with the crucial connection between a generalised affinity with Britain and a special feeling about the significance of the Labour Party itself. This feeling became so deep in him that it is sometimes difficult to separate out the sources of his feelings of national pride. Sometimes it seems he feels it is the special qualities of the Durham miners that have made this country great;* at other times it is the continuities of the political system that appear more

---

* A feeling shared by their leader Sam Watson. Attlee had once considered Watson as a successor to Bevin at the Foreign Office but as Sam never wanted to travel further south than Durham he felt this might be a slight impediment in that job.

important. Often it seems he believes the labour movement itself is almost synonymous with the nation-state of Britain because it encapsulates all the virtues of these islands. This characteristic of Gaitskell's politics was shared with his generation of post-war Labour leaders, with a few notable exceptions just a few years younger such as Roy Jenkins. It binds Harold Wilson, James Callaghan and Hugh Gaitskell much more strongly, as a generation, than many of the other political or party issues that divided them.

The way in which this feeling came to influence Labour politicians is directly related to the extent of the task which faced the Labour government elected in 1945. There had been a rapid recognition, as the war drew to a close and the dimly perceived outline of the bipolar superpower system became gradually clearer, that in the post-war world Britain would need to make a huge effort just to stand still in terms of its international position. Anne Deighton has made the case clearly: the Labour government's foreign policy objective in the immediate post-war period was to maintain an independent role in foreign affairs: 'To assert Britain's own great power status and restore a favourable balance of power in Europe',[30] and 'with the same determination that welfare and nationalisation measures were introduced during this period of financial stringency, the Government sought to try and sustain Britain's status as a great power with an independent role to play as the United States partner in European recovery.'[31] Or as Ernest Bevin summed it up on the British bomb: 'We've got to have the bloody Union Jack on it.'[32]

This situation forced the Labour Party to make some extremely difficult decisions. Was Britain to fight the Cold War and thereby keep a leading place at the head of the global table, or was the Labour government to try to diffuse the Cold War by offering a distinctive third force position by developing an alternative power bloc? This debate resulted in a confrontation between Gaitskell and Bevan on Korean rearmament, followed by arguments on German rearmament and on the place of the UK in the nuclear arms race. Was Britain to have nuclear weapons and, if so, would they be made by Britain or purchased from the Americans? Those who advocated fighting the Cold War through the Atlantic alliance and the United Nations and who supported Korean rearmament, those who supported German rearmament and the British possession of the bomb, preferably made in Britain, believed that Britain could play the part of a political leader of the Western world. The dominant image that

Bevin, Gaitskell, Patrick Gordon Walker and others carried around in their heads was an image of Britain as a great power – as a partner and not a client of the United States. It was an image of global political leadership on one side of a profound ideological struggle.

Those who opposed the 'political leadership' wing of the Labour Party on the issue of nuclear weapons did so on the basis of a profoundly different reading of the dynamics of the Cold War. They believed in Britain's global role no less than did their opponents: they had no less of a patriotic vision than did the *Bevin*ite or the Gaitskellite advocates of political leadership. If anything they had an even greater belief that their country, or perhaps just the labour movement, invariably 'this great party of ours', had the ability and the duty to offer leadership to the world. However, the brand of leadership they were offering was somewhat different: they offered a moral leadership. The best expression of this desire was made in 1951, almost inadvertently by Nye Bevan as he searched for ways to dress his resignation from the Labour government in clothes more fitting than his envy of Gaitskell becoming Chancellor.

> This great nation has a message for the world which is distinct from that of America or that of the Soviet Union. Ever since 1945 we have been engaged in this country in the most remarkable piece of social reconstruction the world has seen. By the end of 1950 we had assumed the moral leadership of the world. [interruption] It is no use Hon. Members opposite sneering, because when they come to the end of the road it will not be a sneer which will be upon their faces. There is only one hope for mankind, and that hope still remains in this little island. It is from here that we tell the world where to go and how to go there . . . there is only one hope for mankind – and that is democratic socialism. There is only one party in Great Britain which can do it – and that is the Labour Party.[33]

When Gaitskell and Bevan considered Britain in relation to the world they were patriotic in both a positive and a negative sense.[34] One dictionary definition of patriotism is the belief in the unique virtue of the national and other characteristics of the people of a nation-state. As J. C. D. Clark has persuasively argued, this can be the ability of people to defy oppression *or their ability to oppress*, which raises the question:

> what form the patriotism should take: should it be a story of achievement, advance, enlightenment? Or should it emphasise a dark side – exploitation,

suffering, poverty? Nothing in the methods of scholarship can answer this question: it is essentially political ... Patriotic history is not a series of sentimental anecdotes of Drake, Nelson or the Battle of Britain, though these can still evoke it. Patriotism is essentially the idea that we are related to 'our' history by something more than contingency; that both the sins and the success of the fathers are visited upon the children unto the third and fourth generation; that we are part of our past, inhabitants not tourists.

If we accept Clark's view that there can be both positive and negative patriotism, then the full extent of the impact and the legacy of the Attlee governments becomes clearer. Speaking in 1937, Attlee had said: 'There is a deep difference of opinion between the Labour Party and the Capitalist parties on foreign affairs as well as on home policy, because the two cannot be separated. The foreign policy of a government is the reflection of its internal policy.' This is a classic statement of a party which has never held a governing majority and still sees itself in a state of struggle with the prevailing political system. But by 1953 Attlee felt 'it is desirable, wherever possible, that, in foreign affairs particularly, Government policy should have the support of all. It strengthens us in giving what I believe is a necessary lead in international affairs.' This is, as Dan Keohane, a historian of Labour's defence policy, noticed, an acute example of the impact of the war on Attlee's perception of international relations. But it is also a reflection of the way in which Attlee's patriotism has been altered from negative to positive. From the struggle to achieve power by the party of the working class to the achievements of the first majority Labour government: it is an astonishingly clear illustration of the impact and manifestation of the responsibilities of power.[35]

More broadly, it is a reflection of what the Attlee government did for the Labour Party: to the solid base of the negative patriotism of the struggle was added an infusion of patriotism and pride in the achievement of the Labour governments. These comments also reflect Attlee's abiding belief that the natural role of the British in world affairs is one of leadership – even if this was only, in his later years, in terms of helping to create a world government.

The Attlee of 1937 and the Attlee of 1953 are united in the conviction that what actually matters is Britain. They are united because they believe there are certain national characteristics that make the British special; and that the British have a responsibility because of their 'specialness' to play a role in world affairs. This vision of Britain that existed in the labour movement dominated the

Labour Party for a generation, and it was a vision that laid the foundations for British perception of its place in the world through the post-war period. The Attlee government changed the way in which democratic socialists thought about Britain: their innate patriotism became a positive feature. It was the achievements of this government – from the nationalisation programme and the housing programme to the NHS; from decolonisation in India to social cohesion; from myths of crime-free streets and ideals of collectivism – to which the Labour politicians of this generation returned again and again. This became a central feature of Gaitskell's political outlook and a central feature of the ethos of the Labour Party.

Gaitskell's contribution to the Attlee governments is, though, more difficult to quantify precisely. There are two kinds of agenda in any democratic government. The first is that of the ongoing management of the state and its apparatus – without which there would be no government – and the smooth running of which is synonymous with 'consensus' government. The second is the ideological agenda of the political party to which the Minister belongs. To an extent, of course, politics is about the way in which the latter attempts to intrude on and change the former. A political judgement on the relationship between a Minister and her or his civil servants might also be about the degree to which the political agenda can be made to influence the flow of the managerial agenda. It seems clear that in the sense of getting civil servants to do what he wanted on the managerial front Gaitskell was a consistent success and would have continued to be a success in a future ministerial career. He managed his departments as a junior Minister well; for example, the doubling of coal output in 1948 and the trebling of coal exports in the same year had partly been achieved by making the apparatus work well. In pushing the civil servants in new directions and changing the notion of the state that needed to be managed, he also achieved considerable success at Fuel and Power, pushing the nationalisation programme through, analysing and drafting the pricing policy for the new industries and applying himself to staffing the management boards of the new state monopolies. These were jobs in which technical ability, attention to detail and perseverance were important and they were also well handled. Gaitskell achieved these things while charming the majority of people who worked with him, but also while making a minimal impact on the wider electorate.

The problem by 1951 was that the ideological agenda of the

government was somewhat exhausted. In his Conference speech before the election that autumn, Bevan stated bluntly that: 'Labour has no sense of defeat'.[36] Even after the election there was a feeling of confidence in the labour movement, with membership rising, and, even while being defeated, Labour achieved its highest ever vote. For Marxist critics of the Attlee governments, like Mark Jenkins, the achievement of the record vote in 1951 was despite and not because of the Labour government's record: 'Labour's record 1951 vote was achieved despite austerity, consolidation, rationing, the use of troops against strikers, imposition of charges on the health service, higher national service to prosecute colonial wars, involvement in Korea, the biggest jump in the retail price index for 10 years and a series of splits at cabinet level.'[37] A list of the achievements of the Labour governments can be set against this list of failings: 'We did what we promised to do . . . to nationalise the Bank of England, the fuel and power industries, inland transport and the iron and steel industry; and this we did in 7 major Acts. We promised a vast development of social services; and faithfully provided, or extended, sickness, unemployment and retirement benefits, maternity grants, widow's pensions and death grants. Free, comprehensive medical service was established.'[38] One can add to Christopher Mayhew's list the demobilisation of the army, the housing programme and the independence of India. Most of the achievements came between 1945 and 1950, most of the failings in 1950 and 1951. Over the troubled period 1950–1, the party's vote increased by nearly 700,000, to reach a total of 13,948,605, and individual membership reached over one million in 1952. As we have seen, the party was defeated by the electoral system, achieving a plurality of votes which, piled up in traditionally Labour areas, produced a minority of seats.[39]

Nye Bevan's assertion that the party had no sense of defeat was based on the hope that the Conservatives would fail in the post-war challenge. Bevan always associated the Tories with high unemployment[40] and believed they would slash public expenditure and force millions back on to the dole. In contrast, Gaitskell's view was that the Tories knew what to do to hold power and he worried about the future political prospects for Labour if the Churchill government simply maintained the agenda created by Attlee. However, the overall mood of the party was confident and the political conflict was set in the context of their expectation of a rapid return to government.

The central question became: what now for the Labour Party?

This formed a key electoral dilemma for the party in the 1950s, and the search for a policy direction was repeated to an extent in the 1980s. The main difference between Labour's two long periods of opposition and policy division was that in the earlier period their legacy was of successful government and the arguments were about how to build on that success. In contrast, in the latter period the problem was a perceived failure of the party in power.

Thus on foreign policy the legacy of the Attlee governments was the clear notion of global leadership but with contrasting views as to how to maintain such leadership. On domestic policy the legacy was of immense achievement, and the debate was whether that achievement should be consolidated and new programmes developed or whether this had only been the beginning and much was still needed to be done.

This argument was central to the historical development of the party. Labour-based movements from the late nineteenth century onwards have suffered from a basic division, with varying degrees of seriousness, between maximalists and minimalists, defined in different ways. In the British context, the Labour Party began as an extension of the trade union movement with a corresponding group of middle-class radicals attached to it and to the Independent Labour Party:

> The Labour Party has always been divided. Whilst intrinsically a creation of the trade union movement, seeking repeal of restrictive legislation, other groups involved in its formation conceived it to be the institution through which a socialist Commonwealth, of whatever kind, might be built.[41]

Tony Crosland, whom Gaitskell first met in 1947, a year after Hugh Dalton had taken the young Crosland, then a fellow of Trinity College, Oxford, under his wing, was to become the leading theorist of the radical right of the Labour Party. He gave a concise summary of the different doctrines which emerged from these two main founding groups, in the opening chapters of his *Future of Socialism,* and concluded that what emerged from this 'brief catalogue' was the 'variety and heterogeneity' from which the modern Labour Party was born.[42] Crosland went on to conclude that

> it is not even surprising that different doctrines should be supported at the same time – Owenism and Chartism, Marxism and Christian Socialism, Fabianism and Guild Socialism. There must always be divergent views on the right emphasis and order of priorities, and these will prevent a

uniformity of thought. The trouble is that some of the divergences are not a matter simply of emphasis or the right priorities. They are fundamental, and the doctrines are mutually inconsistent.[43]

Or, as Gaitskell himself wrote in *Political Quarterly* in 1956:

The British Labour Party has never been encumbered by a precise and rigid collection of dogmas set out in the works of the socialist Fathers. If in discussing socialism we refer to Karl Marx or Robert Owen it is usually for historical interest rather than to produce a quotation which clinches the philosophical argument.

From Crosland's 'divergent and inconsistent theories' there emerged a political party with a political programme. The British political system itself and the need to be electorally viable tended to reduce the utopian and accentuate the practical. The 1945–51 governments exaggerated this process by instituting what Dalton called 'Practical Socialism', thereby defining socialist doctrine in terms of Morrison's maxim that 'socialism is what the Labour Government does.' Interestingly, according to Professor George Jones of the London School of Economics, Morrison used this phrase at an LSE Government Department Seminar chaired by Robert McKenzie in the 1950s.[44]

The result of power was to leave the left of the party stranded in support of the movement for traditional values and the mouthing of 'sacred texts', most notably Clause 4 of the party constitution, but without a clear link to any socialist past. Another consequence was that the mixture of doctrines and their emergence in the policy of the 1945–51 government left the party as a whole rather directionless once it lost power. This opened the way for the 'revisionists' to claim that an appeal to the past was no longer enough and what was needed was a new doctrine for the future.

The political scientist, Patrick Seyd, has suggested that the division in the party between socialists and social democrats can be summed up thus: 'Socialists are committed to the transformation of property relationships and social democrats are committed to the modification of property relationships, "Managing Capitalism set against replacing Capitalism."' This is a clear and useful differentiation between the two main brands of Labour Party ideology, but what underlies both is a vision of Britain that emphasises the backward, the unequal and the poor. The vision of the problem is more or less the same; the prescription for the type of treatment needed is very different. The

Attlee government established an inbuilt majority of social democrats
at ministerial level in the party and among the key trade unions for
a decade, but they also enshrined by their achievements emotional
and linguistic loyalties to the idea of transformation, summed up in
the phrase from Clause 4 about taking control of the means of
production, distribution and exchange.

Social democrats had different policy orientations through time
and have followed different routes, but their objective was to manage
capitalism in such a way as to achieve a fully modern society. The
definition of what constitutes the modern society may change but
it was usually represented by something foreign and/or new: the
differentiation between the modern and the new in social democratic
philosophy is often ambiguous. This may stem from the need to
manage what they perceive to be the chaos of the market. Markets
do not achieve the redistribution objectives that social democrats
feel are essential to bring equality to an unequal but increasingly
affluent society. Left to the market, Britain would continue to divide
between the rich and the poor and continue to be a pre-modern
society.

To bring rational organisation to the chaos of the market it was
necessary to use planning, including the possibility of using physical
controls. The problem was that after the Attlee governments of
1945–51 there was very little mental energy left among the Labour
intellectuals to consider the range of policy options beyond physical
controls. There was also, more fundamentally, a failure to abandon
either the idea of planning in favour of the market, or embrace a
French style of dirigiste machinery of state intervention. Indeed,
some of the wartime planning machinery that Labour dismantled
might have served to promote greater intervention in peacetime had
there not been a significant, though not complete, move away from
planning while the government was in office. This was mirrored by
a move away from wage restraint by the TUC. Such developments
have been analysed by Eric Hobsbawm:

> The wartime dirigiste machinery was dismantled and neither party thought
> we needed a Planning Agency . . . Even though there are signs that under
> Stafford Cripps the necessity for planning was envisaged, and
> the Economic Planning Board was set up, I think most people would
> agree that Cripps was only engaged in short-term operations which
> had not very much in common with planning as otherwise understood.
> Kenneth Morgan perceptively hints at one ideological reason for this.

Social Democrats wanted to distinguish themselves from totalitarian communism, or at least to protect against accusations of being too left-wing, and central planning was indeed identified with this. And the argument that we are not like the communists and therefore we must have freedom and so on was a powerful one.[45]

The pre-war socialist ideas of nationalising the bulk of the economy were thus, along with central planning, discredited. Although forms of indicative and incentive planning could play a part, because they were easier to reconcile with freedom, the overall conclusion the social democrats gradually reached in the years after the Attlee governments was that a new model had to be found. They therefore looked abroad.

Gaitskell and Crosland looked abroad and saw America: they saw the management structure of the 'new' forms of capitalism and they saw the truly global reach of American capitalism. America became, for many of the revisionist social democrats, modernity. While rejecting the inherent inequality of American capitalism and often despising its materialism, nevertheless the notion of managerial capitalism and a 'classless' society based on competition was immensely powerful. The competition would have to be controlled, the wealth redistributed, but the corporation had taken the capitalist out of capitalism. A sub-set of the revisionist social democrats also looked abroad, but much more to continental social democracy. As the 1950s developed they saw the economic miracle of the Six, the reconstruction of Germany on a largely social democratic state model, and they adopted this as their model of modernisation. The EEC, for figures like Roy Jenkins, became modernity.

The left wing of the Labour Party rejected the notion that central planning was necessarily incompatible with freedom or electoral success. They looked east with an at times uncritical acceptance of the image the Soviet Union was projecting. They adopted the idea of the command economy as the model for modernisation – not the creation of a fully planned economy, but the extension of social ownership to the commanding heights of the economy, leaving a small private sector, moving on from what they saw as the bridgehead established by the Attlee governments. The mixed economy of Yugoslavia, with a little of the Soviet Union, minus the gulags, became Modernity. Those who adopted the idea of the command economy, following the dictates of Seyd's distinction, were the tiny socialist minority, among them the communist and Trotskyist fellow travellers, a small but significant number of whom infiltrated the Labour Party in the 1950s.

The left of the party, at least those who were not communist or fellow travellers, which was the vast majority, tried to spell out a socialist alternative which would radically change society, to build on rather than consolidate the achievements of 1945–51. For Bevan and the left, the conflicts in society between property, poverty and democracy were not changed by the war. Bevan's book, *In Place of Fear*, expressed a belief in the power of planning and the need to use the state to control the market so that 'effective social power' will 'pass from one order of society to another.'[46] This watered-down version of the class war was supported by a strong emphasis on the need for participation. 'The ordinary man and woman is called into consultation and is asked to decide what he himself would put first in the national order of things.' Bevan and the left saw state owner-ship rather than demand management as supplying the answer to the problem of full employment, but, to Crosland, growth in the econ-omy and demand management meant that prosperity was assured and the Labour Party could now turn to more social questions.[47]

The left also maintained its faith in public ownership, with modi-fications to make it more accountable, as a form of extending equality, while for Gaitskell and Crosland extending public owner-ship in the already mixed economy was redundant unless it was in the form of competitive public enterprise or government share ownership. Moreover, for Gaitskell the policies of those who wanted to move on to the next stage of socialism and those who were dissatisfied with the achievements of the first instalment were elec-toral suicide. This argument was most clearly stated by Gaitskell's closest ideological ally, Tony Crosland, in *The Future of Socialism* published in 1956. For Crosland, the experience of the war and the post-war Labour governments had discredited the popular assump-tions of pre-war Marxists: 'The belief that the inner contradictions of capitalism would lead to first a gradual pauperisation of the masses and ultimately to the collapse of the whole state, have by now been rather disproved.'[48]

Bevan's fundamentalist formulas prevented him from seeing that the range of possible alternatives to free-market capitalism was now much broader than an overnight transition to socialism. Seyd, though usually sympathetic to the left, supports this view: 'But lacking any extensive research of the structural changes in the British economy [the left] tended to react to initiatives from the right of the Party. General slogans rather than detailed policies became the norm for the Labour left on economic issues.'[49]

The basis of the argument, stressed more by right-wing writers than by the left, was the electoral viability of the Labour programme. Although the vagueness of the left's analysis tended to weaken their arguments on an intellectual level, the appeal of left-wing leaders like Bevan was not primarily intellectual anyway. In contrast the right-wing writers had little popular appeal in terms of inspiring the faithful: 'What is the common factor which Labour people share and which sharply distinguishes us from the Tories? It is Socialism. If it is not that then there is nothing . . . the more we play it down, the less we differ from our opponents and the less reason there is for people to vote for us to get the other lot out.'[50]

Appeals like this were guaranteed to fill halls with the faithful, but the content of the left-wing critique had a basic failing which Gaitskell summed up, harshly: 'Can anyone honestly say that if the Labour Party had chosen a policy which reflected more or less the line of the Communist Party we should have received a larger vote?'[51] The paradox in these intense debates was that, for all their enthusiasm as intellectual wholesalers, these different varieties of Labour thinkers still believed that British democractic socialism could lead the world.

These were the battle-lines of the 1950s. In international and defence policy an idea of political leadership for Britain in alliance with the United States in a global conflict was pitched against the idea of moral leadership by Britain as an alternative to superpower conflict. In domestic policy a view of a fundamentally reformed capitalism demanding consolidation of the advances made by the Labour governments was pitched against the demands for expansion of the public sector at the expense of the private and a continuing march towards transforming capitalism by altering property relationships. Intermingled with these policy issues about the road from 1951 were clashes of the personalities, the lifestyles and the backgrounds of the protagonists.

Gaitskell's path to the Chancellorship had been along an inside track of relatively smooth ascent. In his career until 1950, Gaitskell had actually had little political street fighting to do. But he was now the leader of the anti-communist wing of the party, the champion of the right, and had suddenly acquired the image of something of a political hard man for the way in which he faced down Bevan. In so doing he had reached a remarkable height, but after 1951 he would have to fight month by month for half a decade to take the next leap forward. It was political trench warfare of the bloodiest kind.

7

The Battle with the Bevanites, 1951–1954

Bevanism is an attitude of mind.

Morgan Phillips, 1952

Why can't you be a man and face the music?

Clement Attlee to Nye Bevan, 1954

How can you support a public schoolboy from Winchester against a man born in the back streets of Tredegar?

Nye Bevan to Sam Watson, 1954

Gaitskell was now a member of the opposition and sat on the opposition front bench for the first time. Without departmental responsibility, but still a national figure, he found that the demands of South Leeds asserted themselves. For the next half-decade he devoted himself more directly to dealing with constituency problems than at any other time of his career. By the standards of the time, Gaitskell was a reasonably conscientious constituency member and parliamentary attender. Were he a Labour MP today, however, the extent to which he relied on his friends in the seat, particularly his agent, would be seen as shockingly remiss.

The Gaitskells never owned a house in South Leeds and never stayed there for more than a week at a time. Hugh held monthly surgeries and Dora accompanied him occasionally if there was a particular event which interested her or really required her attendance. She played the role of a good political wife but within fairly strict boundaries that protected her own life and that of her children. George Murray, who replaced George Brett as the South Leeds agent in 1950, sometimes wanted her to visit the constituency more often and sent invitations for various meetings which she turned down.[1] When in the city she would take her own meetings like the Women's Advisory group and Gaitskell would either come along as well or pick her up and say a few words at the end. The latter was especially the case if there was another function running that he could address – so they could divide their attention and cover two Leeds audiences in one afternoon – or, occasionally, if Charles Pannell, a fellow Leeds MP, had managed to get tickets for Leeds United, as in January 1954 when Leeds United were playing Tottenham in the FA Cup.[2]

George Murray frequently tried to get Dora to bring the girls, Cressida and Julia, to the seat, but she seems to have been strict about only allowing the whole family to visit if it did not interfere with school schedules. Dora consistently, as she had in refusing to live in Number 11, protected her family life from the worst intrusions of the political scene. Despite Murray's efforts, by 1957 Cressida, then fifteen, was defending her own time from the responsibilities of politics: 'I am sorry to say that Cressida will not be coming. She is much bothered by exams at the moment and I do not really like to force her.'[3] When they came together they stayed in the more affluent North Leeds with local party members, the Gillinsons. Denis Healey, a fellow Leeds MP, sometimes shared these digs and recalled the Gillinsons in his memoirs: 'Each was an exceptional individual who made a major contribution to the cultural life of the city. Bernard was a natural academic who was compelled to spend his working life running a warehouse business started by his father, a Jewish immigrant from Eastern Europe. He dedicated his spare time to promoting the visual arts . . . and in 1955 David Hockney sold to Bernard his first painting – the excellent *Portrait of my Father*.'[4] Rose Gillinson came from a similar background to Dora: a wealthy Jewish family in St Petersburg who left for Palestine after the revolution. Rose was a great beauty who maintained her Russian connections, and between them, according to Denis Healey, the Gillinsons 'transformed the standing of art in Leeds'.[5] Dora and Rose became great friends and her preference was always to stay with them when in Leeds. Gaitskell's constituents, though, liked it when he stayed in the seat, as he often did when visiting on his own. The Gaitskells also sometimes stayed with the Priors – also active party members – even though their house 'was rather cold'.

When on his own Gaitskell would often stay with the Murrays and enjoy a traditional Sunday lunch with the family.[6] His weekend routine was fairly fixed. He held Saturday surgeries, followed by a rest, perhaps watching a cowboy film at the Murrays' before touring the working men's clubs. On Sunday he might have a second surgery before the general management committee meeting and return to London on an afternoon train. He frequently held his surgeries at either the Middleton Arms or at Number 5 or Number 8 Cambrian Terrace, an attractive row of Victorian houses overlooking a small park. The terrace still stands, though it is surrounded by much newer and less attractive modern housing estates today. From the steps of Number 8, you can look across the M621 urban motorway, which now bisects what was once Gaitskell's constituency, at the 'Gaitskells', a row of early 1960s tower blocks. The area is now a bleak and windswept zone between busy roads and with that empty feel that the 1960s style of slum clearance favoured. The Hulston Working Men's Club and others still exist, standing out as older buildings amongst the more uniform newer estates. Up the hill behind the old constituency office stands a set of back-to-back houses not cleared by the council's bulldozers. They give perhaps something of the feel of how the place must have been in the early 1950s: in the main, still rather bad housing, in a poor district comprising a series of what had until the inter-war period been separate villages, including the mining area of Middleton. But one also gets the sense of a close community, solidly Labour and entirely working class.

It was here, in Cambrian Terrace, that once a month or so Gaitskell met his constituents and tried to help them with their problems. In the evenings, he drank with them and attended their socials and dances. But beyond the form of conscious effort to talk, to write letters and to listen, he thought about the constituency, nurtured it and tried to remain in touch with its developments. For example when he first considered running for the National Executive Committee he asked to be the delegate from South Leeds for the Labour Party Conference. George Murray replied that the party would of course nominate him but some members had questioned whether he would make a satisfactory job of being the local party delegate. Gaitskell replied that he was very anxious to stand, adding, 'I feel that the vote I received last year is sufficient justification for trying again. A number of friends have also told me that they very much hope I will do so. I am certainly prepared to accept the full obligations for the Delegate for South Leeds, to attend a meeting prior to the Conference to discuss the agenda and the attitude to be adopted on the various issues raised, and also of course to report back in full afterwards.'[7]

154

He took the role of representative for the area seriously. Thinking further about the state of the local party he proposed to visit the constituency for a week of political activity in September, to help with a membership drive and generally to improve his personal contacts and profile in the seat. As he wrote to Murray, 'I have been thinking a lot about the constituency recently and wondering whether there was any way in which I could help ... There are various things I could do – factory visits. I have not done any of these for some time and there are at least two places on my list. Secondly, meeting individual members of the Party in the wards.' Murray welcomed the ideas and set up the meetings.[8]

Leeds was an active Labour area with a strong political tradition and Murray was an energetic agent; the combination gave Gaitskell a remarkably solid base. Every year Murray gave the division an end-of-term report on their Member of Parliament, and the esteem in which Gaitskell was held by his agent and the people of his constituency shines through. In the first full year of opposition Murray was reporting that Gaitskell, 'as one would expect', was taking an active role in the party's controversies, and attending the Conference as South Leeds delegate and nominee to the National Executive Committee. Despite his failure to be elected to the NEC, along with 'other old and prominent members ... the value of his realistic and judicial appraisal of the problems which beset our age, and his great ability to meet them was, however, fully acknowledge [sic] by his colleagues in the parliamentary party, and expressed in the large vote given him for the shadow Cabinet elections.'[9] The other purpose of the report was to explain to South Leeds members what Gaitskell was doing when he was not in the constituency. 'Mr Gaitskell has, throughout the year, placed himself at the disposal of Transport House for propaganda work, and almost every week-end has been spent in addressing meetings in the country.'

The following year the local party was still in a generally healthy state: 'a steady effort to increase Individual Membership has been maintained through the year, culminating in a Socialist Week in September. Mr Gaitskell devoted this entire week to propaganda in South Leeds, and visited factories and works, and canvassed in the streets.' The following year, Murray commented that 'constituents continue to come for help and advice to the interviews in three parts of the division. In addition Mr Gaitskell mixes freely with residents in their social life, wherever possible.'[10] This socialising was an important aspect of Gaitskell's relations with the people in South Leeds. He was keen to encourage social occasions, suggesting a regular dinner and dance and supporting the creation of a band to play for the tea dances – though, sadly, the South Leeds Band, from which much had been hoped, had only the year before been disbanded because Councillor Kennally, the leading light, had moved out of the constituency.

Gaitskell's involvement could also be much more directly political and he was capable of what Murray called 'Machiavellian manoeuvres'[11] when any of his people's positions were threatened. This was grassroots politics of the most basic kind, but keeping the constituency under control is a critical part of the life of a British MP.

The secretary of the South Leeds Division Labour Party, the ever loyal and conscientious Murray, had a temporary lapse in confidence at a meeting in June 1953 when facing an attack from within the local party.[12] The issue had developed the previous year when some of the members of the Beeston Ward had signed a petition that went against party defence policy and had joined a communist front organisation called the Assembly of Women, which was on the NEC's proscribed list of organisations deemed incompatible with party membership because of their communist or fellow-travelling connections. Murray had asked for advice and Gaitskell had replied: 'On the Beeston people who signed that petition it seems to me the obvious line to take is to give them a chance of resigning from the Assembly of Women; but if they refuse to do so there is really no option but for the party to expel them.'[13] Murray wrote to the women along the lines Gaitskell had suggested. The Hunslet Ward then passed a vote of censure on Murray as the divisional secretary for exceeding his duty and misinterpreting his instructions as to the type of letter to be sent to the members whose names were reported as being associated with the proscribed organisation.[14] This resolution was subsequently endorsed by the general committee of the ward party.

Councillor Parker said that many people present at the meeting felt that Murray had not followed the instructions he had been given, because he had taken Gaitskell's advice and told the people concerned that they should resign from the Assembly of Women. Murray replied by saying that he *had* followed the instructions and that anyway he was not responsible to individual wards but to the Leeds

City Party as a whole. He implied that this was simply an attempt to undermine his position. The minute book record went on: 'a very full discussion followed in which support for the content of the letters and for Murray was fulsome and a resolution in his support was passed.'

However, the matter was not closed. The city party, considerably to the left of the South Leeds constituency, then advertised for an election agent. Murray could not understand why this had happened and, not getting much support, decided to resign from his post so that the party could appoint a combined secretary/agent. A candidate named O'Connor, unsuitable from Gaitskell's point of view, came forward. Murray seems to have hoped that the Gaitskellite Frank Burnley would be elected secretary and agent. Gaitskell's people were in trouble and the way the member for South Leeds went to work illustrated a grasp of local politics and arm twisting that was quite formidable, especially from someone with a reputation for being remote from grassroots politics.

First, he set about rebuilding Murray's confidence and reasserting his own authority in the seat. He told Murray, in no uncertain terms, that it was up to the candidate to appoint the agent in his own constituency and that this had nothing to do with the city party. He suggested that Murray must have misjudged the mood of the meeting that had caused him to offer his resignation. He then contacted a number of key supporters and got them to help in stiffening Murray's resolve. On his next visit to Leeds he met with Murray and Burnley and they planned their strategy for the general management committee (GMC) meeting, mobilising members to attend and working out what to say. Everything came off almost perfectly. 'I was delighted with the outcome of yesterday's meeting . . . What happened also makes me feel that all your hard work is slowly beginning to show results in the greater confidence displayed towards the leadership in the Divisional Party.'[15] Murray was maintained in his position. While it was a long way from making the Budget speech or flying to Paris for secret meetings with Averell Harriman, this local politics was a crucial part of Gaitskell's political life. A well-ordered local party always gave him a strong foundation in the national battles and he was not above getting his hands dirty in the nitty-gritty lobbying of local members to maintain the dominance of his supporters.

Apart from these political manoeuvres in the divisional Labour

Party, there were dozens of constituency matters to attend to each month, ranging from the numerous speaking engagements and factory visits to his regular advice 'interviews', which gradually as the 1950s progressed became known as surgeries. In these meetings individual constituents could come and seek help from their MP on a range of matters. He was an unusually conscientious member in this respect. Legend has it that, of the four Leeds MPs, Gaitskell saw his constituents most often, followed by Alice Bacon, while Charles Pannell never held a surgery in his West Leeds seat.[16]

The range of constituency problems was immense but often associated with the poor housing in the area. A classic constituency problem cropped up in October 1954 concerning a Mr and Mrs Coy.[17] A quarrel had developed between the Coys and their neighbours, the Butterfields, and the housing manager at the Middleton estate where it took place had already been involved when the constituent took his complaint to Gaitskell. Mr Burton, the housing manager, takes up the tale:

> It seems that Mrs Butterfield has a counter-complaint that Mr Coy adopts a threatening attitude to Mr Butterfield in the street and that Mr & Mrs Coy, together with their step-son, Jack Caleb, have been in the habit of coming home at two o'clock in the morning, singing and shouting and disturbing the neighbourhood. Mrs Butterfield also alleges that they have been abused with foul language for attending to their garden on Saturday mornings, as it is the Coys' habit to lie in bed until mid-day at the weekend. As far as can be ascertained, there is, perhaps, some fault on both sides but the Coy family do seem to be difficult people to get on with . . . The hammering complained of does not apparently go on night after night, but only occurs when Mr Butterfield is repairing a pair of shoes.

The note attached from Gaitskell says, 'the enclosed is, I think, self-explanatory. I do not really know what else I can do.' A few years later two constituents were going through marriage problems. A wife had left her husband with a child, but the husband remained in the council's accommodation. The council's policy was to let the tenancy continue with whichever parent had the child. It put Gaitskell in a tricky position because the husband seems to have approached him and it was the wife who had left the husband. 'We certainly have no particular reason to take sides in this matter because after all both the husband and wife are constituents and, presumably, both are supporters of the Party.'[18] Many of the problems, all of which took up time and energy, were equally intractable. However, there were also some successes.

It is of course difficult to know what difference the intervention of an MP makes in a particular case. In July 1959 a Mrs Burns visited Gaitskell and asked him to help with her son who had been posted to Cyprus. She asked that he be posted back to Britain for compassionate reasons. Gaitskell took the case to the Air Ministry and they agreed to post the soldier to Britain. It is impossible to tell if Gaitskell's letter influenced the decision; perhaps the fact that the family were serious enough to involve their local MP might have helped tip the balance. Certainly the perception among a large number of people was that Gaitskell had helped many individuals over the years in Leeds, by the prestige of his name, his professionalism and his tenacity in pursuing causes.[19]

In turn South Leeds backed its MP on all the great controversies of the 1950s. According to Merlyn Rees, the MP who succeeded Gaitskell, the people of South Leeds could never understand why it was said that Gaitskell found it difficult to mix with working-class people.[20] When out canvassing he would be left behind by the others as he lingered chatting to the housewives; a woman trade-unionist recalls that 'he was pleasant, friendly; you never felt he was talking down to you.' South Leeds gave him a substantial base, direct contact with the people he represented and periodically enjoyable weekends. George Brett's grandson remembers Gaitskell as a very cheerful man, jiving round the house in the morning, and in all the years as a backbencher it is a measure of his dedication that he missed only one Leeds weekend.[21] This solid base was to be vital to him in the years of bitter struggle ahead.

Following the general election defeat of 1951, Gaitskell's house in Frognal Gardens became the centre of a long and successful campaign for the leadership of the Labour Party. Initially it seemed that the leadership would pass naturally for a period to Herbert Morrison before moving to Gaitskell's generation. His feeling when becoming Chancellor had been that the appointment was probably too soon. However, as the battle between Bevan and Gaitskell developed, it became increasingly likely that the leadership would skip a generation. Gaitskell's strategy had two distinct parts. Initially he sought simply to maintain his position at the head of his generation by allying himself to Morrison. Then, after the 1955 election and

Dalton's 'Operation Avalanche',* he set out to win the leadership.

The intriguing question is to what extent this was a conscious strategy for winning the leadership of the Labour Party and gaining the ultimate prize in politics: the premiership. His opponents certainly thought it was a carefully laid plan,[22] and, looked at coolly, with the benefit of hindsight, it reads like a textbook account of how to rise through the Labour Party from the right. However, politics is a more uncertain business than textbook writing. While it is the case that the Gaitskellites were much more open to the charge of being a conspiracy designed to gain the leadership for their campaign than were the Bevanites, in neither case was there a carefully planned forensic operation. The real value of Gaitskell over Bevan as part of a broad strategy for advancement was that Hugh could be counted on to behave in ways that maximised his advantage, while Nye could almost be guaranteed to do something that would undermine his.

Carrying the authority of a former Chancellor of the Exchequer, Gaitskell led the attack on the Conservatives' economic policy. His philosophy of opposition was to combine a limited amount of badgering of the government in party-political terms with an extensive dissection of its policies. As he wrote after a few years experience on the opposition front bench:

> It is sometimes said about the British Opposition that 'Its duty is to oppose.' This does not mean, however, that the Opposition opposes for its own sake. It is simply a way of expressing the critical function of the Opposition. If its criticisms were to become purely destructive it would almost certainly lose ground with the electors.[23]

In his early years he was often genuinely disgusted with the economic policies pursued by Rab Butler. This part of the leadership strategy reached its height in his responses to the 'giveaway' Budgets before the 1955 general election and the economic backtracking forced on the government shortly afterwards.

As early as January 1952 Gaitskell attacked the government in what was to become his typical style of measured criticism. In a speech in Yorkshire he urged vigilance lest the gains of the Attlee years be destroyed by the Tories: 'We must repulse with vigour any

* See p. 219.

attack on the fair-shares principle, which we have done so much to bring to reality in these last six years.'[24] Another example came in July the same year with his indictment of the Tory government as:

1. Breach of promise
2. Pandering to vested interests
3. Reactionary social policy
4. Gross incompetence and muddle of administration.[25]

His endless round of speeches and increasingly effective parliamentary performances, culminating in 1955 in the period after the general election defeat, made him a feared critic of the government through 1953 and 1954. But the speeches did not electrify so much as inform audiences. When he was a Minister his political style lacked a certain bite; in opposition the lecturing tone was simply no match for Bevan. As the years progressed he became increasingly aware of the need to put some blood into his delivery.

Parallel to the extended attacks on the Tories, in and out of the House, Gaitskell was also the central figure in the internal battle between the Bevanites and the leadership. Here again he carefully manoeuvred himself into a stronger and eventually unassailable position. He sought and received the support of the leaders of the key trade union, first by spearheading the anti-communist/anti-fellow-travelling moves of the early 1950s; infamously he recorded in his diary:

> I don't see how one can have strong loyalties with people like George Brown and Alf Robens, not to speak of the T.U. leaders, and continually refuse to do any of the dirty work for them and with them.

In exchange for the 'dirty work' they supported him. In a series of moves he captured in turn the key trade unions, the right of the Parliamentary Labour Party, a section of the constituency parties and finally the leadership. In the process he consolidated his national reputation, and made some strong alliances with leaders of key trade unions which remained, in most cases, a bedrock of his support in the party until the end. He also made some powerful enemies, though not many who carried with them substantial backing at Conference. In this process he displayed a sure political touch, sense of timing and acumen which he was never to repeat. It was a political performance which did not receive the credit it deserved, for energy, for strategy, for political ruthlessness and for sheer nerve. Throughout he was extraordinarily honest in his diary about what he was doing and confessed, as we shall see, at certain crucial points that he felt he had gone too far. But so long as he felt he had been personally consistent, even though to others this might appear an almost reckless consistency, then he could feel that he had been honest. This mattered to him as much as the power he was seeking. But on various occasions during these years the sheer hunger made him lose sight of the larger picture and when the dust settled on the string of political punch-ups there was regret about aspects of the role he had played. He was a basically decent person forced by politics to do questionable things and he suffered for it, but not sufficiently to prevent him from being prepared to do what was necessary to win.

It was not at all obvious in the first months of opposition that he was going to win and he suffered a series of reverses in his position. The Conservative government indicated that they would not be able to spend the full allocation made in Gaitskell's Budget for rearmament: the defence programme was revealed as an indicative plan rather than a physical possibility. It became obvious that, had a little more flexibility been shown by the then Chancellor, the Cabinet need not have split. Seeing the political advantage of driving the wedge further between the former Ministers, the Conservatives did not withdraw the proposal for NHS charges but did revise down the defence estimates.

Churchill also enjoyed himself in the House teasing the Labour front bench that the Member for Ebbw Vale, Nye Bevan, had in fact been right for all the wrong reasons. Churchill also revealed that the Attlee government had an agreement to bomb Manchurian airfields if they were used for bombing British troops in Korea. The combination unsettled the backbenchers and fed Bevan's line that the former government had lost sight of its real domestic and foreign policy goals. There were difficult debates in the House, with Gaitskell having little option but to attack the charges and defend the defence programme; he could hardly have supported all the government's measures or come out wholeheartedly against the programme. In contrast, Bevan was free to say what he pleased, and enjoyed the parliamentary occasions on which he was able to attack the government with relish. For the first few months of 1952 Bevan was in the ascendant.

Labour Party politics in the 1950s were completely dominated by this bitter power struggle, almost unprecedented in its level of personal animosity. When Harold Wilson died in 1995 the obituaries were riddled with references to this period of Labour's internecine warfare. Ian Aitken in the *Guardian* was typical in talking about the 'deep personal hatreds' that existed between the Bevanites and the Gaitskellites: '[Wilson] couldn't stand the so-called "Frognal set" of Gaitskell's rather snooty friends, a group which got its name from the upmarket Hampstead street where Gaitskell lived.'[26]

Differences in the party have arisen frequently in the post-war period, but only rarely have three crucial factors coincided to produce the maximum division. The policy differences have already been set in context, the personalities were Bevan and Gaitskell; and the third factor was the structure of the Labour Party itself. Mark Jenkins described the party as divided between the 'apparatus' and the 'movement.'[27] The party apparatus gained its legitimacy and power from the movement, but remained separate and in some way compromised by its association with the state. Henry Drucker saw the Labour Party as more than simply an instrument for acquiring votes and using power; it was both a party of government and a protest movement.[28] The problem for the British Labour Party was not a careerist leadership, which Drucker identified as the main problem for the German SPD, but an inability to define what the 'implementing of socialism' would actually mean. The party was continually reappraising policy and exposing itself to conflict because it had no agreed idea of what socialism should in practice look like. In the place of a definition of socialism, the Labour Party produced a series of manifesto promises on individual issues.[29] The difference between apparatus and movement and the tendency to make policy through manifestoism both contributed to the atmosphere of division.

However, nothing made the longevity of the internal squabbling inevitable. Of the three elements at work in the party at this time – people, ideas and structures – one predominated and should be blamed for the internal war that led to thirteen years of opposition: that element was, simply, the people who made these arguments prolonged, bitter and divisive. Structures can be adapted to circumstances where there is a will, and at times the party's structures did adapt. Compromises can be reached between opposing ideas: as Crosland argued, the nature of British socialism was a compromise. People, personalities, egos, memories, are what kept the battles alive. The Bevanites attacked the Gaitskellites, and the Gaitskellites defended themselves. In turn, the Gaitskellites counter-attacked the Bevanites and they defended themselves. At times the actual substance of the argument was lost; what became important was winning it. Between the two groups honours are shared equally: the Bevanites' consistent criticism of policy and their refusal to accept the domination of the party by the right provoked the struggle: Gaitskell's protection of Attlee and defence of the official policy prolonged it.

The parliamentary Bevanite group challenged the domination of the Labour Party by the axis of moderate leadership, big trade unions and right-wingers. But who exactly were the Bevanites? There are a number of different ways of measuring their parliamentary strength. The figure ranges from twenty-five hard-core members, which rose to a maximum of fifty-seven over the 1952 defence debates,[30] to forty-seven floating members listed by Jo Richardson, the group's secretary.[31] Richardson's list includes some Keep Lefters – those who had opposed Ernest Bevin's foreign policy back in the first years of the Attlee government – but excludes others, for instance those pacifists who voted with the Bevanites in 1952. The Richardson list can be broken down into leading members, in Bevan's phrase used after the group was disbanded, 'those of us who really matter', and the less vocal Bevanites. The leading Bevanites who eventually came back into the party fold on the defence issue included Richard Crossman, John Freeman, Tom Driberg, Stephen Swingler, Hugh Delargy, Leslie Hale, Bob Stross and A. J. Irvine. There was also a sub-set who started out as Bevanites but who gradually stopped being openly rebellious or supportive of alternative defence policies; they included Harold Wilson, Geoffrey Bing and Desmond Donnelly (who attacked Bevan at Conference in 1954 and was passing details of Bevanite meetings on to Dalton from the very beginning). The final group were the hard core – who mostly became unilateralists and broke with Bevan in 1957 – which included Michael Foot, Jennie Lee, Ian Mikardo, Barbara Castle, Harold Davies, J. P. W. Mallalieu and Emrys Hughes.[32]

The challenge these MPs posed to the leadership took the form of increasingly persistent criticism of the direction of the party after the fall of the Attlee government. But, despite Gaitskell's fears, the group was not organised primarily as a factional bid for the leadership. They were never sufficiently coherent or well organised enough for that; as Foot puts it, 'what was false was the suggestion that all [Bevan's] moves, manoeuvres, protests, resignations, attacks were calculated however ineptly to further his personal ambition: the Deakin/Dalton caricature.' Foot can to an extent be expected to play down his leader's personal ambitions, but John Campbell, generally much more objective about Bevan, also notes Nye's growing disillusionment with politics,[33] the different advice he was receiving from his friends,[34] and the overreaction which the Dalton/Deakin caricature represented.[35] These accounts all refute Gaitskell's belief that Bevanism was above all a conspiracy to gain the leadership for Bevan. Indeed, Crossman,[36] one of the key organisers of the Bevanites, felt that Nye was a reluctant member of the Bevanite group! When a chief conspirator feels the chief pretender is reluctant to play a full part in the conspiracy on their behalf, it tends to undermine the conspiracy theory. Crossman bases this judgement on the fact that after October 1952 Nye tended to avoid meetings. According to Crossman, Gaitskell once said: 'Bevanism is and only is a conspiracy to seize the leadership for Aneurin Bevan. It is a conspiracy because it has three essentials of conspiracy, a leader in Bevan, an organisation run by Mikardo and a newspaper run by Foot.'[37] There was a leader, but he often seemed reluctant to lead. There was an organisation, partly in the form of the Brains Trust, a panel of Bevanite speakers which toured the country holding *Any Questions* style sessions and partly in some consistent Conference resolution drafting and attempts to influence selections. The organisation had a life beyond organising for Bevan's leadership bid and after 1957, when it turned unilateralist, was in effect cut off from its leader.

There was also a newspaper, *Tribune*, which successfully relaunched itself as a weekly in this period and was a guaranteed forum for getting Bevanite views straight into the constituencies. The Brains Trust and *Tribune* had little real impact on the MPs at Westminster and it was the PLP that elected the leader. So where the organisation really counted was in the House and in party meetings. Here they could plan their responses and ensure that the Bevanite view was put across. In both these cases there were periods when they operated effectively but much longer ones when they were arguing among themselves. There is of course the possibility that, while Nye was not consistent, in certain moods he could be conspiratorial and that although he wanted the leadership he lacked the discipline necessary to win it. So, while Bevanism did have some of the characteristics of a bid for power,[38] Nye was always ruining his position in the party by his inability to play on the team. The only time in this period when he really toed the line was right at the end in 1957–60, when any hope of the leadership had disappeared. What emerges from this is the development of Bevan's ambitions over the period rather than a story of a consistent factional attempt to seize the leadership. The real change comes in 1955 with the leadership election and the end of any Bevanite hope for Bevan's leadership of the PLP.

The left's opposition to the Attlee government had been focused on the foreign policy of Ernest Bevin, not the leadership of Attlee.[39] The basis of the 'Keep Left' argument was that the government had been too ready to abandon the idea that 'left can talk to left', in favour of the Cold War. This opposition was neither fully organised nor based on a spontaneous grassroots disillusionment with the Attlee governments. The development of left-wing opposition into the Bevanite group did not materially change its outlook or its organisation, but did enhance its credibility by improving the calibre of its members.

The Bevanite group was not a direct challenge to the leadership but an attack on the complacency of the Labour front bench in the period 1951–5, and a blueprint for left-wing activity in subsequent decades. For the Labour leadership it was insidious because it was unpredictable and a challenge because it was articulate. However, the Bevanites have tended to be vastly overrated, both at the time and since, because of their symbolic value and journalistic prowess. Driberg wrote for *Reynolds News*, Crossman for the *Daily Mirror* and *Sunday Pictorial*, and alongside Freeman for the *New Statesman* and Mikardo and Foot for *Tribune*.

The first challenge came when the party had to vote on the defence estimates that were based on Gaitskell's Budget. Crossman had asked Bevan about the issue in December 1951: 'What attitude should the group take?' 'Oh, I dare say the best thing would be to leave each person to decide for himself.'[40] Crossman goes on, 'So far from being a great strategist and organizer of cabals, Nye is an individualist who, however, is an extraordinarily pleasant member of a group.' Gaitskell's perception was somewhat different. He and Bevan were in a direct race to be the leader of the Labour Party of the next generation, and everything had an impact on that race. When Bevan made an effective intervention at the party meeting before the debate on the estimates, 'the upshot was a definite step back [for Gaitskell] and an advance for him.'[41] Frustrated by the advance of the Bevanites, Gaitskell tried some factional organising of his own. He had first contemplated organising his own group while still Chancellor and had arranged a meeting with some government supporters. Aidan Crawley, John Edwards, Douglas Jay, Patrick Gordon Walker, Frank Pakenham and Woodrow Wyatt all met secretly in Crawley's flat in the summer of 1951. The problem was that as Ministers they could not write articles or campaign against Bevan openly, but they agreed to write letters in the press and speak more in the country. 'But', Gaitskell wrote in August 1951, 'so far as I can see nothing has happened.'[42] After Bevan's strong showing on the defence estimates Gaitskell decided to try again:

> At the next Party meeting there was a discussion on foreign policy, and again they scored some success; so much so that Woodrow Wyatt and one or two others came to me and urged that we should really try and organise some kind of effective opposition. Then we had a meeting in Woodrow's flat. Chris Mayhew, Tony Crosland, Roy Jenkins, Arthur Allen, Alf Robens, Woodrow and myself. We decided that we must get people who could speak well to do so at the Party meetings, especially on defence and foreign affairs. We also tentatively thought of compiling a pamphlet which would contain the answer to Bevan's point of view. The struggle at the Party meetings has continued, with an interval on account of the king's death, ever since; but on the whole the anti-Bevanites have done a lot better, largely owing to the fact that better speeches have been made as a result of urging the right people to make them. Chris, Woodrow, Tony and Roy have all done well, especially the first, and thus set an example to others.[43]

These efforts, however, did not avert a huge setback when fifty-seven Labour MPs voted in the House of Commons against the defence estimates on 2 March 1952. This was an open challenge to the party leadership and an explicit attack on the government's record. The rebellion incensed many backbenchers because it was in direct violation of a PLP decision, and the standard procedure was to accept party discipline once the PLP meeting had voted. The Bevanites' resolution had been defeated at the meeting by 115 to 41 and yet they pressed ahead with abstaining against the party's amendment. The official line for the debate was to accept the estimates but express no confidence in the government's ability to carry them out – itself something of a criticism of Gaitskell. The Bevanites wanted the party to vote against the government.

Michael Foot assumed that all the Bevanites would be expelled for such actions. Gaitskell argued in the Shadow Cabinet for a resolution condemning their actions; for the reimposition of standing orders which had been suspended during the Labour government; and for a written undertaking from the rebels that they would abide by party decisions. Two resolutions were then proposed: Gaitskell's, which he had drafted with Woodrow Wyatt, demanded loyalty and all the rebels' signatures on undertakings; and a compromise resolution, drafted by George Strauss, which simply called for the reimposition of standing orders. The pattern of future battles was set. Gaitskell became the leading hatchet man for the right of the party against the Bevanites; the PLP generally cooled down a few days after the rebellions and wanted a compromise to keep Bevan in the party and avoid expelling the other Bevanites. It should be noted that backbenchers generally were concerned with keeping Bevan in and were less bothered about the fate of the other rebels. In contrast, from this very first open confrontation Gaitskell felt that many in the party were being weak-willed and 'frightened at the prospect of Bevan and some others having to go out of the party altogether. I was naturally quite prepared for this to happen, and indeed there would have been some advantage for it would have left us much freer to attack him.'[44]

Crossman and Foot had written to say that they would accept the compromise, but Bevan made a speech in his constituency that was reported as saying that he refused to recant: 'If they say, "Promise not to do it again", I cannot. If you think what you did was right, you cannot promise not to do what you think right again . . . Is a socialist in danger of being expelled from the Labour Party because he voted against the Tories?'[45] In stark contrast Gaitskell in his weekend speech was trying to maintain a public distance from the internal squabbles in the party. He devoted the speech, a few days before the possible censure and expulsion of up to fifty-seven Labour MPs, to commenting on a string of losses on the reserves. He urged Butler to reveal all the figures of how the sterling area as a whole was going to balance its account with the rest of the world. The speech was fairly straightforward but contained more than a hint of the frustration of no longer being at the centre of things. It pointedly did not add to the internal conflict. It was one of the last times that Gaitskell would show such restraint.[46]

On Tuesday 11 March 1952 the party meeting assembled in the Westminster Hall Grand Committee Room. It was packed. Attlee moved the resolution drafted by the Shadow Cabinet in a lacklustre speech. Bevan replied with some 'knockabout attacks'.[47] Attlee

168

responded to these and the two got into a slanging match.[48] Bevan was trying to put as much blame on Attlee as possible for the split in the party. The compromise amendment was then introduced and carried by 162 to 73. This proposed the reintroduction of standing orders but effectively let the rebels off with little more than a caution. Attlee, however, refused to withdraw the full resolution. Foot believed the intention was to force Bevan and the hardcore Bevanites into refusing to accept the requirement to sign a guarantee on future actions. This would then leave the way open to punish them for this refusal by withdrawing the whip from them.

Gaitskell blamed Attlee for the weakness of his overall performance, but was also shocked when Tom O'Brien and Hector McNeil, usually figures he could count on, spoke in favour of the compromise. O'Brien's speech was the most effective of all. It is likely that Attlee was as surprised as anyone by O'Brien's speech because he had probably called this usually steady trade-union-sponsored MP to support the Shadow Cabinet's line. However, Tom O'Brien was 'off his leash'; he expressed his undying loyalty to Attlee, then attacked the party's defence and foreign policy,[49] before concluding that if the party wanted to commit political suicide they should move from the Committee Room to Westminster Hall 'where public executions could more fittingly be conducted. Then alongside the plaques for Charles I and William Wallace, might be placed another: "On this spot the Labour Party committed suicide aided and abetted by Clement Attlee and Aneurin Bevan."[50] Attlee still refused to withdraw his resolution and it was defeated by 2 to 1. The following week the standing orders were reimposed but the Bevanites had got away remarkably lightly with the first major public rebellion.

While the Labour Party were busy fighting among themselves the Conservative Chancellor, Rab Butler, introduced his first Budget. He labelled it as one to give the country 'solvency, security and incentive.' The excess profits levy that had been discussed in 1951 was introduced at 30 per cent alongside increases in personal allowances. The bank rate was increased from 2.5 per cent to 4 per cent but the widely expected cuts in social services did not materialise.

Gaitskell had opened his attack on Butler in January 1952 with an alternative economic survey of the year. The Tories, he said, were painting a gloomy picture for political reasons, but 'at the same time we must be on our guard against "crisis" talk as an excuse to set back the clock of social progress. While we should not oppose measures which we would have carried out, we must resist strongly any abandonment of economic planning and any return to the stagnation of the 1930s.'[51] He continued the balancing act in his attacks on the Budget. Butler gave him an easy target by cutting food subsidies and Gaitskell effectively showed in the centrepiece of his speech that this would hurt two-thirds of those on low incomes. Yet he did not make simple party speeches in response to any of Butler's Budgets; this led to the birth of 'Mr Butskell'. (Personally, Mr Butskell was Hubert Ashton, Hugh's brother-in-law and Butler's PPS, through whom he communicated with Butler about the timing of debates.) Politically, Mr Butskell was a matter of style rather than substance. The civil servant in him could not very easily condemn wholeheartedly measures that he would have had to implement himself, but more than this he tried to make his responses wide-ranging and constructive. This neatly summed up the difficulties of Gaitskell's position. There were fundamental ideological differences between himself and the Tory government, but they would take time to become clear as the Churchill government shifted the course of the state in their direction. In the short run, Gaitskell's response to Butler was simply to call the measures lamentable and worry that the government hoped to cut demand and increase unemployment so that employers could resist the TUC pressures on wage demands. This proved enough of an attack to satisfy the PLP meeting, which received him well.

Gaitskell made much of the running in the debate on the Finance Bill, but for the first time he was aided by the young MPs Tony Crosland and Roy Jenkins, who were especially good during an all-night sitting. The Hampstead Set had began to take shape.[52] The temporary lull in internal hostilities caused by the debate on the Finance Bill was broken when the issue of Germany came to the fore in May.

The four-power occupation of Germany, established at the end of the war, had turned into a combined occupation of two opposing camps. The Western alliance had made the western half of the country a cohesive democratic unit, but in the eastern sector the Russians crushed all opposition and failed to hold any free elections. The left of the Labour Party felt that not enough effort had been made to reach an agreement with the Russians, that Britain was following too closely the Cold War policies of the United States. The American alliance was so central to Gaitskell's world-view that it seemed necessary to take a full role in the creation of a rearmed and economically viable West Germany, which would be able in turn to take its place in the reconstructed Europe. This was central to American foreign policy. The issue of German rearmament created a strange and temporary alliance between the Bevanites and Dalton, and enabled them to achieve their most important foreign policy success when the Labour Party adopted Dalton's NEC statement of May 1952 which seemed to move party policy towards opposition to German rearmament.[53] The Paris agreements, which compromised on the issue of German rearmament, were eventually passed by the House with only six pacifists voting against.[54] For the Bevanites, opposition to German rearmament was based on the economic consequences of rearmament and the mistaken policy of communist containment, while for Dalton it was based on a fundamental hatred and fear of Germany.[55]

As the party approached the Conference at Morecambe in the autumn of 1952, the revolt on defence estimates, widespread disquiet about German rearmament, criticisms from the left of too tame a response to the first Butler Budget and questions from the right about Attlee's leadership combined to create a stormy political atmosphere.

Meanwhile the Bevanites had been courting the constituencies. In their broken-down *Tribune* van or Gavin Faringdon's Rolls-Royce, they 'would descend on a chosen constituency with a panel of four or five Bevanite MPs – a typical panel might be Crossman, Barbara Castle, Leslie Hale and Stephen Swingler, with Mikardo in the chair – and hold a lively political debate.[56] Every issue on which they made a stand played well with the activist members of the party and up until the Morecambe Conference no one from the right had responded in the press. This was partly because they did not want to lend credibility to what the Bevanites were saying. Attlee especially favoured a dignified silence. It was also because all the press the Bevanites did not themselves write for, from the Conservative papers through the Liberal *Manchester Guardian,* to Labour's *Daily Herald,* were opposed to Bevan and presented the Bevanites as a faction whose objective was to capture the leadership.

Hugh Cudlipp had been threatening Dick Crossman with a massive attack on the Bevanites for two weeks before the Conference. Cudlipp ran the *Sunday Pictorial* and the Labour-sympathising *Daily Mirror* and employed Crossman as a columnist. His article on 28 September in the *Sunday Pictorial* set the tone for the Morecambe

Conference. It was a blistering personal attack on Bevan's vanity, arrogance and spleen, under the headline, 'End the Bevan Myth'. Michael Foot, described in the article as one of the 'bewildered disciples' of Bevan, called the piece 'the nearest the Britain of the 1950s saw to a McCarthyite essay in character assassination'.[57] But simply attacking the Bevanites was not enough for Arthur Deakin, the new leader of the TGWU. Deakin, 'a fierce, breezy, irascible, stout-hearted bison of a man',[58] wanted them to 'get rid of their whips, dismiss their business managers and conform to the party Constitution'.[59] Thus before the Conference started it was clear there was going to be a fight.

Morecambe in October 1952 was very cold and wet and windy.[60] This Labour Conference was the bloodiest since the war, and probably the most divisive until the 1980s. Michael Foot described it as 'rowdy, convulsive, vulgar, splenetic; threatening at times to collapse into an irretrievable brawl'.[61] Dalton felt it the worst, for bad temper and general hatred since 1926,[62] and Gaitskell called it 'extremely hysterical.'[63] On the first day Deakin was booed and Will Lawther, the right-wing president of the NUM, responded to one heckler in a debate on a proposal in favour of industrial action to oppose the Tory government, by telling the delegate to 'shut your gob'. The votes for the NEC were taken on the first night; Jim Callaghan on one side of town phoned Hugh Dalton on the other to commiserate because he thought that Dalton would be voted off.[64] Dalton, characteristically, hoped that Gaitskell would be elected in his place. Morgan Phillips, the general secretary, actually delayed counting the votes until the second day for fear of leaks.

It was at this Morecambe Conference that Gaitskell, as the delegate for South Leeds, ran for the National Executive Committee for the first time. When Labour was defeated in 1951, a great deal of power shifted back from the Cabinet to the NEC, the governing body of the Labour Party. Though formally the Parliamentary Committee or Shadow Cabinet ran the PLP, in opposition the influence of the NEC was much greater than when Labour was in power. Gaitskell did not seem to consider it worth running for the NEC while a Minister, despite Dalton's worry in 1950 that the rising Ministers like Gaitskell had 'no public face at Annual Conference'.[65] But in opposition, and in need of a greater presence in the party and in the country, he sought a place in the constituency section.

All twenty-eight members of the NEC, with the exception of the leader and the deputy leader, were elected annually at the Labour Party Conference. Conference was dominated by the Big Six unions: Transport and General Workers' Union (TGWU), Mineworkers (NUM), Engineers (AEU), General and Municipal Workers (GMWU), Shopworkers (USDAW) and Railwaymen (NUR), who between them controlled 3,029,000 out a total trade union vote of 4,407,000 and a total Conference vote of 5,444,000 votes. Therefore, although Conferences in the 1950s could have a bitterly divisive atmosphere, so long as the leadership controlled the union block vote they were more important as a forum for debate than as a decision-making body.

The NEC had four sections:

1 A trade union section in which twelve members were nominated and elected by the affiliated trade unions.
2 A constituency organisations section in which seven members were nominated and elected by affiliated constituency parties and federations of constituency parties and central Labour parties in divided boroughs.
3 A women's section in which five women were nominated and elected by the whole Conference.
4 A Socialist, Co-operative and professional organisations section in which one member was nominated and elected by the socialist/Co-operative and professional organisations affiliated to the Labour Party.

In addition the Party Treasurer was nominated and elected by the votes of the whole of Conference.[66] The only section not dominated by the block vote was section 2, elected by the constituency Labour parties alone.

When Morgan Phillips finally counted the votes in 1952 he found that the Bevanites had been successful in staging a coup. Barbara Castle transferred to section 2 from the women's section; two of the resigning Ministers, Bevan and Wilson, won places along with the journalists Crossman and Mikardo; and Tom Driberg completed the Bevanite team. Each was a well-known member and Lewis Minkin, the historian of the Labour Party Conference, has stressed that this was a key criterion for election for this section.[67] A combination of the left-wing activism of the constituency parties, the candidates' high profile and some degree of organisation – although by no means to the extent feared by the right – allowed these Bevanites to replace the ex-Ministers Shinwell, Dalton and Morrison. Gaitskell came in as third runner-up with 330,000, which put him far behind Bevan's 985,000 and Castle's 868,000. According to Lewis Minkin, organisation was not decisive in the constituency section elections: 'The Constituency Labour Parties were not impervious to organised influence, but the results of the election to the section were a complex product of inertia, spontaneity and custom as well as organised stimulation.'[68]

The 1952 result illustrated Gaitskell's limited reach in the constituencies. The rest of the Conference illustrated some much harsher political facts. Lawther and Deakin were incensed at the way they had been treated and by the NEC constituency section results, and Lawther told delegates: 'You have the happy assurance that the block vote and the money that is provided will be used in the direction that we think is in the best interests of our membership.'[69] The trade union leaders effectively threw down a gauntlet in response to the Bevanites' triumph: whoever would fight the left would have the support of the block vote and the one seat on the NEC which was in the gift of the trade union leaders: the Treasurership.

Gaitskell picked up Deakin's challenge and set about the dirty work of openly fighting the Bevanites. He was also personally upset by the defeats of former leading members of the government and reacted with a call to arms in tones more reminiscent of southern American senators than former Chancellors of the Exchequer. A mixture of political calculation and emotional reaction lay behind the speech he made at Stalybridge on 5 October 1952. He did not take time to reflect and consult his senior colleagues but instead decided to offer his own public commentary on the events at Morecambe.

In July he had accepted the invitation to speak at Stalybridge as part of the ordinary run of his weekend speeches. Between the routine acceptance and the meeting, the events at Morecambe had considerably darkened his mood and attacking the Bevanites was at the top of his agenda. Gaitskell wrote the speech in the offices of his constituency paper, the *Leeds Weekly Citizen*.[70] He consulted no front bench or close political colleagues but instead talked things over with his local party workers.[71] The context of the times must be borne in mind, as well as the very real fact of the fight between the Labour Party and the Communist Party at local level. What could appear a minor extremist group on the national stage looked different at branch level when it threatened the place of key workers like Murray. On the national and international stage the context was also important. There was a genuine fear of war, as Shinwell's defence debate speech had made clear, and there was a clear ideological and organisational battle between the Labour and the Communist Parties which had deep roots.

Typical of the time was the report in the *Leeds Weekly Citizen* about a meeting of the Communist Party executive under the head-line 'Communists plan new drive inside the Labour ranks'.[72] The report began: 'A new Communist attempt to gain influence within the Labour Party is foreshadowed in a report which Mr Harry Pollitt [General Secretary of the Communist Party] has represented to the Communist NEC.' Pollitt's report, the story claimed, stressed that there was still a need for the Communist Party even though the official policy was now to infiltrate the Labour Party. It continued in McCarthyite terms, substituting the Labour Party for American democracy. Thus, from within the labour movement and most especially from within certain sections of the trade union movement there were well-established precedents for tackling the Communist Party head-on.

Gaitskell had himself already partially broken his self-imposed public silence on the Bevanite dispute in June 1952. In a speech at the National Union of General and Municipal Workers' conference at Whitley Bay on 16 June 1952[73] he had reviewed the points on which the labour movement agreed – the danger of the world situation; the need for NATO and the need to arm NATO; and the need to negotiate for disarmament. The disagreement was about the scale of defence: 'If the critics were only saying that within NATO there should be a review there would be nothing to argue about, for there is going to be such a review every year. But it is one thing to approve of a NATO review and another to insist that we proceed at once to make further arbitrary cuts.' The critics never asked them-selves fundamental questions about where the cuts were to fall, what impact this would have on Britain's allies and what the economic consequences would be. It was a guarded but clear attack on the left. Gaitskell was probably pleased that the *Daily Worker* responded with an attack on him and the way he was destroying the heart of the Labour Party.[74]

However, this was relatively mild and reasoned stuff. Stalybridge was different. No Labour politician had made an out-and-out attack on the Communist infiltrations of the party. No Labour politician had used the language of a witch-hunt, the language of intolerance and of an enemy within. The tone and the content of Stalybridge when delivered by a politician of national standing made a much more dramatic impact than any number of local stories or meetings. 'The defeat of Herbert Morrison for the National Executive is not only an act of gross political ingratitude', Gaitskell told the 450 people gathered in the old theatre,

> but a piece of blind stupidity which, until it is put right, must gravely weaken the Party . . . A most disturbing feature of the Conference was the number of Resolutions and speeches which were Communist inspired, based not even on the *Tribune* so much as the *Daily Worker*. There is no doubt that Mrs Braddock was quite right when she warned us some weeks ago that the Communist Party had now adopted a new tactic of infiltration into the Labour Party. I was told by some well informed correspondents [the journalist Ian Mackay of the *News Chronicle*] that about ⅙th of the Constituency Party delegates appeared to be Communists or Communist controlled. This figure may well be too high but if it should be one in ten or even one in twenty, it is a most shocking state of affairs into which the NEC should look at once.

He went on to attack the left-wing press for putting only one side of the argument on issues like defence and pouring out a 'stream of grossly misleading propaganda with poisonous innuendos and malicious attacks on Attlee, Morrison and the rest of us'. He urged everyone who had supported the last Labour government and who supported the official policy to come forward and put the case.

> Let no one say that in exercising the right of reply to Bevanites we are endangering the unity of the Party. For there will be no unity on the terms dictated by *Tribune*. Indeed its very existence so long as its pages are devoted to so much vitriolic abuse of the Party Leaders is an invitation to disloyalty and disunity. It is time to end the attempt at mob rule by a group of frustrated journalists and restore the authority and leadership of the solid and sensible majority of the Movement.[75]

Gaitskell realised fairly quickly that the phrases 'mob rule' and 'frustrated journalists' were perhaps excessive. In South Leeds the response was mixed. His own closest supporters, with whom he had discussed the speech before delivering it, were one hundred per cent behind him. However, the Hunslet Ward passed the following resolution after the speech: 'This meeting regards Mr Hugh Gaitskell's speech at Stalybridge as unfortunate and regrets that even after a few days' interval, during which his words received wide publicity and approval in the national and local Conservative press, sections of the speech were printed in the *Leeds Weekly Citizen*, the only Labour paper in the city. The meeting feels that canvassers and workers for the Labour cause will not find their task made easier if the paper which is regarded as their own mouthpiece suggests that some of these workers are "Communists or Communist controlled".[76] The next few years of Gaitskell's life inside the Labour Party would be dominated by the unfolding battle which really started with his counter-attack from Stalybridge.

The speech made a big splash. The Tory press enjoyed reporting the Labour Party's difficulties and the Labour press which had been attacked defended itself. *Reynolds News* listed the occasions on which Gaitskell had been invited to write for the paper since the last election and noted his refusals, then focused on the charge that the paper had personally attacked Labour leaders. 'It is a charge', the editor of *Reynolds News* wrote on his editorial page on 19 October 1952, 'which readers of *Reynolds News* will know to be untrue. Whatever the faults of this newspaper, it has always refused to discuss Socialist policy in terms of personalities and has always sought to focus on argument of principle.' In his reply, Gaitskell, conscious of the gathering storm of protest and indignation his speech had provoked, backtracked a little: 'some of the words I used do not apply so much to *Reynolds News*.' But, in the main, he stuck to his guns, especially about the extent to which the line taken in *Reynolds News* was anti-American. After a printed exchange, he and the editor agreed to differ.

Foot summed up the Stalybridge speech as a strange attack from a normally cool performer and noted that 'neither the *Daily Mirror* nor Senator McCarthy himself had ever attempted a vaguer, more unprovable, and therefore more despicable smear.' Ironically, at about the same time Gaitskell was reflecting in his diary on the extent of anti-Americanism in Britain and clearly did not see what he did in Stalybridge as at all in the same league. 'The anti-Communist hysteria takes another form which is especially repugnant to British liberals – the witch-hunt – McCarthyism – the tyranny of the majority. It is indeed probable that if the full truth were known over here about the scale of this movement and the way it seems to permeate the Universities, the Civil Service and business, there would be a really serious revulsion against America.' He concluded that 'on the rational plane it condemns the main argument of the pro-Americans – that America is, after all, a free democratic country, while Russia is a cruel and ruthless dictatorship.'[77]

Bevan had made a rather conciliatory speech at the annual *Tribune* rally on the Wednesday evening of Conference. He teased Arthur Deakin for being a 'softy' compared to Ernie Bevin and said that he 'would rather be attacked in the blunt language with which I am familiar than be surrounded by smoothies'. He also tried to placate those who had been defeated for the NEC.

The combination of Bevan's *Tribune* speech, the Stalybridge speech and the response it provoked and a general outburst of recrimination and argument further motivated the moderates to try to re-establish some sort of equilibrium in the party. Pressure began to mount on both sides to end the dispute. Attlee was intent on some enforcing of discipline but was always flexible enough to leave the rebels a way out. On 11 October, the leader attacked the Bevanites at the PLP meeting:

> What is quite intolerable is the existence of a party within a party with a separate leadership, separate meetings, supported by its own press. It is inimical to effective action in the House. It breeds suspicion and uneasiness throughout the movement. I am certain that the vast majority of the members of the Labour movement throughout the country will agree with me when I say to those concerned: 'Drop it. Stop this sectionalism. Work with the team. Turn your guns on the enemy not on your friends.'[78]

Bevan responded to Attlee's appeal. While he always denied that there was anything approaching a party within a party, he was torn between his natural loyalist instincts and the demands of his friends. A few days after Attlee's speech he exploded at Crossman: 'To continue the [Bevanite] Group now is to perpetuate schism. If you were to continue the Group in these circumstances and I were the Leader, I would have you expelled.'[79] At the PLP meeting on 24 October some clever chairing by Attlee – not calling the Keep Calmers (a group of moderates led by John Strachey), pressing the matter to an immediate vote and curtailing debate – resulted in the passing of an anti-Bevanite resolution. The vote, 188 to 51, was for 'the immediate abandonment of all group organisations within the party other than those officially recognised'.[80] For eighteen months the Bevanites went relatively quiet.

'Is HE here yet?' – Everyone knew, in October 1952,
that *he* was Nye Bevan.

In this phase of Gaitskell's career, which lasted until after the 1955 election, the liberal is little in evidence. The analysis of anti-Americanism which he worked out in his diary (that is, if the people only knew what was happening in the US they would be outraged) was deeply cynical. Was he not outraged? Did the events in America not deserve censure rather than the rather squalid importation of McCarthyite methods to the British scene? But the flow of vitriol was not just one way. *Tribune* repeatedly attacked him both personally and politically. In fact, neither side emerges with much credit from this second round in the Bevan-Gaitskell battle. This was a Labour Party in which fraternal feeling among comrades was often hard to detect and animosity between individuals was often bitter.

Dora backed Hugh in every one of these battles. Ian Mikardo, the leading Bevanite organiser, once described Dora as a great hater,[81] and one can see that in the atmosphere of the time and with this level of personal abuse flying around there was little room for social or emotional understanding between the two camps. It was Dora who compiled press cuttings of attacks on Gaitskell when the *New Statesman* responded to the Stalybridge speech with threats of a writ.[82] But they were more than just separate political camps; these were separate social camps as well.

It is noticeable that Richard Crossman, who mixed with both groups socially, was reluctant to join the social side of the Bevanite group wholeheartedly. The Bevanites were a hard-drinking group, attracted to each by their radicalism, and they bonded through their liking for argument, alcohol and ideas. If the Bevanites were a drunken night in Soho, at the Gay Hussar, with Arthur Koestler shouting at Michael Foot over whisky, or a pub crawl during the Party Conference, and it all ending in a row and a hangover, then the Gaitskellites, as they began to form into a coherent group in these years, were a night dancing at the Café Royal, with Tony Crosland patronising the seriousness of Douglas Jay, too much wine and rich food, and it all ending with an agreement to differ over whose influences were second rate. The Gaitskells gave good parties that were not all politics, and some figures crossed the divide, but in the main these were different sorts of people as well as different sorts of politics.

Christopher Mayhew recalled those 'battles in Committee Room 14 or in the Grand Committee Room with some pride. The debates were conducted on both sides with skill and the votes were sometimes extremely important, capable of decisively changing the policy of the party or the stature of the responsible party leader . . . Sometimes our party seemed to be performing the function of a two-party system all by itself.'[83] The battle between the opposing domestic doctrines was less bitter than that conducted over foreign policy. It is interesting to note that it was foreign rather than domestic policy which tended to dominate the internal battle. This lends support to Drucker's contention that the Labour Party never adequately faced up to the question of what, after 1945–51, implementing socialism meant in practice. The party became in a sense trapped by its own 'consensus'-building achievements and had no effective alternative to competent Tory rule. Its leadership struggled to agree on a distinctive alternative that could outflank the Conservatives and appeal to the electorate now living in relative peace and prosperity, and did not succeed in doing so until after the 1955 election.

The domestic policy debate in the early 1950s was vague. The view of fundamentalists was that, if the electorate were offered a fully socialist programme based on an enlightened form of public ownership and a profound restructuring of society, it would vote for it. The view of the revisionists was that the electorate would not vote for radical change and that anyway society had been so transformed by the Second World War that the Labour Party working within the mixed economy could fulfil a substantial programme of social reform and ensure ever-increasing living standards for the people. These differing opinions underpinned the party divide. The fundamentalist view came to be associated with the Bevanites, but there was very little consistent thinking on these issues. Underpinning the disputes over rearmament were world issues: the Cold War; communist containment; the restructuring of Europe; European unity; and the British 'special relationship' with the United States. These questions tended to dominate the thinking of leading Bevanites and overshadow domestic issues, such as public ownership, especially after the official disbanding of the group in 1952. It is ironic to note that the issue of nationalisation was an increasingly non-controversial one as the divisions on defence and foreign policy deepened.

The leadership effectively controlled the élite of the party, and the policy apparatus, with the exception of occasional upsets at party meetings,[84] but they could not seem to muster the enthusiastic rank-and-file support of the annual *Tribune* rally. Gaitskell did try to organise in the House of Commons in 1952, to get speakers for debates and party meetings. Two years later, to counter the influence of the Bevanite press, after what Dalton described as some wild talk about taking over *Tribune*, Gaitskell was influential in transferring the magazine *Forward*, an old left-wing Glasgow-based publication, from Scotland to London, with Francis Williams as editor and John Harris and George Thomson as staff.[85] This magazine was to be a platform for the views of the revisionists and allowed them a limited access to the constituencies, though it never matched the circulation of *Tribune*.

There were other organisations which came to support Gaitskell's line. The Socialist Union, a commune of Eastern European exiles based in Queen's Park, published *Socialist Commentary*, a quarterly journal of revisionist ideas. Rita Hinden, the editor of *Socialist Commentary*, was later an active member of Gaitskell's Campaign for Democratic Socialism (CDS) and a member of the editorial board of *Campaign*. The revisionists also had access to semi-official party publications, like the Fabian pamphlets, and many sympathisers within the Fabian Society. William Rodgers, the secretary of the

181

CDS, was general secretary of the Fabian Society for much of the 1950s. He was replaced by Shirley Williams as general secretary in 1960. The post was designed to be filled by a Labour Party civil servant and access to publication was open to both left and right. However, the ethos of the society was more in tune with the revisionists than with the fundamentalists.[86]

This tentative organisation was also based on personal friendships and was further enhanced during the leadership election. The people involved tended to follow David Howell's view of the stereotypical revisionist: Oxbridge-educated and with a lifestyle far removed from that of typical Labour voters.[87] The personnel was also remarkably consistent. Until the issues of Europe came to the forefront, the Gaitskellites did not indulge in the schisms which occurred among the Bevanites. Throughout the 1950s and early 1960s the revisionists maintained both unity and discipline.

Despite these patchy Gaitskellite groupings, which certainly attempted to motivate the rank and file in the 1950s, they could not rival the left. It was in part the very power which the right of the party controlled that made their rank-and-file supporters difficult to motivate. They did not need to muster every available member for votes because they could rely on the union block vote. There was also perhaps the arrogance of power, which reduced the time ex-Ministers spent looking after and paying attention to the rank and file. Finally the issues tended to favour the left in terms of 'crowd appeal' and excitement. This was especially the case later in the decade when unilateral nuclear disarmament become a popular cause for rank-and-file members and offered the politically committed plenty of action in the form of the Aldermaston marches and rallies in Trafalgar Square. This might sound like a factious point but it should be remembered that those individuals in society who take part in political activity are a tiny minority and that their motivation can quickly evaporate if they are only offered boring meetings through which to express their enthusiasm. This danger was particularly acute during a period of opposition when the Labour Party at Westminster was largely impotent.

The management of Conference resolutions was also an important area in which organisation could have an impact in policy terms. The domination of the NEC platform at Conferences in the early 1950s was enhanced by the tendency of the committee which decided on the compositing (combining a number of different resolutions into one) to choose for debate the most extreme left-wing resolution. The Bevanites therefore attempted an early distinction between hard and soft left when they tried to get moderate left-wing resolutions with broad appeal accepted. They also tried to influence the wording of composites in favour of motions which at least stood a chance of a decent vote.[88] This and their activity on the NEC and at party meetings was generally more successful on domestic than on foreign policy issues.

In a sense this was due to the 'Clause 4 factor', which made more radical domestic policy propositions harder to oppose than foreign policy because common ownership was enshrined in the party constitution. Moreover, the Labour Party as a whole was more open to left-wing initiatives on the domestic front. Generally, in fact, the party was more left-wing than the revisionists would have liked. The foreign policy criticisms of the Bevanites continued after their gradual decline as a parliamentary group. Indeed it was foreign and defence policy, in the form of the H–bomb, which caused the break between the leading Bevanites, Crossman, Driberg, Freeman, Swingler and ultimately Bevan himself – and the rest of the left.

Bevanite influence in the constituency Labour parties should not be exaggerated. Support for Bevan recorded by Gallup among party members between September 1952 and October 1953 showed a drop of 11 per cent, and this had fallen a further 11 per cent by April 1954 to stand at 24 per cent against 54 per cent for other party leaders. The right's control of the block vote and influence over the apparatus of the party meant that it saw itself as acting in the interests of the whole party, whereas the Bevanites' power base in the local parties meant that any action by the Bevanites appeared as schism, and by extension as a challenge to the central establishment.

The Bevanites functioned both as left-wing critics and as a source of great irritation to the right-wing leadership in the Parliamentary Labour Party and in the unions. They came to represent, for the rank and file, the leadership and values of 'true' socialism which many felt had declined as the party experienced power. But the Bevanites themselves, for example Crossman in his diaries, stressed the difficulty they had in organising in any coherent way.

The fact is that Bevanism and the Bevanites seem much more important, well-organised and Machiavellian to the rest of the Labour Party, and indeed to the USA, than they do to us who are in the group and who know that we are not organised, that Aneurin can never be persuaded to have any consistent or coherent strategy and that we have not even got to the beginning of a coherent, constructive policy. What we have, and it is very important, is a group of MPs who meet regularly, who know and like each other and who have come to represent 'real socialism' to a large number of constituency members. This produces an extraordinary bitterness among those who take the Gaitskell line.[89]

At times the right's obsession with Bevanism reached paranoid proportions and it was the centre of the party, the 'Keep Calm' group, which pulled it back.[90] On the back benches George Strauss, Michael Stewart and John Strachey organised to try to maintain unity; John Campbell, for the most part critical of the Bevanites, agrees that 'the right overreacted in its conviction that Bevanism was a cancer.'[91] Gaitskell himself became more closely associated with the anti-Bevanite stance than any other figure. This was partly by conviction and partly due to political expediency: one of the benefits that flowed from the Stalybridge speech was the breakdown of barriers between himself and Morrison.

With the argument between Gaitskell and Dalton on rearmament and the polarisation of the internal party battle, Morrison had become more important to Gaitskell's career. Though Dalton never stopped backing him, their relationship went through a cool period as long as the issue of Germany was on the scene. Morrison, once he had given up foreign affairs, was the key figure on the right of the party and many expected him to be the next leader. After the dissolution of the Bevanite group in October 1952, the Bevanites ran for the Shadow Cabinet elections and then in November Bevan challenged Morrison for the deputy leadership. He lost by 194 votes to 82 but scraped on to the Shadow Cabinet. Gaitskell again came third in these elections. Bevan was now back on the inside and bound once more by collective responsibility. Morrison now became a keen supporter of Gaitskell, and the suspicions and reserve between the two were broken down. Dalton warned him not to become Morrison's 'Jack in the Box'[92] and not to 'get intriguing with Morrison for him to push out Attlee. Let things run on for a bit.'[93] Gaitskell agreed and was anyway well placed to bide his time. The longer Attlee was leader the better it was for Hugh, and if Attlee should go sooner then he would be well placed if Morrison, already sixty-five, was to be the stop-gap leader. The short-term priority was to improve his party standing and gain access to the NEC.

His best hope for this was the Treasurership. The Treasurer was elected by the whole Conference and a series of leading party figures – Ramsay MacDonald and Arthur Henderson – held the office for extended terms until 1943, when the Conference elected Arthur Greenwood.[94] In 1953 Dalton was planning for Gaitskell to contest the Treasurership if Greenwood retired, and the trade unions had effectively been courted since Stalybridge in 1952 for their support in the election. When Greenwood died in office in June 1954, Morgan Phillips, the general secretary, assumed the job until a replacement could be elected at the Party Conference in the autumn.

Gaitskell had his chance. He saw Deakin for lunch and the first words the TGWU leader said were 'we must nominate you for the Treasurership.' What had started as the dim outline of a political plan in September 1952, and had gradually solidified over the following years, now became a solid alliance. What did Gaitskell promise Deakin for the TGWU block votes and Deakin's influence on other union leaders? Michael Foot speculates that Deakin agreed to back Gaitskell in exchange for an undertaking that Gaitskell would push for Bevan's expulsion from the Labour Party should the opportunity arise. 'Whether a compact in this sense was concluded with Gaitskell is unknown.'[95] Williams understandably picks up on this: 'serious writers usually base charges on evidence not on its absence. There is none.'[96] While it is true that neither participant at this lunch has left a documentary record of a direct deal, Gaitskell did leave one hostage to fortune in his diary when he stressed the need, if working with the trade union leaders, occasionally to do their dirty work.[97] An understanding existed between the two men. There was no spelling out of the specific nature of what Gaitskell would do on the NEC for Deakin in exchange for the votes at the Party Conference. However, the connection between the two is clear and Gaitskell fulfilled Deakin's hopes that he had a hardline ally who would push for the strict application of discipline. They didn't put it in writing but then Arthur Deakin was not the devil, and Hugh was hardly Faust.

Gaitskell initially thought he would be unopposed in the election for Treasurer, but Bevan was again becoming restless and decided that, although he would probably lose, he would challenge Gaitskell. Part of the motivation for this was to split the union vote and attack the entire edifice of the block vote system. He also hoped to show the breadth of his support in the party as against the narrowness of

Gaitskell's. Politically, though, it was a reckless move. He simultaneously surrendered his place on the NEC and ensured he would lose his first direct electoral battle with Gaitskell. Perhaps his vanity was such that he made himself believe he could win. After Deakin delivered the TGWU to Gaitskell, Tom Williamson brought in the AEU and a host of smaller unions followed suit. Bevan's best hope was the miners and he confronted the Durham miners' leader, Sam Watson, a few days after Greenwood's death. He asked the miners' leader directly whom he would back. 'I had to tell him', said Watson, 'that the NUM had already decided that its nominee for the succession was Hugh Gaitskell.' Bevan, realising that any dim hope of winning, indeed of not being crushingly defeated, had just evaporated, exploded at Watson: 'How can you support a public schoolboy from Winchester against a man born in the back streets of Tredegar?'[98]

Gaitskell felt that Watson was personally vital in securing the nomination, and 'the fortunate chance that many others knew me as Minister of Fuel' had also helped.[99] The nominations piled up for Gaitskell but Bevan did not withdraw and, at the Party Conference, was resoundingly defeated.

Gaitskell attended his first NEC meeting as Treasurer of the Labour Party on 29 September 1954, at 5.30 p.m. in the Grand Hotel, Scarborough. He missed only about half a dozen in the remainder of his career. This first session was a dull affair compared to some at which he must have wished he had been present in the recent past and many of which he would be a central part of in the future. Edith Summerskill took the chair, which rotated annually according to length of service. They discussed a coming by-election and the possibility of televising the Party Conference; and Sam Watson requested that there should be no deviation from party policy now that Conference had taken a decision on the issue of German rearmament. The next NEC meeting, back in Labour Party headquarters at Transport House, was held on 27 October and decided who would chair the various policy sub-committees of the Executive. These would be important in the coming years because of their role in detailed policy-making. Gaitskell had a certain advantage as Treasurer and became much more than just an ordinary member of the NEC, because he also became an automatic member of all the sub-committees. He could attend their meetings whenever he needed to. He was also a member of the Special Committee of

Chairmen of Sub-Committees, which managed the work of the various NEC committees. This gave him a good introduction over the next two years to the workings of the party's management body.

Throughout the period 1951—4 Gaitskell had been playing a central role in the party's debates without a voice on its central committee. It is noticeable before his election as Treasurer that he set out to make a splash outside through his weekend speeches, and that after this he had another important way of influencing the party. Though he was, of course, a leading member of the party he had not formally participated in the policy-making process, between 1951 and 1954. This was partly a by-product of his rapid rise. From 1954 onwards Gaitskell was to play a sustained role in Labour Party policy-making.

8

Dirty Work, 1954–1955

You made me the spearhead of a policy in which I did not believe.
Attlee to Gaitskell, 1955

Of course I will – I have every intention of doing so, I am not
going to miss this chance of getting that so-and-so out.
Percy Knight on being asked if he would
move the motion to expel Nye Bevan, 1955

One would get no fun out of politics if one spent all one's
life thinking in terms of the single object of one's own political
success.
Gaitskell, 1955

Gaitskell now had a place on both the main governing bodies of
the Labour Party. The Parliamentary Committee or Shadow Cabinet* gave him a seat on the front bench in the House of Commons
and the National Executive Committee made him part of the
platform at Conference. His place on the NEC also meant that
his already developing contacts with trade union leaders became a
regular fixture of his working life. For much of 1954 and 1955 the
internal world of Labour Party politics dominated his political
activity; it was a period of sustained and gruelling political fighting,
with only intermittent attention being paid to the battle with the
Tories.

However, Gaitskell did try to rise above the quagmire of the
internal war and in his position as Shadow Chancellor he had some
good opportunities for taking the fight to the Tories, particularly
the annual Budget debate. Butler's third Budget outing, in April
1954, was a singularly dull affair in both content and delivery.
The Chancellor himself called it a 'carry-on' Budget, designed to

---

* His vote in the annual Shadow Cabinet polls was as follows: 1952: 179; 1953: 176;
1954: 170; 1955: 184. He rose from third place in 1952 to joint first in 1954 and second in
1955. Jim Griffiths topped the poll in each year.

reaffirm 'our basic policies, rather than marking any major changes of emphasis or direction'. There were very few concrete measures. The highlights were some tax allowances for industry and a reduction in the duty on cinema, theatre and sporting ticket prices by half a penny. It was an interim Budget; even *The Times* called it 'a barren Budget'. In the House of Commons Gaitskell criticised the general direction the Conservative government was taking. He accused them of steering the country to prosperity on 'the backs of those least able to bear the burden'. From the government's point of view nothing was going particularly wrong so there was little incentive to change things.

Shadow Chancellors have the right to reply to the official Budget broadcast. This gave the Treasury portfolio its great advantage as a job in opposition – no other opposition figure except the leader had such an access to the media. From 1954 Gaitskell seems to have taken these opportunities, and broadcasting generally, more seriously. After the débâcle with his fuel and power film he had been a rather cautious broadcaster. However, in 1954 he allowed Tony Benn, then the party's communications whiz-kid, to help with the radio Budget reply. Benn acted as adviser on the presentation and found Gaitskell much more receptive to his ideas than he had been in 1951. Gaitskell allowed him to act as 'producer, script reader, personal private secretary, and general bottle washer' in preparing Labour's radio response. They worked together, with Dora looking on, through an afternoon and into the evening. It is one of the few instances where Gaitskell seems to have allowed himself to be led. Before this broadcast Gaitskell appeared suspicious of the media, after it he felt he had learned something about it, but in 1954 he let the keen young Benn direct him. 'The most extraordinary thing was Hugh's amenability to suggestions.' He accepted almost all the amendments with an appreciative air and was even humanely pleasant and grateful.' Benn modestly felt it to have been 'by far [Gaitskell's] best radio performance yet', and he told Gaitskell so.[1] William Pickles, analysing the Labour Party's television campaign in an internal report on the 1955 election, which included Hugh's Budget talks from this and the 1955 Budget, felt that they had 'rattled the other side enough to produce replies' and to drive them on to the defensive. He also felt that Gaitskell had never failed to project an effective political personality through sound broadcasting.[2]

But this waging of the high political battle with the government

189

was something of an exception in this period. More typical were the events of February 1954 and the renewed row on the issue of German rearmament. In a discussion at the NEC of an 'Interim Memorandum on the German Question at the Berlin Conference', Sam Watson moved 'that the draft statement be adopted'. Tom Driberg and Richard Crossman countered that the statement be referred back. The minutes state that 'considerable discussion followed', which usually means that there was an almighty row. Jack Cooper of the National Union of General and Municipal Workers, fast becoming a Gaitskellite stronghold, on this occasion put forward a compromise by moving that the publication be deferred, but was defeated 11 to 13. The debate moved on to considering amendments and some minor revisions were made before the motion was referred to the International Sub-committee. Crossman returned to the battle on 24 March 1954[3] and proposed a special conference on the issue but was defeated by 15 votes to 7.[4]

Such arguments were hardly unusual but in this case a full account of what took place at the NEC appeared in the *Daily Express*. The report was actually wrong in many respects but there was enough in it that was close to what had occurred at the NEC to accentuate the atmosphere of distrust and division. The right and even the moderate wing of the party disapproved of the briefing of the press about internal and confidential matters – though at different times almost everyone seems to have done it. On the Sunday following the NEC the *Observer* had an even livelier account, this time with the emphasis very much on Attlee's weakness:

> Perhaps the oddest performance came from Mr Attlee. In the Parliamentary Party meeting he gave some people the impression that, although he supported German rearmament, he was hardly an enthusiast. That was not how he behaved at the National Executive. He was, in fact, at his most acid. Mr Crossman, for instance, gave the Executive an instructive lecture on the attitude of the French and Italian Socialists to German Rearmament. When Mr Attlee spoke, he waspishly remarked: 'some people seem to suppose they know what every French and Italian Socialist is thinking.' He had sharp words for Mr Bevan, who had let off a few sprightly quips about the stupidity and dishonesty of some of his colleagues . . . To this Mr. Attlee replied that he would try to speak without accusing anybody of dishonesty. On the general question he said: 'I'm told that this will split the party. Can't help that', he added briskly, puffing on his pipe.[5]

In the renewed atmosphere of distrust and press leaks, the Labour Party was presented with another foreign policy challenge when the House of Commons debated the creation of the South East Asian Treaty Organisation (SEATO). The idea was to form a NATO-type organisation for defence against communist aggression and for mutual economic development in South East Asia. The countries which eventually joined were the US, Britain and France in the northern hemisphere; New Zealand, Pakistan, the Philippines and Thailand in the southern. By the terms of the treaty Laos, Cambodia and non-communist Vietnam were given protection. The US was pressing Britain to sponsor the organisation and give it the same kind of support that NATO received. The key difference was that a 'hot' colonial war was being fought in Indo-China between the North Vietnamese and the French. Before the debate Crossman and Driberg had drafted an emergency resolution on Indo-China for Labour's International Sub-committee declaring opposition to any involvement by the British in the conflict until after a peace conference which had been arranged for October in Geneva. The resolution also deprecated 'all attempts to portray this ghastly civil war, in which both sides are being supported by large-scale foreign intervention, as a crusade against Communism which must be prosecuted until final victory'.[6] This they intended to present to the meeting of the sub-committee at 4 p.m. In between Eden made a statement on his talks with Dulles on this issue which had begun on 11 April.[7] In the background the battle of Dien Bien Phu, the decisive defeat of the French in Indo-China, had been waging since 13 March. When Eden rose in the House of Commons the outcome of this battle was uncertain.

Eden, who was involved in difficult and tetchy negotiations with Dulles, made a general statement about the idea for this South East Asian NATO. He did not commit the government to the plan but indicated that they were under heavy US pressure to help in the region. Attlee responded with equal caution, 'Would the new organisation be free for all to enter, thereby avoiding any misrepresentations about a defence of an obsolete colonialism?' Eden replied mildly; privately he had been fighting hard to prevent the Americans from creating a hard military alliance that could increase Britain's military commitment to the area. However, for Bevan, Attlee's response had been typically weak.

Nye was sitting at the far end of the front bench and pushed his way along to the dispatch box. Gaitskell, presumably sitting on that front bench, as he was present for the debate, watched as Bevan 'nearly trampled his diffident leader'[8] and then 'in a highly excited voice'[9] asked, 'Is the Right Hon. Gentleman aware that the statement which he has made today will be deeply resented by the majority of people in Great Britain? Is he further aware that it will be universally regarded as a surrender to American pressure?' In repudiating the 'whole idea, lock, stock and barrel'[10] he was also repudiating Attlee's leadership – while standing, according to Crossman, literally on the former Prime Minister's toes. Attlee was heard to mutter to himself, 'Just when we were beginning to win the match our inside left has scored against his own side.'[11]

At the Shadow Cabinet later that day Bevan was rebuked by Shinwell and others for his actions. At this and some later meetings Gaitskell let others make the running. It was clear that Bevan's impetuous move was seen by the Parliamentary Labour Party as a fundamental disagreement on policy and a challenge to Attlee. The great irony is that Bevan, as on rearmament in 1951, was broadly right in all the essentials about SEATO, but utterly inept, in terms of the PLP, in his political handling of the situation, not even bothering to co-ordinate his actions with Crossman and Driberg. That Dulles formed a more rigid organisation than the British favoured and that they in turn had to scale down their commitment to it as the war in South East Asia grew worse, was something that at the time could not be known. But that the focus of the argument in the party shifted as soon as the issue was raised from the merits of the debate to the actions of Bevan in the House is testament to Nye's acute lack of political subtlety when it came to the PLP. His defenders would claim, justly, that things cannot always be done by the book, but the problem was that time after time the 'greater truth' of the policy issues involved was obscured by the 'lesser truth' of Bevan's lack of self-control.

At a second Shadow Cabinet the following evening Attlee opened by broadly restating what he had said in the House of Commons. He wanted to maintain the cross-party consensus on foreign policy, but he would also press the government on the particular problems posed by the idea of a collective security organisation in Asia – specifically, the danger of creating such an organisation without the participation of sufficient Asian states. India, for example, had already made it clear she would not take part in SEATO. Further, the purpose of the alliance, if it did not have enough Asian members, could become clouded; it could be seen as an organisation in support of colonialism.

Bevan then stated that he could shorten the meeting. He had decided that, after the recess, he would be returning to the back benches so that he would be free to speak his mind: 'It appears that whenever I open my mouth on the front bench, it gives trouble. Yesterday I was subjected to a most humiliating experience. I do not want to go through that again.'[12]

Gaitskell waited for the chorus of voices which usually accompanied one of these outbursts asking Bevan to reconsider. This time there was silence. Only Attlee spoke: 'Why can't you be a man and face the music?' But Bevan had walked out. Walking down the library corridor, Crossman was briefing Wilson, who had been away, on the recent events. Bevan strolled up and told them he had just walked out on the 'buggers'. They went to have a drink and then along to the party meeting. Bevan took his place at the front of the room on the platform, as he had not yet announced his resignation. Everyone looked at Bevan alone on the platform waiting for the rest of the Shadow Cabinet to arrive, and wondered what was going on. Attlee, Morrison, Gaitskell and the others entered at 6.40 p.m. Attlee made a statement on the SEATO issue. After Bevan had walked out on them, the Shadow Cabinet had sat awkwardly for a few moments, then listened to a long diatribe from Shinwell, before Attlee, to Gaitskell's relief, suggested that in the leader's statement at the party meeting he would mention Bevan's behaviour in the House. When it came to it, Attlee astonished Gaitskell by following his comments on SEATO with an attack on Bevan made with the 'utmost vigour'.[13] This forced the situation and pushed Bevan into announcing his resignation immediately rather than waiting until after the recess.

The resignation decision had some common features with 1951. Bevan had not consulted anyone and was probably in two minds about going, but was ultimately forced by the attack from Attlee to say something: Attlee must have known this. The difference in 1954 was that it was Attlee who was the effective figure pushing Nye to follow his actions and statements to their logical conclusion and not Gaitskell. On this occasion Gaitskell played virtually no overt role. However, it was to be Gaitskell who reaped the long-term benefit from Bevan's exit. The point of policy on which Bevan resigned was concerned with the central debate between political leadership and moral leadership, but the actual focus for the resignation was the behaviour towards the party leader, and for that the Parliamentary Labour Party was unforgiving.

With the Budget tackled but Bevan out of the Shadow Cabinet again, the run-up to the Labour Party Conference promised to be another political maelstrom. However, as in 1951 Bevan, having publicly exploded, then went dormant. He made a great deal of fuss in private but there was no public row until the traditional fallout from the *Tribune* rally at the Conference. Part of the reason for the relative quiet was that the Bevanites were going through one of their periodic bouts of internal blood-letting. Crossman had been increasingly exasperated with Bevan. Wilson had been placed in the awkward position of having to decide, as runner-up, whether or not to take Bevan's seat in the Shadow Cabinet. 'In my innocence', Ian Mikardo recalled to Ben Pimlott, 'I took it for granted that Harold couldn't possibly distance himself openly from Nye by taking that place.' Wilson, of course, had to take the place or be for ever Nye's little dog. He wrote to the press saying that in the interests of party unity he would serve but he was not fooling anyone.[14] Gaitskell heard about the row and noted in his diary that Bevan had met Crossman after the announcement had been made by Wilson. 'So,' Crossman asked, 'you regard Harold as expendable, then, do you?' Bevan replied, 'Yes, and the same goes for you as well.'[15]

Now that Bevan had left the Shadow Cabinet there was a pause in the internal warfare. During the Christmas recess, Gaitskell accepted an invitation to give a speech at Birkbeck College. The college's dedication to adult education was something to which he was attached and the premises were across the road from his old economics department at University College, London. He returned to the Bloomsbury streets through which he had walked so often with Dora and Evan Durbin in the 1930s, but now, in 1954, he was on the threshold of the most politically successful year of his life.

He chose for his subject a 'Defence of Politics'. Interestingly he began by reflecting on the nature of people's perception of politics: 'We must face it. Politics is still looked upon in many quarters as slightly odd, somewhat discreditable, rather silly occupation. Why?'[16] He summed up the public's attitude to politics as one of respect modified by the 'desire to debunk' and said there were two widespread and mutually exclusive criticisms of the major political parties: some felt they were too much in agreement with each other, while others felt that they were too far apart and there was insufficient consensus. On the former charge he was obviously sensitive to his own position. The *Economist* in February had said that 'Mr Butskell is already a well-known figure in dinner table conversation in both Westminster and Whitehall, and the time has come to introduce him to a wider audience.'[17]

His case against the idea of Mr Butskell was straightforward. The British system involved two teams of politicians and the electorate made choices between the two teams at general elections. The difference between the two teams was that 'at present – perhaps one might say almost always – there is one team which tends to favour the status quo and to put the brake on change, which prefers things as they are and is suspicious of radical reform. Call it, if you like, the right-wing party. The left-wing party proposes change and wants to go faster than the other.'[18] Apart from this general difference there are also specific differences, 'today in home affairs the two major differences between the parties arise (A) from a different attitude towards the distribution of income and wealth – which springs from their different philosophies and the different sections of the community associated with them, (B) from a different view of the part to be played by the state in economic life. The Labour Party believes that despite much progress there is still too much inequality in the distribution of wealth and income, particularly wealth . . . The Conservative Party, though seldom vocal on the subject, in practice resists any further change of this kind.' It was necessary for politics to be meaningful for there to be a real choice between the parties and the roots of their politics in different communities ensured this. 'We say firmly that if there is no choice at an election, there is no democracy.'

Though interesting as an early example of his view of the difference between the two parties, with the emphasis on wealth but not on ownership, this was merely a preface to the main point of his speech which was to make the case for well-ordered and disciplined political parties. He led into this by saying that the second kind of criticism of politics was that there was no room for the independent in the two-party system and that the two parties allowed no room for minorities. He conceded that 'both parties are in some way a coalition of interests' but that it is right that Members of Parliament 'are, of course, much less free than individual members. If the Parliamentary Party to which they belong has made a decision, most of them feel obliged to defend that decision, even if they personally disagree with it. Further still up the hierarchy, members of the Executives, either in the parliamentary party or of the national party organisations, have to or should accept much stricter rules about what they may say or write. In the case of the Cabinet this is taken for granted.' It was a clear statement on Bevan's recent behaviour and a coded warning for the future: 'while we all admire a man who follows the dictates of his conscience, I cannot myself agree that the man who puts his own views first and the loyalty to the group second is necessarily right, or better than the man who sacrifices his own point of view for the sake of the group.'[19]

At the Labour Party Conference at Scarborough, Gaitskell's fortunes hung on card votes. Both, this time, went his way. The Executive was supported by 3,270,000 to 3,022,000 on German rearmament and Gaitskell secured his election as Treasurer by 4,338,000 to 2,032,000. On the German question the vote was very tight for the Executive but it was enough because it allowed the real question to be deferred until after the Paris conference. This was reported in the House on 25 October. There was to be a nine-power agreement inviting Germany and Italy into NATO and ensuring a permanent military presence for the US in Europe. This was central to Gaitskell's world-view and the crucial Shadow Cabinet meeting to decide the position of the Labour Party was on 12 November 1954.

Gaitskell considered the Shadow Cabinet debate excellent and engaging. The anti-German rearmament group lost the votes at Shadow Cabinet and as the high tide of Bevanism had receded there was less danger of a reverse of their decision at the Parliamentary Labour Party meeting. The PLP debate was spread over two days; Gaitskell felt it could have been tied up in one with tighter chairing from Attlee. The highlight came on the second day when Reg Paget, a well-heeled backbench Labour MP, attacked the Bevanites' ignorance of foreign policy. Crossman, he said, was the only one who knew anything about foreign affairs, and if the others had known what he wanted they would have violently disagreed. 'The policy is that the victory of Communism is unavoidable, that you may as well lie back and enjoy the rape as best you can, hoping your charms will civilise the victors.'[20] The official line, supporting ratification of the Paris agreements which allowed for German re-armament, was passed by 124 to 72 votes.

If Bevan had let things lie the party might have continued closing the gap with the Conservatives. Instead, to paraphrase Attlee, the outside left attacked his own goal again. Attlee's speech on German rearmament during the official Party Conference debate on foreign affairs warned of the dangers of emotionalism in foreign policy. In general Attlee had blamed Bevan's 'nerves'[21] for his behaviour the year before and clearly was now referring to Nye's unpredictability and tendency to walk out of meetings that were going against him. As if on cue, later in the debate, Bevan, now an ordinary delegate, was reported shouting at Arthur Deakin from the floor.

On the Wednesday evening his own people assembled for the *Tribune* rally and Bevan let rip. 'With all the varied gestures and wit and biting innuendo at his command, he drew every ounce of drama from his situation, presenting a picture of himself as a lone figure striving to save the Party from its leaders and by saving the Party saving the world,' *The Times* reported.[22] Crossman felt it all 'very incoherent, with wild sloshing at unnamed terrible . . . leaders'.[23] There were three sections to the speech: a long opening attack on the press 'prefaced by a statement that he never believed in personal attacks',[24] a shorter assault on the trade unions and then a general attack on the leadership. On the unions he made a direct call to end witch-hunts against supposed Communists. 'We are not going to be intimidated by individual trade union leaders – just a handful of them – going to the rostrum and talking about fellow travellers and about Communists. I say frankly to my friend Ernest Jones: "Drop it. Drop it. We have enough of that from Will Lawther." I say furthermore to Ernest Jones: "In the vote you gave this week you did not represent the miners of Great Britain." He had better learn to behave himself. That is blunt.' It was extraordinary stuff. Bevan was openly attacking the miners for voting for Gaitskell to be elected as Treasurer. But then he came to Attlee's warning about emotional-ism in foreign policy and said that he now knew that

> the right kind of leader for the Labour Party is a desiccated calculating machine who must not in any way permit himself to be swayed by indignation. If he sees suffering, privation or injustice he must not allow it to move him, for that would be evidence of lack of proper education or of absence of self-control. He must speak in calm and objective accents and talk about a dying child in the same way as he would about the pieces inside an internal combustion engine.

Deakin on hearing of the speech commented simply, 'We'll have him out within a year.'[25] Gaitskell seems to have kept clear of the fallout from the speech on *Any Questions* on the Friday evening but in the *Sunday Pictorial* he ended his Conference piece: 'and by the way we do need arithmetic for social progress.'[26]

Was Gaitskell the desiccated calculating machine? The evidence suggests that in fact the adding machine was, as Bevan claimed, a metaphor for the type of leader and the type of politics that he felt were taking over in the Labour Party. If the phrase needs to be understood as referring to people then it meant three people: Clement Attlee, Hugh Gaitskell and Harold Wilson.

The context of the speech suggests that the phrase was a response to Attlee's charge of emotionalism, so in that sense the passage was directed at Attlee. The lack of spirit the party leader had shown in the response to Eden on SEATO was illustrative of a bipartisanship on foreign policy that Bevan distrusted. Attlee's methods of chairing and running things were arid compared to Bevan's fertile political style. The attack on accents and education is suggestive of both Attlee and Gaitskell, but also Harold Wilson, surely the closest thing to a walking adding machine in the party and someone who had recently emerged from Nye's shadow and thereby moved closer to the leadership. When Wilson had taken Bevan's place in the Shadow Cabinet earlier in the year the two had quarrelled bitterly, and Crossman had told Bevan that Wilson was just the sort of man who would succeed Attlee. 'If he's that kind of man, I don't want anything to do with him.' Crossman replied, 'Don't be silly. You've always known that he's that sort of man and the events of the last three days have made no difference to that.' Nye observed that he just wasn't prepared to go through all this nonsense for the sake of political ambition. 'If that's the sort of thing you have to do, I'm not prepared to do it.'[27] Ironically the morning after the *Tribune* speech, Crossman ran into Wilson and found him in 'buoyant form', thinking the whole thing 'splendid'.[28] So the phrase came from a general feeling that the leadership was slipping away from Nye to the cool political operators who would play the game in a way that he would or could not. Among these he included Wilson and Gaitskell. But the phrase stuck to Gaitskell because it suited his public image. Bevan was more than well aware that this phrase did not describe the Gaitskell of private life. He knew Gaitskell's private emotionalism, indeed at times he felt that this was his real failing as a politician; he also maintained that the 1951 rearmament dispute proved that Gaitskell did not know how to count. Apart from the issue of whom precisely Nye had meant, the speech raised the level of personal abuse back up to the heights of the Stalybridge period.

By the time Bevan spoke at the *Tribune* rally a number of people in the Labour Party had already decided that it was time he should be expelled. Any one of his actions since 1951 would not of course have been enough, but the combination plus the background of the resignation from the government built up the feeling against him. Deakin and Williamson and other trade union leaders were clearly in favour of his going. Shinwell, Morrison and Hugh himself felt increasingly that the matter needed bringing to a head. Indeed, Gaitskell had been arguing for such a confrontation on and off since 1951. He was now on the NEC, an important voice on the side of those who favoured punishing transgressors of party unity.

Expelling people from the Labour Party had a considerable pedigree by 1955. Sir Stafford Cripps, Gaitskell's old boss at the Treasury and architect of post-war austerity, had been expelled in January 1939 for advocating the formation of a popular front of anti-fascist parties which would have included the Communists. The NEC gave him the opportunity to state his case before them, but he declined to give the necessary undertakings. Nye Bevan and George Strauss followed Cripps out of the party in April 1939 for similar activity and the same refusal to recant. The whip was withdrawn for only a few months. When the war started, advocating a vigorous resistance to the Nazis seemed less of a crime and all three were readmitted. They had also performed the obligatory recanting and given the requisite assurances about future actions.[29] These expulsions were unusual because the people concerned were essentially Labour loyalists. D. N. Pritt was expelled in March 1940 and J. Platt Mills in March 1948 for 'fellow travelling'; Alfred Edwards in May 1948 for not supporting the nationalisation of steel; Konni Zilliacus was expelled for attacking Cripps's economic policy; and L. J. Solley in March 1949 and Leslie Hutchinson in March 1949 were both on the far left.[30]

The consistency with which those on the left were disciplined provoked one party member to write to Morgan Phillips, the general secretary, in June 1949, 'I have read in a Labour Party publication that the Labour Party is democratic and that the view of every member counts. Does this include the critics of *Bevin*ism?'[31] Party discipline never really applied to those who came from the right of the party in the same way as it did to those on the left.[32]

The British possession of nuclear weapons, the next great foreign and defence policy question to be raised, provided the stage for the concerted attempt to have Bevan expelled. The McMahon Act[33] had forced the British to develop their own nuclear weapons programme in the immediate postwar period. At a time of extreme economic and political crisis the maintenance of Britain's great power status through the ownership of nuclear weapons was to be achieved at any price.[34] This was both in terms of keeping up with the Americans – ensuring that Britain was perceived as being different from other European powers – but also, as the key report on the issue maintained, to provide Britain with a self-defence from possible attack.[35]

The impetus for the programme is best understood through Churchill's three circles. Britain was at the centre of three interconnected circles of Europe, Commonwealth/Empire and the United States. When the Soviets exploded their own megaton weapon in 1953[36] this presented a threat to each of these relationships. Prestige with the Commonwealth and Empire had to be maintained by keeping Britain in the first rank of world powers. This in turn meant that Britain had to make a major contribution to the defence of Europe and play a supportive role to the Americans in their global battle with communism. The problem was that each time the technology took a leap forward the cost of Britain staying in the race also increased and, indeed, began to overtake the resources available.

The alternative to staying in the race was the acceptance of becoming a second rate power, without the political status that the possession of the weapons bestowed; there were thus powerful internal arguments for high defence expenditure levels.[37] Moreover, rearmament was demanded by the USA as Britain's part in the United Nation's intervention in Korea. Gaitskell's part in the maintenance of Britain's world role started as Chancellor in the 'defence and dentures' debate. The relegating of a free health service below rearmament neatly exemplified the Labour Government's adherence to Britain's grand purpose in the world,[38] and to keeping Britain safely in the centre of Churchill's three circles and not committed to one at the exclusion of the other two.

The cost implications of this policy were profound, but any alternative policy would also have entailed heavy expenditure. Part of the appeal of nuclear weapons was that, relatively speaking, they delivered a high level of defence capability at low cost. If Britain were to get rid of her weapons then the question was how would she maintain her global leadership role and meet her existing commitments.[39]

For Bevan[40] this question of existing commitments was central. His powerful speech at the Labour Party conference of 1957, asking the unilateralists if they were prepared to send a British Foreign Secretary naked into the conference chamber was the last best proof of Bevan's attachment to a 'Great' Britain. In contrast, the Bevanites who broke rank with Bevan were prepared to sacrifice Britain's existing network of relations to the cause of unilateralism, some even preaching neutralism.[41] At this stage, Gaitskell felt that virtually any policy of disengagement involved a relative abandonment of Britain's role of leadership. In the debate on the Paris agreements which eventually passed with only six pacifists voting against and both the left and the right of the party abstaining, he had argued that 'defeatism and neutralism' would have the same result as appeasement in the 1930s. He also argued that the idea of a neutralised zone between the Eastern and Western blocs was no more than 'an excellent propaganda word'.[42] From the moment the bomb became a central feature of the political debate he argued that those who opposed it were arguing for British neutralism and should say so.

If the British did not develop their own weapons their only option was to purchase a ready-made and tested system from the Americans. This implied a tacit acceptance of the testing of nuclear weapons which had been a contentious issue since the launch of the British programme in the early 1950s. The problem was that without testing the weapons the deterrent value, especially of new generations of missiles, could not be fully demonstrated. But testing involved risks of radiation poisoning, which was the central popular fear associated with the bomb. The conflict between strategic necessity and popular fear made the issue divisive, complex and politically explosive. British possession or non-possession of nuclear weapons, their testing and the general geopolitical role of such weapons caused the break-up of the Bevanite group and these issues dominated Labour politics almost continuously until 1962. These great issues of state and policy, of the direction and role of Britain as a great power in the world, became obscured in the months that followed. Despite the protestations of nearly all the participants in memoirs and biographies, the final push to expel Bevan, and his action in partly provoking and partly simply giving Gaitskell and the others the opportunity, were about political power struggles.

The fight was renewed when Bevan once more lost his self-control and issued a direct challenge to the authority of the party leader. The decision to manufacture the H-bomb, made in 1953, was finally debated in the House of Commons on 1 March 1955. The party meeting on 24 February approved the Shadow Cabinet's motion which accepted the need for the manufacture of the bomb. However, the motion pointedly did not link it with German rearmament or the demand for talks with the Russians before the ratification of the Paris agreements – options that the Bevanites had been advocating. Attlee had made an excellent speech some months earlier proposing a summit on the new generation of H-bombs and the Bevanites tried to link this with the rearmament issue. Aside from the Attlee speech, Gaitskell and Morrison were much more in control and better prepared for the string of meetings preceding the defence debate than they had been in 1954. In general they managed the Labour Party effectively over these issues and the Bevanites were continually following and reacting to events. The Bevanites were also very disorganised, and were by now constantly arguing amongst themselves.

Bevan himself was clear that there was an opportunity for taking the initiative from the government by combining all the elements – ratification of Paris agreements, H-bomb and summit – into a motion. The PLP meeting, however, rejected this option at the prompting of Gaitskell and Morrison and against the wishes of Attlee. There is little evidence that the motion would have made very much difference to the policy of the party. It would have reopened the question of German rearmament to a fresh debate, but that would have been in the context of forcing the government to discuss the possibility of a summit.

Nevertheless the motion had been rejected by a PLP meeting. Gaitskell considered that the issue was confused and that many people were not sure what they had been voting on, except that they were voting against Bevan.[43] Bevan was furious and collected 100 signatures for a motion to be put down directly in the Commons, demanding a debate on the issues. Gaitskell alleges in his diary that in an attempt to confuse MPs who were asked to sign the motion but who may not have had a great deal of time to read it, the 'harmless stuff' about disarmament was typed using double space at the front and the part contradicting the PLP meeting's decision was pressed together and single-spaced at the end. The point was that Bevan had once more spurned the spirit of the rules of the party. It is important to note, however, that he had not actually broken the standing orders of the party and as a Member of Parliament he was entitled to collect signatures for a motion. At the next PLP meeting on 24 February, Attlee moved a motion on Bevan's conduct: 'That for Members of the Party to take action in direct contradiction to a decision of the Parliamentary Party taken four sitting days previously makes a farce of Party meetings, and brings the Party into disrepute.'[44]

Bevan did not stop there. He did not oppose the manufacture of nuclear weapons by the British, but he opposed first use and the general context in which the policy was being presented. In the debate on the defence White Paper he combined these in an effective exchange with Churchill, pressing the government on the need for talks. But he also put a series of questions to both the government and his own front bench.

> I want my Right Hon. Friends the leaders of the Opposition to answer me, do they mean by that language what the Government mean by the White Paper? Do they mean that nuclear weapons will be used with the support of the British Labour movement against any sort of aggression? I want to know the answer. If my Right Hon. Friend, the Leader of the Opposition, says that this is the interpretation of that amendment, then I do not propose to vote for it this evening . . . The issue is simply this. Are we to conduct a peace policy or a war policy? We could do it. We could meet the Soviet representatives at once. I therefore beg the Government to measure up to the magnitude of this problem. Let the Prime Minister do deeds to match his great words; not attempt to delude the country by the majesty of his language but inspire it by the dedication of his behaviour. That is what we want from him. We want from my Right Hon. Friends the leaders of the Opposition an assurance that the language of their amendment, moved on our behalf, does not align the Labour movement behind that recklessness; because if we cannot have the lead from them, let us give the lead ourselves.[45]

Bevan sat down at 6.19 p.m. Attlee rose to reply at 8.40 p.m. He ignored Bevan's speech and concentrated on the substance of the debate. Nothing could have been calculated to incense Bevan's vanity more than being ignored. As the leader of the party ended, Bevan shot to his feet: 'There is a matter on which Hon. Members on this side of the House would like to have some clarification. The amendment which had been moved by the Opposition speaks about the deterrent effect upon aggression of the threat of using thermo-nuclear weapons . . . What we want to know is whether the use of the words to which I have referred in our amendment associates us with the statement that we should use thermonuclear weapons in circumstances of hostilities, although they were not used against us.' Attlee replied that he was talking in general terms and that 'deterrents, by the possession of thermonuclear weapons, are the best way of preventing another war.' Bevan retorted: 'That's no answer, that's no answer.' At 10 p.m. the amendment was called and Bevan sat with sixty-two other Labour MPs abstaining.

The questions which then buzzed round Westminster were: who had Bevan meant when he said that they should give the lead? Did he mean the Labour Opposition against the government? Foot maintains that his body language suggested just that. Or did he mean the Bevanites should give the lead to the Labour Party that Attlee and the other leaders had failed to give? How would the Shadow Cabinet react? Could the party expel sixty-two MPs, and, if not, how could they only expel Bevan?

On 7 March the meeting of the Shadow Cabinet seemed to offer a resolution of the issue by actually conceding the main policy point and deciding to put a motion down pressing the government on the need for talks. This impression lasted for twenty-four hours until news of the second decision of that meeting was made public. Chuter Ede opened the meeting by proposing that they withdraw the whip from Bevan.

This posed some problems for Gaitskell at this stage. The voting for the 1955 Treasurership election was taking place among the trade unions and he had to balance the general political benefits of expel-ling Bevan with the personal problems this might present to him in this election. He felt that 'sooner or later he would have to go, but I was not sure whether this was the right moment.'[46] Callaghan, Morrison, Edith Summerskill, Philip Noel-Baker and Shinwell all spoke strongly in favour of withdrawing the whip. Alf Robens, Hugh Dalton and Attlee all said that on balance they were against. Dalton stated that if they gave Bevan the opportunity he would himself resign from the party and that this would be preferable to the Shadow Cabinet recommending expulsion. Callaghan challenged Dalton, arguing that this was 'too clever by half'. Dalton responded, 'Better to be too clever by half than too stupid by three-quarters.' The vote was taken and by 9 to 4 they decided to recommend the withdrawal of the whip from Nye Bevan.

Until the vote Gaitskell was in two minds on the issue. On the one hand he felt that Bevan's behaviour had been intolerable and that the Labour Party could not continue down this road. Moreover, he had already placed himself in the hands of the trade union leaders to an extent and they favoured expulsion. Negotiations were at an advanced stage with Deakin, Ernest Jones, Tom Williamson and others to increase the number of trade union members affiliated to the party and thereby increase the trade unions' financial input through the political levy.[47] The number of members that any particular union chose to count as affiliated to the party could vary. 'By custom, some unions, the Shopworkers for example, scrupulously calculated an exact figure which, however complicated, bore some resemblance to the variation in levy-paying. Others named an approximate figure which did not change over a decade. Political considerations also played a part. Committed support for the anti-Bevanite forces undoubtedly motivated the Transport and General Workers [Deakin] and the General and Municipal Workers [Williamson] to raise substantially their affiliated membership when the Treasurership contest was at its height in 1955.'[48] Affiliated members also equalled votes.

The first layer of the political judgement Gaitskell had to make was whether a public attempt to expel Bevan would result in a corresponding split in the union votes for Gaitskell in the Treasurership. This possible loss in votes could be partially, but only partially, offset by increased affiliation. The second layer was whether the trade unions would find another champion if he did not press for the full measures against Bevan. The third layer was that once the whip was withdrawn the party might decide to go no further. This he judged to be the worst possible outcome. It would merely be a rap over the knuckles which would take months to achieve and would leave the party divided just before a general election. Once the process was started it had to be completed. The Shadow Cabinet had taken the first step by recommending the withdrawal of the whip. Gaitskell now fell in with the hardliners: if the Shadow Cabinet had made the decision then it would have to be done; once the die was cast there was little further reflection on it until the end. Characteristically, once set on a certain path he stuck to that path and tried to achieve as many of his objectives as possible until it was obvious that he could go no further: it was head down into the dirtest politics of his career.

Bevan now fell ill and his summoning before the party meeting to respond to charges was delayed until 16 March. In the meantime Nye sat up in bed receiving people who urged various courses of action on him.[49] Barbara Castle, Tony Greenwood and Richard Crossman arrived on Friday 13 March at the farm in the Chilterns which Nye had purchased the previous year. Barbara suggested that he apologise to Attlee over the weekend – to which he responded by 'shouting like a petulant child, "I won't! I won't!" '[50] But eventually, after much persuasion, he issued a statement that what he had said and done was not a direct challenge to the personal authority of Attlee.[51]

Gaitskell decided to reply to this statement in his weekend speech. In contrast to Stalybridge when he had simply shown the text to local party workers, this time he checked what he planned to say with Alf Robens and Douglas Jay and read it over the phone to Dalton. In his diary Dalton recalled, 'We both think something emphasising Bevan's conduct in the House on 2nd March (Ruth [Dalton] says, most people don't realise this at all) . . . Hugh and I are both a bit apprehensive that Attlee may weaken as this goes on. Today is only Saturday, and they have till Wednesday!'[52]

In Doncaster the same Friday Gaitskell made his sharpest anti-Bevanite speech since Stalybridge. He said that 'people who thought they were so right and the party so wrong' should realise that 'the only course open to them was to get out.' The speech was widely and correctly reported as a shot in defence of Attlee after Bevan's interruption of Attlee on the floor of the House of Commons on 2 March. The issues Bevan's actions raised were profoundly concerned with loyalty to the Labour Party: 'I do not see how this sort of thing can possibly be regarded as anything else but a direct challenge to the elected leader of our party and therefore an affront to the party itself which elected him.' After this speech Gaitskell was seen, not unreasonably, as the chief right-wing prosecutor.[53] He did not, as Williams shows, ask all the questions at all the meetings, but he was the key factor determining that the party pursued Bevan much further in 1955 than in 1952.[54]

On Tuesday 17 March the Shadow Cabinet assembled to plan their strategy for the meeting with Bevan, fixed for the next day. The

'*But are you sure the best way to heal a rupture is cutting the patient
in half, Dr Edith? – Vicky's view of the Great Expulsion of 1955.*

chief whip produced confident predictions of the voting, especially if
it were turned into a vote of confidence in Attlee's leadership. Gaitskell was worried that Attlee would not show sufficient strength
in presenting the leadership case to maximise the vote.[55] Dalton
commented, 'so it turns primarily on the Little Man tomorrow. If
he's firm, he'll win, and by a firm majority.'[56]

Bevan, recovered from his flu, ate a good dinner at the Ivy with
close Bevanite friends the night before the inquisition.[57] Attlee
opened the Parliamentary Labour Party meeting. Though Committee Room 14 was full it was noticeable that there were a significant
number of absences for illness, diplomatic or otherwise. Gaitskell
had met with Dalton for half an hour on 10 March. They decided
to prepare a brief for Attlee for the PLP meeting and to give this
to Robens to hand to the leader – Attlee was always more sensitive to working men and would take it better from Robens.[58] The
brief was drafted by Gaitskell and duly passed on. Attlee began the
meeting by stating that he had no intention of allowing publication
of lists of the way in which MPs voted: this was an attempt by the
Bevanites to 'throw a spanner in the works'.[59] It was item 1 on
Gaitskell's brief for Attlee.[60] Then he went on to list the charges
against Bevan in detail,[61] not just for his conduct on 2 March but

for the events surrounding the SEATO debate in April 1954 – items 4–11 on Gaitskell's brief. In fact, Attlee simply read Gaitskell's brief through from beginning to end before adding that the party should remember what had happened to the Liberals.[62] He then sat down.

Bevan rose and attacked the 'hatchet-faced men sitting on the platform' who were the real threat to the leadership. He attacked George Brown for his part in a 1947 conspiracy against Attlee and he attacked Gaitskell for his Doncaster speech. There was no sign of an apology to Attlee. In turn, Attlee showed no sign of making it an issue of confidence until the very end when he said weakly, 'Yes, of course it is a vote of confidence – necessarily so.'[63] A compromise motion calling for the censuring of Bevan, Gaitskell's initially preferred option, was defeated by 138 to 124 and the Shadow Cabinet's proposal to withdraw the whip was passed by 141 to 112 votes. For the press it gave Bevan a minor victory because the Chief Whip's predictions of much bigger majorities had leaked.

Bevan had now had the whip withdrawn. The Parliamentary Party informed the National Executive Committee of this decision. It was for the NEC to decide if Bevan should now be expelled from the party. Attlee was in favour of leaving him hanging on a thread for a while[64] and had told Leslie Hunter that he was set against expulsion.[65] Gaitskell was worried that they would end up with the worst of all worlds and that the unions would refuse to increase the affiliated members unless a proper stand was taken. He and Alf Robens went to see Attlee to complain about his lack of leadership. Attlee, in a very unpleasant interview, snapped at them, '"You made me the spearhead of a policy in which I did not believe." Whereupon we both said, "Why didn't you make that plain at the time and take a strong line?" "Well," he said. "we took the vote." I said, "You don't take a vote in the Cabinet. Surely if you had really felt that way you should have made it plain that you were not prepared to go through with it."'[66]

Gaitskell had argued his way into the centre of the move to oust Bevan. That 'reckless consistency' had again taken over. Dora urged him to reconsider and not go too far in isolating himself.[67] But he took the lead in persuading the NEC to decide on expulsion. He had already played a fairly central role, and now he pushed on to the next stage. Whether it was the right thing to do or not seems to have slipped from his mind. But he focused on the idea of a six-month suspension as the way to achieve some sort of settlement of the issue without hopelessly dividing the party. Electorally, it is difficult to see how this was much better as an option than full expulsion, but it was an achievable goal.

He met Sam Watson at the Russell Hotel and they agreed that Bevan had to be expelled and that Attlee had to support this.[68] He then lobbied Deakin and Williamson to go and see Attlee and try to secure his agreement to, at the very least, a six-month suspension from the party. Gaitskell was surprised to find 'Tom . . . much more vehement, and it took me some time to persuade him even to consider anything short of flat expulsion.'[69] But the six-month plan was eventually considered. The main sticking point became whether the unions would oppose Attlee and press for some kind of action above and beyond an apology. The key figures assembled a few days later at St Ermin's hotel. The financial arrangements for the increase in affiliation became entangled once more with the issue. Tom Williamson and Arthur Deakin ended dinner favouring defying Attlee and holding out for full expulsion; the compromise of suspension was lost. There was again no direct fix, but Gaitskell in his own diary record shows the way in which the hardening line among the trade union leaders moved him away from the idea of some sort of compromise. He began to feel that full expulsion was a possibility. 'I went home a good deal more encouraged and determined to try it out', – that is, to have Nye Bevan expelled from the Labour Party in defiance of the wishes of Clement Attlee.

Despite the battles Gaitskell never completely lost sight of the merits of his chief rival. It was probably during this crisis that Gaitskell had to attend one of his regular XYZ dinners in the House. He was accompanying his friend and guest, Lady Brook, through the House of Commons when Nye Bevan passed them on the stairs. Helen Brook, wife of the banker Robin Brook and a friend from the 1930s, recalled to Philip Williams that she made a derogatory comment about Bevan. 'It was the only time Hugh ever ticked me off. He said, "Helen, that's not the way to talk about a great man and a great politician" – although he was fighting him. He really gave me a lecture.'[70]

Deakin, Williamson and Ernest Jones went to see Attlee and pressed the case for expulsion. Attlee evaded the issue and tried to talk about the weather.[71] Following a meeting of the Finance and General Purposes Committee on the next afternoon Gaitskell continued to sound out the trade union members of the Executive.

They did not seem to believe that Attlee would not support the motion. The problem for Gaitskell was persuading them that he might not and finding someone to propose the motion. Jack Cooper of the General and Municipal Workers and he decided to try Percy Knight of the Seamen's Union who was Vice-Chair of the NEC in 1954–5. '"Well, Percy, we have decided that you will have to move the expulsion tomorrow." Percy said, "Of course I will – I have every intention of doing so, I am not going to miss this chance of getting that so-and-so-out."'[72] Weeks of lobbying and arm twisting came to a head at the NEC meeting. Gaitskell indisputably led the attack in this meeting, stating that, if the party did not expel Bevan, the 'Tories would certainly claim that he was indispensable, and indeed the future leader of the Party . . . they would use this in the Election.' Attlee again manoeuvred his way through the situation by proposing that Bevan appear before a sub-committee of the NEC to answer the charges. It was a classic ploy to pull the party back from full expulsion but nevertheless to make it appear that they had reprimanded Bevan. The moderate unionists and a few others who had previously backed the hard line deserted Hugh. Attlee's amendment was passed by 14 to 13 votes.

The special sub-committee of the NEC convened on Tuesday 29 March 1955 at 10.30 a.m. in Transport House.[73] The ball was now with Bevan, and the committee's task was to seek assurances from him as 'to his future conduct as a member of the party.' Edith Summerskill was in the chair; the rest of the committee comprised Attlee, Gaitskell, Griffiths and Castle from the PLP and Percy Knight, Jack Haworth and Jack Cooper from the trade unions. Bevan joined the meeting and read his statement, 'a really abject apology' according to Crossman.[74]

> The charge is that in what I have done and also in the way I have done it I have created difficulties for Mr Attlee and caused him embarrassment in his position as the Leader of the Party. This was certainly never my intention. But if my action or speech could lend themselves to the interpretation that such was my motive, then I am sincerely sorry and I apolgise to Mr. Attlee for any pain I may have caused him.

Jack Cooper and Gaitskell pressed him to give assurances on attacks on trade union leaders, on his refusal to accept majority decisions and the existence of an organised group within the party with its own press. Apart from this Gaitskell said little. Nye neatly side-stepped each of these in turn and then turned the tables on the committee by advocating that the Shadow Cabinet should be selected by the party leader. 'He instanced the fact that when Mr Attlee formed his government in 1945 he did not include many of the members who had previously served as elected members of the Parliamentary Labour Party Executive' (as the Shadow Cabinet was then known). Bevan turned to Gaitskell at one point and admitted that it was 'difficult for an ex-Cabinet Minister to be both a statesman and a protagonist for new or minority opinions and he agreed that those around the table, including himself, had greater obligations than many members of the Party.' That Gaitskell, though not the chief interrogater at this meeting, was identified even more strongly than Morrison with the moves to get Bevan out was then plainly illustrated. Gaitskell asked Bevan, '"Would you agree that it was a bad thing for the Party if members attack the leaders, and if so, will you agree not to do this in future?" He said, "I refuse to answer that question. It is a trap." Whereupon there was a sort of uproar and everybody tried to rush in to keep us apart.'[75]

At the Executive meeting the next day a resolution by Jack Cooper endorsing the withdrawal of the whip, noting Bevan's assurances to the sub-committee and warning him that 'it will take drastic action against future violations of Party disclipine', was passed by 15 votes to 10. Bevan was safe from expulsion but had still had the whip withdrawn.

Gaitskell had devoted a huge amount of time and political energy to attempting to manage the expulsion of Bevan and he had failed to achieve that objective. What is striking is both his determination to do what the trade union leaders wanted done and his own reservations about the policy he was pursuing. Bevan behaved irresponsibly, rudely and with considerable petulance at times but he was always internally consistent; he followed his emotions down a number of dead ends but always seemed reasonably sure why. Gaitskell did what he had to do in some of the dirtiest politics – on both sides – in the history of the Labour Party up to this time, but in the end he admitted to his diary that Bevan's position had been strengthened more by the failure to expel than it would have been by an initial censure motion. He also felt that Attlee's position with the right had slipped and that the 'whole thing may be regarded as a stalemate'.

His friends were telling him that his own position was considerably set back by his conduct. Roy Jenkins, Tony Crosland and Woodrow Wyatt wrote to him at the height of the battle, urging him to broaden the base of his support.[76] But politically at least he had consolidated his hold on the right and ensured his re-election, with a vastly increased majority because of the increase in the number of affiliated members, as Treasurer at the Labour Party Conference. He was, though, honest in his own conclusion on the issue:

> I always find it difficult to behave in these matters in the subtle way which my own friends seem to expect. I don't see how one can have strong loyalties with people like George Brown and Alf Robens, not to speak of the T.U. Leaders, and continually refuse to do any dirty work for them and with them. But undoubtedly had I foreseen, as I should have done, where Clem's original attitude would lead us, I should have thrown my weight on the first day against withdrawing the Whip and in favour of the censure motion . . . We might be said to have gained some ground after heavy casualties . . . the right wing is rather dispirited, and looking at it personally, my own position is no doubt weaker . . . I must say that I do not and cannot regard that as the only thing that matters. One would get no fun out of politics if one spent all one's life thinking in terms of the single object of one's own political success.[77]

The decision to reprieve Bevan was made on Wednesday 30 March. On 15 April the Tories announced a general election: the outside world stubbornly intruded into Labour's private wars.

The failed attempt to expel Bevan and Nye's actions in provoking it broke up the Bevanites. Crossman had opened channels to Gaitskell during the crisis, Wilson was hovering and other moderate Bevanites were disillusioned with their champion. The full-blown schism was over. The eventual outcome of the Bevanite challenge belied the intensity with which the conflict was conducted in the 1950s. The domestic differences were largely ironed out and Bevan quickly came to an accommodation with the leadership in the year after the 1955 election. However, the maximalist versus minimalist and the political versus moral leadership controversies surfaced again in the early 1960s, and in the governments of Wilson and Callaghan. The symbolic stance of the Bevanites was represented in the person of Foot as leader and in the Labour manifesto of 1983, the first time a maximalist programme had been presented to the electorate, and the electorate resoundingly rejected it.[78] Following this defeat Neil Kinnock was elected leader of the Labour Party. Kinnock's style of leadership was not unlike that of Hugh Gaitskell – he led from the front. He also engaged in an extended battle with a maximalist group in the party, the Militant Tendency. The comparison can be taken one stage further. In the same way that Hugh Gaitskell tried to dominate his party by a speech at Conference, so Neil Kinnock asserted his authority over the party at the 1985 Bournemouth Conference. In so doing he aligned himself with Gaitskell's view that the priority for the Labour Party should be the pursuit of power and that compromise on policy was a necessary expedient in winning power, but the clearest connection between the Kinnock of the 1980s and the Gaitskell of the 1950s was the perception that a disciplined and unified party was essential to electoral victory.[79]

9

The Top of Labour's Greasy Pole, 1955

This is the biggest act of political deceit for 20 years.
Gaitskell, October 1955

In my view, the issue of the leadership is settled for twenty years.
Harold Wilson to Hugh Gaitskell, December 1955

Prior to the general election of 1955, despite being primarily inward-looking for much of the pre-election period, the Labour Party did not suffer from a lack of popularity in the country. Gallup polls conducted during the 1951–5 Parliament showed that out of the 42 months between November 1951 and May 1955 the Labour Party held a lead in 28 months ranging from 10 per cent in July 1952 to 0.5 per cent in October 1954, and held a virtually unbroken lead until January 1955. Even at the height of the Bevanite controversy, during 1952, the Labour Party held an average lead of 6 per cent.[1] It also had a front-bench team comparable in experience, quality and profile to the Conservative front bench. The record membership figures and increases in the level of trade union affiliations in the early 1950s provided sound, if not exactly flourishing, finances.[2] In the early 1950s a certain amount of complacency developed in the administration of the party. Gaitskell was to comment when elected Treasurer that the job had not really been done for ten years,[3] which meant that the Labour Party's organisation was in places poor and inefficient. But this should not be exaggerated. The Labour Party was not in bad shape. It did not even suffer in the main from its recent record of internal division and strife.

Nevertheless the Conservatives started the 1955 campaign with most of the advantages and few handicaps. Eden had taken over from Churchill and made only minor changes in the Cabinet. The Churchill and Eden governments gave the Conservatives a powerful domestic legacy to exploit in the general election. The governments

214

had not introduced a full-blooded capitalist economy and could therefore put themselves forward as one-nation Tories. Their key advantage was the generally favourable economic conditions, as Anthony Seldon, an historian of that government, sums up: 'the economy was run at full employment with a minimal rate of wage or price inflation; without, after 1952, balance of payments difficulties, and in the absence of a wages policy.'[4] Although problems of over-stimulation of the economy were to occur in the summer, for the election in May the economic picture was sound. Moreover, the Conservatives had not returned to confrontation with the unions but had reached a state of industrial harmony when Walter Monckton had been appointed by Churchill specifically to deal with the trade union leaders. Most of the union trouble was caused by unofficial strikes of which there were a number through the election period, but these strikes were over differentials and other industrial issues associated with affluence, rather than a product of industrial militancy. The *Observer* commented at the time of the 1955 election: 'In the economic field Britain is very prosperous, the prosperity is widely diffused, with full employment and higher wages than ever before.'[5] The welfare state and social services had been left untouched and even expanded in some areas. Macmillan was highly successful in the public relations for his house-building programme. The Chancellor, Rab Butler, introduced a giveaway Budget before the election which caused many problems later but provided a surplus of some £140 million to be distributed by reducing the base rate of income tax and by increasing personal allowances.[6] The standard rate was cut from 9s. (45p) to 8s. 6d. (42.5p), the single person's tax allowance was raised by £20 to £140 and there were selective cuts in purchase tax.

In his Budget speech, Butler had declared that 'We are one of the most heavily taxed nations in the world . . . I should very much like to give some help to the family man.' Gaitskell attacked this notion and dissected the figures to show that the effect on the family would be marginal. In his broadcast he stated: 'I know some of you will say: "Of course, that's natural enough, richer people pay more taxes. If you reduce the taxes obviously they are going to get more benefit." Personally I do not look at it that way. I do not see the logic of that argument. I think the Chancellor, if he has money to give away, should ask himself, "Where can I do good? Who really needs the help most? Where does the shoe pinch?"'[7] A newspaper strike, which ended two days after the Budget, followed by the arrest of Ruth Ellis for the shooting of David Blakeley, kept the newspaper coverage and analysis of the Budget to a minimum. This coincided with a general Conservative strategy of minimising the political heat to keep the turnout low.

The internal Labour report on the election highlighted Tory prosperity as a major problem for the party.

> Thousands of industrial workers, skilled and unskilled, are able in many parts of the country to earn on piece work or overtime up to £15 or £20 per week, and it is quite possible that a lot of these people, whilst they would not in any circumstances vote Tory, are happy about the present position and had no inclination to secure a change of government at this time. Despite the rising cost of living, they have been able, during the last few years, to purchase a television set and perhaps a washing machine or cleaner. Increased allocation of new cars on the home market has reduced the price of second-hand models, and more and more people have obtained cars for the first time in their life. There has been full employment and – so far as the man in the street is concerned – every prospect of it continuing.[8]

Moreover, the Conservative governments had done little during the Parliament to weaken their electoral chances.

In contrast, Labour continued until a month before the election to shoot itself in both feet. As the opposition to a government that had pursued a successful domestic policy, the Labour Party had a difficult task and the election was fought and won by the Conservatives on domestic issues. The Labour Party could have adopted various electoral tactics. They could have attempted to make the election a choice between individuals rather than policies, to promote an efficient team able to run the country better than the Conservatives. They could have challenged Conservative policy and offered either radical or moderate alternatives to set the agenda for the campaign, putting the government on the defensive and mobilising discontent. They also needed their share of luck or gaffes from the government.

The Labour Party managed to achieve few of these objectives. It was difficult to promote the image of a team when a leading player, Bevan, organised his own meetings and failed to keep in touch with Transport House. (Though he was, in Crossman's phrase, conventionally loyal at election times.)[9] The Labour Party came up with a programme that was neither distinctive nor original – 'a rehash of an indigestible dish' was Hunter's description of the manifesto.[10] Most Labour candidates concentrated on attacking the Tories rather than advocating their own policies because on some issues the difference was technical and difficult to get across.[11] Eden was highly successful at playing down the election and thereby keeping Labour's full electoral strength away from the polls. There was also the overwhelming problem that most people thought the result was a foregone conclusion: 'the absence of doubt about the outcome may have been largely responsible for the tranquillity.'[12]

Gaitskell's own election tour started on 9 May 1955 in Attleborough near Norwich. He made a series of speeches in Norfolk where he stressed local farming issues (basing his speeches on an agriculture pamphlet by George Brown), the state of the economy and the repayment of post-war credits – all of which received local and national coverage. From Norfolk he travelled north to Shipley, Newcastle upon Tyne and Sunderland, and on 16 May stopped off at his Leeds South constituency where he called the Tories' claim that Labour would bring back rationing a lie.[13] This was the main excitement of the campaign. The Tories produced and distributed thousands of miniature imitation ration books, arguing that if Labour were re-elected they would reintroduce physical controls of commodities and rationing.

Gaitskell went on from Leeds for a tour of Yorkshire, trying to increase his range of attacks on the Tories but generally finding rather apathetic audiences. At Keighley on the 18th the Tories were 'hysterical'[14] and talking 'moonshine' (the local paper called this one of the best-attended meetings of the campaign), on the 19th at Brighouse the Tories were the 'two-scare' party rationing and the cost of the Labour programme),[15] on the 22nd at Hebden Bridge Butler's statement on price rings was 'worth nothing at all'. On the 23rd Gaitskell was attacked by the Financial Secretary of the Treasury for gambling that he could use the Tory system to introduce socialist measures including increased taxation.[16] After responding vigorously to the charge, he was somewhat bizarrely attacked by Colin Welch in the *Daily Telegraph* as a demagogue.[17] He was back in Leeds for polling day, when the *Daily Herald* reported his attack on the Tories: 'They have always fought the people's progress.' He also pledged that Labour would bring steel and road haulage back into public ownership – key features of the undigestible dish. It was all rather tame and did little to improve his already low opinion of electioneering.

A low turnout in an uninteresting campaign produced the expected Tory victory. After the defeat Gaitskell felt there were three main reasons: the economic situation as it 'strikes the ordinary voter', the superior Tory machine and dissension within the Labour Party.[18] He had warned, in a speech to the Amalgmated Society of Woodworkers, that indifference could turn into hostility. The internal Labour post-mortem broadly endorsed his opinions.

With the defeat of Labour in 1955, after a nationally disappointing and poorly focused campaign, the attention of the party became centred on Attlee's retirement. Attlee received little blame for the defeat; as he was an elder statesman, the party campaign had in fact featured his experience, with an election poster carrying the message 'Four Power Talks. Send Attlee.' The pipe and the cherry blossom cottage may not have looked particularly impressive on television, but the full-blooded political post-mortem of 1959 was not foreshadowed in 1955. Attlee was neither temperamentally nor intellectually prepared for such a battle.

The post-election analysis, such as it was, tended to blame division within the Labour Party and the Conservatives' success with the economy.[19] The NEC inquiry concluded that 'the result was extremely disappointing, although it must be remembered that the circumstances surrounding the election were more than a little difficult. The overlap between it and the local elections [at which the Conservatives made substantial gains] was, for one thing, very unfortunate'; this meant that, organisationally, 'effective work' for the general election did not begin until 12 May.[20] But it was more than just a slow organisational response.

Dalton recorded in his diary: 'This is my 10th general election and, counting two byes, my twelfth Parliamentary. And it was the most tedious, apathetic, uninteresting and, I think, worst organised of them all.'[21] Gaitskell ranked causes of defeat as the economy, dissension and organisation.[22] Wilson's report on the party echoed this, but Attlee felt that the Conservatives had won because 'they had taken over as their own policies that which Labour had preached and practised from 1945 on.' In fact, the tax cuts and business incentive policies of the Butler election Budget, the general trend away from regulation of the economy and the emphasis on selective tax reforms to aid particular sectors, like cotton, were actually moving the political economy of the UK down a very different road after 1951 than Gaitskell would have taken if he had remained Chancellor.

Full employment had been maintained and there had been no major assault on the nationalised industries, but even here the electoral impact was difficult to judge. Would an increase in the level of unemployment in traditional heavy industries, for example, have done anything more than fulfil Crossman's fear that in 1955 there would be another plurality of Labour votes but minority of seats?[23] The general election of 1955 illustrated the beginning of substantial shifts in the political, social and economic structure of Britain. These were dimly perceived by the politicians of the time; Morgan Phillips, the general secretary, spoke in his election report of Tory prosperity. Tony Benn saw that people in his Bristol East seat were 'better off and the end of most shortages has enabled rationing to be ended on everything but coal. There has been no unemployment. A family in a council house with a TV set and a car or motorcycle-combination on hire purchase had few reasons for a change of government.'[24] The affluent society, and the profound political challenge this presented to the Labour Party, was arriving.

It also presented a generational challenge. The Conservatives had changed leader immediately before the election and in so doing had switched generations. The prelude to the 1955 leadership contest had been long and often bitter. The general expectation before the 1955 election was that Morrison, after twenty years of service to the party, would step into office for a short time and then be superseded by a younger leader; the prospect of Bevan leading the Labour Party after the expulsion crisis of March and the parliamentary row of April 1955 was thought to be remote.

However, the possibility of winning the leadership concentrated Bevan's mind and although he was torn between the role of romantic rebel, the course favoured by his wife Jennie Lee, and respectable leader, the course favoured by most of the other Bevanites, he knew that if he was to stand a chance of winning the leadership he had to delay the contest until the memory of the expulsion crisis had receded.[25]

In the week after the election the expected leadership contest opened when Dalton launched 'Operation Avalanche'. Feeling tired and depressed at the prospect of another long period of opposition and desirous of finding ways to help his young friends, he resolved to 'break the log-jam of ancients on the Parliamentary Ctee'.[26] 'Operation Avalanche' was a typical piece of Dalton scheming; the letter he wrote declared, 'I myself have decided not to be a candidate for our Shadow Cabinet in the new Parliament and I hope that a number of my fellow veterans will decide likewise.'[27] He handed the letter to Desmond Donnelly to pass on to Crossman for leaking to the *Daily Mirror*.

It had been clear for some time that Attlee would retire, but it took considerable effort on behalf of his friends to persuade Gaitskell that he should run. At the height of the election campaign, Frank Pakenham predicted in the *News Chronicle* that Gaitskell would be the next leader of the Labour Party.[28] In June Roy Jenkins, at a private dinner, put the case for running 'with all the force' he could command.[29] But Gaitskell held on to the idea of a short Morrison leadership.

The Margate Conference and an emergency Budget in October were great opportunities for Gaitskell and beauty contests for the prospective candidates. Gaitskell clearly realised the need to distance himself from the image that the Bevanites had built of him as the hard-faced inquisitor who had tried to destroy Bevan. On 23 May, writing in *Daily Herald,* he stated that 'the central Socialist ideal is equality . . . a classless society – one in which the relations between all people are similar to those existing within one social class.' This was the precursor, during the election campaign, of his 'Why I am a socialist' speech at the Labour Party Conference at Margate.

The party assembled at the seaside on Monday 10 October, 'in an atmosphere of such utter and complete boredom as I cannot describe', according to Crossman.[30] On Tuesday afternoon, in what was supposed to be a private session with a report by Harold Wilson on party organisation, a row flared up about the attempt to expel Bevan from the party. Bill Webber, a Gaitskellite trade-unionist, denounced Wilson and the left for losing the Labour Party the election. Bevan responded by arguing that the electorate had not been offered a proper socialist alternative or a real campaign of socialist education.[31] 'It was a brilliant and spontaneous *tour de force* and as Nye returned to his seat he was nearly mobbed by the delegates.'[32] Gaitskell witnessed the explosion of support for Bevan in the hall as the delegates rushed to surround Nye. It was not so much that the party had been split again as that the distance between the two in their relationship with the party was made obvious. Later, Morrison replied in a quiet, modest speech stressing the achievements of the Labour governments of 1945–51 and holding the hall. Gaitskell confided to Leslie Hunter that he had greatly admired the speech and did not feel he could match it. His two main rivals for the leadership had dominated, in their different ways, the conference hall. The leader of the Labour Party was not elected by Conference but Gaitskell would hardly have been human, let alone a politician, if he had not felt the need to compete. But how to do it? His main speech to Conference was about the achievements of nationalised industries; it was full of statistics; it was, in short, one of his lectures. These could be effective, as the speech at the TUC in 1951 had shown, but he was no longer a Chancellor of the Exchequer, he no longer had to be quite so cautious in his presentation. However, it started ordinarily enough: the one short joke he allowed himself, among a welter of statistics, was that 'you need a calculating machine to work them out.' The audience laughed, and Gaitskell looked up from his pages of notes. He noticed Bevan with his friends at the back of the hall enjoying the joke.[33] Something in him switched a gear, he departed from his notes and for one of only half a dozen times in his career so far he spoke directly off the cuff about the need for greater equality and planning, and then explained:

> I am a socialist and have been for 30 years. I became a socialist quite candidly not so much because I was a passionate advocate of public ownership but because at a very early age I came to hate and loathe social injustice, because I disliked the class structure of our society, because I could not tolerate the indefensible differences of status and income which disfigure our society, because I hated poverty and squalor . . . rewards should not be, as they still are, dependent upon the accident of whether you happen to be born of wealthy parents or not . . . I am a socialist because I want to see fellowship, or if you prefer fraternity, while [preserving] the liberties we cherish. I want to see all this not only in our country but over the world as a whole. These to me are the socialist ideals. Nationalisation is a vital means, but it is only one of the means by which we can achieve these objects.[34]

Hunter saw Nye Bevan red-faced and furious at the back of the hall muttering, 'Sheer demagogy, sheer demagogy', as the delegates and the platform gave Hugh a one-minute-long ovation.[35] Summing up the week, Crossman felt that 'a considerable shift of power and change of constellation took place within the leadership . . . a new Centre is forming.'[36] Letting his personality come through at Margate, Gaitskell stunned many delegates with the power of his performance, opened many people's eyes to his character and consolidated his standing with a significant section of the constituency parties. But the PLP elected the leader, and it was the assault on Rab Butler in the House of Commons and Morrison's failure in the ensuing censure debate that counted for more than verbal pyrotechnics at Party Conference.

Soon after the Conservative government returned to power the balance-of-payments situation began deteriorating and the need for taking demand out of the economy became acute. It was clear that there would be a supplementary Budget reversing the tax cuts of the spring, and this was in fact introduced on 26 October with increases in purchase tax, profits tax and cuts in housing subsidies.

Gaitskell mustered his arguments for such a devastating political attack on Butler that it forced the Conservative Chancellor's removal from the Treasury. Hugh began to build up with a speech in Leytonstone saying that it was 'virtually certain' that Mr Butler was 'going to reverse the policy he adopted for the purpose of winning votes'. He went on: 'that kind of politics is unworthy of our country and unworthy of the Chancellor of the Exchequer himself. He cannot blame us if we say these things.' He said he feared the supplementary Budget would be the 'signal for the beginning of an onslaught on the welfare state'. When the measures were introduced in the Commons, Gaitskell's performance was reported by one MP to have been 'stupendous – it changed the whole atmosphere of House.' 'He made the speech of a lifetime from his party's point of view and well merited their vociferous applause.'[37] The April Budget, he said in the Commons, had not been intended to produce economic incentive but the incentive to vote Tory. The April Budget was 'a masterpeice of deception', and Butler behaved in a 'manner unworthy of his high office. He began in folly, he continued in deceit and has ended in reaction.'[38]

The *Observer* political diary recorded the 'Demise of Mr Butskell'. 'Mr Gaitskell has slain his alter ego in one of the more ferocious assaults of recent times.' It went on, 'there is a sense in which Mr Gaitskell's speech might have been composed by two people. The first part is by the man we all know – playful, ironic and admonitory. The second is in quite a different key – vituperative, angry and relentless. The impression that most people carried away was that he was determined not merely to wound but also to kill.' Gaitskell had been building up to this speech for months. The *Telegraph* felt that 'Mr Gaitskell transgressed the bounds of Parliamentary propriety when he accused Mr Butler yesterday of deceit.' The question, the *Observer* journalist asked himself, was why did he do it? 'When the PLP met after Mr Butler's speech there was not a man present who did not feel a surge of overweening jubilation.' For the first time the real passion behind Gaitskell and his palpable anger at the Budget came through: yet the ground had been carefully prepared. The key to the performance was the way in which his most powerful weapons worked together. His analytical mind delivered an intellectually devastating attack on Butler while his passion commanded the House of Commons and his genuine disgust at the auctioning of the election allowed the two to blend into an assault that finished off the Chancellor and galvanised the opposition. Moreover, it all took place before the audience that was about to elect a new leader of the Labour Party.

On 2 November he wrote in the *Daily Herald*: 'I am quite unrepentant. Our arguments are sound: our accusations justified to the hilt. Their record over these last six months is disgraceful. There is only one thing to be done. Hit that record hard and go on hitting.' He continued to press home his case in broadcasts, in the press and through the debate on the Finance Bill. The Gaitskellite team was complemented by Harold Wilson, and produced 'the first effective fighting Opposition we've known for a long time'.[39]

Immediately after the general election Gaitskell had indicated that he would not oppose Morrison in the leadership race. He then said that he would not do so if there was any chance of Bevan winning by a split right-wing vote. As Bevan's prospects seemed to pale, his supporters urged on him the need to dish Bevan by settling the leadership question once and for all, not allowing it to drag on through a stop-gap Morrison leadership. Many swung behind Gaitskell in the debates on the Finance Bill, but Patrick Gordon Walker, a close associate of Morrison, who had initially favoured a short leadership by Morrison followed by Gaitksell, changed his attitude at the Margate Conference: 'I . . . found a strong trend amongst MPs in Hugh's favour. (1) HM would be too old to lead the Party. (2) The Bevanites would back HM. (3) We should settle the leadership once and for all.' Finally, in early November, Gaitskell decided to run against Morrison and arranged to lunch with him and tell him that he would withdraw his support. He dreaded the occasion but told Roy Jenkins that it had gone 'remarkably well'. Morrison appeared not to take the idea seriously and, almost patting him on the head, said, 'Of course, my boy, you go ahead if you want to, you'll be out on the first ballot.'[40]

Speculation now mounted on Attlee's future. Dalton had excluded Attlee from his appeal for older members to stand down but Attlee was ready to retire and, at the first Shadow Cabinet meeting and the first PLP meeting after the election, he offered to resign. Bevan had sought to delay the leadership race, and Nye was the first and most vocal voice to call on Attlee to stay on, while Morrison was silent. Attlee agreed to stay and recorded in his diary that night, 'This is almost certainly the end of Morrison.'[41] The delay was bad for Morrison because his age counted against him and he therefore needed a quick election before the effects of the generational changes caused by the Dalton letter could be felt. The initially delayed departure of Attlee was further put off because the parliamentary session was extended. In August 1955 Attlee, now aged seventy-two, had a stroke and in September in an interview with Hugh Cudlipp, just before the Party Conference, he restated his desire to retire and specified that his successor should be neither Morrison nor Bevan by indicating that he did not want a 'Victorian, or a futile left-winger'.[42] By November speculation was almost out of control.

Both Gaitskell and Morrison did well at the Margate Conference of 1955 but more importantly Gaitskell was able to score heavily in the parliamentary debates on the Finance Bill which repudiated much of the giveaway Budget that had preceded the election.[43] As the Labour leader was elected solely by the Parliamentary Labour Party at this time, this success and the destruction of Butskellism counted for more than his 'Why I'm a socialist?' speech at the Conference. As Wilfred Feinburgh, writing in the *New Statesman*, had put it before the election: 'After Hugh Gaitskell had replied to Butler there remained little to be said about the Budget. Gaitskell did more than disturb the equanimity of the Chancellor, which is in itself a feat: he also disposed of Butskellism.'[44] But, overall, it remained a confused and fluid situation.

Leadership races have since become a standard part of British politics, but in the 1950s they were more of a novelty. Eden had simply emerged as Churchill's successor as Prime Minister some months before and the Labour Party had not had a contest for twenty years. With the electorate comprising the rather fickle PLP, the jockeying for position was clearly a delicate matter. The great fear for the right was that Bevan would slip into the job if Gaitskell and

Morrison opposed each other and split the centre and right vote. Gaitskell wanted to be sure that he would not 'upset the applecart' by running, but had to balance his well-developed sense of loyalty to Morrison with his own political career. People run for the office of leader from a number of different motivations. It is an important way of putting a marker down for the future, as Morrison seemed to be saying to him at their lunch: That's fine – you cut your teeth this time, and who knows about the future. Hugh consulted with his friends. The idea of a Morrison caretaker leadership followed by Hugh had certain problems. It would make Morrison essentially a lame-duck leader and there would then be an extended leadership campaign. The pressure to settle the leadership question once and for all favoured Gaitskell's candidature.

On 11 December 1955, Gordon Walker recorded in his diary, 'I am feeling very miserable because I have decided to back Gaitskell against Morrison for the leadership of the party. I dearly love Herbert and he can never understand. He will regard me simply as a turncoat, someone who has jumped on the bandwagon.'[45] Walker was adamant that 'the party must renew its leadership. The men of 50 must take over – and we must absolutely and evidently finish Bevan.'

According to Attlee's biographer the old leader was not particularly close to or keen on Gaitskell and would perhaps have preferred Bevan if he had played more effectively on the team.[46] But Attlee certainly did not want Herbert Morrison and as loyalty was the virtue he favoured most he was perhaps moderately in favour of the arch-loyalist Gaitskell. Attlee clearly felt that Gaitskell would win. All the signs before the actual election were in Gaitskell's favour. Perhaps the most significant challenge was the plan originally favoured by Dalton to have Jim Griffiths, himself a veteran MP and former Colonial Secretary, elected as a stop-gap leader.[47] Dalton became disillusioned with this option when it became clear that Griffiths was himself too old and that Gaitskell had a chance of winning in his own right first time.[48] Jay identified in December 1955 a landslide in favour of Gaitskell in the Parliamentary Party, because of his performance in the House.[49] Attlee resigned on 7 December sure that the Labour Party was in good heart and that his resignation would unleash no new divisions.[50] With a keen group of supporters ranging from young members to the wily old Dalton, Gaitskell was in a commanding position. It is not so much that Gaitskell did not overtly campaign as that he did not need to.

Gaitskell seems to have been a little ambivalent about his success or failure:[51] he knew that if he failed this time he would still be in the running in the future, especially if Morrison was to win, but he was told throughout by Jay that after the finance debate it was in the bag, so he could afford the luxury of a laid-back attitude. As a professional politician he knew he had to stand and, despite this hint of ambivalence, he of course wanted to win. The election campaign had only one twist and it was a twist that made his discussion not to campaign and intrigue openly seem highly astute.

Back in February 1954 a political correspondent on the *Observer* had written that a group of Bevanites unhappy with Attlee's leadership had 'suggested that Mr Bevan should approach Mr Morrison with the idea of forming an unholy alliance to oust Mr Attlee from the leadership. Once again Mr Bevan refused and there were mutterings off stage that certain people were dragging their feet.'[52] The idea was now reintroduced by Dick Stokes and other Morrison supporters. Morrison and Bevan met in the smoking-room of the House of Commons for a drink on 3 November: 'for which, [Brown] thinks Bevan paid! Donnelly next morning on the phone confirmed this!'[53] On the Thursday afternoon, with nominations due to close the next day, Bevan announced he would withdraw if Gaitskell agreed to do the same, giving Morrison a free ride and presumably Bevan the deputy leadership.

As Gordon Walker put it, 'It looked like a shady deal. This did much to put my heart at ease about supporting Hugh.'[54] Not even Foot could defend the idea either in *Tribune* or in his biography of Bevan. Douglas Jay, Gaitskell's unofficial (non-)campaign manager, initially thought it was a very clever move but opinion turned against such a cynical manoeuvre. The alliance between the old and bitter rivals achieved nothing, except perhaps a slight increase in Gaitskell's support. The end result was a substantial victory for Gaitskell, who won an absolute majority on the first ballot: Gaitskell 157, Bevan 70, Morrison 40. Crossman, at a by-election in Torquay, felt that 'every Labour person now feels we have a Leader and can say who the next Prime Minister will be and they all feel this makes a difference.'

The celebrations were played down by Gaitskell as he attempted to keep Morrison as deputy leader, but Morrison refused and resigned. This, combined with earlier resignations, meant that between May and December 1955 Attlee, Morrison, Dalton, Chuter Ede, Manny Shinwell, W. Glenvil Hall, Frank Soskice and William

Whiteley had all disappeared from the Shadow Cabinet.[55] The period also saw the final break-up of the Bevanites, Crossman, Castle and Wilson being furious with Bevan for his intrigues with Morrison. The leadership election ended the Bevanite schism, marked the change of generation and provided the basis for a period of relative calm and unity within Labour ranks as the Conservative Party faced its profoundest crisis since taking office in 1951, the Suez invasion. In the new year the deputy leadership was won by Jim Griffiths. Dalton recorded in his diary: 'I feel a little like a Creator who rested and beheld his handiwork after much hard labour and saw that it was good. Vacancies due to Attlee's and Morrison's departure from Shadow Cabinet filled by Tom Fraser and Kenneth Younger. Hugh Gaitskell leader, Jim Griffiths wonderfully loyal Deputy, and other younger people on the Shadow Cabinet, of which the average age is now fifty-two – younger than that of Tory Cabinet.'[56]

Party unity was ensured by an accommodation between Bevan and Gaitskell during 1955–6 which culminated in the Gaitskell-Bevan axis of 1957–9. This unity at the top of the Labour Party was generally reflected, in the movement as a whole, in the honeymoon period after the leadership election. However, vocal criticism of party policy, from the inside and outside of the Labour Party itself, continued in the late 1950s through 'Victory for Socialism', a revival of Bevanism, and through the Campaign for Nuclear Disarmament. Thus at no time in the 1950s was the party lacking some form of left-wing organisation which was more or less hostile to Gaitskell and the Gaitskellites.

In winning the leadership Gaitskell reaped harvests from his tough political life since the fall of the Attlee government. The trade-union-sponsored MPs were 'behind him almost to a man'.[57] Of the ninety-five sponsored MPs, thirty-four came from Sam Watson's miners, fourteen from Arthur Deakin's Transport Workers and five from Tom Williamson's General Workers, providing just under a third of his final vote. The right was split but many, especially younger members, supported him; and the centre from which Morrison might once have hoped to gain support had crumbled.

Those who had fought the Bevanites with him sent in their congratulations that the long struggle for the leadership had been victorious, Woodrow Wyatt writing that through 'your steadfastness and courage . . . you have been a rock in moments of despair. Without you the Parliamentary Party would have jumped off the deep end as well as the rank and file.'[58] The ex-Bevanites also emerged, Crossman writing: 'I am *unqualifiedly* glad that you are now the Leader. I am also even gladder that there is now no fence with each of us on his own side. Personally – and because I like Dora very much – it is nice to feel we can be friends again. But I want you also to know that I am not a bandwagon kind of person. My value to the party, so far as I have one, is as an awkward independent ideas man.' To which Gaitskell replied, 'Nobody in their senses could possible accuse you of jumping *on* to bandwagons. On the contrary I could make out something of a case against you for jumping off rather than on, at some moments during the last 10 years!'[59] Bevan himself took longer fully to accept the decision. As Morrison was walking out after the vote, Gaitskell turned to Nye and said, 'Nye, we haven't got on in the past, but if you accept this vote, as I would have had to accept it if it had gone the other way, I promise you I will not be outdone in generosity.' Bevan replied with congratulations and the hope of higher office before withdrawing to his farm at Ashbridge to brood. 'Gaitskell and Gaitskellism offended against everything in his spirit and vision', according to Foot.[60] As for Gaitskell himself, he gave much of the credit for his elevation to Bevan: 'The leadership came my way so early because Bevan threw it at me by his behaviour. Ask yourself about the Labour Party now – if not me then who? Qualities? Perfectly ordinary ones – intelligence, hard work, capacity for getting on easily with people and some moral courage. Of course there are great weaknesses – don't I know! But the whole subject is boring.'[61]

Gaitskell was the youngest party leader of the century and had only entered the House ten years before. Attlee led the party for twenty years so there was every chance that he would lead the party into the 1960s and lead the country before long. Bowra wrote from Oxford, 'Look after your health and drive Sir Antony [*sic*] to a loony bin as soon as you can before he drives everyone else.' His new friend, Ann Fleming, wrote, 'If we have to have a Labour Party, it is as well you should lead it.'[62]

10

Hinterlands

We spoke of ethics and [G. E.] Moore. Hugh says to love, and to be loved, is much the biggest thing in the world.

Hugh Dalton, 1952

The Platitude From Outer Space – that's Brother Nigel. He'll end up in the Cabinet one day, make no mistake.

Jimmy Porter, *Look Back in Anger*, 1956

A. J. P. Taylor once argued that the Second World War did not end until 1956. In Britain, symbolically at least, it did not end until ration books were withdrawn in 1954. The Conservative Party's victory in the 1955 general election was widely seen as an indication that prosperity was beginning to be felt. The disruption of people's lives by the massive readjustment to peace and austerity of the late 1940s and early 1950s was giving way to a more settled pattern of life and experience. There was a fleeting moment after the Coronation of Queen Elizabeth II when people even spoke of a new Elizabethan Age: 'We felt we were on the crest of everything going right, with a young Queen looking to the future, not looking back. The feel of it was real, but in the end it lacked substance.'[1] Yet this establishment Elizabethanism was not to be the spirit of the age. Against it came the first flushes of rebellion: 'A new generation of novelists, poets and playwrights were beginning to challenge the metropolitan and Oxbridge establishment, while a rising group of self-consciously provincial intellectuals were beginning to make a more critical assessment of the nation's cultural life.'[2] Much of the social revolution which was associated with the 1960s had deep roots in the beginnings of the 'age of affluence' in the 1950s.

'Youth' broke into the national consciousness with the Teddy boys spreading out of the slums of South London to become a national phenomenon; and the newspapers became obsessed by the activities of the 'Chelsea set'. This new mood was also reflected in various cultural styles and fads. Art schools flourished, the jazz of the twenties was much in vogue with the middle class and there were the first stirrings of the post-war generation of designers and artists. In November 1955, a month before Hugh was elected leader, Mary Quant and Alexander Plunkett-Green opened the first Bazaar in the King's Road:

> The following year, a 19-year-old grocer's son, John Stephen, came down from Glasgow to open his first clothes shop for teenagers, moving shortly afterwards to Carnaby Street in Soho. And, on a wider front, nothing more clearly indicated the influence of this blossoming youthful obsession with fashion than the speed with which, in 1957, the waistless, Twenties-style Sack dress and the new knee-length 'short skirt' were able to sweep away the last remnants of the New Look.[3]

1956 was the year of the 'Angry Young Men', epitomised by Jimmy Porter in John Osborne's *Look Back in Anger*. It was also the year of *Rock around the Clock* and the skiffle craze. Contradicting Larkin's view that sexual intercourse began in 1963, Kenneth Tynan's review of *Look Back in Anger* 'had singled out Jimmy Porter's "casual promiscuity" as one of the ways in which he was typical of Britain's post-war youth':

> Of all sections of society, the progressive intellectuals gave the 'sexual revolution' and the 'New Morality' the most fervent welcome. As they proclaimed the need for a new 'honesty' and 'realism', and the need for 'emancipation' from 'Victorian, bourgeois morality', they believed that, in the wake of contraception and feminine emancipation, a new attitude to sex was becoming possible.[4]

In popular music, art and literature and in social attitudes new generations and new ideas were beginning to break through the grey mist of post-war austerity. Affluence brought new cultural and social constructions that politicians had to try to deal with. But politicians are also people and, as the new leader of the Labour Party began the search for a new political direction for the Labour Party in response to the new society it faced, so Gaitskell the man lived through the changes and these changes were in turn reflected in his own life.

Politically, the election of the new leader gave the Labour Party a chance to stress the new generation coming to prominence in its own leadership and to contrast this with the decidedly ageing Conservative Party. Gaitskell tried to articulate the change in generations that had taken place in his first speech as leader, warning of the dangers of stale slogans for the Labour Party and urging the need for fresh thinking.[5] He followed this in his first broadcast as leader by stating that he and most people in the Labour Party regarded nationalisation as a means to an end and not an end in itself. He told a meeting in Liverpool shortly afterwards that nationalisation was not the only form of public ownership.[6]

It was clear that a new generation of Labour leadership was intent on moving the agenda forward. Tony Crosland and others produced an analysis of post-war capitalism as daring and 'new' as any of the social or artistic features of the changing times. The emerging revisionist analysis set out to push Labour away from its obsession with ownership and towards a coherent response to post-war affluence.

As Gaitskell prepared to face his first parliamentary session as leader he told Robert Carvel that the Labour Party was going to offer vigorous opposition throughout the session; the policy would be one of attack.[7] In his first month as leader he assailed the government on Cyprus, on 'the lunacy' of Butler's financial policy and on the Middle-Eastern policy. The press was generally supportive, the *Guardian* for instance, saying: 'It is a good measure for a month's leadership. Mr Gaitskell, it is plain, intends to make things "whizz" as the boy said about the fireworks. He has vigour, courage, and pugnacity.'[8]

The role of leader raised both Gaitskell's profile and the professional demands on his time. The political world was Gaitskell's chosen world, but it never entirely defined him. Denis Healey's friends used to tell him that his problem was the opposite of that of a politician like Mrs Thatcher: he had too much hinterland.[9] Gaitskell did not have too much. There was sufficient drive to get him to the very top, a drive he shared with Thatcher but which was lacking in Healey, but he did not have Thatcher's lack of personal or intellectual breath. He had his hinterland and it mattered to him a great deal. There were at least four distinct areas of his personal life that allowed him a range of experience away from the daily drudgery of politics; each provided protection and different kinds of rewards; each was affected differently by his election as leader.

The first and most important part of his private life was represented by the bricks and mortar of Number 18 Frognal Gardens. Gaitskell's immediate family – Dora, his daughters Julia and Cressida, and his mother and stepfather who shared the house – were the first refuge he sought from politics. Here was a settled extended family life that Hugh could dip into when the time allowed; it was a world in which he could completely relax. He and Dora regularly and successfully entertained. They gave parties – often with dancing – to a wide range of different people. On these occasions, outsiders were struck by the difference between his public and private personas. Barbara Castle has described how she discovered the private nature of her bitter political opponent:

> I also found he could be a jolly man in private life. I came across this facet of him by accident when I was invited by one of Hugh's coterie to a social evening in his house. I went out of curiosity and found Hugh holding court with relaxed boyishness among his friends, perched on the edge of the kitchen table, cracking jokes.[10]

Frognal also meant his garden. He had developed an interest in growing vegetables, out of necessity, in the austere days after the war. Although he had little time for it, it remained an interest, which he continued when he had the chance. His daughter Julia still has the certificate he received as a president of the Tree Growers' Association.[11]

Within the orbit of Frognal Gardens, we should place the second part of the hinterland: the private pursuits of music, reading and entertaining. He was fairly conventional for his time and class in his reading and listening habits, but a little more modern in his tastes than most. He would relax at the end of a day with a whisky, a book and a record of a female jazz vocalist, perhaps Ella Fitzgerald or Billie Holliday. The book might be poetry, perhaps Shakespeare's *Sonnets* or Yeats, or maybe a modern novel. He also liked Trollope and Wodehouse. Books were important to him. Williams recounts that 'there was great excitement when he found a copy of Meredith's sonnet sequence *Modern Love* in Norman's Hampstead secondhand bookshop; in 1959, he wrote quite a long comment on an analysis of it by an Oxford undergraduate friend of Julia's.'[12]

The Gaitskells were also involved, in a minor way, in the arts having helped to found a small gallery for the sale of reproductions.[13] The Rosses, friends from Bloomsbury in the 1930s – Gaitskell met Dora while working on Amyas Ross's election campaign in Marylebone – started the business in Soho Square selling imported prints. The Gaitskells invested at the outset, primarily to help their friends, and the business boomed.[14] Hugh liked paintings, being knowledgeable but not an expert, and collected a little, giving a friend a Matisse, enjoying the work of Van Gogh, Paul Klee and Picasso. He also bought new works. In the summer of 1961 he was strolling through an open-air exhibition on the edge of Hampstead Heath and spotted three pieces that he liked. Maurice Mann, the artist, brought them to Frognal Gardens and Gaitskell wrote out a cheque. The three paintings were a nude, a still life and a portrait of a Parisian girl. The nude turned out to be Lady Coldstream, the wife of Sir William Coldstream, head of the Slade art school. When the papers asked her what she thought of hanging in the hallway of the leader of the opposition, she told them, 'I don't really mind.'[15] Despite buying and investing, painting does not seem to have had the same fascination for Hugh as poetry or jazz.

The rediscovered traditional jazz of the 1920s had been imported into Britain during the war by US troops. It became a predominantly middle-class craze in the post-war years, established in a 'number of West End clubs, suburban pubs and provincial dance halls':

> the traditional jazz cult . . . also attracted a significant number of somewhat self-consciously unconventional former public schoolboys, such as the Etonian Humphrey Lyttelton and George Melly . . . [the traditional jazz fans had a] reverence for a particular Romantic image of America.[16]

Though perhaps not a full blown 'cultist' because of his passion for dancing, Hugh was one of these 'unconventional' former public schoolboys. One Saturday morning in 1956 he set out on a record-buying expedition with Cressida, his fourteen-year-old younger daughter, to HMV on Oxford Street. The record store was crowded with shoppers and Gaitskell had trouble getting anyone to help him. Eventually a young woman found him a cubicle so that he could listen to the records he had chosen, Cressida wandered off and the leader of the opposition began to dance 'to the rhythm'. The sound-proof cubicles had glass doors and it was not long before he was recognised. The door was opened and Elaine Burton, the Labour MP for Coventry, surprised him dancing on his own. 'She said, "I must tell you what the girl has just said to us. She said, 'Do you know, I believe the Chancellor of the Exchequer is next door.'"'[17]

Hugh was one of those enthusiasts who like to listen to their own records at other people's parties. There were shades here of that urge to improve people that Elizabeth Pakenham had remarked on while they were at Oxford. Ann Fleming once invited him to a small

233

dance with a live band. Hugh turned up with his favourite recordings under his arm and the band had to be hastily 'smuggled out of sight'.[18] George Murray approved of his taste and asked Hugh to bring his records for the annual constituency garden parties.[19] He was not unusual in carrying his music with him. Susan Crosland recalls a night at Tony's flat when Kingsley Amis arrived armed with his favourite jazz records in a special black case. Susan's first husband proceeded to get into a 'violent altercation' with Amis over whether Coleman Hawkins or Lester Young was the superior tenor saxophonist and the evening ended badly.[20] Thus Gaitskell was not alone in his seriousness about jazz or his desire to educate people about its quality.

Gaitskell kept his life neatly ordered in emotional and intellectual compartments and thus had the enviable ability to relax completely and become absorbed in whatever he was doing. One part of Gaitskell enjoyed life and wanted to have fun – that was the part that was caught dancing that Saturday morning. But there had been precious little fun for him in the first half of the 1950s. Dora complained that she actually saw less of him than when he had been in government.

Gaitskell was a domesticated man, as this tale from the *Yorkshire Post* illustrates:

> The tap was running, the good hot water was flowing over the stack of plates ready for treatment. One by one the man in shirt sleeves took them up, dipped them first in the bowl of soapy water and then under the tap and placed them carefully in the rack not without having made sure, by holding them against the light, that they were really clean and sparkling . . . Then at last the model house worker put on his coat, surveyed the scene and withdrew. The Minister of Fuel and Power had finished the washing up.[21]

But it was Dora who ran the home. The centre of their house was the large kitchen with a central dining table, Dora's desk and sewing basket. This small, dark-haired, fiercely loyal woman worked hard to maintain the house and bring up Cressida and Julia. However, there was a great deal more to Dora than simply a quiescent political wife and 'homemaker'.

She had worked in publishing before the war, but once Hugh was in the House of Commons she devoted herself to being a political wife. She 'dwindled into a wife' before growing again after his death and pursuing an active political career through the United Nations and in the House of Lords. Dora took great pride in the fact that she had joined the Labour Party at the age of sixteen, and she had a passionate interest and engagement with politics. As she said in 1958: 'I have always been a socialist. Even at school I used to join Labour meetings. For me it seemed a perfectly natural thing to do.'[22]

Dora sometimes managed to accompany him on his 'political tours' – public relations exercises that became increasingly popular as the 1950s progressed. These illustrated both her desire to spend as much time as practically possible with him and her own perception of the political role of a wife. As she explained: 'That's the point of going round the country with my husband. It's a chance to answer back, to argue. And to be together.' As a rule she enjoyed being with Hugh when he made a big speech, 'I have a sort of sentimental theory that there's a sort of telepathic communication between husbands and wives on these occasions – and that the wife can give the man additional strength. It's not rational I know.'[23] Dora frequently canvassed with Hugh in South Leeds, as well as taking part in all the mundane activity that keeps political parties going, from licking envelopes to opening bazaars.

The fierceness of her loyalty to Hugh often made her appear – to his political opponents – the key figure pushing him down particular factionalist roads. In public she 'would bridle when a hostile question was flung at her husband'[24] and during a meeting in Nottingham she actually stormed off the platform and challenged a group of communist hecklers, giving them a dressing down. One of them, Geoffrey Staniforth, responded by telling her that they were the communist part of the Labour Party, to which Dora responded: 'You are nothing to do with us. Labour is a democratic socialist party.'[25] In private she would challenge his critics and was much more conscious of who were and were not his political friends. Of the two, Dora was if anything the more factional. Richard Crossman, who was fond of her, acknowledged this trait in her character.

> We took Dora Gaitskell down by car to the Coventry annual bazaar on Friday and heard a splendid lot of gossip. Dora's line is that she doesn't influence Hugh about politics in any way, though she has very strong views of her own. She certainly does, particularly about people, whose failings, whether real or imaginary, she sees with great clarity.[26]

Dora herself admitted that she found it difficult to combine friendships and politics, but:

I am not one of these women who refuses to speak to anyone who disagrees with her husband. If you never spoke to people who disagreed with you politically, there would be a terrible silence on many occasions. I always like to wade in and have a jolly good argument. And I do. Then I feel better.[27]

This willingness to take on Gaitskell's critics was characteristic of her approach. When Vicky did a particularly unflattering cartoon, Dora buttonholed him at Conference and gave him a tongue-lashing for his lack of respect. When the journalist Henry Fairlie wrote that Gaitskell hated Macmillan, Dora rebuked him: 'Not true, not true,' she said, 'you should not have written it.' Henry Fairlie couldn't get a word in in his own defence.[28]

When Gaitskell became Chancellor, Dora greeted the increase in their public profile with some trepidation: 'I am not a public woman and I'm terrified of opening bazaars. I can talk and write but when I have to speak in public I just seem to dry up.'[29] However, as the years went on she made more and more public appearances, gradually gaining in confidence. She made her first full-blown public speech in June 1958, though she had frequently made the odd polite remark at a meeting before this. She told a conference of 800 women from forty-one East Midlands constituencies that planning was essential to prosperity, and she went on: 'I don't make a practice of public speaking for two reasons – one is that I have very little time to learn and the other is that I am afraid of becoming a tape recorder for my husband – and giving a poor carbon copy of his speeches'.[30] But she also made some good political points on this and other occasions. In this speech she stated: 'In this complex economy of ours we say that planning is the only thing if we want more prosperity, fair shares and greater equality. One of the good things done by the Labour Government was to make inequality a word that the Tories are afraid to use.'[31] A year later she was pleading for purchase tax relief on items that made housework easy and attacking Tory Budgets: 'Up to now, in Tory Budgets, the Chancellor has usually given away a few things in one Budget, waited a few months then taken them back.'[32]

Though she actively disliked public speaking, she forced herself to become better at it. When Hugh lost his voice, Dora would give the speech.[33] When the press needed an interview for a piece on politicians' wives, Dora would give the interview and generally made a good impression. She was a rather formidable women, who could

1 The 'very proper' Hugh in a studio portrait and (2) his schoolfriend
John Betjeman in the woodwork room at the Dragon

3 A thespian Dragon – Hugh, second from back row, fourth from the right,
in a school production of *The Merchant of Venice*

The Big Five in the Labour Government of 1945–51 and the two leaders of the next generation. 4 *From left to right:* Ernest Bevin, Foreign Secretary, Clement Attlee, PM, and Herbert Morrison, Home Secretary. 5 Nye Bevan, Minister of Health, with Hugh Dalton, the Chancellor and Gaitskell's mentor. 6 Stafford Cripps who succeeded Dalton as Chancellor and who was in turn replaced by Gaitskell

Power. 7 The National Coal Board is launched in January 1947. Manny Shinwell, Gaitskell's first ministerial boss at Fuel and Power, is on the left. 8 Against bitter opposition, electricity is nationalised and Gaitskell makes a point of celebrating an extension of electricity supply in Leeds in 1948. 9 Stepping out of the Treasury, Gaitskell presents the Gladstone box on the day of his one and only budget

The leadership election. 10 'Have a go if you like, my boy' – Morrison shrugs off Gaitskell's challenge. 11 'Neither an Edwardian nor a futile left-winger, so it had better be you': Gaitskell with Attlee. 12 'How many votes do you need?' Arthur Deakin, head of the TGWU and Hugh's key backer. 13 'He threw the leadership at me' – Hugh's judgment on beating Nye for the leadership

The Hampstead Set on the march: 14 Uniformed Denis Healey and Roy Jenkins. 15 Woodrow Wyatt as Labour MP for Birmingham, Aston. 16 The first Gaitskellite: Douglas Jay. 17 Tony Crosland, the intellectual power house of revisionism and the Hampstead Set

18 The Gaitskell family in 1959, just after the General Election was announced

19 Mr and Mrs Ian Fleming. Ann Fleming was previously married to the 2nd Viscount Rothermere

'Doing the Folks' Gaitskell-style. 20 At Lymington in 1961: Hugh comes second in the sack race but wins in the egg and spoon; (21) with his Trade Union backers, the miners in 1957 and (22) with Leeds constituents.

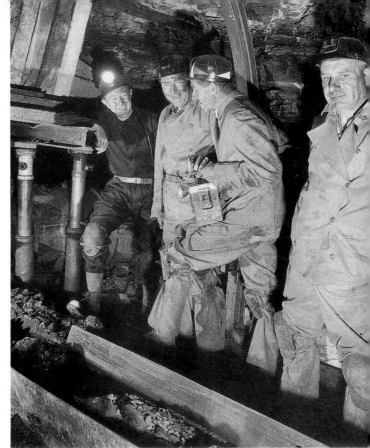

A life-long passion for dancing. 23 Gaitskell spins with a keen-looking Margaret Herbison, 1957 Party Chairman; (24) a contented-looking Lady Korsah, wife of the Chief Justice in Ghana and (25) a rather more reluctant partner, 1959 Party Chairman, Barbara Castle

hold her own in any situation. While staying with the royal family in 1951 Dora had joked with the King. 'He said to her at one point, "I wonder what he has got in his box for us? I hope it will not be terrible." Dora replied, "I don't suppose it will be as bad as all that. After all he is rather right wing." This the king thought a tremendous joke.'[34]

However, there were strict limits to the extent to which she would allow the family to be sacrificed to the party. For instance, not accompanying Hugh on one occasion in 1961 for an important speech because 'Cressida has a vital exam at the end of November and I feel she really does need a bit more attention. She may be 18, but that doesn't mean she doesn't require some attention from her mother. At times like this I feel rather torn.'[35] The amount of time Hugh himself had to spend with Cressida and Julia was always limited by the pressures of work. What was lodged firmly in Julia's memory was the holidays, often in Pembrokeshire or Dorset, and later in France, Italy or Yugoslavia. These provided precious opportunities for Gaitskell to relax with the family and spend time with his growing daughters. Julia remembers the holidays as very special occasions, and also recalls being taken to a matinée and an evening production of Shakespeare at Stratford upon Avon.[36] But these moments are memorable partly because Gaitskell was so often absent working.

It was the combination of protecting the pleasant domestic world of Frognal Gardens and being a pugnacious political supporter that made Dora such a vital part of Hugh's life. She defended their space, and the time that he allowed for their marriage, from intrusion. When he was made Chancellor they faced the choice of taking 11 Downing Street as their home. In a revealing interview, one of her first, she talked to Maurice Wiltshire from the *Daily Mail* about the decision to stay in their own house:

> It would have been an awful upheaval. For a long time I thought it would be compulsory and I dreaded it. I have only been there twice to tea with Isobel Cripps and Ruth Dalton, but I never considered the place from the viewpoint of having to live there ourselves. I asked Isobel Cripps what they gave you when you moved into No. 11. She told me the Crown supplied plate, linen, silver and heating but no staff except for the public rooms. I was horrified, I could see it would be expensive . . . I've only got a little Swiss girl and a weekly help.[37]

Dora was thus a private champion who gradually developed a

public role by necessity rather than choice. She had a significant dialogue with Hugh on politics – particularly when it came to personalities. As he reached the very top of the party and the factionalism and the cycle of meetings increased, Dora's role as close political associate, antenna and truculent supporter was correspondingly enhanced, whilst her role as a partner, perhaps, diminished.

The third section of the hinterland comprised his friends. These came in two varieties: a strong set of old friends from the pre-war life in Oxford and Bloomsbury, and some others who were mainly outside politics and offered a relief from it. The second set were political friends and these became increasingly the rising stars of the revisionist wing of the Labour Party: Tony Crosland, Roy Jenkins and Woodrow Wyatt. There were also already established friendships with fellow politicians like Douglas Jay, Patrick Gordon Walker and Frank Longford. Finally, especially after he became leader, there were diplomatic and press contacts who were congenial enough to cross over into friendship.

The most important group was the Hampstead Set, sometimes later called the Frognal Set. This comprised the mostly younger MPs who were working out the revisionist response to the changes brought about by the war, and slightly older political supporters like Jay. The relationship extended beyond politics and the group shared, and enjoyed, a vigorous social life. As John Vaizey recalled:

> It was this social life, which was in all truth not at all grand, centred on [Gaitskell's] house in Frognal, a smart part of Hampstead – itself rising in the social scale throughout the 1950s – that led to charges that he was the centre of a coterie of exclusive, smart and supercilious young men. As a description of the usually tiresome Tony Crosland and the Roy Jenkins who had not yet discovered duchesses and was barely beyond plonk, let alone into claret, this was ludicrously inapt.[38]

Inapt or not, the charge of cliquishness troubled Gaitkskell's old champion Dalton. For Gaitskell the concept of leadership was not simply to reconcile the opposing sides but to educate the Labour Party, by force of argument. Dalton in the last years of his life warned Gaitskell against too close an association with a particular group in the party, even if such a group was necessary to a leader who was trying to command from the front, and urged him to widen his contacts with the back benches.[39]

At the centre of the Hampstead Set were Roy Jenkins and Tony

Crosland. Jenkins began as an Attlee man and did not get to know Gaitskell until after the Attlee government had fallen – though he supported him as Chancellor and sided with him against Bevan when the resignations came.[40] While Jenkins progressed from admirer to colleague to friend, in the course of 1951–3, Crosland was already well established in the leader's affections.

Dalton had brought them together and Gaitskell took immense care in encouraging Crosland in his writing and in his political career. In a way he became Crosland's champion, just as Dalton had previously been his. When Harold Lever mildly teased Crosland on his performance in a Budget debate – 'my Honourable Friend is a typical academic: if the grandfather clock happened to strike midnight on a sunny afternoon, he would put out the cat, put on his pyjamas and go to bed' – Crosland laughed it off, but Gaitskell, running into Lever, burst out, 'That was heinous what you did to Tony.'[41] Later, after Crosland had ill-advisedly abandoned his South Gloucestershire seat for what Dalton and others felt to be a better bet in Southampton, and ended up losing, Hugh worked hard to get Tony back into the House. When Kenneth Younger, the MP for Grimsby and a colleague of Gaitskell's from the Attlee government, came to see the leader to tell him he did not intend to stand again, 'Gaitskell devoted exactly one sentence to expressing regret before asking Younger whether he thought the seat could be won by Tony Crosland.' It was an uncharacteristically insensitive response from Gaitskell, but also an illustration of what Tony meant to him:

> The two men admired, loved and maddened one another. The bonds between them were far stronger than mutual censure. They shared what might be called an egalitarian attitude to people, their manner unaffected by someone's position . . . Both men threw themselves into their work. Both had a large capacity for enjoyment. Both viewed power as a vehicle for putting principles into practice, not as an end in itself. The main and continuing contention between them was Tony's concern that Hugh was insufficiently radical for a left-wing leader.[42]

Roy Jenkins and Tony Crosland were the closest to the leader among the younger Labour MPs, but the nature of their relations with him differed slightly. In Jenkins's own judgement, Gaitskell liked him because he had so many interests outside politics.[43] For Crosland the relationship was more about politics, but mostly about mutual admiration. In both cases, bonds of friendship held even in times of disagreement, and this was in part due to Hugh's recurring desire to defy the maxim that 'there are no friends at the top'.

As Party Treasurer after 1954 and leader after December 1955, Gaitskell could, and did, attend any of the sub-committees of the NEC that he wished. A typical month would have featured a set of committee meetings grouped around the middle week. Policy and Publicity, International and Organisation met on consecutive days in the middle of the month, the NEC and Finance towards the end and the Commonwealth at the beginning. So in any one week there were at least two of these meetings, usually taking much of a morning or an afternoon. There were at least twice-weekly meetings of the Shadow Cabinet and frequent evening PLP meetings. When the House of Commons was sitting there were regular attendances at debates and any one of those commitments could produce further meetings or smaller study and discussion groups on particular policy areas. At weekends, there was constituency business once a month and often weekend meetings twice or even three times. On average Gaitskell seems to have had one weekend off each month.

The Frognal house was well placed for easy commuting down to the Embankment and though there were frequent evening functions he could make it home easily enough. Dora would often wait up and next day they would breakfast together, silently, devouring the morning papers. There would often be a mid-morning start in the House but he was usually up much earlier. A friend of Julia's remembers Hugh up at 7 a.m. one weekend, reading all the newspapers.[44] To sustain such a workload one has to be basically fit. While he did get a little exercise through gardening, he was lucky to have a sound constitution and abundant energy.

This energy had been devoted since 1945 to an unrelenting political rise. He put his head down and pushed his way to the top. It was not an easy rise, though it was rapid. He had immense ambition and enjoyed the attention that each climb in his career brought. Hugh was a basically jovial and positive man, but, apart from official engagements and the odd night out, the 1940s and early 1950s had not featured a great deal of fun. In 1955 he seems to have looked up from the climb. He was pushing fifty, leader of the Labour Party, probably the next Prime Minister, with an election a full Parliament away and the demands of the opposition lightening a little with the closing of the Bevanite schism. For a time it made sense to try to have a little more fun. He accepted more invitations – indeed the diary begins to read much more like an engagement diary than a political document – and went out more.

Dora and he had what appeared to have been a conventionally happy marriage until the mid-1950s. As these years of effort and toil proceeded, however, Hugh began to look elsewhere for escape from the political life. It may have been that they reached an agreement of sorts. Their courtship and marriage had not, after all, been entirely conventional and one suspects that if Gaitskell had been in a different profession their marriage would not have been conventional either. Whatever the private arrangement, silent acceptance or states of ignorance that existed, Gaitskell's natural attraction to and for women reasserted itself in the mid-1950s. He sought ways of escape from the political grind, and he sought a certain reconnection with the fun-loving side of his character. After a decade of dominance by the 'Durbin side', which had carried him to the very top in politics, the 'Bowra side' began to come through again. As he wrote to his daughter, Julia, at Oxford:

> You know what a pleasure lover I am. So you must not expect a puritan outlook from me! Pleasure is not only all right but good so long as it is not too selfish or too undermining of one's capacity to do whatever it is one can do . . . if you have too much of it (in the crude sense) you react against it & look round for a little monasticism.[45]

The Labour Party could always be relied upon to deliver the necessary monasticism. The pleasure came with what Williams called 'light-hearted' flirting with attractive women,[46] and even Gaitskell's usually very strait-laced published diary contains references to the attractive women he came across. He was aware of women, he liked their company and he was good at listening and making people feel they were the centre of his attention.[47] Political opponents spoke of the playboy side to Gaitskell[48] and he gave a great deal of attention to his personal appearance: in fact, his vanity is apparent in virtually all the surviving photographs of him and in the recollection of people who worked with him.[49] All these characteristics were part of him and were connected with the aspect of his character that loved society. When he became leader of the opposition, the scope to enjoy this side of this life was greatly enhanced and he made the most of it. He worked hard, but, as the 1950s wore on, he also played increasingly hard.

His connections with London 'society' were partly through his family, partly through friendships, either from the 1930s or from various other stages of his career, for example film people from the Board of Trade days, and partly from some of the bankers involved with the XYZ Club.

He always loved good food, and wine or whisky, in a congenial atmosphere. In the 1940s Dora and he escaped to the Gargoyle Club when they could. The Gargoyle had been very much the 'in' place in the 1930s, its glory had faded a little by the 1950s, but it was still the only club that suited the different tastes of both Burgess and Maclean: 'It was said of the Gargoyle that on a good night there were more lords lying drunk under the tables than there were remaining upright on the banquettes of all the plusher establishments put together.'[50] Nights dancing in the Gargoyle became rarer as lunch and dinner parties became more frequent – either at Crosland's flat, where Hugh was usually the only other politician, or with Roy and Jennifer Jenkins or other friends. Hugh liked gossip, both political and social, and, as his diaries occasionally reveal, he revelled in good stories, anecdotes and jokes.

While Gaitskell did not entirely embrace the social revolution that was stirring amid the new affluence, he was undergoing his own liberation from post-war austerity and reconnection with some of the aspects of life that he had had little chance to indulge in his hectic schedule since the 1930s. The final part of the hinterland comprised his women friends. He seems to have been a sexually active man before his marriage and always attracted female admirers and friends. Even Williams alludes to the the fact that, while many men 'could not penetrate the curtain of reserve behind the courteous affability', there were women who denied that any reserve existed.[51] In embracing a more social existence he never lost sight of his political position, but, in turn, that position contributed to the range of possibilities for fun because it markedly increased the number of invitations he and Dora received. These came from embassies, from colleagues and from a variety of social and political hostesses; included amongst them was one from Ann Fleming.

Ann Fleming had been married to the newspaper magnate, Lord Rothermere, and through him developed an interest in the worlds of newspapers and politics. She tinkered with the *Daily Mail* for a while during this marriage. But she soon tired of Rothermere and after a long and complex courtship married Ian Fleming – at that point on the verge of unleashing the thoroughly unpleasant, rather sadistic, misogynist James Bond upon the world. Bond, immensely popular from the outset, was a fictional creation who had certain characteristics in common with his creator. Ian Fleming was an equally unpleasant, highly misogynistic and sado-masochistic Old Etonian.[52] Ann was a bright and interesting Tory hostess, who escaped from her husband's relentless adultery by pursuing a vigorous social life of her own.

> Ann had been called a political hostess, sometimes the last of the political hostesses, but this was true only in the simple sense that she was often a hostess to politicians. She had no axe to grind, was not plotting to further one man's career or destroy another's. Policy was not altered under her roof, suitable allies were not subtly thrown together . . . Power attracted her but she did not want it for herself. When a new figure rose to prominence, she would be intrigued to meet him; but if he turned out to be pompous or banal, boring in any way, the interest evaporated.[53]

Her parties were a fixture of the social scene in London from about the mid-1940s. She was an accomplished and attractive hostess. Gaitskell's rise in the Labour Party attracted her attention and the invitation was issued. Gaitskell and Fleming also shared a connection through their mutual friend, Maurice Bowra.

It was the 'Bowra side' of Gaitskell that was attracted to this world of conversation, wit and upper-class frivolity. It was not so much that Fleming showed him a world on which he had turned his back – the upper middle class of his own family were as distant from Ann Fleming's set as were the Durham miners – but that she offered him an escape from the endless cycle and frequent drudgery of Labour politics. She was exciting, sophisticated and amusing. His initial attraction for her was partly his social and political position: having had the idea of gaining access to power through the *Daily Mail* while married to Rothermere, now she liked the idea of gaining access to a central political leader. Andrew Lycett, Ian Fleming's latest biographer, speculates that she

> considered it a challenge to wean him from his puritanical socialist principles to an enjoyment of the more overt pleasures in life . . . she promoted Gaitskell with Beaverbrook and ensured that his policies received favourable *Express* group newspaper coverage in any internal Labour Party dispute with the left wing . . . the political hostess who split the Labour Party and kept the Labour right wing in business: it is an interesting and not implausible thesis.[54]

Unfortunately, the thesis is implausible in just about every respect. Gaitskell was not a 'rather dry' socialist who needed weaning from puritanism, but a person with an immense appetite for life and commitment to socialist politics who was not open to such 'weaning'. The frequent references to food in his diary and his tastes at Oxford testify to the fact that he needed no introduction to how to live. The *Express* group was largely irrelevant to the internal Labour battles of the 1950s and 1960s and its support or otherwise for the Labour right made no difference whatever to the outcome of the battles. Beaverbrook continued his relationship with the ex-Bevanites and Gaitskell kept his distance until the Common Market gave them common cause.[55] Finally, the idea that this 'political hostess' kept the Labour right in business is simply ludicrous. In fact, Gaitskell's attachment to Ann and to the 'Café' society she represented did him harm with his party rather than any good; even Tony Crosland worried about it.[56] Politically Ann meant nothing. She appealed to another part of his self entirely, and his ability to keep separate people who appealed to different parts of him had been illustrated over and again in his life. Fleming represents the extent of the conflict between the public and the private in Gaitskell's life, his struggle with himself about what he actually wanted from life. It grew from an acquaintance to an affair in which friendship rather than passion predominated[57] and seems to have lasted until the end of his life.

Lycett is not alone in speculating about the political impact of the relationship between the leader of the Labour Party and this society hostess. 'We cannot automatically regard Gaitskell's relationship with a leading aristocratic lady, who mixed in high Tory circles, as irrelevant to Gaitskell's thinking; especially as the Labour leader was, at the time, involved in bitter controversies within his working-class party.'[58] It is not the duplicity entailed by Gaitskell's affair that bothers Ben Pimlott. The problem is essentially tribal; Fleming was a Tory, she was 'one of them'. 'He did not kiss duchesses, like MacDonald, but nearly all his intimate friends, within the party and outside it, came from his own milieu. He was more often to be seen at Belgravia lunch parties and at the celebrations of Café society than at trade union socials.'[59]

Gaitskell was not especially unusual in mixing with people from his own milieu, or having friends or going to lunch parties. The Hampstead Set were mainly from public school backgrounds, but Gaitskell's political contacts extended well beyond the close Hampstead network. He did not have Harold Wilson's image of the common touch because he did not change either his accent or his manners to reflect the company he was in. He also went to more than his share of trade union socials, nationally and especially in Leeds, but insisted, rightly, that he was also entitled to a life beyond politics. For Gaitskell that life involved a great deal more dancing and jazz than lunches in Belgravia. The picture of Gaitskell being sucked into a Tory world and turning his back on the class to which he was committed underestimates the man. Gaitskell did not stop doing any of the political and social things he had been doing in the 1940s and 1950s, in what would be considered 'respectable' Labour terms: he simply added an increasing number of the kind of social engagements that appealed to his need and ability to find personal fulfilment through fun. His relationship with Ann belonged to the compartment that wanted to enjoy and indulge itself; it was not a significant and new part of his life and was not to the exclusion of other things. The connection between this relationship and his attempt to expel Nye Bevan, or the revisionist policy of *Industry and Society*, or the later attempt to replace Clause 4, is non-existent. Britain was changing, growing more affluent, beginning to enjoy the peace, and Gaitskell relaxed a little along with everyone else.

The other side of the question is why Ann Fleming fell for Gaitskell. Here it is only possible to speculate because her letters on the subject, and the stories that she told, were generally defensive and derogatory of Hugh and of herself and her feelings. Typically upper-class English, she tried to cover the distance between her self-image and her feelings with sarcasm. But in the difference between Gaitskell and Ian Fleming we can perhaps see the attraction.

Hugh himself professed to liking the Bond books. When the *New Statesman* attacked Ian Fleming's works, Gaitskell defended them:

> As you know I am a confirmed Fleming fan – or should it be addict? The combination of sex, violence, alcohol and – at intervals – good food and nice clothes is, to one who lives such a circumscribed life as I do, irresistible.[60]

But while he might have liked the books there is little similarity between the two men, except perhaps the curious coincidence that both had more successful older brothers whom they followed through school. Ian Fleming enjoyed humiliating people, was incapable of loyalty and had serious emotional problems derived from his complex and destructive relationship with his mother; and he had a feeling of inferiority towards his brother which seems to have crippled him (whereas Hugh had quickly transcended similar feelings in his own childhood). Such problems led to a marked tendency in Fleming towards sadism and general unpleasantness in his personal relationships. The contrast with Hugh could not have been more profound. Ann Fleming might have been initially attracted to the leader of the opposition as a lunch guest: she had an intimate friendship with a gentle and loving man, a refuge from what appears to have been a sad and empty marriage.

The relationship began with the acceptance of an invitation to a party in April 1956, though Hugh does not seem to have shone in rather lively company: 'We had a jolly dinner, the Gaitskells, Bonham Carters, Boothby and Randolph; Violet wrote to me and said that "of the brass in your orchestra Boothby was more matured than Randolph Churchill." '[61] From then on Gaitskell began to enjoy his visits to these parties. In November, at the height of Suez, 'Mr Gaitskell came to lunch and fell in love with Diana [Cooper], he held her hand – apparently when he was at Winchester he fell in love with Felicity Tree so they had much to talk about. He had never seen cocktails with mint in them or seen a magnum of pink champagne, he was very happy. I lied and told him that all the upper class were beautiful and intelligent and he must not allow his venom to destroy them.'[62] The friendship developed and they became lovers – meeting in the late 1950s in Crosland's flat – but Ann never lost her slightly mocking tone towards him and he continued to play the part of suitor.

Hugh's hinterland consisted of his family – Dora, Julia and Cressida – his male friends (both political and unpolitical), jazz and poetry, and his women friends, most importantly Ann Fleming. Each of these hinterlands was affected by his election as leader. Dora and the children saw less of him; he had less time for his private pleasures of music and books. The non-political friends were somewhat squeezed out, simply because of the pressure of time, though the pace of his working and social life was such that he seems to have done well in maintaining a wide circle of friends. The political friendships were complicated, despite his consistent attempt to keep political and personal relations separate, by his newly powerful position. He had to reconcile the demands of friendship with the need to balance the political wings of the party. Finally, his election opened up new social worlds to him and having achieved so much, and at such a cost in time and effort, he seems to have looked for ways of filling the store of fun in his life: he found a source in the society life of Ann Fleming and her set. Just at the moment when these possibilities for greater pleasure were opening up, Britain was descending into the worst political crisis since the end of the war; and the beginnings of a social and political revolution, dimly perceived before the events of the summer and winter of 1956, were becoming starkly obvious:

> Outwardly it seemed that little had changed. Deep in the national psyche, however, was the knowledge that a very real watershed had been passed. Attitudes to the outside world and to authority, the relations between class and class, England's fundamental view of herself – a whole web of complex sentiments and assumptions that had been built up over hundreds of years – had been irreparably undermined. The dam had burst.[63]

Gaitskell's role as leader of the opposition, as the dam burst on the old England and ushered in the new, was to be pivotal.

11

Suez, 1956–1957

I want Nasser destroyed.
                    Eden to Anthony Nutting, March 1956

I could not regard an armed attack on Egypt by ourselves and
the French as justified by anything which Nasser has done so far
or as consistent with the Charter of the United Nations.
                    Gaitskell to Eden, 8 August 1956

You can't beat an Englishman when he's straight.
                    Irish tram-driver on hearing Gaitskell's
                    broadcast of 4 November 1956

I don't see how the case against the Government could have been
put better than you put it.
                    Edward Boyle to Gaitskell, 30 January 1957

Napoleon called Egypt the most important country in the world.
For Britain it had long been of vital strategic interest because of
Ferdinand de Lesseps' canal. This provided the most direct route to
the Indian Empire. Disraeli had purchased a 44 per cent stake in the
canal for the British government in 1875. As Empire turned to
Commonwealth, the importance of the canal increased rather than
diminished because of the oil it carried. However, in the post-war
world the fact that British troops still patrolled the banks of the canal,
within the sovereign state of Egypt, was an increasingly irritating
anachronism for the Egyptians. Under the terms of the Canal Users'
Treaty of 1888, these arrangements were due to end in 1969.

Negotiations for the withdrawal of troops from the Egyptian bases
and over the future of the Sudan had been taking place, off and on,
since October 1946. However, the tension between Egypt and
Britain, already strained by the creation of Israel in 1947, was heightened after General Neguib, an Arab nationalist, deposed King Farouk
in a coup in July 1952. After the Sudanese were granted self-
government and Neguib had in turn been deposed by Colonel

248

Nasser, an agreement was reached on 20 June 1956: all British troops were to be withdrawn from the Canal Zone.

As part of the treaty for withdrawing from the Egpytian bases, both governments reaffirmed their commitments to the 1888 convention which guaranteed the free navigation of the canal. The Egyptian Bases Agreement caused deep splits in the Conservative Party and a small Suez Group formed who criticised the Foreign Secretary, Anthony Eden, for selling out to Nasser. They talked of the Egpytian Bases Agreement as the scuttling of the British Empire.

After the agreement to withdraw British troops from Suez, Anthony Eden became increasingly obsessed by Nasser. There is some evidence that as early as the spring of 1956 Eden had decided that Nasser would have to be crushed. After winning the election of 1955, Eden faced a difficult period under attack at home. From the left came Gaitskell's parliamentary assault on the Butler Budgets and from the right the attacks from the Suez Group. Moreover, a fresh area of colonial conflict had broken out in Cyprus, and Eden was similarly caught between condemnation from Gaitskell for his harsh treatment of the nationalists in Cyprus and demands for a hard line from the right of the Conservative Party. All these combined to undermine Eden's position.

On 1 March 1955, King Hussein of Jordan had sacked General Glubb and other British officers who ran the Jordanian army. The Egyptian government had long been pushing anti-British propaganda and Hussein's action seemed to imply that the British position was now under threat in Jordan too.[1]

Anthony Nutting, Minister of State at the Foreign Office, was with Eden on the evening he learned of Glubb's sacking and Eden 'put all the blame on Nasser'.[2] A few days later Nutting sent the Prime Minister a note on his views for retrieving the situation in the Middle East and Eden phoned him at the Savoy Hotel where he was having dinner:

> [the Prime Minister said] 'I suppose you think it's negative to want to get rid of Nasser.' So I said, 'well frankly I do because I think if you get rid of Nasser you'll get chaos in Egypt.' He said, 'I don't care if there is chaos in Egypt, I want Nasser destroyed', and this over an open telephone line too at the Savoy Hotel.[3]

This extraordinary outburst was followed by a more considered debate on British policy options in the Middle East at Cabinet on

21 March 1956. The Foreign Secretary, Selwyn Lloyd, outlined the strategy for a new approach to the Middle East which assumed that Egypt was a hostile power. This included a series of moves designed to undermine Nasser's position: bringing Iraq and Jordan closer together; withdrawing support for the Aswan High Dam project; withholding of military supplies and the blocking of sterling balances. In all this, concluded the Foreign Secretary, 'we should need the support of the United States Government. The first task would be to seek Anglo-American agreement on a general realignment of policy towards Egypt.' The Prime Minister then said:

> It might not be easy to secure United States support for a new policy on these lines. We must, however, do our utmost to persuade them of the importance of checking Colonel Nasser in his bid for leadership of the Arab world.[4]

Following this Cabinet, Selwyn Lloyd asked to see Gaitskell at the Foreign Office. Lloyd informed Gaitskell that military planning was taking place between the United States and Great Britain with respect to the Middle Eastern situation. Gaitskell warned Lloyd that 'in his view the Americans were hopeless and he thought in an election year there was not the slightest chance of the Americans taking any action, whatever the extent of the emergency.'[5] Gaitskell pressed Lloyd on the need to supply arms to Israel and came away with the impression that 'it was quite clear that they [the Government] have got fed up with Nasser and Egypt generally.'[6]

At this point the extent of the co-operation between the British and Americans was limited but both powers were increasingly dissatisfied with Nasser and with the financial help they had agreed to give him. Foster Dulles, the American Secretary of State, shared Lloyd's reservations. The largest single commitment was to the Aswan High Dam project. The US, Britain and the World Bank were committed to providing $270 million on condition that Nasser found $900 million. With Egypt courting the Eastern bloc the British and US governments wondered why they were giving financial aid to a potentially hostile power. By April both governments had more or less decided to let the aid 'wither on the vine' but no announcement was made.[7]

In September 1955 Nasser announced that he had concluded a deal to use the revenue from the harvest to purchase $150 million worth of arms from Czechoslovakia. In May 1956, Nasser recognised

Communist China. In June the Russian Foreign Minister was present in Cairo at the celebration for the withdrawal of British troops. The combination of the movement towards Russia and the arms shipments from Czechoslovakia risked a destabilisation of the Middle East and the possibility of the frequent border skirmishes between the fledgling Israeli state and her Arab neighbours developing into a full-scale war. For the British, this threatened their closest ally in the area, Jordan. For the United States this undermined the basis of their policy of giving aid to Egypt in an attempt to keep Nasser within the Western orbit.[8] Dulles and Eisenhower, under pressure from Congress,[9] had had enough. At Cabinet on 17 July, Lloyd informed his colleagues that the Americans had decided to inform the Egyptians that they were withdrawing support for the project. Lloyd concluded his statement, with a typical understatement: 'This might well lead to a deterioration in our relations with Egypt with serious consequences for our trade.'[10]

On 26 July 1956, President Nasser of Egypt made a speech in Alexandria:

> Arab nationalism progresses. Arab nationalism triumphs. Arab nationalism marches forward; it knows its road and it knows its strength. Arab nationalism knows who are its enemies and who are its friends. Arab nationalism realises that its existence depends on its unity and its strength lies in its nationalism . . . In the past we were kept waiting at their offices – the offices of the British High Commissioner and the British Ambassador. Today since our political freedom has been achieved . . . they take us into account.[11]

He defended his recent arms purchases from the Russians and attacked the US for refusing to support the Aswan High Dam scheme. Speaking to the Americans was like 'sitting in front of Ferdinand de Lesseps'. At the moment he mentioned the words 'de Lesseps', Colonel Mahmoud Yunis and his team of police moved into the Suez Canal Company's offices in Ismailia, Suez and Port Said. Nasser continued, 'Instead of the Canal being dug for Egypt, Egypt became the property of the Canal and the Canal Company became a state within a state. But now the days of alien exploitation are over the Canal and its revenues would belong entirely to Egypt.' He then read the terms of the decree nationalising the Suez Canal.[12] His purpose was to replace the capital the Americans were refusing for the Aswan High Dam scheme with capital from the Canal

Company. However, it was not an economic decision but a political one. Nasser's judgement was that the West would not respond. He gambled that with the US in an election year, the French not prepared to act alone and the British too stretched to do anything for at least two months, he could get away with it. Thus Nasser became the symbol of Arab nationalism.

In Downing Street Eden was hosting a reception for the King and the Crown Prince of Iraq; Gaitskell was also a guest. Eden's private secretary informed the Prime Minister of Nasser's speech at about 10 p.m. Eden summoned the American Chargé d'Affaires, the French Ambassador and Chiefs of Staff – two of whom were actually at the dinner. At about 10.45 p.m. Eden approached the King of Iraq who was sitting talking to Gaitskell. 'I want you to know – and I think the Opposition should know as well – what Nasser has done tonight. He has made a speech announcing that he is going ahead with the Aswan Dam, that they cannot get any foreign money, but that, nevertheless, they are going ahead, and, in order to finance it, they are taking over the Suez Canal Company, and will collect . . . substantially increased . . . dues from ships using the Canal.'

Gaitskell asked what he was going to do. Eden said he was getting in touch with the American Ambassador and taking the matter to the Security Council. Gaitskell asked, 'Supposing Nasser doesn't take any notice?' Selwyn Lloyd, who had been standing near by, said, 'Well, I suppose in that case the old-fashioned ultimatum will be necessary.' Gaitskell replied that he thought they ought to act quickly, whatever they did, and that, as far as Great Britain was concerned, public opinion would almost certainly be behind them. But 'I also added that they must get America into line.' Gaitskell turned to the King and the Crown Prince and asked them what they thought. The Crown Prince replied, 'We had better send for our Prime Minister too – that's the constitutional position.'[13] (Unknown to Gaitskell the last visitor to Downing Street that night was Sir Alexander Cadogan, formerly Eden's Permanent Under-Secretary at the Foreign Office and in 1956 a director of the Suez Canal Company and Chairman of the BBC.)[14]

Around midnight Eden, Selwyn Lloyd, Lord Salisbury, Lord Kilmuir, Douglas–Home, the French Ambassador, the American Chargé d'Affaires, and the Chiefs of Staff – Mountbatten, Templar and Dermot Boyle – met in the Cabinet Room. The scene must have been quite extraordinary as they were all in full evening dress, the Prime Minister in knee breeches and Lord Salisbury wearing the Garter.[15] The Chiefs of Staff were instructed to prepare plans for an invasion of Egypt. Lloyd, heeding Gaitskell's words of 11 April and of a few hours earlier, took the American Chargé d'Affaires, Andrew Foster, to one side and told him that he felt the only solution would be for a Western consortium to take over the canal by force if necessary and run it.[16]

Foster communicated these thoughts, which were not entirely out of line with the conclusions reached at the March Cabinet, directly to Eisenhower. However, there was no mention at this stage, in the presence of the Americans, of Britain acting alone and the fact that Foster was present at this meeting adds strong weight to the case that Eden wanted, if at all possible, to act with American support.

Yet within twenty-four hours it was clear that Eden wanted to act whatever the circumstances. He had been set on a confrontation with Egypt since the beginning of the year: the nationalisation of the Suez Canal gave him the pretext for preparing a military response. From this July night until the bombs began to fall on Port Said in November, Eden searched desperately for a further pretext to put the plans into action. At each turn between July and November the Americans thwarted him by opening up new opportunities for a diplomatic solution.

Gaitskell's response was quite different. Within forty-five minutes of the British Prime Minister hearing of the nationalisation of the Canal, the leader of the opposition was warning him that the British government could not take action on its own. Gaitskell did not, in this first conversation, emphasise the need for the British government to act in accord with the UN Security Council because Eden had already told him that the British would be taking the issue to the Council. But, according to Eden's memoirs, this was very much a first reaction, or at least something that he felt Gaitskell and the King of Iraq might want to hear. 'Though we favoured', Eden later wrote, 'using every method of conciliation, we were not convinced that it was wise to begin by a reference to the Security Council.'[17] Later Gaitskell was to feel that throughout Eden had been economical with the truth in his dealings with the opposition, and that this began in the very first conversation.

However, this first action also illustrates Gaitskell's basic willingness to pursue a bipartisan foreign policy. The Suez crisis might have been very different if Eden had tried to bring Gaitskell into his confidence. Much of the venom in Gaitskell's later attacks on the government came from the way he was personally misled by Eden; a little better management of the leader of the opposition might well have pushed him towards those in the Labour Party who believed you could not oppose the government when British troops were involved in military action. It was not easy for Gaitskell to take the stand that he eventually did, since it offended his sense of patriotism and his belief in the need for Britain to pursue a role of world leadership. Anthony Eden's ruthless dishonesty gradually reduced Gaitskell's options down to outright opposition.

Later on the morning of 27 July the British Cabinet met.[18] The issue was no longer merely a legal one but one of international importance and it was agreed that the government's policy should be to bring the canal under international control of 'Powers interested in international shipping and trade by means of a new international Commission on which Egypt would be given suitable representation'.[19] This would be accompanied by diplomatic pressure, a note of protest and by concerted actions with the French and American governments. 'The next question the Government faced was the crucial one. Should we be prepared in the last resort to use force to dislodge Colonel Nasser from the Canal?' Eden, recounting this Cabinet meeting, goes on in his memoirs:

> It was our intention first to bring the maximum political pressure to bear upon him. The means would be worked out in the tripartite [with French and Americans] talks of the next few days. Economic weapons were also at our disposal and the Chancellor of the Exchequer had prepared financial measures which were to come into operation at midnight that night. But economic and political pressures alone might not succeed in checking Nasser and re-establishing international control over the Canal. From the start we had to prepare to back our remonstrances with military action.[20]

If Britain failed to hold the canal, the Prime Minister feared that there would be a domino effect, that it would lead to the loss 'one by one of all our interests and assets in the Middle East and, even if we had to act alone, we could not stop short of using force to protect our position if all other means of protecting it proved unavailing.'[21]

Following the dramatic events on the evening of 26 July, Gaitskell put down a private notice question to the Prime Minister on the 27th:

Mr Gaitskell: asked the Prime Minister whether he had a statement to make on the reported action of the Egyptian Government in regard to the Suez Canal.

The Prime Minister: Yes, Sir. The unilateral decision of the Egyptian Government to expropriate the Suez Canal Company without notice and in breach of the Concession Agreements, affects the rights and interests of many nations. Her Majesty's Government are consulting other Governments immediately concerned, with regard to the serious situation thus created. The consultations will cover both the effect of this arbitrary action upon the operation of the Suez Canal and also the wider questions which it raises.

Mr Gaitskell: On this side of the House, we deeply deplore this high-handed and totally unjustifiable step by the Egyptian Government. Has the Prime Minister in mind to refer this matter to the Security Council? Has he yet come to any decision on that point? In view of the seizure of the property of the Suez Canal Company and the vague statement about future compensation, will he bear in mind the desirability of blocking the sterling balances of the Egyptian Government?

The Prime Minister: . . . As regards the Security Council, I would rather not say what action the countries concerned – we are in consultation, naturally, now with them – would wish to take, whether in the Security Council, or immediate diplomatic action, or whatever it may be.[22]

Thus Gaitskell's first public intervention stressed the need to go to the Security Council. In the first twenty-four hours of the crisis Gaitskell had stated in public and in private the twin pillars of his policy: the issue should be dealt with through the United Nations, and the Americans needed to be on board for any British policy to stand a chance of success. He stood by these from the first twenty-four hours to the last. But he was let down, as we shall see, by his inadequate command of presentation, by the tightness of his definition of responsible politics and by his tendency to behave as though he were in government. His over-emotional response to the growing duplicity of the government also let him down, but he was totally consistent in terms of his basic response to Nasser's actions. Eden, suffering from progressive mental and physical collapse,[23] chose not to hear what even close colleagues who disagreed with him were saying. As for the words of the leader of the opposition, Eden heard what he wanted to hear: from 27 July, Eden recalled Gaitskell's condemnation of Nasser's action but not the question about the Security Council. It was a pattern that was to be repeated again and again. As Eden wove an increasingly opaque web of deceit around his actions so he increasingly misrepresented what Gaitskell was saying. Eden wrote to Eisenhower:

> My colleagues and I are convinced that we must be ready, in the last resort, to use force to bring Nasser to his senses. For our part we are prepared to do so. I have this morning instructed our Chief of Staff to prepare a military plan accordingly. However, the first step must be for you and us and France to exchange views, align our policies and concert together how we can best bring the maximum pressure to bear on the Egyptian Government.[24]

This relatively moderate tone, with its final paragraph stressing the need for co-operation, was flatly contradicted in an embassy telegram sent at 2 a.m. on 31 July from Robert Murphy, a senior State Department official dispatched to London by Eisenhower. Murphy told Eisenhower that after long discussions with Eden and Macmillan he was requested to tell the President that the 'British Government has decided to drive Nasser out of Egypt. The decision they declare is firm. They expressed simple conviction military action is necessary and inevitable. In separate conversations each said in substance they ardently hoped the US would be with them in this determination, but if we could not they would understand and our friendship would be unimpaired. If we were with them from the beginning chances of World War III would be far less than if we delayed.'[25] Following this rather alarming telegram, Eisenhower replied to Eden later on 31 July:

> I hope that you will consent to reviewing the matter once more in its broadest aspects. It is for this reason that I have asked Foster [Dulles] to leave this afternoon to meet your people tomorrow in London . . . the step you contemplate should not be undertaken until every peaceful means of protecting the rights and the livelihood of great portions of the world had been thoroughly explored and exhausted. Should these means fail, and I think it erroneous to assume in advance that they needs must fail, then world opinion would understand how earnestly all of us had attempted to be just, fair and considerate, but that we simply could not accept a situation that would in the long run prove disastrous to the prosperity and living standards of every nation whose economy depends directly or indirectly on East-West shipping.[26]

It was a clear private message to Eden to slow down and an unequivocal indication that at this stage the Americans were not on board. Eden was now entirely committed to war[27] but Eisenhower had equally clearly indicated that the Americans would not support that war. The *New York Tribune* correspondent, lunching with Gaitskell, made the same point that Eisenhower had stressed in his letter to Eden, but turned it to the domestic political situation in the US where a presidential election was pending. When Gaitskell questioned why a strong line by the Republicans would be unpopular, Don Cook responded, 'Well, they don't think of it that way. All they know is that they have promised peace and prosperity, and that everything would be spoilt if there is no peace.'[28]

Eden had arranged three-power talks to start in London the following day. Publicly the government condemned Egypt's actions, and Britain and France imposed economic sanctions on all Egypt's foreign exchange and trade operations. The Suez Canal Company's assets in London were protected, arms sales with Egypt suspended, and the Admiralty and the War Office took a series of precautions, with the object of strengthening the position in the eastern Mediterranean and Britain's general ability to deal with any situation that might arise. At the same time Eden stated that single-power control of the canal was totally unacceptable.[29]

Gaitskell met with his Shadow Cabinet on Monday 30 July. As far as they knew all the options were still open: the American, French and British governments were meeting to discuss the situation. The Shadow Cabinet therefore decided to bide their time and await the outcome of the talks. After Eden had made his statement in the Commons, Gaitskell met with the Israeli Ambassador, Elath. In January 1953 Gaitskell had visited Israel for the first time, to give a series of lectures at the Hebrew University in Jerusalem, and he had strong personal and family links with the country. Now the Ambassador sought to make it clear to Gaitskell that Israel's fears were that Nasser's ultimate aim was the destruction of the Jewish state, whether he won or lost his gamble with the canal: 'Israel was now entering on her most critical period.' He told Gaitskell that there had been further talk about the possibility of a preventive war against Egypt, but that they had rejected this idea. The Foreign Office had been in touch with the Ambassador and 'begged him not to make any fuss either to thank them for what they were doing or to intervene in any way at all.' Gaitskell asked Elath what the Israelis wanted the British to do. Elath replied:

> it was essential that we should make Nasser see that this kind of thing did not pay, even if it involved some sacrifice to ourselves. He thought, therefore, we should adopt every kind of economic measure open to us . . . it was essential on the political side to show a firm front. This could be done best by helping our friends, not only Israel but also, for instance, Iraq. Arms should be provided both for Israel and for the Baghdad Pact as well.[30]

He did not feel the Soviet Union would get involved, but asked for Gaitskell's firm backing for strong action against Nasser and for aid to Israel in case the Egyptians attacked. Gaitskell could support all this, but was worried that the government would take his approval of military action for granted. He was prepared to back the government in certain ways but there was a strict limit to the line he would take. Unknown to him, however, the Israelis were already contemplating linking a military action of their own with any British or French action.[31]

That evening, 30 July, Gaitskell and the deputy leader, Jim Griffiths, went to see Eden. He wanted to clarify the situation and ensure that the off-the-cuff remarks about fully supporting the government which he had made at Downing Street on the 26th were put in proper context. The Shadow Cabinet had also raised the issue of not appearing too bellicose.[32] Gaitskell then made it completely clear to Eden, with no ambiguity, the circumstances under which he would support the government:

> there were certain circumstances in which force would be appropriate, it had to be in self-defence or, at any rate, in circumstances which could be properly justified before the United Nations . . . I gathered that there were going to be some troop movements in the near future of a precautionary kind because, said Eden, it was possible that Nasser might do some foolish thing, and we had to be ready . . . [Eden then mentioned the proposal for international control of the canal.] . . . I said, 'What happens if he doesn't [accept this]? Do you then use force?' Eden replied, 'Well, I don't want to take that hurdle yet.' I had already made it plain, I may say, that I doubted whether we could support force merely on those grounds.

In fact the Prime Minister had already taken that hurdle. He had made clear to Eisenhower and to the Cabinet that the failure of the internationalisation of the Suez Canal would lead to intervention and that military planning and preparations were under way. It is likely that Eden was consistent from that first night when the news broke in wanting to have his war. But what Gaitskell knew as of 2 August, the day of the first full House of Commons debate on the Suez situation, was that, on the one hand, the peaceful option was being attempted (but that any Western weakness might result in an attack on Israel) and, on the other, that Eden might abandon the peaceful option if the Labour Party appeared too ready to accept the use of force.

Before the debate he had a long talk with Denis Healey. Healey was an acknowledged international affairs expert who had come through the international section at Labour HQ and was now an MP. Gaitskell relied on him for solid foreign policy advice and support. Healey was much more anti-government and 'more pacifist, more neutralist' than Hugh had expected. He then met with the Foreign Affairs Steering Committee and gave its members a lecture on foreign policy. They did not impress him in the least. One member he judged 'rather a stupid man'; another was a 'softy'; the third was Tony Benn who, 'although talented in many ways, a good speaker and a man of ideas, had extraordinarily poor judgement. He is the last person in the world I would go to for advice on policy.'[33]

In the Shadow Cabinet no one objected to Gaitskell's proposal to condemn Nasser, but they insisted that he must stress that they did not condemn the fact of nationalisation, only the failure to do it within the United Nations orbit. George Brown told him, 'It will be an awkward speech to make, but somehow or other you will find your way through.'[34] Of all these talks before the debate on 2 August the one with the Israeli Ambassador, urging a strong line on Nasser, seems to have had the most impact on Gaitskell.

Eden asked to see him on the morning before the debate to tell him that the government would not say much in the House that day because of the three-power talks. Gaitskell again pressed him on the use of force. Gaitskell thought Eden said, 'I only want to keep open the possibility of force in case Nasser does something else.' Eden later said he had stated, 'I only want to keep open the possibility of force in case or if Nasser did something else.' Douglas Jay also met Gaitskell before the debate and told him of rumours flying round the *Daily Herald* office, which we now know to be true, that military plans were being made to seize the canal. Gaitskell simply could not believe that Eden would be so 'reckless and foolish'.[35]

Jay persuaded him to put a line in his speech about the United Nations. Up until his talk with Jay he had not done so because he was so sure that the use of force without recourse to the UN was out of the question. Gaitskell thus walked into the Chamber thinking that Eden had reassured him again that there would be no unilateral use of force by the British and simply not believing that Eden would be stupid enough to try to defy the world. His speech took this for granted, attempting to be supportive of the British and helpful to Israel by attacking Nasser. The problem was that the speech did not measure up to the occasion and the general line of Labour speakers, mostly from the right of the party and mostly supporting the idea of the use of force, compounded the political error.

The problem with the speech was that, although he made plain that Labour would not support the government in the use of force except in accordance with the United Nations Charter, Gaitskell also said:

> while I have not hesitated to express my disagreement with the Government in their policy in the past, I must make it abundantly plain that anything that they have done or not done in no way excuses Colonel Nasser's action in seizing the Canal . . . [Nasser] wanted to challenge the West and to win. He wanted to assert his strength. He wanted to make a big impression. Quiet negotiation, discussion around a table about nationalising the Company would not produce this effect. It is all very familiar. It is exactly the same that we encountered from Mussolini and Hitler in those years before the war.[36]

For every sentence talking of Britain not breaching international law and isolating herself in the United Nations, there were paragraphs attacking Nasser's expansionism and the threat to Israel. All the main points were there in the speech but what stuck in the memory were the allusions to appeasement and the dictators of the 1930s.

The Suez Group – diehard Tory extremists – jumped over each other to welcome the speech and the support it offered for the government. Even worse, leading Labour figures and influential backbenchers like Herbert Morrison, Reginald Paget and Frank Tomney spoke in support of the use of force. Only one left-winger spoke openly against it. The impression left was that the Labour Party had backed the government and that Gaitskell had not come out against the use of force. This impression, held by the left and by the Suez Group, was wrong. The words are there in Hansard: 'We must not, therefore, allow ourselves to get into a position where we might be denounced in the Security Council as aggressors, or where the majority of the Assembly were against us.' But they have been drowned by the subsequent braying of the Tory mob and were obscured at the time as the left responded to the continued military build-up by demanding a peace protest movement and not a bipartisan foreign policy.

Gaitskell's role as leader of the opposition in such a situation was unenviable. He knew more than most of his colleagues about what was going on and, with his own experience over Korea and Persia, he would have assumed that the government was being straight with him. Thus, as far as he knew, all the options were still open. He had to combine the need to be an opposition leader, to offer alternative policy options and the need to scrutinise the government's actions with the desire, which he always felt, to be a responsible politician. It was an immensely complex role which demanded skill and, above all, a certain coolness and detachment. It was not sufficient in such circumstances simply to get the words right – the message needed to be clear.

The root of Gaitskell's failure in the Commons debate was not merely a 'lapse in communication';[37] it was indicative of his general political approach to opposition. The debate was a 'political' as much as a 'state' occasion. He needed to strike a balance between being a responsible statesman who did not bring comfort to the enemy and being a party leader who gave warning that there were limits to Labour's tolerance. He was not the government and therefore did not need to do the government's job of appearing firm in front of Nasser. He could stand back from the 'state' occasion and look at the politics, follow the consequences of the use of force through to their logical conclusion and ensure that the government was clear that if it took lines that the Labour Party opposed they would split the country. This he failed to do. It was also a genuine consciousness of history that prevented him.

Nasser was an aggressor; the Egpytian government was authoritarian; and a small state that he cared about, Israel, was potentially under threat, so the forces pushing him towards caution and statesmanship were strong. But there are different ways of being a statesman; simply supporting the government's policy is one, offering the vision of alternatives and spelling out the consequences of extremist actions by the government, is another. In these respects the speech was not all it could have been, but it is important not to go too far in condemning Gaitskell's initial stance on Suez.

The Conservative government and the Suez Group bitterly attacked Gaitskell for years to come for changing tack from his initial hostility to Nasser, to opposing the use of force. The charge of dishonesty should lie where it deserves to lie: at Anthony Eden's door. He lied to Gaitskell, misled the House of Commons and launched this futile and rather pathetic adventure in 'posthumous' imperialism. The right of the Conservative Party viciously attacked Gaitskell in the years after Suez for his supposed duplicity and submission to the Labour left. If he changed his mind, and the evidence suggests that in fact he was entirely consistent in his beliefs, though fluctuating occasionally in emphasis, then he was responding to events and to the realisation that the Conservative Prime Minister was lying to him about the enterprise on which Britain was engaged. If, after the troops had gone in to the Canal Zone in defiance of the world, he had carried on making speeches similar in the balance of their content to the July speech, he would not have survived as leader of the Labour Party.

As he sat down in July, given the state of his knowledge and the assurances that he thought Eden had given him, his speech was still a politically weak one. However, the only meaningful charge that can be made against Gaitskell is not that he then changed his mind but that he stopped playing at being the government, and started doing his constitutional job as leader of the opposition; not unnaturally, the Conservative government did not much care for the new Gaitskell.

The result of the tripartite talks was the summoning of a conference of Suez Canal users. Foster Dulles thus introduced the first in a series of diplomatic delaying tactics. The American objective was to prolong the negotiations into the winter. After mid-November it would be difficult to launch any kind of military operation until the spring. By then the election would be out of the way and if a diplomatic solution had not by then been found the American administration would have had considerable more freedom of movement. Moreover, in the short run Dulles felt that no action could be taken without some attempt at a diplomatic solution.[38]

As the three-power talks broke up, Gaitskell was preparing to leave for Pembrokeshire on one of his precious family holidays and decided to write to Eden seeking to clarify the position further.

> Gaitskell to Eden: At our first meeting you said, if I recollect rightly, that you would 'prefer to take that hurdle when you came to it', and yesterday I understood you to say that you only wanted to be free to use force if the conference did not succeed in its object and if Colonel Nasser 'did something else'. In the course of my speech I uttered some warning words about the circumstances in which force was and was not justified. But I deliberately refrained from putting the hypothetical question in public 'Was it proposed to use force to compel Nasser to accept the International Control Scheme?' . . . But in view of the reports in the Press this morning [that Britain would use force] . . . I feel I must repeat to you privately the warnings I have already uttered . . . While one or two members of the Party indicated in the debate that they would support force now, this is, I am pretty sure, not the general view.[39]

> Eden to Gaitskell: I understand your reasons for speaking as you did and that your attitude about the use of force must depend on the exact circumstances. As regards my own position, that must rest on what I said publicly in the House last Thursday. I think that what I said privately to you was that I only wanted to be free to use force if the Conference did not succeed in its object or if Colonel Nasser 'did something else'. Certainly the Government's attitude to the use of force would also have to depend on the circumstances at the time. I am very glad that the debate last Thursday showed such a wide measure of agreement.[40]

The day before Eden sent this letter, the British dispatched the parachute brigade to the Middle East and on the 8th Eden broadcast to the nation and extended the range of those he was misleading: 'We do not seek a solution by force, but by the broadest possible international agreement.' Jay was reminded of the way in which Hitler had spoken of Beneš as he listened to the broadcast.[41] Gaitskell was increasingly worried about the extent of the military preparations that were going on. On the 7th, Jay and Healey had written, with Hugh's strong support, to *The Times* questioning the continued preparations. On the 9th Eden wrote to Gaitskell again, telling him that the acceptances for the first London conference were going well and ignoring entirely the widespread press speculation about the use of force. Given Eden's role in advancing the military preparations, the letter is almost patronising in the way it ignores the debate which was raging in political circles.[42] Gaitskell replied to Eden on the 10th, supporting Jay and Healey and trying to force the Prime Minister to come clean on substantive issues at stake.

Lest there should still be doubt in your mind about my personal attitude, let me say that I could not regard an armed attack on Egypt by ourselves and the French as justified by anything which Nasser has done so far or as consistent with the Charter of the United Nations. Nor, in my own opinion, would such an attack be justified in order to impose a system of international control over the Canal, desirable though this is. If, of course, the whole matter were to be taken to the United Nations and if Egypt were to be condemned by them as aggressors, then, of course, the position would be different. And if further action which amounted to obvious aggression by Egypt were taken by Nasser, then again it would be different. So far what Nasser has done amounts to a threat, a grave threat to us and to others, it certainly cannot be ignored; but it is only a threat, not in my opinion justifying retaliation by war.[43]

Robens and Griffiths met Eden on the same day and there was more stonewalling from the Prime Minister. They warned him, in the same terms as Gaitskell's letter, that the opposition would reject the use of force. Jay kept telling Gaitskell that he was hearing from Ewar, the diplomatic correspondent of the *Daily Herald*, that the government was planning a military operation. Each day the Foreign Office Information Department held drinks with diplomatic correspondents and through this channel word was leaking about military preparations.[44] Finally, Gaitskell broke off his holiday and returned for a meeting of the Shadow Cabinet on 13 August. On the previous evening Nasser had announced that he would not be attending the London conference. Despite these private exchanges of letters, the press still very much associated Gaitskell and, by extension, the Labour Party with the use of force. The Shadow Cabinet therefore decided to issue a statement emphasising the warnings that had been made in Gaitskell's speech. Bevan, who had advocated the internationalisation of all waterways, astonished Gaitskell by urging that no mention be made of this idea: 'You will be surprised to hear this from me but I think it would be a great mistake to say anything at the moment which would embarrass the Americans.'[45]

They drafted and issued the statement. It declared that Nasser's nationalisation was not wrong in itself but that the way in which it had been done caused great anxiety; it opposed the use of force except under the United Nations Charter; and it demanded the recall of Parliament. In Cabinet Eden presented his talks with Robens and Griffiths in the best light he could: 'They considered that any international action should be considered at a special session of the

United Nations and that the new authority should be set up under that Organisation. They had, however, recognised that if any new incidents occurred, such as interference with ships using the Canal, a new situation would arise in which force might be justified.'[46] However, in his memoirs he recorded the moment rather differently: 'their retreat then began amid a clatter of excuses.'[47] Dulles felt that at this point support for intervention was minimal and after having dinner with Macmillan, who was again stressing the need to compel Nasser to accept international control, he told Eisenhower that the attitude of the Labour Party was a hard blow for the government and, on balance, made the use of force more likely because it ruled out a bipartisan approach.[48]

The next evening Gaitskell had dinner with André, of the French embassy, and found out about divisions in the government on the issue of force. With the diplomatic activity intensifying, in the days before the London conference, Gaitskell slipped away for two days with his family before returning to London for the conference which opened on 16 August. Foster Dulles put forward the proposal for an international board to run the canal and there followed a month of intense diplomatic activity.

The extent of Eden's delusions about Gaitskell's view, and the attitude of the Labour Party at this point in the crisis, was made clear in an after-dinner meeting between Eden, Selwyn Lloyd, Menzies, the Australian Prime Minister, Aldrich, the American Ambassador and Dulles. This took place 19 August. By this stage Gaitskell had had numerous meetings and written a series of letters, and the Shadow Cabinet had issued a public statement, all making clear that he and the Labour Party would not support the unilateral use of force. Dulles had already told Eisenhower this was the case. But when Dulles raised the problem of public opinion at this meeting Lloyd and Eden said that this was not the case, that the public, except the left-wing Labour element, was behind the government. Eden had refrained from building up public support for action but was sure that when the chips were down the British people would rally:

> Eden at the end of the meeting drew Ambassador Aldrich aside and asked him to assure [Dulles] that he (Eden) was completely satisfied that Gaitskell would stand with the Government in the use of force ... This was the second time Eden had made this statement privately to the Ambassador.[49]

It is impossible to tell if Eden really believed this. Probably he felt that whatever the circumstances in which the British became involved in conflict then Gaitskell would have supported him. If they had gone in after a conference, with the backing of the United Nations and in league with the US, then Gaitskell would have supported British troops in action. But what actually happened was different.

The London conference ended on 23 August. Menzies was sent to Egypt to persuade Nasser to accept the conference proposals. The idea was for the operation of the Suez Canal to be handed to an international board and to allow free passage through the canal by all powers. By implication this included Israel. The conference had split, with Russia, Indonesia, India and Ceylon proposing a compromise, but under strong British pressure the final terms which were to be put to Nasser were for a Western-dominated board. Nasser, as Eden had hoped, rejected the plan. But as Menzies did not reach Cairo until 3 September this all took up more of the time before the military option would be ready.[50] As Menzies was preparing to set off, Eden was telling Dulles that he could not keep the military on stand-by indefinitely and 'the present plans are to move in a week or ten days unless the situation definitely clears up.'[51] Again, this state of readiness was unknown to Gaitskell.

On 26 August, writing in *Reynolds News*, Gaitskell unambiguously presented the Labour case yet again. The London conference had made clear that the world would not accept the imposition of an international control of the canal by Britain and France by force: 'It was a very foolish line. For it turned world opinion against us and gave Nasser exactly the propaganda material he wanted ... The conference had produced a distinct cooling off. This is all to the good ... for these achievements the chief credit goes to Mr Dulles.'[52] This public praise for Dulles's role was followed by a private meeting with the Secretary of State in which Gaitskell pushed the line that the Labour Party would not back the use of force and urged the Secretary of State to publicise the background to the cancellation of the loan to Nasser for the Aswan Dam which had precipitated the initial crisis, feeling that this would help public opinion with respect to the US.[53]

In parallel to the diplomatic activity the military preparations also continued. At the end of August the French stopped informing London and Washington of arms shipments to Israel, which comprised in this period some sixty jet fighters,[54] and French troops arrived in Cyprus. Nasser rejected the Menzies proposals on 9 September. The British military operation was basically ready to begin. Eden had to judge whether or not the rejection of the Menzies conference was a sufficient pretext for intervention. Dulles now came up with yet another diplomatic delaying tactic. On 2 September, while resting on Duck Island, Lake Ontario, he had drafted a plan for an association of canal users as an alternative to the eighteen-nation proposals which Nasser rejected or the use of force. This proposal was fully worked out by the Americans in the days that followed and the Suez Canal Users' Association (SCUA) was announced in the Commons on 12 September. At the same time the CIA's Watch Committee reported, in detail, on British military preparedness.[55]

With reports appearing in the US press on the military preparations of the Israelis and French,[56] Eisenhower was asked at a press conference on 11 September whether the US would back Britain and France if they resorted to force. Eisenhower replied, 'This country will not go to war ever while I am occupying my present post unless the Congress . . . declares such a war.'[57] Eden responded the next day. The House of Commons had been recalled to debate Nasser's rejection of the eighteen-power plan, and the Prime Minister now announced Dulles's Suez Canal Users' Association. Eden, having had to accept SCUA, in the hope of getting the US back on board, now presented it as a military as well as an organisational commitment. He announced the SCUA in exactly the terms that had been agreed with the French and the US governments:

> I must make clear that if the Egpytian Government should seek to interfere with the operations of the Association, or refuse to extend to it the essential minimum of co-operation, then that government will once more be in breach of the Convention of 1888. In that event, Her Majesty's Government and others concerned will be free to take further steps as seem to be required either through the United Nations, or by other means for the assertion of their rights.[58]

This was generally felt to imply that the government would use force if necessary. Gaitskell was rather wrong-footed by the announcement of the Canal Users' Association – everyone had been expecting the government to be announcing the referral to the United Nations – but he replied that the points at issue between the government and the opposition were, specifically, 'the attitude of the Government to the use of force as a means of solving this dispute and concern the closely related question of the Government's attitude to the United Nations and the United Nations Charter . . . I want to emphasise with all the strength that I can that [the approach to UN must not be] to go through the formalities so that we may thereafter resort to force.' Towards the end Gaitskell asked, 'What does the Government mean by other means? We have waited six weeks to try and get clarity on this.' Receiving no reply he tried again:

> Is [the Prime Minister] prepared to say on behalf of Her Majesty's Government that they will not shoot their way through the Canal?
>
> The Prime Minister: I said that we were in complete agreement with the United States Government about what to do . . . We propose to ask for that co-operation [from the Egyptian government;] if they do not give it, they are, in our view, in default under the 1888 Convention but if they are so in default, we should take them to the Security Council.[59]

For the first time since the night of 26 July, Eden had accepted the need to take the matter to the United Nations. George Thomson, writing in Gaitskell's *Forward* journal, noted that he had 'never seen a clearer or more outstanding victory of Opposition over Government'.[60] Gaitskell's performance and speech, according to his old school friend Mallalieu, were the 'noblest speech he had ever heard'. Barbara Castle and Richard Crossman thanked God that he had not repeated the mistakes of 2 August, but thought he 'was like an opera singer who is supposed to reach a high note and then just fails to do so'.[61] The censure motion was put to a vote and the government won by 321 to 251 votes. Dulles, at a press conference in Washington, asked about Eden's mention of force, replied that the United States 'did not intend to shoot its way through the Canal'.

The opposition had the government on the defensive. Eden was now somewhat trapped between the diplomatic and the military timetables. Dulles's plan made the immediate use of force impossible. There were many potential difficulties with SCUA and there was, of course, no guarantee that Nasser would reject the plan. Indeed, Gaitskell felt that if it were presented to the Egyptians as giving them control over the 'daily operation' of the canal 'while leaving to an international council specific matters such as freedom of passage, tolls, development, and possibly the larger question of investments in Egypt' this would overcome Nasser's reluctance to accept a

Western-dominated arrangement.[62] He also felt that the United Nations would be the best way of achieving this settlement. If SCUA developed along these or other lines it would be unacceptable to the British. With the Americans making what he considered 'weak' statements Eden fell back much more on the French. Eden in consultation with the French now decided that the matter should be presented to the Security Council, in the hope that Nasser could be made to defy a resolution worded against him.

Between 19 and 20 September the second London conference was held and plans were devised for the SCUA, which was to have had its first meeting on 1 October. On 23 September the British and French finally referred the Suez dispute to the UN Security Council and on the same day the Israeli Prime Minister, David Ben-Gurion, referring to the French, said that Israel would soon be able to rely on 'a true ally'. The clouds of evasion from the government on the use of force were beginning to clear a little to reveal the outline of military collusion between Britain, France and Israel. However, so long as the matter was at the United Nations, there seemed little possibility of military action.

At the Labour Party Conference Gaitskell mustered his forces. It was becoming clearer almost by the day that the crisis would have to come to a head. Reports of possible collusion trickled out in late October and early November but so far there were only the continuing troop movements to judge by. The government had now agreed to raise the issue with the UN. Gaitskell rose at the Party Conference and tried to shift the balance of the argument. Instead of relegating the issue of force to a few perfunctory paragraphs he made it the centre of his speech. There were no more comparisons of Nasser and Hitler. 'The crucial issue of force' was not a question of being pro- or anti-Nasser but of working within the United Nations Charter to achieve a peaceful settlement. On 5 October this became much more likely, as progress at the UN towards agreeing to Six Principles on which SCUA could be made to work seemed to be being achieved by Lloyd in New York:

> In sum, Egypt was now willing to negotiate an agreement which gave the maritime powers substantially all that they were asking. The Suez Canal Users' Association, or its equivalent, would now have a real job of work to do as the organised representative of the users and, without prejudice to Egypt's right of ownership, would be able to safeguard the interests of its members ... After two and a half months of bitter

exchanges, it seemed that agreement had finally been reached that the Suez Canal would be run as a partnership between Egypt and the users.[63]

Anthony Eden was in danger of losing the chance for his war. With America opposed to the use of force the only other real option was to use SCUA as a pretext, but now the UN seemed to have resolved the outstanding issues on this. But at the Conservative Party Conference Eden returned to the issue of the use of force. Eden said:

> President Eisenhower in his press conference on Thursday is reported to have said that you must have peace with justice, or it is not peace. I agree with those words. We should all take them as our text. That is why we have always said that with us force is the last resort, but it cannot be excluded. Therefore, we have refused to say that in no circumstances would we ever use force. No responsible Government could ever give such a pledge.[64]

He was cheered to the rafters by the Conservative Party Conference. The window of opportunity for peace was closed at that Conference; now Eden was renewed in his desire to find a pretext for war. As soon as it appeared that SCUA might actually provide the diplomatic solution, along the lines advocated by Gaitskell, Eden needed another pretext. Then, on a glorious autumn day at Chequers, representatives from the French government supplied it. In Cabinet on 3 October, Eden had said how impressed he was with the Mollet government's uncompromising attitude towards the Suez situation.[65] 'Now the French representative, Gazier, asked Eden what would be Britain's reaction if Israel were to attack Egypt. Eden replied that this was a very difficult question ... "But would you resist Israel by force of arms?" Gazier asked. To this Eden replied with a half-laugh that he could hardly see himself fighting for Colonel Nasser!'[66]

Three days later Eden and Selwyn Lloyd travelled to Paris to discuss the arrangements for joint military action against Egypt. On 16 October the *Washington Post* reported French troops assembling in the Marseille-Toulon area. They were informed that they were going overseas but not to Algeria. *Time* reported that American diplomats had lost all contact with their London and Paris counterparts in the Middle East. The meeting which decided on the course of collusion took place in Paris on 16 October 1956. Selwyn Lloyd, Anthony Eden and the Chiefs of Staff held a meeting in London before the Prime Minister and Foreign Secretary flew to Paris for talks with Mollet and the French Foreign Minister, Pineau. On the

18th Sir Walter Monckton, known for his longstanding opposition
to intervention in Egypt, resigned from the Defence Ministry. On
the 20th Selwyn Lloyd stated that Britain and France had gone to
the 'limit of conciliation'.

As Eden was being given the pretext he needed for his war with
Nasser by the French at Chequers, Gaitskell was preoccupied by
private grief. His mother, who had stayed during the week in a flat
in the Frognal house and at weekends in a cottage in the village of
Milland, died on 16 October. Gaitskell's long rebellion against his
family and their coolness about his marriage to Dora had both faded
with the years. Mrs Wodehouse, who had married an old Burma
hand like her first husband, Arthur Gaitskell, and a cousin of P. G.
Wodehouse to boot, had become a Labour loyalist and used to
call her son 'the Minister'. She frequently attended the House of
Commons, not just for the big occasions like his one and only
Budget. She was a lively woman who became a little difficult in

later life. Julia remembers a certain rudeness to waiters but she and Hugh became close again and her death, especially at such a time, caused immense emotional strain for him. As Gaitskell buried his mother, the British government proceeded with their plans.

From 22 to 24 October, French, British and Israeli government officials assembled at Sèvres and worked out a scheme for intervention.[67] The plan was for the Israeli forces to attack Egypt on 29 October, supported by the French, across the Sinai. The British and French would then issue appeals to the Egyptian and Israeli governments to halt all acts of war.

> In addition, the Israeli Government will be notified that the French and the British Governments have demanded of the Egyptian Government to accept temporary occupation of key positions along the Canal by Anglo-French forces. It is agreed that if one of the Governments refused, or did not give its consent within twelve hours, the Anglo-French forces would intervene with the means necessary to ensure that their demands are accepted.[68]

In other words, the French, British and Israelis agreed to fulfil their own national interests in collusion with each other at the expense of Egypt, the rule of law, the United Nations and most of the structures of democratic government. During the discussion Lloyd did mention that 'important sections of public opinion in Britain, in some Commonwealth countries and in particular in Scandinavia set much store by a peaceful solution' but this, along with other reservations from Lloyd, was brushed aside; the meeting at Sèvres was a council of war. The Watch Committee reports on the 28th had warned the American administration of Israeli mobilisation but tended to suggest that this would be for an attack on Jordan.[69] French military movements also featured but not British. At 11.17 on the morning of 29 October a telegram was sent from the US Department of State to the embassy in France.[70] It concluded that there would be an Israeli attack on Egypt, assisted by the French and possibly the British.

On the 29th, supported by the French air force, Israeli armour and paratroopers invaded Sinai. The British Mediterranean Fleet, with the invasion force on board, moved east from Malta toward Cyprus on a 'communications exercise'. Eisenhower appealed to the Security Council. The next day the Anglo-French ultimatum to Israel and Egypt was issued. Nasser rejected the ultimatum and ordered a full mobilisation. Eisenhower appealed to Britain and France to await United Nations action. Britain and France vetoed the Security Council decision. British bombers began operations against Egypt. In meetings in Washington, Eisenhower's initial reaction was that 'those who had started this operation should . . . boil in their own oil' but he cooled and as early as 4.25 p.m. on 30 October was instructing his officials to look into ways to 'help meet the British shipping problem'. However, he broadcast on 1 November condemning British and French action.[71]

Gaitskell was presenting a television award when he was informed that Israel had mobilised; his physical tension as the news came through was something that stuck in Malcolm Muggeridge's mind. All the usual channels were closed between the government and the opposition. The opposition had been given fifteen minutes' notice of the ultimatum to the Egyptians. This was, in many ways, the final humiliation for Gaitskell. Eden had consistently lied to him in public and private; the passionate hatred he felt for this kind of political conduct, in this kind of way, resulted in a series of intense, at times tearful public interventions. It was as though much of what he had fought for since 1945, the maintenance of Britain's place in the world, the Anglo-American alliance, not to mention truth, integrity and decency in public life, were being sacrificed on the altar of Eden's damaged ego. At times, over the next week, Gaitskell could not control the anger, the emotion and the physical pain he felt at what was happening. On day one of the military operation, 29 October, there was no statement in the House of Commons by Eden. Pineau was asked by an aide, 'Is it war?' He replied, 'I cannot tell you yet.'

The next day, the Anglo-French ultimatum having been delivered, Eden issued a statement but made no mention of bombing. Newspaper reports began appearing saying that the whole operation had been co-ordinated between the British, French and Israelis, that British bombers from Cyprus had attacked Egyptian airfields and that the British and French had vetoed the Security Council resolution calling for ceasefire, the first time the British had used the veto. Gaitskell returned to the attack:

In taking this decision the Government, in the view of Her Majesty's Opposition, have committed an act of disastrous folly whose tragic consequences we shall regret for years. [Hon. Members: Oh] Yes all of us will regret it, because it will have done irreparable harm to the prestige and

reputation of our country. Sir, this action involves not only the abandonment but the positive assault upon the three principles which have gov-
erned British foreign policy for, at any rate, the last ten years – solidarity
with the Commonwealth, the Anglo-American Alliance and adherence
to the Charter of the United Nations. I cannot but feel that some hon.
Gentlemen opposite may have some concern for these consequences . . .
Even worse is the effect on the third pillar of our foreign policy which
has now been so wantonly attacked by the Government – our support
for the United Nations. Indeed, it is our attack upon the principles and
the letter of the Charter which is the reason that our action has been so
coldly, indeed hostilely, received by both the Commonwealth and the
United States.

The NEC met on the morning of 1 November and there was complete unanimity on the idea of the National Council of Labour – an
umbrella organisation of the various parts of the labour movement –
taking over the Suez Action Group and directing demonstrations and
a campaign against the government. Tony Benn had already phoned
the Movement for Colonial Freedom and had them book Trafalgar
Square for a rally to be held at the weekend and this was now handed
over to the Labour Party.[72] The Labour Party's campaign was to focus
on the slogan 'Law not War'. The National Council of Labour issued
an immediate statement calling on the British government to cease all
military measures in Egypt, and to support the demand made in the
UN for an immediate ceasefire and withdrawal of Israeli troops. The
campaign against Suez was launched.

Posters, leaflets and meetings were organised throughout the
country. Telegrams flooded in. The Microcell Shop Stewards
Committee called for a general strike;[73] the Woolwich Arsenal shop
stewards wrote in expressing their horror and grave concern.[74] About
80 per cent of the letters sent to the general secretary, Morgan
Phillips, supported Labour's stand against the operation. Those that
did not generally came from older members, who, while not fully
endorsing what Eden was doing, felt it wrong not to support the
government of the day in a time of crisis.[75] Somebody returned one
of the 'Law not War' leaflets to Morgan Phillips at Transport House,
and in the section asking people for more details they had scribbled:
'If Bevan ever becomes Prime Minister then this country will one
day be another Hungary. "Think on these Things." And God bless
Anthony Eden. And down with Labourites.'[76]

On 5 November amid worldwide condemnation and widespread

speculation about collusion, British and French paratroopers landed at Port Said. With British troops in action, opinion in the country moved behind Anthony Eden's adventure. Precedent had it that the opposition was briefed when military action was taking place. Churchill and Eden had been kept fully informed of the events in Korea. Gaitskell, however, received no such courtesy from Eden over Suez. Nevertheless it took immense courage for Gaitskell to continue to condemn the government once military actions had begun; and he went even further.

When Eden announced that he would broadcasting to the nation on the evening of Sunday 4 November, Gaitskell demanded a right to reply. He phoned Tony Benn, whose policy advice he may not have valued but whom he trusted on broadcasting, and told him he would be making a broadcast and needed all the arrangements made. Benn rang the Director of Sound Broadcasting at the BBC, Harman Grisewood, to ask for studio time. Grisewood asked him what broadcast he was talking about and Benn told him that the Prime Minister was speaking and Gaitskell would be replying. Grisewood was outraged and said that this was an 'unwarrantable assumption': Eden was making a ministerial broadcast and there was no automatic right to reply. Mr Benn would have to go through 'the usual channels'. That meant the Chief Whips, Herbert Bowden for Labour and Edward Heath for the Conservatives. Consultation through the usual channels was time-consuming and time was a critical factor: British bombers were destroying the Egyptian air force and the invasion force was mustering. Benn pressed on. The government, he said, would almost certainly refuse a broadcast and if that happened Labour would press the BBC for a decision. Grisewood responded, 'That is quite impossible, we shall all be in bed.' Benn said that was intolerable and somebody had to be available to give Gaitskell an answer that night. Grisewood relented and said he would arrange for Sir Alexander Cadogan, the Chairman of the BBC and a director of the Suez Canal Company, to be on stand-by with a response. Benn reported back to Gaitskell, who then had Bowden call Edward Heath. Heath said that they could not know if they would have wanted to reply until they had heard the broadcast so he could not give a response. Gaitskell was becoming increasingly angry and exasperated. Then Benn suggested they put out a press release saying that Gaitskell would be replying on Sunday at 10 p.m. This would give them a no-loss situation:

This statement was instantly taken up by the press and appeared in the ITA news flash at 6 p.m. It was an exceptionally cunning move for whatever happened the headline was as damaging to the Government. Either it would be 'Eden gags Gaitskell', 'BBC gags Gaitskell', or 'Gaitskell beats Eden's gag', or 'Labour beats BBC gag on Gaitskell'.[77]

The news release forced the government's hand and they agreed to the broadcast but not before some high drama, which, if the situation had not been so tense, would have had an air of farce. Gaitskell was in Frognal Gardens with Dora listening to Eden's broadcast. Herbert Bowden was at home in Leicester. Grisewood was at Broadcasting House and Cadogan was by his telephone at home. A courier was at Number 10 ready to take the text of Eden's speech to Gaitskell by 11 p.m. so that he and his advisers could confirm the arrangements with the BBC and work on their own script; then notice of the broadcast could be given in the morning news programmes. It made sense for everything to be arranged that night. Eden spoke between 10 and 10.15 p.m. Everyone was kept waiting until 11.30 for the text and Heath's judgement was that the broadcast had been 'quite impartial' but the Conservatives would not object if Gaitskell wanted to reply. Bowden, having heard this from Heath, now phoned Grisewood to make the arrangements. Grisewood rang Cadogan, who said it was too late to make a decision that night and they would have to wait until the morning.

Bowden phoned Gaitskell and told him of the BBC's stonewalling. Gaitskell rang Grisewood, demanded Cadogan's home phone number and in a rage tried to speak to him to demand a response. But Cadogan had had enough and refused to answer his phone. Gaitskell was furious. However, in the morning Cadogan agreed to the broadcast. The episode, apart from the delay involved, was quite trivial but it illustrates the breakdown of the 'usual channels' and normal courtesies during the crisis; it might in itself have been a minor humiliation for Gaitskell, leader of the opposition, to be left hanging on the phone by a public servant like Cadogan, but it was indicative of the establishment closing ranks against him. He was to endure much worse.

On Sunday 4 November, in Downing Street, Eden was meeting with the Cabinet and by a majority decision they agreed to ignore all appeals for a ceasefire and press on with the operation. In Egypt the Suez Canal had been blocked. In the Treasury, perhaps $50 million in reserves had been lost in the last forty-eight hours; estimates of the cost of replacing the oil that normally came through the canal were between $500 million and $700 million a year. At midnight on Saturday the news of Anthony Nutting's resignation from the government was released. Tony Benn bought all the Sunday papers and arrived at Hugh Gaitskell's house at 11 a.m.

Later that morning, Tony Benn, Woodrow Wyatt and Hugh Gaitskell assembled in Frognal Gardens to work on the script for the broadcast. Meanwhile David Wedgwood Benn was in the *Daily Herald* office phoning through news as it came in. The Benn brothers and Woodrow Wyatt were Gaitskell's private office at this critical moment of the crisis. While Wyatt and Benn read the newspapers and answered the phone, Gaitskell worked on the text of his broadcast. By 2.30 the draft was finished and Dora served them lunch. It was a friendly and amusing meal, the adrenalin and the sense of history affecting them all. Benn felt that 'that house at that moment was one of the centres of the world.' They arrived at the studio at 6.30 p.m. and Gaitskell rehearsed. The technicians, in 'contrast to their usual lolling and whispering', stood silently and listened. At 9.00 Gaitskell finished the rehearsal, realised he had to cut five minutes, and deleted an entire passage. At 9.55 he read it through once more for mistakes. At 10 the red light flashed and Gaitskell spoke:

> It has been a tragic, terrible week. Indeed a tragic and terrible day with the news coming in about Hungary. It's been, I think, by far the worst week for the world and for our country, since 1939. Last Monday evening came the news of the Israeli attack on Egypt . . . I'm not going to try to apportion the blame – that's really the job of the United Nations. But what should we have done? That's the real question.

He went on to attack the government for obstruction in the United Nations; for breaking international law; for being the aggressor against Egypt. Taking each of Eden's justifications in turn he dismissed them as groundless:

> What are the consequences? We have violated the Charter of the United Nations. In doing so, we have betrayed all that Great Britain has stood for in world affairs. Since the war, at least, we have supported every stand against aggression . . . A deep, deep division in the Commonwealth . . . This is not a Labour Party matter – it touches the whole nation – all those who care for the rule of law in international affairs.

Britain should now support the United Nations Assembly resolution demanding a ceasefire and the acceptance by both sides of a United Nation police-keeping force; the government should abandon the idea of solving the problem by force. Until this point, much of what Gaitskell said had been unanswerable. It was to be repeated over and again in the debates in November and December and would lead, along with a series of other factors, to the resignation of Eden. These other factors, particularly the financial drain that made the adventure unsustainable, were on balance more significant; but in the long run, especially in the Commonwealth, Gaitskell's impassioned appeal opened the way for the rekindling of Commonwealth links and alliances. However, the ending of his broadcast showed the extent to which the issue had become something personal between him and Eden, and connected to the way Eden had behaved. As Crossman put it, 'One can't actually make people desert if one is their enemy – unless, of course, they are crooks and psychopaths – and the more you encourage them to do so, the more you stiffen their morale.'

> Only one thing can save the reputation and the honour of our country – Parliament must repudiate the Government policy. The Prime Minister must resign. The Labour Party cannot alone achieve this. We are a minority in the House of Commons. So, the responsibility rests with those Conservatives who like us are shocked and troubled by what is happening and who want a change. I appeal to them especially. Theirs is a difficult decision, but I want to say to them that our purpose too, in this matter, rises above Party – I give them indeed this pledge. We undertake to support a new Prime Minister, in halting the invasion of Egypt, in ordering the cease-fire, and complying with the decisions and recommendations of the United Nations. In that way only, believe me, can the deep divisions in the country on this matter be closed. I appeal to those who can bring this about, to act now and save the reputation of our country and the future peace of the world.[78]

This powerful attack and the follow-ups in the House of Commons effectively divided the country and injured Eden at home. Then around the world the financial markets, led by the Americans, attacked the pound. These global darts opened up the wounds. The United Nations condemned the aggression. At the Suez Committee on 4 November Macmillan threw up his hands and said, 'Oil sanctions. That finishes it.' When after another forty-eight hours America opposed an approach to the IMF to stop the run on the reserves, even Eden realised the game was up. The combination of blows crippled Eden. From 7 November, Butler and Macmillan were in charge and Eden effectively had a mental and physical breakdown. The government was forced to accept a humiliating ceasefire.

When the ceasefire was announced, Gaitskell greeted the news at a packed peace meeting in the Royal Albert Hall by saying that the pause in the fighting was one of the 'greatest triumphs for democracy the world has ever known'. During the past week Labour had been determined to 'tell the world that in Britain the Government did not represent the true views of the people. And the people had responded with passioned and determined protests against the policy of the Eden government.' He demanded that Britain must now resume free negotiations with Egypt and other parties, and urged the withdrawal of British forces from Egypt: 'We must abandon the monstrous idea that we can solve the Suez problem by force.'[79]

The reviews of his Suez performance were of course mixed. The strength of Tory feeling was summed up in May 1957 by a profile by Henry Fairlie in the *Daily Mail*. Headlined the 'The Case against this Man', it began:

> Mr Gaitskell's behaviour during the Suez crisis has earned him more public discredit more quickly than any other politician, at least since the war. No Labour leader is more bitterly hated by the Conservatives, or more distrusted by the general public ... When the Suez Canal was flowing through Sir Anthony Eden's drawing-room – so the accusation goes – Mr Gaitskell was playing political ducks and drakes in its muddy waters. National interests were thrown overboard in order to keep the Labour ship afloat.

Fairlie rightly went on to state that there was no truth in the charge but that Gaitskell was hated by the Conservatives as a traitor to his class and mistrusted as an intellectual. For Fairlie, Gaitskell's main quality was courage and he recalled talking to Gaitskell immediately after the Morecambe Conference in 1952:

> Straight from the conference room, over a cup of coffee he said to me: 'There is only one thing we have to do in the next few years and that is keep the Labour Party behind the Anglo-American alliance.' ... But, basically, Mr Gaitskell's problem is one that concerns himself alone. He is absorbed by the exercise of power and by his own reactions to its exercise. No politician is more introspective about his political actions.

This could be a source of weakness and if it is allowed to become so it will destroy him as it destroyed Sir Anthony Eden's political genius.

Michael Foot gives rare praise to Gaitskell in his description of the Suez debates:

Indeed, the speeches of Gaitskell and Bevan throughout the crisis – the combination of Gaitskell's relentless, passionate marshalling of the whole legal and moral case against the Government's expedition to Suez and Bevan's sardonic and reflective commentary upon it – complemented one another and constitute together the most brilliant display of opposition in recent Parliamentary history.[80]

While British bombers destroyed the airfields of Egypt – evoking starker images of Mussolini in Abyssinia than Nasser had ever done – more echoes of 1930s-style international relations were heard as Russian tanks crushed the revolt in Hungary. The 'tragic day', 4 November 1956, was a defining moment for many on the left. The repercussions of the Soviet attack on Hungary were to be felt for years, in many bitter arguments, in former Communist Party members who now turned to the Labour Party, and in the final disillusionment of many who had given the great experiment the benefit of the doubt even after the Nazi-Soviet Pact of 1939.

The Hungarian uprising began on 23 October 1956, when police attempted to arrest students demonstrating against the deposing of the reformist leader, Imre Nagy. Nagy's rise to power and a parallel revolt in Poland resulted from a general weakening in the structures of Stalinism following the Soviet dictator's death in March 1953. Not being able to rely on the Hungarian military, the Soviet Union discovered by 28 October that they could not put down the rebellion with the forces at their disposal inside the country; by this stage some 10,000 people had lost their lives. The Soviet troops withdrew from Budapest and regrouped. Nagy requested United Nations intervention, announcing that Hungary had left the Warsaw Pact and was now neutral. The United States decided, after the earlier events in Poland, not to intervene militarily in the region; the Western alliance therefore did not respond. It has even been suggested that the US actually informed Khrushchev, through Tito, on 2 November that 'the Government of the United States does not look with favour upon governments unfriendly to the Soviet Union on the borders of the Soviet Union.'[81] Either with or without this American blessing, the Soviet troops counter-attacked on 4 November, bombing Budapest and reinvading Hungary. Tony Benn recorded in his diary: 'the last day of freedom in Budapest and the agonising goodbye to Mr Nagy in his dramatic appeal to the world. Then the Hungarian national anthem and total, total silence.'[82] By the time the USSR had installed a new government, 30,000 people were dead.

For Gaitskell, Hungary had a strong personal resonance. While he was not aware that the US had given *carte blanche* to the Soviet Union (or that the Soviets had withdrawn advisers and aeroplanes from Nasser), he was aware that it was impossible for the British to condemn the Soviet action in trying to crush a regime that had defied it. Moreover news of a brave group of democratic socialists being crushed by force brought back memories of Vienna. The Soviet Union's actions in Hungary, more perhaps than any others in the post-war period to this date, also confirmed all that Evan Durbin had felt about the nature of Russian communism. Gaitskell had long since been convinced that his old friend was right, but the brutality of the events in Hungary must have brought home to him the extent to which Durbin's contention that Soviet communism and freedom were incompatible, and that there was no real difference between the totalitarianism of Nazis and that of the Soviet regime, was vindicated. The passion and vigour with which Gaitskell fought unilateralism and neutralism in the years to come had many roots: the 30,000 killed in Hungary and the arguments of his old friend that this was an inevitable outcome of totalitarianism were two of them.

Events now moved fast on the British scene. Gaitskell's broadcast of 4 November, with its call for Suez rebels among the Conservatives to combine with the opposition and replace Eden, effectively ruled out, as Crossman had predicted, a full-scale split in the Conservative Party. This was not May 1940. One of the Tory rebels phoned by Richard Crossman told him, 'Country before party, Dick. I beg you to stop the "Eden Must Go" campaign, since this will make it impossible to get rid of him.'[83] Faced with the force of Gaitskell's denunciation and Eden's climbdown in the House of Commons, not to mention the undermining of the American alliance, isolation in the UN and condemnation by the bulk of the Commonwealth, the British Conservative Party rallied around their leader. By 5 November, Eden had received 200 telegrams of support from Conservative Party organisations around the country. The local Conservative association in Hampstead 'convened a special meeting to deplore the "objectionable broadcast" of the area's most famous political resident'. This was an early taste of the concentrated attack that Gaitskell was to suffer from the Tories for the next two years.[84] On 5 November the ceasefire was announced and the Conservatives began their long retreat from Suez.

Macmillan effectively pulled the plug on the military operation. In Cabinet on 7 November he switched from being one of the key hawks to being a dove and 'counselled that the operation must be terminated'.[85] The Cabinet agreed that, in 'order to regain the initiative and to re-establish relations with those of the United Nations ... in sympathy with our aims, we should agree ... to stop further military operations.'[86] The losses from the reserves for November were expected to be some $300 million.[87] In Cabinet on 28 November, the Chancellor informed his colleagues that there was no longer any option but a speedy withdrawal because, in essence, 'all the money was gone':

> It would be necessary to announce, early in the following week, the losses of gold and dollars which we had sustained during November. This statement would reveal a very considerable shock both to public opinion in this country and to international confidence in sterling. It was therefore important that we should be able to announce at the same time that we were taking action to reinforce the reserves both by recourse to the International Monetary Fund and in other ways. For this purpose the good will of the United States Government was necessary; and it was evident that this good will could not be obtained without an immediate and unconditional undertaking for withdrawing Anglo-French forces from Port Said.[88]

The economic repercussions continued well into 1957, with 'the Treasury reporting the loss of $30 million in one week' in March. It took much of that year to rebuild any kind of economic confidence. As Lewis Johnman, the historian of the economics of the Suez crisis, concludes: 'There can be little doubt that Treasury advice over Suez was accurate and that, had it been accepted, a political and economic (and perhaps military?) fiasco could have been avoided.'[89] But the advice was not given to the rest of the Cabinet or the Suez committee.

Johnman also questions Harold Macmillan's role in the crisis. If the Treasury was warning of the consequences on the pound of the intervention, did Macmillan brief his colleagues fully? If he had, would Eden have listened? 'Perhaps it is too Machiavellian to see Macmillan's role in Suez as a bid to oust Eden but it was Macmillan who became Prime Minister in 1957.'[90]

12

The Future of Socialism

The pursuit of truth to the bitter end.

Gaitskell, 1953

Socialism is about equality.

Gaitskell, 1956

Candidly, I doubt whether the public ownership plan is a positive and saleable proposition.

Gaitskell, 1957

The political fallout from Suez quickly began. After 12 or 13 November 1956 Anthony Eden was effectively no longer operating as Prime Minister. The policy priority for the Conservative government was to get the Americans back on board. In the telegram traffic and the records of meetings for the endgame of Suez, only Macmillan, Butler and occasionally Selwyn Lloyd figure.[1] On 23 November, five days before the Cabinet that decided on withdrawal, Eden left Britain for Jamaica to try to recover his health. Lady Eden judged that her old friend Ann Fleming's house would be a safe place for her husband to get some rest. Alan Lennox-Boyd contacted Ann and asked if their house, Goldeneye, was free. Finding that it was, amid much melodramatic secrecy, the Prime Minister left for his holiday:[2]

> The Party reacted with incomprehension and the press was again hostile; Randolph Churchill went so far as to say that the only historical parallel for the British troops now abandoned in Egypt was the German army at Stalingrad, 'but even Hitler did not winter in Jamaica'. Such polemics did terminal damage to Eden's reputation.[3]

On 3 December, Selwyn Lloyd – flanked, according to his biographer, on one side by Macmillan and on the other by Butler[4] – came to the House of Commons to announce the unconditional withdrawal of British troops from Egypt.[5] On 5 December, Bevan concluded the House of Commons debate:

It will take us very many years to live down what we have done. It will take us many years to pay the price. I know tomorrow evening hon. and right hon. Members will probably, as they have done before, give the Government a vote of confidence, but they know in their hearts that it is a vote which the Government do not deserve.[6]

However, Bevan's gentle response gave the Tories one of their more powerful weapons to use against the opposition, portraying Nye as the statesman over Suez and Gaitskell as the hysterical and inexperienced leader following his party. Typical was the *Daily Telegraph* on 1 January:

Since last August, Mr Gaitskell had broken all records for lithe agility. Now he gives us a message for the New Year, and the theme of his message is the duty of the Opposition to attack the Government for its action in Egypt. One can almost hear the deep tolling of Wordsworth's bell: 'Stern daughter of the voice of God.' It would have been more effective if Mr Gaitskell's conception of duty had been consistent from the beginning . . . No one really wants the Opposition to 'gag itself at a time of crisis'. But we have a sorry example of the present Opposition's behaviour when the gag is withdrawn. Pecksniff has never been a very popular character in this country. When the Leader of the Opposition pontificates on 'our duty to speak out', the ordinary citizen is tempted to adapt the words of an immortal satire: 'Chuck it, Gaitskell.'[7]

When Eden slunk back into the House of Commons on his return from Goldeneye, only a single Conservative backbencher responded by waving an order paper. Eden's position was now untenable; shortly after Christmas he resigned on grounds of ill health.

Gaitskell watched the events from an unfortunately timed lecture tour of the United States. He would have preferred Butler as Eden's replacement because he already had the measure of him from the years of replying to his Budgets. Harold Macmillan, however, outplayed Rab in the manoeuvres that followed. Such was the confusion in Conservative Party politics at the end of Suez that the leadership was decided in the end by the fact that 'the hostility to Butler on the right was infinitely deeper than any resistance to Macmillan on the left.'[8] Macmillan's speech to the party meeting that elected him by acclamation head of the Conservative Party – he had already been appointed Prime Minister by the Queen – suggested the lines his premiership would take and the challenge this would present to Gaitskell:

> I hear a lot of talk about the Left and the Right. To the broad stream of our philosophy there are many tributaries. Indeed we are always adding to this flow as the parties of the Left break up into a kind of delta of confusion . . . We do not believe much in expelling people. I think that is a good thing, because I, no doubt, would have been a candidate for expulsion many years ago. It is this tolerance which makes us not only a national Party but a Party at the roots of whose philosophy lies the conviction that we are all in the same boat, with common problems to solve and a common destiny before us.[9]

Macmillan had set out his stall. His first priority would be to rebuild the unity of the Conservative Party and then to approach the country with a combination of one-nation Tory rhetoric and policies designed to extend affluence. As John Turner argues, 'During 1958 he embraced expansion and encouraged his Chancellors to a series of measures which had the effect of overheating the economy . . . at that point Macmillan's government were committed to demand-management as their main economic policy.'[10] This was coupled with a concerted attempt to rebuild Britain's world position by putting life back into the 'special relationship' with the United States and readjusting the relationship with the remains of the Empire and the disgruntled Commonwealth. Macmillan began as soon as he was elected: 'By a series of imaginative political strokes he has managed to make the whole Suez story seem irrelevant.' He took the wind out of the sails of the divisions in the party, according to Fairlie, 'by including in his Government the two most formidable young advocates of the opposing points of views on Suez, Sir Edward Boyle and Mr Julian Amery', and by introducing 'into practical politics the whole conception of political and economic unity with Europe'.[11]

The confident moves with which Macmillan rebuilt the Tory Party in the run-up to the general election of 1959 left Gaitskell languishing some paces behind. But the Labour Party faced deeper challenges which at times handicapped Gaitskell's ability to take on Macmillan.

As has already been discussed, the very success of the Attlee governments gave rise to many problems, the most compelling of which was how the Labour Party was to move on. There were different kinds of responses. For some, the Attlee governments represented a beach-head in the invasion of capitalism: the task was to break out of this beach-head and gain control over the remains of the private sector. For others, the achievements of the Attlee governments had settled the domestic balance of the economy: the mixed economy was the new reality and the challenge was the effective management of the mixed economy to promote greater equality – an objective which might or might not be achieved by gaining greater control in the form of nationalisation.

This second school came to be known as the 'revisionists', after Eduard Bernstein's classic text revising Marxism.[12] The irony was not lost on Tony Crosland, one of the key players among the revisionists. Some years later, when helping to organise the Gaitskellite Campaign for Democratic Socialism, Crosland used to add Bernstein's name to lists of possible supporters. Revisionism was a mixture of economics, political philosophy, practical proposals and party propaganda. Gaitskell embraced it, helped to shape it and championed it practically; his theoretical contribution was, however, rather more limited.

Gaitskell always began his analysis of British socialism by considering its roots. Thus, in a *Political Quarterly* piece published in 1956, on the 'Economic Aims of the Labour Party', he opens by reminding readers that Labour 'has never been encumbered by a precise and rigid collection of dogmas set out in the works of the socialist fathers.'

Similarly, in his *Recent Developments in British Socialist Thinking* he distances the party from Marx: 'Marx provided some, but by no means the most influential of these ideas'[13] in the early days of the Labour Party:

> Such influence as Marx had at this time was indirect, and extremely limited ... If one reason for the small impact made by Marx was the impatience of the British with too much theory, another was the importance of Trade Unionism. In the first half of the 19th century, the Trade Unions, suppressed, persecuted, operating at a time of intense industrial depression and before the arrival of political democracy, took part from time to time in revolutionary activities. But after the collapse of Chartism in the 1840s they settled down and became organisations for securing better working conditions and the highest wage rates they could squeeze from employers.[14]

The trade unions made the Labour Party but they did not do so alone. In 1927 his *Chartism* essay argued for the importance of middle-class leaders in working-class movements; in his 1956 essays he extended this idea to the role of groups within the labour movement whose job it was to provide ideas and inspiration.

The two most important were the Independent Labour Party and the Fabian Society. The ILP provided 'both the emotional inspiration and the driving force', while the Fabians offered 'the most important intellectual contribution'.[15] Gaitskell's primary interest was in the intellectual contribution of the largely middle-class Fabians. In assessing the contribution of the early Fabians, he singled out the Webbs' notion that any kind of state intervention was socialism and criticised the concept of the 'inevitability' of socialism, which he argued was inspired less by historical determinism than by a desire to make socialism seem 'respectable'. This respectability was challenged by the development of guild socialism. But, overall, the Fabian contribution was vital to beginning the process (which he saw himself as continuing) of devising detailed policy approaches to achieve the broad objectives of the Labour Party. However, before the gradualist road was embraced the party went through a 'growing process' in the radicalism of guild socialism.

For Gaitskell the relationship between the trade unions and the Labour Party was central and immutable. The critical development was after the First World War when G. D. H. Cole's guild socialism was abandoned in favour of the democratic road. This process reflected the evolutionary nature of the nexus between the political and the industrial movement:

> In the history of the British Trade Union and Labour Movement one can trace a certain oscillation between industrial and political action. For a period of years the greatest effort and activity is thrown into the struggle for political rights and legislative reforms; the emphasis then changes, a disillusionment with politics sets in, and the hopes of the workers become concentrated on the industrial front as trade unionism grows and becomes more militant in the fight for higher wages and better working conditions.[16]

Guild socialism represented a period of political action by the industrial wing, and was completely different from Fabianism both in 'method and in ultimate objectives'. The central failure of guild socialism was its rejection of the Fabian thesis that the way to win power was gradually, by democratic means. In contrast, Cole's guild socialists regarded the gradualist road as an unacceptable compromise with capitalism. The working-class victory would come through the class war, and not through the ballot box.

The reason for the central difference in objective was that the goals of the political movement and a politicised industrial movement were different. The guild socialists were opposed to public ownership by the state, because they believed that this would perpetuate 'the wage system' and therefore make no fundamental difference either to the status of the workers or to the economy in which they were employed: they would only be exchanging one master for another; capitalist employers would go, but state bureaucrats would take their place. Instead of this, the guild socialists wanted to do away with the 'wage system' altogether by transferring the ownership and control of industry not to the state but to the workers organised in their trade unions. After the transfer of power, the workers would form producers' guilds in their respective industries, whose job it would be to organise and manage production.

Gaitskell was utterly dismissive of these ideas: they were a 'nostalgic, pre-capitalist ideology reminiscent of the socialism of Robert Owen'. But his rejection went deeper: guild socialism, like syndicalism, was 'anti-rational and emotional, it was expressed often in extravagant and abusive language, especially when it was criticizing other socialist but democratic doctrines, such as those of the Fabians.'[17] This 'emotional response' would of course have left no role for the technocrats; the working class would, in this utopia, have managed without the middle-class intellectuals. One can almost feel Hugh shuffling uneasily as he responded to these ideas: where was the role for him in such a labour movement? Thankfully, he concluded, the ideas were utopian; and, in the face of the 1920s depression and the failure of a series of industrial lock-outs culminating in the general strike, guild socialism, and Gaitskell's first mentor, G. D. H. Cole, were discredited. The labour movement rejected the revolutionary road because

> The leaders of the Unions never thought in terms of revolution at all; although there was serious unemployment, the economy was never near collapse; the power of the Government was more than adequate to defeat any attempt by the workers to 'take over' the factories; and finally the overwhelming majority of the people were entirely against revolution. All this, insofar as it was not apparent before, became crystal clear at the time of the General Strike. There could not have been a more vivid illustration of the absurd 'myth' of syndicalism that at the right moment capitalism would of itself collapse.[18]

For Gaitskell there could have been no more effective exposure of the emotional, anti-rational outlook of guild socialism than the 1926 general strike. The moment which turned the young Oxford undergraduate into an active socialist was dismissed by the mature Gaitskell as an emotional, anti-rational action, which compared badly with both the cautious planning of democratic socialism and the ruthless logic and professional techniques of the Bolsheviks. The residual good sense of the labour movement saved it from being mesmerised by the moment:

> Having been brought to the brink and seen what lay ahead, the British Labour Movement lumbered decisively away. Thereafter it became accepted that political objectives must be fought for through the Labour Party and the ballot box, while the unions concentrated on their traditional function of improving the wages and conditions of their members.

This was the great transitional phase. From it emerged the fully worked-out programme for a Labour government. Responsibility and respectability were embraced in the name of gradual change; emotionalism, romanticism and anti-rationalism of the mass industrial movement seizing power were dismissed. In rejecting the latter, Gaitskell was also rejecting the idea of transforming capitalism in 'one go'. Gaitskell's rationalism became fixed on the possible economic problems faced by the community and how they could be tackled. In assessing the work in turn of Dalton, Tawney, Jay and Durbin, he was working out the democratic socialist approach to reforming the economy: the central objective of reform was equality; the means were economic theory.

Gaitskell's daughter Julia remembers three books as centrally important to her father: Shakespeare's *Sonnets*, Tawney's *Equality* and Durbin's *Politics of Democratic Socialism*. The appeal of Tawney was based on his ethical attack on modern capitalism:

> His main thesis is that private property to be justified must be associated with some function, and its owner therefore performing with it and through it some task of social value. When this is not so, it is positively harmful to society, not only because of the toll involved in the income which it draws, but also because of the social conflicts created by the fact of some people receiving something for nothing.

This system was simply wrong and should be changed by the intervention of the state. The nature of the state intervention and the best way of changing the existing circumstances to make society more ethically organised was the essence of Gaitskell's socialism. In 1931 Tawney had suggested three key questions in the consideration of whether or not an industry should be nationalised: Were the industries basic? Were they monopolies? Did they require to be re-organised?[19]

As the Attlee governments developed, these questions were refined – particularly the need to reorganise the industry to promote greater efficiency. While these specific 'efficiency' arguments came forward, the general 'egalitarian' arguments originally associated with nationalisation fell into the background. There were two reasons for this. Equality could be advanced by other means, such as the welfare state and progressive tax, and Labour had accepted the notion of paying compensation to the private owners of industry because this was the only course compatible with a gradualist approach. Gaitskell continued:

> It is impossible to justify confiscating the property of particular classes of owners without regard to their wealth but simply because they hold shares in the industries which happen to be selected for nationalisation; and in fact no party which proposed to act in such an arbitrary way would have much prospect of being elected to power in Britain.[20]

The first major stride forward had been the creation of the nationalised industries on Herbert Morrison's model. In parallel there were other types of intervention involving Keynesian ideas of demand management. But Keynes on his own had not been enough. What was also needed for a socialist government were physical controls and planning:

> There was, of course, no question of maintaining the whole war-time apparatus of control. This would in any case have been impossible because it depended for its successful operation, amongst other things, on a large volume of direct government orders, and on the goodwill and readiness to co-operate of the business community – neither of which were likely to continue in peace time. But the question remained – what controls should be retained, temporarily or permanently?[21]

The basis on which the use of physical controls should be used at any one time must depend on circumstances:

> I would be inclined, myself, to the view that the key physical controls in the private sector, without which we could not carry out a full employment policy, were foreign exchange, import and building licensing and price controls, but we should aim at normally confining ourselves to these. This means that we should try to adjust our monetary and credit policy so as to make it unnecessary to have many other controls except occasionally the allocation of a scarce raw material.[22]

The management of the mixed economy became essentially concerned with the way to distribute the spending and the growth generated by the combination of planning and progressive taxation. There were certain problems with ever-increasing taxation; therefore:

> our strategy in the next stage towards greater equality ought to be directed not to narrowing still further the differences in earned income so much as at three other matters – 'expenses', education, and the distribution of unearned income and property from which it is derived. For I believe that these are three of the major causes of inequality to-day and that in tackling them we should enjoy a good deal more popular support than by proceeding along the more familiar road of higher taxation on incomes – earned and unearned alike.[23]

Each of these problems was essentially derived from affluence. As Crosland put it, there had been a change in the nature of capitalism:

> Such primary poverty as remains will disappear within a decade, given the present rate of economic growth; and the contemporary mixed econ-

omy is characterised by high levels of both employment and productivity and by a reasonable degree of stability. In other words the aspirations relating to economic consequences of capitalism are fast losing their relevance as capitalism itself becomes transformed.[24]

Gaitskell echoed this notion of reformed capitalism in his work. He criticised the early Fabian emphasis on the taxing of land on the grounds that the nature of the ownership of land had substantially changed since the war:

> No doubt if it assumed that all land owners are weathly aristocrats who have inherited their property, to tax their heritage seems fair enough, but the justification would then really be due to the scale of their wealth and the fact that they inherited it rather than to the type of property they owned. But no such assumption can nowadays be made. In a modern economy property is constantly changing hands. There is nothing to prevent a man switching the form in which he holds his wealth from land to banks to securities and vice versa. The owners of developed land may thus include people of very different levels of wealth, insurance companies which invest the premiums paid by millions of individuals, building societies and other corporate bodies. It is difficult to justify picking on such a miscellaneous group of people for special attack.[25]

What is striking when reading Crosland and Gaitskell's work in this respect is the confidence they expressed that the economic problem of wealth creation had been solved. This optimism is matched by an astonishing faith in the power of indicative planning and demand management. But Crosland also believed that it was the affluence of the new society which had contributed to the defeat of a backward-looking Labour Party and that if the party were to win it had to stress modern visions of socialism, like social welfare, and not harp on about 'nationalising the commanding heights of the economy'.

The new society, brought about by the development of world markets in the twentieth century and by the Second World War, had produced a new economic organisation. Crosland called this the 'mixed economy', to imply a mixture of state and private ownership, and he was adamant that the Labour Party must adapt its vision of socialism to this new situation if it was ever going to win power. This idea was not by any means confined to the revisionists of the Labour Party. It formed a central tenet of the pluralist view of society represented in the writings of Professor Galbraith and Professor Lipset. Ralph Miliband in his critique of these pluralist ideas sums up the post-capitalist argument: 'This was a belief, not simply in the occurrence of major changes in the structure of contemporary capitalism, which are not in question, but in its actual transcendence, in its evolution into an altogether different system and, needless to say, a much better one.'[26]

In this brave new world, a new problem was created by the possible effects of high taxation. While more efficient taxation of inheritance and state ownership (though this did not necessarily mean having control) were favoured as a sound policy for equality, there was also the danger of reducing the amount of money available for investment, which in turn would effect growth and could represent 'a lion in the path towards greater equality'.

> Our modern socialist is therefore in favour of those who save and wants to penalise those who dissave. Finally, he is also impressed with the extent to which capital gains free of tax have preserved inequality, and he feels that the British system here is out of date and anomalous with other countries, such as the USA and Sweden.

There are, then, strict limits to what a democratic socialist can do. These limits are the democratic system. While some writers such as Harold Laski might, Gaitskell argues, consider defying the democratic structures, the majority view was put by Durbin in *The Politics of Democratic Socialism*.

> In this book, Evan Durbin stated with remarkable clarity the true connection between Socialism and Democracy, showed how impossible it was to achieve the former without the latter and drew out the full political implications of this. He continued with a devastating critique of the central Marxist doctrines which he completely rejected. He cut through the veil of sentimentality and ignorance which caused many British socialists and others before the war to combine violent protests about the Nazi atrocities with a stony silence about what was happening in Russia. With great courage and prescience he emphasised the appalling similarity between the two regimes – even devoting a complete appendix to a comparison of the cruelties perpetrated by each. His book was unfortunately not finished till the outbreak of war, and therefore never received the publicity it deserved. Even now it is still far the best treatment of the subject available.[27]

Implicit in the acceptance of the democratic system was the need to present new ideas in ways that would be attractive to the electorate. The Labour Party needed modern policies that were derived from the broad ethical approach and which were capable of securing support and connecting in some way with the electorate. Durbin's thesis naturally led to the need for modernisation in policy and presentation: there was little point in being a democratic party unless you set out to win elections.

This combination of new and traditional thinking, when combined with the achievements of the Attlee governments, produced something of an identity crisis for the left: 'Labour Governments have been in power and have found responsibility harsher and quite different from anything they expected, while full employment and social security have destroyed the rationale of much of the old emotional enthusiasm.' For both working-class and middle-class activists the success of the Attlee governments in fulfilling many of the demands of the 1930s created a psychological barrier against accepting the need to change socialism. The experience of government, the very creation of a partially socialist society, meant that many of the old dreams were dead. Crosland realised that revisionism, which pointed this out, was resented:

> Now the certainty and the simplicity are gone; and everything has become complicated and ambiguous . . . 90% of resolutions at Party conference today are Quixotic tilts at objects still hopefully seen as 'outrageous giants of that detested race'. Unfortunately there are too few Sancho Panzas to point out that they are really windmills.

Crosland saw the way out of the confusion and the first step in re-establishing the agenda of socialism as the production of a modernised definition of socialism. Gaitskell was to latch on to this later when he asked for a revision of the Labour Party's basic aims. Crosland believed that the only constant element, 'common to all the bewildering variety of different doctrines which had been known as socialism', consisted of certain 'moral values and aspirations'; and people had called themselves socialists because they shared these aspirations. Therefore a belief in the 'possible future that designates socialism' rather an attachment to a particular set of means was what was important.[28]

The values that Crosland identified were as follows: a protest against the material poverty and physical squalor which capitalism produced; a wider concern for social welfare for the interests of those in need or oppressed or unfortunate from whatever cause; a belief in equality and the classless society and especially a desire to give the worker her or his just rights and a responsible status at work; rejection of competitive antagonism, an ideal of fraternity and co-operation and a protest against the inefficiencies of capitalism as an economic system. Gaitskell echoed many of these concerns directly in his 'Amplification of Aims' and in his speech at the post-mortem Conference after the 1959 general election.

The most obvious omission from this list of socialist values was the question of the 'ownership of the means of production, distribution and exchange'. As socialism was not defined in the Marxist terms of ownership, adherence to nationalisation was not a key criterion of socialism. Moreover, simply as a means to an end – the end not specified – nationalisation could, Gaitskell and Crosland argued, be used to justify types of society which had little to do with British socialism. Ownership was not central to socialism; but social welfare aspirations and equality were. It is hardly surprising that some writers, like Jay, were to take this to its logical conclusion and demand a change in the party's name.

If, following Patrick Seyd's view, socialism is defined as transforming property relationships in capitalism then there is little to tie Gaitskell and Crosland's ideas to this somewhat abstract notion of socialism. However, if democratic socialism is defined as modifying property relations and managing capitalism, then these ideas become central to this political philosophy for the next two decades: indeed, they defined this philosophy in a way it had not been defined before.

The contemporary image of a revisionist or a moderniser implies a certain flexibility, an ability to travel lightly encumbered by core beliefs: it evokes images of throwing babies out with the ideological bathwater. The first generation of revisionists were rather different – though it did not always seem so to their more traditional opponents at the time. Both Gaitskell and Crosland were very limited in the range of their revisionism. There is a distinctive nature to their political philosophy, and the way in which they related to it, that makes it understandable more as a faith than as an ideology. At heart, though capable of immense leaps forward in their thinking, leaps that left many of their colleagues floundering, both men had a core of fundamentalist feeling not shared by all of their close associates. Both – Gaitskell even more than Crosland – had a deep attachment to the Labour Party as an institution; both revelled in its history as a distinctive democratic movement and leaned on it for a part of their personal identities: they were team players but their support for the team was not contingent. Though Crosland was once to threaten divorce, they could not imagine belonging to another institution, another political party.

Macmillan was making the political running in the period 1957–9 and rebuilding the Conservative government – but that did not mean that Gaitskell and his supporters had any more sense of defeat than in 1951. As far as they were concerned, they would govern and when they did it would be on their own terms, as a majority and taking substantially different directions from those pursued by Macmillan and Butler. The Conservatives might employ the same kinds of mechanisms but their destination was different. Gaitskell caught the sense of the difference and the root of the faith, in an introduction he contributed to the re-publication of Evan Durbin's *Politics of Democratic Socialism*. Describing the ideas and arguments of the 1930s, he wrote:

> The most fundamental ideal of those who share this outlook was social justice – but it was an ideal in no way inspired by class hatred. They were equally devoted to democracy and personal freedom. They believed in tolerance and they understood the need for compromise. They were for the rational and practical and suspicious of large general ideas which on examination turned out to have no precise content.

The vital phrase in this quotation is 'large general ideas which on examination turned out to have no precise content'. Though ideas are what matter – a position Gaitskell shared with Bevan and Crossman – the difference was that they did not matter for the beauty of them, as it often seemed was the case with Bevan, or for the arguments you could have about them, as was often the case for Crossman. Political ideas did not matter for their poetry. They mattered if they worked. Ideas – or theories, or economic policies, or even defence policy drafts – needed to be tested against experience and needed to be capable of verification by demonstration – either in numbers or in argument. Gaitskell's introduction to Durbin goes on:

> They were realistic in politics and critical of armchair politicians who, not understanding what the British electorate was really like, were forever making bad political judgements. Above all, while accepting the ultimate emotional basis of moral valuation, they had great faith in the power of reason, both to find answers to social problems and to persuade men to see the light. They were for the pursuit of truth to the bitter end, through

the patient and unswerving application of logical thought. They wanted no barriers to obstruct the free working of the mind or to blunt the sharp edge of intellectual integrity.[29]

Social problems were amenable to solution by the application of logical thought. Every question, even the question of why one person was poorer than another, was capable of being answered and capable of being solved by the action of the state. The philosopher, A. J. Ayer, a friend of Gaitskell, introduced the notion of logical positivism to Britain in 1936 in his *Language, Truth and Logic*. While Gaitskell was at UCL, Karl Popper, another key figure in popularising and building on these ideas, was teaching at the LSE. Ayer's and Popper's ideas, in different ways, influenced Gaitskell's thinking. Bryan Magee, then a young Gaitskellite, argued that Popper could actually replace the 'garbled mixture of Marxism and liberal-minded opportunism which passes for political theory on the democratic left'. In a later study of Popper he offered a striking analogy between the philosopher's ideas and the revisionists' approach:

> Organisations and institutions of every kind have to be looked on as machines for implementing policies. And it is as difficult to design an organisation so that its output is what you want as it is a physical machine. If an engineer designs a new machine but his design is not right for the purpose; or if he is adapting an already existing machine, but has not changed it in all necessary ways; then what will come out of it cannot possibly be what he wants: it can be only what the machine can produce ... this is true of a great deal of organizational machinery ... The implementation of every policy needs to be tested: and this is to be done not by looking for evidence that one's efforts are having the desired effect but by looking for evidence that they are not.[30]

Gaitskell's chosen machine was the Labour Party. He was tied to it by emotional links that flowed from the way he had grown up in the movement. Moreover, he was tied to it by intellectual links which meant that he believed that only a majority Labour government was capable of achieving the changes he was interested in making in society. For Gaitskell, democratic socialism had evolved to a point at which the tools existed to promote a more equal society through a combination of public ownership (in a wide variety of forms and decided upon a basis of efficiency); demand management (with an awareness of the disincentive effects of high taxation); and physical controls, either through indicative planning (national plans and targets) incentives or, if necessary, through directive measures (further nationalisation). These policies for equality were to be conducted through a mixed economy in which the 'capitalist' class had largely been replaced by the managerial class. It was to be implemented by a Labour Party that was a coalition of the political party and the trade union movement, which had long ago abandoned the transformatory or revolutionary road for gradualism and embraced the democratic road. With the apparatus in place for changing society, the tools of modern economic and social theory, and with the labour movement united as a force for gaining, through democratic means, the levers of power, society would gradually improve as growth provided the surpluses to spend on social welfare and greater equality. The problems would be in finding the right kinds of policy to implement – making the machine work – and ensuring that the society created was ethically based, but also fun to live in.

The mature version of Gaitskell's socialism filled various roles in his life. He had neither faith in God nor time for metaphysics; his approach to philosophy, as to politics, was practical. Yet at heart the combination of a belief in the limitless possibility of logical exploration of the world's problems, and a belief in the efficacy of economic theory, amounted to a faith. It was a somewhat paradoxical faith in reason. This great confidence in the ability of the application of reason provokes a powerful image of the Wizard of Oz: behind the façade of technological wizardry, of 'Whitehall knows best', of national plans and economic models, would sit Prime Minister Gaitskell, ruling with a majority in Parliament, pulling the Keynesian levers and pushing the planning buttons, to improve everyone's life and make the world a happier, more equitable place.

Apart from generating ideas and debating with Crosland, Gaitskell's major contributions to the development of revisionism were inspirational and practical. He was inspirational in terms of his personal relationships with revisionist writers and politicians, like Healey, Crosland, Jenkins and Jay, and in the way he led the party by trying to educate it. He was practical in his prolonged battle through Conference and the NEC to get revisionist policy accepted by the Labour Party.

Gaitskell's most important contribution was practical. In this field there arose the most controversy and while he functioned in the service of his revisionist friends – for example, finding Crosland his seat at Grimsby[31] – he occasionally got himself into trouble with the left. Ideally, perhaps a Labour leader should, like Attlee, have no close political friends; or, like Wilson, surround himself with cronies. Gaitskell's period as leader, between the two 'dealers' Attlee and Wilson, appears as a break in the Labour Party's continuity and a period of brinkmanship leadership. The contrast with Attlee could not have been greater. H. G. Nicholas, in describing Attlee's electioneering at the time of the 1950 election, also sums up his style of leadership:

> [Attlee's electioneering style] was merely the natural expression of the Prime Minister's habits and personality, there can be no doubt that it was a *tour de force* of unassuming advertisement. The family car, pre-war and far from de luxe. Mrs Attlee at the wheel, no entourage beyond the indispensable detective, the roadside stops ahead of schedule, Mrs Attlee would catch up on her knitting and Mr Attlee would do a crossword.[32]

As Philip Williams has written: 'Gaitskell was a sharp contrast to Attlee – both far more gregarious and far more willing to give a strong and early lead. When the second habit brought him under furious attack and he fell back on the few friends he could trust, he acquired a much exaggerated reputation for cliquishness.'[33]

Frustration at the way in which the left tended to dominate party meetings inspired Gaitskell before he became leader to form an organisation to rival the left. This had not amounted to very much outside Parliament, but inside the Parliamentary Labour Party and in the House of Commons they seemed to have had some success. The main targets of these organisations were Bevan and the Bevanites. The nature of the practical help which Gaitskell gave his friends is revealing. There was no single and consistent organisational expression of revisionism before the creation of the grassroots Gaitskellite movement, the Campaign for Democratic Socialism, but there was most certainly a champion for the cause ready to fight at any opportunity. In so appearing he perhaps undermined his effectiveness as a non-partisan leader, above the fray and representative of all sections of the party, but he was being more consistent with his style of politics at normal times like these than in the honeymoon period of conciliation before the 1959 election.

Equality was the issue over which Gaitskell's first major policy initiative was carried through and in this Gaitskell achieved a remarkable degree of consensus. He did so by fudging the wording. The study group on equality developed a series of policies that responded to the idea of the changed nature of capitalism. These new ideas were argued out in a group which was headed by Gaitskell but included Nye Bevan, Barbara Castle, Frank Cousins and Herbert Morrison. Two of the major insights derived from Gaitskell's and Crosland's new thinking featured in these discussions. First, because full compensation was paid when Morrisonian nationalised industries were created, this form of public ownership had little effect on the actual distribution of income: wealth flowed in the form of interest rather than dividends but it still flowed to the same group. Second, this traditional form of intervention made no allowance for the changed nature of capitalist enterprises, particularly the way in which the private sector was dominated by large companies where the managerial class was more important, in terms of controlling the company, than either an individual capitalist or groups of shareholders. In this circumstance, and for various other reasons connected to the failure of the traditional nationalised industries to generate surpluses for reinvestment, what was needed was state shareholding in major companies and competitive public enterprises.

The first draft proposals resulting from these discussions were presented to the NEC in June 1956[34] and produced an immensely radical set of policies. The private sector was dominated by 'a few hundred large companies' which controlled half the nation's resources. According to the study group's statement, there had been a separation between ownership and control:

> The immediate problem that confronts us is to ensure that these great concentrations of private power are not abused. The managers and owners of private industry should be trustees responsible to the nation; in more than one sense, all business is the nation's business. But the mechanisms of control which are supposed to operate on the private sector are clearly inadequate.[35]

Shareholders no longer had any control over the companies and because a small number of firms dominated certain sectors – like chemicals, oil refining, motor cars and synthetic textiles – they could virtually fix prices and continued to expand out of retained profits. For some sectors the power of trade unions in a situation of full employment limited the potential of these companies to exploit employees:

> Other methods of [control] are therefore necessary . . . In some cases it may be possible to disperse economic power through vigorous anti-

monopoly measures. But where this is not possible, we have to develop forms of public accountability, ownership and control, which will ensure that economic power is exercised only in the public interest.[36]

Buried in this paragraph was the undertaking to intervene in the top 200 or so companies to control private profit:

> The conclusion of the document was clear: the whole sector could be brought into public ownership, over any timescale that the Party leaders thought politically acceptable. And since Gaitskell had himself claimed that 'socialism is about equality' and that existing inequalities of wealth and income were unacceptable, the sooner private ownership was contracted and public ownership extended, the sooner would Gaitskell's own goal of greater equality be reached.[37]

If the document had been adopted as Labour Party policy as it stood, possibly with greater detail about the way in which the top 200 companies would be brought into public ownership – probably by the compulsory purchase of shares rather than the payment of compensation (a sort of reverse privatisation process) – it would have amounted to far more than a consolidation of the beach-head. The radical potential was very much in the detail. Though Nye Bevan and Frank Cousins (of the TGWU) were on the drafting committee, their battle was against a return to Morrisonian shopping lists of nationalised industries rather than the detail of the proposals being drafted, and as they were often absent from the meetings they largely missed the radical potential contained in the detail of the first draft.

The study group on equality worked through the year and Crosland was brought in to draft what would become *Industry and Society*. When it was finally published in July 1957 it had undergone significant changes, not least reflecting Gaitskell's concern with electoral presentation. However, the analysis of the private sector was more detailed but the argument was essentially the same. The number of key firms had increased from several hundred to 500 and in the middle sections the case against the large enterprises, drafted by Peter Shore, who was then in the Labour Research Department, was put just as bluntly as in the earlier document:

> large firms . . . have clearly achieved an independent life and purpose of their own. So much so that one must now ask the question: is there a case, in these large firms, for private ownership in its present form? Is there, indeed, any case at all for private ownership of these firms?

Shore's answer was that shareholders no longer had control, capitalists no longer took risks in investing so should not enjoy rewards, and companies did not invest their retained profits. Therefore, in reformed capitalism, since all the main functions of private capital had been removed, there was no need for the capitalist. Private ownership of large companies was simply perpetuating inequality:

> In the past, socialist thinkers argued that the value of land increased steadily and automatically over the years, thus bringing to its owners a completely unearned increment. This led to proposals for the public ownership of land, or for tax measures designed to remove this unearned income . . . it can [now] fairly be said that many of the characteristics once ascribed to land are now possessed by the equity shares of industry.

At this point, according to Peter Shore's account, the pen of Tony Crosland takes over from his own. The implication of bringing the top 500 companies into public ownership is replaced by the milder conclusions that shares would be purchased by taking death duties in shares as well as cash, through programmed share purchases by the National Superannuation Fund:

> It is not, of course, any part of our intention that the Government should indulge in a wildly inflationary scramble for shares. But where convenient opportunities present themselves, there is no reason whatever why public ownership of industrial shares should not be increased.

Profit would accrue to the state and not to private shareholders and profit could be either invested or used for social expenditure.

From the perspective of the 1990s, Peter Shore's idea that, possibly at a stroke or more likely gradually, the state should bring into public ownership through share purchases the top 500 companies, as well as Tony Crosland's idea that the state should gradually build up a shareholding in the major public companies, both appear more like further invasions into capitalism than safe consolidations of the Attlee beach-head. At the time, however, despite Bevan's and Cousins's tacit support, the left of the Labour Party were outraged by this retreat from public ownership.

When the statement was presented to the Labour Party Conference, Bevan was clearly embarrassed to be associated with the conclusions of *Industry and Society*. *Tribune* had condemned it on publication as a 'maze of qualifying clauses' and Jennie Lee called it 'Too Pink, Too Blue and Too Yellow'.[38] Ellis Smith, a 'disappointed ex-Minister', organised a circular letter to *Reynolds News* condemning the policy. In response, Charles Pannell put together a more prestigious group and showed the list of names to Gaitskell, 'who at once began trying to redraft their letter'.[39] More generally the left were outmanoeuvred. Cousins was not about to split the Labour Party on the issue of nationalisation at the Party Conference, and Bevan was reluctant to champion the cause. Foot 'was at his most blaring demagogic' in attacking *Industry and Society* but Bevan 'made a long statesmanlike speech'[40] and *Industry and Society* was endorsed by 5 million to 1.3 million votes.

For Gaitskell, the toned-down conclusions that Crosland had inserted provided a politically effective fudge. If the Conservatives focused on Shore's part of the statement, then Gaitskell could stress that the only specific commitments on nationalisation were road haulage and steel – if the left attacked the lack of commitment to taking over the commanding heights, then the ambiguity of the idea of purchasing shares in companies that were failing the national interest could be played up.

The left were reduced to muttering about commanding heights; *Industry and Society* was perceived to have been a triumph for the revisionists. Stuart Hall, in the *New Left Review* in 1960, summed up:

> The ideological battles have long since been joined and won. First Gaitskell assented; and then, one after another, the up and coming intellectuals in the leadership . . . By the time *Industry and Society* appeared at Brighton in 1957 the picture of reformed capitalism, the managerial revolution and applied Keynesian economics which Mr Crosland described had already begun to be extended across the face of official policy.[41]

Despite this perception, *Industry and Society* was actually a rather limited victory for modernisation. The words were fudged and any Labour government could have used them to introduce a full-blown extension of nationalisation in both new and traditional forms. Indeed, Gaitskell was not privately averse to his own shopping list of industries, favouring machine tools, aircraft and possibly chemicals and urban land.[42] The radical right of the 1950s actually had much more in common with the 'commanding heights' left then either of them imagined or could see at the time. They were bickering about the degree and form of public intervention in the state, about the role of a National Enterprise Board and about whether or not the capitalist or the private ownership of shares was sustainable or necessary. Both groups were arguing over the best means of organising society to promote equality and to intervene in order to change, generation on generation, the physical distribution of wealth. While the left might not have been quite as sanguine as Crosland on the changed nature of capitalism, both agreed that there would always be a private sector. The focus of the debate was about the extent and nature of the increased role for the public sector: the extent to which the state should be enlarged. Revisionism as a credo was a belief in the efficacy of state intervention; it was radical only in so far as it set limits on that efficacy and advocated new ways of achieving that form of control. It was a debate within a concept of political economy that has almost entirely disappeared.

After the Brighton Conference in 1957 the Labour Party's domestic policy was fixed and there was little further debate until after the 1959 election. The debate that had taken place, though passionate at the time, appears with hindsight to have been about different formulations of the same basic approach, at least as far as the leading parliamentarians were concerned. The other major debate at Brighton in 1957 could not so easily be settled; though Gaitskell achieved the votes he needed to go into the election with something approaching a coherent policy, the fundamental differences of approach on nuclear weapons could not so readily be patched over.

13

Chasing Supermac, 1957–1959

We are grown-up people and need not go in for that kind of
pretence.
> Gaitskell to Andrei Gromyko, 1956

I was astonished that serious men could conduct serious meetings
in such silly clothes surrounded by so much humbug.
> Khrushchev, on being shown the House of Lords, 1956

The Leader emerges from the husk of the ordinary politician.
> Crossman on Gaitskell, 1959

There will be no increase in the standard or other rates of income
tax under the Labour Government so long as normal peacetime
conditions continue.
> Gaitskell, 1959

At the beginning of 1956, Gaitskell met his Shadow Cabinet for a
pep talk. Alf Robens, James Callaghan, Tony Greenwood, Dick
Stokes and George Brown were summoned to the leader of the
opposition's room in the House of Commons and lectured on the
necessity for teamwork. He told them that he wanted a 'young and
energetic team' in which each member had a job to do, so that 'we
can prepare ourselves for the desperate and dangerous business of
government.'[1] Following Attlee's innovation, he gave each member
of the Parliamentary Committee a government department to
shadow. Defining their responsibilities also meant that the spectacle
of Bevan talking over the leader – as he had done with SEATO –
would not be repeated.

When a delegation came to see Gaitskell to ask him what his
attitude would be to Bevan, he hedged: it was up to Nye to join
the team.[2] This was a difficult moment in Gaitskell's leadership. If
Bevan stayed outside the leadership he could be the focus for
rebellion at any time. If he were brought in, then the left would
lose its leader and the party would be much easier to manage. In

306

retrospect, the left had already moved away from Bevan; and Bevan was semi-detached from domestic politics and increasingly concerned with his farm. However, at the time it seemed that the prospects for a *rapprochement* were not good. In private Bevan was worrying about the impact of power on Gaitskell:

> The more I reflect on Gaitskell the more gloomy I become and the more I dread the ordeal before me if ever he becomes Prime Minister. With that power and authority in his possession it will be difficult to brake his reactionary impulses and compel him to make concessions early enough. Even the thought of the effort needed to influence him to the right courses makes my spirit sink.[3]

Apart from Bevan's private grumbling, Gaitskell enjoyed an initial honeymoon with the party and made a number of strategic moves to keep the internal opposition quiet. Harold Wilson had already been brought in as Shadow Chancellor and though Gaitskell never trusted him – 'he was a cold fish' – he felt he could be controlled because he knew the need for loyalty. Gaitskell also had a fluctuating accord with Crossman; politically the other Bevanites did not matter. His real political goal was to bring Bevan into the fold.[4] After Jim Griffiths had been re-elected deputy leader of the party, Gaitskell decided to offer Bevan the colonies as his shadow portfolio. Before he had the chance, Bevan made another of his periodic wild attacks on the leadership, this time on the idea of a 'team' and on the revisionists:

> Play inside the team indeed! When you join a team in the expectation that you are going to play Rugger, you cannot expect to be enthusiastic if you are asked to play tiddlywinks . . . You would have thought that some of these people had only just arrived in the socialist movement. You would have thought that the history of the socialist movement began when they came into it. The history of the socialist movement looks as though it is beginning to end when they came into it . . . Do we now burn books? Don't we need to bother with William Morris, or Karl Marx, or Keir Hardie?

As an attack on the substance of revisionism and the writings of Gaitskell and Crosland it was a poorly aimed shot. But Bevan was not attacking the substance of what they said; he loathed the way that they said it. Like the 'desiccated calculating machine' attack, Bevan hated the medium, even while, in more considered moments, he appreciated the importance and the relevance of the message.

307

How was Gaitskell to respond to the challenge in this speech? On Valentine's Day, the Tuesday after the speech quoted above, he sent for Bevan. Jim Griffiths and Gaitskell waited in the leader's office. The pattern of being summoned to the 'headmaster's study' had already been established. Bevan, thinking himself the 'errant schoolboy' for his weekend speech, defiantly 'swaggered' in. Gaitskell said, 'Come along, Nye, come and sit down.' Nye sat. Gaitskell went on: 'Allocation of jobs'. Nye was wrong-footed. Gaitskell then said: 'We would like you to take the Colonies.' So surprised and pleased was he by this turn of events that he 'proceeded to talk in a more sensible and rational manner than I have heard him do for a long time'. The only awkward moment was when he said he would have wanted Foreign Affairs. Gaitskell tactfully ignored this. Bevan then admitted that he did not know a great deal about the subject. 'This is a very rare admission from Mr B!':

> 'Well, you'll learn a lot – it's a job with a lot of work attached to it. But it's something to get your teeth into. You didn't really have much scope when you were doing the Ministry of Labour.' He agreed with all this. . . . We are giving him a job which is an interesting one, with plenty of Parliamentary scope, with travelling . . . If, despite this, he refuses to work in the team, and goes on behaving as he has been doing recently, sooner or later he will simply get himself out of the Party . . . I have a feeling that his pride will always make it very difficult indeed for him to work in a team under my leadership, or indeed under anybody else's who is now on the scene.[5]

Gaitskell was proved wrong. During the Suez crisis Bevan eclipsed the official spokesman, Alf Robens, and in November Gaitskell made him Shadow Foreign Secretary. The Gaitskell–Bevan axis was forming. At the Party Conference in 1957 it was made firmer by Bevan's emotional repudiation of unilateralism. The political *rapprochement* was accompanied by an attempt at personal reconciliation. Gaitskell took his daughter Julia for a visit to Bevan's farm in Asheridge on a weekend in late November 1957. While Jennie Lee showed Julia the view, Gaitskell and Bevan went for a long walk together.[6] But they never became close: Gaitskell gave Bevan respect and saw him as a great man undone by his ego; Bevan never really understood Gaitskell, though increasingly he gave recognition to his political courage. Yet neither empathised with the other; if they had managed to connect in a more collaborative way they would have made, as they did for the briefest of moments over Suez, a formidable team.

While Bevan was being brought on board, Gaitskell consciously set out to enhance his own reputation in foreign affairs. The central question of the period was the relationship with the communist world. Gaitskell's attitude to the Eastern bloc and the Soviet Union was fundamentally hostile; that attitude was hardened after Hungary. However, he also maintained that the West needed some flexibility in its response to the East if there was ever going to be an opportunity for bringing freedom to the Soviet Union's satellite states. Gaitskell's first encounter with the Soviet leaders occurred in May 1956 when Malenkov, the Minister of Power, visited London to prepare the ground for a visit by Khrushchev and Bulganin.

On the evening of 29 March 1956, Gaitskell arrived, characteristically late, for a reception at the Soviet embassy. Dora came to pick him up at 7.45 p.m. to take him on to a party at the Croslands' and in the course of the conversation they teased the Soviet Ambassador, Malik, that they had never met his wife. He responded by taking them up by lift to his private quarters. A small group then assembled in the Ambassador's living-room. With Malenkov and the Ambassador and his wife were Andrei Gromyko and his wife and various other officials. As soon as they got into the living-room the Ambassador turned on the television, with the volume up high.

Tea was served and there followed two hours of informal conversation which ended with an exchange of invitations for a party at Frognal Gardens to be followed by a further dinner at the embassy. Hugh and Dora went on to the Croslands' flat and invited Roy and Jennifer Jenkins, the Jays, Frank Soskice and others to join them for the party which was to be held the next Friday. This proved an equally informal and successful affair: 'The Russians duly arrived bearing gifts – books for the children and some vodka and brandy for us. Quite a successful party followed in which I left the others who had not met him to talk to Malenkov.' At 7.15 the Russians returned to the embassy and, having got rid of their other guests, Dora and Hugh followed, bearing their own gifts – a scarf, some good scent, four Dior earrings and a copy of Evan Durbin's *Politics of Democratic Socialism,* which Gaitskell had inscribed. Next there was dinner at the Soviet embassy:

> I was given lots of caviare (Dora didn't do so well and I noticed the women didn't seem to eat much of it) followed by Schaslik and a fruit sweet. There was lots of vodka and brandy, also some Swedish wine.

Once again, the television seemed to be going most of the time until Dora asked for it to be turned off. We couldn't help wondering whether there was some microphone device – or alternatively, whether it was to obscure the noise of the conversation. After dinner we sat on the sofa and easy chairs and another long discussion followed ... We left about midnight – all very friendly despite the frankness of the talks.[7]

What struck Gaitskell during the conversations was the openness of Malenkov compared to Gromyko and the Ambassador. The Soviet Minister asked detailed questions about the British party system, the British attitude to Russian foreign policy, the Middle East, the position of the Communist Party in the UK and the class structure. In his responses Gaitskell explained the role of the parliamentary opposition in a democracy but seems to have had trouble getting across the idea that although there was a large measure of agreement on foreign policy – 'the Conservatives had taken over the policies of the post-war Labour government' – the opposition was free to take a different attitude from the government. Apart from the international relations aspects of the conversation, Gaitskell criticised the Soviet links with the Communist Party in the UK. When Gromyko denied such links, Gaitskell told him, 'We are grown-up people and need not go in for that kind of pretence.'[8] Malenkov questioned him closely on the class system and Gaitskell conceded: 'Our trouble was that prosperity had made too many workers vote Tory.' Throughout their conversations Malenkov stressed that the collective leadership had come to stay in the Soviet Union, denying the generally held idea that the real successor to Stalin had not yet emerged.

Gaitskell circulated a full record of these conversations – extraordinarily rare in this period of the Cold War – to key colleagues and to the Prime Minister and Foreign Secretary; he also mentioned the business of the television set, concluding with Dora's and his uncertainty as to whether it was for or to cover up a bug, or 'just a bad habit [the Ambassador] had picked up in America'.[9]

Malenkov's visit was followed by Khrushchev's, which was much less successful all round. It was Khrushchev's first visit to London: he enjoyed being taken to Buckingham Palace to see the Changing of the Guard and the way the English 'paid tribute to their past' but simply could not understand the House of Lords:

When we visited the House of Lords, the chairman [Lord Chancellor] came out to meet us wearing an absolutely comic outfit. He had a red gown and a red robe and a huge wig. He showed us the seat from which he chaired sessions of the House of Lords. It was nothing but a sack of wool! I was astonished that serious men could conduct serious meetings in such silly clothes surrounded by so much humbug. I couldn't help smiling as I watched this bizarre theatrical spectacle.[10]

Gaitskell first met the Soviet leaders at the embassy and was introduced by Malik; he told Khrushchev that he had had interesting conversations with Malenkov. Khrushchev replied, 'Yes. You seem to have made a great impression upon him.' Gaitskell replied, 'Well, he made a great impression on us too.' There followed a rather grand reception with caviare and pink champagne.* Gaitskell remarked that Khrushchev was like a rather 'agreeable pig', to which Jim Griffiths replied, 'Yes, Animal Farm.'[11] In response to Khrushchev's speech, Gaitskell said: 'while there was this division between Communism on the one side and Capitalism on the other, perhaps they might like to try a compromise – namely, democratic socialism.'[12]

At each stage in the subsequent meetings Gaitskell tried to make substantive points on issues such as human rights. With junior members of the delegation like the cultural attaché, Mikhailov,[13] he came up against a stone wall on anything beyond pleasantries, and with the senior members the hostility to democratic socialists was plain. Gaitskell felt ethically bound first to address the issue of those social democrats whom he thought were imprisoned† in Eastern Europe and then press on to other issues, but he did not get the chance at this meeting.

In one memorable exchange with Khrushchev he urged that the Soviet Union stop working through Communist Party front and fellow-travelling organisations but instead use ones like Chris Mayhew's Anglo-Soviet Group which was operated through the British Council. The Soviet leaders questioned why there was such an objection to leading people like the Dean of Canterbury, Dr Hewlett Johnson. Gaitskell replied that they did not approve of Johnson; 'most people regarded him as a lunatic as well.' This

---

* Sadly Gaitskell did not record in what size bottles the champagne came, otherwise this might have challenged Ann Fleming's claim, see p. 248.

† A footnote in Khrushchev's memoirs comments: 'Gaitskell annoyed Khrushchev by handing him a list of East European Socialist politicians who had vanished, asking him to find out what had happened to them (they had all, of course, been shot. (*Khrushchev Remembers* (Sphere, London, 1971), p. 376).

was not, Gaitskell recorded, 'terribly well received'.[14] Khrushchev then launched into a tirade against the British labour movement, criticising the fact that whenever British trade-unionists visited the Soviet Union they only ever reported the shortage of toilet paper. When Khrushchev had finished his attack, the private secretary came to tell them that their time was up, the meeting then broke up and Gaitskell had no opportunity to present his list of social democrats who were missing. These meetings had been hosted by the Prime Minister at Chequers. The following Monday, it was the Labour Party National Executive Committee's turn to act as host.

In briefing the Soviet Ambassador, Gaitskell and Griffiths made it clear that in the question period after the meal they would raise the issue of the social democrats imprisoned in Eastern Europe. The Ambassador responded, 'Oh, must you bother about a small thing like that?' Jim Griffiths retorted: 'It is not a small thing to the people concerned.' The scene was set for what became a legendary encounter between the Labour leaders and Khrushchev.

George Brown, fast becoming a key member of the Shadow Cabinet and a close associate of Gaitskell's – but not someone who could hold his drink or his temper if provoked – was teasing Khrushchev's son and toasting Khrushchev as the 'big boss'. Khrushchev replied that George Brown looked like a little boss himself.[15] There were not supposed to be any speeches, just questions at the end of the meal, and the presentation of the list of imprisoned social democrats. But Brown was now involved in a running banter with the Soviet leader, while at the other end of the table Gaitskell and Robens were trying to persuade Bulganin that there would not be a revolution in Britain. As Khrushchev recorded in his memoirs, by this stage the 'English whisky' was flowing.[16] Edwin Gooch, a trade-unionist and chairman of the Labour Party that year, made a short speech to which Bulganin made a good-natured reply.[17] There was then a pause, due to Gooch's 'poor chairing', and Jim Callaghan led a call for Khrushchev to speak.[18] From the beginning Gaitskell had planned to avoid allowing Khrushchev to make a speech but events were now beyond his control and the Soviet leader delivered an hour-long harangue against the West. Crossman recalled this speech in his diary later:

> He seems to be a boss and a bully, who doesn't believe in world expansion
> with his brain but will practise it in a quite sincere way to make Russia safe.
> I will never forget his contemptuous attitude to us, his couldn't-care-less
> suggestion that we should join the Russians because, if not, they would
> swat us off the face of the earth like a dirty old black beetle.[19]

Such sentiments – and the generous quantities of alcohol that had
been consumed – contributed to the explosive atmosphere. George
Brown kept responding as the translation came through and, when
Khrushchev started talking about the pre-war alliance system and
defended the 'Stalin-Ribbentrop pact', Brown, busy filling his pipe,
muttered, 'May God forgive you.'[20] At that point Khrushchev
rounded on him: 'What did you say?' People sitting around Brown
tried to keep him quiet. But Khrushchev insisted, and so Brown
repeated what he had said and explained precisely what he had
meant. 'At this, absolute pandemonium broke out.'[21] Gaitskell tried
to make a conciliatory reply, but he felt honour-bound to bring up
the subject of the imprisoned social democrats, which worsened
Khrushchev's mood further; he replied: 'If you want to help the
enemies of the working class, you must find another agent to do it.'
At this Sam Watson and Nye Bevan, though more quietly than
Brown, joined in the general argument. Bevan asked who the
enemies of the people were and how their guilt had been established.[22] After some more general arguing, Khrushchev got up and
left, saying to the Foreign Office man outside that he had wasted
an evening.[23]

The next day at the Speaker's lunch the Soviet leader refused to
shake hands with Brown and said that he had not met people like
this for thirty years. As Foot commented, 'It was a novelty to meet
people who called themselves Socialists, talked about freedom and
dared to argue with him.'[24] However, Khrushchev credited Gaitskell
with tact for his part in the evening and when saying goodbye shook
his hand. The next day Gaitskell and Griffiths had their final meeting
with the Soviet leaders.

Khrushchev announced that they would be publishing an account
of the evening back in Russia. Gaitskell countered by saying that in
that case they would publish one in England. (Neither did.) Then
Khrushchev remarked that he had said nothing new in his speech.
Gaitskell asked:

'Do you believe in being blunt? Do you agree that other people, therefore, have the right to be blunt in reply?' Khrushchev said, 'Yes.' 'Well, Mr K, believe me, everybody on our side thought you said several things that were very new indeed', implying that it was a pretty shocking statement.

When Khrushchev renewed the argument about the pre-war position, Gaitskell decided to cut the meeting short, asking the Russians how much time they had left before they had to leave. At this Khrushchev's mood lightened: 'Well, it's no use going over it; let's forget all about it; let's put all personal recrimination on one side; and let us look forward to friendship in the future.' Then, holding Gaitskell's hand for a long time, he continued: 'Well, perhaps sometimes after a quarrel, relations are better.' They all agreed that it had cleared the air. Gaitskell then made the Soviet leader burst out laughing by saying that if he could only get to know George Brown better he would realise they had a lot in common: 'You are both very outspoken, you are both fairly abrupt, you are both very strong.'[25]

The dinner with Khrushchev and Bulganin made little difference to the Labour Party's relations with the Soviet Union. Throughout, Gaitskell had shown that he had few illusions about the nature of the Soviet regime; but he did not always respond with a simple Cold Warrior position and reflected his increasing sophistication in international relations. The subtlety and skill with which something was retrieved from the Khrushchev visit was reflected a year later when Gaitskell made two major interventions in international relations. The first was an idea which was never implemented, the second one was debated on and off until overtaken by events in 1961.

Gaitskell's first intervention came out of his fifth trip to the US. During his visit he proposed in a speech to the Trades Union Congress in Atlantic City that every member of the United Nations should donate 1 per cent of its national income as aid to the Third World through the UN. He said: 'I realise the Russians might refuse. Well, if they do, the world will draw the conclusion that they are more concerned with spreading Communist propaganda and infiltration than with providing genuine economic assistance.' Nothing came of this bold idea, though it was discussed in UN circles for a number of years.

Gaitskell's second intervention took place the following January when he gave a series of lectures at Harvard and outlined his boldest ever initiative in foreign affairs. Working closely with Denis Healey, who did some of the drafting,[26] Gaitskell produced some radical ideas which he continued to press until the Berlin Wall was erected in 1961.

The events in Hungary had shown that the new openness signalled by Khrushchev's speech to the twentieth Communist Party Congress, condemning Stalin, was limited in its operation. In his first Godkin lecture Gaitskell summed up the challenge this represented:

> To us, then, the challenge of co-existence is not merely how to avoid a third world war, not merely how to settle international disputes peacefully, to live and let live, not merely how to conduct an ideological struggle against totalitarian communism, but how to do these things and also to bring to those people who do not enjoy them the benefits of liberty and true self-government.

He went on to stress the central role of the United Nations, but maintained that there were two prevalent attitudes to the UN which tended to alter depending on the issue which was being faced: either the UN was a useless talking shop or it was supposed to solve the world's problems. When the UN clearly reflected world opinion, as over Suez, it should be supported by states honestly desiring to follow the principles of the UN Charter. Gaitskell, while not condoning the actions of Israel, did not condemn a preventive war against the Arab states. However, he also maintained that, if the veto had not been applied by the French and British, then collective action could have been taken to prevent war in the Middle East on 30 October 1956. Yet while the veto remained, and while states continued to use the UN only when they needed to, the UN's potential would remain limited.[27]

The limitations of organisations like the UN increased the relevance of collective security bodies like NATO.

> For my part I have never looked on the balance of power as an evil thing which is itself the cause of war. The balance of power is simply an attempt to ensure that no one power or group of powers occupies such a dominating position that the temptation to indulge in aggressive war against others is overwhelming. If the balance is there, runs the doctrine, then it will provide a deterrent against attack.[28]

This balance of power, Gaitskell argued, was best maintained by organisations like NATO, but central to the balance of the power was the involvement of the United States. The building up of NATO had also been accompanied by a considerable strengthening of other ties between America and Europe, within Europe itself, and between

Britain and Europe. Gaitskell saw each of these developments as important for collective security. He especially mentioned the OEEC, the Council of Europe, the Coal and Steel Community and the Euroatom project. On the horizon, but not welcomed or rejected in these lectures, was the 'suggestion of a common market for some countries and a free trade area for many more'.[29]

> The European movement may not have made as much headway as its supporters desired, but it has certainly achieved some change in outlook. The European people today feel closer to one another than ever before. This would probably not have happened without the basic Atlantic Alliance – NATO.

With these developments in mind, and in the context of the changes in the Soviet Union, especially the idea of a coexistence between the communist and the democratic world, what was needed was a bold change of policy. This Gaitskell envisaged as a sweeping disengagement in the heart of Europe, allowing for a zone in central Europe that was demilitarised and nuclear free. The Gaitskell Plan called for the demilitarisation of Central Europe – Poland, Hungary, Czechoslovakia and East and West Germany – the reuniting of the two Germanys and the creation of this area as neutral buffer between East and West.

> It is time we launched our own peace offensive. It must be a genuine one, however, as I believe the neutral zone plan to be. We need not fear a new relaxed atmosphere. On the contrary experience has shown that while there has been some weakening in the unity of the West since the Soviets developed the tactics of co-existence the effects behind the Iron curtain have been far greater.

Partly in response to Gaitskell's bold plan, on Saturday 12 October 1957 Gaitskell was given a letter from Khrushchev by an official of the Soviet embassy. The letter from Khrushchev was an offer to join with France and the USA in renouncing the use of the force in solving disputes in the Near and Middle East. Referring to Gaitskell's plan for disengagement, Khrushchev wrote: 'Now there are signs of a certain narrowing of the gap between the views of the Labour Party of Great Britain and the Communist Party of the Soviet Union on a number of important questions concerning peace.'[30]

On the Sunday, Haakon Lie, Chair of the Norwegian Labour Party, who had received a similar letter, flew to London to discuss it. Jim Griffiths, Morgan Phillips and Hugh Gaitskell met Lie at

Frognal Gardens. After discussions with these men and then with Bevan, it was decided to contact the Foreign Office and a meeting was arranged with the Prime Minister. An interim reply was then sent to Khrushchev. Initially reluctant to make the correspondence public they decided to publish it after similar letters had appeared in the European press.

Morgan Phillips and the others drafted a quick response noting that the matter should be considered by the UN Security Council and followed this with a longer response after the NEC had met. They pointed out to Khrushchev that they could not, as an opposition, enter into negotiation with a foreign government, rejecting much of the content of the Khrushchev letter and declining the invitation to a meeting.[31]

Gaitskell returned to the idea of disengagement a year later. In March 1958, in an interview with the London correspondent of the *New York Times*, he put forward a slightly different version of his five proposals on disengagement.

1 Gradual withdrawal of all foreign military forces from East and West Germany, Poland, Czechoslovakia and Hungary.
2 An agreement to limit and control conventional forces permitted to the nations covered by the agreement. No nuclear weapons to be allowed them.
3 Reunification of Germany in freedom.
4 The conclusion of a security pact by the Great Powers guaranteeing the frontiers of the countries in the neutral zone.
5 Withdrawal of West Germany from the Atlantic Alliance, and of Poland, Czech and Hungary from the Warsaw Pact.

Contemporary responses were mixed in Britain and America, but with hindsight the plan appears bold and imaginative:

> the interest of this is that these remarkable non-confrontational policies were being put forward by this man who was so passionately committed to NATO, total western resistance to the Soviet Union during the cold war, and West German membership of NATO. He argued the case for disengagement on the grounds not of emotion, but of realism . . . this remains the more original and innovative phase of his views on foreign affairs.[32]

Though he continued to argue for the adoption of the Gaitskell Plan, such initiatives were gradually overshadowed by the issue of nuclear weapons.

★

The Suez period and the years leading up to the general election of 1959 saw the blurring of the internal party lines which had character-ised the early years of the decade. Frank Cousins (the new general secretary of the TGWU), Bevan and Gaitskell combined over the policy document *Industry and Society* opposing Morrison's commitment to a shopping list of industries that Labour would nationalise. The concept of nationalisation envisaged before the Second World War was gradually eroded as the party attempted to meet the challenge of Tory affluence.[33] In the foreign and defence field the old alliances broke up as Bevan bitterly parted from his rank-and-file supporters over the unilateralist debates of the 1957 Conference. Crossman described the 1957 Conference as a monumental success for Gaitskell.[34] Gaitskell's agent wrote to congratulate him:

> Your leadership and guidance has played no small part in the decisions taken. I do hope both you and Cressida are fully recovered from effects of the flu . . . Mattie is dying to ask you what you have done to Nye.

To which Gaitskell replied:

> The conference did go extraordinarily well. We really had some luck for a change. And undoubtedly the silly press helped us by playing up all the difficulties beforehand, I think I told you I thought this might happen. Of course, I will tell you – and Mattie – all about it when I see you.[35]

Although the Bevan–Gaitskell axis had been developing over the *Industry and Society* policy, its flowering, such as it was, dates from this Conference. The accord between the two leaders did not mean that either abandoned his respective style or that they became particu-larly close; it did, however, provide a united front in the House of Commons and in the country.[36]

Bevan still criticised Gaitskell's leadership, but only in private,[37] and the public schism between the two was not repeated. Gaitskell needed to keep the Labour Party united and balance the needs of effective opposition with party-political gain. He was handicapped by the constraints of continued opposition which made the last years of the 1955–9 Parliament dull,[38] and by Mikardo's and Foot's attempt to revive Bevanism in a new grassroots organisation, Victory for Socialism. Gaitskell's reaction was to meet Victory for Socialism head on. At the NEC he urged that they inform local parties that it was unconstitutional to associate with VFS. A letter warning CLPs not to associate with VFS was dispatched and the leaders were brought in for a grilling as to their intentions. Gaitskell warned them that 'a national organisation composed of like-minded people, with an Executive, annual conferences and branches, existing not only to discuss policy but also to propagate views seemed to go beyond the limits of what was permissible.'[39] This initial show of strength was welcomed in the press, but VFS continued to organise.

The internal stability of the Labour Party had not been helped by the bus strike of July 1957. This dispute, like the strikes at the time of the 1955 election, was seen as reflecting badly on the Labour Party's image of a forward looking and modern organisation. Even a sympathetic account of the strike, by Frank Cousins's biographer, acknowledges the skill with which Macmillan used the dispute against the Labour Party.[40] The bus strike presented Gaitskell with a difficult political situation: Ian Macleod, Minister of Labour, refused to intervene and Gaitskell attacked him for forcing a showdown between the two sides: 'If the strike is unnecessary, it should have been possible for the two sides to come to an agreement. If Mr Macleod says the strike is unnecessary why has he not intervened to bring the two sides together?' On 4 June, after the strike had collapsed costing the TGWU £1,170,000, Sir John Elliot, chair of London Transport, called it a flop. Gaitskell responded: 'That in the first instance, whatever the effects of the strike, it is a very provocative thing to say . . . If you want to encourage the strike to go on you cannot do better than to describe it as a flop. It is bound to be a challenge to those concerned.' It was the classic dilemma for the leader of the Labour Party during an unpopular strike: if he condemned the strikers he might gain some support from the press but would be attacked from inside the party; if he supported the strikers then the Tories could use this against him with marginal voters. Indeed, Macleod scored heavily off Gaitskell when the issue was debated in the House of Commons. The bus strike was one of the first great industrial confrontations between a union and a government: Cousins lost, but it was a watershed in post-war industrial relations.

The bus strike may have damaged Labour's 'image' in the run-up to the general election, but it was not a decisive issue. However, the fact that Macmillan shrewdly held out until October 1959 was devastating for Labour's chances. In the country this period saw the revival of the left as activists turned to CND, which was launched in January 1958, and by the leftward swing of the TGWU under Frank Cousins. For the Conservative-inclined sections of the press, the new bogeyman on the left was Cousins, who, after initially working with the Bevan–Gaitskell axis, began to move in an increasingly militant direction after January. In any case the Conservatives were 'engaged in a public relations campaign on a scale that was altogether new to British politics'.[41] In effect the government fought a twenty-seven-month election campaign, spending around £500,000 during the period from June 1957 to September 1959 on nation-wide poster campaigns. The Labour Party, in contrast, spent only £102,000 from late 1958 to the spring of 1959.[42] Internally there was unease about the gap between the two parties. In March, A. J. McWhinnie, a *Daily Herald* journalist, minuted the Labour Party Campaign Committee about the need for a better press and publicity machine:

> The Tories, apart from the large Press staff at Central office, have 10 thoroughly trained, schooled news reporters acting as Press Officers in each of 10 regions. Most of them get £1,500 to £1,750 a year plus a car and sufficient expenses for them to meet, mingle and entertain and steer newspapermen . . . I've seen it work.[43]

In modern language, McWhinnie was saying that the Labour Party did not have enough spin doctors.

The Conservatives successfully weathered an economic storm, abandoning deflation as the election approached. For the Labour Party the period between the 1958 Budget and the election saw the opening moves in the unilateral disarmament dispute. The crisis in Labour defence policy was caused by the formation of CND as a pressure group dedicated to the unilateral renunciation of nuclear weapons, and by the Duncan Sandys's defence White Paper which moved British defence policy towards an increasing reliance on nuclear rather than conventional weapons. These twin pressures made precarious the delicate compromise on defence policy devised after the 1957 Conference. Cousins and other union leaders supported unilateralism and in July 1959 the TGWU delegate conference adopted a defence policy which was largely opposed to the official Labour Party policy of the non-nuclear club.

Gaitskell replied to the open challenge from Cousins[44] and displayed his schoolmasterly tone publicly in a speech at Workington on 11 July 1959:

The problems of international relations . . . will not be solved by slogans, however loudly declaimed, or by effervescent emotion, however genuine, [but by] very hard, very clear, very calm and very honest thinking . . . our Party decisions on these matters are not dictated by one man whether he be the Leader of the Party, our spokesman on Foreign Affairs, or the General Secretary of the Transport and General Workers' Union. They are made collectively.

In the same speech he stated his view of Conference sovereignty and its limitations, identifying – a year before the 'Fight, fight and fight again' speech – his willingness to campaign openly to reverse decisions of Conference:

we should argue out and settle ultimately in our Conference the great issues of policy. But it is not right that a future Labour government should be committed by Conference decisions one way or the other on every matter of detail for all time . . . A Labour government will take into account the views of Conference . . . but Annual Conference does not mandate a government.[45]

An internal Labour Party poll directly after the TGWU decision tested voters' reaction: 'Do you see the Labour Party as a party severely split by disagreement on important issues or as a party which is basically united but determined to discuss issues openly?' In response to this question, 44 per cent replied that it was split, 29 per cent that it was united.[46] Yet Crossman found Gaitskell invigorated by the contest and was impressed by him at this time: 'The whole talk was that of a man who is rather rapidly growing up, growing tougher and growing stronger.'[47] Such optimism reflected strength of character rather than political reality.

Hugh and Dora, Bevan, David Ennals and other Labour officials left for a visit to Eastern Europe in August 1959. But Macmillan was, as usual in this period, a step ahead. Gaitskell had been going to take up Khrushchev's invitation in late 1958 but then the leader of the Hungarian rebellion, Nagy, was shot by the Soviets and Gaitskell's trip was postponed. Macmillan stepped in; he and Selwyn Lloyd arrived in Moscow in February 1959, generating headlines around the world. As Gaitskell wrote to a friend, 'It's all very chess like & unreal isn't it? That's the trouble when you have a super tactician like Macwonder.'[48] It was a chess game Gaitskell frequently lost.

The Russian trip was a prolonged repeat of the London dinner:

rows, poor publicity and too much vodka. Relations between the members of the Labour delegation were sound but there was little warmth. Bevan had been reluctant to make the trip, having visited Russia many times before. Khrushchev was about to leave for the first trip to the United States by a Soviet leader and was therefore little concerned with the Labourites. There was a general division in the group between the Gaitskells, who wanted to go dancing, and Bevan, who did not: 'Suddenly the whole slightly purposeless, slightly claustrophobic, too official, too alcoholic expedition to Moscow was interrupted by news from London. Harold Macmillan announced the date for the general election – 8 October.'[49] There had been a successful trip to a collective farm on the last day and a great deal of vodka and brandy had been consumed. The press wanted an interview with the party leader but Hugh could not be raised and Bevan took the questions. They stalled the press for three hours – it must have been quite a hangover – before Gaitskell came down to 'mumble a short prepared statement'.[50] As Foot notes, not a word of this incident, nor a later one in which two political correspondents found Gaitskell much the worse for whisky outside the House of Commons,[51] ever reached the press.[52]

Arriving back in London Gaitskell met with his press adviser, John Harris, at Heathrow airport – in the VIP Gents – and received a briefing and a copy of the draft of the manifesto.[53] Gaitskell then went straight to the TUC conference in Brighton. After a bloody row between members of the TUC General Council and Crossman over who should go to the airport, the three knights on the General Council met the leader of the opposition off the plane and shepherded him for the rest of the day. The leader made a forceful and well-received speech: 'Believe me,' he told them, 'any leader of the Labour Party would not be worth his salt if he allowed himself to be dictated to by the trade unions.'[54] It was not until the evening on the flight back to London that Gaitskell could get down to business and begin rewriting Morgan Phillips's draft of the manifesto.[55] From this first night back in Britain until polling day on 8 October, the pace was unrelenting.

Crossman took over the redrafting of the manifesto that Friday and Saturday; then he and Gaitskell met the NEC to discuss the manifesto and the broadcasting group to plan the radio and television campaign. Both meetings produced problems. In the NEC, Gaitskell first 'tore the economic paragraphs' of the manifesto apart and then after the Executive had agreed a draft began to make further changes:

> At three points he repudiated what the Executive had wanted, in particular writing in all sorts of qualifications on further nationalization, which would have taken months of debate before the Election. I think he was impressed by the way the job had been done, but he still read every page and made about twenty amendments.[56]

Tensions were evident between the broadcasting team who had been working since December 1958 on new formats for the broadcasts and background films, and Crossman, who was appointed head of the Campaign Committee. Gaitskell banged heads together and forced them to work as a team. This was to be Gaitskell's campaign. Crossman commented that Gaitskell's personality had been transformed since he came back from Russia: 'He has suddenly become a television star, a political personality in his own right – confident, relaxed, a Leader – with Nye as a rather faded elder statesman behind.'[57] On 22 September Tony Benn was amazed at the crowds at a public meeting addressed by the Labour leader:

> The size of the crowd and the tremendous reception given to Gaitskell surprised us all. He was on top of his form and made a really grand, clear, forceful speech . . . Afterwards police with linked arms had to hold back the crowd to let his car go back to the Grand Hotel.[58]

The Labour campaign of 1959 was better organised, financed and fought than the 1955 campaign. The Conservatives initially attempted to keep the election quiet, as they had successfully done in 1955, but the Labour Party – the leadership and the membership – fought a vigorous campaign which demanded a response. Gaitskell, appearing in all the television broadcasts and in an exhausting national tour, spearheaded the campaign. Crossman headed a committee which co-ordinated the effort by taking charge of 'the Research Department, which issues campaign notes, and of the television and radio and the leaflets, as well as trying to impose the general policy direction on the campaign'.[59]

Despite the efforts of the Labour Party, the dominant issue was, from the outset, economic well-being. Labour began well and the organisation in place at the beginning had improved especially in preparations for the broadcasting side of the battle. The election was much more strenuously contested than in 1955 and aroused much greater national interest. In 1955 the Transport House campaign team were answering about fifteen letters a day; in 1959 they dealt with ninety a day. Labour held daily press conferences and supplied 90–100 journalists with daily copy – a tactic which proved so successful that the Conservatives had to follow suit; they have taken place at each subsequent election.

Gaitskell also featured in the main television innovation: a series of studio-style debates sent out live. The production team consisted of Alasdair Milne from the BBC, and Tony Benn, Woodrow Wyatt and Chris Mayhew from the Labour Party. These lively and well-received programmes reached audiences of between 12 and 13 million. Gaitskell had to manage the two 'prima donnas', Crossman and Benn, who were competing for control of the programmes, Crossman from the Campaign Committee at Transport House, Benn actually making the programmes.

Gaitskell hardly had time to visit Leeds during the campaign but he wrote to George Murray: 'Julia would like to come to help in the constituency during the campaign. I have not settled exact dates with her but I think she could probably come for the week before we arrive. I imagine you will wish her to do canvassing and possibly make brief appearances at any meetings you may be organising. She is not used to speaking but may be able to utter a few words. All that, however, could be settled on the spot. It can do no harm for her to be with you. I think she will enjoy it and we shall probably get some publicity out of it as well.'[60]

Gaitskell threw everything, physically and emotionally, into the race and produced a stunning campaigning performance that inspired the party. It was a political coming of age in many ways. More people saw the warmth and the passion than before. The internal survey conducted by the Campaign Committee asked 200 candidates, MPs and party workers what they thought of the leadership: there was much praise for the campaign and the leadership. Such expressions as 'brilliant', 'the best campaign in history', and so on, were frequent.[61] Crossman recorded: 'For months he was no bloody good because everyone said he was no bloody good. Now everyone says that Gaitskell is very good indeed and he becomes very good indeed, so that I can watch the godhead emerging from the man. Yes, one can actually watch it. The Leader emerges from the husk of the ordinary politician.'[62]

On 22 September 1959 the *Daily Mail* published a poll showing the Tories' lead cut from 7 per cent to 3.5 per cent. As polls reflected opinion three or four days before, this showed the initial impact of the campaign. Staff at Transport House and Gaitskell himself began to believe that Labour could win. Other people also seemed to have picked up the idea. On 20 September, Dora had woken up to find that an enormous lawnmower had been delivered. As she explained in the *Sunday Pictorial*, characteristically charming the journalist and getting a good press: 'People are always sending things – and of course, they all have to go back . . . the mower arrived because a picture was published showing my husband using one. No letter. No phone call. Nothing. Just an enormous great mower sitting there on my front lawn.'[63]

Gaitskell gave fifty speeches in eleven days, touring the country before appearing in his constituency for the end. However, in the middle of the campaign, with the tide of opinion seeming to move in his favour, he gave the Conservatives the opening they needed for their counter-attack. He was warned over the weekend of 26–27 September by John Harris that the Conservatives would be counter-attacking on the cost of Labour's programme, particularly the pledge to increase pensions. In a bid to divert attention from this scare, Harold Wilson, when asked by Woodrow Wyatt in the second broadcast put out on the BBC Light Programme on 22 September, how Labour would pay for their programme stated that 'They are going to be paid for not out of increased taxation but out of increased production.'[64] After consulting with Wilson and deciding to state it even more plainly, in a speech at Newcastle on 28 September, Gaitskell repeated the pledge that there would be 'no increase in the standard or other rates of income tax under the Labour government so long as normal peacetime conditions continue'. There had been some talk, according to Crossman, of Wilson actually proposing on television the following week that the Labour Party would introduce a tax cut if elected[65] and Wilson did make a pledge on purchase tax three days later in the *News of the World*. All these statements were designed to kill the Tory scare that the Labour programme would have to be financed out of higher taxation:

> it killed the scare – but at the same time it provided the Tories with an opening to challenge not only the financial policy of the party but the integrity of the leadership.[66]

Macmillan recorded:

This gave me an opening for a mocking retort: 'Mr Gaitskell . . . introduced only one Budget, fortunately for you . . . He was faced with having to raise something like £400 millions in extra taxation . . . What did he do? . . . He put 6d on the income tax . . . and for good measure he put a charge on spectacles and teeth under the health service.[67]

Rab Butler followed up with 'The Labour slogan seems to be this – "a bribe a day keeps the Tories away".'[68] Gaitskell's pledge on income tax on 28 September was followed by a repeated pledge by Wilson on purchase tax on 1 October and then Morgan Phillips, on 5 October, 'nonchalantly let out, on a background paper on the cost of living, a firm pledge to reduce purchase tax on essentials'. Not only did this provide the Conservatives with fertile ground for attack, but this ground grew and grew, and the emphasis of the campaign shifted from the Labour attacks to the cost of the Labour programme:

From then on, however forthright were our attacks, in the eyes of the general public, as influenced by the right-wing press, Labour was on the defensive. The Conservatives, who had not effectively challenged our policies, succeeded in blurring the image of the party's integrity. From then on all the Tories' anti-Labour propaganda was effective and the image that had been presented in the first ten days was substantially obliterated.[69]

All Gaitskell had actually said in his speech was that he could run the economy better than Macmillan. He believed that he could pull the Keynesian levers and push the planning buttons and produce more growth than the Conservatives had done, and he believed when he said it that the people would accept it. When responding to Macmillan's 'You've never had it so good' speech, he stressed the production failures:

In the field of production the years since 1955 have, without any shadow of doubt, been by far the worse period we have had since the war. Since the last election there has been virtually no expansion of production whatever. That is simply not good enough where people expect a steady increase in living standards and where we have to play our proper part in world affairs.[70]

It is characteristic that Gaitskell, knowing himself to be the better economist, believed he could do better.

On the last Sunday before the election Gaitskell learned that a Gallup poll had put the two parties neck and neck. His final sound and television broadcasts were judged by Crossman to be excellent,[71] and when they were done Gaitskell returned to South Leeds for three days' final campaigning in his own seat. In a three-cornered fight his majority came down by 500:

Gaitskell (Lab.)	24,442
Addey (Con.)	12,956
Meeks (Lib.)	4,340
Majority	11,486

He watched the other national results coming in. First to declare was Billericay, which had been targeted by groups of Labour Party workers from West and East Ham, but was held by a Tory majority of 4,000. The two Salford seats were held with swings to Labour. Then Battersea South and Watford were both held by the Conservatives; then a Tory gain at Acton – after which it became increasingly clear that Macmillan would have a majority.[72] Gaitskell conceded defeat on television – the first party leader to do so – before the polls had closed. When the full results were known, Gaitskell and the Labour Party were faced by an impregnable Tory majority of 100.

Gaitskell's tax pledge was not the cause of the defeat in 1959 but it took the swing out of the campaign. Labour probably could not have won, even with a flawless campaign in 1959, but they might have reduced the Conservatives' majority and, given the run of by-election success in the following Parliament, that would have made the task of gaining a majority in 1964 that much easier. Labour's internal post-mortem, as in 1955, identified prosperity as the major cause of the Conservatives' win. It is difficult to argue with that judgement. Macmillan's performance in rebuilding the Conservative Party and bringing them through to a victory in 1959 was remarkable and it is difficult to see what Gaitskell could have done differently in order to have won.

It did not seem like that at the time, and the 1959 election defeat caused a profound internal battle about the ideology and the image of the party. However, at root it represented the ending of an era. It is difficult to recreate the world that was the Labour Party and the labour movement in the 1950s: proud, confident, socially and politically a cohesive unit. The activists might not ever have been a majority of working-class Labour voters but they had been a substantial presence; George Murray's annual reports on Gaitskell's own

Leeds South constituency show how deep and how far the social change, represented in Macmillan's majority, was cutting into the Labour movement:

> 1955: Boundary changes had left the constituency untouched, though the South Leeds Band from which much had been hoped only the year before had been disbanded because Councillor Kennally had moved.

> 1956: Each successive year the position deteriorates because of our failure to recruit young members. We who have inherited Socialist ideals from our Fathers have failed to inspire our Children. An organism that cannot reproduce must in time die.

> 1960: Our failure to win popular support in the General Election, with an excellent policy, a greatly improved organisation, and a more equal share of publicity – thanks to T.V. – than ever before, came as a profound shock to most of us, particularly as the last Tory government seemed to us, the most incompetent, and immoral government of the century . . . It has now become obvious beyond doubt that we have lost touch with the people we seek to serve. We either do not offer the things they want or we fail to tell them of our purpose in terms they understand.[73]

The decade of division which closed with this election defeat had seen the Labour Party lose three general elections in a row. After the defeat of 1951 there had been an expectation that power would be regained at the next election. After the defeat of 1955 attention had focused on the leadership of Clem Attlee. There was nothing to distract the party after the defeat of 1959, and a period of bitter internecine warfare followed. In the course of this warfare both sides organised campaigns to pursue their favoured policies, and for the first time the right wing of the Labour Party took the battle to what had been traditionally seen as the stronghold of the Labour left – the constituency Labour parties.

Gaitskell travelled back to London and issued a statement through Transport House:

> We have suffered neither a landslide nor a disaster but a setback. We had hoped to win 40 or 50 seats. We have instead lost 23. But the swing against us is a very small one – three people in every 200. The losses are at the margin only. They can be recovered. If a small swing makes a big change in the majority, so will a small swing towards us eventually restore our position . . . So I give this message to all Labour supporters. After a setback we still represent nearly half the nation. We are a great party and

a great power for good in the world. Our ranks are unbroken. We have attacked – and on this occasion we have been repulsed. We shall attack again and again until we win.[74]

14

Clause 4, 1959–1960

To secure for the workers by hand or by brain the full fruits of
their industry and the most equitable distribution thereof that may
be possible upon the basis of the common ownership of the means
of production, distribution and exchange.
   Clause 4, part 4, of the Labour Party constitution, 1918–95

The picture posed . . . is of a coven of old Wykehamists converg-
ing in the dark of Mr Gaitskell's house in Frognal Gardens.
                              Ivan Yates, 18 October 1959

What kind of tripe is a mixed economy? Where he is going at
the end, I do not know. I hope I am not there when he is.
   Mr K. Brown, Bury and Radcliffe constituency Labour party

When Gaitskell got back to Transport House to draft his press notice
on the election result, he was physically and emotionally exhausted.
On the Monday evening before polling he had been drafting his
Cabinet, confident that Labour would win. Richard Crossman, meeting him that evening, recorded:

> He was obviously dead tired and on the edge of an emotional collapse
> . . . he was over-quiet, not tense but somehow slumped, and the draft
> [statement on the result] he produced consisted of double negatives. 'It
> isn't true that we shall not go forward', and suchlike. I substituted a few
> positives and a last sentence saying we shall fight and fight and fight again
> until we win, which he used straightaway . . . on the television . . . The
> poor man was subjected to that strain, too.[1]

In a matter of hours, however, Gaitskell had begun to pull himself
together. Dora suggested to Crossman that they get Hugh away for
a holiday and Crossman invited them down to the country. But
Gaitskell had other ideas: he wanted to talk things over with his
friends and colleagues and begin thinking about the future. Dalton
rang and spoke to Dora, asking her how she felt: 'Very angry with
the electors and very proud of Hugh,' she told him. Then Hugh
came on the phone: 'Come round on Sunday morning and I'll try

to get some of the intelligent young men along, built round John Harris.' Dalton phoned Tony Crosland and invited him round to the Gaitskells'.[2] Later, Hugh Gaitskell spoke to Tony Benn and asked him to join them.[3] He also contacted Jenkins and made him cancel a lecture tour of the United States so that he would be available in the post-election period; he did not give specific instructions but just seemed to want him around. Jenkins recalls: 'This is a clear indication that Gaitskell intended to strike while the iron was hot in an attempt to reform the Labour Party, and wanted to have members of his praetorian guard around, both for moral sustenance and in order to prospect the ground over which he might or might not advance.'[4]

So an informal 'post-mortem' was held at Gaitskell's house at 18 Frognal Gardens on the weekend after the election.[5] The actual events have been much disputed. Present at the gathering were three generations of right-wing Labour politicians: Hugh Dalton, Tony Crosland, Patrick Gordon Walker, Douglas Jay, Roy Jenkins, Herbert Bowden and John Harris. In the evening Gaitskell was given dinner by Woodrow Wyatt – which rather shocked Crossman when he heard about it[6] – and Tony Crosland, and during the day Douglas Jay and Tony Benn visited the house. Nye Bevan was invited but didn't come, and Harold Wilson, as usual, was underestimated and ignored. It seemed, therefore, that only the Hampstead Set were meeting to plan a response to the election.[7]

Michael Foot's account makes clear that from the outset this week-end of meetings was perceived by the left to be the launch-pad for 'a bold initiative' which was being 'set in motion by the right wing of the Party, and it does appear that the lever which helped to let it loose was pulled at that Sunday night meeting in Frognal Gardens.' Foot concludes that 'the idea was to erase the working-class image of the Party, to remove the "danger of fighting under a label of a class that no longer exists"; to seize the moment to carry forward the revisionist ideas of recent years no longer solely by relentless pressure but by a coup d'état.'[8]

It would perhaps have been better if Gaitskell had taken charge and organised his supporters' response to the defeat; but such a calculated strategy singularly failed to materialise. In consequence the views of his friends emerged piecemeal during the weeks that followed. Ironically, this lack of control actually contributed to the impression in left-wing circles, among trade-union MPs and Labour

Party officials that what was taking place was an organised response, which had as its object the fundamental reform of the party. This was highly detrimental to the chances of success for Gaitskell's more considered reaction to the defeat which he worked out after consulting all sections of the party. The whispering campaign by the left, especially regarding the proposal to break links with the trade unions, turned many in the Labour Party against any form of substantive change.

What actually occurred during the weekend has tended to be obscured by what was thought to have happened. Many of those who took part in the discussions were naturally, after a long campaign and a substantial defeat, rambling and punch-drunk.[9] Among the various themes they touched on were nationalisation's effect on the result, the possibility of a Lib–Lab Pact and the reform of Clause 4; Douglas Jay said he was thinking about writing an article for *Forward*.[10] Dalton summarised the conversations in his diary:

> Party constitution might be revised, some new formula on public or common ownership substituted for the 1918 text. Party constitution might also be changed by having National Executive elected by Unions, local Parties regrouped regionally and Parliamentary Party with shift of authority towards Parliamentary leadership . . . Hugh very wisely listens more than talks to groups like this.[11]

Crosland warned Gaitskell against changing Clause 4, while Woodrow Wyatt tended to favour its reform. There was no mention of the unilateralists. Roy Jenkins recalls the weekend as an informal inquiry into why the election had been lost:

> A general consensus among those who were present was that there were about four reasons for it. One was the unpopularity of nationalisation, one was the unpopularity of trade unions, one was the unpopularity of Labour local councils and [one was that] the party was slightly too stuck in an old-fashioned proletarian groove. A certain amount of germination of ideas that led on to the Clause 4 battle took place. The whole debate was conducted much more casually than conspiratorially.[12]

So a group of politicians met over a weekend and had a series of casual, confused and rather depressed conversations. The left, however, charged that over this weekend a revisionist agenda was devised for a revolution in the ideological shape of the Labour Party. This was to be achieved by abandoning the commitment to nationalisation, breaking the links with the trade unions and even forging an alliance with the Liberal Party. While all these possibilities were discussed during the weekend – such a defeat bred some extreme reactions – they did not form part of an agreed agenda. The irony of the left's paranoia runs even deeper because Gaitskell's own thinking was not clear enough immediately after the election for him to have invented such an plan – as is shown in his conversations during the ensuing week.

In fact it was Fleet Street and not Hampstead that was the main source of the 'hidden agenda' – in the form of Ivan Yates's article in *Reynolds News* on Sunday 11 October 1959. It was Yates who produced the analysis of the election which fitted the left's allegation much more closely than did Douglas Jay's. Yates was a member of 'the Group' – an informal Gaitskellite debating society that had met through the 1950s – and had close associations with younger members of the party; but he was not a member of the Hampstead Set and had not been at Frognal Gardens during the post-mortem weekend.

In his article, Yates stated that Labour had lost the election, 'to put it bluntly, because the electors did not like its face. They didn't like one thing above all, its close links with the Unions . . . the block vote and strikes official and unofficial.' To strengthen his case he pointed out that the left had been particularly critical of the block vote system at the height of the Bevanite rebellion, and claimed that a *Tribune* pamphlet of four years earlier, which had advocated the reform of the block vote system, had been printed but not published. As well as advocating a change of policy on nationalisation, Yates called for a reform of the constitution, especially Clause 4: 'the phrase committing the Party to the nationalisation of all the means of production, distribution and exchange should be scrapped. No one any longer believes in it literally.'

The response to Yates's article was generally hostile. The editor of *Reynolds News*, William Richardson, stated in an editorial that he opposed breaking the links with the unions.[13] Three hostile letters were printed alongside Yates's next article, in which he made no apology but played down the idea of breaking the links with the unions while stressing the need to revise Clause 4. He also ridiculed the left-wing view of the post-mortem weekend:

> The picture posed . . . is of a coven of old Wykehamists converging in the dark of Mr Gaitskell's house in Frognal Gardens. We see them plotting

333

round the fire where the cauldron bubbles merrily away. There is Woodrow Wyatt eating devilled kidneys off silver plate. Tony Crosland's in the kitchen boiling himself an egg. While in a corner of the sitting room Mr Gaitskell himself cuts a rug . . . I don't suppose it's quite like that but Hugh Gaitskell does have his friends round and they did come round just after the election; they even, believe it or not, discussed politics and thought up some ideas.[14]

On the Monday evening after Yates's article, Roy Jenkins appeared on *Panorama* and questioned the future of nationalisation, arguing that at the very least the party should drop the idea of steel nationalisation.[15] Four days later came the publication of Jay's article in *Forward*. However, it was not under instructions from the 'coven of Frognal Gardens' that the article was produced; in fact Jay had been asked by the editor of *Forward*, Francis Williams, to write a piece about the election. Jay's plan had been to write up the impressions of his local party workers in Battersea; and so on the Friday after the post-mortem weekend Jay had travelled round the constituency interviewing ordinary activists. His article was a record of what 'some people who had really canvassed felt about the election'. Between these conversations with the party workers and the publication of the article, however, two events occurred. First, Francis Williams persuaded Jay to put his name to the article; because Jay was so closely associated with Gaitskell, he was then widely assumed to be flying a kite for the leader. Second, Jay spoke to Eric Fletcher, the Labour MP for Islington North, who persuaded Jay that nationalisation had been a major issue in the election. Jay's article of 16 October questioned the future of nationalisation in Labour's policy and suggested changing the party's name to 'Labour and Radical'.[16]

The notorious *Forward* article, when it is re-read today, appears a mild essay in reform rather than a broad manifesto for revolution. Indeed, as Jay pointed out in his memoirs, many of the charges made against it at the time were false. The article did not propose a break with the trade unions but it did advocate moving the Labour Party Conference to May so that the appearance of its simply rubber-stamping TUC proposals would be reduced. This criticism of the relationship between the Labour Party and the trade unions seems rather lame; the link was disliked for other, more profound reasons that Jay did not mention in his article, such as the block vote and the support of unpopular strikes. Nor did the article propose the abandonment of all forms of public ownership, but it did recommend that no new state monopolies be created – very much in line with some of the discussions associated with *Industry and Society* but implicitly questioning the nationalisation of the steel industry. The proposal to change the name of the party – by adding 'Radical' or 'Reform' to 'Labour' – now seems at most a cosmetic public relations exercise rather than the attempted *coup d'état* that the left tried to make it appear. The most controversial ideas put forward by Jay were to leave steel nationalisation out of future party policy, a scheme which Gaitskell opposed, and to transform the NEC into a federal body, eliminating the section elected by the Labour Party constituency activists – which Gaitskell contemplated, along with a series of other institutional reforms, but then rejected.

After the *Forward* article was published, Eric Fletcher made a speech supporting Jay which was reported on the front page of the *Observer*: 'Jay's diagnosis is correct. Talk of nationalisation lost us the election more than any other factor.' Shirley Williams was invited by the *Sunday Times* to give her view on the same day. She supported Jay on nationalisation, arguing that 'nationalisation is probably the single most unpopular plank in Labour's policy', but she felt that 'a break with the unions is a counsel of despair'.[17]

The left's other charge against Gaitskell, which also came from Fleet Street, was the talk of a pact with the Liberals. In fact, as this story dominated the front pages of the Sunday papers after the election, it must have been discussed on the Sunday of the post-mortem weekend. The drift of these articles was that the country needed a 'union of radicals' and that Joe Grimond, the Liberal Party leader, was prepared to do a deal; the *Sunday People* went so far as to report meetings at the highest level between Labour right-wingers and leading Liberals.[18] Jay's suggestion that the party change its name to Labour and Radical fed this speculation.[19] Woodrow Wyatt, who attended the post-mortem weekend, had advocated this plan, but Gaitskell had rejected it out of hand.

In the following week Gaitskell visited Crossman at his farm, telling him that 'in his view we couldn't afford to lose the next Election . . . Then there really would be a growth of the Liberal Party and a split.' But he also remarked: 'We must let the pendulum take us in and carry nothing which stops it swinging our way. It wasn't iron and steel and road haulage, the specific pledges, but the general threat to nationalize 600 firms which lost us votes this time.'[20] By his aim to 'carry nothing' he meant more than discarding

unpopular policies: in the course of a six-hour conversation he proposed a complete revision of the constitution, redefinition of aims
and a federal structure; but he was against dropping nationalisation
or breaking the links with the unions. During the rest of the week
he held various meetings, including one with Bevan, and put forward
schemes for reforming the party's organisation. It is intriguing that
in these early conversations his emphasis seemed to be on élite
structure, the NEC and the Shadow Cabinet, rather than on ideology. Bevan proposed that the Shadow Cabinet be appointed by the
leader rather than elected, but Gaitskell was not at all keen on this
idea because he felt he could get his way in any case and 'nomination
would make him too open to blame for everything that went
wrong'.[21]

Yates had said three things would come out of the meeting of
the 'coven': 'One, that Douglas Jay should write an article. Two,
that Roy Jenkins should take over from Harold Wilson as shadow
Chancellor, Mr Wilson becoming some sort of super organisation
man and shadow Leader of the House. Three, that Dick Crossman
should carry on in the future the work he did during the election
in charge of Labour's campaign committee.'[22] However, Jay's article
provoked Crossman to move back into his old role of troublesome
rebel. As far as Wilson was concerned, Gaitskell was questioning his
future, and Crossman reported all his conversations with Gaitskell
to Wilson; moreover, the rumours sparked off Wilson's fears and
partially rekindled the Bevanite alliance of Barbara Castle, Harold
Wilson and Dick Crossman. These rumours were compounded
when the *Sunday Times* ran a story that Wilson was going to be
replaced by Roy Jenkins, who, on seeing the report on his rearranged
lecture tour in the US, called it 'an agreeably flattering bit of nonsense'.[23] Wilson later claimed that but for this episode he would not
have challenged Gaitskell for the leadership: it infuriated him.[24]

Gaitskell's standing within the Parliamentary Labour Party was
not outwardly affected. On 21 October he faced his first PLP meeting
since the election and received a standing ovation. Douglas Jay's
Forward article was denounced, and Crossman felt this meant the
Jay–Jenkins line had been defeated.[25] A few days later Wilson, sensing
the way the wind was blowing, became the first leading party figure
to come out publicly against the proposals when he opposed 'frenzied
attempts to trim the party's sails to the electoral wind'.[26]

The controversy which arose in the weeks after the general election merged into the longer-term debate about the future of the Labour Party. The wider debate centred on two main interrelated questions: what was the best way for the Labour Party to achieve power and what was the best way of building on the achievements of the Attlee governments? On the revisionist wing of the party the most influential response to these questions came from a market researcher, Mark Abrams, who held the view that Labour had lost the election because it was too left-wing and outdated.[27] Dr Abrams's analysis appeared in the summer of 1960 in *Socialist Commentary*, under the title 'Why Labour Has Lost Elections', but the findings were fed to Gaitskell the previous winter.[28] His main conclusions seemed to support Douglas Jay's contention in his *Forward* article that relying on the working class was an electorally dangerous tactic. The survey provided additional material to suggest that attachment to the Labour Party on the grounds of its standing for the working class was

> a fragile bond . . . Already almost two-thirds of the Labour Party's working class supporters consider themselves to be outside the working class (the outstanding identification mark of the Labour Party) and another quarter, while admitting their working class general status, distinguish themselves clearly from the Labouring classes.[29]

Part 4 of Abrams's study concentrated on young voters who had come on to the electoral roll while Labour were in opposition. The study did not offer much more hope here:

> If we ignore the 10 per cent whose political views were so uninformed that they could not be described even as leaning towards any party, then it appears that 52 per cent of young people today are Conservatives, 43 per cent are Labour supporters and 5 per cent are Liberals. This Conservative lead has two sources; 35 per cent of all working-class young people are ready to identify themselves with the Conservative Party, and only 10 per cent of middle-class young people support the Labour Party. Further, when the young people were asked what they most liked or disliked about the Labour programme, 47 per cent of the 18–24 age bracket didn't know, but of those who did express a dislike, 26 per cent identified nationalisation.

Although this negative image of nationalisation owed much to the powerful anti-nationalisation propaganda carried by newspapers, by television and even in cinemas,[30] Abrams's conclusion concerning young people in 1959 was straightforward: 'There is among young people today a complex of barely conscious Conservative sympathies which have still not yet fully expressed themselves in overt Party affiliations.'

Abrams's conclusion that nationalisation was unpopular was disputed by the left wing of the party and this difference in opinion can be seen by comparing the campaign committee's report on the election with that of the General Secretary. The campaign committee's report, drafted by Peter Shore under Richard Crossman's close guidance, commented: 'Few voters of any party think that [nationalisation] is an important issue, and it is best dealt with as part of the expansion theme rather than on its own.'[31] In contrast, the section in Morgan Phillips's report as General Secretary stated:

> Nationalisation. This was far and away the most frequently mentioned liability . . . The majority thought that it was the Tory propaganda campaign, together with the actual performance of the nationalised industries, which had created a public impression that nationalisation had failed . . . the promise to purchase shares was too easily represented as an intention to nationalise anything and everything without putting it first to the electorate.[32]

However, neither wing of the party denied that the better-financed and longer Conservative campaign had undermined Labour's efforts from the start. Many newspapers mentioned that the Conservatives had begun to fight their campaign some years before the election, while Labour had only really started in the weeks after the dissolution of Parliament. The combined effects of Wilson's reorganisations[33] and Crossman's campaign committee could not match the Conservative Party's long-term offensive. Although Labour's campaign in 1959 was well received, the need for modernisation in both policy and presentation permeated the post-election wrangling on both the right and left.

It was against this background, amid cross-currents of debate, that Gaitskell planned his speech for the post-mortem Conference. Since the election he had not stopped to rest but had spent his time collecting opinions from key figures in the party; and he decided to use his speech at the Conference to outline his plan for constitutional reform. The particular tactical choice of Clause 4 was Gaitskell's own. He did not want to abandon the emotional force of the old formulation, but he was keen to remove the uncertainty about the extent to which the party was dedicated to large-scale nationalisation, and believed he could achieve this by replacing the existing clause with a new statement of the party's aims. In 1950, 1952 and 1955 he had attacked or agreed with attacks on Clause 4, so after a long period of consultation and prompted by Ivan Yates and others he chose his own ground.

Despite his talks with left-wingers, Gaitskell had underestimated the romanticism of the party while overestimating the force that logical argument would have in persuading Conference delegates of the merits of his case. He also suffered from the fact that word of his intention had leaked out. On 12 November Charles Pannell, Sam Watson and Bill Webber warned Gaitskell that trade-unionists would not accept a change to Clause 4. Among his close friends, Douglas Jay, Roy Jenkins, Tony Crosland and Dora all opposed the change; only Patrick Gordon Walker supported it.

On 14 November, in a private meeting at Oxford, he tried out his ideas on Marcus Lower, an Oxford city councillor, Ron Owen, a member of the university's extra-mural department, Brian Walden, also at the extra-mural department, and Julia, Gaitskell's daughter. They gave the ideas a cautious but not hostile reception.[34] Four days later Dalton wrote to Gaitskell: 'Jay's *Forward* article gave it all a bad start, and struck the tuning fork for all the Gregorian Chants of the Old Believers.' Most of Gaitskell's friends were now urgently warning him that events since the election made the possibility of change more remote: the trade unions were hardening in their opposition to any alteration to the constitutional settlement of the party; the 'kites' had so outraged the left and the trade-union MPs that other reforms suffered guilt by association. On 24 November, Charles Pannell urged Gaitskell to drop the whole thing or at least to show the speech to Bevan before he delivered it. In consequence, the night before Gaitskell was due to give the speech he showed it to John Harris and Nye Bevan. Harris then showed it to Jay. Jay said it would cause trouble but Bevan – either maliciously or not – did not raise a single objection. Gaitskell was determined to bring about a change: 'If he provoked a storm it was not for lack of warning.'[35]

On Saturday 28 November 1959 Gaitskell delivered the speech to the Party Conference in Blackpool. The circumstances were unfavourable. There was no platform position: Gaitskell spoke for himself alone. Even his initial procedural decision to push the reforms through Conference was probably mistaken. Over defence, as we shall see, he could challenge Conference sovereignty by advocating a policy which had joint TUC and NEC backing and therefore isolate his opponents. On Clause 4, however, there was no platform lead because NEC investigations into the constitution, promoted as much by Morgan Phillips as by Gaitskell himself, were only to begin after Conference. Gaitskell was facing a hostile Conference without the protection of either the block votes or other sections of the party. Moreover, Crossman's opposition, coupled with the alleged plot against Wilson, had revived factionalism within the Parliamentary Labour Party.[36]

Barbara Castle as chair had opened the Conference with a call to arms for the fundamentalists:

> Are we prepared to affirm that what Nye has called 'the commanding heights of the economy' must be publicly financed under public ownership? Of course this does not mean we want to nationalize everything from atomic energy to pin-table saloons. But it does mean that the community must control, inspire and finance new industrial developments.[37]

Gaitskell spoke later on the first day. The key section of his speech argued that Clause 4 in its current form was inadequate and 'lays us open to continual misrepresentation . . . It implies that we propose to nationalise everything, but do we? Everything? Every little pub and garage? Of course not. We have long ago come to accept . . . a mixed economy . . . the view . . . of 90 per cent of the Labour Party – had we not better say so instead of going out of our way to court misrepresentation?' Then Gaitskell went on to list what he regarded as the socialist aims which should form the basis of a new Clause 4:

> First, we express what G. D. H. Cole once called 'a broad, human movement on behalf of the bottom dog' . . . Thus, at home, our first concern is naturally for the less fortunate – the old, the sick, the widowed, the unemployed, the disabled and the badly housed; abroad, it is reflected in a deep concern for the well-being of people much, much poorer than ourselves, badly in need of help. Secondly, we believe in social justice, in an equitable distribution of wealth and income. Thirdly, we believe in a 'classless society' – a society without the snobbery, the privilege, the restrictive social barriers which are still far too prevalent in Britain today. Fourthly, we believe in the fundamental equality of all races and all peoples . . . we believe quite simply in the brotherhood of man. Fifthly, British socialism has always contained an essential element of personal idealism – the belief that the pursuit of material satisfaction by itself without

spiritual values is empty and barren and that our relations with one another should be based not on ruthless self-regarding rivalry but on fellowship and co-operation. Sixthly, we believe that the public interest must come before private interest. Finally we believe that these things must be achieved with and through freedom and democratic government.[38]

There were hostile interruptions from the floor.[39] From the platform there was muted applause from Dick Crossman, Tom Driberg and Nye Bevan, but none from Tony Greenwood, Ray Gunter, Ian Mikardo and Eirene White.[40]

The speech that followed Gaitskell's contained a bitter attack and included the memorable peroration: 'We have a capitalist economy, and where is this tripe getting us about a mixed economy which is non-existent? Engels many years ago wrote, "Nothing is; everything is becoming." What kind of tripe is a mixed economy? Where he is going at the end, I do not know. I hope I am not there when he is.'[41]

The rest of the debate was by no means completely hostile; Dick Taverne, Denis Howell and Douglas Jay, all later involved in the CDS, made speeches in defence of the leader, though Taverne was the only speaker to support Gaitskell specifically on the reform of the constitution. However, the feeling that it was sacrilege to touch Clause 4 was plain and what Crosland termed the 'antediluvian opponents of change' received the better reception. The *Observer* of 29 November 1959 described Gaitskell's reception as confused, a feeling echoed by Jay about his own speech, while Michael Foot seemed 'to inspire the hall' and was cheered. In contrast Tom Driberg and Ivan Yates in *Reynolds News* gave Gaitskell a much better press, reporting enormous cheers at the end, ignoring Castle's speech as chairman and claiming that Foot was the only openly critical speaker. Of the other speakers, Yates singled out Shirley Williams, Denis Healey and Tony Benn. Harold Hutchinson also commented on Williams's speech in the Monday edition of the *Daily Herald* and strongly backed Gaitskell. Aside from this, Yates's coverage was atypical. Tom Driberg described it as the worst Conference since Morecambe in 1952 and attacked Gaitskell's speech: 'No socialist has ever suggested that this [Clause 4] means state ownership of everything down to every home, car, TV set and toothbrush, and if the Tories misrepresent it as meaning that they will misrepresent any formula we devise instead of it.'[42]

By the final day the party seemed hopelessly divided and Nye Bevan rose to close the debate:

> I used to be taught as a boy, not at university but even in Board school, one of Euclid's deductions: if two things are equal to a third thing, they are equal to each other. Yesterday Barbara quoted from a speech which I made some years ago, and she said that I believed that socialism in the context of modern society meant the conquest of the commanding heights of the economy. Hugh Gaitskell quoted the same thing. So Barbara and Hugh quoted me. If Euclid's deduction is correct they are both equal to me and therefore must be equal to each other. So we have a kind of trinity – I am not going to lay myself open to a charge of blasphemy by trying to describe our different roles.

After this opening emphasis on unity, repeated throughout the speech, Bevan actually laid out a fundamentally different perception of the role of public ownership and a different basic definition of democratic socialism; he also put forward what with the benefit of hindsight now appears an almost absurd view – but one that Wilson shared – that the challenge to Britain would not come from capitalism:

> The challenge is going to come from Russia. The challenge is not going to come from the United States. The challenge is not going to come from Western Germany nor from France. The challenge is going to come from those nations who, however wrong in many fundamental respects . . ., nevertheless are at long last being able to reap the material fruits of economic planning and public ownership. That is where the challenge is coming from, and I want to meet it, because I am not a Communist, I am a Social Democrat . . . I believe that this country of ours and this movement of ours, despite our setbacks, nevertheless is being looked upon by the rest of the world as the custodian of democratic representative government.[43]

It was Bevan's last speech at Party Conference and it summed up the main elements of his political faith: that the future belonged to collectivism, not to the market, and that the eyes of the world were focused on the actions of the Labour Party. In other moods Bevan could be a moderniser and believe that the mixed economy might provide the surplus needed for foreign aid, but in this mood he was set square against change. Socialism was nationalisation and nationalisation was socialism: it was the only way to meet the challenge of the command economies of the Eastern bloc.

The thrust of Gaitskell's arguments, on the other hand, was that the challenge was coming from the West and not from the East. Bevan and Castle were out of tune with a number of influential foreign socialist parties, broadly wrong in their economic analysis and entirely misguided in their electoral analysis. Gaitskell's political tactics were questionable, but he was much more in tune with the radical thinking and modernisation that was sweeping through other socialist and social democratic parties in those years. The German Social Democrats had shown the way with the abandonment of their constitution and the adoption of a reformed set of principles centred on the idea that

> The modern economy has a variety of forms. It should, therefore, not be subjected to a uniform structural scheme. It is possible neither to put the whole economic system under the law of free competition, nor to choose socialisation of all the means of production as a desirable structural scheme for today's economy. When the economy is left to itself, under the guise of 'free competition', it becomes the victim of various interest groups. When the economy is compressed into a few mammoth organisations – be they private property, common property, or state-owned property – not only the development of free enterprise is threatened, but the freedoms which employees and consumers enjoy, are also endangered . . . private ownership of the means of production deserves protection and encouragement so long as it does not obstruct the creation of a just social order.[44]

The Canadian equivalent of the Co-operative Party had also recently adopted a new national programme, which carefully defined the terms of extending public ownership:

> Enlargement of the publicly owned sector of our economy:
> (1) where it is necessary to facilitate economic planning, as in transportation and communication and basic iron and steel;
> (2) where it is necessary to break the stranglehold of private monopoly.[45]

The Norwegian Labour Party adopted a similarly flexible approach:

> In the field of economics, society must take the steps that are necessary to obtain the objective, viz, maximum production and fair distribution. This calls for different solutions in the different branches. In a number of cases the State should take over economic activity. In other cases it is natural to have undertakings run by local authorities, operating separately or in groups. In many spheres it is a sound policy to carry on production

and trade on a co-operative basis. Finally, there are some cases where society will be best served by private enterprise.[46]

Internationally, some democratic socialist parties were increasingly recognising the mixed economy, putting Keynesian demand management and indicative planning ahead of nationalisation and regarding economic aims as one among a set of principles to which the party was committed. Gaitskell's intention was to achieve similar flexibility in the British Labour Party by reforming Clause 4. Gaitskell was right in his objectives in 1959, for unless he changed the destination of the labour movement he had little hope of revitalising its image. Without a fundamental ideological shift along the lines then being carried out in the German SPD, the Labour Party would retain its quixotic tilt, ensuring that the possibility would always exist for the 'antediluvian opponents of change' to claim that they represented the real soul of the party. Labour's disappointing electoral performance on those occasions when policies were adopted which reflected Clause 4 – the 1983 general election being the clearest example – illustrates the degree to which Gaitskell's instincts had been well-founded.

Politically, however, he was wrong to have chosen Clause 4 as his target for change and arrogant in his presumption that, if he simply indicated the direction, the party would meekly follow. His didacticism at Blackpool backfired badly. On 29 November Bevan spoke of challenging Gaitskell while Wilson was actively plotting. Reaction was almost universally hostile, mostly questioning Gaitskell's tactics. Healey, Brown, Strachey, Freeman and Jenkins (who described the choice of Clause 4 as appalling) all told him in no uncertain terms that he had been wrong.[47]

In response Gaitskell changed tack a little when he appeared on *Panorama* on 30 November:

> If you were to say to me, 'Really we've got to accept the colour bar, because you'll never get into power if you don't', I should say, 'Well, in not very polite language, Go to hell ... that's absolutely against my principles ... But if you say to me 'I think your argument for nationalising the machine tool industry is rather weak', I would say, 'Well, I'll discuss that with you.'

With the Labour Party defeated in the general election and in turmoil over the Clause 4 speech, and with an ailing Bevan having been replaced as leader of the left by Harold Wilson, a series of

'Not even within stabbing distance
of Gaitskell's back,' says Mr Foot.

public challenges to Gaitskell's position as leader began. From Christmas 1959 until the summer of 1962 there was a consistent assault on his leadership of the party, and Ian Mikardo recalled that the objective was to remove him as leader.[48] At the point at which the campaign against him was gathering steam, Gaitskell, travelling under the name 'Mr Thornton', left for Jamaica via Canada and New York. He desperately needed a rest after the pace of the election but his choice of holiday destination was not conducive to a stress-free period. He wanted to stay at the Flemings' house but because of the legend of Eden's retreat there after the Suez crisis 'his party said he could not come to Goldeneye because everyone would make jolly jokes'.[49] Instead he stayed in the Governor's residence, but was still anxious, given the political storm he had left behind, that the press would be filled with gossip. Fleming wrote to Evelyn Waugh about Hugh's visit:

> I went rafting with him and he is blind and deaf to natural beauty like poor you and poor Sparrow, but he is a much stronger swimmer, and the river being in spate he disappeared for several minutes, and we were about to form a human chain when he rolled onto the shore like an amiable hippo . . . I dare not write my funniest story because you're so indiscreet.[50]

This story was probably about their trying to dodge the *Daily Express* reporter who had heard of Gaitskell's visit. Ann sent a telegram asking Beaverbrook to intervene so they could have some peace: 'Express pursing [sic] Hugh please darling Max prevent Goldeneye publicity urgent, passionate love and gratitude Annie.'[51] Fleming was kept out of the *Express*, but Gaitskell was not. On 17 January 1960 the *Sunday Express* reported that the leader of the Labour Party had been turned away from a private resort; the next Sunday's front page carried a blistering attack on his leadership from Michael Foot – 'Mr Gaitskell will have to go' – and Eden's criticism of Gaitskell in his newly published memoirs: Gaitskell's election, Eden wrote, was a 'national misfortune'.[52] Gaitskell replied to Foot through the *Daily Herald* journalist Charles Bray on 20 January: 'It would be improper and undignified for me as leader of the Labour Party to reply to such things ... particularly from someone incapable of winning his own constituency' (Michael Foot had lost his seat in Plymouth Devonport in 1955 and had failed to regain it in 1959).

The bitter press campaign was still raging against him, when news reached him of Bevan's illness and he abandoned his attempt at a holiday and came home early. Bevan, who had assumed the deputy leadership after the election and Jim Griffiths's retirement, was diagnosed as having cancer and returned, in ignorance of this, to his farm at Asheridge in February. He never resumed a full political role; his health deteriorated after Easter and he died on 6 July 1960.[53]

Thus Bevan was off the political stage as Gaitskell's leadership descended further into crisis. In February 1960, facing a hostile campaign by *Tribune*, Gaitskell continued to fight back. On 13 February in a speech at Nottingham he restated his view that Clause 4 needed to be revised, and he attacked the 'small professional anti-leadership group', while also stressing that he supported public ownership. Support came from the ever faithful George Murray in Leeds, who wrote to him: 'Your speech last weekend has done a power of good, and should rally some of the more timid among your supporters.'[54] To which Gaitskell replied: 'I am glad you liked the speech. It has done good down here as well. But we are by no means out of the wood yet.'[55]

Under the headline 'Mr Gaitskell Changes his Tune', *Tribune* welcomed the Nottingham speech as the 'most important declaration of his life'. The *Spectator* called the speech a 'withdrawal from his Blackpool position' which would 'only make his task of rallying moderates behind him even more difficult'. *The Times* carried the headline 'Mr Gaitskell Calls for More Public Ownership'.[56]

On 24 February the NEC had an acrimonious discussion in which Harold Wilson declared that if Gaitskell continued to make speeches about Clause 4 then he too would do so. Gaitskell argued that he had made the Nottingham speech only because he had been attacked by Michael Foot and therefore needed to respond. Bessie Braddock and Jim Callaghan called for restraint and an end to speeches. Jim Boyd, a trade union leader, then made a passionate plea for loyalty to the party.[57]

After this NEC the left ceased their frontal assaults, as some MPs and trade-unionists came out in support of the beleaguered leader. There had been a marked silence from much of the front bench in this period. This silence and the lack of co-ordination by Gaitskell's supporters inspired Dick Taverne and Bill Rodgers to take action. Rodgers recorded in his unpublished 'History of the CDS': 'During the whole of the Clause 4 dispute leading members of the Parliamentary Party who supported Hugh Gaitskell had made weekend speeches without telling . . . either Hugh or each other.' Nobody in the Parliamentary Labour Party had tried to 'mobilise sympathetic opinion in the rank and file'. No one had issued instructions; the initiative came from Rodgers himself and he recruited Taverne as co-sponsor. They tapped into the network provided by the activists known as 'the Group' and other contacts to organise a letter of support produced on 3 February and signed by fifteen candidates all under forty.[58]

Encouraged by this but still hampered by vocal opposition, Gaitskell gave more ground. His plan had originally been to replace Clause 4 with a new statement of aims including such issues as colonial freedom and racial harmony but omitting the specific aim of widespread nationalisation. On 3 March Gaitskell told Sam Watson that although he would have preferred to adopt the statement of aims as a replacement for Clause 4 he was prepared to see it alongside the existing clause, as an amplification.

Even this concession proved to be inadequate. Gaitskell accepted a series of amendments in a 'second reading' style of debate at the NEC meeting on 16 March to discuss constitutional reform. Morgan Phillips made it clear that he thought the time had come to rewrite the constitution – indeed he had been arguing for this since the previous July[59] – and he circulated a document which he thought would bridge the gap between Clause 4 and the 'Amplification of Aims', the statement now formally presented by Gaitskell. Barbara

Castle moved the key amendment which changed Gaitskell's phrase 'it believes that further extension of common ownership should be decided from time to time . . . according to circumstances' to read: 'through an expansion of common ownership substantial enough to give the community power over the commanding heights of the economy'. Castle's amendment was accepted by 22 votes to 1; the amended 'Amplification of Aims' was adopted with only one vote against. This result would have been a draw and the old and the new 'testaments' would both have been incorporated, but any constitutional change had to be ratified by Conference. This same meeting of the NEC received sixty-three resolutions from constituency Labour parties protesting against any amendments to Clause 4. In the following months it became clear that the trade unions as well as many CLPs would oppose revising the constitution and the new testament would become simply a statement of aims published by the NEC.

In order to ratify changes to the constitution, the trade union conferences had to endorse a resolution decided on by the NEC. Gaitskell could not command a majority of the key trade union executives: he had no organisation for lobbying these bodies, and the right and centre of the party were apathetic. Once the executives had been mandated, the union vote was established. Further, since there was no Gaitskellite organisation trying to influence the shape and content of the NEC, Gaitskell was not guaranteed a majority even on this body. Thus Gaitskell was defeated in his attempt to ditch Clause 4.[60]

Gaitskell and the Hampstead Set learned their lesson. Up and down the country ordinary party members who supported the leadership also took note of the way Gaitskell had lost his battle. But at the trade union conferences votes began to swing against the leadership, and the prospect arose of the leader being defeated both on his constitutional reform and on his defence policy. The question this posed to Gaitskell's supporters was clear: how long could the leader last?

15

Ban the Bomb, 1960

There are some of us, Mr Chairman, who will fight and fight
and fight again to save the Party we love. We will fight and fight
and fight to bring back sanity and honesty and dignity, so that
our Party with its great past may retain its glory and its greatness.
                                                          Gaitskell, 1960

The reform of Clause 4 was very much a part of the revisionist
project, but the question of defence belonged to broader foreign
policy issues on which there was less unity among the Gaitskellites.
Indeed, their differences on foreign policy would eventually divide
them. For Roy Jenkins, the growing unity of Europe was central; in
contrast Douglas Jay opposed Britain's involvement in the European
Economic Community and Tony Crosland was developing a pose
of studied boredom with the subject. However, on defence matters
the right of the party was in general agreement about the importance
of NATO.

Some of Gaitskell's close associates were very anti-communist.
For example Christopher Mayhew had worked in unison with the
Foreign Office to close down the Anglo-Soviet friendship societies,[1]
and others, like Patrick Gordon Walker, supported Britain's retention
of an independent nuclear deterrent,[2] although privately Walker
urged Gaitskell not to make an overt commitment either way: 'On
all matters I said we should say that an opposition could not know
and must keep its hands free.'[3] All the Gaitskellites were united on
the need to retain nuclear weapons within NATO until they could
be negotiated away multilaterally.

The case for unilateral nuclear disarmament was rejected because
it was seen as unrealistic. Some of the younger Gaitskellites had felt
sympathetic to the Bevanites in the early 1950s and now understood
the passions of the Campaign for Nuclear Disarmament but believed
that the natural conclusion of unilateralism was neutralism.[4] The
foundation for this rejection of unilateralism was a belief in the
Atlantic alliance and collective security. The pro-Americanism of

349

Crosland, Gaitskell and the younger supporters of Gaitskell was based on their experience and interpretation of the Cold War and was compounded, after November 1960, by the election of the young and dynamic President John F. Kennedy. In fact two of the younger Gaitskellites, David Marquand and Bernard Donoughue, were in the USA until late in 1960, Donoughue having worked for the Kennedy campaign.[5] The depth of Gaitskell's pro-Americanism shocked Denis Healey in 1962 when Gaitskell declared that the US had as much right to prevent a Soviet base in Cuba as the UK would have if it had been in Ireland.[6] Events like the Cuban missile crisis, which were to encourage the unilateralists in their conviction of the necessity for nuclear disarmament, caused the modernisers to stress instead the need for strength. In this sense the rejection of unilateral nuclear disarmament could be presented as being in line with the revisionist agenda.

One side in the debate believed that the only possible consequence of the possession of nuclear weapons was genocide; the other felt that the consequence of surrendering these weapons would be world domination by a repressive Soviet system. It was hardly surprising that the debate was often expressed in highly emotive terms. Bill Rodgers, looking back after thirty years, summed up his view of the way in which Labour Party meetings on defence were conducted: 'Quite often the motions on unilateralism had been carried because someone had stood up in a meeting and said, "I want to say, Mr Chairman, that I think nuclear weapons are awful and for the sake of my children and my grandchildren I propose we vote against nuclear weapons", and the Chairman said "Anyone against?" '[7] Even the NEC discussions featured similar sentiments. In March 1958, Edith Summerskill began her discussion of the draft statement on Labour's defence policy: 'The question before us was one of human survival.'[8] Conversely, the multilateralists would attack CND for being neutralist, pacifist and communist – Mayhew later described it as a fellow-travelling organisation[9] – and maintained that if Britain were unilaterally to abandon nuclear weapons the country would be defenceless against the Soviet Union.

These two entrenched positions tended to obscure the areas which were available for compromise. Richard Crossman, and later Walter Padley, tried to find forms of words that would be acceptable to both sides.[10] The future of Britain's independent deterrent was the aspect of the defence debate that was most open to compromise:

Gaitskell did not believe in the independent nuclear deterrent as a matter of principle and was fighting for the retention of weapons within NATO.

Back in April 1957 Duncan Sandys had published his Defence White Paper.[11] The task Sandys set himself was to reduce the size of Britain's defence spending by increasing her reliance on nuclear rather than on conventional weapons.[12] The original commitment to the bomb had been made by Attlee and Bevin in 1947, despite the arguments of Dalton and Cripps that Britain could not afford the expense of independent weapons development.[13] The Prime Minister had been adamant: 'It had, in theory at least, an overriding claim to the physical and human resources at the disposal of central government.'[14] The development of the bomb between 1945 and 1958 illustrated perfectly the powerful dynamic of the arms race: 'In October 1952, British nuclear capability was, roughly speaking, where the Manhattan Project had been in July 1945 and Kurchatov's team in the Soviet Union in August 1949. Within weeks of Monte Bello, the Americans tested a thermonuclear device. In the summer of 1953 the Soviets exploded a device in the megaton range.'[15] The British scientists were off again chasing the H-bomb, which they succeeded in exploding in 1957. This opened the way for 'co-operation with the Americans', which in turn became 'purchasing from the Americans'. In the end Cripps and Dalton were proved right: Britain could not afford to join the race.

The purpose of the British bomb was 'to bolster the nation's political power'.[16] The debate on nuclear weapons involved a series of initial questions. Should nuclear weapons play a role in British defence policy? If the answer was no, then was Britain to have a 'hawkish' level of conventional weapons spending? One of the chief reasons Sandys put forward for the nuclear defence policy was that it would save money, which did not prove to be the case, but the unilateralists rarely advocated increases in conventional weapons spending.[17] If the answer was no, did this mean a reworking of British treaty commitments? Bevan clearly felt that it did and he rejected this option,[18] whereas Frank Cousins was prepared to follow it through,[19] and some of the unilateralists were openly advocating withdrawal from NATO and a move to neutralism.[20]

If, on the other hand, the answer to the question whether British defence should include nuclear weapons was yes, then should Britain develop its own weapons and produce its own enriched uranium?

As has been said, some of Gaitskell's associates wanted to maintain the British deterrent. However, if Britain was not going to develop its own weapons then should it purchase them from the US? Whether Britain developed its own system or merely purchased one, the question arose of whether or not the weapons should be tested. The issue of British testing of nuclear weapons had been debated throughout the 1950s since the first test at Monte Bello in 1952. Opponents of the tests saw them as an unnecessary increase in the amount of radiation in existence and a threat to human and animal life. Moreover, the tests were relatively easy to oppose if the system was to be purchased from the United States because the United States rather than Britain would have to carry them out.

These and other related questions were debated at the annual Labour Party Conference in motions which either broke the questions down or put them together. Motions calling for multilateral disarmament usually also called for a worldwide effort to end wars; these were perfectly acceptable because they committed the party to nothing. There were also resolutions demanding unilateral disarmament or a pacifist defence policy. It was relatively straightforward for Gaitskell to oppose these types of resolutions, which were usually moved on a single issue or drafted by a single affiliated body. When resolutions were composited, by being grouped together with motions on diferent issues from various different organisations, problems could arise.

Opposition to nuclear weapons could be advocated by calling for an end to the manufacture and testing of nuclear weapons, or a ban on the use of British airspace for overflying by planes carrying nuclear weapons, or an end to the stockpiling of nuclear missiles. If such calls were coupled with a demand that China be included in the UN and that conscription be restricted, Gaitskell could agree to the ending of tests, to including China in the UN and to the abolition of conscription; but he was bound to oppose an end to the manufacture of the weapons and airspace restrictions because he was still committed to the British bomb and the NATO alliance. Motions calling for China to be admitted into the UN were carried regularly between 1955 and 1961 when part of general composite resolutions but were defeated between 1955 and 1959 when part of unilateralist composites.[21] Moreover, resolutions which if they had been implemented by a Labour Government would have meant virtual unilateralism were passed before 1960. A resolution demanding an end to testing and manufacture, passed every year from 1956, when coupled in 1957 with a demand for a decrease in defence spending and a call for 'progressive' disarmament,[22] would have amounted to the dismantling of much of British nuclear defence.

These were issues loaded with symbolism, and voting was based on much more than the mere wording. Even the person introducing the motion or composite could make a difference to the platform's attitude, as in 1960 when Frank Cousins moved the TGWU resolution.

Labour had gone into the 1959 general election campaign with resolutions passed by Conference advocating a nuclear defence policy based on opposing the testing of the weapons, calling for worldwide disarmament, for decreases in defence spending and reductions in the period of conscription.[23] The unilateralist motion of 1958 had been defeated by 4.5 million votes and there was no full Conference in 1959.[24]

The trade union conferences which took place between Easter and August 1960 had two main propositions before them: the revision of the constitution; and unilateral nuclear disarmament. Union delegations to Labour Party Conferences were mandated to vote on resolutions according to the decisions made at the trade union conferences. However, the system was wide open to abuse. Bill Carron, the leader of the Amalgamated Engineering Union (AEU), was famous for casting his vote at Conference in contradiction of the way he was mandated, by claiming a wider mandate from the membership, or for casting the AEU vote twice for opposing resolutions.[26] Frank Cousins cast the TGWU vote for unilateralism in 1960 with no mandate from his union to do so.[27] The delegation from the National Union of Railwaymen which cast 272,000 votes at the 1960 Conference had been swung to the unilateralist resolution by a single vote on its executive.[28] All sides of the party agreed that the system was unfair, unrepresentative and outdated but would only say so when suffering defeats. The Bevanites had attacked the union block vote in 1952 but by 1960 were defending it.[29] Whereas Gaitskell never demurred during the period from 1955 to 1959 (when the platform did not sustain a single defeat), at Scarborough he called the system unrepresentative.[30]

The main difference between the two sides in the debate was that the left had national organisations putting its case, Victory for Socialism and CND, and in *Tribune* a weekly newspaper spreading the word; CND also produced model resolutions for constituency Labour parties to put forward and collaborated on the compositing of resolutions so that they could concentrate their efforts on one or two key votes. There was no equivalent organisation promoting multilateralism.

The undermining of Gaitskell's position by opposition to his reform of Clause 4 was compounded by the stirrings of revolt on unilateralism. Early in 1960 twenty-four Labour MPs signed a unilateralist motion in the House of Commons. On 1 March forty-three MPs led by Crossman and Wigg abstained on an official Labour defence motion.[31] Gaitskell was being attacked for not responding more quickly to the news, leaked on 26 February, that the Government were going to cancel the Blue Streak missile system, leaving Britain without a modern means of delivering its independent deterrent. In private Gaitskell gave only tentative support to the British bomb and had misgivings about it on financial and technical grounds, but he was reluctant to say so in public.[32] His reluctance meant that the Labour Party was in danger of supporting a deterrent that the government might have abandoned.

This coincided not only with the trade union conferences but also with the Aldermaston march and with opinion polls showing a rise to 33 per cent of support for CND (which was as high as 41 per cent among Labour voters). The Communist Party had belatedly leapt on to the unilateralist bandwagon and its influence swung the Electrical Trades Union's 140,000 votes against the official policy.[33]

On 1 March, Gaitskell asked questions in the House on rumours that Blue Streak was to be cancelled.[34] Rather than attacking the government for a failure to manage the nation's defences – as his colleagues were to do later – Gaitskell played at being Prime Minister. His target was the neutralism of CND and he repudiated calls for Britain to stay out of the nuclear game now that it appeared that there was no effective deterrent available. He stated that the leader of the opposition did not have sufficient information to make judgements on these kinds of policies. Nevertheless the intervention, no matter how cautious, had opened a debate on the future of the deterrent. Gaitskell, however was exhausted, and on April 1 he left for a socialist international conference and missed the full Blue Streak debate. His decision to go on a vacation at this time was roundly condemned.[35]

This also strengthened an underlying concern that Gaitskell tended to display ambivalence on critical issues until he had decided on his course or was faced with a crisis. For those who campaigned on disarmament issues throughout the 1950s this caused some disquiet. Philip Noel-Baker, the leading multilateralist campaigner of the period, expressed his frustration at Gaitskell's attitude to James Meade: 'I have never been able to make Hugh Gaitskell take a real interest in disarmament. Whenever I say to him that the only way out with the unilateralists is by running multilateral disarmament very hard he always says "Yes", and then has a perfunctory half sentence or half paragraph in the next speech. But when I have tried to urge debates in the House in which he and Healey should take part he always says "What is there to say?" '[36]

While Gaitskell was away, the Easter trade union conferences were held and the Co-operative Party, with a 'growing Communist influence', voted unilateralist by 3 to 1.[37] USDAW, the shopworkers' union, emulated the Carron technique by passing an orthodox motion by 62,000 and a unilateralist one by 19,000. Walter Padley, the general secretary, thought he could have swung the vote but had to speak in the Clause 4 debate instead. USDAW had 329,000 votes at Conference.

Meanwhile, in the debate in the House of Commons on the cancellation of Blue Streak, George Brown and Harold Wilson, without consulting Gaitskell – who was now in Haifa – moved towards a rejection of the independent nuclear deterrent. The debate was a censure motion calling on the government to hold an inquiry into the 'circumstances surrounding the initiation, continuance and cancellation of Blue Streak'. George Brown laid into the government in general and Duncan Sandys in particular: 'I do not believe it is unfair to say that the decision to go forward with Blue Streak must be a blunder of an unprecedented size.' He was careful to concentrate his fire on the particular type of system – 'fixed-site liquid-fuelled rockets' – rather than the principle of Britain's deterrent. Nowhere in the speech did he mention Britain's capacity to deliver its bombs using the V-bomber force. The passage which caused comment ran:

> I fear that a gap, during which we shall not have a credible means of delivering an independent British deterrent, seems now to be inevitable. We must remember that it is the credibility outside that matters and not the self-delusion in which we engage inside. The argument for main-taining an independent British deterrent for basic political reasons is one

thing when you have it . . . *the argument for going back into the business once we are out is altogether different.*[38]

In fact all George Brown was saying was that once the Blue Streak system was cancelled the arguments changed. Since he ignored the existence of the V-bombers and their free-fall H-bombs, his contention that the deterrent was inoperative was actually false. The impression was created, however, especially in an atmosphere that was increasingly hostile to the weapons, that the Labour Party was moving towards the repudiation of the British bomb. Wilson's knockabout summing-up of the debate added to the impression: 'Like so many other rather pathetic individuals whose sense of social prestige outruns their purse, he is left in the situation at the end of the day of the man who dare not admit he cannot afford a television set and who puts up the aerial instead. That is our situation, because without an independent means of delivery, the independent nuclear deterrent, the Right Hon. Gentlemen's short cut to national greatness is an empty illusion.'[39] There was virtually no difference in the policy but Gaitskell saw it as a challenge to his leadership.

He also reacted angrily to the attacks on him for his absence. Speaking in his constituency on May Day he explained that the date of the conference at Haifa, where he had had interesting talks with Asian and African leaders, had actually been moved so that he could open the Commons debate. If he had not attended it, the left would have attacked him for the 'rebuff to the Indians, the lost opportunities of giving a British lead etc. etc.' 'But of course this little professional, anti-leadership group, whose journal only survives on rows within the Party, would have attacked me just as bitterly if I had at the last minute broken my promise to go to the International.'[40]

Wilson's speech, however, did reflect his growing independence. Having been quiet between 1955 and the election in the hope that his childhood fantasy of being Chancellor of the Exchequer would come true, Wilson was now actively plotting against Gaitskell. With the leader's position weakening, Wilson sensed his chance; but he was also very badly managed by Gaitskell. Ironically, while Gaitskell took immense care and patience with working-class figures like George Brown, Alf Robens and Jim Griffiths and enjoyed strong personal friendships with trade-unionists such as Sam Watson, Bill Webber or Arthur Deakin, he tried his best to avoid Harold Wilson.

In the same way that Crossman could never see Gaitskell without thinking of the affable schoolboy from Winchester, Gaitskell could never see Wilson without seeing a second-rate economist with a knife in his hand.[41] Above and beyond this, Wilson, who was only slowly learning how to use his wit, was also rather dull. Crossman was possibly less reliable but was always interesting. Being dull was, perhaps, Wilson's greatest crime in Gaitskell's eyes. One story – and the glee with which it is recorded in Hugh's diary – illustrates what bored Gaitskell about Wilson. It was New Year's Eve 1950 and the Gaitskells were giving a successful party. Alf Robens's wife Eva, slightly drunk, was 'getting more and more restive because of what she regarded as the phlegmatic behaviour of those present . . . [she] looked hard at Harold Wilson and said, "You come from North of the Trent, don't you? Surely you know how to behave!" And then proceeded to fling her arms around him and kiss him passionately, to his very great embarrassment. As he had just then been giving a lecture on why the ladies could not obtain nylons – which was full of statistics but all very sober – this incident gave great pleasure.'[42] The idea of lecturing on nylon statistics after the New Year had been drunk in was anathema to Gaitskell; but, more than this, Wilson had so negligible a hinterland that there was little to connect with. They were too closely competitive politically to be able to scheme together; too similar in background to be a leadership team and too different to be friends. Wilson felt socially inferior – rather needlessly, given that the Hampstead Set were not really as grand as he seems to have thought them to be – and personally unsympathetic to Gaitskell's tastes. Perhaps if Hugh had been in a full 'Durbin' phase they might have become closer, but by 1960 Gaitskell wanted more from intimacy than an intellectual or political association: he wanted a little fun. Wilson had nothing to offer, and was anyway seen by the Gaitskellites as the enemy.

While Gaitskell was attacking his left-wing critics in Leeds on May Day, the AEU, with Carron this time outmanoeuvred, voted unilateralist by 38 to 14, taking another 697,000 votes away from Gaitskell. George Brown as official defence spokesman was trying, with Crossman, to find a form of words that could be the basis of a compromise. Gaitskell told a meeting of close supporters that a unilateralist resolution was bound to be passed at Conference. In contrast Frank Soskice, Patrick Gordon Walker, Roy Mason and Michael Stewart held out for the British deterrent.

Gaitskell faced defeat on two central policy positions. The left of the Labour Party was in the ascendant and baying for the leader's blood; the right and centre were on the defensive; and the Tory government were off the hook as the country watched the Labour Party tearing its leader apart. The revisionists' strength had gradually weakened over the past year. In the background to the drama on the national stage, Gaitskell's friends and his supporters at the grass roots of the party had watched the unfolding of the year with increasing dismay. Their response was finally to organise.

Gaitskell, Tony Crosland, Roy Jenkins and Patrick Gordon Walker met in London on 12 May 1960. The discussion centred on how to deal with the defence question, and whether it was time to split the party:

> Crosland said that if G took this line how many would he carry into opposition? He could not hope for 100. 'Perhaps 10' said G who became very angry and rounded on the other 2 sharply and implied that I was a 'fudger' of principle. [Crosland] said this would be like the ineffective right-wing breakaway in French party – purely intellectual with supporters like Tomney and Bellenger.[43]

The wounds of Suez were evident in Gaitskell's vehemence that he would not, as he told Gordon Walker, falter on defence; he insisted on 'provocative clarity'. In the evening he dined alone with Hugh Dalton. His old mentor doubted whether they could stop the slide to unilateralism now that the AEU had voted in favour. The miners and the NUR would follow, and Gaitskell would be defeated on both the bomb and Clause 4: 'then could Hugh go on as Leader?' Gaitskell tried to cheer Dalton up a little, saying it was not as bad as all that, and if he had to resign he would sit below the gangway and many in the PLP would follow: 'He would tell the P.L.P. that he couldn't go on as Leader. He didn't know whom they'd choose. The new official leadership and front bench wouldn't be impressive. I asked him if his constituents in Leeds were firm. He said Yes.'[44] Gaitskell had in fact written to his agent: 'The AEU vote is pretty depressing. But at least last Sunday's speech got a tremendous press and in a sense, the reaction in the House of Commons is at present not unhealthy. As you can imagine, I intend to go on fighting.'[45]

At this stage, though, he was not sure what form that fight would take. But the fairly desperate private talk had been reflected among younger supporters, and Dick Taverne, a prospective candidate at the time, recalls a conversation between himself and Bill Rodgers, then general secretary of the Fabian Society:

I remember going to a young Fabian conference in Wilton Park, travelling in the train with Bill, and one of us said to the other . . . 'If the Labour Party goes on like this there is no point in belonging to it any more. Let's give it one last try, can't we organise something?'[46]

So the depression was accompanied by a growing feeling that they must organise in the face of what was perceived to be the skilled organisation of the left, in the form of CND, *Tribune* and the orchestration of resolutions to the Party Conference.[47] Mikardo always claimed the left was much less organised than the right supposed; but the perception on the right of the party was that they were competing with a skilled and highly organised left wing.[48] They concluded that the only way of defeating such an organisation was to set up a rival. This was not to be based, as in the past, on the PLP, or the official channels of Transport House, but was to operate unofficially, through the constituency Labour parties. For the first time the right wing of the party was going to take the battle directly to the membership.

Brian Walden was organising in Oxford: 'a group within the university and the City Labour Party was meeting because of their concern with the activities of CND supporters within the City Labour Party.'[49] This connected with a larger London group. In fact, from about 1954 a number of younger Labour Party members, including candidates and councillors, had been meeting together in an informal debating society known as 'the Group'. Bill Rodgers reviewed the early years in his diary in 1957: 'We started three years ago with about eighteen members of whom perhaps 6–8 generally attended. Now we are up to two dozen or so and the newcomers are more active.'[50] Rodgers had organised the Group to ensure that some of his Oxford contemporaries did not lose track of politics.[51]

There was a feeling among these young Labour activists that there was a great deal of support that simply needed to be 'rallied' in defence of the leader. Rodgers and Taverne had sent a letter of support to Gaitskell at the height of the Clause 4 battle in February. That these generally loyalist figures were contemplating openly conducting factional organisation, after all the fights against Bevanism in the 1950s, illustrated the extent to which the events inside the Labour Party since the defeat of 1959 had produced a crisis on the right of the party.

Philip Williams, Ron Owen and Brian Walden now proposed the

creation of a Gaitskellite pressure group to Tony Crosland in Nuffield College. Crosland's reception of the idea was 'wildly enthusiastic' and he informed Walden and the others about the London group that had been established. The London group, which was planning a meeting on 27 June,[52] was described as 'entirely middle-class in composition'. Crosland invited the Oxford people to come to London and lay out their plans to a combined meeting of the two groups. The new organisation, christened 'The New Group', would be based on local groups and enlarged through personal contacts. There would be no problem with finance: 'Crosland guarantees all the money we need for a venture of this kind.' 'Emphatically this is going at first to be democratic centralism, there is going to be no bloody nonsense about constitutions and executive committee etc. We are all privates and generals at the same time.'

The idea of a 'democratic centralist' organisation with local groups was dangerously like a party within a party, or indeed a new party. The depth of depression reached at this stage of 1960 among the right-wing supporters of Gaitskell is disclosed again in a letter written by Walden describing Crosland's reactions to his proposals:

> Crosland appealed passionately that we go for Labour Party members, and Labour sympathisers. He did not discount the possibility that eventually the Labour Party would split, and then the role of the New Group would change, but for the moment he wanted us to do what you and I have already discussed, namely build ourselves up as a new given factor within the Labour Party.

The picture Walden paints in this letter may have been partly a result of his tendency towards disingenuous over-dramatisation, as in 'For the pioneers this is going to involve a complete sacrifice of personal interest, and advancement within the present Party', but it is revealing just how far Crosland was prepared to take the logical consequences of Gaitskell's potential long-term defeat on Clause 4 and defence.

> *Above all else* this is not going to be a wholly middle-class talking shop. We want no windy discussions on minute matters of policy, and we do want working class, no class, any class members, trade unionists, local councillors, GMC delegates, non-GMC delegates, ward members, non-ward members – the whole bloody lot.[53]

The conversation with Crosland generated a fever of enthusiasm in Walden; schemes, plans and possibilities opened in front of the young lecturer. It is possible that something would have come of this encounter if the links had not been made with the London group. It is much more probable that, like a million other alcohol-fuelled political-planning sessions, it would have evaporated with the world put to rights but nothing changed. It was only when experienced political organisers, like Rodgers and Taverne, were involved that something substantial emerged.

For Bill Rodgers the campaign began on a day in Easter Week 1960.[54] Rodgers had resigned as general secretary of the Fabian Society in January 1960 and taken a job with the Consumers' Association.[55] Having made the decision to leave his job in the Fabian Society he felt 'free to take a more public position' by organising a letter of support for Gaitskell on 3 February. While he was still serving out his notice,[56] he arranged a meeting with Tony Crosland at the Two Chairmen pub in Dartmouth Street, across the road from the Fabian Society headquarters. Rodgers's account of this meeting made plain the personal difficulties his plans gave him:

> I said then that I felt personally in a dilemma. I had decided to leave full-time politics and had in mind that I would not play a very active part at least until the next general election. On the other hand, it now seemed to me, in view of the Clause 4 dispute, that this was really the time to rally more seriously than ever before people of like minds. I raised with Tony the whole question of liaison on the right in the light of our experience of the Clause 4 dispute and of my letter to Hugh Gaitskell.

Rodgers lamented the fact that *Tribune* had succeeded in making left-wing policy appeal to young people by giving them a direct input into an organisation and allowing them to meet 'leading *Tribune* figures socially'; there was 'real cohesion on the left'. Finally he told Crosland what he wanted to see happen: 'Was it possible to get some sort of continuous liaison on the right from Hugh Gaitskell at the top, through Members of the Parliamentary Party, to candidates and key workers in the constituencies?'[57]

In further discussions they decided to assemble a group in London to discuss what should be done.[58] This became the Campaign for Democratic Socialism. Present at the London meeting were representatives from inside and outside the House of Commons.[59] The non-parliamentarians included Dick Taverne, Rodgers's co-organiser of the letter of 3 February and co-organiser of the Group. There was also Ivan Yates, another leading light of the Group and the author of articles supportive of Gaitskell over Clause 4 in *Reynolds News*, who was active on the steering committee of CDS until he left to join the *Observer* in 1961. Finally there was Michael Shanks, also a Group member, industrial editor of the *Financial Times* and author, in 1961, of the revisionist tract *The Stagnant Society* which sold 60,000 copies and was the first in a series of Penguin Specials along the lines of 'What's wrong with Britain'.[60] Shanks, in common with other CDS organisers, had spent time in the United States[61] and shared Rodgers's impatience with the lack of organisation on the right of the Labour Party. He became an active member of the steering committee and later the editorial committee of the CDS newsletter, *Campaign*.

From the Commons came the four leading members of the Hampstead Set. Rodgers later offered his own verdict on the contributions of Douglas Jay and Roy Jenkins: 'Douglas Jay, although always willing to help, didn't play a leading part. Roy Jenkins kept in continuous contact, was always very willing to help and served on committees, but he was perhaps less close to us in the crucial months than some others.' Roy Jenkins suggested they also invite Denis Howell. Howell had been elected for Birmingham All Saints in 1955 but had been defeated in 1959[62] – his defeat had been Dalton's biggest disappointment[63] – and was therefore out of the House working in public relations.[64] He was seen as a considerable grassroots operator in the Birmingham area and became the main organiser for the Campaign for Democratic Socialism among the trade unions and constituency Labour parties around the country.[65] The two key figures were Patrick Gordon Walker and Tony Crosland. Gordon Walker kept Gaitskell informed of what was happening in the CDS and in the liaison committee set up with the trade unions on the selection of parliamentary candidates. But it was Crosland who became the most deeply involved in the early phase of the CDS.

Tony Crosland was the link and the motivator for both small groups of Gaitskellites who had begun to gather in London and Oxford. There was a general consensus among the CDS organisers, from Rodgers and Taverne down, that Crosland was the ideological inspiration. In the very early period he was also the link between the different groups and therefore the main inspiration. Brian Walden, writing the first outline plan for the CDS in May 1960, remarked: 'The only policy the group will have is this . . . an acceptance of modern political, social and economic realities as exemplified

in the writings of Crosland and Galbraith.'[66] Rodgers later described
Crosland's effect on the early period of the Campaign:

> Throughout the period of preparation before the launching of the Cam-
> paign Tony Crosland's role was crucial. Not only did he give the intellec-
> tual lead reflected in the Manifesto: he also showed a single-mindedness
> of purpose and discipline which most of us had previously believed he
> had not possessed. It was he who kept us at it when we met, mainly at
> his flat, refusing, for example, to let us have a drink until we had done
> three hours solid work. He had the authority to keep us together and
> although he in no way dominated the group he gave it a lead without
> which much less would have been done.[67]

Taverne echoed Rodgers's feelings about Crosland: 'The person who
I think contributed most after Bill [Rodgers] was Tony Crosland.
At the meetings we went to he was the driving force. He would
constantly say "Look, forget about all this talk about intellectualism.
We are apparatchiks." '[68]

A manifesto of approximately 600 words was to be prepared by
the Oxford group and Crosland. This was to be circulated to 'carefully selected individuals'. It would be released to the press and carry
the name and address of Frank Pickstock an Oxford CDS activist.
Once the manifesto was public the 'spontaneous formation of groups
would be mentioned'. Until this stage, which would be after the
Party Conference, lists of supporters should be prepared and 'planned
spontaneity ought to be the aim in all arrangements, with the emphasis on grass-roots origin'.[69]

Since Pickstock had not attended the meeting, Rodgers sent him
an account of what had been agreed:

> There was unanimous approval for starting an organisation. I confess that
> this surprised me because I had expected more caution from the MPs.
> The only doubt was whether it might be regarded as a Party within a
> Party and come under a general proscription – or make it more difficult
> to deal with VFS [Victory for Socialism], if this was necessary at any time.
> But it was thought that this could be avoided, especially as personalities
> would not be involved: in any case, some risk was worth running other-
> wise the right would remain unorganised and exposed.[70]

He was also frank about the nature of the proposed spontaneous
growth. 'This spontaneous growth would, of course, result from
your plans carefully laid in advance.'

Throughout the planning stage the organisers' primary concern was not to be seen as exclusively middle class and intellectual. The power of this accusation when used by the left against them was significant, but would not greatly have affected their ability to organise and campaign. Their natural constituency would not have been primarily concerned with the class composition of the group but with the power of the argument. Apart from everything else, the left itself was dominated by middle-class intellectuals. What is striking is the extent to which it was the CDS organisers who felt insecure about presenting themselves as a middle-class group. They were not comfortable with each other and latched gratefully on to Frank Pickstock as a figure to give them some credibility and authenticity as part of the Labour Party. This kind of insecurity about their own role in the party was directly related to the symbols that Gaitskell had been attacking in the Clause 4 debate. They were in fact surrendering to the same type of prejudice and mythology which had defeated the 'Amplification of Aims'.

This in turn had an impact on the drafting of their manifesto, which attempted no demolition of icons without having a good stab at trying to replace them. It tried to shift the party away from an attachment to the Marxist texts by stressing the role of an alternative set of sacred texts and writers derived from the history of British radicalism. The CDS did not consider that adherence to an imagined past might be considered a handicap for a supposedly radical party; they simply felt that the imagined past should be the right one. The revisionists claimed that they approached contemporary issues in a contemporary way, based on the critical application of policy approaches free of the intellectual baggage of the left. In fact, they simply approached these problems with their own set of intellectual baggage, less encumbered, but resilient none the less. Moreover, this baggage contained a significant dose of belief in planning, physical controls, economic intervention, selective and innovative social ownership and progressive taxation. The drafting of the CDS manifesto went on through the summer. As drafts shuttled to and from Oxford and London, the political hostilities deteriorated further.

Gaitskell could still occasionally escape from the grind, as this letter from Ann Fleming to Evelyn Waugh shows:

> We had a very jolly dinner here to mix Oliver Lyttelton Chandos with the Gaitskells and Tony Crosland; you wouldn't have approved but Oliver was very happy and stayed till 2.30 a.m. to perfect his mimicry of my left-wing friends.[71]

But in the main the internal battle dominated. On 31 May the TUC and NEC each appointed drafting committees of four people to devise the new Labour Party defence policy. At the end of the first meeting of the drafting committee, which discussed a draft by Crossman, Brown, Healey and and Morgan Phillips, Gaitskell got himself added to the committee. Crossman, however, felt that without Gaitskell's presence they could have persuaded Frank Cousins to accept the compromise. Brown and Crossman produced a draft that Cousins could accept but which fudged the key issue by making no reference to the retention of nuclear weapons within NATO. Gaitskell opposed this draft, and the trade-unionists 'exposed [Crossman's] semantic shams as hopelessly fragile' or, as Crossman put it: 'Every word, every comma, was niggled at and disputed, either for minutiae of drafting points or, more often, in demand for a more nuclear-warrior-like presentation.' Inside the International Department, David Ennals remembers the bruising, pugnacious tone of these meetings and Gaitskell's relentless pedantry. Gordon Walker felt that Gaitskell was being self-destructive, Gaitskell that the party was intent on suicide. Not since the days of the 'Bevan expulsion' crisis was Gaitskell so deep in the trenches of internal warfare.

During this debate Frank Cousins made it clear to Bill Webber that he felt that NATO should have no nuclear weapons at all, but Cousins was isolated in his opposition and the draft was accepted. Crossman recalled: 'All those four hours rowing, wrangling, for nothing except to make sure that Frank Cousins was against us.'[72] Dora later told Geoffrey Goodman:

> Hugh did not hate Frank or anything like that. He never hated anybody. There are very few people against whom Hugh felt real hostility, Frank was not one of them – but I think Frank did dislike Hugh. Frank, I think, always felt that Hugh was never really a socialist at all. He clearly felt that Hugh was an intruder in the Movement. Frank was one of those who felt that you couldn't be a true socialist unless you were working class, Hugh wasn't working class and he never pretended to be either.[73]

For his part Frank Cousins agreed with Dora's assessment, but added that Gaitskell was an 'intellectually honest man who may have been driven to extremes by the force of his own case – as I too sometimes was'.[74]

Labour's existing nuclear policy already pledged the party to no further British tests, no first use and no joint European deterrent;

Britain would in future contribute to defence through conventional means and would cease to be an independent nuclear power. As a result of this meeting phrases were added about loyalty to NATO and political control of nuclear weapons.

Gaitskell was now armed with a policy statement endorsed by the TUC and the NEC and he made a series of speeches, urging the unions to vote against the TGWU unilaterist resolution and for the official defence policy. His speech at the conference of the National Union of General and Municipal Workers (NUGMW) on 23 May was acclaimed as his best outside the House. The *Manchester Guardian* described it as the most impassioned speech of his career.[75] It was the classic Gaitskell lecture on the defence issue: the Labour Party Conference should not dictate to a future Labour government; did unilateralism mean pacifism or neutralism; and if Britain gave the lead who would follow that lead? After the speech, which the chairman declared was the finest he had ever heard, adding, 'There is really nothing more to be said', the NUGMW decided to cast its 650,000 votes against unilateralism by 260 votes to 80. Then the Post Office Workers, with 160,000 votes, gave Gaitskell victories on both defence and on Clause 4. The Railway Clerks and Woodworkers also came out in support of the NEC and the Yorkshire NUM voted for the TUC–NEC nuclear policy by 75 votes to 19.

On Clause 4 the tide was turning the other way: USDAW had accepted the statement of aims but not as an amendment to the constitution; the NUGMW had accepted it, but by a much smaller majority, 204 votes to 132. The AEU and the Yorkshire NUM both voted to retain the existing Clause 4. In early July the NUM as a whole voted against a change in Clause 4 by 354,000 votes to 326,000, and voted against unilateralism by 470,000 votes to 201,000. On the other hand, the National Union of Railwaymen went with the left on both issues, by 66 votes to 11 and by 39 votes to 38 repectively, carrying 272,000 votes with them, as did the Building Workers, Boilermakers and Electricians.[76]

Victory for Socialism latched on to the defiance of Conference implicit in Gaitskell's speeches even before Scarborough. On 20 June VFS issued a call for Gaitskell to resign from the leadership in the interests of the party, condemning his leadership as a 'source of weakness, confusion and disunity'. Gaitskell decided to test his strength with the Parliamentary Labour Party and ensure that the PLP supported him, whatever happened at Scarborough. The Chief

Whip introduced a confidence motion at the PLP meeting on 30 June:

> This meeting of the Parliamentary Labour Party expresses its full confidence in the Leader of the party and condemns in the strongest possible terms all attacks from whatever quarter and calls on all members to show by their actions and words their unity and loyalty to the party.

John Stonehouse proposed the addendum: 'and accordingly expresses the hope that decisions when taken will be loyally accepted'.

Gaitskell closed the two-hour debate with one of his most effective PLP speeches. Replying to criticism that he did not spend enough time in the smoking room, he said that he would have liked nothing more than a 'leisurely gossip in the smoking room' but for the last few months he had been without a deputy leader and there was simply not the time. In response to the charge that he could find time for the XYZ Club, he pointed out that he had dined there only three times in the last five years.

> The Labour Party was a difficult party to lead. It was not made easier when the Leader sitting on the Front Bench had to listen to attacks from people behind him which only encouraged the people opposite. It was nevertheless the responsiblity of the leader to lead.

Gaitskell disowned Douglas Jay's article of October 1959 in *Forward*, saying that although Jay had been a friend for thirty years he had not been in touch with him before the *Forward* article was written, and he had not agreed with all of it. It was a skilful performance, delivered with noticeably more warmth than his usual PLP meeting speeches. The vote was decisive:

For Mr Gaitskell	179
Against	7
Abstained or left meeting	18
Absent	53
Total PLP	257[77]

Of the fifty-three who were absent, seven sent in sick notes expressing support for Gaitskell. This meant that the worst-case scenario, in which all the other absentees and abstainers would have voted against, would have been 186 votes to 71 against, a substantial margin which roughly reflected the 1955 figures from the last contested leadership election. The minority of seven who voted against were: Sydney Silverman, Stephen Swingler, Harold Davies, Will Griffiths, Konni Zilliacus and J. P. W. Mallalieu; Manny Shinwell abstained. The left were attracted to Stonehouse's amendment, hoping they could broaden its meaning to include resolutions passed at Conference.

While the PLP meeting had gone well for Gaitskell, and Chris Mayhew throughout this long and difficult year kept telling him that the PLP mattered more than anything else,[78] the union conferences continued to go against the Labour leader. By July there was a mandated majority of 1,700,000 trade union votes against reforming the constitution. On 13 July, at a special meeting of the NEC, the proposed amendment of the constitution was dropped and it was agreed that the 'Amplification of Aims' would simply be published separately. This was a case of bowing to the inevitable but it also avoided the possibility of the platform being defeated on both defence and constitutional reform. Rather than take a similar course on defence, however, Gaitskell ensured there would be a confrontation leading to a 'Who runs the party?' debate.

In July, at the Durham Miners' Gala, usually a good forum for him, Gaitskell spoke passionately of the need for loyalty. Large meetings of miners always seem to have influenced Gaitskell. If there was some sort of benchmark for him it was the attitude of the miners: they backed him on the bomb but opposed him on Clause 4. That he never should have raised Clause 4 was a judgement that Dora believed her husband eventually shared:

> I think that in the end he realised that, too, although he never doubted he was right in principle. He was never a great nationaliser, he never regarded nationalisation as an end in itself, only a means. He was in favour of various forms of State intervention in the economy but he never regarded nationalisation as a major principle at any time of his life. Hugh was a reformer, never a revolutionary socialist.[79]

As in the early 1950s the outside world occasionally intruded into Labour's internal war. When Gaitskell was in deep trouble in early June, Macmillan confided to his diary: 'One begins to wonder whether Gaitskell will be able to survive and ride the storm. I should be sorry if he went, for he has ability without charm. He does not appeal to the electorate, but he has a sense of patriotism and moderation.'[80] After the vote of confidence on 30 June there was some relief in Number 10 because, 'on the whole, Gaitskell suits us pretty well'.[81] However, Gaitskell's response to Macmillan's appointment of Lord Home as Foreign Secretary dented Macmillan's complacency a little. When the story first leaked, Gaitskell told the *Observer*:

> Nowadays when foreign affairs are so tremendously important the Foreign secretary ought without question be answerable in person to the House of Commons, which unlike the House of Lords, is elected by the votes of the British people. To appoint a member of the House of Lords to this vital post would be undemocratic and entirely inappropriate to modern conditions.[82]

He demanded a debate in the House of Commons and made what Macmillan judged to be his most effective speech in the Commons.

When the House rose, the Gaitskells managed to get away for a two-week holiday in Yugoslavia, with A. J. Ayer and his family: 'We had a good holiday in Yugoslavia and enjoyed it very much indeed.'[83] Hugh's daughter Cressida delighted Marshal Tito with her calypso guitar music.[84] For once this was the only kind of headline the trip generated. However, the ever attentive *Daily Express*'s William Hickey column did note that even if Gaitskell survived as leader he might leave the Labour Party because Tom Mahoney, who had just become membership secretary of the Hampstead ward, had discovered that the Gaitskells had not paid their subscriptions. As soon as they were back Hugh paid up the £3 subscription for Dora, himself and the girls. Another light moment was provided by a short speaking tour around London, which ended with Hugh dancing calypso with a West Indian woman in Notting Hill. She said later, 'He is a very good dancer.'[85]

Much more typical of this 'summer of the bomb' was the series of speeches in which Gaitskell rehearsed the themes of his Conference speech. At Battersea in September the *Telegraph* – which, having now forgiven him for Suez, consistently gave him a good press – reported that 'a new aggressive Gaitskell emerged yesterday in defence of the Labour Party's official policy on nuclear weapons'.[86] The *Yorkshire Evening Post* quoted a clear indication that defiance was already his intention: if the Conference voted for unilateralism, Gaitskell said, 'I do not believe that either the millions of our supporters in the country, still less the British people as a whole, will accept it for one moment.'[87]

On his return from holiday, he wrote to Murray: 'South Leeds is quite sound but it is only right and proper that I should be there and explain just what the dangers ahead are.'[88] The dangers were now increasingly obvious. Estimates before the Conference showed a majority of one million among union votes and a majority of one million among constituency Labour parties for unilateralism. The *Daily Mail* gave Gaitskell a 50 per cent chance of surviving Conference. During the previous month Gaitskell had trailed the possibility that he would defy Conference. He had contemplated resigning the leadership and taking up the position of 'the prince across the water'. His supporters had an organisation ready to fight for his ideas in the grass roots of the movement and, if necessary, be already in existence if the party should split. Nobody expected the events at Scarborough to make all that much difference because nobody expected Gaitskell to deliver the most effective speech by a Labour leader in the post-war period.

As Conference convened, everyone felt that for the first time the leadership was about to face a major defeat. Tony Benn made one last attempt to broker a compromise. At exactly 10 o'clock on Saturday 1 October he knocked on the door of Hugh Gaitskell's suite at the Royal Hotel in Scarborough. Hugh was wearing a dark blue shirt with no tie and blue trousers; he looked 'dejected and bored and had the longest face', and he regarded Benn with 'intense distrust'. Dora recalled Benn

> trying to persuade Hugh not to press with his argument but to seek a compromise. He begged Hugh to change his mind. Well, perhaps in that sense Hugh was inflexible. But he would not compromise on what he regarded as an issue of great principle. Nor did he have any illusions about what was at stake.[89]

Benn remembers him being intent on having a confrontation with the left, whatever the issue, and insisting that he would not be dictated to by Frank Cousins. He told Benn, 'You are a very talented young man, but you have no political judgement and you don't realise that sometimes silence is golden.'[90] Cousins gave Benn an equally unhelpful reception: 'If you think you can save that man in this way, you've made the biggest mistake of your life'.[91] There would be no compromise. Both sides had decided on the need for a confrontation: the left was disillusioned with Gaitskell's leadership and frustrated by the months of argument; the right was ready for a fight.

Gradually the emotional aspect of Gaitskell's personality had seeped through into his public persona. On Clause 4 his intellectual aspect had been given free rein. Before the election defeat in 1959, he had played the party game, agreeing compromises on domestic policy, ensuring unity in the party in the run-up to the election, preventing his supporters from organising to compete with VFS and trying to bring a united party to power. He failed, and the failure freed him. David Marquand has argued:

> After 1959, perhaps because he reckoned that he now had nothing to lose, the romantic broke free. He would now pursue truth to the bitter end; he would no longer allow barriers of prejudice to obstruct the free working of the mind; putting his faith in the power of reason, he would try to persuade his party to see the light.[92]

This is a convincing explanation for his insistence on reform of Clause 4. Gaitskell tried to lead but the party would not follow; emotionally he now felt the party might not be worth leading. But the pull on his love for the party was stronger than the pull away from politics. Moreover, the arena had changed from the constitution to the defence of the realm. Romanticism could bring him so far, and rationalism now reasserted itself; yet it was not a barren or dry rationalism, but a passionate belief that Britain could not abandon its role in the world. This alone was sufficiently important for him to remain leader in order to fight for it. He believed that if CND won the Labour Party would be finished. He was also fighting for his own political survival: if CND won he too would be finished. It was a monumental combination: career, party, country. But there was more. He was a dedicated Atlanticist. What would happen to NATO if Britain withdrew into neutrality? Would the US withdraw from Europe? Gaitskell thought he was arguing to try to save his country from pacifism, the Western Alliance from neutralism and the Labour Party from permanent electoral oblivion as well as his career from ending.

On 2 October the NEC voted 17 to 4 against compromise with Frank Cousins and 13 to 7 to oppose the TGWU resolution.[93]*

---

* The resolution rejected a defence policy based on the threat of the use of strategic or tactical nuclear weapons and called for ending the manufacture of bombs, banning the transportation of nuclear weapons by aircraft in British airspace and the closing of nuclear bases.

Cousins persuaded his own union to vote, without a mandate, for unilateralism.[94]

The night before the speech Gaitskell rehearsed the main points, for the first time since his maiden speech, in front of Dora. Neither had much sleep. At 4 a.m. he finished drafting the peroration. John Harris saw the body of the speech but not the ending. Dora remembered that night:

> He certainly had no idea that the voting would be so narrow. He expected a much heavier defeat and he had no illusions whatever about the outcome of such a defeat. He would have had to quit as party leader and go to the back benches.[95]

The debate on foreign policy and defence opened on 5 October with the presentation of the joint TUC–NEC document, *Policy for Peace*, by Sam Watson of the NUM and the NEC. Watson attacked the attempts by Richard Crossman and George Brown to paper over differences, made it plain from the outset that any victory for unilateralism would be hollow and bluntly stated: 'The final arbiters of the future of this party do not sit in this conference, but are the British electorate and the British people.'[96] The main thrust of this and the other speeches on behalf of the platform was that the differences between the two sides were not minor ones but that they boiled down to whether Britain should leave NATO if it refused to disarm unilaterally or whether Britain should stay in NATO but without its own nuclear weapons. The debate then took a curious turn, with a resolution from ASLEF, which was eventually remitted, opposing the training of German troops in Britain.

The AEU resolution was then introduced and seconded by Ian Mikardo and things started to warm up. In a short emotive speech Mikardo made clear the basis of the unilateralist case, which echoed throughout the debate: an emotional appeal based on the destructive power of the weapons followed by doubts about the aggressive intent of the USSR and attacks on the theory of deterrence. Mikardo was followed by Cousins, who introduced the TGWU composite resolution. He added to the Mikardo case the view that as the Labour Party had lost three elections in a row the presentation of a new policy to the British electorate would actually help the Labour Party electorally.

After the presentation of resolutions, Conference moved to a general debate, which was opened by Philip Noel-Baker. Noel-

Baker's speech was one of the most powerful, not the less effective because he had just received the Nobel Peace Prize; the case he made for multilateral disarmament carried a great deal of authority. George Brown followed with a forthright defence of the NEC's position: 'Britain has to be defended in the conditions which exist today and not those which we wish existed today.'

Back came the unilateralists with Michael Foot introducing the question of control, in a sharp, passionate speech:

> Is there any lady, mother or grandmother who can step to this microphone, who can take part on the platform, who can listen peacefully in the galleries and not be fully conscious that when the die is cast today, irrespective of whether we have a Labour government within the next four years or not, human destiny is being decided?

The unilateralists used emotive language and extravagant arguments to put their case. The multilateralists countered with logic and with what, like Denis Healey, they saw as the fallacies of the unilateralist argument: 'The unilateralists are saying . . . that we have got to give a lead. The question I ask you is: if we give a lead, who is going to follow?' The atmosphere and the tension grew as the main event approached. The hall was airless and hot, the television lights adding to sense of theatre.

Just before 3 p.m. Gaitskell started speaking. His face was white from the tension and the heat. As always perfectly dressed in a dark three-piece suit, he had a small sprig of white heather in his left lapel. Harold Wilson, sitting two seats to his left, leaned back in his chair, sucking his pipe. He had played little part in the drama to date but what he was about to hear convinced him of the need to challenge Gaitskell for the leadership.

Gaitskell began by praising the debate and listing all that the two sides agreed on, which was much, before changing tack and launching into his attack on unilateralism and his advocacy of the 'Policy for Peace'. He initially concentrated on the abandonment of the British deterrent before turning, as Denis Healey and Sam Watson had done, to the question of the Western alliance and NATO. He made it clear that possession of the bomb by Britain was not a matter of principle: 'I have never taken the view that the decisions made originally by the Labour Government in 1947 to manufacture our own atom bomb . . . were the kind of things which involved us in a matter of principle.' He accused the unilateralists of cloaking their real intentions by not coming out and saying they were prepared to see Britain withdraw from NATO: 'If you are a unilateralist on principle, you are driven to becoming a neutralist.' The middle section of the speech outlined the platform's objections to the particular motions in detail. Finally he turned to the consequences of defeat and finished his speech with an extremely powerful challenge and a call to arms:

> The place to decide the leadership of this party is not here but in the parliamentary party . . . It is perfectly reasonable to try to get rid of somebody . . . who you think is not a good leader . . . What would be wrong . . . and would not be forgiven, is if, in order to get rid of a man, you supported a policy in which you did not wholeheartedly believe.

Gradually the audience began to respond more and more to the salvoes from Gaitskell. The 'crackle of interruptions pierced the atmosphere' and grew to the proportions of an 'artillery barrage' as he reached the peroration:[97]

> Supposing all of us, like well-behaved sheep, were to follow the policies of unilateralism and neutralism, what kind of an impression would that make upon the minds of the British people? . . . What sort of people do they think we are? Do they think we can simply accept a decision of this kind? Do they think we can become overnight the pacifists, unilateralists and fellow travellers that other people are? I say this to you: we may lose the vote today and the result may deal this party a grave blow. It may not be possible to prevent it, but I think there are many of us who will not accept that this blow need be mortal, who will not believe that such an end is inevitable. There are some of us, Mr Chairman, who will fight and fight and fight again to bring back sanity and honesty and dignity, so that our party with its great past may retain its glory and its greatness.

Gaitskell sat down sweating profusely as the hall exploded into two-thirds of sustained cheering and applause and one-third booing or silence. After the singing of 'For he's a jolly good fellow' the results of the votes were announced. Gaitskell had lost. The joint NEC–TUC policy on defence was defeated by 297,000 votes. The TGWU resolution, which Gaitskell took to espouse unilateral disarmament, was passed by just 43,000 votes. The AEU resolution, in favour of which seventy-nine other organisations withdrew their resolutions, was passed by 407,000 votes. This last resolution was the most straightforwardly unilateralist. Yet, as Dora described it, 'he smiled until he almost laughed' because the majorities against him were only a third of what had been predicted. Significantly Gaitskell had been particularly effective in swinging constituency Labour parties.

Emerging from the conference hall, Gaitskell was besieged by the media and gave a string of television and radio interviews. By coincidence the TGWU were holding their annual dinner that night, to which by tradition the leader was invited. As the evening news bulletins completed their interviews Frank Cousins and Hugh Gaitskell found themselves in the same television studio. Both must have been exhausted but Gaitskell looked drained and dejected. Cousins went over to him: 'Hugh, don't take it this way for heaven's sake. Come down to our union dinner and have a drink and let's forget about it for a while. After all, we've still got to work together to get a Labour Government.' Gaitskell replied, 'That's very nice of you, Frank, I'd be happy to come. Can Dora come too?' 'Of course she can,' Cousins said.[98] Nance Cousins, Frank's wife, whom Gaitskell had described the night before as 'very left',[99] was sitting next to George Brown when Cousins and Gaitskell walked in. Brown told her to stand up and receive her leader. She refused. They started to shout at each other. The top table was now in a state of confusion. Some people were clapping. Some people stayed sitting down. Others were watching the fight. For the next year the rest of the Labour Party mirrored the top table at the Transport Union dinner.

On the morning after the vote, still in his dressing-gown, Gaitskell met with John Harris and told him that this morning he had started 'planning operations at the grass roots to reverse the decision'. He also wrote a sketchy note of his 'Objects: This year desperately good organisation needed.'[100]

16

The Fight Back, 1960–1961

At the moment I feel more planned against than planning.
>Gaitskell, October 1960

There certainly isn't anything conspiratorial about us.
>Bill Rodgers on CDS, 1960

After talking to Lord Salisbury, Lord Lambton and Anthony Runt,
I conclude that some Conservatives hate Harold Macmillan as
much as some socialists hate Gaitskell.
>Ann Fleming to Evelyn Waugh, 7 November 1960

Gaitskell's friends were as surprised as his enemies by the power
of the Scarborough speech. From the Shadow Cabinet down to
constituency level, the force of the argument, the manner of its
delivery and the passionate leadership it offered combined to galvan-
ise people into action: here was a leader worth fighting for. That
the fight could have been avoided, that the defeat was as much to
do with the abortive Clause 4 reform as with defence issues, and
that with a little more skill the party could have been kept together
were now irrelevant. Many who had contemplated leaving the party
or forming some kind of centre grouping now felt that it was worth
staying inside and bringing Labour back from the edge; what mattered now was winning the defence debate and then fighting for the
election of a majority Labour government. Gaitskell himself organised a campaign against the unilateralists on three levels: parliamentary, trade union and constituency. The objective of the campaign
was to defend himself from any further challenge to his leadership
and reverse the Scarborough defence vote by the biggest majority
possible.

On the evening of the defence debate Patrick Gordon Walker
had assembled a group of Gaitskellite MPs in his hotel room:

The word had been put out by Albu that absolutely reliable people should
meet in my room. Present: Mayhew, Albu, Crosland, S. Irving, Horace

King, Gerry Reynolds, Reg Prentice, Jack Diamond and one of two more. We decided to set up an organisation in the Ply [Parliamentary] Party – a machinery of communication. Gerry Reynolds, should be the link between me and Gaitskell – and the reliable ones in the Party. The purpose would be to co-ordinate action instead of dissipating our forces. There was very strong feeling in favour of this – and of getting rid of Harold Wilson.[1]

This group, under cover of being the Campaign for Multilateral Disarmament, became the Gaitskellite caucus in the Parliamentary Labour Party. They organised attendance at PLP meetings, drafted speeches for debates, put down parliamentary questions and collected signatures for motions. They also lobbied on Gaitskell's behalf in the leadership elections in 1960 and 1961.

The first open challenge came from Anthony Greenwood. A strong unilateralist, he made the initial move by resigning from the Shadow Cabinet on 14 October 1960 to fight Gaitskell for the leadership. Once a contest was made inevitable the left wanted the strongest possible candidate to oppose Gaitskell. That meant Harold Wilson.

The week that followed Greenwood's resignation witnessed what Richard Crossman described as 'the most elaborate fencing and man-oeuvring I have experienced in the long and dreary history of the last nine years'.[2] The result, after an extraordinary meeting between Wilson and Crossman on a sleeper at Euston Station,[3] was Greenwood's withdrawal and Wilson's running as an anti-unilateralist and unity candidate.[4] The Commons group lobbied hard and Crosland appointed himself Gaitskell's chief of staff:

> These are my immediate reactions to the Wilson decision: (1) Object. In the next 10 days, we have one single over-riding object: to make sure that his vote is as low as possible, and yours as high as possible. Our possibilities over the next 12 months will depend entirely on this, & to achieve this we must resort to any degree of chicanery, lying etc.[5]

A fight with Anthony Greenwood would barely have caused Gaitskell to break sweat. Gordon Walker, Crosland and the others realised that Wilson was a much more serious challenge. As Crosland pointed out, the size of the result mattered if the overall fight back was to be a success. Dora found the whole fight and the bickering tawdry; 'if Nye had been here none of this business would ever have happened'.[6] Yet Wilson had little choice but to challenge Gaitskell if he was to remain at the head of his generation of MPs.

In the leadership ballot Gaitskell defeated Wilson by 166 votes to 81, thereby consolidating his hold on the Parliamentary Labour Party and gaining PLP endorsement for his defiance of Conference. This vote was a crucial morale booster but the fight was a long way from over. Gaitskell's mood fluctuated in the months that followed. At a party for the American election in November, he carefully avoided wearing a button for either Nixon or Kennedy until someone suggested he wear both, to which he replied that he did not want to look like Harold Wilson.[7] At the annual London Labour Party dance at the Lyceum Ballroom, just the kind that Hugh liked best, 'Barbara Castle asked Harold Wilson if he could rock and roll, he said no so they waltzed.'[8] And Gaitskell, who had of course given a speech in the earlier part of the evening, arrived late and in a police car. His car had been towed away for illegal parking, so the police took pity on him and gave him a lift. While Desmond Donnelly had gone to Vauxhall to pick up Hugh's car, Hugh danced the night away. According to the *Express*, 'His crowning achievement was, I thought, an energetic hands-knees-and-boomps-a-daisy, from which he finally emerged breathless and somewhat dishevelled to observe: "what a wonderful night."'[9]

But at other times his mood was more sombre. Ann Fleming recalled meeting him in those days and finding him tense: 'I sometimes walk with him in remote parks, he wears dark spectacles and tells me his problems.' She, characteristically, could not take his political troubles seriously: 'my mind wanders and I watch the spring mating of the ducks – when I hear him say "By the way, that's top secret", I ask him to tell me that bit again, but it's seldom very exciting – and by the way, that's all TOP SECRET.'[10] Jenkins described him at this time as being 'fed up'. Even though the ground had really begun to shift back to him after his defeat of Wilson, he could still have dark moments – not least because of the sheer toil of the fight. The credibility of his leadership had not been regained without an immense effort. Yet again, he put his head down and ploughed into the dirty politics of the factional battle.

Gaitskell's closest trade union associates met in a co-ordinating committee each month. Before the meeting of the General Council of the TUC, he dined with his friends – each diner at a different location.[11] While Gaitskell lobbied the union leaders, trying to find procedural ways of challenging the unilateralist vote, he used his speeches to swing the argument in the body of the party. These meetings were critical in building the perception among the moderate union leaders that Gaitskell was essential to the electoral success of the Labour Party and that they needed to organise in his support. Gaitskell also offered conciliation, conceding that he had made mistakes and that the attempted reform of Clause 4 had been too radical a move, and coupling that admission with every kind of pull on the union leaders' natural sense of loyalty.

He tried to combine factional speeches with attacks on the government. The pre-election economic upturn had created strong inflationary pressure and Heathcoat Amory, the Chancellor, had been forced to introduce a credit squeeze by increasing the bank rate and restricting the amounts available for hire purchase. Gaitskell focused on this, demanding the end of the squeeze and the dropping of restrictions on car purchases;[12] accusing the government of planning its regional policy only for electoral success;[13] using a party-political broadcast on 4 December to lament the government's lack of economic dynamism and its policies aimed at making things easy for the 'Get Rich Quick Boys'.[14] He attacked the growth in the concentration of the ownership of newspapers at a Labour Party rally in Portsmouth in November.[15] At each of the public meetings where these speeches were made he faced questions and demonstrations about the bomb. Not since the Suez crisis had he found it so hard to get a proper hearing from his audiences.

Moreover, after Scarborough, partly because of the speech and partly because of the demonstrations, every Gaitskell meeting was news: he attracted crowds and controversy. At times the sheer hatred directed towards him shocked those accompanying him; people would spit and shout abuse, and on some occasions there was a real threat of physical violence.[16] Four unilateralists were arrested outside one meeting in his Leeds constituency.[17] At virtually every meeting he was heckled, and the process of giving speech after speech in such circumstances must have been soul-destroying and exhausting. But at other meetings his supporters and neutral people in the crowd drowned out the boos of the CND enthusiasts and gave Gaitskell a sympathetic and at times enthusiastic response. One such meeting was at Bingley in Yorkshire where the following exchange occurred:

Q: Can Mr Gaitskell give some explanation to justify the immorality of his retaining the leadership of a party to whose policies he is opposed?
A: I did not retain the leadership. I was elected to it by a large majority.

For a while he was unable to continue as the crowd packing the hall clapped and cheered, completely obliterating the noise from one small section of hecklers.[18]

In his speeches Gaitskell consistently stressed the policy for peace, arguing that it was the neutralism of CND policy rather than British possession of the deterrent that was the problem. He also tried to broaden out the debate a little. The *Guardian* of 12 December 1960 reported him outlining other efforts which Britain should be making in foreign policy:

1. Pressing strongly for a new attitude by the West to Communist China.
2. Putting forward and backing a plan for a zone of controlled disarmament in Central Europe.
3. Keeping the cold war out of Africa.
4. Trying to clear up the confusion and conflicts in NATO.

In addition to his formidable programme of speeches, he had an organisation fighting for him on a seat-by-seat, ward-by-ward, union-by-union basis: the Campaign for Democratic Socialism. The grassroots campaign was ready to launch in September 1960. Bill Rodgers drafted a set of possible questions and answers for the press launch – including, for example, the following:

Q: Some years ago the Bevanites were censured for being a Party within a Party. Aren't you setting out to be that?

A: Not at all, on the contrary we believe that we represent the great *majority* of opinion within the Party . . . There certainly isn't anything conspiratorial about us.

Q: How representative are you really? Aren't you the intellectuals again – London and Oxford?

A: That isn't the conclusion that I would draw from the list of signatories. We are very varied in our interests and backgrounds. What we have in common is considerable service to the Labour Movement in one capacity or another – as Parliamentary candidates (two of us as MPs) and in local government, for example. We are a pretty good sample of what a constituency Labour Party looks like.

In the short term Scarborough was a slight inconvenience as well as an opportunity. Rodgers realised that support for Gaitskell's defence policy was critical to the credibility of the CDS but that this had to be balanced by ensuring that the CDS did not appear to be the splitters. In the launch statement issued immediately after the press conference the tightrope walking this involved was well illustrated:

This is clearly not splitting the Party or introducing new divisions but *rallying it round its own central tradition*. Of course, we want unity – everyone does – but on whose terms? Time and time again there has been a compromise in response to the cry of unity: and time and time again the left has failed to respect it. *One prominent member of the NEC now believes that unity consists of standing against Mr Gaitskell for the leadership. Someone else yesterday spoke of 'a new statement of policy' on defence.* What has either of these done to campaign for united support for the agreed policies and for Mr Gaitskell in the past? There are deep differences on defence that have to be thrashed out. We *have had enough of those who face both ways.*

The effect of the vote at Scarborough had been predicted; the impact of Gaitskell's speech had not. His defiance appealed to CDS organisers like Taverne who had never wanted a compromise on Clause 4: 'It was deliberately not a Gaitskell fan club ... it wasn't until Hugh Gaitskell's speech at Scarborough that we then said, "Of course now there is no question whatsoever, from now on the cause we believe in is personally identified with Gaitskell and the issue we must fight is now CND and unilateral disarmament because that is the issue we may be able to win."' Philip Williams reacted to the events of the Conference directly: 'It's all ghastly – but at least we shouldn't have to worry much now about momentum ... After this week I am sure we ought to revise para 1 as well as 4 of the Manifesto if only for topicality.' After a redrafting by Tony Crosland and Frank Pickstock the opening paragraph read:

> We are long-standing members of the Labour Party who are convinced that our Movement cannot afford another Scarborough. Rank-and-file opinion must now assert itself in support of Hugh Gaitskell and of those Labour MPs – the great majority – who are determined to resist and then reverse the present disastrous trend towards unilateralism and neutralism.

Ten days after the initial launch, Pickstock drafted a progress report for Gaitskell. The initial mailing of the CDS manifesto was in duplicate form with 500 going out from Pickstock's office at the Oxford University Delegacy for Extramural Studies: the response had been excellent, support was coming in from all around the country and from all sections of the Labour movement.

The launch received a positive press. Victor Knight, in the *Daily Mirror*, stressed the value of the manifesto and quoted two paragraphs in full. The *Daily Sketch*, under the headline 'Stand and Fight', quoted directly from the organisers' statements and answers:

Alderman Pickstock said, 'We are the NCOs and the platoon commanders of the Party. We are after the people whom we think will stand and fight.' . . . 'We are the rank and file,' said Mr Rodgers . . . 'There are no MPs on the list of signatories,' said Mr Howell, 'because this is a grass root organisation.' He said that Mr Gaitskell knew nothing beforehand about the manifesto and agreed that it was a declaration of hostilities against Victory for Socialism, 'Call us Victory for Sanity' . . . The sentiments it expresses and the people who have launched it are just those Mr Gaitskell will appeal to in the next four weeks. Mr Rodgers said, 'We have to begin to do what we don't like to do – begin to fight.'

The Times reported that a manifesto had been issued by a number of members of constituency Labour parties and then it simply reprinted the bulk of it with no other comments. In contrast the *Manchester Guardian* gave the story front-page coverage and in the longest article to appear the day after the launch reflected all the views the organisers hoped to put across at the news conference. But the most positive reaction came from one of the organisers, Ivan Yates. Writing in *Reynolds News* Yates warmly welcomed his own organisation:

> The silent majority had to assert itself if the Party was not to perish, *'We were not prepared – as long standing and responsible members of the Party – to see this.* We decided to make some demonstration of our own. We discovered a very similar group in Oxford that had been convened by Alderman Pickstock and joined with them and one or two others including Mr Denis Howell. We agreed *as a first step in our campaign* to publish a Manifesto and rally support. We approached a number of active rank and file people in the Party and they agreed to sign. We didn't want to take a final decision until the Party conference but of course Scarborough settled it.' Of course Scarborough did not settle it, it had already been decided to go ahead.[19]

CDS was an effective and well-run organisation; it was also well financed, and this led to allegations that the CIA had backed the CDS and Gaitskell. These allegations were published in *Militant* in February 1977 and based on the findings of the US Senate's Church Committee in 1976.[20] There were a number of CIA front organisations operating within the labour movement at this time; for example, the Trade Union Press Agency and others provided information to labour attachés at the American embassy. Such 'liaising' was the most substantial connection:

Information on individuals, on political parties, on labour movements, all derived in part from liaison. Certainly, the difficulty and long-term nature of developing assets was largely responsible for the CIA's initial reliance on liaison. The existence of close liaison relationships inhibited developing independent assets. First, it was simply easier to rely on information that had already been gleaned from agents. Regular meeting with local officials allowed CIA officers to ask questions and to get the information they needed with minimum effort.[21]

This was by far the most important and regular means of gathering information. The labour attachés at the US embassy were regular attenders at the parties and gatherings of Labour politicians in the 1950s.[22] Joe Godson, attaché from 1952 to 1959, was particularly close to Sam Watson and Sam Berger, his replacement, was a great friend of Denis Healey.[23] For much of the period it was not necessary to influence policy on defence; when it was, there is no evidence that the Gaitskellites required much help from the CIA; but there is plenty of circumstantial evidence that they regularly had contact with CIA officials. Informally, links existed, and formally Gaitskell spoke on platforms funded by the CIA-backed Congress for Cultural Freedom. *Militant*'s charge centres on the paragraph following the one quoted above from the Church Committee report, which states:

Financial support to individual candidates, subsidies to publications including newspapers and magazines, involvement in local and national Labour unions – all of these interlocking elements constituted the fundamentals of a typical political action program. Elections, of course, were key operations, and the Agency involved itself in electoral politics on a continuing basis. Likewise, case officers groomed and cultivated individuals who could provide strong pro-Western leadership.

Given the revelations about Soviet support for sections of the left, it is tempting to wonder what was wrong with CIA support for sections of the labour movement that opposed communism. The invidiousness of the charge is that Gaitskell and the Gaitskellites would not have enjoyed the support that they did in this and other battles without CIA backing. This argument can of course be turned round: would CND and the *Morning Star* have received the support that they did without KGB backing? The point is that there was a global ideological conflict at the time, and Gaitskell's strong perception was that he and the other Atlanticists were on the same side in that war as the Americans. However, there are some factors that point towards it being unlikely that the CIA funded the CDS.

The CIA was faced with strong Communist Parties in France and Italy, and had its largest presence in West Germany. In Britain the leaders of the two major parties for the whole of the period were dedicated to the Western alliance. It is unlikely that the British labour movement would have been a long-term priority for CIA anti-communist covert operations. It is highly probable that the CIA would have kept a close eye on the British labour movement and would have been intensely worried by the events at Scarborough. The only evidence so far produced to support the claim is the connection between the Church Committee's mention of the funding of labour movements and the fact that the CDS was a pressure group. Once that connection is made, it is then simply repeated from book to book. There is no evidence that it was CIA gold which funded Gaitskell's fight back, though if it had been needed it would have been forthcoming.

It was not needed because CDS was in fact bankrolled by Charles Forte and other businessmen through the offices of Jack Diamond, Labour MP for Gloucester. Diamond had been raising money to finance research since the mid-1950s when he made a large profit out of steel shares and wanted to use the money to help Gaitskell as leader. No previous leader had that kind of independent support; it funded Tony Crosland for a year's research on the co-operative movement, and on the development of new ideas.[24] Diamond now performed the same role in the fight back against unilateralism. Rodgers described Diamond's role in his history of the CDS as follows:

> I had known Jack for nine years and had worked closely with him when he was Treasurer of the Fabian Society. But he was not thought of in a political capacity: he was the technician – in particular the technician who knew how to raise money.
>
> As far as I can remember we did not consult him at all until after the Manifesto had been published. Certainly he was not approached to contribute towards the cost of publishing the Manifesto. We raised £200 from amongst the 25 or so people who had been responsible for launching it. However, he must have been approached as soon as the Manifesto was published and I think it was by Tony Crosland. From then on I was in close contact with him and he became the main organiser of funds not only for us but for any claimants amongst supporters of Hugh ... Jack worked on the principle that if you wanted to raise a lot of money, and

to do so quickly, you should go to the few people with a lot of money to spare ... The key occasion was a dinner given by Charles Forte in the Café Royal early in 1961. Hugh was there and Jack, Patrick Gordon Walker, Fred Hayday and myself. There were I think no more that half a dozen of us but from this something over £5000 was raised.

Diamond was consistent in his efforts on the Campaign's behalf. The initial donation recorded in the accounts as £5,500 was 'from Jack Diamond' for the period 1 December 1960 to 31 December 1961. Expenditure was reduced in 1962; Rodgers estimated it to be £2,500 and expected the following year to be approximately the same. The vast majority of these funds came through Jack Diamond. At the height of the Campaign's activity in 1960–1 income from sources other than Diamond amounted to £1,652 out of a total income of £7,153; donations from other sources amounted to £868, and the sale of publications provided £134. The proportion derived from Jack Diamond, and in turn from business interests that were well disposed towards the Labour Party, hardly reinforces the image of the CDS as a grassroots movement. These figures can be put into perspective by comparing them with figures from CND, which had a total income of £14,367 for the same period, and the Fabian Society, which had an income of some £10,000. With Forte's support the CDS set to work.[24]

The objective was to maximise the majority for the TUC–NEC document, *Policy for Peace*, defeat the TGWU Conference resolution and neutralise the AEU; once that had been achieved the Gaitskellites tried to influence candidate selections, elections to the NEC and the general policy direction of the Labour Party. They provided briefing and propaganda material, circulated approved amendments and resolutions and established contacts in all the major unions.

Out of the seventy-three unions listed by Hindall and Williams in their 1962 analysis of the voting at Scarborough, the CDS was active in twenty-six.[25] In general the CDS first established who it was necessary to contact in each trade union, then either approached these individuals directly or encouraged others to do so. In addition, small groups were assembled and the multilateralist case was put to them, either by local supporters or by the trade union organisers of the Campaign. According to Denis Howell – the key CDS lobbyist – it was not made explicit that the speakers were from the CDS, but 'everyone knew what was going on.'[26] A similar technique was applied to the constituency Labour parties; 'Tea Meetings' were organised at which small groups of activists heard the multilateralist case.[27] Most important were those unions that Gaitskell and the Trade Union Committee thought could be persuaded to switch their policies: the AEU, USDAW, NUR, Foundry Workers, Vehicle Builders, Metal Mechanics and ASLEF,[28] with a total block vote of 1,419,000.[29]

The armoury that the Gaitskellites employed consisted of the quality of Gaitskell's leadership, the multilateralist case, the pressure for unity being applied throughout the trade union movement and the organisational resources available for getting their message across. This message was based on the agreed TUC–NEC *Policy for Peace*, which advocated an international multilateralist case, with NATO retaining its weapons, but a national unilateralist case, with Britain giving up its independent deterrent.

The first target was the Amalgamated Engineering Union.[30] It was the AEU that had sponsored the most straightforwardly unilateralist motion at the 1960 Party Conference, which had achieved the largest majority against the platform.[31] The structure of the AEU was more complex than that of most unions and therefore at once more difficult and easier to lobby: more difficult because one body within the union could override the other, easier because the AEU could be made to face both ways.[32]

The CDS was helped considerably by the support of the union's President Bill Carron; Jim Boyd, a member of the executive council and one of the three national organisers; and Jim Conway, who had signed the CDS manifesto. These highly placed officials operated within the union and supplied CDS with a list of the delegates to the AEU national committee, the TUC conference and the Labour Party Conference. Rodgers obtained the delegate lists from Bill Carron and additional names from Bill Webber, both of whom were regularly meeting with Gordon Walker and Gaitskell to co-ordinate policy.[33] Rodgers and Howell then scrutinised the list to identify those delegates who should be contacted and sent briefing material. The analysis was presented in columns in which Patrick Gordon Walker, Jim Boyd and the other CDS officers made notes which formed a 'picture' of each delegate was built.[34] It was a fairly rudimentary form of analysis, mainly just a tick or a 'no' with occasional comments. In early 1961 eighteen possible or definite supporters of the official defence policy were identified and approached. Of the eighteen, fourteen who were deemed to be in favour of the official policy received copies of the newsletter *Campaign*, defence statements and a letter.[35] The other four were thought to be unreliable, largely through a lack of information or because information had come from only one source which could not be confirmed.

Once a delegate had been identified as an opponent he received no material from CDS, thereby ensuring that knowledge of outside interference was kept to a minimum. There were two categories of opponents in the AEU, the communists and the unilateralists. There had been a prolonged fight against the communists within the union who had concentrated support in certain areas.[36] In the run-up to the AEU conference the CDS mailed circulars and lobbied individuals, and on the national stage Gaitskell spoke frequently, urging a reverse of the vote. As the AEU assembled, Rodgers jotted down his prediction at the end of the AEU national committee delegate list:

FOR 14, PROBABLY FOR 4, POSSIBLY FOR 9
CP AGAINST 14, PROBABLY AGAINST 9
NO INFORMATION 2[37]

He was almost exactly right: 'The unilateralist resolution was defeated by twenty-eight votes to twenty-three with one abstention.'[38] Now 697,000 votes were lined up behind Gaitskell.

Another large union that had voted against Gaitskell at Scarborough was USDAW, the Union of Shop, Distributive and Allied Workers. The annual delegate meeting of USDAW presented a complex problem for the CDS because the general secretary, Walter Padley, was sponsoring a compromise defence policy that he had worked out with Richard Crossman.[39] Padley asked the CDS supporters proposing the official policy to withdraw it in favour of the compromise he was putting forward. However, the CDS intervened and stiffened the resolve of its supporters in USDAW and ensured that the official policy was put to a vote. It was passed, and another 329,000 votes lined up. This, in combination with the AEU decision, started the bandwagon rolling as well as ensuring the maximum possible majority for the official defence policy.

The CDS started from a very hopeful position in the National Union of Railwaymen because the decision to mandate delegates to vote for unilateralism had been made by a majority of only one.[40] In May 1961 Rodgers was being assured by Solly Pearce, editor of the *Leeds Weekly Citizen*, that 'the NUR is in the bag or will be when it meets. It is thought that about 27 of the 75 delegates can be described as left.'[41] Much as in the AEU, detailed lists of the delegates to the NUR annual general meeting were compiled with notes on the delegates' views on the defence issue. There were a number of sources of information on the others.

Despite this CDS activity the NUR failed to pass either *Policy for Peace* or a unilateralist resolution. The unilateralist resolution was defeated 39 votes to 37, and there was a tie on the multilateralist resolution, which was declared as not carried.[42] But in the end Gaitskell got these votes because Sidney Greene, the general secretary of the NUR, cast 254,000 votes for the official policy on the basis of these inconclusive votes.

Gaitskell's foot soldiers had an easier time among the smaller unions. The Metal Mechanics' Union held their conference in Birmingham, and Denis Howell visited the executive in the pub next door to their headquarters in Birmingham. He reminded them of their sons in National Service and asked them if they were going to send them into battle without the proper weapons; 'They went back to their executive meeting and voted against unilateralism.'[43]

Bill Rodgers even drafted speeches for the Transport Workers' conference, though they knew there was no chance of reversing their decision. One paragraph in a speech stated:

> It has been said that there has been outside interference in the affairs of this union, that delegates who disagree with the general secretary have been got at by some body or another. All I want to say is that I have certainly not been got at. No one has ever told me what to think and they aren't going to do so now.[44]

In parallel to the battle over the defence vote in the unions, the CDS was active in the constituency Labour parties. The purpose of this activity was fourfold. First, the CDS aimed to maximise the vote in favour of the official defence policy at the Blackpool Conference of 1961 by ensuring that the psychologically important total of CLPs voting for the leadership was high. Second, they hoped to increase the votes for friendly candidates in the constituency elections to the National Executive Committee, which had, since the early 1950s, been dominated by the left. Third, they wanted to motivate supporters of the CDS to take part in the selection of parliamentary candidates. Finally, the Campaign's general objective of educating the Labour Party in the ideas of revisionism and modernisation needed support from rank-and-file members.

The Campaign for Democratic Socialism quickly established a national network of supporters, since initial publicity for the launch of the CDS manifesto led rapidly to the compiling of a card index of supporters around the country. The most committed of these became constituency 'whips' responsible for organising other like-minded individuals and for disseminating CDS propaganda. An inner group of 'whips' became regional representatives responsible for reporting on a group of constituencies.

In April 1961 Rodgers drafted a memorandum to regional representatives about *Organisation in the Constituencies* in which he summed up the activity of the first six months of the Campaign: 'In practice, CDS probably has supporters in 400 constituencies and this should rise to 500 by the end of May, which must be our target organisationally.'[45] A measure of the support for CDS after its launch was given in the first issues of *Campaign*, the official CDS newsletter. In the first three editions the number of offers of support was presented in a box accompanied by the words 'Up and Up, we have now received —— separate offers of support from key Party workers.' The figures given in the box were 2,373 in February 1961, 2,751 in March 1961, 2,856 in April 1961 and 3,011 in May 1961.[46] The breakdown of this support across the country was not uniform and tended to be concentrated in urban areas.[47] In Glasgow, Birkenhead and Leeds the organisation duplicated that of a constituency Labour party, with chairmen, vice-chairmen, whips, press officers and women's sections.[48]

Edward Janosik's study, *Constituency Labour Parties in Britain*, based on research in the period 1962–3, revealed a number of the problems that the CDS came up against from the outset of its activity in the constituencies in 1961. A majority of constituencies surveyed by Janosik were led by individuals who favoured a more left-wing policy,[49] especially on nationalisation.[50] But Gaitskell's problem was not only the dominance of the left but the ingrained tendency of constituency Labour parties to be swayed by a particular policy view:

> Moderate or left-wing opinion so completely dominated some constituency parties that opposition to the prevailing view was abortive. Even though minority opinions were freely expressed they were seldom accepted . . . Under these circumstances there is justification for the belief that parties with a narrow range of policy views might unwittingly discourage those with divergent opinions from becoming active in Party affairs.[51]

To mobilise right-wing party members, information, propaganda, encouragement and ideas continued to flow from the Red Lion Street office of CDS throughout 1961 and 1962. At times the advice would be specific, particularly in the form of resolutions for the Party Conference. Model resolutions were offered on defence, such as the following one circulated in January 1961:

> This organisation, recognising that Britain should remain a member of NATO and that the western alliance should not renounce nuclear weapons while the Russians retain theirs, urges the Labour Party to intensify its efforts to bring about all-round multilateral disarmament.[52]

Keeping CDS supporters in touch and trying to match CND organisationally were aspects of CDS activity that could be described as 'practical politics'. The other side to the conflict with the left and indeed the conflict with the Conservatives was winning the ideological argument. The main weapons the CDS employed to get its ideology across were *Campaign* and the contributions supporters made to the revisionist journal *Socialist Commentary*.

The idea of a newsletter emerged from the early planning discussions. Tony Crosland, Philip Williams and Bill Rodgers worked out the details in November and December 1960. In addition to the officers of the CDS a number of MPs and supporters contributed – such as Tony Crosland, Tom Bradley, Patrick Gordon Walker and Roy Jenkins. Non-MPs who did much of the writing included Tony King, Philip Williams, Michael Shanks, David Marquand, Bernard Donoughue and Anthony Dumont. Rita Hinden, the editor of *Socialist Commentary*, was also active on the committee and other members of the editorial board of *Socialist Commentary* also wrote for *Campaign*, including Allan Flanders and Anne Godwin. In October 1963 it was proposed to publish the names of all the contributors to *Campaign* in a special last edition. In addition to those already mentioned the list of contributors included J. Richardson, Ivan Yates, Alan Fox, Douglas Jay, Uwe Kitzinger, David Saunders, George Jones, Peter Pulzer, John Vaizey, Evan Luard, J. B. Cullingworth and David Shapiro.[53]

The content of *Campaign* as it emerged during 1961 was developed alongside the task of the CDS. The objective of *Campaign* was clear to Rodgers:

> We then provided briefing, in a sense we tried to match *Tribune*. *Tribune* every week always telling the activists in the constituency parties which

motions they should be putting down – which issues they should be advancing, a marvellously effective campaign and in our very moderate way we produced *Campaign* from February 1961.[54]

The first twelve issues were dominated by the defence policy. Only one article appeared that was critical of the Conservatives;[55] in contrast each issue contained attacks on the left. The favoured targets of the CDS writers were Frank Cousins, instances of Labour Party bodies rejecting CND, and, after May 1962, a series of articles highlighting the increasing extremism of CND. However, the tone of *Campaign* was never predominantly negative; indeed a great deal of space was devoted to getting the CDS case across.

The overall impression that *Campaign* tried to convey was of a responsible organisation concerned with a range of policy issues and defending the leadership against irresponsible elements on the left of the party. There were frequent quotations from Gaitskell and other multilateralists on the defence issue, but these were accompanied by analysis of world events not directly concerned with defence. On all of these questions the writers took positions which were in broad agreement with the front bench of the party and also, for example with regard to the controversy over the treatment of communist prisoners held by the Greek government, used a subject to attack the left. Defence-related matters tended to follow the run of events and offer the Campaign's opinions. Up to the Blackpool Conference the articles which did not directly attack CND were concerned with putting across the official policy. After Blackpool the defence issue became centred on the negotiations that led to the Test Ban Treaty. In these articles and in an article advocating the surrendering of the British independent nuclear deterrent, *Campaign* took a markedly anti-nuclear line to emphasise the genuine nature of the multilateralist commitment to nuclear disarmament. The article attacking the deterrent opened with a sharp attack on Macmillan's policy:

> In spite of Macmillan's doubletalk, the Nassau conference between him and President Kennedy marked the final, humiliating collapse of the defence policy which the Tory Government has followed for nearly three years. Since the spring of 1960, the British deterrent . . . has been independent in name only. The failure of Blue Streak showed that a country of Britain's size cannot afford to remain an independent nuclear power in any meaningful sense, without an intolerable strain on its resources. But the Tories refused to face reality. They clung to the myth of the independent deterrent, and hoped to prolong the life of Britain's

ageing force of V-Bombers by buying Skybolt missiles from the United States.

As the next general election neared, attacks on the Tory government and the Liberal Party were stepped up. From November 1962 to July 1963 each edition contained a diatribe against the Conservative government. Taken together they were a concerted critique of the Macmillan years, ranging from the government's economic and social policies to the appointment of Lord Hailsham as Minister for the North East, culminating in a 'Macmillan must go' front page in July 1963. Preparation for the general election also inspired a series of articles on Labour's domestic programme, which chimed in with the general critique of the Conservative governments being put forward by the Labour Party, but offered the Campaign's particular, if not very distinctive, view. These articles characteristically centred on the official party policy statement, *Signposts for the Sixties*. This was analysed in a series of five articles from September 1961 through to March 1962. The underlying assumption was that increased economic growth would enable a Labour government to improve social services and education. The CDS attitude reflected mainstream Labour thinking of the early 1960s, thereby illustrating the extent to which Gaitskell was in control of the domestic policy of the Labour Party. There was little in *Signposts for the Sixties* that was not in line with general revisionist principles.

Gaitskell was particularly keen to influence the composition of the NEC. A brief was prepared for circulation to the CDS regional representatives. After outlining the details of the voting procedure and the composition of the NEC, it then suggested five tasks that the 'whips' could undertake:

1. Discover NOW the date of the meeting of your General Management Committee when the decision on which candidates to support will be taken;
2. *Ensure well in advance* that there will be a good attendance of delegates and ensure *on the day* that they attend;
3. Let these delegates know about the candidates so they may be able to judge who best to support;
4. Acquaint yourself with the procedure to be followed at the meeting so that you can take steps to see that candidates are fairly considered;
5. Allocate responsibility for putting forward names and getting them seconded so that your GMC has them all before it. DO NOT LEAVE ANYTHING TO CHANCE.[56]

The brief went on to outline the different procedures used by the local parties in deciding whom their annual Conference delegates should be mandated to vote for. This detailed brief was accompanied by the CDS slate of candidates and notes on their virtues. In 1962 this concentrated on four candidates. The CDS slate was composed of Jim Callaghan, described as 'outstanding amongst existing members',[57] and Denis Healey, Chris Mayhew and Patrick Gordon Walker as candidates who had won 'substantial support' in the past. Ian Mikardo and Tom Driberg were singled out as members of the NEC who least deserved support.

There was a minor increase in the votes for right-wing candidates proposed by the constituency Labour parties during the CDS years, but the overall left-wing domination of the CLP section of the NEC was not affected, the only non-left-wing candidates who featured being Tony Benn and Jim Callaghan. The other places were taken by the old Bevanite MPs, Barbara Castle, Harold Wilson, Tony Greenwood, Dick Crossman, Tom Driberg and Ian Mikardo. If the figures for the top twelve places are taken then an increase of approximately a third was achieved in right-wing votes for 1962 and 1963. Only Jim Callaghan and Denis Healey managed to improve their standing and the hold of the left on the constituency section of the NEC was not affected.

The ability of an internal party group like CDS to influence the selection of parliamentary candidates was very limited, but this was another area in which Gaitskell was keen to see action.[58] Each constituency Labour party was technically an independent part of the Labour Party with other affiliated organisations like trade unions and the socialist societies attached to it at the local level. Candidates were nominated by these organisations or sponsored in the case of trade unions. Sponsorship could be an important consideration when the local party was short of money, and trade unions could increase their number of delegates to the local party at the time of selections and thereby swamp a meeting. Labour Party headquarters maintained two lists of candidates which were circulated to the local parties, an A list of candidates sponsored by trade unions and a B list of unsponsored candidates. However, any Labour Party member could attempt to gain adoption as a candidate.

External influence could be exerted on constituencies at the initial stage when the timing of the selection was fixed, when the short list of candidates was being drawn up and even at the time of the selection conference. The regional organiser could influence events at each stage of these proceedings and as a last resort the NEC could withhold approval of the candidates after selection. This last procedure was rarely used. The period in which the CDS was active in this field has been described as 'the high point of central control'.[59]

The position of CDS as both an independent and a loyalist organisation made the relationship between the Campaign and the Labour Party's regional organisers a sensitive issue. The scope for organisers materially to effect the outcome of selections was limited, although, as Shaw has put it, 'between overt manipulation and absolute neutrality lay sufficient territory to allow organisers if they so chose to exert a significant degree of influence'.[60] The regional organisers involved were Donald Alger, John Anson, Jim Cattermole, Ron Hayward, Jim Raisin, Len Sims and Reg Wallis.[61]

The Labour Party organiser most overtly supportive of the CDS was undoubtedly Jim Cattermole in the East Midlands region. He took an active view of his role in the parliamentary selections in his area and helped when he could with 'sound' or CDS candidates. His role was valued by Rodgers; he was one of the 'key supporters' consulted in August 1961 when the future of the CDS was under review, and he also helped in getting resolutions for the Party Conference adopted by constituencies in his area.[62] Donald Alger was also in sympathy with the Campaign in general and Rodgers in particular but he seems to have operated in a less overt way than Cattermole, preferring to go through MPs like Gordon Walker rather than straight to the CDS. Alger, the Northern Area organiser, supplied Patrick Gordon Walker with a complete list of the selections that were due in his region and this was passed on to Rodgers. However, his personal regard for Rodgers was clear in their correspondence over Rodgers's prospects for adoption at the by-election at Stockton. Alger offered advice but also stressed that Labour Party regional organisers could not use 'their influence to get a person nominated'.[63] The position with Alger was further complicated when his wife wrote to Rodgers asking for help with finding a candidate for their local party at Hexham; Rodgers replied recommending Edward Pearce.[64] John Anson, the Yorkshire Area organiser, also supplied lists of candidates through Gordon Walker and seems to have been generally well disposed towards the Campaign.[65] In contrast, Len Sims, who also supplied information, did so with a marked reluctance: 'I have been holding back on Parliamentary selection conferences in the hope that our internal difficulties would be resolved and candidates chosen for their ability as candidates rather than for being "pro" or "anti".' However he was broadly sympathetic to the CDS. Reg Wallis was asked to supply comments on lists of trade union delegates to the Blackpool Conference. There is no evidence in the CDS Papers that Ron Hayward was involved and he has denied any involvement,[66] but Rodgers and Cattermole maintain that his role in the early 1960s was very different from his subsequently careful career.[67]

The relationship between CDS and the central organisation, especially the National Agent's Department, was complex. The Colne Valley by-election is probably the best example of the complexity of this relationship and the limitations of the Campaign's activity in the selection of parliamentary candidates. The by-election contains all the main elements: it was held in what was then a safe Labour seat; there were plenty of candidates; the local CDS contact was very active and the liaison committee was formed comprising CDS, the Chief Whip and the trade unions. The by-election was occasioned by the death of the sitting MP, W. Glenvil Hall, in October 1962.[68] Florence Price, a highly active local party member and CDS supporter, immediately contacted Rodgers.

> I wonder if you could suggest to me a few names of people whom you would recommend for consideration? If you could suggest some former members who are at present out of Parliament but would be prepared to return, I think that might be preferable – as we shall be up against a very strong Liberal candidate who has nursed the constituency for something like 6 years.[69]

Rodgers's first thoughts were Ian Winterbottom, who had been MP for Nottingham Central from 1950 to 1955, and Shirley Williams, who had contested three seats in the past. In his reply to Price he pushed Williams harder than Winterbottom.

> She is an old friend of mine and in the opinion of many people outstanding amongst the younger women in the Labour Party. I know that she would make a first rate candidate and she would be a great asset in the House of Commons.[70]

A week later he contacted Ian Winterbottom and Shirley Williams and suggested they get in touch with Florence Price.[71] After the NEC had set the date for the special meeting of the local party, Price asked Rodgers for more names of possible candidates,[72] whereupon

Rodgers proposed Harry Waterman and Dick Leonard, also offering some practical help: 'It may be that I will be able to give you some advice after your meeting this Sunday. If you cared to let me have the names of anyone who was mentioned there I could probably indicate to you whether they are worthy of support.'[73] Having met all the people Rodgers put forward, Florence Prince decided to back Ian Winterbottom,[74] who in fact was emerging as the official candidate. This was decided at a meeting on 6 November 1962 of the secret liaison committee that tried to co-ordinate the activity of the leadership and the CDS in candidate selections. Rodgers reported to Gaitskell: 'Meeting consisting of Patrick Gordon Walker, the Chief Whip, Fred Hayday, Denis Howell and I to discuss Colne Valley, agreeing that Ian Winterbottom was the right choice but noting also that Mrs Price had shown interest in Dick Leonard as a second string.'[75]

Three weeks later George Brown informed Rodgers that Merlyn Rees was now the official candidate.[76] Although Winterbottom was generally favoured, there were worries that he was too old,[77] and George Brown had not been present at the earlier meetings. Brown had been appointed chairman of the NEC Organisation Committee, responsible for selections, in March 1962, 'in a deliberate move to step up the importance of the post and place the Party machine more firmly at the service of the Parliamentary leadership'; along with the National Agent's Department he was taking a keen interest in selections.[78] In the three weeks between the meeting of the secret liaison committee and Brown's bombshell, the CDS had been active in pushing Winterbottom, whom Rodgers regarded as the choice of the leadership, while at the same time not deterring other CDS favourites from entering the contest. The object was, if possible, to have a completely 'sound' list, but specific assistance was limited. Co-ordination, through Fred Hayday, of the lobbying of the only union that was strong locally, the Textile Workers, was something Rodgers could do. Florence Price supplied the lists of local union activists whom Hayday then contacted, in the hope of gaining information and encouraging nominations for candidates backed by the CDS.[79]

The main left-wing candidate for the seat, Pat Duffy, was also busy lobbying and by the time of the special meeting he had been nominated by seven organisations. At the beginning of this meeting the Yorkshire regional organiser, John Anson, announced that two of the local ward branches which had submitted nominations had done so without informing their memberships. In both cases the branch secretary had simply filled in the form, and both branches had nominated Pat Duffy. The meeting was in uproar and Anson's intervention, designed to discredit Duffy, was to backfire badly. Price sent Rodgers a full account of the meeting and detailed the left's response to Anson's announcement:

> Attacks were made on John Hare – he was too old – on Roy Hattersley – he was the regional office blue-eyed boy and had ambitions to become MP for all Yorkshire – but the real fury came at the end for Winterbottom. He was a company director and a gentlemen farmer, so we couldn't possibly ask working class socialists to support him; his membership of a trade union was simply to put himself right with the rules in order that he could stand as a Labour candidate: people educated at public schools were not socialists and the final blow was 'People don't vote for a chap just because he sits up straight on a horse!' Winterbottom's long service to the Labour movement was put to the meeting, his undoubted ability and success when he was in the House – but to no avail. He was defeated by one vote.[80]

Florence Price responded by trying to force his inclusion on the ballot at the following Sunday's meeting. Her final efforts to get Winterbottom on to the short list, which included Dick Leonard and Merlyn Rees, were blocked by Sara Barker, the National Agent, who argued that the local party executive had agreed the short list and the leadership's choice, Rees, was already on it.[81] When the selection meeting finally took place Merlyn Rees put up a good fight against Pat Duffy but Dick Leonard's performance was reported by Price to have been disappointing. The voting in the first ballot was: Bishop 2, Duffy 66, Hare[82] 12, Leonard 1 and Rees 52; in the second it was Duffy 69 and Rees 63. Naturally disappointed, Price decided to dedicate herself to 'getting the left-wing element voted off the Executive Committee'.[83] The Colne Valley by-election was won by Duffy, but the seat was eventually lost at the 1966 general election.

The events illustrate the difficulties the CDS faced when dealing with George Brown. There had been problems earlier in the year when Brown 'took Bradley out of Bristol without warning or consultation'.[84] Brown's action over Colne Valley angered Rodgers sufficiently for him take the unusual step of sending a full account directly to Gaitskell.

The answer clearly is – and Denis Howell and I agreed on this with George on Monday – that liaison must take place at a very early stage. Miss Price was quick off the mark and we were ready to help her at once. Experience has told us that it is essential to move at once in a case like this. In future Denis will consult with George at the beginning. This ought to avoid this sort of muddle ... I understand that Sara Barker is irritated with us over Colne Valley. I don't believe she has any reason to be but frankly if she devoted more attention to the Lancashire seats the dividends could be great.

Gaitskell replied judiciously:

As you say, there is no doubt about the source of the trouble which is inadequate liaison sufficiently early on. I spoke yesterday to Patrick Gordon Walker and the Chief Whip about this and I think more satisfactory arrangements will now be made.[85]

This story also reveals the ambiguous role CDS was playing in the selection procedure. Although it had no official position as an organ of the Labour Party – which was partly why there was a conflict with the National Agent[86] – it was operating in support of the leadership and had direct contact with the Leader of the Labour Party, the Chief Whip and other top officials. It was not supposed to be Gaitskell's private army, yet it was only Gaitskell's intervention that prevented Sara Barker from pressing for a full inquiry into the Campaign's activity – an inquiry that might have exposed the direct links between the CDS and the leadership.[87] As is clear from Rodgers's letter to Gaitskell, the situation caused considerable frustration.

An area in which CDS had some success, and which was a by-product of Rodgers's particular attachment to younger politically active people, was the encouragement of younger candidates. A number of those active in the 'Counterblast' youth section of the CDS became parliamentary candidates through 'the good offices of Bill Rodgers' and CDS. George Jones, who as a research student at Nuffield College had helped with the initial mailings, became the prospective parliamentary candidate at Kidderminster. He in turn supplied Rodgers with the names of other young hopefuls including Robert Skidelsky, Tom Nossiter, Harold Lind, Edward Pearce, John Gyford and Colin Pepworth.[88] Another leading light of the Counterblast group, David Saunders, was adopted as candidate in Peterborough. The chairman of Counterblast, Stephen Haseler, was still under twenty-one and so was too young for adoption as a candidate.[89]

Gaitskell's supporters were successful in the by-elections that were held during the 1959–64 Parliament. Denis Howell was the first to win a seat. He had been MP for Birmingham All Saints between 1955 and 1959 and secured the nomination for the Small Heath by-election in March 1961. His nomination had little to do with the direct involvement of CDS but was a tribute to his network of local contacts.[90] Dick Taverne won the by-election at Lincoln in March 1962 after Hugh Gaitskell had suggested him to the retiring member, Geoffrey de Freitas, a keen CDS supporter who in turn helped Taverne with introductions in the constituency:[91]

> I received a telephone call one day from John Harris, who was Gaitskell's aide at the time, asking me whether I was still interested in standing for Parliament . . . Gaitskell suggested me for the seat for two reasons; firstly, he was keen to see leading younger figures of CDS brought into Parliament and Bill Rodgers and myself were the two most obvious candidates. Secondly, it was thought I would be a suitable horse for the Lincoln course . . . The fact that I was an officer of CDS personally recommended to Geoffrey by Hugh Gaitskell and duly selected for the seat later created a myth about my selection conference . . . It is firmly believed by some, and has been reported in the *New Statesman*, that my election was somehow 'rigged' and that I was foisted as a right-winger on an unwilling left-wing local party.[92]

For a short time after news of the by-election was announced there had been a conflict between Rodgers and Taverne, who both had designs on the seat, but Rodgers withdrew in favour of Taverne. In turn Taverne had received the aid of the local CDS whip, Ken Rawding, who had helped gain a nomination from a ward. The short list at Lincoln had comprised solely CDS or 'sound' candidates, Terry Boston, Neil Macdermott and Arthur Bottomley, all of whom eventually found their own seats. Taverne was the youngest candidate when he was selected.[93] So, even if the selection conference was not actually fixed, the local party was only offered a choice between Gaitskellite candidates, all of whom had been chosen by the leadership and the CDS; for the left in the local party this amounted to a rigged contest. One man walked out of the selection meeting.[94]

At the other by-elections held during the active life of the CDS, more supporters of the Campaign were elected: Niall Macdermott at Derby North; Tom Bradley at Leicester North East; Guy Barnett at Dorset South; Merlyn Rees at Leeds South; Will Howie at Luton;

Terry Boston at Faversham and Bill Rodgers at Stockton-on-Tees. Tam Dalyell, who spoke on CDS platforms, was also returned for West Lothian in the period. Thus of the twenty-seven by-elections won or held by Labour, from Denis Howell's victory onwards, eleven were won by CDS candidates. The CDS continued to try to influence selections until the election of 1964 and then closed down.

From the Scarborough Conference in October 1960 until the Blackpool Conference in October 1961, Gaitskell's own campaign had been continual. He had made more speeches, had co-ordinated with Tony Crosland and Patrick Gordon Walker in their work in the constituencies and trade unions, and had tried to keep up the attack on an increasingly faltering Conservative administration.

On the Sunday after the Scarborough Conference George Murray had secured a supportive resolution from Gaitskell's South Leeds party:

> This meeting expresses its pride and confidence in the Leader of the Labour Party, the Right Hon. Hugh Gaitskell, MP for South Leeds, and congratulates him on his fine speech at the Labour Party Conference, which correctly reflects the views of the Members of the South Leeds Constituency Labour Party, and of the great majority of Labour supporters in the country. It further pledges full support for the reversal next year of the Scarborough Conference decision on unilateral disarmament.[95]

A similar resolution was passed by the Middleton Labour Party. However, Gaitskell also had his opponents in South Leeds CLP – in particular Mrs Beryl Dobbins and her husband, who organised a few others, including ex-Communist Party members, to write to Emrys Hughes in the House of Commons opposing the Polaris missile system.[96] But this was a minor irritant: whatever happened in the party, Gaitskell's seat was safe. At the end of 1960 he had issued a New Year message:

> We say goodbye to 1960 without a pang. Let us look to the future instead. As for the defence dispute, it is tempting to pretend that it does not exist. But that is just unreal. There are big issues at stake here; and when people feel that they may involve the whole future of the party, it is no use trying to cover them up. But these are three things at least that we can all do. We can conduct the discussion in a friendly and courteous manner without introducing personalities. We can confine the argument within its true limits and avoid manufacturing differences which do not really

exist. We can insist that the dispute should not prevent us in any way from doing our job as a great Party – at present in Opposition but determined to win power again.[97]

One fairly typical weekend for Gaitskell at this stage of the fight back went like this: Friday: Talk to Nottingham University Socialist Society; Belper CLP dinner. Saturday: Private meeting of Leicester party workers; regional conference at Derby; Lincoln Co-operative Society dinner; annual reunion of Lincoln Labour Party. Sunday: Press conference at Grimsby, followed by private meeting in Alexandra Ward; tea with Scunthorpe party workers and another private meeting.[98] At meetings usually Gaitskell was met with a picket outside, was heckled inside during the proceedings, but received an ovation or at least applause from the vast majority of the people present at the end.[99]

On 17 January 1961 he went to the United States for a short trip, to visit old American friends and allies including Averell Harriman, Chester Bowles and Adlai Stevenson.[100] He also had his first meeting with Kennedy, reporting:

I was tremendously impressed by Mr Kennedy. He was so relaxed it was difficult to realise that this was a man who was on the eve of taking up the biggest job in the Western world; he was open minded on all the subjects we discussed.[101]

During the trip he met up with Ann Fleming for an evening's dancing – Ian being in bed ill – but managed to miss Kennedy's inauguration gala and Frank Sinatra singing for the President through one of his periodical strokes of practical bad luck: this time being stuck in snow for five hours.[102]

Back in Britain he returned directly to the fight. Even his report on the US trip stated that many Americans were worried about the possibility of the Labour Party going neutralist.

Armed with the new *Policy for Peace*, endorsed by the Shadow Cabinet, the personal campaign and the CDS operation both moved up a gear. The government also provided a few more openings. Selwyn Lloyd, the new Chancellor of the Exchequer, had introduced a partial relaxation of the hire-purchase restrictions; then Enoch Powell, the Minister of Health, annouced an 11 per cent rise in NHS costs and the doubling of prescription charges to deal with the increase. The relief with which Gaitskell embraced the opportunity to attack the Macmillan government was clear. A statement by Macmillan that the Conservatives were a classless party gave him the opening:

> Now and then the Tories come out with a bit of propaganda that is positively sublime in its remoteness from truth. Their latest effort, that the Tory Party is not a class party, is breathtaking. Not a class party, when half the Cabinet were educated at Eton?[103]

Gaitskell was mainly a reactive opposition leader at this stage – which tended to maximise his moderate tone. Take the case of aiding Kuwait when it was threatened by Iran in the early 1960s. A typical Gaitskell line of sense and statesmanship had to be maintained, but it did take the sting out of the attack: 'Speaking as a representative of the Labour movement, we do not intend to allow the imperialism of the past to return again. So let us make clear the distinction between doing what we were pledged to do – rendering help which I think we had to do – and in remaining there for our own ends.' The ruler of Kuwait had invoked the agreement recently made, and asked for Britain's help. 'If you make agreements – and it is for the government of the day to make them – your word as a country would not be worth very much if, within weeks of signing that agreement, when the other party invoked that agreement and asks for your assistance you turn your back on them.' Gaitskell may have been speaking good sense, but any rhetoric was absent on matters of this kind. On domestic issues, from spy scandals to Macmillan's 'You've never had it so good', Gaitskell was on easier ground:

> The economic weakness of Britain was blazoned abroad. The Tories have had ten years in which to prove their theory that if you leave it to private enterprise, it will all come right. Now everyone knows it is a complete and absolute flop. We would have lost the war on the philosophy of 'I'm alright Jack' just as we are now losing the peace. The mentality behind wildcat strikes and takeover bids has quite a lot in common. How Mr Lloyd in particular has the face to ask for wage restraint is hard to understand, for such an appeal means that people have to accept income distribution as it is. You will only get a response if there is a general feeling that the way things are shared out today is fair, or at least that the government are doing their best to make it so.[104]

The distance between 1961 and 1945 is not so great: it is still all about fair shares for all.

The corner had been turned in the spring, when the trade union conferences began to reverse their votes. In the early summer of

1961 predictions began to appear in the press that Gaitskell would win at Blackpool. In July the *Observer* forecast that the defence dispute would 'fairly probably' have come to an end by the end of the year and *The Times* felt that the tide of opinion in the country was turning in Labour's favour.[105]

By September, Gaitskell's sense of confidence was growing, but he did not let up in his meetings and speeches. At Birmingham he said he was delighted with the spirit of the party:

> I shall be disappointed if we do not see an improvement from now on. There is a growing feeling that the government is becoming more and more discredited and a conviction that the Labour Party has very largely overcome the difficulties created by internal dissension in the past two years. The main desire of party members is to get down to the job of winning public support in order to win the next election.[106]

That desire and Gaitskell's task were made much easier when the official defence policy was overwhelmingly passed at the Labour Party Conference at Blackpool in October: the internal fight back was completed.

17

'A Thousand Years of History'
1962–1963

I don't believe in faith. I believe in reason and you have not shown me any.

Gaitskell to Jean Monnet, 1962

If we go into this we are no more than a state in the United States of Europe, such as Texas and California.

Gaitskell, 1962

I inevitably felt a little more sympathy with those who had differed from him in the past!

Roy Jenkins, 1962

The European issue came to the centre of the political stage in the midst of Gaitskell's battle on unilateralism. In July 1961 Macmillan launched Britain's bid for entry to the European Economic Community. In March Britain had applied to join the European Coal and Steel Community (ECSC) and Euratom. From then until September the pace of talks accelerated. Gaitskell's initial handling of the issue caused few problems for his friends: he had approved a compromise which accepted the principle of membership providing the conditions of entry guaranteed various national interests. However, signs of unrest soon became apparent. Roy Jenkins was the first to show dissent. In response to the conditions which Harold Wilson laid down in the House of Commons as being essential to the Labour Party's acceptance of EEC membership, Jenkins resigned from the front bench. Despite the powerful advocacy of close friends like Jenkins, Gaitskell, while continuing to state his belief in European unity and keeping a well-balanced tone in his statements on the particular merits of the Community, turned increasingly against the bid for entry.

The conditions that Macmillan intended placing on Britain's entry seemed to Gaitskell to undermine the position of the

Commonwealth; yet he feared the prospect of another huge split in the Labour Party so soon after the 1960–1 battle over defence, and the possibility of another five years in frustrating opposition. The consequence, in the autumn of 1962, was a markedly anti-Community broadcast, followed by Gaitskell's second most famous speech to Conference.

The place of the European conflict in the internal politics of the Labour Party was not straightforward. It did not fit into the left–right divide as this had expressed itself since 1951 in the differing views of the best way for Britain to maintain her global leadership role, or over the defence issue at the Party Conferences of 1960 and 1961, or over the future of public ownership and Clause 4 in the aftermath of the 1959 general election. The essence of the Common Market issue was the nature of Britain's relationship with the rest of the world, but this involved no clear-cut question of moral versus political leadership. If the Conservative government were successful in taking Britain into the European Community (thereby rejuvenating the flagging Macmillan administration), Britain's relationship to the Commonwealth and the 'special relationship' with the United States would need to be reconsidered. But this did not immediately rule out EEC membership for those who believed the UK could provide political leadership. Moreover, while moral leadership had little role in such an economic association – which threatened to weaken the Commonwealth – many on the left initially favoured the EEC on grounds of international co-operation.

There was another layer of complexity. The Bevanite disputes of the 1950s had often centred on defence and foreign policy issues – most notably German rearmament – but these were only part of a much broader debate concerning Britain's post-imperial position in the world. The left's attitude to these questions tended to be coloured by an anti-American perspective, while the right of the party, and Gaitskell in particular, nurtured a strong Atlanticist bias. In a sense Gaitskell viewed the possibility of closer integration of Western European nations in terms of the wider security implications inherent in the Cold War. Both Nye Bevan and Gaitskell shared a residual belief in Britain's global responsibilities, especially where the Commonwealth was concerned.[1] To an extent they regarded the development of the European Community as something of an irrelevance in the context of this global role. On the other hand, Gaitskell's younger colleagues like Roy Jenkins increasingly believed that

Britain's future lay in achieving closer links to the Community because they thought Britain could not sustain its international role and therefore needed to develop a more realistic sense of its position in the world. For the first time since the war a powerful lobby in the Labour Party was arguing against the idea of Britain having a global leadership role and proposing a strategic readjustment: cutting the international cloth to fit the domestic economic reality.

These divisions in the Labour Party highlighted the general problems for British politicians caused by the detailed progress of European integration through the stages of the Council of Europe, the European Coal and Steel Community and the Treaty of Rome – establishing the European Economic Community of the Six.[2] There were three main dimensions to the debate. The peculiarity of Britain's post-war position comprising the sterling area as an economic unit, the Commonwealth as a political entity, and the 'special relationship' with the United States, had to be balanced with Britain's role as a European power. In turn the conflict between Britain's role as a European power and as a world power created other difficulties. Given the other roles the UK was called on to play, what would be its real commitment to the Community? From a European perspective the suspicion arose that a United Kingdom only partially committed to the Community would not be able to make a positive contribution. On the other hand the dynamic being created on the Continent forced British politicians to ask themselves if they could afford not to join the Community.[3]

This led naturally into the second main problem: the form the association of nations should take. Many in the Labour Party saw the 'capitalist' association represented by the Treaty of Rome as an external force that might prevent a future Labour government from planning the British economy – a factor that heavily influenced Douglas Jay.[4] The counter-argument was that only if the progressive force of the British Labour Party was present in the institutions of the European Community would it develop along lines in tune with democratic socialism. Related to this was the disagreement over the effect that the EEC would have on existing trading patterns. The pro-Marketeers maintained that entry would open up the markets of Europe but, as long as safeguards were built in, this would not adversely affect the Commonwealth. The anti-Marketeers believed that the gains in European markets would not offset the losses in the Commonwealth markets.

The Labour Party faced these complex questions posed by the European Community during a period in which it was dealing with and then recovering from deep divisions over Clause 4 and unilateralism. There was no certain way of predicting on which side of the European debate the protagonists in the other debates would fall. Those on the left tended to be anti-European except for those who came from an ILP background, who tended to be in favour of the Community as an international organisation. Among the Gaitskellites the pro-Marketeers were a majority but there was an effective minority of anti-Marketeers, including leading figures like Douglas Jay. Stephen Haseler estimated the position of 'revisionist' MPs as dividing roughly 75 per cent pro-Common Market and 25 per cent anti-Common Market.[5] In the Parliamentary Labour Party as a whole there was a majority of anti-Marketeers.

In the party at large, opposition to the Community was widespread. Uwe Kitzinger, a keen Gaitskellite and advocate of British entry to the Community, observed:

> As freedom of movement clashes with xenophobia, so the problem of supranationalism touches the deeper suspicions against the outside world. In defence Britain has long abandoned independence; in economics, a country as heavily dependent on the rest of the world can only ever be master of its own fate to a very limited degree; but the formal merger of decision-making procedures, the absence of a formal veto on proposals by a body on which the British government is not itself formally represented, go against the grain even of many who on most other grounds would like to see Britain join the Community.[6]

Inside the Labour Party the way these feelings were expressed reflected the underlying characteristics of the movement. Edward Janosik found that among his sample of leading members of constituency Labour parties in 1963 'three out of four respondents were either strongly or moderately opposed to the idea of entry, while less than one respondent in five gave moderate or strong support'.[7] The reasons the respondents gave for opposing entry tended to reflect the main issues in the wider debate:

> To most respondents, France and Germany were dominating the Market and would continue to do so. De Gaulle and Adenauer were not admired by CLP leaders, who considered them old, inflexible and very conservative. The Treaty of Rome was, by its phraseology a 'capitalist device' since it assumed the existence of competitive economies in the member

states. British membership in EEC would make achieving socialism in Britain more difficult, and would prevent a British government from directing industry to areas of persistent unemployment. Although a number of respondents referred to the fact that both De Gaulle and Adenauer were Roman Catholic and attributed the conservatism of both men to their common religious persuasion, only one, an MP, viewed the whole Common Market proposal as a 'Catholic Plot'. He noted that President Kennedy, also a Roman Catholic, was urging British entry into EEC, and concluded his comment by saying meaningfully: 'It is called the Treaty of Rome, you know, and we all know what is in Rome.' The general impression gathered was that Labour Party members in general objected to the ideology of the Treaty of Rome, to its supra-national implications, and to the nations and the leaders who concluded it.[8]

Broadly speaking, in relation to the leader the Labour Party was divided in more or less the opposite way to the division over the defence issue, with the moderate trade union MPs and the leader this time siding with most of the left wing. By contrast with the defence issue, when Gaitskell could count on an overwhelming majority in the PLP, if he had come out in favour of the Common Market he would have faced a battle with all sections of the Labour Party: the PLP, the trade unions and the constituency Labour parties. On the other hand if he came out against the Common Market he risked alienating his more loyal supporters. One leading Gaitskellite maintained later that Gaitskell's stance on Europe was primarily designed to unify the party.[9]

Gaitskell's own view on the Community was based on an acceptance of the underlying aspirations of the European movement tempered by a deep suspicion of the implications for Britain if it joined. This view manifested itself most clearly in a profound concern about the precise terms of entry:

> From the start not only the Opposition but the Government as well were not in favour of 'going in and trying to get the best possible terms' but only for 'going in if certain conditions were fulfilled' . . . we certainly took the conditions very seriously and always meant to stand by them. There were two reasons for this attitude. First, I myself and my leading colleagues all happened to believe and still believe that the arguments of principle were fairly evenly balanced for and against and that the balance would be tipped in favour of our entry only if our conditions were fulfilled. Secondly, this policy of making our final judgement depend on conditions was the only one which could have been accepted by the Party as a whole. If I had urged unconditional entry (thus going further

than the Government) there would have been bitter opposition from a minority which was basically hostile to our entry. If I had urged opposition whatever the terms this would also have been bitterly opposed ... In either case, there would have been a major split in the Party, which, following the great dispute on defence, would have been fatal to our prospects.[10]

Moreover, he felt that the chances of de Gaulle actually agreeing to British entry were remote. As Dora recalled:

Hugh knew we hadn't an earthly chance of getting in. He was convinced of that after talks with the French. He was not against the Common Market in principle, but he argued that the economic case was not proved and he was a great believer in the Commonwealth. He felt it was a factor of stability in the world.[11]

With these considerations in mind he insisted on the most rigid terms; believing that the talks would fail, he had nothing to lose by arguing that Britain must maintain its vital interests. The conditions Gaitskell outlined for membership were guarantees for British agriculture; a fair deal for the European Free Trade Association (EFTA) partners; the ability for Britain to plan its own economic policy; and the safeguarding of the Commonwealth. However, in a party-political broadcast on 8 May 1962 Gaitskell leaned a little towards the Community. In a well-balanced account that summed up the arguments on both sides, stressing the 50–50 nature of the economic debate, he put the political argument in fairly positive terms:

You hear people speaking as though if we go into the Common Market, on the basis of the Treaty of Rome, that this is the end as far as an independent Britain is concerned. That we're finished, we are going to be sucked up in a tunnel of giant capitalist, Catholic conspiracy, our lives dominated by Adenauer and de Gaulle, unable to conduct any independent foreign policy at all. Now frankly, this is rubbish on the basis of the Treaty of Rome.[12]

Having dismissed the gloomy picture he went on to make the case that, without Britain and its Commonwealth links, the Community would be a much more introverted organisation:

If we go in and make it a kind of link between the Commonwealth and Europe, and if Europe were also to adopt the kind of modern attitude that I think we should be adopting, that would be a tremendous step forward. And I'll go further than that, if we don't go in, if we stay out, you might get a very tightly formed state in Europe with high tariffs, inward looking, rather reactionary, and conservative and nationalistic in its attitude. If we can prevent that by going in I think we've certainly done a good job.[13]

Between May and September 1962 the details of the conditions became known, and as the Macmillan government became firmer in its support for entry, so Gaitskell's position hardened against the Common Market. He foresaw a long set of negotiations ending in the French veto. From the strict neutrality of his early stance, through his mildly positive broadcast in May, he now came out clearly against the conditions as negotiated by the Macmillan government. In another political broadcast on 21 September 1962 he stated:

> There is a case for entry. And it's like this: if we don't get in there is a possibility that the six countries will form themselves into a European State, and there is a danger that this state's policy could be reactionary, nationalistic and possibly dangerous to peace as well. And the idea is that if we go in, we could prevent that. We might be able to persuade the Six and the others to let in the rest of Western Europe, Scandinavian States, and Austria and Switzerland. We might have a loose association which would be outward-looking, in favour of low tariffs, progressive in its foreign policy and its home policy, anxious to help under-developed countries, supporting the United Nations. This would be certainly a force for good in the world, and it would be a great ideal. But what is really involved in this is building a bridge between the Commonwealth and Europe; and we cannot do that if we destroy the Commonwealth by our entry. And if by our entry we are committed to European Federation or anything of that kind, we do destroy the Commonwealth. And if by our entry the economic damage to the Commonwealth countries is so serious the links are all broken, and the Commonwealth fades out, we cannot do it either.[14]

On the day the broadcast was televised, the executive committee of the CDS wrote to Hugh Gaitskell asking him to maintain neutrality on the European issue:

> The maintenance of the official benevolence of the Party towards the Common Market will give time for those of us who are for, as well as those who are against, to crystallise problems and opinions in the coming months in a fairly amicable spirit. [15]

Gaitskell replied that he did not 'think anything in your letter was inconsistent with the statement of the Commonwealth Labour leaders', going on to restate the view he had expressed in his broadcast: that it was necessary to join the Common Market to prevent undesirable developments in Europe but that Britain should only go in on the best possible terms. He continued:

> At the same time, we have all along insisted that certain conditions must be fulfilled. Perhaps the most important of these is the safeguarding of our ties with the Commonwealth. I do not see how anybody can possibly believe that this condition is fulfilled by the terms so far negotiated and set out in the White Paper . . . It is, of course, possible to argue that the condition should not be laid down but it has been laid down not only by us but by the Government as well . . . From all this I think you will see that you have no reason to fear that we shall take an out and out anti-Common Market line. Our attitude will be precisely the same as it has been in the last fortnight – simply that the terms as at present negotiated are not good enough and we must have better ones.[16]

At the same time that Pickstock, the secretary of the CDS, wrote to Gaitskell he made the Campaign's views clear in similar letters to George Brown, Denis Healey and Herbert Bowden, the Chief Whip.[17] Gaitskell's letter did not allay the anxiety of Bill Rodgers, the main organiser of the Gaitskellites, and on 25 September he circulated a letter to key supporters stating the problem presented by Gaitskell's change of stance:

> As we see it, the position is that the leadership of the Party has given the impression both within the Party and to the general public that Labour is now flatly against entry to the Common Market.
>
> It is not simply a question of insisting on adequate terms; we all want the best terms Britain can get. The danger is in saying that the Commonwealth is the supreme consideration and implying that Britain really has little in common with Europe. Labour's position may not have been stated in precisely this way but equally Hugh Gaitskell has expressed no positive sympathies at all towards Europe. Everyone believes that he has come down off the fence against the Common Market.
>
> This means that within the next few days everything must be done to persuade the leadership of the Party that there is a very substantial body of most loyal supporters who would regard a firm commitment against entry to the Common Market as a disaster. We do not ask Labour to declare unequivocally in favour of the Common Market. What we must do is redress the balance against the anti-Common Marketeers and try and bring Labour back to a balanced position again. If this is not achieved by next week's debate we believe that the consequences for the Labour Party could be far reaching.[18]

Jean Monnet described the process of European integration as a journey to an unknown destination. Roy Jenkins brought Monnet to meet Hugh Gaitskell at a meeting of the XYZ Club hosted by Jack Diamond in April 1962.[19] Gaitskell interrogated Monnet about the effect of tariffs on particular Commonwealth countries and was unimpressed by Monnet's answers. Finally Monnet protested, 'You must have faith', to which Gaitskell replied, 'I don't believe in faith, I believe in reason, and you have not shown me any.'[20]

The debate on the European Community is often presented as being polarised between pro- and anti-Marketeers. It is almost as though these opinions were generated instantly and in isolation from wider political discourse. However, the way in which Gaitskell developed his attitude to the EEC was representative of a kind of agnosticism characteristic of many in the Labour Party in the late 1950s and early 1960s. For many there was a lack of faith in the idea of the European Community, but also an acceptance or a rejection of the process of integration. Gaitskell, although initially felt to be sympathetic to the Community, and indeed never opposed in principle to Britain's joining, eventually rejected the particular terms secured by Macmillan in his first bid for entry. This disguises a more general ambivalence on his part to Britain's role in the process of European integration.

For key periods in the story a substantial section in the Labour Party expressed agnosticism on this question – ranging from Tony Crosland's studied boredom with the subject, to more agonised attempts to reach a conclusion, such as those of Denis Healey. It was a feeling reflected generally in the electorate and among many of the constituency Labour parties. Such ambivalence did not neatly match the character of later battles where the issue became almost a test of loyalty to the party. For the committed European the idea of abstaining on the vote for entry in October 1971 was anathema. However, for many others the reason for voting against entry was not a firmly held ideological opposition to the European Community but because it was a Conservative government that was introducing the measure and it called for opposition for opposition's sake. Moreover, for some, like Michael Foot, the Heath government was not just a Conservative government but 'one of our most reactionary governments – since Lord Liverpool's day'.[21] In contrast, when Gaitskell eventually came down against supporting the terms of entry to the Community, he did so in a finely balanced way and his obvious exasperation with the subject was representative of opinion in both political parties at the time.

As Gaitskell prepared for the Party Conference of 1962, agnosticism mingled with political calculation; his faith in the Commonwealth and belief in Britain's global role conflicted with loyalty to his supporters and an instinct that the British bid would in any case be rejected. He prepared the text for his speech in secret. George Brown, his deputy leader and strongly pro-Market, would be winding up the Conference debate and he asked to see Gaitskell's text. Gaitskell kept saying 'Yes' but not producing the text. Brown kept asking to see the text. Finally, he turned up at Hugh's hotel room in Brighton late on the night before the speech was to be given. Hugh let him in and sat down again at his table, covering up the text with some other papers. Brown said, 'You know, I'm getting a bit suspicious of what you are going to do tomorrow. You obviously aren't going to show me your speech, and I'm asking myself, Why? You are not going to switch the line are you?' Gaitskell put his arm round his deputy and assured him, 'You know me better than that. I'd never do a thing like that.' Brown concluded: 'And I have no doubt that is how he thought of it at that moment. Anyway, we all went to bed.'[22]

In the weeks after Conference a critical difference emerged among his supporters between those who had actually been in the hall and those who had only read the speech afterwards.[23] As with all of Gaitskell's other great speeches, unless you heard and saw the passion you could never recapture the impact. Just before the Conference Gaitskell had met two sympathetic trade-unionists, Fred Hayday and Bill Webber, and had assured them, 'Don't worry, wait till you hear what I say. I intend to speak to my friends.'[24] Gaitskell rose to open the debate at 10 a.m. on 3 October 1962. Conference was in another airless, over-heated hall: this time the Brighton ice-rink.

The centre of Gaitskell's case was rather contradictory. He insisted that the debate had to be based on the facts, especially the economic facts: 'I say this to start with, because I do not think the level of argument in the Press has been all that high . . . I also prefer to rely on facts.'[25] But the most effective passages in his speech came from pure emotion, for example in discussing the prospects for a federal Europe:

We must be clear about this: it does mean, if this is the idea, the end of Britain as an independent European state. I make no apology for repeating it. It means the end of a thousand years of history. You may say, 'Let it end', but my goodness, it is a decision that needs a little care and thought. And it does mean the end of the Commonwealth. How can one seriously suppose that if the mother country, the centre of the Commonwealth, is a province of Europe (which is what Federation means) it could continue to exist as the mother country of a series of independent nations? It is sheer nonsense.

Gaitskell also foresaw the extension of majority voting from economic to political issues and a faster pace of integration. He finished his speech by laying out the terms that he thought would be acceptable:

If we carry the Commonwealth with us, safeguarded, flourishing, prosperous, if we could safeguard our agriculture, and our E.F.T.A. friends were all in it, if we were secure in our employment policy, and if we were able to maintain our independent foreign policy and yet have this wider looser association with Europe, it would indeed be a great ideal. But if this should not prove to be possible; if the Six will not give it to us; if the British Government will not even ask for it, then we must stand firm by what we believe, for the sake of Britain and the world; and we shall not flinch from our duty if that moment comes.[26]

He spoke for 105 minutes. The Common Agricultural Policy, he said, was the most devastating piece of protectionism ever invented. Britain had to have the right to veto. The Commonwealth had fought with Britain at Vimy Ridge and Gallipoli. How long before the Treaty of Rome was a military alliance? The British should be allowed to drink its national beverage, tea, as they liked. Britain would lose its independent foreign policy. A British government would lose the right to implement its own economic policies. The people should be consulted; the idea that the government could make these decisions, that the top people knew best, was 'an odious piece of hypocritical supercilious arrogant rubbish'. Nobody coughed, stirred or smoked. Sweat was running off his nose by the time he finished. His collar was soaking wet.

In the hall the ovation was 'unparalleled',[27] although Bill Rodgers stayed firmly in his place and Dora said in dismay: 'But all the wrong people are clapping.' Wilson suggested the speech should be printed and Cousins said the Transport Workers' Union would pay for it. Douglas Jay described the effect of the speech from the point of view of an anti-Marketeer: 'It was unique among all the political speeches I ever heard; not merely the finest, but in a class apart, even from Gaitskell's Suez speeches. It can only be described as an intellectual massacre. Nobody had anything else to say. For its uniqueness rested in its ring of truth.'[28]

In this speech Gaitskell unified private passion and public political vision. What he said was based on a mix of economic judgement and political calculation; the way that he said it came from deep inside him. It was an almost entirely antediluvian vision, based on the shakiest grasp of economic or political reality, but as a political performance it was his finest hour. He had mastered his private capacity for emotion and moulded it into a political weapon which, supported by his intellectual capability, and the shock tactics of the unexpected message, left his political opponents and friends floundering in his wake. There would have been a diminishing return if he had tried too many of these kinds of political performances but this one, sure to be within eighteen months of an election, was perfectly timed, perfectly delivered. Its message unified the party. Those in favour of Britain joining were isolated; but, in the main, the pro-Marketeers were tied to Gaitskell, and the need for a majority Labour government, by threads of loyalty that even these 105 minutes could not sever. The speech delighted those who wanted to see the party united to take on the Tories and silenced those who remained implacably opposed to Gaitskell's leadership but had been denied any grounds for continuing the assault. Moreover, it was a policy that had immense popular potential, and, if his hunch proved right, the political cost would be zero because de Gaulle was about to reject the British bid anyway.

The political circle was completed when Hugh and Dora Gaitskell invited Frank Cousins and his wife to a private dinner at Frognal Gardens. The Cousinses had been to one of the Gaitskells' parties before, but, remarked Dora, 'Frank didn't much like some of our friends. He didn't think they were working-class; he thought them a bit stuffy and intellectual.'[29] So dinner on 12 November 1962 was for just the four of them. After one of Dora's good meals they discussed old battles and agreed to work together.

Brighton in 1962 buried for ever the image of Gaitskell as a gentle-minded Wykehamist who lacked the final few inches of steel necessary for the political kill. His instincts, his didacticism and his reckless pursuit of the truth could let him down, at times he lacked the tactical edge of a Wilson or the easy populism of a Bevan, but at Brighton he showed he had that strain of brutal effectiveness that was necessary to conquer and command the Labour Party.

Gaitskell united the party behind his leadership in a single speech. However, in the process he left many of his friends confused and angry. Anthony Howard, writing in the *New Statesman*, saw Brighton as 'as ruthless a power struggle as has been seen for a long time in a British political party'.[30] If Gaitskell was talking to his friends then he was trying to persuade them that they were wrong, just as he had tried to persuade the left by force of rational argument that they were wrong on Clause 4 and defence. But the way in which he did it raised a number of questions. Anthony Howard described the impact on the pro-Marketeers:

> Why did the Labour Party leader decide to go as far – sparing the feelings of none of his former associates in the process? There is some evidence that at first he may not quite have realised how intransigent the opposition of his former friends would turn out to be. But once he realised this he clearly made his decision that if they could not be shaken they must be destroyed . . . The proof of it was to be seen in the well-known faces which could be noticed primly sitting down on the ex-officio benches as the rest of the Conference rose to give Hugh Gaitskell the greatest ovation of his career. Men like Jack Diamond and Bill Rodgers (Roy Jenkins had the sense to stand up and make a brave shot at making the best of it) certainly looked angry; but they also looked beaten and betrayed.[31]

After the Conference Gaitskell acknowledged the misquiet among his supporters by meeting a small group of them in private on 21 October 1962 at Bill Rodgers's house. He made plain in this meeting that he had never seen himself as a pro-European.[32] As late as July 1962, however, he had been prepared to give as strong a lead against the left on the European issue as he had successfully done on unilateralism.[33] But once the detailed terms were known he felt duty bound to oppose entry because the government was behaving in a 'shabby' way and was prepared to enter on any terms.[34] He made plain that he thought the Common Market 'had nothing to do with the basic principles for which CDS stood'. He regarded the matter as 'a bore and nuisance and it always had been . . . As the evening wore on, he showed increasing signs of weariness. A number of those present thought this reflected his regret that he'd been forced to take the stand on an issue about which he cared little.'[35]

Once he had taken the stand, as Roy Jenkins acknowledged, his old friends discovered that, when opposing Gaitskell rather than supporting him, what had seemed like courage became stubbornness:

> I inevitably felt a little more sympathy with those who had differed from him in the past! Courage could be interpreted as inflexibility and an aggressive respect for rationality as a tendency to equate little points and big ones. Yet, by and large, he appeared just as impressive as a temporary opponent as he had so long done as an ally and leader . . . Nor did this difference make close personal relationships with him impossible. At first I thought it would, but that was under the shock of a sudden break in a long habit of agreement. But then he made it clear that he was still faithful to his old rule of the primacy of private relations. For the last few weeks of his active life we were back on terms of closest friendship.[36]

The way in which Gaitskell made up his mind on the question of Europe and the debates it generated in the Labour Party reflect a number of key factors in how the European issue was handled in the Labour Party between 1961 and 1970. First, the actual issue of the European Community was part of the ongoing party-political discourse, both inside the Labour Party and between government and opposition. Gaitskell partly accepted the view that it was a matter that transcended party politics, but only partly. It was also, clearly, a matter on which he could unite the party in opposition to the Macmillan government. Second, the approach to the actual European question was at best grudging, at worst agnostic. The key passage in his speech was a series of 'Ifs': If the Commonwealth could be safeguarded . . . If the EFTA countries could be brought in, and implicitly if it could be an inter-governmental organisation . . . If, in other words, the Community was a different entity and could be proved to be a different entity, then Gaitskell was prepared to believe in it. By the same token his objection was based not on the principle of entry but on the particular terms secured by the Conservative government. It was a political choice, made to unite the party midway through a Parliament against a government that was increasingly in trouble and had staked much of its reputation on the possibility of joining the Community. Behind the rhetoric of the Conference speech and behind the political expediency, there was a core of ambivalence. In this ambivalence Gaitskell was not alone, as Bernard Donoughue has pointed out:

Wilson was always mildly anti-European, in the sense that he seemed not to like continental Europeans, their style of life or their politics. He was basically a north of England, non-conformist puritan, with all the virtues and the inhibitions of that background. The continental Europeans, especially from France and southern Europe, were alien to him . . . Despite this background, Harold Wilson decided from October 1974 that a 'yes' position was the most practical choice. As a statesman – which was part, but only part of his complex personality – he knew that Britain must be centrally placed in Europe's future. As a party leader, he saw it as the best way to hold Labour together – because the antis would not leave the party over Europe, but the pros would. As a shrewd politician, he saw the pro position as the most likely winning one . . . Mr Heath had taken the British Establishment into Europe. Harold Wilson took in the British people.[37]

The Labour Party was more strongly united by Gaitskell's speech on Europe than it had previously been under his leadership. This unity was sealed at the private dinner with Cousins on 12 November. After they had agreed to work together, Gaitskell began to consider the shape of his Cabinet. He would bring in the left, with Crossman and Castle, and said to Frank Cousins, 'We are going to be very short of talent; will you come into a Government?' The TGWU leader replied, 'Let's not rule it out.'[38]

Gaitskell's New Year message, reported in *The Times* on 1 January was upbeat.

The Party is now faced with the greatest challenge of the last ten years – the challenge of responsibility: I believe we are now ready to meet it. More and more people are turning towards us, and with more and more confidence as the weeks and months go by. We have to earn and confirm that confidence by the way we behave – by remaining united; by being honest with ourselves and with others; by applying in our traditional fashion Socialist ideals with practical common sense; above all, as always, by the simple, hard, devoted work which has made our movement what it is.

Gaitskell's personal popularity had overtaken Macmillan's in April 1962 and the Labour Party overtook the Conservatives in February 1963. Many contemporary commentators were predicting a Labour victory. Gaitskell was beginning to sketch out his administration. If an election had been called on the issue of Europe after Brighton, then Gaitskell would almost certainly have won it. But there was no need for Macmillan to call an election; he could hang on for almost another two years. Anything could have happened in that time.

Gaitskell's career reached its height in the weeks after Brighton. There are two contrasting accounts of how he came to dominate the Labour Party to such an extent. The first version is that he did so by being a 'ruthless machine politician'. This view was unfailingly held by his political opponents like Michael Foot, intermittently held by Nye Bevan and consistently documented in the pages of *Tribune*. Gaitskell's meteoric rise to the leadership and dominance of the right and centre of the party was the product of a series of Machiavellian manoeuvres by a clever politician, skilled in the manipulation of mandates at party meetings and conferences. It was based on the patronage of powerful friends rather than ability or roots in the labour movement. The victim of this public-school-educated, latter-day Borgia was Nye Bevan.

Nye's inheritance was stolen from him in stages. In the first, Gaitskell used his influence with Hugh Dalton to get the chancellorship – over the claims of Bevan and to a lesser extent Wilson. Then as Chancellor he isolated Bevan by refusing to surrender anything of the rearmament package demanded by the Americans and thereby irritated Bevan into an emotional, untimely and politically suicidal resignation. Once his main younger opponent was out of the way he moved against Herbert Morrison. Capitalising on Attlee's hatred of Morrison he sold his soul for Arthur Deakin's block votes. This culminated in his spearheading the attempt to have Bevan expelled from the party. Gaitskell's 'dirty work' failed but he still managed to get himself elected as Treasurer and move from there to defeat Morrison and Bevan for the leadership. He opened his leadership with a brief conciliatory period in which he consolidated his position in the PLP by his opposition to Suez, the accord on domestic policy in the form of *Industry and Society*, and his reaching an accommodation with Bevan. He succeeded in cutting the head off the left and leaving the Bevanites stranded and isolated on everything but defence.

However, the conciliation ended when the Labour Party lost the 1959 election – partly because of a gaffe on taxation by Gaitskell himself. This removed any hint of restraint from Gaitskell and he planned and nearly executed a coup against the basic ideological faith of the party. He wanted to rid the party of socialism and turn it into the Liberal Party Mark 2 or a new version of the American

Democrats. His defeat on this issue was followed by the rejection of the joint NEC–TUC *Policy for Peace* and the passage of unilateralist resolutions from the AEU and the TGWU at Scarborough: the movement repudiated his leadership. Faced with this overwhelming rejection of his views by the Labour Party Conference, he responded by launching both a clandestine and a public campaign to overturn the votes and attack the sovereignty of Conference. Using CIA-backed organisations he threatened, forced, interfered with and blackmailed the trade unions to make them change their minds. Triumphant in 1961, he repaid his loyal supporters by turning on them and cynically opposing British membership of the European Community to provide the basis for a unified party in the run-up to the general election.

On the one hand he was a Machiavellian, ambitious, driven, Cold Warrior who imposed charges for teeth and spectacles, stole the leadership, lost the 1959 general election, proved his tactical ineptness by failing to carry the reform of Clause 4 and finally deserted his followers. On the other he was a dry, priggish, social democrat who failed to appreciate the poetry of politics, in Barbara Castle's phrase a 'passionate philistine' whose ambition in life was to follow the Treasury brief and whose attachment to socialism was an accident. As Prime Minister he would have turned the Labour Party into an administrative tool of the Civil Service, designed to uphold the maxim of his close friend, Douglas Jay: 'Whitehall knows best.' Gradualism would have ground to a halt. Personally, his stubbornness, pedantry and emotionalism would have limited his abilities in the top job. His lack of imagination in oratory and policy-making would have made any government he led a pedestrian, intellectual, middle-class affair that would have turned the trickle of activists leaving the party into a flood. His Atlanticism would have pushed Britain into a disastrous involvement in Vietnam. Personally, his increasing flirtation with an aristocratic world and his longstanding relationship with Ann Fleming suggested a cosiness with the establishment that was entirely incompatible with the leadership of a radical government. Finally, all that was wrong with Gaitskell was summed up in Michael Foot's most serious charge: Hugh Gaitskell couldn't stand Venice.

The alternative version can be called the 'best Prime Minister this country never had' view of Hugh Gaitskell. It is most effectively expressed in Philip Williams's biography and in the memoirs, recollection and writings of his friends, notably Roy Jenkins and Douglas Jay; but it is a view shared by a sizeable number of left-of-centre people who came to political consciousness and maturity in the 1950s and early 1960s.

Gaitskell was not born into the Labour Party but he was representative of those who chose it on the basis of ethics and a belief that the world could be made a more equitable place by the twin innovations of the inter-war years: Keynesianism and planning. He reached the top of the Labour Party on the strength of his intellectual ability and awareness of the newly emerging economic analysis.

Appointed by Attlee as soon as his health had recovered after the war, he rose rapidly through the government, eventually leading his generation. During his brief period as Chancellor he fought to maintain Britain's role in the world by delivering its part of the rearmament programme. He was also brave enough to hold out against Bevan for the imposition of charges on teeth and spectacles in the first attempt to bring some rationality to the ever expanding expenditure on health. Bevan's emotional resignation was a misfortune but it did not materially affect the prospects of the government, which increased its popular vote at the 1951 election. In contrast to Bevan's rebelliousness and organisation of a party within a party, Gaitskell was loyal to Attlee's leadership and consistent in his anti-communism. Although perhaps going a little over the top in his speech at Staleybridge, he nevertheless was only saying out loud what many others were thinking. Once he was committed to a course of action, his relentless application of intellectual honesty forced him on to take events to their logical conclusion, even if this was unpalatable, or damaging to his own interests.

One instance which he quickly came to regret was the attempt to expel Nye Bevan from the party in 1954. Bevan had been behaving in an increasingly unacceptable way and the last straw was a direct contradiction of Attlee in the House of Commons during a debate. The parliamentary committee's initial response was to ask for an apology. Attlee failed to provide any lead and when Bevan refused to apologise Gaitskell decided that he would have to go. Once the die was cast in his mind he had to follow it through; he lobbied hard for a vote to expel but was later thankful when he failed.

He recovered from this failure and was elected leader of the Labour Party by a clear margin. Although Herbert Morrison was inconsolable after the announcement of the vote, Bevan reached an accord with the leader and they worked closely together over Suez and in the run-up to the 1959 election. The election campaign of 1959 was a personal triumph for Gaitskell, with enthusiastic crowds all over the country. This lulled him into a false sense of security and made the blow of electoral defeat doubly harsh. Rather than stopping and resting, coasting for a few years before rejoining the fight, he did not take a holiday but launched into a whirlwind round of consultations with friends and colleagues. The task he set himself was the modernisation of the Labour Party and after much discussion he decided to attack Clause 4 because of its symbolic statement of the party's transforming aim.

Again, once he had made the decision to deliver to the British labour movement the equivalent of the Bad Godesberg agreement, he would not be dissuaded. His defeat on this merely confirmed, for him, the need for modernisation. It had been a tactical mistake to choose this particular piece of text but the basic idea was sound. He never advocated either a break with unions or a change of the party's name but he did want a restatement of the party's basic aims. The objectives of the November 1959 speech in which he laid down his socialist vision were largely fulfilled. As Jenkins wrote in his essay on Gaitskell in the collection of appreciations edited by William Rodgers in 1964: 'No one looking at the Party today could doubt that Gaitskell, in a long-term sense, had won his battle.' His attempt to marry the party's language with the reality it offered in power failed; but the Labour Party's basic policy position had been modernised. His honesty was again made plain when after much agonising and analysis he decided that the terms offered to Macmillan for British entry into the EEC were unacceptable. Although his friends were disappointed, their loyalty was undiminished, and had he lived they would have served him loyally in government and helped him renegotiate acceptable terms.

This courageous, aggressively rational, exceptionally bright, charismatic leader would never have made the tactical, personal and ideological mistakes that Harold Wilson made, because he had an overriding quality that Wilson lacked: integrity. He would not have baulked at making decisions that were good for the country even if they were bad in the short term for his party. In other words he would have devalued early rather than late. His private self was a loving, jovial man, who had a separate part of his life for pleasure and friendship which he kept isolated from the public persona. A

Gaitskell administration would have been socially more radical in issues such as divorce law, homosexual age of consent and abortion, more competent in the management of the economy – not requiring the energy wasted in the Department of Economic Affairs – and more effective in maintaining economic confidence.

The endless fascination of Hugh Gaitskell was that he had elements of all of these things. He was the Wykehamist who loved to dance, the civil servant who wanted power and the socialist who loved socialites. He inspired passionate devotion and passionate hatred. The key to the puzzle was in the barrier between the public and the private. Gaitskell believed in separating the public man from the private man but the events of his political career and the times in which he lived demanded a greater integration of the two which pushed him further away from the high-minded Wykehamist of the 'Butskell' caricature, towards a well-rounded and mature politician with the potential to dominate.

The relentless application of logic was also characteristic of his personal career. He was an extremely ambitious man whose public and private lives have a certain driven quality which is almost zealous. In some ways he was a little too engaged, and suffered from an urgent need to be in control. Some politicians like to be loved and some like to be feared; Gaitskell wanted to be in control, to be master of the situation, and this was reflected in his desire to be master of himself. Controlled passion best describes the force he brought to the crucial political battles of his life.

Control was also crucial to his view of how the country should be run. When made Chancellor he told William Armstrong that he wanted to see Britain evolve towards the US system by removing the divisiveness and unpredictability of politics and having the economy fine-tuned by experts who could manage it for the benefit of all. That, in essence, was Gaitskell's socialism. He opposed the left because he felt their political economy was not properly worked out, was incoherent and not good economics, since it did not have sufficient faith in the new economics to be effective in practice.

Overlaying his personal struggles and his political obsession with power was his deep patriotism. The values he believed in, the values that Britain represented to him, were universal values from which the whole world could benefit. In his view Britain deserved a world role because British culture had much to offer. Gaitskell liked 'abroad' in small doses, though he was not such a little Englander as Douglas Jay – he spoke excellent German and had good foreign contacts – but his most characteristic political position was his attitude towards the Common Market: control over his country's destiny.

The Labour Party was, of course, the wrong party for someone so attached to control. His primary political failure was in managing the Labour Party. Arguably, the Labour Party can best be managed by gaining its affection from the centre left. Gaitskell won the party's respect but it was not until 1962 that he gained a widespread and somewhat grudging affection; his failure in this regard always limited his scope for action. His desire for control was also displayed in a recurrent pedantry that could be infuriating.[39] His concentrated emphasis on the task in hand when coupled with his well-developed didactic streak was probably his worst fault; it suggested a lack of breadth of vision and it held the greatest dangers for him if he had ever become Prime Minister. Yet his main qualities were also derived from this rather obsessive personality: his bravery and honesty.

Gaitskell did not retreat from the challenge of Cousins and *Tribune*, he did not accept the compromise of Crossman and Padley, but instead created his own policy which fudged the central issue of the British nuclear deterrent but ensured that he had sufficient scope to fight on the principle of NATO's possession of nuclear weapons. He then set his own terms for defeat and minimised them by the effectiveness of his speech. Rather than attacking all the resolutions hostile to the NATO alliance, he concentrated on defeating the unilateralist TGWU resolution, on neutralising the AEU and on passing *Policy for Peace* by the biggest majority possible. Although *Policy for Peace* was multilateralist and stressed the need for NATO to have nuclear weapons, it was opposed to the independent British nuclear deterrent.

Whether, once he was in government, Gaitskell would have honoured this policy any more than Wilson did is highly questionable; he had resisted the commitment to abandon the British bomb for a long time on the grounds that in opposition it was impossible to have such policies because of the lack of information. However, *Policy for Peace* was not designed primarily as a document for government. It was introduced at the start of the Parliament effectively as an internal document designed to isolate the unilateralists by achieving as wide a consensus as possible on international multilateralism and the need to stay in NATO.

Gaitskell's contribution to the history of the Labour Party up to the winter of 1962–3 had been mixed. Positively he had aided the defeat of Marxism/communism both intellectually and organisationally – temporarily removing the influence of command models for economic organisation from the Labour Party's dialogue, and promoting revisionism as a radical doctrine of social change and improvement. In the process he had brought idealism and principle to the centre and right of the party, proving that the heroes of the left were not the only socialists who could hold their convictions with courage, idealism, consistency and honesty. The Labour Party had accepted policy options that were achievable and practical – not by defining any particular programme but by advocating a general reforming approach which attempted to deny Crossman's thesis of the Labour Party as crisis management and move towards Wilson's thesis of Labour as the natural party of government. After 1951 he had taken Labour down the route to political leadership and the social-democratic objective of a humanely managed capitalism: in sum he had given the Labour Party a taste for power and for government.

In the deficit column should be entered a streak of intolerance which did much to darken the atmosphere in those days. This intolerance was revealed in disciplinary matters, both with MPs who would be summoned to the leader's office and throughout the party, and in the failure to compromise unless the compromise was strictly on his terms. If one agreed with his policy, this intolerance, as Jenkins admitted, came across as bravery and honesty; if one disagreed, it came across as stubbornness and pedantry. He was also wrong on occasion: he was wrong on the level of rearmament, and on teeth and spectacles charges in 1951 (though right in the attempt to limit social expenditure); his attitude to Europe was locked in a vision of Britain's role in the world that owed more to the 1950s than to the 1960s.

In the final analysis Gaitskell was immensely well qualified to lead a British government and he would have led from the front like a Thatcher. But he would have suffered from an inability to delegate which might have cost him an overall vision of the direction of the government, though he would have been in charge. The accord with Cousins suggests that he might have been able to manage the left, but there has to be a big question mark over how long he could have done so. At heart he would have trusted to the experts and to his own economic ability – he would have been his own Chancellor rather than his own Foreign Secretary – and a lot would have depended on his ability to manage the economy better than Wilson. With the left hardening in their opposition to the EEC, it is hard to see how he could have changed his policy on this and kept the party together. If he had managed to deliver more growth then this would have been used effectively; and, if he had managed to avoid an overt commitment to the Americans in Vietnam, the Commonwealth might well have developed under his leadership.

A Gaitskell government – if he had won the 1964 election – would have resembled the Wilson government but would have moved faster and probably further along the road of social and cultural modernisation. The economic record might have been better but unless Gaitskell had devalued earlier – something that as the main architect of the 1949 devaluation he would have been reluctant to do – it might equally have ended up much the same. There would have been less of a breach of promise because the nature of the promise would have been different; he would not have suffered the same frenzy of expectations that Wilson endured, and this, above all else, might have given him a better chance.

In June 1962 Hugh Gaitskell had had the first sign of serious illness since the heart attack in 1945: he blacked out after recording a television programme. He had shoulder pains but rarely seems to have complained, although in the second half of 1962 he did finally cut down on some of his workload. He seems to have had some sort of sustained influenza and checked into the Manor House Hospital for a full examination. The winter of 1962–3 reminded many of the winter of 1947 – the year Gaitskell made his first mark on public life.[40]

Ann Fleming visited him on 21 December 1962 in the Manor House and recorded that after a complete check-up he was declared to be perfectly well. However, he was already seriously ill, and reports hinted that he might not be able to resume his duties until Easter. He did manage to return home for Christmas, but on 4 January 1963 he cancelled a tour of heavy-unemployment areas which he was due to make with George Brown. John Harris was handling all the press announcements and stated: 'Mr Gaitskell's pleurisy is taking longer to cure than was expected.' The following day his doctors issued a statement: 'Mr Gaitskell has been admitted to the Middlesex Hospital with a recurrence of a virus infection involving the bases of the lung, causing pleurisy and pericarditis. The condition although serious is not giving rise to immediate anxiety.' Pericarditis is inflammation of the pericardium, the smooth membrane which surrounds the heart. Pleurisy is inflammation of the pleura, the membrane which covers the lung. Press reports about his condition began to circulate in earnest only quite late in the day. On 16 January *The Times* carried a report about 'some anxiety'. Dick Taverne telephoned his brother who worked at the Middlesex: 'I hear you have old Hugh staying with you, how is he?' 'Well, actually,' the doctor replied, 'he isn't too good. I don't think he is going to make it.' Taverne was completely shocked. The report on the 16th indicated that Hugh's condition had deteriorated in the last twenty-four hours.

For most of that time Dora was at his side, her calm and dignity impressing many people at the hospital. George Brown cut short his tour of the north and flew back to London to see Gaitskell on the 17th. But despite his courage, his strength and his will to live, all of which impressed the doctors and nurses who treated him, his condition gradually worsened.

The letters in the constituency file tell their own story. His forthcoming January weekend was cancelled by the secretary on 9 January.[41] Dora wrote to George, 'Hugh was very pleased to see your letter and he asked me to write and thank you all for your good wishes and your sympathy. Of course, we will let you know how things are going but, as you say, it really is important to see that he has plenty of rest before going back to work.' Murray wrote again on the 12th: 'I have been greatly relieved by the latest reports from Transport House. It would seem that a turn for the better has come. I do hope this will be maintained. We have all been greatly worried.'[42]

On the evening of the 17th, the hospital contacted Scotland Yard, who rushed in an artificial kidney to cleanse Hugh's blood. His body had been attacked by lupus erythematosus, a disease of the immune system which affects different organs of the body generally or can lead to a collapse of the whole system. Gaitskell was unlucky: the disease was rare in men of his age. It was also extremely difficult to treat. Ann Fleming came to see him again on the 16th, and later wrote to Clarissa Avon, 'I mind very much more than I could have imagined, and I am sure it need not have happened. Two days before he died I felt impelled to go to the Middlesex Hospital and with much courage demanded to see Dora; she said she had complete faith in all ten doctors – how can one like ten doctors?'[43] This point and other minor criticisms were subsequently made: that the announcements had not been made early enough about the seriousness of the situation, that Gaitskell had not been transferred from the trade union hospital at Manor House to the better-equipped Middlesex early enough, and so on. They must have hurt Dora badly. In truth everything that could have been done had been done; and one can guess that Gaitskell's very courage and will to live may have prevented the announcements from being too pessimistic. Moreover, the final crisis came relatively quickly. The pressure of the renal and other infections on his heart was simply too great. He was resting peacefully around 9 p.m. on the evening of 18 January when he made a sudden movement. Dora had barely left his side, and she and his sister Dorothy and brother Arthur were with him. She called for one of his doctors, Walter Somerville, but Hugh died at 9.10 p.m. from extreme pulmonary congestion. Dora was with him. His daughters, Cressida and Julia, had visited him during the day. He was laid in the Church of England chapel in the basement of the hospital and Dora returned to Frognal Gardens at about 11 o'clock that night.

Because of the suddenness of the news and the relatively short illness, the response was perhaps more genuine and spontaneous than it might otherwise have been. In fact, it was a remarkable outpouring of national grief and feeling that transcended party-political divides, and there was a real feeling for this man who had been in the prime of his political career: so centred on his goals and, as he had clearly shown in the previous three years, so committed to his goals.

The press obituaries were generally united. George Gale wrote in the *Daily Express*: 'Who among the Labour party leaders can now, now that Hugh Gaitskell is dead, challenge Harold Macmillan? There is none. This is the measure of Gaitskell's greatness. This is also the measure of his loss.' Harold Hutchinson in the *Daily Herald*, a long-time supporter: 'I believe he would have been one of the great Prime Ministers. He was human enough to enjoy the approval and the ovations which greeted him in the last year or so of his life. He enjoyed the access which his position gave him to the men of power in all parts of the world.' William Barkely (the *Daily Express*): 'In politics "Gaitskell at Brighton" was becoming as famous as "Burke at Bristol". His memorable speech last October demanding better conditions for entry into the Common Market was one of the dozen times in my life when a speaker totally dominated his audience.

Never mind the argument.' The writer of the 'London Letter' column in the *Guardian* praised the Hampstead Set: 'Mr Gaitskell's group of friends . . . shared a gusto about the arts and an almost obsessive determination to keep up with the new generation. In his other interests as in politics, Mr Gaitskell was very much a contemporary man. He took great pride in his dancing.' The *Daily Telegraph* leaders: 'There was nothing of envy or malice anywhere in his nature.' Roy Jenkins in the *Daily Mail*: 'He was deep in politics. It was his life and his purpose. He never played it as a game. In every battle which he fought he was convinced and involved.' Or, as Cassandra simply put it: 'Everything was within his grasp – except life itself.'

Macmillan moved the adjournment of Parliament, the only time for the death of a leader of the opposition who was not Prime Minister; Butler recorded his surprise at how moved he was when he heard the news. Many ordinary Labour Party members were in tears. The shock of the news and the feeling that he was so close to the premiership were significant.

At Transport House the trickle of telegrams and messages that had started when he was first admitted to hospital became a flood. 'Would you please convey to Mrs Gaitskell & her family our deep sympathy, and that our efforts are now even more determined than ever to quickly see the results of all the good work put in by the late Brother Hugh.' 'A great friend of the miners. A tragedy. much loved.' The socialist parties in Israel, Switzerland, Denmark, Holland, Italy and France, the Spanish workers in exile and many others – individuals or organisations – expressed the same sentiments, all with the message of the frustrating of such a potent man at the moment when he was about to achieve power. The telegram from the Israeli Labour Party, filed in the Labour Party Archive, was typical, but perhaps even more passionate:

> Head bowed in reverence. Hugh Gaitskell was outstanding Spiritual leader noble and ennobling personality who combined within himself qualities of strength of vision and ability translate vision into reality. His belief in the victory of free socialism his unbounded loyalty to the mission of the British Labour Party made him respected beloved Leader of British working masses and united around himself all sections of British Labour Party.

However, even in the moment of his death the dogged head of criticism was not silent. Despite the wave of feeling, there were

429

those who continued to point out his weaknesses. The *Financial Times* was barbed: 'He was known as a little vain, and despite his many courageous fights, always felt criticism keenly, especially press criticism. A deeply emotional man, he occasionally let his heart rule his head, especially in the course of a speech for he could be an impassioned orator though he was never a phrase maker.' The *Daily Telegraph*, although kind in parts, also stated that the 'Labour Party may find leaders with more fire and personality than he had'. But such comments were few and far between in the immediate aftermath.

On 24 January 1963 the regional organiser for the Yorkshire office wrote to George Murray about the selection conference for a new candidate for South Leeds – such is politics.[44] The minute book for the next constituency meeting began with a few moments' silence for 'a man, dear to us all', and went on to discuss arrangements for the nominations.[45]

'It is the tradition not only of the stage but of politics also that the show must go on.'[46] The process of selecting a candidate for a safe Labour seat combines the need of the locality with the demands of the national party in a sometimes uneasy and conflictual relationship.[47] When the seat has been represented by a leader of the Labour Party then the demands are even higher. Prospective candidates in this kind of selection need perhaps more than most to combine national potential with local connection. The short list comprised Francis Booth, a local politician, city councillor and branch secretary of the NUGMW – Gaitskell's most loyal union; Stanley Cohen from the Leeds South East CLP, another local politician and member of the TSSA; Gerald Kaufman, locally educated and then a journalist on the *Mirror*, who was nominated by the local branch of Paole Zion; Victor Mishcon, a Labour lawyer who had fought Leeds North West in the 1950 election; Harry Waterman, another lawyer and member of the Leeds West CLP. Finally there was Merlyn Rees, the candidate with the least claim to a local connection but perhaps the greatest potential to be a national figure. George Murray recorded in his annual report:

> On 31st March, 1963, 72 delegates assembled in East Hunslet Labour Club to select a Candidate from a short list of six. At the second ballot Merlyn Rees had 51 votes to Victor Mishcon 32 votes, and was declared to be the candidate on the financial responsibility of South Leeds Labour Party.[48]

Rees was duly elected at the by-election. Dora had been approached about taking the seat but refused. In the first months her life was inevitably dominated by Hugh's death; then she rebuilt it and enjoyed a long and distinguished career in the United Nations and the House of Lords. She wrote to Charles Pannell, a solid Gaitskellite, in March 1963:

My dear Charlie

I have been answering more of my letters about Hugh and read yours again and I am so moved. You always stood by him in the difficult days when he was so alone and had to take so much from the Party. I can never forget this and will always have a very warm corner in my heart for you. I am going out quite a lot and it helps to wear a brave face and it eases the pain to see friends. But there are so many tears – it seems they will never stop.[49]

18

Epilogue

Gaitskell would be the first to be shot outside the Houses of
Parliament as a traitor to the working class.
                              Khrushchev's alleged attitude to Gaitskell

Our problem is that it seems that our campaign slogan would be:
Better George drunk than Harold sober.
                                                    Bill Rodgers, 1963

I was not born into this party. I chose it.
             Tony Blair after winning the Clause 4 ballot, 1995

A few months after Gaitskell died, the American President John F.
Kennedy was shot in Dallas. There had been an unprecedented
outpouring of feeling when Gaitskell died, partly because of the
suddenness of his death and partly because of the poignancy of it
coming when the Labour leader seemed to be on the threshold of
power; that feeling was now overshadowed in the more profound
shock caused by Kennedy's assassination. From the moment the
bullets were fired in Dallas an industry was born. It was based on
the creation of the Kennedy myth of unfulfilled promise and on the
endless new theories of who killed the President. By the end of the
1960s, the 'Kennedy industry' had substantially expanded. In contrast, Gaitskell's sudden death generated only a cottage industry of
outlandish theories, while the debate on Gaitskell's political legacy
fluctuated unevenly over the decades that followed.

The stories about Gaitskell's death began to emerge in the 1960s,
the brevity of the final illness being the pretext for a number of
conspiracy theories. These varied in detail: one had Gaitskell
poisoned by the Polish, another had him infected while in India.
The main theory settled down as follows. On 23 December 1962,
after he had already complained of being unwell and had had the
first blackout, he visited the Soviet consulate to obtain a visa for a
planned visit to Moscow. He was kept waiting and was served tea

and biscuits.[1] These biscuits contained hydralazine, a drug which produced lupus-like symptoms and which, according to a 1956 article in a Moscow journal, could be used for assassination.[2] On the evening after the visit to the consulate Gaitskell was taken ill again and was admitted to the Middlesex Hospital on 4 January. He apparently told one of the doctors about the tea and biscuits. A Soviet defector, Anatoli Golitsin, told his British handlers that just before coming over he had heard that the KGB was planning to kill an opposition leader and an Israeli intelligence source had informed the British intelligence officer Peter Wright about the method to be used. These theories were given credence because James Angleton, the somewhat insane head of American counter-intelligence, trusted Golitsin. Peter Wright went down to the Porton Down Chemical Defence Establishment to try to verify the method and came up with the hydralazine idea. In October 1971 the story surfaced in the *News of the World*, though it was credited to a later defector, Oleg Lyalin, rather than Golitsin.[3] The reason Gaitskell was assassinated was to make Harold Wilson leader.

The theory runs like this: Gaitskell was a dedicated Atlanticist who would keep Britain in the US orbit; Wilson was a KGB agent who would shift the UK away from the Americans. Moreover, Khrushchev hated Gaitskell and had told a Polish defector, 'If communism were to triumph tomorrow Gaitskell would be the first to be shot outside the Houses of Parliament as a traitor to the working class.'[4] Peter Wright fuelled the speculation as best he could through the 1970s during his campaign against Wilson.

Each part of the myth of Gaitskell's murder is based on some grain of truth but the sum of the parts is an elaborate and rather ludicrous fantasy. Taking each stage in turn, Gaitskell was already ill when he was supposed to have been poisoned in the Soviet consulate on 23 December. Indeed, this part of the story is in itself unlikely: having been discharged from the Manor House Hospital for Christmas, Gaitskell is supposed to have immediately gone to the Soviet consulate to get a visa for a trip which he cancelled two days later. But all this is beside the central point: Harold Wilson was not a KGB spy. Moreover, until James Callaghan entered the leadership race, described below, it was not at all certain that Wilson would have won. Indeed it seemed more likely that George Brown would have gained the leadership, which makes the strategy of killing Gaitskell at best high risk, at worst farcical. Wilson was not a unilateralist;

surely, if logic is applied, the Soviets would have at least favoured a unilateralist leader if they had wanted the Labour Party to move to the left. But would it have been in the Soviet Union's interests for Britain to disarm, given that the arms race was an essential element maintaining the Soviet regime? This leaves the only stated motive for killing the Labour leader Khrushchev's alleged violent dislike of Gaitskell, but did Khrushchev really hate him so much that he wanted him dead? The evidence from their various meetings suggests not; even if he did dislike him, is it credible that personal dislike would push the General Secretary of the Communist Party of the Soviet Union to have the Leader of Her Majesty's Opposition murdered? Finally, what are the sources for these allegations? Golitsin, a widely discredited defector, and Peter Wright, a man obsessed with Harold Wilson. The Gaitskell conspiracy, more prosaic than the various accounts of the Kennedy assassination, is merely a footnote to support the more outlandish fantasies generated by the Cold War. The political repercussions of Gaitskell's death, however, were of much greater significance.

As Susan Crosland bluntly stated: 'As is the custom, before Hugh Gaitskell's body was cold others were moving into positions to determine who would succeed him.'[5] According to Dick Taverne:

> There were two [meetings to discuss the succession],[6] an initial one in Jack Diamond's flat, but the elaborate analysis of who we should back was at Tony Crosland's flat at Bolton Gardens ... what happened there was that there was a lot of analysis of the candidates. George Brown had certain weaknesses which could be regarded very seriously. That Jim Callaghan was inexperienced and some said shallow. And that Harold Wilson won't put a foot wrong, win us the next elections but would then run the party into the ground, and nobody supported Harold, but the votes were divided between those who backed Callaghan which certainly included Tony Crosland, George Thomson and yourself [indicates Jay] and those who felt that in the end there was only one person of real calibre whatever his faults and that was George Brown and that was really the rest of us.[7]

Ever since he had fought Gaitskell in 1960, the left had only one possible candidate: Harold Wilson. There seems to have been some muted discussion of Wilson's candidature among the Gaitskellites. Dick Taverne later recalled:

> I remember ringing up Bill [Rodgers] and saying, 'What the hell do we

434

do if he dies?' We both then agreed that we weren't exactly necessarily sure that we would vote for George Brown but that we might even feel that Harold Wilson was the only alternative and in fact Tony Howard wrote an article about it because he got wind of it, saying that some of the young CDS people are even thinking about electing Harold Wilson.[8]

A similar story was recalled by David Marquand:

I have it so strongly in my mind that I think it must be true: a lunch I had with Bill in the House of Commons dining room and it was just before Gaitskell died and indeed before he was even ill. And I am almost certain that I said in the curious way you sometimes do: 'Just suppose Hugh was to fall under this fatal bus, what would happen?' And Bill, I am 95 per cent convinced, said to me: 'Well, of course, it would have to be Harold.'[9]

Anthony Howard actually wrote: 'At least one prominent member of the right-wing CDS is on record as saying in a first shock reaction to Mr Gaitskell's illness: "I suppose there's nothing for it – if anything happens to Hugh, it'll just have to be Harold."'[10] However, once the meetings were arranged and the Gaitskellites began to get over the shock of the leader's death, the more senior MPs asserted their influence. The discussions produced a split. Tony Crosland, George Thomson and Douglas Jay felt they could not back George Brown as potential Prime Minister, but most of the group decided to back Gaitskell's deputy; most did it with little enthusiasm but out of a sense of loyalty, as Bernard Donoughue reported: 'I met Bill immediately after, or very soon after, that key meeting and Bill said to me, "Our problem is that it seems that our campaign slogan would be: Better George drunk than Harold sober".'[11]

George Brown then undermined his own position by the heavy-handed tactics he employed in the race. Crossman recalled:

The Callaghan candidature was precipitated by the strong-arm methods of the Brownites, combined with the agonised awareness of some of Gaitskell's closest friends that, if Harold Wilson was an odious and impossible man, George Brown was plain impossible.[12]

These 'strong-arm' methods included 'some crude appeals . . . made to honour, some fairly rough threats . . . issued that men would lose their Shadow jobs and chance of office if they voted wrong'.[13]

The basis of the Brown campaign was that the followers of Gaitskell had a duty to support the choice of the majority of the group. Crosland described this as 'gang mentality',[14] the problem being that the unifying element, Gaitskell's leadership, was now removed. Crosland and others pressed Callaghan to stand as an alternative to Brown; Crossman and the Wilsonites of course supported this because it split the anti-Wilson vote. In the first ballot Wilson had 115 votes to Brown's 88 and Callaghan's 41. Wilson only needed 8 of Callaghan's votes in the second ballet to win: in the end he got 29 of them and was elected leader of the Labour Party on 14 February 1963.

The effect of Gaitskell's death and the split at the top of the Gaitskellite group over the succession had its effect at the grass roots. Some, like George Jones, expressed their disillusionment: 'We knew the left was still there and Wilson was seen as our enemy.'[15] The private discussions on how to deal with the new leader produced more uncertainty. In the main the MPs, especially Tony Crosland and Roy Jenkins, were unwilling to deal with Wilson. Those outside the House of Commons took rather a different view. Philip Williams wrote to Tony Crosland to sound him out about an approach to Wilson:

Of course it will be a distasteful operation . . . I'd be very sorry, but not too surprised if you or some others dropped out of politics now; but if you stay in you have to take the world as it is and not as we'd like it to be (as we have so often said to the left). This is not only my view but that of every CDS non-MP I've spoken to . . . Bernard Donoughue . . . and (I'm told) David Marquand.[16]

Wilson naturally viewed the Gaitskellites with the utmost suspicion. Crossman recorded the following conversation in his diary:

'But shouldn't you train up one of these bright new men to be your P.P.S.?' I asked. 'Which one?' Harold said, looking at me sharply. I thought rather desperately and said, 'Dick Taverne is voting for you in the second ballot.' 'But what reason have I to think he is trustworthy?' Harold said sharply. 'Oh, no reason at all, but what reasons have you to think him untrustworthy?' 'I don't give people jobs if I don't know whether they are trustworthy,' he said.

Wilson's distrust of the Gaitskellites in CDS never dissipated over the years. In 1969 after the death of Stephen Swingler, the Minister of State at the Department of Health and Social Security, Wilson and Crossman discussed who should succeed him.

Epilogue

When I was asked whom I wanted I said, 'Roy Hattersley, of course'. Harold said, 'You can't have him, partly because Barbara can't do without him and partly because he is disloyal and belongs to the wrong side. I must have the political balance kept. We must have another left-winger, and Reg Freeson is on the left.' 'Well,' I said, 'I must consider competence and Roy Hattersley and Dick Taverne, both of whom I know are CDS, are the only two.' Harold said, 'Oh, do be serious, that's impossible.'[17]

Further discussion ensued; Crossman still did not want Freeson. The second discussion produced a remarkable exchange between Wilson and Crossman:

He had further reports. Roy Hattersley had made three disloyal remarks recently and we couldn't promote him. What about other people? 'Well,' I said, 'do a few remarks matter?' We cast around and I suggested Dick Taverne. He said, 'Have you lost all your political antennae that you fail to remember what our loyalties are? Dick Taverne, he is a silken, treacherous member of the CDS group, he is most unpopular in the Parliamentary Party. If you have him it will be a betrayal of all we stand for. I am amazed at your forgetting.' I said, 'It's not I who have forgotten, Harold. I think these young men have forgotten their past. I know Roy Hattersley is no more loyal to Roy Jenkins than he is to you. He is just an able young man on the way up and I think Dick Taverne has rather more loyalty and decency about him. He is a loyal Jenkins supporter but he is not going to be disloyal to you in his job for me.' Then Harold said, 'It's out of the question.' 'Look,' I said, 'can I perhaps move David Ennals from Health?' 'Yes,' said Harold, 'you can, and put somebody else into the Health side in his place. What about Shirley Williams?' I said, 'Shirley Williams is much more CDS than Roy Hattersley or Dick Taverne.' 'But she is a woman, it would suit you. Shirley Williams, that's a good idea.' I don't know what to think.[18]

Other members of CDS were luckier than Dick Taverne; Bernard Donoughue in particular managed to escape his past in Harold Wilson's eyes, becoming his chief policy adviser.[19]

The government which Harold Wilson formed in October 1964 was a masterly balancing of interests. Inheriting a Shadow Cabinet still dominated by former supporters of Gaitskell, Wilson had only limited room for manoeuvre, but used it effectively. Within the Cabinet, Wilson was faced by Jim Callaghan[20] and George Brown,[21] his two opponents in the leadership contest and numbers two and three in the government. The leading revisionist MPs also found places in the government: Tony Crosland went to the Department of Economic Affairs as George Brown's number two;[22] Roy Jenkins went to the Ministry of Aviation;[23] Douglas Jay went to the Board of Trade,[24] Patrick Gordon Walker went to the Foreign Office,[25] Jack Diamond became Chief Secretary to the Treasury and Herbert Bowden was made Lord President. Further down the ministerial batting order, the Gaitskellites continued to be represented: Bill Rodgers and Maurice Foley were Under-Secretaries at the DEA; Niall Macdermott was Financial Secretary to the Treasury; Denis Howell was Under-Secretary at Education and Science and Chris Mayhew became Minister for the Navy. Later, Dick Taverne, Austen Albu, Edmund Dell, Jim Boyden and Roy Hattersley all found places in the administration. While this did not preclude factional activity, it did minimise the danger of such action.

Even before George Brown's emotional resignation from the government, the leadership of the scattered Gaitskellite group had moved to Roy Jenkins, who was also one of Gaitskell's executors and the designated official biographer.[26] From the late 1960s onwards the future of the Gaitskellites, who increasingly styled themselves as social democrats, became wedded to the European debate, Crosland and Jay parting company with the rest on this issue.

The experience of the Wilson government, and the left-wing backlash which followed in the early 1970s,[27] left the already scattered and divided Gaitskellites stranded. In some ways the early 1970s were a rerun of the 1950s, except that the 'floor' of Conference achieved many more victories over the 'platform'. In response to the political polarisation of much of the membership there were calls to revive the right-wing organisation. However, when Dick Taverne faced his deselection, after defying the whip to vote for British entry to the EEC,[28] many of the old campaigners held back from openly helping the Democratic Labour Party launched by Taverne to fight and win the by-election he had forced: Bill Rodgers's wife went to Lincoln to assist Taverne, but Rodgers himself felt the move was premature.[29] For others the record of the Wilson government needed to be defended and the European Community was not the central issue. For these revisionists the future could still lie within the Labour Party.[30] From the time of the vote for entry to the European Economic Community on 28 October 1971, when sixty-nine Labour MPs voted with the Heath government, the paths between those whose primary cause had become the EEC and those who shared Gaitskell's exasperation with the subject increasingly diverged.

Epilogue

The Labour Party was perhaps saved from immediate division by the unexpected electoral victory of 1974.[31] Once again Wilson had to blend the warring factions into a government and the leading social democrats continued their ministerial careers. In marked contrast to the 1964–70 government, when the only active right-wing organisation was the Labour Committee for Europe, the 1974–9 governments saw the formation of the Manifesto Group of MPs in 1974; the grassroots Social Democratic Alliance, run by the former chairman of the CDS student wing, Stephen Haseler, in 1975; and finally Bill Rodgers back in the chair of a right-wing pressure group in the Campaign for Labour Victory in 1977.[32]

The crisis on the right of the party, already compounded by Jenkins's resignation from the deputy leadership in 1972, was made worse by his resignation from the government. Having been offered the job of President of the European Commission in January 1976 he had held on to fight for the Labour Party leadership before eventually going to Brussels in 1977.[33] Tony Crosland, although he had split with many of his old colleagues over the European issue, was still seen as a potential leader. His tragically early death in 1977 again left the social democrats leaderless. The 1979 defeat of the Callaghan government precipitated a further leftward swing in the Labour Party, particularly in the make-up of the Parliamentary Labour Party. An indication of this change was the fact that not a single MP of the 1979 intake joined the right-wing Manifesto Group in the House of Commons. Despite the efforts of the Campaign for Labour Victory, there was no 'unilateralist' issue to fight on, and no leader to offer unqualified support. There was no logic to the events of the early 1980s that would have brought the remnants of the Gaitskellite group back into a powerful position in the Labour Party. Perhaps the last hope was to get Denis Healey elected as leader. When he was defeated in the leadership election by Michael Foot, many of the old Gaitskellites still active in British politics gave up the battle for the Labour Party and left to establish the Social Democratic Party.

The idea that there was a consistent development from the factionalism of the 1950s and early 1960s to the succession of the SDP is mistaken.[34] The political circumstances were radically different by 1981. Gaitskell provided an emotional bond between some of those who set up the SDP. But when they had been young Gaitskellites they had been overtly loyal to the Labour Party and operated by

439

motivating those elements in the Labour Party who favoured unity behind the elected leader.[35]

The extent of the Gaitskellites' failure to maintain this motivation and achieve a permanent impact on the Labour Party was finally illustrated by the division of 1981. This failure was tied into the nature of support for the Gaitskellite pressure groups like the CDS. The support into which the 1960 CDS manifesto tapped was substantial, but it was conditional on the particular circumstances of the early 1960s and the threat these circumstances posed to the future prospects of the Labour Party for those active within it. For many it was also conditional on the leadership of Hugh Gaitskell. In contrast, the circumstances of 1981 found a majority of activists inside the Labour Party supportive of the policies that the social democrats found most disagreeable – withdrawal from the European Economic Community, unilateral nuclear disarmament and reform of the party constitution to elect the leader by an electoral college. The constituency that the social democrats needed to rally in 1981 was largely outside the Labour Party.

The launch of the SDP ensured successive electoral victories for the Conservative Party. It also had an impact on the Labour Party. Neil Kinnock's election as leader in 1983 began the process of recovery. Kinnock owed his loyalty to the tradition of Nye Bevan but he employed the tactics of the revisionists and he led in the style of Hugh Gaitskell. Without abandoning the basic beliefs and ideological framework of democratic socialism the party pulled itself slowly and painfully back on track for electoral success. Neil Kinnock succeeded where Gaitskell had failed. He employed better tactics over a longer period, but, more important, the labour movement – the trade unions as well as the Labour Party – had lost the confidence born of the Attlee governments and the years of free collective bargaining. The devices used in the Kinnock years to retreat from the 1983 manifesto – the speech at the 1985 Conference, the policy review – were Gaitskellite to the core. In the 1985 speech Kinnock attacked that which was thought sacrosanct; in the policy review he attempted a thoroughgoing revisionism of party policy.

In the pantheon of Labour heroes, however, Gaitskell's status stayed stubbornly low in the 1970s and 1980s. Michael Foot and Neil Kinnock traced their ancestry through the Nye Bevan line – Kinnock hated the comparisons with Gaitskell. However, when John Smith was elected, Gaitskell's position improved. Smith had cut his

440

political teeth working with Gaitskellite organisations like the CDS, so with his election as leader the office passed back to the house of Gaitskell. Smith took pride in his Gaitskellite past and shared some of the same ideological instincts, particularly that part of Gaitskell's ideology summed up as 'the pursuit of power to put principles into practice'. They shared the view that a party in a mature democracy should have certain basic principles which inform its policy formation, but that from that point on everything was secondary to achieving power to put those policies into practice. It was an ideology that lacked the romance and rhetoric of Nye Bevan. It was an appeal that went against the dominant feeling on the left. Leaders like Smith and Gaitskell telling the party that it could not remake Britain in a socialist image because the British people did not want it were not welcome. But neither Kinnock nor Smith repeated Gaitskell's tactically inept attack on Clause 4, though we know that Kinnock at least supported the idea of replacing it; it took the general election defeat of 1992 and another change of leader before that was open to change.

Thatcherism had forced the Labour Party to admit overtly what it had acknowledged covertly since 1945 – that a Labour Government would have to manage capitalism. Gaitskell rigorously argued in his Clause 4 speech for the aims and values of the party, the destination of the party in power, to reflect achievable aims and realisable values in society as it existed and not as the party might have liked it to exist. He felt that to do this he had to replace the summation of the party's theology – Clause 4 – with a new statement not centred on property relationships. He was not the leader and they were not the times in which to do this. Gaitskell could no more lead the Labour left against its emotionalism and ideology than could Nye Bevan over the bomb in 1957. It took the electoral humiliations of 1983, 1987 and 1992 to convince many of the truth of Gaitskell's assertion in 1955: 'Can anyone honestly say that if the Labour Party had chosen a policy which reflected more or less the line of the Communist Party we should have received a larger vote?' Too many people in the Labour Party believed for too long that if only the British people were offered the undiluted possibility of the fulfilment of Clause 4 then the party would be swept to power.

But the Clause 4 challenge was more than just an honourable failure. The idea that a democratic socialist party should have sacred texts is nonsensical. Theology of objective is a sure route to the maintenance of the status quo; it leaves a utopian future as an excuse for the failures of the present. Theology of means is the route to reaction. To be still advocating state nationalisation of monopolies on the 1945 model in the 1990s is pure reaction. Gaitskell's revisionism offered a process for asking of each institution and relationship in our society: What is it for? Who does it benefit? Should it be changed? Crucially, though, there was always a final question and a standard against which action was interpreted: how can it be used to achieve greater equality? The method or mechanism could vary but the objective was fixed. Tony Blair's election to the leadership of the Labour Party thus marked the point at which the Gaitskellite Labour Party was finally transcended; the point at which the revisionist approach became focused on the creation of a different kind of society to that envisaged by Gaitskell's generation: equality was no longer the objective of Labour in power.

As the history of the Labour Party has unfolded since January 1963, so there have been a number of manifestations of Hugh Gaitskell to add to the views of him abroad in his lifetime. The first picture to come into focus was the Mr Butskell caricature of the 1950s – which took a more concrete form in the 'desiccated calculating machine' image of the anti–unilateralist. At the very end of his life and in his death, the man came through the image as both hero and lost leader for a generation of radically minded people. The hero was given his monument in Philip Williams's official life, finally published in 1979. After this, with the Labour Party dividing and the SDP quietly claiming his mantle, he descended into political obscurity. As collectivism ended and the Labour Party switched from the intellectual powerhouse of post-war contemporary history to the intellectual hoarder of other people's ideas, so Hugh Gaitskell slipped from political actor and influence, into history: the kinder, gentler, more tolerant and more egalitarian world he tried to make, and was then robbed of the opportunity of making, slipped with him.

Notes

ABBREVIATIONS

Attlee	Earl Attlee Papers
CAB	Cabinet Papers, PRO
CDS	Campaign for Democratic Socialism Papers
FO	Foreign Office
FRUS	Foreign Relations of the United States
HDD	Hugh Dalton Diary (ed.) Ben Pimlott
HGD	Hugh Gaitskell Diary (ed.) Philip Williams
Labour	Labour Party Papers
Leeds	South Leeds Constituency Labour Party Papers
LPACR	Labour Party Annual Conference Reports
LSE	London School of Economics
NEC	National Executive Committee Minutes and Papers
PGWD	Patrick Gordon Walker Diary (ed.) Robert Pearce
PRO	Public Record Office
RCD, 1979	Richard Crossman Diary (Cabinet) (ed.) Janet Morgan
RCD	Richard Crossman Diary (Backbench) (ed.) Janet Morgan
T	Treasury Papers, PRO
TBD	Tony Benn Diary, 1940–1962 (ed.) Ruth Winstone

Preface and Acknowledgments

1 Philip Williams, *Hugh Gaitskell: A Political Biography* (Cape, hardback, 1979) and *Hugh Gaitskell* (OUP, paperback, 1982). Also Philip Williams (ed.), *The Diary of Hugh Gaitskell* (Cape, 1983).

Chapter 1   Dragon, Wykehamist, Socialist, 1906–1928

1 Alan Bullock, *The Life and Times of Ernest Bevin*, vol. 1 (Heinemann, 1960), p. 2.
2 Anthony Howard, *RAB: The Life of R. A. Butler* (Cape, 1987), p. 5.
3 Lady Longford in interview with author.
4 HDD, 29.5.52, p. 589.
5 Kenneth Harris, *Attlee* (Weidenfeld & Nicolson, 1982), p. 3.
6 *Picture Post*, 7 April 1951.
7 John Wilson, *CB: A Life of Sir Henry Campbell-Bannerman* (Constable, 1973), p. 510.
8 Philip Williams, *Hugh Gaitskell: A Political Biography* (Cape, 1979), pp. 5–6.

9 Ivan Yates, 'The Lessons of Gaitskell's Early Years', *Observer*, 20 January 1963.
10 *Rudyard Kipling's Verse*, Inclusive Edition (Doubleday, 1927), pp. 378–9.
11 *Picture Post*, 7 April 1951.
12 Ibid.
13 John Betjeman, *Summoned by Bells* (John Murray, 1976), p. 43.
14 *Picture Post*, 7 April 1951; quoted in a slightly different version in Williams, *Gaitskell*, p. 7.
15 Jonathan Gathorne-Hardy, *The Public School Phenomenon, 597–1977* (Penguin, 1979), p. 31.
16 Jennifer Sherwood and Nikolaus Pevsner, *Oxfordshire* (Penguin, 1974), p. 166.
17 John Wakeford, *The Cloistered Elite* (Macmillan, 1969), p. 55.
18 Richard Crossman, *The Charm of Politics* (Hamish Hamilton, 1958), pp. 116–17.
19 Lord Longford in interview with author.
20 *Picture Post*, 7 April 1951.

21 Tam Dalyell, *Dick Crossman: A Portrait* (Weidenfeld & Nicolson, 1989), p. 18.
22 Roy Jenkins, *The Times,* 18 January 1973.
23 *Picture Post,* 7 April 1951.
24 Williams, *Gaitskell,* p. 9.
25 Quoted in Philip Williams, *Hugh Gaitskell* (paperback, OUP, 1979), p. 12.
26 Lord Jay in interview with author.
27 Quoted in Williams, *Gaitskell,* p. 10.
28 *Picture Post,* 7 April 1951.
29 Roy Jenkins, *The Times,* 18 January 1973.
30 Lucille Iremonger, *The Fiery Chariot: A Study of British Prime Ministers and the Search for Love* (Secker & Warburg, 1970).
31 Hugh Berrington, 'Review Article: The Fiery Chariot: British Prime Ministers and the Search for Love', *British Journal of Political Science,* 4 (1970), pp. 345–69.
32 Lady Longford in interview with author.
33 Lord Longford in interview with author.
34 Hugh Gaitskell, 'At Oxford in the Twenties', in Asa Briggs and John Saville (eds), *Essays in Labour History in honour of G. D. H. Cole* (Macmillan, 1967 edn), p. 6.
35 Mark Amory (ed.), *The Letters of Ann Fleming,* 'To Evelyn Waugh, 28 November 1958', p. 223.
36 Hugh Gaitskell to his mother, 15 December 1927, quoted in Williams, *Gaitskell* (paperback), p. 14.
37 Lady Longford in interview with the author.
38 Maurice Bowra in William Rodgers (ed.), *Hugh Gaitskell* (Thames & Hudson), p. 21.
39 Williams, *Gaitskell,* p. 18.
40 Lord Longford in interview with author.
41 Hugh Gaitskell to his mother, 5 May 1926, quoted in Williams, *Gaitskell* (paperback), p. 21.
42 Hugh Gaitskell 'At Oxford in the Twenties', p. 10.
43 Hugh Gaitskell, *Chartism* (Longmans, 1929).
44 Margaret Cole, in W. T. Rodgers (ed.), *Hugh Gaitskell 1906–1963* (Cape, 1964), p. 38.
45 Hugh Gaitskell to his mother, 20 May 1926, quoted in Williams, *Gaitskell* (paperback), p. 23.
46 Williams, *Gaitskell* (paperback), pp. 25–6.
47 Lady Longford in interview with the author.
48 Ibid.
49 Quoted in Williams, *Gaitskell,* p. 25.
50 Williams, *Gaitskell* (paperback), p. 33.
51 Quoted in Williams, *Gaitskell,* p. 24.
52 Quoted in Williams, *Gaitskell,* p. 26.
53 Hugh Gaitskell to his mother, 5 March 1928, quoted in Williams, *Gaitskell* (paperback), p. 36.

Chapter 2 An Unorthodox Academic, 1928–1939

1 Hugh Gaitskell to Arthur Gaitskell, 13 November 1928, quoted in Philip Williams, *Hugh Gaitskell* (OUP, 1982), p. 46.
2 Hugh Dalton, *High Tide and After* (Muller, 1962), p. 426.
3 Quoted in Ben Pimlott, *Hugh Dalton* (Cape, 1985), p. 223.
4 Pimlott, *Hugh Dalton,* p. 221.
5 Michael Postan, in William Rodgers (ed.), *Hugh Gaitskell* (Thames & Hudson, 1964), p. 51.
6 Robert Skidelsky, *John Maynard Keynes: The Economist as Saviour, 1920–37* (Macmillan, 1992), p. 449.
7 Skidelsky, *Keynes,* p. 447.
8 Hugh Gaitskell, *Recent Developments in British Socialist Thinking* (Co-Operative Union, 1956), pp. 20–1.
9 Gaitskell, *Recent Developments,* p. 21.
10 Elizabeth Durbin, *New Jerusalem* (Routledge & Kegan Paul, 1985), p. 70.
11 Denis Healey, *The Time of My Life* (Penguin, 1990), p. 37.
12 Ben Pimlott, *Frustrate their Knavish Tricks* (HarperCollins, 1994), p. 98.
13 Harold Laski, *The Danger of Being a Gentleman* (George Allen & Unwin, 1939), p. 57.
14 John Strachey, *The Theory and Practice of Socialism* (Victor Gollancz, 1936), p. 7.
15 LSE: Evan Durbin papers, file 2/2.
16 Durbin, *New Jerusalem,* p. 110.
17 Ibid.
18 David Horner, 'The Road to Scarborough: Wilson, Labour and the Scientific Revolution', in Nick Tiratsoo (ed.), *The Wilson Governments, 1964–70* (Pinter, 1993), p. 50.
19 Jenkins, *The Times,* 18 January 1973.
20 Issac Kramnick and Barry Sheerman, *Harold Laski: A Life on the Left* (Hamish Hamilton, 1993), pp. 334–45.
21 Quoted in Durbin, *New Jerusalem,* p. 83.
22 Pimlott, *Dalton,* pp. 222–3.
23 Quoted in Durbin, *New Jerusalem,* p. 82.
24 Pimlott, *Dalton,* p. 223.
25 Durbin, *New Jerusalem,* p. 113.
26 See LSE: for example, Durbin papers, 4/6, Political theory, 1940ca–1950ca.

27 Quoted in Francis Ludwig Carstrem, *The First Austrian Republic 1918–1938: A Study based on Britain and Austria* (Gower, 1986), p. 182.

28 Williams, *Gaitskell* (paperback), p. 60.

29 CAB: FO 371, 18351, Memo by E. H. Carr, 26 February 1934.

30 *Daily Herald*, 23 October 1950.

31 Naomi Mitchison, *Vienna Diary* (Victor Gollancz, 1934), p. 9. Gaitskell is Sam in the diary.

32 Mitchison, *Vienna Diary*, p. 65.

33 Ibid., p. 75.

34 Philip Williams, *Hugh Gaitskell* (Cape, 1979), p. 58.

35 *Daily Herald*, 14 April 1951.

36 Majorie Brett, in W. T. Rodgers (ed.), *Hugh Gaitskell* (Thames & Hudson, 1964), p. 68.

37 Ibid., p. 71.

38 Douglas Jay in interview with author.

39 Witness Seminar Transcript, Contemporary Record, Vol. 7, N2, ANT 1993, pp. 374–5.

Chapter 3   Whitehall Irregular, 1939–1945

1 Peter Hennessy, *Whitehall* (Fontana, 1990, Chapter 3, 'Hitler's Reform', gives a full account of the wartime mobilisation of which Gaitskell was a part, pp. 88–120.

2 Graham Greene, 'Men at Work', in *Twenty-One Stories* (Penguin, 1970), pp. 62–9.

3 Hugh Gaitskell to Christopher Mayhew, 23 September 1943, letter shown to author by Lord Mayhew.

4 Roy Jenkins, *The Times*, 16 January 1973.

5 Susan Crosland, *Tony Crosland* (Cape, 1983), p. 13.

6 Denis Healey, *The Time of My Life* (Penguin, 1990), p. 44.

7 Ben Pimlott, *Harold Wilson* (Harper-Collins, 1992), p. 70.

8 W. N. Medlicott, *The Economic Blockade, Vol. 1* (HMSO and Longman, 1952), p. xi.

9 Ibid., p. 13.

10 PRO: FO 837/N1328/069.

11 Hugh Dalton, *The Fateful Years* (Muller, 1957), p. 280.

12 HDD, 10 April 1940, p. 326.

13 PRO: FO 837/24/N1328.

14 Ben Pimlott, *Hugh Dalton* (Cape, 1985), p. 277.

15 PRO: FO 837/13/N1326.

16 M. R. D. Foot, *SOE in France* (HMSO, 1966), pp. 6, 18.

17 Quoted in Pimlott, *Dalton*, p. 296.

18 M. R. D. Foot, *SOE in France* p. 18.

19 Tam Dalyell, *Richard Crossman* (Jonathan Cape, 1992), p. 59.

20 Quoted in Charles Edward Lysaght, *Brendan Bracken* (Allen Lane, 1979), pp. 205–6.

21 HDD, 25.7.41, Quoted in Pimlott, *Dalton*, pp. 321–2.

22 Dalton, *Fateful Years*, p. 296.

23 David Marquand, *The Progressive Dilemma* (Heinemann, 1983), p. 83.

24 Quoted in Philip Williams, *Hugh Gaitskell* (Cape, 1979), p. 99.

25 Peter Hennessy, *Never Again* (Cape, 1992), p. 102.

26 Pimlott, *Dalton*, p. 351.

27 Williams, *Gaitskell*, p. 110.

28 Pimlott, *Dalton*, p. 354.

29 Paul Addison, *Churchill on the Home Front* (Cape, 1992), p. 348.

30 Hennessy, *Never Again*, p. 102 and n63.

31 Addison, *Home Front*, p. 349.

32 Pimlott, *Dalton*, p. 357 and Addison, *Home Front*, p. 349.

33 Pimlott, *Wilson*, pp. 77–81.

34 Williams, *Gaitskell*, p. 122.

35 Ibid.

Chapter 4   Building the New Jerusalem, 1945–1949

1 Peter Hennessy, *Never Again* (Cape, 1992), pp. 79–80.

2 Lewis Minkin, *The Labour Party Conference* (Allen Lane, London), p. 21.

3 Richard Cockett, *Thinking the Unthinkable* (Fontana Press, 1994), p. 91.

4 Ibid., p. 93. In 1980 Professor Hayek wrote to Paul Addison and commented, 'I am afraid there can be little doubt that Winston Churchill's somewhat unfortunately phrased Gestapo speech was written under the influence of *The Road to Serfdom*.' Paul Addison, *Home Front*, p. 383 and n.

5 Cockett, *Thinking the Unthinkable*, p. 87.

6 Hennessy, *Never Again*, p. 83.

7 Quoted in Isaac Kramnick and Barry Sheerman, *Harold Laski, A Life on the Left* (Hamish Hamilton, 1993), p. 483.

8 LSE: Durbin, 1/5, Peace and War, Syllabus of a special course of three lectures on The Causes of War, by E. F. M. Durbin, Oxford University Extra Mural Department, 1937.

9 Philip Williams, *Hugh Gaitskell* (Cape, 1979), p. 125.
10 HGD, 6.8.45, p. 5.
11 Hennessy, *Never Again*, pp. 56, 86 and Paul Addison, *Home Front* (Cape, 1992), p. 385.
12 Michael Foot, *Aneurin Bevan, 1945–1960* (Granada, 1975), p. 13.
13 *New Statesman and Nation*, Saturday 28 July 1945, Volume XXX, No. 753, p. 49.
14 *New Statesman and Nation*, Saturday 4 August 1945, Volume XXX, No. 754, p. 71.
15 *Spectator*, Friday 17 August 1945, No. 6112.
16 Hennessy, *Never Again*, p. 56.
17 HGD, 6.8.45, p. 5.
18 HGD, 6.8.45, p. 7.
19 He only held the job for short time as he could not give it sufficient attention.
20 John Hersey, *Hiroshima* (Penguin Books, 1946), p. 13.
21 HGD, 8.8.45, p. 16.
22 HGD, 13–24.8.45, p. 19.
23 HDD, 15.5.46, p. 371.
24 Quote from Dalton in HDD, 15.5.45, p. 371, details from Ben Pimlott, *Harold Wilson* (HarperCollins, 1992), p. 98, Philip Ziegler, *Wilson: The Authorised Life* (HarperCollins, 1993), p. 53 and HGD, 12.8.47, pp. 22–34.
25 HGD, 12.8.47, p. 23.
26 Douglas Jay, *Change and Fortune*, 1980, p. 152 as quoted in Jim Tomlinson, 'Mr Attlee's supply-side socialism', *Economic History Review*, XLVI, I (1993), pp. 1–22.
27 Jim Tomlinson, 'Mr Attlee's supply-side socialism', *Economic History Review*, XLVI, I (1993), p. 9.
28 The exchange was widely reported: *The Times*, 19 April 1948; *Manchester Guardian*, 28 April 1948; *Daily Herald*, 3 May 1948; *Daily Graphic*, 3 May 1948 and *Daily Express*, 8 May 1948.
29 *George Wigg by Lord Wigg* (Michael Joseph, 1972), p. 129.
30 Hennessy, *Never Again*, p. 103 and Douglas Jay, in W. T. Rodgers (ed.), *Hugh Gaitskell* (Thames & Hudson, 1964), p. 90.
31 HGD, 12.8.47, pp. 28–9.
32 HGD, 4.12.47, p. 47.
33 *Daily Express*, 27 October 1947.
34 HGD, 4.12.47, p. 47.
35 *Daily Express*, 5 August 1946.
36 *Yorkshire Post*, 22 August 1948.
37 *Daily Telegraph*, 24 July 1948.

38 *Manchester Guardian*, 3 May 1948.
39 Williams, *Gaitskell* pp. 151–2 and HGD, 30.1.48, p. 53.
40 Douglas Jay, in Rodgers (ed.), *Hugh Gaitskell*, pp. 91–2.
41 This and earlier quotes from T. A. B. Corley, 'Oil companies and the role of government: Britain, 1900–75' in Geoffrey Jones and Maurice Kirby (eds.), *Competitiveness and the State. Government and Business in Twentieth-Century Britain*, MUP, p. 168.
42 *Daily Express*, 7 July 1949.
43 HGD, 29.7.49, p. 118.
44 David Marquand, *The Progressive Dilemma, From Lloyd George to Kinnock* (Heinemann, 1991), p. 123.
45 Attlee: 87, fols 69–74.
46 HGD, 20.9.48, pp. 82–84.

Chapter 5   Chancellor for Dentures and Defence, 1949–1951

1 HGD, 24.1.51, p. 228; 30.4.51, p. 241 and 9.11.51, p. 284 for instance.
2 HGD, 21.9.49, p. 133.
3 HGD, Document No. 5, pp. 153–4.
4 Peter Hennessy, *Never Again* (Cape, 1992), p. 387.
5 Morgan, *Labour in Power 1945–1951* (Oxford University Press, 1984), p. 402.
6 Hennessy, *Never Again*, p. 387 and Douglas Jay in W. T. Rodgers (ed.), *Hugh Gaitskell* (Thames & Hudson, 1964), p. 95.
7 Morgan, *Labour in Power*, p. 402.
8 HGD, 27.1.50, p. 162.
9 Ibid., pp. 161–2.
10 HGD, 21.3.50, p. 166.
11 Speech at Oxford, 1 February 1950.
12 Jim Tomlinson, 'Mr Attlee's supply-side socialism', *Economic History Review*, XLVI, I (1993), p. 11.
13 Quoted in Peter Stanford, *Lord Longford: An Authorised Life* (Heinemann, 1994), p. 258.
14 *Daily Mail*, 3 February 1950.
15 HGD, 21.3.50, p. 165.
16 *Daily Herald*, 4 February 1950.
17 *Manchester Guardian*, 7 February 1950.
18 *Daily Express*, 11 February 1950.
19 *The Times*, 13 February 1950.
20 *Manchester Guardian*, 16 February 1950.
21 *Cleckheaton Independent*, 18 February 1950.
22 John Campbell, *Nye Bevan, A Biography* (pbk) (Hodder & Stoughton, 1994), pp. 212–13.
23 Leeds: 22, Election Expenses.

24 HGD, 21.3.50, p. 167.
25 Quoted in Hennessy, *Never Again*, p. 389.
26 HDD, 25.2.50.
27 Philip Ziegler, *Wilson* (HarperCollins, 1993), p. 53.
28 HDD, 27.1.50, p. 466.
29 HDD, 4.4.51, p. 518.
30 HDD, 27.1.50, p. 466.
31 Ibid.
32 *Manchester Guardian*, 7 June 1950.
33 HGD, 11.8.50, p. 193.
34 *Daily Mail*, 14 September 1950.
35 Ibid.
36 HGD, 23.4.48, p. 59.
37 HGD, 26.5.50, p. 184.
38 *Observer*, 1 October 1950.
39 *Daily Worker*, 20 October 1950.
40 HDD, 27.1.50, p. 466.
41 PRO: T171/400, Gaitskell to Cripps, 10 March 1950, quoted in Morgan, *Labour Government*, 1984, p. 410.
42 *Observer*, 20 October 1950.
43 Philip Williams, *Hugh Gaitskell* (Cape, 1979), p. 190.
44 HGD, 26.5.50, p. 185.
45 HGD, all quotes on US trip from pp. 201–11.
46 Attlee: 119, 145–6, 15 April 1951: text of tribute to Bevin.
47 Edwin Plowden, *An Industrialist in the Treasury, The Post-War Years* (Andre Deutsch, 1989), p. 104.
48 Michael Foot, *Aneurin Bevan* (Granada, 1975), p. 298.
49 Clem Attlee, *The Granada Historical Records Interview*, 1967, p. 44.
50 Foot, *Bevan*, p. 296.
51 Quoted in Foot, p. 297.
52 Ben Pimlott, *Harold Wilson* (Harper-Collins, 1992), p. 157.
53 HGD, 3.11.50, p. 215 and 5.1.51, p. 221.
54 Pimlott, *Wilson*, p. 157.
55 Quoted in Williams, *Gaitskell*, p. 236.
56 *Daily Mirror* and *Evening Standard*, 20 October 1950.
57 HGD, 3.11.50, p. 216.
58 PRO: CAB 128/18 CM (50), 67th conclusion.
59 Present were:
Clem Attlee, Chair
Herbert Morrison, Lord President of the Council
Viscount Addison, Lord Privy Seal
Viscount Jowitt, Lord Chancellor
Manny Shinwell, Minister of Defence
Nye Bevan, Minister of Health
James Griffiths, Secretary of State for the Colonies
Ernest Bevin, Secretary of State for Foreign Affairs
Hugh Dalton, Minister of Town and Country Planning
Viscount Alexander of Hillsborough, Chancellor of the Duchy of Lancaster
Chuter Ede, Home Secretary
George Isaacs, Minister of Labour
T. Williams, Agriculture and Fisheries
Hector McNeil, Secretary of State for Scotland
Patrick Gordon Walker, Secretary of State for Commonwealth Relations

Also present:
Maurice Webb, Minister of Food
William Whiteley, Parliamentary Secretary, Treasury
Hartley Shawcross, Attorney-General
Jim Callaghan, Parliamentary and Financial Secretary at the Admiralty

Secretariat:
Sir Norman Brook
Mr A. Johnston
60 Hennessy, *Never Again*, p. 404.
61 See for example, Anita Inder Singh, 'Britain, India and the Asian Cold War, 1949–54', in Anne Deighton (ed.), *Britain and the First Cold War* (Macmillan, 1990), p. 226.
62 PRO: T237/82, 'Note of meeting between Prime Minister and American Ambassador on 24th July 1950'.
63 PRO: CAB 129/41, CP (50), 181, 31 July 1950.
64 PRO: CAB 128/18 52nd conclusion, Tuesday 1 August 1950.
65 PRO: CAB 129/41, CP (50), 181, 31 July 1950.
66 Edwin Plowden, *An Industrialist at the Treasury* (Andre Deutsch, 1989), p. 99.
67 Foot, *Bevan*, p. 305.
68 Plowden, *An Industrialist at the Treasury*, p. 100.
69 Ibid., p. 104.
70 HGD, Document No. 7, p. 208.
71 PRO: CAB 128/18, CM (50), 12 December 1950 and CM (50) 87, 18 December 1950.
72 Alec Cairncross (ed.), *The Robert Hall Diaries, 1947–1953* (Unwin Hyman, 1989), p. 155.
73 PRO: CAB 129/44, CP (51) 20, 19 January 1951.
74 *Manchester Guardian*, 22 January 1951.
75 *Daily Express*, 22 January 1951.
76 Hennessy, *Never Again*, p. 410.
77 *Observer*, 29 January 1951; *Daily Herald*,

29 January 1951; *The Times*, 29 January 1951.
78 *Sunday Times*, 28 January 1951.
79 Hennessy, *Never Again*, p. 410.
80 HGD, 30.4.51, p. 240.
81 HGD, 21.3.50, p. 174.
82 HGD, 21.3.50, p. 174.
83 John Strachey, obituary of Gaitskell, *Sunday Times Weekly Review*, 20 January 1963.
84 Foot, *Bevan*, p. 292.
85 Robert J. Jackson, *Rebels and Whips* (Macmillan, 1968), lists 8 domestic and 31 foreign revolts during the Attlee governments. These were unorganised. Stephen Haseler, *The Gaitskellites* (Macmillan, 1969), pp. 19–20.
86 HDD, 4.4.51, p. 518.
87 HDD, 6.4.51, p. 519.
88 HDD, 5–6.4.51, pp. 518–19.
89 PRO: CAB 128/19 CM 9 April 1950.
90 HDD, 6.4.51, p. 520.
91 HGD, 30.4.51, p. 245; HDD, 10.4.51, p. 523.
92 HGD, 30.4.51, p. 246.
93 HGD 30.4.51, p. 247 and fn.
94 Williams, *Gaitskell*, p. 253.
95 HGD, 30.4.51, p. 251.
96 *Glasgow Herald*, 11 April 1951.
97 *Evening Standard*, 11 April 1951.
98 *Daily Graphic*, 11 April 1951.
99 HGD, 4.5.51, pp. 256–7.

Chapter 6   The Road from 1951

1 John Campbell, *Nye Bevan, A Biography* (Hodder & Stoughton, 1994), p. 255.
2 HDD, 16.9.51, p. 554.
3 Morgan, *Labour in Power* (Oxford University Press, 1984), p. 471.
4 HGD, 8.8.51, p. 264.
5 Peter Hennessy, *Never Again* (Cape, 1992), p. 421.
6 Attlee: 127, 41 Text of speech by Gaitskell 8/10/51.
7 HGD, 10.8.51, pp. 267–8.
8 HDD, 30.10.51, p. 566.
9 HGD, 10.8.51, p. 269.
10 Philip Williams, *Gaitskell* (JCape, 1979), p. 270 and note 12.
11 HGD, 9.11.51, p. 274.
12 *Daily Mirror*, 5 September 1951.
13 HGD, 9.11.51, p. 275.
14 HDD, 16.9.51, p. 553.
15 Hennessy, *Never Again*, p. 422.
16 Williams, *Gaitskell*, p. 283.
17 Morgan, *Labour in Power*, p. 480.
18 TBD, 31.10.51, p. 159.
19 David Butler, *The British General Election of 1951* (Macmillan, 1952), p. 48.
20 HGD, 23.11.51, p. 307.
21 LPACR, p. 120.
22 HGD, 16.11.51, p. 291.
23 HGD, 16.11.51, p. 293.
24 HDD, 30.10.51, p. 567.
25 Williams, *Gaitskell*, pp. 146, 285.
26 Ibid., p. 288.
27 Maurice Bowra in W. Rodgers (ed.), *Hugh Gaitskell* (Thames & Hudson, 1964), p. 20.
28 *Daily Sketch*, 19 January 1963.
29 HGD, 30.1.48, p. 53.
30 Anne Deighton, 'Towards a "Western Strategy": The Making of British Policy Towards Germany, 1945–46', in Anne Deighton (ed.), *Britain and the First Cold War* (Macmillan, 1990), p. 67.
31 Ibid., p. 54.
32 Peter Hennessy, *Whitehall* (Fontana, 1990), p. 713.
33 Aneurin Bevan, House of Commons, 21 April 1951.
34 Special Feature: 'History, the Nation and the Schools', *History Workshop Journal*, Issue 29, Spring 1990, Introduction, Anna Davin, pp. 92–4.
35 Quotations are from *The Labour Party in Perspective*, (Gollancz, 1937), pp. 226–7; quoted in Dan Keohane, *Labour Party Defence Policy since 1945* (Leicester University Press, 1993), p. 1.
36 Campbell, *Bevan*, p. 267.
37 Mark Jenkins, *Bevanism, Labour's High Tide and the Democratic Mass Movement* (Spokesman Books, 1977), p. 115.
38 Christopher Mayhew, *Party Games* (Hutchinson, 1969), p. 42.
39 Figures quoted from David Butler and Gareth Butler, *British Political Facts 1900–1985* (Macmillan, 1986), p. 152.
40 Campbell, *Bevan*, p. 279.
41 Alan Warde, *Consensus and Beyond: The Development of Labour Party Strategy Since World War Two* (Manchester University Press, 1982), p. 1.
42 C. A. R. Crosland, *The Future of Socialism* (Cape, 1956), p. 45.
43 Ibid., p. 87.
44 I am grateful to Professor Peter Hennessy for giving me the source of this quote.
45 Eric Hobsbawm, 'Britain: A Comparative View', in Brian Brivati and Harriet Jones (eds), *What Difference Did the War Make?* (Pinter, 1993), pp. 22–3.
46 Michael Foot, *Aneurin Bevan* (Granada, 1975), p. 371.

47 Warde, *Consensus and Beyond*, p. 79, quoting Nye Bevan, *Democratic Values*, Fabian Tract 282, London 1950, p. 11.
48 Expanded on in 'The Transition of Capitalism' in Richard Crossman (ed.), *New Fabian Essays* (Turnstile Press, 1952).
49 Campbell, *Bevan*, p. 266. Patrick Seyd in *The Rise and Fall of the Labour Left* (Macmillan Education, 1987), p. 13.
50 Bevan, *Tribune*, 3 December 1954.
51 Gaitskell, *Tribune*, 24 June 1955.

Chapter 7: The Battle with the Bevanites 1951–1954

1 For instance, see who came for the dinner in January 1953 of the Leeds Jewish Representation Council. Leeds: 13, Gaitskell to Murray, 29 December 1953.
2 Leeds: 13, Gaitskell to Murray, 23 December 1953.
3 Leeds: 13, Gaitskell to Murray, 9 July 1957.
4 Denis Healey, *The Time of My Life* (Penguin, 1990), p. 141.
5 Ibid., p. 142.
6 Leeds: 13, Gaitskell to Murray, 8 January 1958.
7 Leeds: 13, Gaitskell to Murray, 2 April 1953.
8 Leeds: 13, Gaitskell to Gaitskell Murray, 22 May 1953.
9 Leeds: 18, 1953–1968, Secretary's Annual Reports, 1953.
10 Leeds: 18, 1953–1968, Secretary's Annual Reports, 1953.
11 Leeds: 13, Murray to Gaitskell, 25 July 1953.
12 Leeds: Murray to Gaitskell, 16 June 1953.
13 Leeds: 13, Gaitskell to Murray on 2 February 1953.
14 Leeds: 2/4 Minute books of the South Leeds constituency party, 1947–54.
15 Leeds: 13, Gaitskell to Murray, 13 July 1953.
16 Healey, *The Time of My Life*, p. 154.
17 Leeds: 13, Burton to Gaitskell, 1 November 1954.
18 Leeds: 13, Gaitskell to Murray, 8 January 1958.
19 Leeds: 13, Burns exchange of letters, July 1959.
20 Merlyn Rees in interview with author.
21 Philip Williams, *Hugh Gaitskell* (Cape, 1979), p. 309.
22 Barbara Castle in interview with author.
23 Leeds: 17, Hugh Gaitskell, 'A Note on Opposition in the Older Democracies',

a paper delivered at 'Representative Government and Public Liberties in the New States', an international seminar organised by the Congress for Cultural Freedom, Rhodes, Greece, 6–13 October 1958.
24 *Manchester Guardian*, 4 January, 1952.
25 Speech at Poole, 20 July 1952.
26 *Manchester Guardian*, 25 May 1995.
27 Mark Jenkins, *Bevanism, Labour's High Tide and the Democratic Mass Movement* (Spokesman Books, 1977), p. 13.
28 H. M. Drucker, *Doctrine and Ethos in the Labour Party*, George Allen & Unwin, 1979), p. 1.
29 Described by Drucker as manifestoism in Drucker 1979, pp. 91–4.
30 Hansard 5th Series Vol. 497 Col. 559–60.
31 Quoted in Jenkins, *Bevanism*, pp. 309–11.
32 Other members: Donald Bruce, George Craddock, F. E. Jones, Archie Manuel, Ellis Smith, John Timmons, Tudor Watkins, Edward Yates, Will Griffiths, George Roberts, Richard Acland, Marcus Lipton, Thomas Williams, Geoffrey Roberts, Cecil Poole, Julian Shaw, David Weitzman, Maurice Orbach, Julius Silverman, John Baird, C. R. Bence, Fenner Brockway, J. Carmichael, Ernest Fernyhough, Malcolm McMillan; John Rankin and Walter Marlow.
33 John Campbell, *Nye Bevan* (Hodder & Stoughton, 1994), pp. 284–5.
34 Ibid., pp. 303–4.
35 Ibid., p. 255, *see also* RCD, 21.1.52, p. 63 and 3.3.54, p. 290.
36 RCD, 21.1.52, p. 63.
37 RCD, 24.3.55, pp. 409–10.
38 Ibid.
39 See Geoffrey Wakeford, *The Great Labour Mirage: An Indictment of Socialism in Britain* (Hale, 1969), and Jonathan Schneer, *Labour's Conscience: The Labour Left 1945–1951* (Unwin Hyman, 1988).
40 RCD, 17.12.51, p. 53.
41 HGD, 21.3.52, p. 311.
42 HGD, 10.8.51, p. 272.
43 HGD, 21.3.52, p. 311.
44 Ibid., p. 313.
45 Michael Foot, *Aneurin Bevan* (Granada, 1975), p. 362.
46 *Manchester Guardian*, 10 March 1952.
47 RCD, 11.3.52, p. 93.
48 HGD, 21.3.52, p. 313 and RCD, 11.3.52, p. 93.
49 RCD, 11.3.52, p. 93.

50 Foot, *Bevan*, p. 363.
51 Quoted in *Guardian*, 4 January 1952.
52 HDD, 29.5.52, p. 588.
53 HDD, 2.5.52, pp. 585–6 and RCD, 29.4.52, pp. 102–3.
54 HGD, 12.11.54, pp. 348–9.
55 HDD, 1.7.52, pp. 592–7.
56 Campbell, *Bevan*, p. 272.
57 RCD, 26.9.52, p. 141 and Foot, *Bevan*, p. 376.
58 Foot, *Bevan*, p. 350.
59 LPACR, 1952, p. 127.
60 HDD, September, p. 598.
61 Foot, *Bevan*, p. 376.
62 HDD, September, p. 598.
63 HGD, 1952–4, generally, p. 331.
64 HDD, September, p. 598.
65 HDD, 14.9.50, p. 486.
66 L. Minkin, *The Labour Party Annual Conference* (Allen Lane, 1978), p. 243.
67 Ibid., p. 244.
68 Ibid., p. 245.
69 Quoted in Barbara Castle, *Fighting all the Way* (Macmillan, 1993), p. 206.
70 Williams, *Gaitskell*, p. 304.
71 Leeds: 13, Brenda to George Murray, 1 July 1952.
72 *Leeds Weekly Citizen*, 28 December 1951.
73 *Guardian*, 17 June 1952.
74 *Daily Worker*, 21 June 1952.
75 Note of a speech by the Rt Hon. Hugh Gaitskell CBE, MP at Stalybridge on Sunday 5 October 1952, in South Leeds Constituency Labour Party Archive.
76 Leeds: 13, Gaitskell to George Murray, 12 September 1952.
77 HGD, Document 9, p. 320.
78 Labour: GS/LS/67i.
79 RCD, 14.10.52, p. 157.
80 Labour: GS/LS/67i.
81 Mikardo in interview with author.
82 HGD, Document 10, p. 325.
83 Christopher Mayhew, *Party Games*, Hutchinson, 1969, p. 102.
84 See R. K. Alderman, 'Parliamentary Discipline in Opposition: The Parliamentary Labour Party 1951–1964', *Parliamentary Affairs*, Volume 21, 1968, pp. 124–35.
85 Transcript of Witness Seminar on CDS, held at the Institute of Contemporary British History, Lord Jay.
86 See R. H. S. Crossman (ed.), *New Fabian Essays* (Turnstile Press, 1952). This gives a good indication of the balance of the society.
87 D. Howell, *British Social Democracy* (Croom Helm, 1976), p. 234.
88 RCD, 27.9.52, pp. 144–5.
89 RCD, 4.12.51, pp. 47–8.
90 See Hugh Thomas, *John Strachey* (Eyre Methuen, 1973), p. 269; Foot, *Bevan*, p. 392; RCD, 29.1.53, pp. 196–7 and HGD, 12.11.54, p. 349.
91 Campbell, *Bevan*, p. 275.
92 HDD, 17.7.52, p. 593.
93 HDD, 29.10.53, p. 616.
94 Labour: NEC minute, 23 June 1954.
95 Foot, *Bevan*, p. 434.
96 Williams, *Gaitskell*, p. 328.
97 HGD, 2.4.55, p. 401.
98 Foot, *Bevan*, p. 435.
99 HGD, Summer and Autumn 1954, p. 335.

Chapter 8 Dirty Work, 1954–1955

1 TBD, 7.4.54, p. 179.
2 Labour: NEC, June 1955, 'The General Election 1955', Appendix IV, 'Notes on Labour Party Broadcasting and Television', by William Pickles.
3 Labour: NEC, Minutes EC8, 1953–54.
4 Labour: German rearmament, NEC, 24 February 1954, EC 7 1953–54.
5 *Observer*, 28 February 1954.
6 RCD, 21.4.54, p. 311.
7 Anthony Eden, *Full Circle* (Cassell, 1960), p. 95.
8 Michael Foot, *Aneurin Bevan* (Granada, 1975), p. 427.
9 HGD, Spring 1954, p. 327.
10 RCD, 21.4.54, p. 311.
11 Foot, *Bevan*, p. 428.
12 HGD, Spring 1954, p. 327.
13 HGD, Spring 1954, p. 329.
14 Ben Pimlott, *Harold Wilson* (HarperCollins, 1992), p. 185.
15 HGD, Spring 1954, p. 330.
16 Hugh Gaitskell, *In Defence of Politics*, The Foundation Oration delivered at Birkbeck College, 1954, p. 3.
17 *Economist*, 13 February 1954.
18 Gaitskell, *In Defence of Politics* p. 6.
19 Ibid. p. 13.
20 HGD, 12.11.54, p. 349.
21 HDD, 14.4.54, p. 624.
22 *The Times*, 31 September 1954.
23 RCD, 1.10.54, p. 351.
24 RCD, 1.10.54, p. 351.
25 Text and Deakin quote from Foot, *Bevan*, p. 447.
26 *News Chronicle*, 3 October 1954.
27 RCD, 21.4.54, p. 314.
28 RCD, 1.10.54, pp. 351–2.
29 Labour: GS/LS/10ii.
30 Labour: GS/LS/11ii.

31 Labour: Maurice Evans to Morgan Phillips, 19 June 1949, GS/LS/6.
32 There is a full and excellent account of the management of the Labour Party in Eric Shaw, *Discipline and Discord in the Labour Party* (Manchester University Press, 1988).
33 K. Morgan, *Labour in Power* (Oxford University Press, 1984), pp. 280–4.
34 Peter Hennessy, *Whitehall* (Fontana, 1990), p. 716.
35 Brian Cathcart, *Test of Greatness: Britain's Struggle for the Atom Bomb* (John Murray, 1994), p. 12.
36 Hennessy, *Whitehall*, p. 772.
37 Morgan, *Labour in Power*, p. 284.
38 Ibid., p. 280.
39 M. Dockrill, *British Defence Since 1975* (Basil Blackwell, 1988), p. 70.
40 Foot, *Bevan*, pp. 572–3.
41 Philip Williams, *Hugh Gaitskell* (Cape, 1979), p. 609.
42 *News of the World*, 26 September 1954.
43 HGD, 19.3.55, p. 365.
44 Labour: GS/LS/67ii.
45 Foot, *Bevan*, p. 460.
46 HGD, 19.3.55, p. 368.
47 HGD, 9.11.54, pp. 343–4.
48 L. Minkin, *The Labour Party Annual Conference* (Allen Lane, 1978), p. 91.
49 Foot, *Bevan*, p. 464.
50 RCD, 15.3.55, p. 400.
51 Foot, *Bevan*, p. 464.
52 HDD, 12.3.55, p. 649.
53 *Yorkshire Post*, 14 March 1955.
54 Williams, *Gaitskell*, p. 344.
55 HGD, 19.3.55, p. 371.
56 HDD, 15.3.55, p. 651.
57 Foot, *Bevan*, note p. 466.
58 HDD, 10.3.55, p. 648.
59 Foot, *Bevan*, p. 467.
60 HGD, Document 12, p. 375.
61 Foot, *Bevan*, p. 467.
62 Ibid., p. 467.
63 Dalton has this as 'We should have to consider our position', HDD, p. 653.
64 HGD, 19.3.55, p. 383.
65 L. D. S. Hunter, *The Road to Brighton Pier* (Arthur Barker, 1959), p. 104.
66 HGD, 19.3.55, p. 385.
67 Williams, *Gaitskell*, p. 342.
68 HGD, 19.3.55, p. 384.
69 HGD, 19.3.55, p. 385.
70 Williams, *Gaitskell*, p. 343.
71 HGD, 25.3.55, p. 388 note.
72 HGD, 25.3.55, p. 389.
73 Labour: GS/LS/64.
74 RCD, 31.3.55, p. 413.
75 HGD, 2.4.55, p. 398.
76 HGD, Document 13, pp. 394–5.
77 HGD, 2.4.55, p. 401.
78 See Austin Mitchell, *Four Years in the Death of the Labour Party* (Methuen, 1983).
79 See Michael Leapman, *Kinnock* (Unwin Hyman, 1987), pp. 104–5.

Chapter 9   The Top of Labour's Greasy Pole, 1955

1 Anthony Seldon, *Churchill's Indian Summer* (Hodder & Stoughton, 1981), pp. 441–3.
2 Michael Pinto-Duschinsky, *British Political Finance 1830–1980* (American Enterprise Institute, 1981), pp. 155–78.
3 HGD, 9.11.54, p. 344.
4 Seldon, *Churchill's Indian Summer*, p. 177.
5 *Observer*, 8 May 1955.
6 *New Statesman*, 23 April 1955.
7 *Listener*, 28 April 1955.
8 Labour: The General Election 1955, NEC/June 1955, p. 5.
9 RCD, 26.4.55, p. 419.
10 Leslie Hunter, *The Road to Brighton Pier* (Arthur Barker, 1959), p. 112.
11 Labour: The General Election of 1955, NEC, June 1955, p. 6.
12 David Butler, *The British General Election of 1955* (Macmillan, 1955), p. 91.
13 *Herald*, 17 May 1955.
14 *Telegraph*, 19 May 1955 and *Keightly News*, 21 May 1955.
15 *Daily Worker*, 20 May 1955.
16 *Daily Sketch*, 23 May 1955.
17 *Telegraph*, 23 May 1955.
18 *The Times*, 3 June 1955.
19 R. J. Jackson, *Rebels and Whips: An Analysis of Dissention, Discipline and Cohesion – British Political Parties* (Macmillan, 1969), p. 138 and Geoffrey McDermott, *Leader Lost* (Frewin, 1972), pp. 88–94.
20 Labour: NEC report, p. 6.
21 HDD, 26.5.55, p. 671.
22 Philip Williams, *Hugh Gaitskell* (Cape, 1979), pp. 353–4.
23 RCD, 3.5.55, p. 420.
24 TBD, June 1955, p. 182.
25 K. Harris, *Attlee* (Weidenfeld & Nicolson, 1982), p. 535.
26 Ben Pimlott, *Hugh Dalton* (Cape, 1985), p. 622.
27 Quoted in Pimlott, *Dalton*, p. 622.
28 *News Chronicle*, 19 May 1955.
29 Roy Jenkins, *Life at the Centre* (Macmillan, 1991), p. 111.

30 RCD, 15.10.55, p. 447.
31 Michael Foot, *Aneurin Bevan, Vol. II* (Granada, 1975), p. 478.
32 RCD, 15.10.55, p. 448.
33 Williams, *Gaitskell*, p. 356.
34 LPACR, p. 175.
35 Hunter, *Brighton Pier*, pp. 142–3.
36 RCD, 15.10.55, p. 449.
37 *Yorkshire Post*, 27 October 1955.
38 House of Commons Debates, 1955, cols 390–408.
39 RCD 2.12.55, p. 453.
40 Jenkins, *Life at the Centre*, p. 113 and Williams, *Gaitskell*, p. 363.
41 Harris, *Attlee*, p. 536.
42 Ibid., p. 539.
43 Bernard Donoughue and George Jones in *Herbert Morrison: Portrait of a Politician* (Weidenfeld & Nicolson, 1973), p. 538, contrast Gaitskell's success in the House of Commons with Morrison's failure. In the main their account of the leadership election agrees with Gaitskell's biographer, Williams, pp. 537–41, and is reinforced by a contemporary observer, Leslie Hunter, in *The Road to Brighton Pier* (Arthur Barker, 1959), pp. 158–9, pp. 162–4 and pp. 170–1.
44 *New Statesman*, 30 April 1955.
45 PGWD, 11.12.55, pp. 226–7.
46 Harris, *Attlee*, p. 543.
47 Pimlott, *Dalton*, p. 601.
48 Quoted in Pimlott, *Dalton*, entry for end of October 1955, p. 674.
49 Douglas Jay, *Change and Fortune* (Hutchinson, 1980), p. 245.
50 Harris, *Attlee*, p. 541.
51 Jay, *Change and Fortune*, p. 245 and Williams, *Gaitskell*, p. 361.
52 *Observer*, 24 February 1954.
53 HDD, 3.11.55, p. 676.
54 PGWD, 16.10.55, p. 226.
55 This was in part due to Hugh Dalton's 'Operation Avalanche'. Dalton wrote to the *Daily Mirror* encouraging his older colleagues to stand down, 'I myself have decided not to be a candidate for our shadow cabinet in the new Parliament and I hope that a number of my fellow veterans will decide likewise,' quoted in Ben Pimlott, *Hugh Dalton* (Jonathan Cape, 1985), p. 622.
56 HDD, 2.2.56, p. 677.
57 Williams, *Gaitskell*, p. 369.
58 HG Papers, P99, Wyatt to Gaitskell, 13.10.55, quoted in Williams, *Gaitskell*, p. 369.
59 HG Papers: RCD to HG, Thursday, reply

Boxing Day: filed RCD, quoted in Williams, *Gaitskell*, p. 370.
60 Foot, *Bevan*, pp. 494–5.
61 Williams, *Gaitskell*, p. 371.
62 Ibid., p. 368.

Chapter 10 Hinterlands

1 Lord Harewood quoted in Robert Hewison, *Culture and Consensus, England, art and politics since 1940* (Methuen, 1995), p. 86.
2 Ibid., pp. 86–7.
3 C. Booker, *The Neophiliacs* (Collins, 1969), p. 40.
4 Ibid., pp. 42–32.
5 *Manchester Guardian*, 24 January 1956.
6 *Manchester Guardian*, 24 January 1956; *Daily Telegraph*, 28 January 1956 and *Sunday Times*, 12 February 1956.
7 *Star*, 24 January 1956.
8 *Manchester Guardian*, 4 January 1956.
9 Denis Healey, *The Time of My Life* (Penguin, 1990), p. 564.
10 Barbara Castle, *Fighting all the Way* (Macmillan, 1993), p. 192.
11 Julia McNeal in interview with author.
12 Philip Williams, *Hugh Gaitskell* (Cape, 1979), p. 373.
13 Roy Jenkins, *The Times*, 18 January 1973.
14 Williams, *Gaitskell*, p. 37.
15 *Daily Sketch*, 21 July 1961.
16 Booker, *The Neophiliacs*, p. 37.
17 HGD, 28.2.56, p. 454.
18 John Vaizey, *In Breach of Promise* (Weidenfeld & Nicolson, 1983), p. 29.
19 Leeds: HG to Murray, 22 June 1955.
20 Susan Crosland, *Tony Crosland* (Cape, 1982), p. 85.
21 *Yorkshire Post*, 12 December 1955.
22 *Guardian Journal* (Nottingham), 9 June 1958.
23 *Express*, 20 June 1962.
24 *Daily Sketch*, 19 January 1963.
25 *Daily Express*, 8 May 1961.
26 RCD, 21.11.56, p. 550.
27 *Sunday Express*, 23 October 1960.
28 *Sunday Pictorial*, 20 January 1963.
29 *Daily Mail*, 23 October 1951.
30 *Guardian Journal* (Nottingham), 9 June 1958.
31 Ibid.
32 *Yorkshire Evening Post*, 6 April 1956.
33 *Daily Mail*, 6 February 1961.
34 HGD, 4.5.51, pp. 250–1.
35 *Sunday Express*, 23 October 1961.
36 Julia McNeal in interview with author.
37 *Daily Mail*, 23 October 1951.

38 Vaizey, *In Breach of Promise*, p. 29.
39 HDD, Easter Recess April 1958, pp. 688–9.
40 Roy Jenkins, *A Life at the Centre* (Macmillan, 1991), pp. 83, 91.
41 Susan Crosland, *Tony Crosland*, p. 65.
42 Ibid., p. 88.
43 Jenkins, *A Life at the Centre*, p. 103.
44 Tim Cook in interview with author.
45 Williams, *Gaitskell*, p. 376.
46 Ibid., p. 376.
47 HGD, for instance, 4.5.51, p. 250 and 4.6.56, pp. 532–3.
48 Barbara Castle in interview with author.
49 For instance TBD, 7.4.54 and David Ennals in interview with author.
50 Douglas Sutherland, *Portrait of a Decade: London Life 1945–55* (Harrap, 1988), p. 217.
51 Williams, *Gaitskell*, p. 378.
52 See John Pearson, *The Life of Ian Fleming: Creator of James Bond* (Coronet Books, 1966) and Andrew Lycett, *Ian Fleming* (Weidenfeld & Nicolson, 1995).
53 Mark Amory (ed.), *The Letters of Ann Fleming* (Collins Harvill, 1985), pp. 42–3.
54 Lycett, *Fleming*, p. 296.
55 Anne Chisholm and Michael Davie, *Beaverbrook: A Life* (Hutchinson, 1992), pp. 517–18.
56 Susan Crosland, *Tony Crosland*, 1983, pp. 107–8.
57 Amory (ed.), *The Letters of Ann Fleming*, p. 210.
58 Ben Pimlott, 'The Future of Political Biography', in *Frustrate Their Knavish Tricks*, (HarperCollins, 1994), p. 156.
59 Ibid., p. 96.
60 Pearson, *Fleming*, p. 410.
61 Amory (ed.), *Letters of Ann Fleming*, 'To Evelyn Waugh', 4 April 1956, pp. 181–2.
62 Ibid. to Evelyn Waugh, Saturday 24 November 1956, p. 186.
63 Booker, *The Neophiliacs*, p. 117.

Chapter 11   Suez, 1956–1957

1 Anthony Eden, *Full Circle* (Cassell, 1960), p. 347.
2 Anthony Nutting, *No End of a Lesson* (Constable, 1967), p. 18.
3 Churchill College Archive: 'The day before yesterday', SELO 6/202: David Elstein interviewing Anthony Nutting, 207, take 1, p. 12.
4 PRO: CAB 128/30, Minute of Cabinet, 21 March 1956, p. 5.
5 D. R. Thorpe, *Selwyn Lloyd* (Jonathan Cape, 1989), p. 201.
6 HGD, 20.4.56, p. 493.
7 Thorpe, *Lloyd*, p. 201.
8 'The Record on Suez', *Manchester Guardian*, November 1956, p. 2; Roy Fullick and Geoffrey Powell, *Suez: The Double War* (Leo Cooper, 1979), pp. 2–11 and Thorpe, *Lloyd*, pp. 213–14.
9 Nutting, *No End of a Lesson*, p. 44.
10 Thorpe, *Lloyd*, p. 214.
11 Speech by President Nasser at Alexandria announcing the nationalisation of the Suez Canal Company, 26 July 1956.
12 Anthony Nutting, *Nasser* (Constable, 1972), p. 145.
13 HGD, 20.7.56, pp. 552–3.
14 Tony Shaw, 'Eden and the BBC during the Suez Crisis: A Myth Re-examined', *Twentieth Century British History*, Volume 6, Number 3, 1995, p. 323.
15 Fullick and Powell, *Suez*, p. 13.
16 Ibid., p. 13.
17 Eden, *Full Circle*, p. 426.
18 PRO: CAB 128/30 pt II, 27 July 1956.
19 Ibid.
20 Eden, *Full Circle*, p. 427.
21 Ibid.
22 House of Commons Debates, vol. 557, cols 777–80.
23 Nutting, *No End of a Lesson*, pp. 26, 32, 107, 133, 158, 159, 165.
24 Eden, *Full Circle*, p. 428.
25 FRUS, 1955–1957, pp. 60–61.
26 PRO: Prem 11/1098 Eisenhower to Eden. 31 July 1956.
27 The Americans estimated that the British would take six weeks to be ready. FRUS, 1955–1957, Memorandum of Conference with President, White House, 31 July 1956, 9.45 a.m., p. 63.
28 HGD, 30.7.56, p. 559.
29 Eden, *Full Circle*, p. 434.
30 HGD, 30.7.56, p. 560.
31 FRUS, 1955–1957, Telegram from the Department of State to the Secretary of State, at London, 1 August 1956, p. 100.
32 HGD, 30.7.56, p. 558.
33 HGD, 2/3.8.56, p. 567.
34 HGD, 2/3.8.56, p. 568.
35 Anthony Gorst, ICBH Oral History Project on Suez, interview with Douglas Jay.
36 House of Commons debates, Volume 557, cols 1609–17.
37 Philip Williams, *Hugh Gaitskell* (Cape, 1979), p. 423.

38 FRUS, 1955–1957, message from the Secretary of State to the President, 2 August 1956, pp. 110–11.
39 HGD, Document No. 17, pp. 570–1.
40 Ibid., p. 572.
41 Gorst interview with Jay.
42 HGD, Document 17, p. 574.
43 Ibid., p. 575.
44 Gorst interview with Jay.
45 HGD, 22.8.56, p. 581.
46 PRO; CAB 128/30 part II, Minutes of Cabinet Meeting, 14 August 1956.
47 Eden, *Full Circle*, p. 445.
48 FRUS, 1955–1957, Message from Secretary of State to the President, 19 August 1956, pp. 231–2.
49 FRUS, 1955–1957, Memorandum of a conversation at the Ambassador's residence, London, 19 August 1956, pp. 233–4.
50 Nutting, *Nasser*, pp. 54–5.
51 FRUS, 1955–1957, Memorandum of a conversation between Secretary of State Dulles and Prime Minister Eden, 10 Downing Street, 24 August 1956, p. 285.
52 *Reynolds News*, 26 August 1956.
53 HGD, Document 18, pp. 588–90.
54 *Observer*, 11 November 1956.
55 FRUS, 1955–1957, Memorandum by the Secretary of State, 2 September 1956, pp. 351–2; Appendix to Watch Committee Report No. 318, 5 September 1956, pp. 378–80; Secretary Dulles' Proposal for a Suez Canal Users' Association, 9–18 September 1956, pp. 448–55.
56 But not the British, see Tony Shaw, 'Government Manipulation of the Press during the 1956 Suez crisis', *Contemporary Record*, Volume 8, Number 2, 1994.
57 Nutting, *No End of a Lesson*, p. 62.
58 Eden, *Full Circle*, p. 482.
59 House of Commons Debates, vol. 558, col. 297.
60 Quoted in Williams, *Gaitskell*, p. 429.
61 RCD, 14.9.56, p. 513.
62 FRUS, 1955–1957, summary of developments in Suez situation, 11 September 1956, pp. 474–5.
63 Nutting, *No End of a Lesson*, p. 77.
64 Eden, *Full Circle*, p. 508.
65 PRO; CAB 128/30 pt II, Cabinet Meeting, 3 October 1956.
66 Nutting, *No End of a Lesson*, p. 77.
67 Keith Kyle, *Suez* (Weidenfeld & Nicolson, 1991), pp. 565–6.
68 Churchill College: SELO 6/202, Suez, meetings at Sèvres, 22–25 October, narrative, Donald Logan, 24 October 1986, p. 2.
69 FRUS, 1955–1957, Special Watch Report of the Intelligence Advisory Committee, 28 October 1956, pp. 798–800.
70 FRUS, 1955–1957, Telegram from the Department of State to the Embassy in France, 29 October 1956, pp. 815–16.
71 FRUS, 1955–1957, Memorandum of a conference with the President, Washington, 30 October 1956, pp. 873–4.
72 TCB, 31.10.56, p. 193.
73 Labour: GS/Suez/65.
74 Labour: GS/Suez/71.
75 Labour: e.g. GS/Suez/1117.
76 Labour: GS/Suez/56.
77 TBD, 3.1.56, p. 199–200.
78 RCD, 7.11.56, p. 539 and HDD, Document No. 20, pp. 619–22.
79 *New Statesman*, 10 November 1956.
80 Michael Foot, *Aneurin Bevan* (Granada, 1975), pp. 516–17.
81 Brian McCauley, 'Hungary and Suez, 1956: The Limits of Soviet and American Power', *Journal of Contemporary History*, Volume 6, 1981, pp. 777–800.
82 TBD, 4.1.56, p. 201.
83 RCD, 7.11.56, pp. 541–2.
84 John Ramsden, *The Age of Churchill & Eden 1940–1957* (Longman, 1995), pp, 310–13.
85 Lewis Johnman, 'Defending the Pound', in A. Gorst, L. Johnman and S. Lucas (eds.), *Post-war Britain 1945–64.* (Pinter, 1989), p. 174.
86 PRO: CAB 128/30 pt II, Cabinet Meeting, 6 November 1956.
87 Johnman, 'Defending the Pound', p. 174.
88 PRO: CAB 128/30 pt II, Cabinet Meeting, 28 November 1956.
89 Johnman, 'Defending the Pound', p. 179. For the military side, see Anthony Gorst and W. Scott Lucas, 'Suez 1956: Strategy and the Diplomatic Processes', *Journal of Strategic Studies*, December 1988.
90 Johnman, 'Defending the Pound', p. 179.

Chapter 12   The Future of Socialism

1 FRUS, 1955–57, Volume XVI, pp. 1162–229.
2 John Pearson, *The Life of Ian Fleming* (Coronet Books, 1966), p. 391 and Andrew Lycett, *Ian Fleming* (Weidenfeld & Nicolson, 1995), pp. 302–3.
3 J. Ramsden, *The Age of Churchill and Eden* (Longman, 1995), p. 316.

4 D. R. Thorpe, *Selwyn Lloyd* (Cape, 1989), p. 256.
5 House of Commons Debates, Volume 559, 3 December 1956, col. 877.
6 House of Commons Debates, Volume 559, 5 December 1956, cols 1268–83.
7 *Daily Telegraph*, 1 January 1957.
8 Ramsden, *Churchill and Eden*, p. 324.
9 Quoted in Ramsden, *Churchill and Eden*, p. 326.
10 John Turner, *Macmillan* (Longman, 1994), p. 270.
11 *Daily Mail*, 19 January 1957.
12 See Leopold Labedz, *Revisionism*, Library of International Studies (George Allen & Unwin, London 1962).
13 Hugh Gaitskell, *Recent Developments in British Socialist Thinking* (Co-operative Union, 1956), p. 2.
14 Ibid., pp. 3–4.
15 Ibid., pp. 5–6.
16 Ibid., p. 11.
17 Ibid., p. 13.
18 Ibid., p. 14.
19 Ibid., p. 25.
20 Ibid., p. 24.
21 Ibid., p. 30.
22 Hugh Gaitskell, 'The Economic Aims of the Labour Party', *Political Quarterly*, 26 (1956), pp. 5–18.
23 Gaitskell, *Economic Aims*, p. 16.
24 C. A. R. Crosland, *The Future of Socialism* (Cape, 1956), p. 105.
25 Gaitskell, 'Recent Developments', p. 8.
26 Ralph Miliband, *The State in Capitalist Society* (Quartet Books, 1969), p. 11.
27 Gaitskell, *Recent Developments*, p. 40.
28 Crosland, *Future of Socialism*, pp. 99–101.
29 Hugh Gaitskell, 'Foreword' in Evan Durbin, *The Politics of Democratic Socialism, An Essay on Social Policy* (Routledge & Kegan Paul, 5th Impression, 1957), p. 9 – quoted in David Marquand, *The Progressive Dilemma* (Heinemann, 1991), pp. 134–5 – Professor Marquand also goes on to make the connection with 'positivist rationalism'.
30 Bryan Magee, *Popper* (Fontana Press, 1982), pp. 76–7.
31 Susan Crosland, *Tony Crosland* (Cape, 1982), p. 88.
32 H. G. Nicholas, *The General Election of 1950* (Frank Cass, 1968), pp. 93–4.
33 Philip Williams, 'Changing Styles of Labour's Leadership', in Dennis Kavanagh (ed.), *The Politics of the Labour Party* (George Allen & Unwin, 1982), p. 57.
34 NEC Minutes, 25 January 1955, Study Group on Equality, Draft Policy Statement, Re. 78/June as revised.
35 Labour: Study Group on Equality, Draft Policy Statement, Re. 78, June 1956 (revised), pp. 13–14.
36 Labour: Study Group on Equality, Draft Policy Statement, Re. 78, June 1956 (revised), p. 15.
37 Peter Shore, *Leading the Left* (Weidenfeld & Nicolson, 1993), p. 66.
38 J. Campbell, *Nye Bevan and the Mirage of British Socialism* (Weidenfeld & Nicolson, 1989), p. 329.
39 Philip Williams, *Hugh Gaitskell* (Cape, 1979), p. 448.
40 RCD, 4.10.57.
41 *New Left Review*, Volume 1, Number 1, 1960, p. 18.
42 Williams, *Gaitskell*, p. 449 and n46 p. 890.

Chapter 13   Chasing Supermac, 1957–1959

1 HGD, 9.1.56, p. 409.
2 HGD, 9.1.56, p. 409.
3 Quoted in J. Campbell, *Nye Bevan and the Mirage of British Socialism* (Weidenfeld & Nicolson, 1989), p. 328.
4 HGD, 9.1.56, p. 410.
5 HGD, 6.2.56, pp. 442–3.
6 Private information.
7 HGD, Document No. 16, pp. 482–3.
8 HGD, Document 16, p. 488.
9 HGD, Document 16, p. 491.
10 Edward Crankshaw (ed.), *Khrushchev Remembers* (Sphere Books, London 1971), p. 374.
11 HGD, 20.4.56, p. 497.
12 Ibid.
13 HGD, 20.4.56, p. 500.
14 HGD, 22.4.56, p. 504.
15 HGD, 23.4.56, p. 507.
16 Crankshaw, *Khrushchev*, p. 375.
17 HGD, 23.4.56, p. 507.
18 George Brown, *In My Way* (Victor Gollancz, 1972), p. 72 and HGD, 23.4.56, p. 507.
19 RCD, 6.11.57, p. 624.
20 Brown, *In My Way*, p. 72, though Gaitskell thought he said, 'May God forgive him' meaning Stalin, HGD, 23.4.56, p. 508.
21 Brown, *In My Way*, p. 73.
22 Michael Foot, *Aneurin Bevan* (Granada, 1975), p. 503.
23 HGD, 23.4.56, p. 509.
24 Foot, *Bevan*, p. 502.
25 HGD, 23.4.56, p. 513.

26 Denis Healey in interview with author.
27 Hugh Gaitskell, *The Challenge of Co-existence* (Methuen, 1956), pp. 13–27.
28 Ibid., p. 37.
29 Ibid., p. 41.
30 Labour: Covering letter to comrade Gaitskell, main text to the Executive Committee of the Labour Party of Great Britain, 11 October 1957 from N. Khrushchev, First Secretary of the CC CPSU and the Central Committee of the Communist Party of the Soviet Union.
31 Labour: NEC Minutes, 23.10.57. MP to Khrushchev. 23 October 1957.
32 Kenneth Morgan, 'Hugh Gaitskell and International Affairs', *Contemporary Record*, Volume 7, Number 2, Autumn 1993, p. 318.
33 This issue is fully discussed in Tudor Jones, 'Revisionism in the Labour Party', *Contemporary Record*, Volume 5, Number 3, 1992.
34 RCD, 4.10.57, p. 615.
35 Leeds: 13, Murray to Gaitskell, 7 October 1957 and Gaitskell to Murray, 11 October 1957.
36 Campbell, *Nye Bevan*, pp. 327–40.
37 For example RCD, 25.3.59, p. 743.
38 They were also quieter in terms of revolts inside the Labour Party. There were 15 revolts recorded in the House of Commons between 1951–1955 as against 9 in the 1955–1959 Parliament. Recorded in R. J. Jackson, *Rebels and Whips* (Macmillan, 1968), p. 114 and p. 152.
39 Quoted in Eric Shaw, *Discipline and Discord in the Labour Party* (Manchester University Press), p. 314, n29.
40 Geoffrey Goodman, *The Awkward Warrior, Frank Cousins, His Life and Times* (Davis-Poynter, 1979), pp. 177–91.
41 David Butler, *The British General Election of 1959* (Macmillan, 1960), p. 17.
42 Ibid. p. 21 and p. 28.
43 Labour: NEC Minutes, Labour Party Press and Publicity Needs, Campaign Committee, 10 March 1959.
44 RCD, 17.7.59, p. 767.
45 Williams, *Gaitskell*, p. 504.
46 Labour: General Election of 1959, Report of the Election Sub-Committee, NEC, 28 October 1959.
47 RCD, 13.8.59, p. 770.
48 Quoted in Williams, *Gaitskell*, p. 519.
49 Foot, *Bevan*, p. 620.
50 Williams, *Gaitskell*, p. 521.
51 Private information.
52 Foot, *Bevan*, p. 620.
53 Williams, *Gaitskell*, p. 521.
54 TUC Annual Report, 1959, p. 460.
55 RCD, 15.9.59, p. 777.
56 Ibid. p. 778.
57 RCD, 22.9.59, p. 780.
58 TBD, 22.9.59, p. 313.
59 RCD, 22.9.59, p. 779.
60 Leeds: 13, Gaitskell to Murray 11 September 1959.
61 Labour: General Election 1959, Report by the Secretary, p. 59.
62 RCD, 24.9.59, p. 780.
63 *Sunday Dispatch*, 20 September 1959.
64 Ben Pimlott, *Harold Wilson* (Harper-Collins, 1992), p. 222.
65 RCD, 30.9.59, pp. 781–2.
66 Labour: Report of the Election Sub-Committee, General Election 1959, NEC 28 October 1959, p. 3.
67 Harold Macmillan, *Pointing the Way, 1959–1961* (Macmillan, 1972), p. 11.
68 Macmillan, *Pointing the Way*, p. 11.
69 Labour: Campaign Report, p. 3.
70 *Eastbourne Evening Argus*, 29 May 1959.
71 RCD, 5.10.59, p. 785.
72 HDD, 8.10.59, p. 693.
73 Leeds: Frank Murray Annual reports on Gaitskell, South Leeds, CLP Papers, 18, 1953–1968, Secretary's Annual Reports.
74 Labour: Statement issued by Hugh Gaitskell, 9 October 1959, Press Office, Transport House.

Chapter 14   Clause 4: 1959–1960

1 RCD, 19.10.59, p. 788.
2 HDD, 9.10.59, p. 694.
3 TBD, 10.10.59, p. 317.
4 Roy Jenkins, *A Life at the Centre* (Macmillan, 1991), p. 129.
5 Hugh Dalton, *High Tide and After* (Muller, 1962), p. 467. The account in his diary is specific: Ben Pimlott (ed.), *The Political Diary of Hugh Dalton* (Cape, 1986), entry for 11 October 1959, p. 694, states that the meeting took place on the Sunday. Susan Crosland, *Tony Crosland* (Cape, 1982), p. 92, and Philip Williams, *Hugh Gaitskell: A Political Biography* (Cape, 1979), p. 538, call it a farewell dinner for Dalton; Lord Jenkins and Lord Jay in interview with author deny it was a dinner for Dalton; Ben Pimlott (ed.), *Hugh Dalton* (Macmillan, 1985), p. 633, mentioned the meeting but not as a dinner for Dalton. In fact it was unlikely that a dinner for Dalton would have been held so long after he actually gave up his

seat for Jim Boyden, and Dalton makes no mention of it.

6 RCD, 19.10.59, p. 788.

7 The sources for the reconstruction of the post-mortem weekend are: Pimlott, *Dalton*, p. 633 (who does not mention Harris); Williams, *Gaitskell*, p. 538, and Pimlott (ed.), *Dalton*, entry for 11 October 1959, p. 694 (who do); Crossman 1981, entry for Monday 19 October 1959, p. 788; Foot, *Bevan*, p. 628, mentions Gaitskell's visit to Bevan, but does not mention the invitation to Frognal Gardens; Lord Jay in interview with author.

8 Michael Foot, *Aneurin Bevan* (Granada, 1975), pp. 630–2.

9 Susan Crosland, *Tony Crosland* (Cape, 1982), p. 92.

10 Lord Jay in interview with author.

11 HDD, 11.10.59, pp. 695–6.

12 Lord Jenkins, interview with author.

13 *Reynolds News*, 18 October 1959.

14 Ivan Yates, *Reynolds News*, 18 October 1959.

15 RCD, 19.10.59, p. 789.

16 This account of the *Forward* article incident is drawn from Lord Jay, interview with author, and Lord Jay, *Change and Fortune* (Hutchinson, 1980), pp. 271–5.

17 *Observer*, 18 October 1959, and *Sunday Times*, 18 October 1959, p. 10.

18 *Sunday People*, 11 October 1959, front page: 'Is it a Lib–Lab Deal?'

19 *Forward*, 16 October 1959.

20 RCD, 19.10.59, p. 789.

21 Ibid., p. 790.

22 *Reynolds News*, 25 October 1959.

23 Jenkins, *Life at the Centre*, p. 131.

24 Ian Mikardo, interview with author; RCD, 21.10.59, pp. 793–4, and entry for 9.12.59, p. 804; Ben Pimlott, *Harold Wilson* (HarperCollins, 1992), pp. 226–7.

25 RCD, 21.10.59, p. 794. Crossman does not record who denounced Jay and Jenkins.

26 Pimlott, *Wilson*, p. 226.

27 *Socialist Commentary*, May–July 1960.

28 Mark Abrams in interview with author.

29 Subsequent quotations are from Mark Abrams, *Socialist Commentary*, May 1960 –July 1960.

30 David Butler, *The British General Election of 1959* (Macmillan, 1960), p. 17 and pp. 241–55, especially p. 254 for the non-Conservative Party campaign against nationalisation.

31 Labour: Report of Election Sub-

Committee, General Election 1959, NEC 29 October 1959, p. 8.

32 Labour: General Election 1959, Report by the Secretary, p. 43.

33 Eric Shaw, *Discipline and Discord in the Labour Party* (Manchester University Press, 1988), p. 81.

34 CDS Papers: Origins File.

35 Lord Jay in interview with author and D. Jay, *Change and Fortune* (Hutchinson, 1980), p. 277. For Pannell see Williams, *Gaitskell*, p. 544 and quote is from Williams, *Gaitskell*, p. 550.

36 RCD, 19.12.59, p. 804.

37 Quoted in Barbara Castle, *Fighting all the Way* (Macmillan, 1993), p. 317.

38 LPACR 1959, p. 111.

39 The report of the conference is in LPACR 1959, quotations in order of appearance in the text are from pp. 111–12, 119–20, 117–18, 120–1.

40 RCD, 9.12.59, p. 803.

41 LPACR 1959, p. 114, Mr K. Brown, Bury and Radcliffe constituency Labour party.

42 *Observer*, 29 November 1959; Harold Hutchinson, in *Daily Herald*, 30 November 1959; Ivan Yates and Tom Driberg, in *Reynolds News*, 29 November 1959.

43 LPACR 1959, p. 151.

44 *A Design for a New Socialist Platform*, Social Democratic Party of Germany, August 1958.

45 *The National Programme of the Co-operative Commonwealth Federation*, adopted by the Canadian National Countil in January 1957.

46 Principles and Purposes adopted by the Congress of the Norwegian Labour Party, 1959.

47 RCD, 25.11.59, pp. 802 and 804 and Williams, *Gaitskell*, pp. 558 and 560.

48 Mikardo in interview with author.

49 Mark Amory (ed.) *The Letters of Ann Fleming* (CollinsHarvill, 1985), p. 250.

50 Ian Fleming to Evelyn Waugh, 26 January 1960, Goldeneye, Jamaica.

51 Quoted in Lycett, p. 363.

52 *Sunday Express*, 17 January 1960 and *Daily Express*, 19 January 1960.

53 Campbell, *Nye Bevan*, p. 368.

54 Leeds: 13, Murray to Gaitskell, 16 February 1960.

55 Leeds: 13, Gaitskell to Murray, 18 February 1960.

56 *Tribune*, 19 February 1960, front page; *Spectator*, 15 February 1960; *The Times*, 13 February 1960.

57 Labour: GS/CMR/57i–iii.
58 CDS: Rodgers, 'History of the CDS'.
59 Labour: Memorandum from Morgan Phillips to Hugh Gaitskell, The Parliamentary Labour Party and the Constitution, GS/CMR/40.
60 NEC Minutes for 16 March 1960, section number 85, pp. 21–2.

Chapter 15   Ban the Bomb, 1960

1 CDS Witness Seminar Transcript, Mayhew, ICB.
2 Philip Williams, *Hugh Gaitskell: A Political Biography* (Cape, 1979), p. 587.
3 PGWD, pp. 1–3.
4 Jay in CDS questionnaire, Taverne in CDS questionnaire, Marquand in interview with author and Rodgers in interview with author.
5 Marquand and Donoughue in interview with author, and Witness Seminar Transcript.
6 Williams, *Gaitskell*, p. 694.
7 CDS Witness Seminar Transcript, Rodgers, ICBH.
8 NEC Summary Report of International Committee meeting, 6 March 1958.
9 CDS Witness Seminar Transcript, Mayhew, ICBH.
10 RCD, 20 May 1960, pp. 846–8; Williams, *Gaitskell*, pp. 583–91; Minkin, *Labour Party Conferences* (Allen Lane, 1978), p. 107.
11 *Defence: Outline of Future Policy* (HMSO, April 1957), Cmnd 124.
12 Michael Dockrill, *British Defence since 1945* (Basil Blackwell, 1988), pp. 65–81.
13 Kenneth Morgan, *Labour in Power* (Oxford University Press, 1984), pp. 280–4.
14 Peter Hennessy, *Whitehall* (Fontana, 1990), p. 716.
15 Ibid., p. 772.
16 Morgan, *Labour in Power*, p. 284.
17 Dockrill, *British Defence Policy Since 1945*, p. 70.
18 Foot, *Aneurin Bevan, Volume 2, 1945–1960*, pp. 572–3.
19 Williams, *Gaitskell*, p. 609.
20 For example *NATO or Neutrality*, a Young Fabian Publication (May 1961), makes the case for a neutral Britain.
21 F. W. S. Craig (ed.), *British General Election Manifestos, 1918–1979* (Political Reference Publications, 1982), pp. 131–48 and pp. 248–71.
22 LPACR 1957, p. 163.
23 Craig, *British General Election Manifestos*, p. 136.
24 LPACR 1958, p. 178.
25 L. Minkin, *The Labour Party Annual Conference* (Allen Lane, 1978), p. 3.
26 Ibid., pp. 177–9.
27 Ibid., p. 96. The TGWU resolution of 1958 represented a break with the official policy but not a mandate for full unilateralism.
28 Keith Hindell and Philip Williams, 'Scarborough and Blackpool: An Analysis of Some Votes at the Labour Party Conferences of 1960 and 1961', in *Political Quarterly*, Volume 33, Number 3, July–September 1962, p. 309.
29 CDS Papers: 'Conference must decide' leaflet issued by Victory for Socialism.
30 LPACR 1960, p. 201.
31 House of Commons, Motions and Questions and Orders of the Day 1959–1960, January and February, No. 58, 17 February 1960, p. 1894a; Hansard Fifth Series, Volume 619, 1 March 1960, cols 1158–1167.
32 CDS Witness Seminar Transcript, Lord Jay, Denis Healey in letter to author and Williams, *Gaitskell*, p. 557, ICBH.
33 Willie Thompson, Letter to author.
34 Hansard Fifth Series, Volume 618, 1 March 1960, cols 1144.
35 John Marullus, *Tribune*, 29 April 1960, 'The invisible leader'.
36 Churchill College Archive: Noel-Baker Papers: Correspondence 1959–1964, NBKR, 2/124, Noel-Baker to Meade, 7 January 1961.
37 Williams, *Gaitskell*, p. 580.
38 Hansard Fifth Series, Volume 622, 26 April 1960 Cols 228, emphasis added by author.
39 Hansard Fifth Series, Volume 622, Cols 330.
40 Labour: Text of Speech by Hugh Gaitskell, at May Day meeting in Leeds Town Hall on Sunday 1 May.
41 Pimlott, *Wilson*, pp. 220–1.
42 HGD, 27.1.50, pp. 161–2.
43 PGWD, 12.5.60, p. 259.
44 HDD, 12.5.60, pp. 698–99.
45 Leeds: 13, Gaitskell to Murray, 5 May 1960.
46 CDS Witness Seminar Transcript, ICBH, and Taverne interview with author.
47 CDS Witness Seminar Transcript, ICBH, Magee, Donoughue, Rodgers and Taverne.
48 Ibid.

49 Brian Walden, an ex-student of Nuffield College and at the time tutor-trainee in the extramural department, recruited Alderman Frank Pickstock for this anti-left pro-leadership group. On Wednesday 11 May the first discussion of a broader new group took place between Walden and Pickstock. While travelling together to North Staffordshire they discussed the state of the party, 'and agreed that there was no future in it for us if the present inability to resist its lunatic left, pressure groups like CND, and its inability to adjust itself to the present day continued'. Rather than confining themselves to Oxford they considered that 'as a despairing effort' they should 'sound out possibilities' of forming a 'centre group to express the mass of moderate opinion'.

50 Unpublished diary quoted in letter to Michael Summerskill, 18 January 1990.

51 Bill Rodgers in a letter to Michael Summerskill, 18 January 1990.

52 CDS: Rodgers CDS History, the decision to hold a further meeting with an enlarged group was presumably taken at the first meeting of 16 May.

53 CDS: Walden to Pickstock, 18 May 1960, emphasis as original, preceding quotations in this section are from the same letter.

54 CDS: Rodgers' CDS History, p. 1, Witness Seminar Transcript and Rodgers in interview with author. This quote, in roughly similar form, occurs in all three.

55 He was sacked shortly after the publication of the manifesto, by Caspar Brook, the Director of the Consumers' Association, who objected to his association with the Campaign, CDS: Rodgers CDS History, p. 11.

56 Shirley Williams replaced Rodgers at the Fabian Society so was mainly neutral during the active period of the CDS, Williams in interview with author.

57 CDS: Rodgers' CDS History File, pp. 3–4. Neither Windlesham, Communication and Political Power (Cape, 1968), nor Seyd, Factionalism in the Labour Party – a Case Study of the CDS (unpublished MPhil. Thesis, Southampton, 1968), mention this meeting in detail, Haseler, The Gaitskellites (Macmillan, 1969), mentions it (p. 209), but only in passing. S. Crosland, Tony Crosland, mentions it (p. 100) and quotes from Rodgers without giving the source as the CDS history.

58 CDS: Rodgers' CDS History, p. 4, there is no minute of this very first meeting among the papers.

59 Lord Windlesham, Communication and Political Power, Patrick Seyd, Factionalism in the Labour Party – a Case Study of the CDS (unpublished MPhil Thesis, Southampton, 1968), and S. Haseler, The Gaitskellites (Macmillan, 1969), were unaware of this meeting and the 26 June meeting; they give the first meeting as the 27 June. In fact by 27 June much of the planning had already been done.

60 The Stagnant Society (Penguin, 1961). John Barnes, 'From Eden to Macmillan' in Ruling Performance, edited by Hennessy and Seldon (Blackwell, 1987), p. 105.

61 After Oxford he was a lecturer in economics in the USA.

62 Returned at by-election for Birmingham Small Heath, March 1961.

63 HDD, 8.10.60, p. 693.

64 Windlesham, Communication and Political Power, p. 99, CDS: Origins File, Howell to Rodgers, 30 September 1960, headed paper. His company was simply called Denis Howell, Public Relations and was run from Birmingham.

65 Windlesham, Communication and Political Power, p. 95.

66 CDS: Untitled File, Walden to Pickstock, 18 May 1960, this letter is the first recorded plan of how the CDS was going to develop and is contained in an untitled File in the CDS papers, it was not available to previous writers on the CDS.

67 CDS: Rodgers' CDS History File, p. 6.

68 CDS: Witness Seminar Transcript, ICBH.

69 CDS: Origins File, Minute of first meeting, 27 June 1960.

70 CDS: Untitled File, Rodgers to Pickstock, 29 June 1960.

71 Mark Amory (ed.), The Letters of Ann Fleming (CollinsHarvill, 1985), p. 255.

72 RCD, 1.6.60, pp. 856–7.

73 Geoffrey Goodman, The Awkward Warrior (Davis Poynter, 1979), p. 254.

74 Ibid., p. 254.

75 Manchester Guardian, 24 May 1960.

76 All voting figures compiled from Williams, Gaitskell, pp. 592–3 and Hindell and Williams, 'Scarborough and Blackpool' p. 309.

77 All reports in preceeding pages of PLP meeting on 30 June from Daily Telegraph, 30 June 1960.

78 Chris Mayhew in interview with author.

79 Quoted in Goodman, Awkward Warrior, p. 249.

80 Macmillan diary, 19 June 1960, quoted in Harold Macmillan, *Pointing the Way* (Macmillan, 1972), p. 232.
81 Macmillan, *Pointing the Way*, 30 June 1960, p. 232.
82 *Observer*, 7 July 1960.
83 Leeds: 13, Gaitskell to Murray, 7 September 1960.
84 *Star*, 23 September 1960.
85 *Daily Telegraph*, 24 September 1960.
86 *Daily Telegraph*, 26 September 1960.
87 *Yorkshire Evening Post*, 26 September 1960.
88 Leeds: 13, Gaitskell to Murray, 12 September 1960.
89 Quoted in Goodman, *Awkward Warrior*, p. 271; see also TCB, 1.10.60, p. 344.
90 TCB, 1.10.60, p. 345.
91 Ibid.
92 David Marquand, *Progressive Dilemma* (Heinemann, 1991), p. 135.
93 Williams, *Gaitskell*, p. 593, p. 595 and p. 607.
94 L. Minkin, *The Labour Party Annual Conference* (Allen Lane, 1978), p. 96.
95 The debate can be found in LPACR 1960, pp. 170–201.
96 Williams, *Gaitskell*, p. 613.
97 Goodman, *Awkward Warrior*, p. 273.
98 Ibid., p. 277.
99 To Tony Benn, hinting that she was a fellow traveller, TCB, 1.10.60, p. 344.
100 Williams, *Gaitskell*, p. 623.

Chapter 16   The Fight Back, 1960–1961

1 PGWD, 9.10.60, p. 270 – this meeting was not, as indicated in the published version of Gordon Walker's diary, the beginning of CDS.
2 RCD, 19.10.60, p. 884.
3 RCD, 19.10.60, p. 886.
4 Philip Williams, *Hugh Gaitskell: A Political Biography* (Cape, 1979), p. 625.
5 Susan Crosland, *Tony Crosland* (Cape, 1982), p. 103.
6 *Daily Express*, 30 June 1960.
7 Williams, *Gaitskell*, p. 627.
8 *Evening Standard*, 19 October 1960.
9 *Daily Express*, 20 October 1960.
10 Mark Amory (ed.), *The Letters of Ann Fleming*, to Evelyn Waugh, 25 March 1961, p. 281.
11 Williams, *Hugh Gaitskell*, p. 632.
12 *Daily Telegraph*, 10 November 1960.
13 *The Times*, 28 November 1960.
14 *The Times*, 4 December 1960.
15 *Observer*, 27 November 1960.
16 Douglas Jay in interview with author.
17 *The Times*, 10 December 1960.
18 *Daily Telegraph*, 12 December 1960.
19 Quotes from the CDS organisers on these pages are taken from CDS: Origins File, notes for press conference and basis of statement by WTR at press conference, 18 October 1960. The newspaper reports of the launch all appeared on 19 October 1960 except Ivan Yates in *Reynolds News* which appeared on 23 October 1960.
20 'Who Backed the Gaitskellites', *Militant*, 18 February 1977.
21 *Supplementary Detailed Staff Reports of Foreign and Military Intelligence*, Book IV, *Final Report of the Select Committee to Study Governmental Operations with Respect to Intelligence Activities* (United States Senate, US Government Printing Office, Washington, 1976), p. 49 (Church Committee).
22 HGD, 14.10.54, pp. 339–40.
23 Denis Healey, *The Time of My Life* (Penguin, 1990), p. 113.
24 Lord Diamond in interview with the author and Rodgers, CDS History, pp. 14–17.
25 CDS: Trade Unions, Brown File and Red File.
26 Denis Howell in interview with author.
27 Denis Howell in interview with author.
28 CDS: Trade Unions, Red File and Brown File.
29 Williams, *Political Quarterly*, 33, 3, July–Sept., 1962, p. 309.
30 Ibid.
31 LPAR 1960, p. 202.
32 L. Minkin, *The Labour Party Conference* (Allen Lane, 1978), pp. 175–6.
33 Denis Howell in interview with author and CDS: Trade Unions, Red File, AEU Delegate List.
34 CDS: Trade Unions, Red File, AEU Delegate List annotated.
35 CDS: Trade Unions, Red File, Rodgers did a mailing to the AEU supporters on 30 March 1961 enclosing 'A short note of information and arguments on defence and a copy of the joint Labour Party–TUC policy statement'. This was a follow-up to the week before when copies of *Campaign* had been dispatched. They were sent to Jones of Merthyr Tydfil, Richards of Cwmbran, Butler of Coventry, Careless of Crewe, Smith of Consett, Aitken of Kilmarnock, Flowers of Dumbarton, Maley of Renfrewshire,

Shelton of Leicester, McColl of Glasgow, Calder of Kendal. At the same time Hooley of Chilwell was sent *Ten points on defence* and *Campaign*. In April, Ramsden of Chapel Fields and Sharpe of Barton-on-Humber, were approached. Red File, Rodgers to Ramsden, 13 April 1961.

36 Minkin, *The Labour Party Conference*, p. 180.

37 CDS Papers: Trade Unions, Red File, AEU national committee delegate list, back page.

38 Minkin, *The Labour Party Conference*, p. 191.

39 On the Padley–Crossman plan see RCD, entry for 23 February 1961, pp. 929–34 and p. 950 and Williams, *Hugh Gaitskell*, pp. 643–4.

40 CDS: Witness Seminar Transcript, ICBH, Rodgers. Confirmed in Williams, *Hugh Gaitskell*, p. 593 and Woodrow Wyatt in *The Sunday Times*, 30 October 1960, see Windlesham, *Communication and Political Power* (Cape, 1961), p. 139.

41 CDS: Trade Unions, Red File, Pearce to Rodgers, 4 May 1961. The *Leeds Weekly Citizen* was a consistent supporter of CDS.

42 Seyd, *Factionalism in the Labour Party*, p. 145 and Windlesham, *Communication and Political Power*, pp. 139–40.

43 Denis Howell in interview with author.

44 CDS: Untitled Red File, Transport Workers' speeches, copies of eleven are on file.

45 CDS: *Organisation in the Constituencies*, Rodgers, 6 April 1961.

46 A comparision could be made with figures for the Fabian Society, although there was considerable overlap in membership and CDS people were only asked to 'support' the Campaign, not to 'join'. The Campaign actually received more offers of support than the Fabian Society had members. In 1960 the Fabians had 2,586 members and in 1961 2,711: *Fabian Society Annual Report*, July 1960 to June 1961, p. 2.

47 CDS: Supporters Lists File, assorted lists of supporters for the period from the launch up to November 1961. The numbers in brackets are the numbers of supporters in each constituency given in this file. An analysis of the geographical location of 1,563 CDS supporters illustrates this. The main centres of activity among these supporters were: Birmingham (53), Birkenhead (42), Bristol (51),

Cambridge (29), Glasgow (85), Kent (69), Leeds (111), London (146), Manchester (90), Nottingham (28), Oxford (49) and Sheffield (41).

48 CDS: Supporters Lists File, Howell to Rodgers, undated for Glasgow details: chairman, Alex Cameron; joint secretaries, John Urhart, John Smith and Mrs Clayton, agents for each constituency. Howell to Rodgers, undated for Birkenhead details: chairman, Richard Kimberley; vice-chairmen, John Davis and Stuart Robinson; women's section, Dorothy Tomlinson; press officer, Walter Smith. Solly Pearce to Rodgers, undated, for Leeds details: organiser, Denis Matthews; Yorks organiser, Harry Waterman; divisional whips for each constituency, trade unions, Alfred Smith.

49 Edward G. Janosik, *Constituency Labour Parties in Britain* (Pall Mall Press, 1968), p. 29, states that 54% favoured a move slightly or sharply to the left and 46% favoured the status quo or a move to the right.

50 Ibid., p. 31.

51 Ibid., p. 103.

52 CDS: CDS Hand-outs, Circular letter, 11 January 1961.

53 CDS Papers: Campaign Letters (consent to publication), undated list.

54 CDS: Witness Seminar Transcript, ICBH, Rodgers.

55 *Campaign* 8, August–September 1961, 'Selwyn Lloyd's Wage Pause'.

56 CDS: To Lie with Minutes, 'Voting for the National Executive Committee,' undated.

57 CDS: To Lie with Minutes, 'National Executive Committee: Annual Ballot 1962,' undated.

58 Jim Cattermole and David Marquand interview with author.

59 Eric Shaw, *Discipline and Discord in the Labour Party*, (Manchester University Press, 1988), pp. 96–100.

60 Shaw, *Discipline and Discord in the Labour Party*, p. 108.

61 Seyd, *Factionalism in the Labour Party*, 1968, p. 197.

62 CDS: Labour Party Organisers, Rodgers to Cattermole, 9 May 1961.

63 CDS: Labour Party Organisers, Rodgers to Alger, 6 December 1961 and Alger to Rodgers, 12 December 1961.

64 CDS: Parliamentary Candidates (General), Rodgers to Mrs D. Alger, 21 July 1961.

65 CDS: Parliamentary Candidates (General), Anson to Gordon Walker, 27 April 1961.
66 CDS: Labour Party Organisers, Gordon Walker to Reg Wallis, 16 March 1961 and Shaw 1988, p. 331.
67 Jim Cattermole and Bill Rodgers in interview with author.
68 CDS: Parliamentary Candidates (General), Price to Rodgers, 15 October 1962.
69 CDS: Parliamentary Candidates (General), Price to Rodgers, 15 October 1962.
70 CDS: Parliamentary Candidates (General), Rodgers to Price, 16 October 1962.
71 CDS: Parliamentary Candidates (General), Rodgers to Winterbottom, 24 October 1962 and Rodgers to Williams, 24 October 1962.
72 CDS: Parliamentary Candidates (General), Price to Rodgers, 18 October 1962.
73 CDS: Parliamentary Candidates (General), Rodgers to Price, 25 October 1962.
74 CDS: Parliamentary Candidates (General), Price to Rodgers, 2 November 1962.
75 CDS: Parliamentary Candidates (General), Rodgers to Gaitskell, 5 December 1962.
76 CDS: Parliamentary Candidates (General), Rodgers to Gaitskell, 5 December 1962.
77 CDS: Parliamentary Candidates (General), Rodgers to Bowden, 8 November 1962.
78 Shaw, *Discipline and Discord in the Labour Party*, p. 98.
79 CDS: Parliamentary Candidates (General), Rodgers to Hayday, 8 November 1962.
80 CDS: Parliamentary Candidates (General), Price to Rodgers, 28 November 1962.
81 CDS: Parliamentary Candidates (General), Price to Rodgers, 12 December 1962.
82 A local candidate.
83 CDS: Parliamentary Candidates (General), Price to Rodgers, 11 December 1962.
84 CDS: Parliamentary Candidates (General), Rodgers to Gordon Walker, 16 March 1962.
85 CDS: Parliamentary Candidates (General), Rodgers to Gaitskell, 5 December 1962 and Gaitskell to Rodgers, 7 December 1962.
86 Shaw, *Discipline and Discord in the Labour Party*, p. 114.

87 Ibid. and Seyd, *Factionalism in the Labour Party*, pp. 209–10.
88 CDS: Possible Parliamentary Candidates, Jones to Rodgers, 11 November 1961.
89 CDS: Possible Parliamentary Candidates, Rodgers to Haseler, 8 August 1962.
90 Bill Rodgers in interview with author. The impression is underlined by the work Howell did for CDS in the local area.
91 Dick Taverne in interview with author.
92 Dick Taverne, *The Future of the Left, Lincoln and After* (Cape, 1974), p. 26.
93 Ibid.
94 See John Ramsden and Chris Cook, *By-Elections in British Politics* (Macmillan, 1973).
95 Leeds: 13, Resolution in support of Gaitskell, Sunday, 9 October 1960.
96 Leeds: 13, Copy of letter, 2.11.60.
97 Press Release of New Year Message, PS/78 released from Transport House, 30 December 1960.
98 *Daily Telegraph*, 7 January 1961.
99 For example, see *Manchester Guardian*, 9 January 1961 and 16 January 1961.
100 *The Times*, 18 January 1961.
101 *Daily Telegraph*, 19 January 1961.
102 *Manchester Guardian*, 24 January 1961.
103 *Observer*, 11 February 1961.
104 *The Times*, 31 July 1961.
105 *The Times*, 10 July 1961.
106 *Manchester Guardian*, 18 September 1961.

Chapter 17 A Thousand Years of History, 1962–1963

1 Michael Foot, *Aneurin Bevan, 1945–1960, Volume II* (Poynter-Davis, 1975), p. 575.
2 For the development of the European Community see, William Diebold, *The Schuman Plan* (Praeger, 1959), Edward Fursdon, *The European Defence Community: A History* (Macmillan, 1980) and Stephen George, *An Awkward Partner: Britain in the European Community* (Oxford University Press, 1980).
3 The best recent study on this is David Reynolds, *Britannia Overruled, British Policy And World Power in the 20th Century* (Longmans, 1991), for a synthesis of the developing role of Britain in the 20th century, especially Chapter 8, 'Circles 1955–1970', pp. 202–26.
4 For the debate on the Community inside the Labour Party see L. J. Robbins, *The*

eluctant Party: Labour and the EEC 1961–1975 (G. W. and A. Hesketh, 1979).

5 Stephen Haseler, *The Gaitskellites* (Cape, 1969), p. 228.

6 Uwe Kitzinger, *The Challenge of the Common Market*, (Basil Blackwell, 1961), pp. 150–51.

7 Edward G. Janosik, *Constituency Labour Parties in Britain* (Pall Mall Press, 1968), p. 42.

8 Ibid.

9 Denis Howell in interview with author.

10 Williams, *Gaitskell*, p. 705. Quoting Gaitskell's letter to Kennedy.

11 Quoted in Geoffrey Goodman, *Awkward Warrior* (Davis Poynton, 1979), p. 337.

12 CDS: Common Market Correspondence File, Hugh Gaitskell, A Party Political Broadcast on behalf of the Labour Party, 8 May 1962, transcription from broadcast.

13 Ibid.

14 CDS: Common Market Correspondence, Hugh Gaitskell, The Common Market – Text of a television broadcast, 21 September 1962, reproduced in *This Week*, 4, 30, 27 September 1962, p. 158a.

15 CDS: Common Market Correspondence, Pickstock to Gaitskell, 21 September 1962.

16 CDS: Common Market Correspondence, Gaitskell to Pickstock, undated copy.

17 CDS: Common Market Correspondence, Pickstock to George Brown, 21 September 1962, a note on this letter indicates that letters were sent to Healey and Bowden.

18 CDS Papers: Common Market Correspondence, Rodgers, 25 September 1962.

19 Jack Diamond in interview with author.

20 Campbell, *Nye Bevan* (Weidenfeld & Nicolson, 1985), p. 71.

21 Witness Seminar, 'The Labour Committee for Europe', *Contemporary Record*, Volume 7, Number 3, 1993, Lord Jenkins of Hillhead quoting Michael Foot, p. 391.

22 George Brown, *In My Way* (Weidenfeld & Nicolson, 1972), p. 218.

23 CDS: Common Market Correspondence: Rodgers to Smith, 15 October 1962 and Williams to Rodgers, 10 October 1962.

24 CDS: Common Market Correspondence: Rodgers to Williams, 10 October 1962.

25 LPACR, p. 155.

26 Ibid.

27 Ibid.

28 Douglas Jay, *Change and Fortune* (Hutchinson, 1980), p. 286.

29 Quoted in Geoffrey Goodman, *Awkward Warrior*, p. 340.

30 *New Statesman*, 5 October 1962, p. 438.

31 Ibid.

32 Williams, *Gaitskell*, p. 702, there is no record of this meeting in the CDS Papers.

33 Williams, *Gaitskell*, p. 712.

34 Ibid., p. 728.

35 Susan Crosland, *Tony Crosland* (Jonathan Cape, 1983), p. 111.

36 J. Campbell, *Roy Jenkins: A biography* (Weidenfeld & Nicolson, 1983), p. 72.

37 Bernard Donoughue, 'Renegotiation of the EEC terms: A witness account,' in Brian Brivati and Harriet Jones (eds.), *From Reconstruction to Integration, Britain and Europe since 1945* (Leicester University Press, 1993), pp. 204–5.

38 Quoted in Geoffrey Goodman, *Awkward Warrior*, p. 340.

39 Lord Ennals in interview with author.

40 Richard Cottrell in interview with author.

41 Leeds: 13, Skeller to Murray, 9 January 1963.

42 Leeds: 13, Murray to Beryl, 12 January 1963.

43 Mark Amory (ed.), *The Letters of Ann Fleming: To 'Clarissa Avon'* (Collins Harvill, 1985), 30 January 1963, p. 321.

44 Leeds: 13, Anson to Murray, 24 January 1963.

45 Leeds: 2/3 Minute book, 1954–63, Minutes of meeting, 7 February 1963.

46 Leeds: Frank Murray annual reports on Gaitskell, South Leeds, CLP Papers, 18, 1953–68, Secretary's Annual Reports.

47 Leeds: 14, 1963, Correspondence, File re nomination conference for Leeds South Parliamentary Party. As Murray recorded in his annual report.

48 Ibid.

49 Letter from Dora Gaitskell to Charlie Pannell, Pannell papers, House of Lords Record Office, PAN8, Letter dated 10 March.

Chapter 18 Epilogue

1 Chapman Pincher, *Too Secret, Too Long* (St Martin's Press, New York, 1984), p. 473.

2 Roland Perry, *The Fifth Man* (Sidgwick and Jackson, 1994), p. 279.

3 Ben Pimlott, *Harold Wilson* (Harper-Collins, 1992), p. 711.

4 Pincher, *Too Secret*, p. 474.

5 Susan Crosland, *Tony Crosland* (Cape, 1982), p. 115.

6 *New Statesman*, 1 February 1963, 'The Making of a Premier', Anthony Howard, gives the dates as 21 and 22 January 1963. Howard's articles formed the basis for Anthony Howard and Richard West, *The Making of the Prime Minister* (Cape, 1965).

7 CDS: Witness Seminar Transcript, ICBH, Taverne.

8 Ibid.

9 CDS: Witness Seminar Transcript, ICBH, Marquand.

10 Anthony Howard, 'Labour's Duel at the Top', *New Statesman*, 8 February 1963, p. 174.

11 CDS: Witness Seminar Transcript, ICBH, Donoughue.

12 RCD, 8.2.63, p. 969.

13 RCD, 8.2.63, p. 970.

14 Crosland, *Tony Crosland*, p. 116.

15 CDS: Witness Seminar Transcript, ICBH, Jones.

16 Crosland, *Tony Crosland*, p. 117.

17 RCD, 1979, p. 511, entry for Wednesday 19 February 1969.

18 RCD, 1979, p. 513, entry for 20 February 1969.

19 Donoughue was initially employed by Wilson to monitor opinion polls before being appointed a senior policy adviser to the Prime Minister. See Bernard Donoughue, *Prime Minister* (Cape, 1987), p. 1 and p. 78.

20 Callaghan was Chancellor from 16 October 1964 to 30 November 1967 and Home Secretary from then until the election in 1970.

21 Brown was First Secretary at the DEA from 16 October 1964 to 11 August 1966 and Foreign Secretary until 6 March 1968 when he resigned.

22 Crosland was Minister of State at the DEA 20 October 1964 to 27 January 1965 and then Secretary of State for Education and Minister for Local Government and Regional Planning.

23 Jenkins went from Aviation to the Home Office in December 1965 and then became Chancellor in November 1967.

24 Jay stayed at the Board of Trade until August 1967 when he was sacked for his position on the Community.

25 Gordon Walker lost his seat in 1964 but Wilson appointed him Foreign Secretary anyway. He could not sustain this position after losing the Leyton by-election. He was eventually returned in 1966 and was Minister without Portfolio.

26 George Brown gave his reasons for resigning as the 'Presidential' style of government introduced by Harold Wilson. George Brown, *In My Way* (Weidenfeld & Nicolson, 1972), p. 161.

27 L. Minkin, *The Labour Party Annual Conferences* (Allen Lane, 1978), p. 336.

28 Dick Taverne, *The Future of The Left* (Cape, 1974), p. 64.

29 Ramsden and Jay, in Cook and Ramsden, *By-Elections In British Politics*, 1973, p. 279, state that Roy Jenkins tried in vain to persuade Taverne not to force a by-election, but many were well disposed. Bill Rodgers in interview with author.

30 This position was exemplified by Tony Crosland in *Socialism Now* (Cape, 1974).

31 Geoffrey Williams and Alan Williams, *Labour's Decline and the Social Democrats' Fall* (Macmillan, 1989), p. 104.

32 This right-wing activity was in part a reaction to the organisation of the left of the Labour Party. A full account of this grassroots organisation is contained in Patrick Seyd, *The Rise and Fall of the Labour Left* (Macmillan Education, 1987).

33 Roy Jenkins, *European Diary 1977–1981* (Collins, 1982), pp. 2–6.

34 Williams and Williams, *Labour's Fall* sets out to give this impression.

35 Although things might have been very different if Gaitskell had been defeated on the defence issue in 1961 and forced to resign the leadership. Some of the Gaitskellites contemplated leaving politics if Gaitskell were defeated. It is unlikely that a major realignment of the centre-left would have taken place in 1961, but many would have questioned their futures in the PLP. Without this core of revisionist MPs it is arguable that the swing to the left of the 1960s and 1970s would have been faster and gone further. This exercise in counter-factual history is unprovable, but the existence of a solid group of moderate MPs in the House of Commons in the 1960s and 1970s significantly slowed the rise of the left.

Select Bibliography

1 Private, institution, organisation and state papers
Clement Attlee, Bodleian, Oxford
Campaign for Democratic Socialism, Private collection
Bill Carron, Churchill College, Cambridge
CND, *The Left in Britain: the Campaign for Nuclear Disarmament*, Microfiche, Harvester Press, 1977
G. D. H. Cole, Nuffield College, Oxford
Frank Cousins, Warwick Modern Record Centre
Tony Crosland, British Library of Political and Economic Science
Hugh Dalton, British Library of Political and Economic Science
Evan Durbin, British Library of Political and Economic Science
Fabian Society Papers and Annual Report, 1927–1964, Nuffield College, Oxford
George Brown, Bodleian, Oxford
Patrick Gordon Walker, Churchill College, Cambridge
The Group, Private Collection, Summerskill Collection
Hansard, House of Commons Debates, 1945–1963
Alastair Hetherington, British Library of Political and Economic Science
Labour Party Annual Conference Reports, 1927–1964, British Library of Political and Economic Science
Leeds South Constituency Labour Party, West Yorkshire Record Office
Herbert Morrison, Nuffield College, Oxford
National Executive Committee, Labour Party, Minutes and Papers; NEC sub-committee minutes and papers, National Museum of Labour History
Philip Noel-Baker, Churchill College, Cambridge
Charles Pannell, House of Lords Record Office
Morgan Phillips, National Museum of Labour History
Public Record Office, Kew

Cabinet Minutes and Conclusions (CAB)
Prime Ministers Papers (PREM)
Ministry of Fuel and Power (POWE)
Treasury (T)
Foreign Office (FO837) for Ministry of Economic Warfare
Emanuel Shinwell, British Library of Political and Economic Science
Trade Union Papers, Warwick Modern Record Centre
Ronald Waterhouse, Private Collection
Philip Williams, Nuffield College

2 Publications by or about Hugh Gaitskell

Gaitskell, H. *Chartism*, WEA, London, 1927.

Gaitskell, H. *Labour and the Common Market*, Labour Party, London, 1962.

Gaitskell, H. *Recent Developments in British Socialist Thinking*, Co-Operative Party, London, 1956.

Gaitskell, H. *The High Cost of Toryism*, Labour Party, London, 1956.

Gaitskell, H. *In Defence of Politics*, Birkbeck College Foundation Oration, London, 1954.

Gaitskell, H. *The Challenge of Co-existence*, Methuen, London, 1957.

Foot, M. 'Hugh Gaitskell', in *Loyalists and Loners*, Collins, London, 1986.

Marquand, D. 'Hugh Gaitskell: The Social Democrat as Hero', in *The Progressive Dilemma*, Heinemann, London, 1991.

Pimlott, B. 'Hugh Gaitskell', in *Frustrate their Knavish Tricks*, Harper-Collins, London, 1994.

Shore, P. 'Hugh Gaitskell: 1955–1963', in *Leading the Left*, Weidenfeld & Nicolson, London, 1993.

Vaizey, J. 'Hugh Gaitskell', in *Breach of Promise*, Weidenfeld & Nicolson, London, 1983.

Haseler, S. *The Gaitskellites*, Macmillan, London, 1969.

McDermott, G. *Leader Lost*, Frewin, London, 1972.

Rodgers, W. T. (ed.) *Hugh Gaitskell 1906–1963*, Thames & Hudson, London, 1964.

Williams, P. *Hugh Gaitskell: A Political Biography*, Cape, London, 1979.

Williams, P. (ed.) *The Diary of Hugh Gaitskell*, Cape, London, 1983.

3 Labour Party and Fabian Society publications

Crossman, R. H. S. *Labour in the Affluent Society*, Fabian Society, London, 1960.

Jenkins, R. *The Labour Case*, Penguin, London, 1960.

Jenkins, R., and Jay, D. *The Common Market Debate*, Fabian Tract 341, Fabian Society, London, 1962.

Labour Party, *Industry and Society*, 1957.
Labour Party, *Labour and the Common Market*, 1962.
Labour Party, *Labour and the Scientific Revolution*, 1963.
Labour Party, *Labour Believes in You*, 1949.
Labour Party, *Policy for Peace*, 1961.
Labour Party, *Signposts for the Sixties*, 1962.

4 Oral sources

Interviewees: Austen Albu, Ivan Alexander, John Barnes, David Benn, the Rt Hon Tony Benn MP, Lord Bonham Carter, Dr Peter Catterall, Lord Borrie, Jim Boydon, Dr Jeremy Bray MP, Roger Broad, Tyrell Burgess, Dr David Butler, Dr Larry Butler, Dr Stephen Byrd, Sir Alec Cairncross, Baroness Castle, Brian Cathcart, Jim Cattermole, Dr Richard Cockett, Dr Gerard Daly, Conrad Dehn, Lord Diamond, Professor David Donnison, Lord Donoughue, Bruce Douglas Mann, Dr David Edgerton, Lord Ennals, the Rt Hon Michael Foot, Professor M. R. D. Foot, Reg Freeson, Sir Martin Gilbert, Lord Gladwyn, Anthony Gorst, Alec Grant, Kenneth Harris, Professor Stephen Haseler, the Rt Hon Roy Hattersley, Lord Healey, Group Captain David Hobart, Dr Martin Holmes, Ben Hooberman, Lord Houghton, Dr Andrew Howard, Lord Howell, Lord Jay, Lord Jenkins of Hillhead, Lord Jenkins of Putney, Dr Lewis Johnman, Professor George Jones, Dr Harriet Jones, Dr Tudor Jones, Lord Kennet, Keith Kyle, David Lane, Alan Lee Williams, Dick Leonard, Roger Liddle, the Earl of Longford, the Countess of Longford, Ivor Lucas, Dr Dickson Mabon, Alec McGiven, Julia McNeal, Colin McIntyre, Bryan Magee, Professor David Marquand, Lord Mayhew, Lord Mellish, Ian Mikardo, Lord Oram, Dr Nick Owen, Sir Leo Pliatzky, Professor Ben Pimlott, Lord Prentice, Virginia Preston, Dr Stephen Proctor, Professor John Ramsden, Dr Huw Richards, Lord Rodgers, Lord Merlyn-Rees, Sir Kenneth Robinson, Lord Sainsbury, Siemon Scammell-Katz, Dr Anthony Seldon, Dr

Geoffrey Sell, Dr Patrick Seyd, Dr Alan Shipman, Lord Soper, Peter Stephenson, Michael Summerskill, Lord Taverne, Andrew Thomas, Mike Thomas, Lord Thomson, Dr Willie Thomson, Polly Toynbee, Professor John Turner, Dr Frank Trentman, David Vaughan Williams, Sir Ronald Waterhouse, Professor Donald Watt, Baroness Williams, Daniel Wincott.

Archivists at: Bodleian Archive, North Yorkshire Archives Service, House of Lords Record Office, Labour Party Archive, Modern Records Centre, LSE Archives, New York Public Library, Churchill College, Nuffield College and University College.

Anthony Gorst, Institute of Contemporary British History Oral History Project on Suez, ICBH.

Witness Seminar Transcripts published as Brian Brivati and Daniel Wincott (eds), 'The Evolution of Social Democracy in Britain', Special Edition of *Contemporary Record*, vol. 7, No. 2 (autumn 1993): 'The Campaign for Democratic Socialism 1960–1964', pp. 363–85; 'The Labour Committee for Europe', pp. 386–416; and 'The Launch of the SDP 1979–1981', pp. 417–64 (full text version held at Institute of Contemporary British History).

5 Periodicals and newspapers

Campaign, Cleckheaton Independent, Daily Express, Daily Graphic, Daily Herald, Daily Mail, Daily Telegraph, Daily Worker, Economist, Encounter, Evening Standard (London), *Guardian, Guardian Journal* (Nottingham), *Leeds Weekly Citizen, Listener, Manchester Guardian, New Left Review, New Statesman and Nation, News Chronicle, Observer, Reynolds News, Socialist Commentary, Spectator, Star, Sunday Dispatch, Sunday Express, Sunday Pictorial, Sunday Times, Times, Tribune, Yorkshire Evening Post, Yorkshire Post.*

6 Autobiographies, biographies, diaries and memoirs

Amory, M. (ed.) *The Letters of Ann Fleming*, Collins Harvill, London, 1985.

Attlee, C. *The Labour Party in Perspective*, Victor Gollancz, London, 1949.

Benn, T. *Years of Hope, Diaries 1940–62*, ed. Ruth Winstone, Hutchinson, London, 1994.

Bevan, A. *In Place of Fear*, Heinemann, London, 1952.

Select Bibliography

Campbell, J. *Nye Bevan and the Mirage of British Socialism*, Weidenfeld & Nicolson, London, 1989.

Crosland, S. *Tony Crosland*, Cape, London, 1982.

Dalton, H. *Call Back Yesterday: Memoirs 1887–1931*, volume 1, Frederick Muller, London, 1953.

Dalton, H. *The Fateful Years: Memoirs 1931–1945*, volume 2, Frederick Muller, London, 1957.

Dalton, H. *High Tide and After: Memoirs 1945–1960*, volume 3, Frederick Muller, London, 1962.

Donoughue, B. *Prime Ministers*, Cape, London, 1987.

Donoughue, B., and Jones, G. W. *Herbert Morrison*, Weidenfeld & Nicolson, London, 1973.

Foot, M. *Aneurin Bevan: A Biography*, volume 1: *1897–1945*, Mac-Gibbon & Kee, London, 1962.

Foot, M. *Aneurin Bevan: A Biography*, volume 2: *1945–1960*, Davis-Poynter, London, 1973.

Harris, K. *Attlee*, Weidenfeld & Nicolson, London, 1982.

Healey, D. *The Time of My Life*, Penguin, London, 1990.

Horne, A. *Macmillan 1957–1986*, Macmillan, London, 1989.

Howard, A. *RAB: The Life of R. A. Butler*, Cape, London 1987.

Jay, D. *Change and Fortune*, Hutchinson, London, 1980.

Jenkins, R. *A Life at the Centre*, Macmillan, London, 1991.

Kramnick, I., and Sheerman, B. *Harold Laski: A Life on the Left*, Hamish Hamilton, London, 1993.

Lee, J. *Tomorrow is a New Day*, MacGibbon & Kee, London, 1963.

Macmillan, H. *Pointing the Way 1959–1961*, Macmillan, London, 1972.

Macmillan, H. *At the End of the Day 1961–1963*, Macmillan, London, 1973.

Macmillan, H. *Riding the Storm 1955–1959*, Macmillan, London, 1971.

Mayhew, C. *Party Games*, Hutchinson, London, 1969.

Mikardo, I. *Back-Bencher*, Weidenfeld & Nicolson, London, 1989.

Morgan, J. (ed.) *The Backbench Diaries of Richard Crossman*, Hamish Hamilton and Cape, London, 1981.

Morgan, J. (ed.) *The Crossman Diaries: Selections from the Diaries of a Cabinet Minister 1964–1970*, Book Club Associates, London, 1979.

Pearce, R. (ed.) *Patrick Gordon Walker: Political Diaries 1932–1971*, Historians' Press, London, 1991.

Pimlott, B. *Harold Wilson*, HarperCollins, London, 1992.

Pimlott, B. *Hugh Dalton*, Cape, London, 1985.

Pimlott, B. (ed.) *The Political Diary of Hugh Dalton*, Cape, London, 1986.

Shinwell, E. *The Labour Story*, Macdonald, London, 1963.

Skidelsky, R. *John Maynard Keynes: The Economist as Saviour, 1920–1937*, Macmillan, London, 1992.

Sutherland, D. *Portrait of a Decade: London Life, 1945–1955*, Harrap, London, 1988.

Thomas, H. *John Strachey*, Eyre Methuen, London, 1973.

Williams, F. *Nothing So Strange*, Cassell, London, 1970.

Wright, A. *R. H. Tawney*, Manchester University Press, 1987.

Ziegler, P. *Wilson: The Authorised Life*, HarperCollins, London, 1993.

7 Secondary sources

Abrams, M., and Rose, R. *Must Labour Lose*, Penguin, Harmondsworth, 1960.

Addison, P. *The Road to 1945*, Cape, London, 1975.

Adelman, P. *The Rise of the Labour Party 1880–1960*, Longman, London, 1986.

Allen, V. L. *Power in the Trade Unions*, Hall, London, 1954.

Anderson, P. *Towards Socialism*, Fontana, London, 1963.

Bartlett, C. J. *British Defence Policy East of Suez 1947–1968*, Oxford University Press, Oxford, 1973.

Bartlett, C. J. *A History of Post-War Britain 1945–1974*, Longman, London, 1977.

Bealey, F. W. *The Social and Political Thought of the Labour Party*, Weidenfeld & Nicolson, London, 1970.

Beer, S. H. *Modern British Politics*, Faber, London, 1965.

Beloff, M. *The Party System*, Phoenix House, London, 1958.

Beloff, M. *Trade Union Leadership*, Phoenix House, London, 1957.

Bence, D., and Branson, C. *Roy Jenkins: A Question of Principle*, Moat Hall, London, 1982.

Berrington, H. *Backbench Opinion in the House of Commons 1945–1955*, Pergamon Press, Oxford, 1973.

Bogdanor, V., and Skidelsky, R. *The Age of Affluence 1951–1964*, Macmillan, London, 1970.

Booker, C. *The Neophiliacs*, Collins, London, 1969.

Select Bibliography

Boyd, F. *British Politics in Transition 1945–1963*, Pall Mall, London, 1964.

Braddon, R. *Suez: The Splitting of a Nation*, Collins, London, 1973.

Bradley, I. *Breaking the Mould*, Martin Robertson, London, 1981.

Brook, S. *Labour's War: The Labour Party during the Second World War*, Oxford University Press, Oxford, 1992.

Butler, D. *The British General Election of 1951*, Macmillan, London, 1952.

Butler, D. *The British General Election of 1955*, Macmillan, London, 1955.

Butler, D. *The British General Election of 1959*, Macmillan, London, 1960.

Butler, D. *The British General Election of 1964*, Macmillan, London, 1965.

Cairncross, A. *Years of Recovery*, Metheun, London, 1987.

Cairncross, A., and Watts, N. *The Economic Section 1939–1961*, Routledge, London, 1989.

Cathcart, B. *Test of Greatness: Britain's Struggle for the Atom Bomb*, John Murray, London, 1994.

Cole, H. B. *The British Labour Party*, Pergamon Press, Oxford, 1977.

Cook, C., and Stevenson, J. *The Slump*, Cape, London, 1977.

Crosland, C. A. R. *The Conservative Enemy*, Cape, London, 1962.

Crosland, C. A. R. *The Future of Socialism*, Cape, London, 1956.

Crosland, C. A. R. *Socialism Now and Other Essays*, Cape, London, 1975.

Crossman, R. H. S. (ed.) *New Fabian Essays*, Turnstile Press, London, 1971.

Darby, P. P. *The Long Retreat: A Short History of British Defence Policy 1945–1970*, Macmillan, London, 1972.

Dockrill, M. *British Defence Policy since 1975*, Basil Blackwell, Oxford, 1988.

Drucker, H. M. *Doctrine and Ethos in the Labour Party*, George Allen & Unwin, London, 1979.

Durbin, Eliz. *New Jerusalem*, Routledge & Kegan Paul, London, 1985.

Durbin, E. *The Politics of Democratic Socialism,* Routledge & Kegan Paul, London, 1947.

Eckstein, H. *Pressure Group Politics*, George Allen & Unwin, London, 1960.

Epstein, L. D. *British Politics in the Suez Crisis*, Pall Mall, London, 1964.

Foote, G. *Labour Party Political Thought*, Croom Helm, London, 1982.

Frankel, J. *British Foreign Policy 1945–1973*, Oxford University Press, Oxford, 1975.

Gardner, H. *Leading Minds: An Anatomy of Leadership*, Basic Books, New York, 1995.

Grooms, A. J. R. *British Thinking about Nuclear Weapons*, Frances Pinter, London, 1974.

Hall, P. G. *Labour's New Frontiers*, André Deutsch, London, 1964.

Harrison, M. *Trades Unions and the Labour Party since 1945*, George Allen, London, 1960.

Hennessy, P. *Cabinet*, Blackwell, Oxford, 1986.

Hennessy, P. *The Hidden Wiring*, Cassell, London, 1996.

Hennessy, P. *Never Again*, Jonathan Cape, London, 1992.

Hennessy, P. *Whitehall*, Fontana, London, 1990.

Hennessy, P., and Seldon, A. (eds) *Ruling Performance*, Basil Blackwell, Oxford, 1987.

Hester, S. *Defence and the Parties*, British Atlantic Publisher, London, 1977.

Hindess, B. *Parliamentary Democracy and Socialist Politics*, Routledge & Kegan Paul, London, 1983.

Holland, S. *The Socialist Challenge*, Quartet Books, London, 1975.

Howard, A., and West, R. *The Making of the Prime Minister*, Cape, London, 1965.

Howarth, T. E. B. *Prospect and Reality: Great Britain 1945–1955*, Collins, London, 1973.

Howell, D. *British Social Democracy*, Croom Helm, London, 1976.

Hunter, L. D. S. *The Road to Brighton Pier*, Arthur Barker, London, 1959.

Janosik, E. G. *Constituency Labour Parties in British Politics*, Pall Mall, London, 1968.

Jay, D. *Socialism in the New Society*, Cape, London, 1962.

Jenkins, M. *Bevanism, Labour's High Tide, the Cold War and the Democratic Mass Movement*, Spokesman Books, London, 1977.

Johnson, F. *Defence by Committee*, Oxford University Press, Oxford, 1960.

Johnson, F. *Defence by Ministry*, Duckworth, London, 1980.

Select Bibliography

Jones, J. B. *Labour and the British State*, Clarendon Press, Oxford, 1985.

Kaufman, G. *The Left*, Anthony Blond, London, 1966.

Kavanagh, D. *The Politics of the Labour Party*, George Allen & Unwin, London, 1982.

Kitzinger, U. *The Challenge of the Common Market*, Basil Blackwell, Oxford, 1961.

Lucas, S. *Divided We Stand*, Hodder & Stoughton, London, 1991.

McKie, D., and Cook, C. *The Decade of Disillusion*, Macmillan, London, 1972.

McKenzie, R. *Trade Unions and the Government*, Cape, London, 1960.

Miliband, R. *The State in Capitalist Society*, Quartet Books, London, 1969.

Miliband, R. *Parliamentary Socialism*, George Allen & Unwin, London, 1961.

Minkin, L. *The Contentious Alliance*, Edinburgh University Press, Edinburgh, 1991.

Minkin, L. *The Labour Party Annual Conference*, Allen Lane, London, 1978.

Minnion, J., and Bolsover, P. *The CND Story*, Allison & Busby, London, 1983.

Morgan, K. *Labour in Power 1945–1951*, Oxford University Press, Oxford, 1984.

Nicholas, H. G. *The General Election of 1950*, repr. Frank Cass, London, 1968.

Pierre, A. J. *Nuclear Politics: The British Experience 1939–1970*, Oxford University Press, Oxford, 1972.

Pinto-Duschinsky, M. *British Political Finance 1830–1980*, American Enterprise Institute, Washington, 1981.

Pimlott, B. *The Politics of the Labour Party*, Allen & Unwin, London, 1982.

Punnett, R. M. *Frontbench Opposition*, Heinemann, London, 1973.

Ramsden, J. *The Age of Balfour and Baldwin 1902–1940*, Longman, Harlow, 1978.

Ramsden, J. *The Age of Churchill and Eden 1940–1957*, Longman, Harlow, 1995.

Ramsden, J., and Cook, C. *By-Elections in British Politics*, Macmillan, London, 1973.

473

Robbins, L. J. *The Reluctant Party: Labour and the EEC 1961–1975*, G. W. and A. Hesketh, Ormskirk, 1979.

Rodgers, W. *The Politics of Change*, Secker & Warburg, London, 1982.

Rosecrance, R. N. *Defence of the Realm: British Strategy in the Nuclear Epoch*, Columbia University Press, London, 1968.

Seldon, A. *Churchill's Indian Summer: The Conservative Government 1951–1955*, Hodder & Stoughton, London, 1981.

Shanks, M. *The Stagnant Society*, Penguin, Harmondsworth, 1961.

Shaw, E. *Discipline and Discord in the Labour Party: The Politics of Managerial Control in the Labour Party 1951–1987*, Manchester University Press, Manchester, 1989.

Snyder, W. P. *The Politics of British Defence Policy 1945–1962*, Ernest Benn, London, 1964.

Stephenson, H. *Claret and Chips*, Michael Joseph, London, 1982.

Strachey, J. *Contemporary Capitalism*, Victor Gollancz, London, 1956.

Strachey, J. *On Prevention of War*, Macmillan, London, 1962.

Taverne, D. *The Future of the Left*, Cape, London, 1974.

Tawney, R. H. *The Acquisitive Society*, George Bell, London, 1945.

Taylor, A. *The Trade Unions and the Labour Party*, Croom Helm, London, 1987.

Titmuss, R. M. *Essays on the Welfare State*, George Allen & Unwin, London, 1962.

Titmuss, R. M. *Income Distribution and Social Change*, Allen & Unwin, London, 1962.

Warde, A. *Consensus and Beyond: The Development of Labour Party Strategy Since World War Two*, Manchester University Press, Manchester, 1982.

Wilson, H. H. *Pressure Groups*, Secker & Warburg, London, 1961.

Windlesham, Lord, *Communication and Political Power*, Cape, London, 1966.

Williams, G., and Williams, A. *Labour's Decline and the Social Democrats' Fall*, Macmillan, London, 1989.

Wright, A. *British Socialism: Socialist Thought from the Late 1880s to the 1960s*, Longman, London, 1983.

Index

Index

Index

Index

Index

Home, Alec Douglas, Lord 89,
252, 369
Horder, Lord Thomas 65, 71
Howard, Anthony 416, 435
Howell, David 182
Howell, Denis 341, 362, 382,
385, 388, 396, 398, 399,
400, 438
Hughes, Emrys 164, 400
Hulston Working Men's Club
154
Hungary 280–1, 309, 315, 321
policy on 316
Hunt, Henry 18
Hunter, Leslie 208, 217, 220
Hurst, Sir Alfred 57
Hussein, King of Jordan 249
Hutchinson, Harold 104, 341,
428
Hutchinson, Leslie 199

IIC see Industrial Intelligence
Centre
ILP see Independent Labour
Party
IMF see International
Monetary Fund
Independent Labour Party 145,
288, 407
India, independence 143, 144
Indo-China war 191
Industrial Intelligence Centre
(IIC) 46
Industry and Society 245, 302,
304, 318, 335, 419
International Monetary Fund
(IMF) 97, 282
Iran crisis 125–8, 130
iron and steel, nationalisation
75
Irvine, A.J. 164
Irving, S. 376
Israel 248, 257–8, 266, 269,
270, 272, 273
Israeli Labour Party 429

Jamaica 284, 345
Jamieson, Addie Mary see
Gaitskell, Addie Mary
Jamieson, George (grandfather)
5, 8–9
Janosik, Edward 389, 407
Jay, Douglas 32, 69, 84, 94,
104, 167, 291, 309, 336,
390, 420, 434, 435, 459n,
460n, 467n
The Socialist Case 30

on Attlee government
74–5
and CDS 362
on change of party name
296
checking speech 206
and Common Market 406,
407, 414–16
on defence 349
election prediction 90
on fuel crisis 77
on nationalisation 332, 335,
336, 339, 367
others' opinions of 95
response to election failure
331, 333
at Winchester 8, 9
on NEC sub-committee 34
relationship with HG 238,
299, 421
role in devaluation 84, 85
in Shadow Cabinet 438
social activities 180
and Suez crisis 259–60,
263
supporting HG 41, 225, 226,
341
in war 45
Jebb, Gladwyn 53, 55
Jenkins, Jennifer 242, 309
Jenkins, Mark 144, 163
Jenkins, Roy 69, 140, 223, 309,
336, 344, 390
and CDS 362
and Common Market
405–6, 412, 416
on defence 349, 358
on HG 9, 10, 59, 74, 378,
421, 422, 425
looking to Europe 148
on nationalisation 334, 339
obituary of HG 429
President of European
Commission 439
relationship with HG 87,
238, 242, 299
resignation on EEC 404,
439
response to election failure
331, 332
in Shadow Cabinet 438
supporters 437
supporting HG 167, 170,
212, 220
unwilling to deal with
Wilson 436
Jenkinson, A.J. 25

Johnson, Dr Hewlett 311–12
Johnston, Eric 98
Johnstone, S.J. 47
Jones, Ernest 197, 205, 209–10
Jones, George 146, 390, 398,
436
Jordan 249

Kahn, Richard 27
Kaldor, Nicholas 84, 96
Katz, Milton 126
Kaufman, Gerald 430
Keeling, George 20
Keep Calm group 179, 184
Kennally, Councillor 156,
328
Kennedy, John F. 350, 391,
401, 408, 432
Keohane, Dan 142
Keynes, John Maynard 25, 27,
34, 55, 76, 292
Keynesian theory 26–7, 29,
30, 62, 63, 421
Khrushchev, Nikita 280, 306,
309, 310–14, 315,
316–17, 321–2, 432,
433, 434
Kilmuir, Lord 252
King, Horace 376–7
King, Tom 390
King's College, Cambridge 7
Kinnock, Neil 212, 440–1
Kitzinger, Uwe 390, 407
Kleinfeld's (Fitzroy Tavern)
32–3
Knight, Percy 188, 210
Knight, Victor 381
Koestler, Arthur 180
Korda, Alexander 60, 81
Korean War 105–11, 126,
140, 200, 275
Kulscar, Ilsa 37
Kurchatov, Igor 200, 351
Kuwait 402

labour movement 289, 290
changes in 137–8
economic theories 28
people attracted to 23–4
Labour Party:
action to help Austria 36–7
alliance proposed with
Liberals 332–3, 335
alliances 41
attempts to expel Bevan
from 185, 188, 199, 200,
204, 208–12

483

Index

Index

Index

Index

Thorne, Will 19
Time (magazine) 270
Times 189, 197, 263, 346, 382, 418, 427
Tito, Josip Broz 280, 369
Tomlinson, George 72, 119
Tomlinson, Jim 75
Tomney, Frank 260
Tots and Quots 31, 34
Townsend, Audrey 15
Trade Union Congress (TUC) 125
  action to help Austria 36–7
  Conference 322
  joint defence policy with NEC 340, 365, 366, 372, 374, 385, 386, 420
  speech at 128–9
  wage policy 147, 170
Trade Union Press Agency 382
trade unions:
  affiliation to party 205
  attempts to get Bevan expelled 174, 185, 188, 199
  and Clause 4 332–48
  communists within 387
  confrontation with 215
  dominating Conference 173
  fighting communism 137
  gaining support from 185–6
  general strike 16–18
  HG working with 188
  influence on 420
  Labour Party developing from 145
  legal position 4
  NEC seat 174
  power 301
  proposal to break links with Labour Party 332–48
  relationship with Labour Party 288–90
  sponsored MPs 227
  and Suez 274
  votes at Conference 353, 366, 386
Trades Dispute Act 4
Transport and General Workers Union (TGWU) 68, 173, 186, 205, 227, 319, 320, 353, 366, 372, 375, 385, 388, 414, 424

Treaty of Rome 406, 407–8, 414
Tree, Felicity 246
Tribune 165, 166, 171, 226, 304, 346, 359, 361, 390–1, 419, 424
  rally 178, 181, 197
Truman, Harry S. 106, 111
TUC *see* Trade Union Congress

UCL *see* University College, London
Union of Shop, Distributive and Allied Workers (USDAW) 173, 355, 366
United Nations 126, 264–5, 267–8, 269, 270, 277–8, 282, 314, 315, 352
  Dora's career with 431
  Security Council 106, 127, 128, 253, 255, 269, 272–3, 317
United Nations Relief and Rehabilitation Administration (UNRRA) 56–7, 60
University College, London (UCL) 25, 40, 60
USA:
  aid from 107–10
  alignment with 349–50
  alliance with 170–1, 281, 284, 371, 383
  attacking pound 278
  Blue Streak missile 354, 355–6, 391
  feelings against 177–8
  HG's visits to 99, 100–2, 109–10, 129, 286, 314–16
  in Korean War 105–11
  loan from 76
  as model 148
  rearmament demands 106–13, 200
  relationship with 420
  during war 51–2
  EEC and 405, 406
  and Soviet Union 280–1
  and Suez 250, 251–3, 255, 256–7, 262, 264, 265–7, 268, 269, 272
  in Vietnam 426
USDAW *see* Union of Shop, Distributive and Allied Workers

USSR:
  HG's visits to 321–2
  in Hungary 280–1
  theories of conspiracy in HG's death 432–3
  threat from 108–9, 111
  US support 280–1
  visit of leaders to London 309–14

Vaizey, John 238, 390
Vallance, Aylmer 18
Vansittart, Sir Robert 48
VFS *see* Victory for Socialism
Vicky (cartoonist) 236
Victory for Socialism (VFS) 227, 318–19, 353, 363, 366, 371, 382
Vienna 35–8
Vienna School 14, 15
Vietnam 191, 420, 426

Walden, Brian 339, 359–60, 362
Walker, Patrick Gordon *see* Gordon Walker, Patrick
Wall Street Crash 19
Wallis, Reg 394, 395
Wansborough, George 32
War Office 52–3
Washington Post 270
Waterman, Harry 396, 430
Watson, Sam 139n, 186, 190, 209, 227, 313, 339, 347, 356, 372, 373, 383
Waugh, Evelyn 345, 364, 376
WEA *see* Workers' Educational Association
Webb, Beatrice 16
Webb, Sidney 16
Webber, Bill 220, 339, 356, 365, 413
Welch, Colin 217
Wells, G.P. 31
White, Eirene 341
Whiteley, William 227
Wigg, George 76, 354
Williams, Francis 31, 32, 181, 185, 206, 334
Williams, Philip xv–xvi, 9, 10, 20, 209, 300, 359–60, 381, 390, 420, 436, 445
Williams, Shirley 182, 335, 341, 396, 437
Williamson (accountant) 32
Williamson, Tom 186, 205, 209–10, 227

491